W9-BBE-293

THE NAZI DICTATORSHIP

THE NAZI DICTATORSHIP

A Study in Social Pathology and the Politics of Fascism

by

FREDERICK L. SCHUMAN, PH.D.
ASSISTANT PROFESSOR OF POLITICAL SCIENCE
UNIVERSITY OF CHICAGO

SECOND EDITION, REVISED

NEW YORK · ALFRED · A · KNOPF

1936

Manufactured in the United States of America

Published April 22, 1935
Second Edition, Revised, May 11, 1936

TO

DONALD ROBERT

PREFACE TO THE SECOND EDITION

On March 29, 1936, the German electorate marched once more to the polls to "endorse" the Nazi régime by electing the "Reichstag of Freedom and Peace." The totalitarian ballot with its single circle opposite the name of Hitler afforded no opportunity to vote against the dictatorship. Dissenters and abstentionists were warned that they would be regarded as traitors. On election Sunday, police and Storm Troopers admonished tardy voters to perform their civic duty. These pressures were supplemented by the propaganda machine, with its shrewd manipulation of xenophobia and militaristic nationalism and its adroit dramatization of the lowest possible emotional denominators of the mob mind. In the result all records for unanimity were broken. Of the eligible voters (Jews were disfranchised), 98.95 per cent cast ballots. Of these, 44,389,140, or 98.79 per cent of the total, voted according to orders. Only 542,898, or 1.21 per cent, dared to disobey by casting "invalid" ballots. Germany was "united." The pending shop-council elections, which might have conceivably led to a different result, were cancelled as unnecessary. Der Führer, having won renewed mass support by violating treaties and challenging the Powers, could count upon further support for new violations and challenges. The following that wavered in the face of impoverishment and gave only feeble cheers for anti-Semitism and racial mysticism could still be relied upon to shout itself hoarse under the spell of sabre-rattling, goose-stepping, and the brutal diplomacy of the *fait accompli*.

What is of greater import, the Rhineland *coup* of March 7 has now become an unqualified victory for the Reich. For the third time the Powers have responded to Nazi defiance exactly as the defenders of the Weimar Republic responded prior to 1933—with fear, idle protests, naïve faith in new promises, a willingness to compromise, a blind and muddled grasping after straws, and chronic internecine quarrels which destroy all possibility of a united front and paralyse all will to action. However long and tedious the current negotiations may be, the Rhineland remains in the hands of the Reichswehr and will be rendered impregnable to French attack. Whatever compacts Downing Street may make with the Quai d'Orsay, Britain will never fight Berlin unless France, Belgium, or The Netherlands is invaded. Such invasion has now been rendered superfluous for the attainment of the goals of Nazi diplomacy. France, having surrendered strategic domination of the Rhine, can be checkmated while the German war machine prepares to move in the direction of Vienna, Prague, Memel, Reval, Warsaw, and Kiev. Paris can no longer give effective military aid to Czechoslovakia or the U.S.S.R. in the event of German attack.

Hitler has thus won the early engagements of the next war without firing a shot. Not only is French hegemony ended and the French bloc broken, but the League system of collective security has probably been dealt a fatal blow by the refusal of the British Cabinet to honour the obligations of Locarno by supporting sanctions against Germany. Fascist imperialism is the beneficiary. The forces of liberalism and peace have again abdicated before the Nazi menace. In Konrad Heiden's apt phrase, *Das Zeitalter der Verantwortungslosigkeit*—the Epoch of Irresponsibility—stumbles toward catastrophe.

These tragic developments were forecast in the first edition of this work. The events of 1935–6 have substantiated the analysis of the NSDAP there set forth. The Third Reich moves inexorably toward ends predetermined by the dynamics of Fascism. The slow strangulation of monopolistic economy, coupled with the suicidal and homicidal tensions of collective paranoia and megalomania, has driven the dictatorship toward ever greater intolerance at home and ever accelerated preparations for war abroad. Under these circumstances, no extensive revision of these pages has been required. Minor errors have been corrected and a section has been added on the happenings of the past year. Alfred Rosenberg will doubtless continue to deplore this book and to feel regret that so good an "Aryan" as its author should succumb to "Jewish influences." It is the author's hope that others will continue to find it an honest and accurate account of the German Fascist State.

March 31, 1936 F.L.S.

PREFACE

The phenomenon of Fascism has stimulated the writing and publication of an impressive number of histories, descriptions, eulogies, and indictments. This literature has increased manyfold since the political upheaval of 1933 in Germany. None of the studies of German Fascism thus far published, however, offers a comprehensive and definitive analysis of both the Nationalsocialist movement and the new Nazi State. There has not yet appeared an adequate account of the almost incredible events of the "revolution." Neither is any full and critical treatment available of the organization, philosophy, and strategy of the NSDAP, despite the highly useful treatises of Konrad Heiden, Ernst Ottwalt, E. A. Mowrer, Calvin Hoover, Mildred Wertheimer, and other commentators.

The present work aspires to meet these needs. It attempts to analyse and evaluate recent and contemporary German politics in terms of the concepts of a Political Science which is not merely descriptive of political ideas, public behaviour, and governmental institutions. A realistic Political Science must concern itself with the social contexts of power relationships, with the established procedures for the distribution of material and psychic values in society, and with the value hierarchies which emerge and persist in the body politic. It must likewise endeavour—now more than ever in the twilight of old ideologies and State-forms—to disclose the effects of economic change upon social deprivations and insecurities and to reveal the consequences of insecurities for the invention and propagation of political symbolisms. Institutionalizations of power are meaningful only against the background of these underlying configurations. The processes of politics, in the narrower sense, can be dealt with intelligently only in terms of the struggle for power between social groups and in terms of the basic weapons of power in all cultures: violent and non-violent coercion; emotional conditioning or conversion through propaganda; and the wise and masterly distribution of material emoluments. The present volume is concerned with the use of these weapons by the NSDAP in its struggle to conquer and retain power in the Reich, with the economic and psychological genesis of German Fascism, and with its implications for the social order in Germany and throughout the world.

No effort to apply this approach to the Nazi Dictatorship can be wholly comprehensive, since the new Totalitarian State has politicalized all aspects of communal life. Considerations of space have required the omission of much manuscript material (some of it published elsewhere in articles and monographs) dealing with the earlier politics of the Weimar Republic, the Church conflict, the foreign policy and the international economic and political position of the Third Reich, and various social aspects of the new dispensation. In most other respects, however, this book is intended to be a reasonably complete study of the politics of Nazi Germany.

A wholly definitive study is still impossible, since many indispensable sources of information, such as the party archives and accounts, are closed to scholars. With regard to many events, judgments must be based upon admittedly incomplete evidence. These difficulties, which always beset the student of contemporary politics, are aggravated here by the determined and well-organized efforts of the new German régime to discourage incisive research into its methods and objectives and to misrepresent many of its goals and techniques for reasons of political expediency. Deception is a political imperative in all government. In the Third Reich it is an applied science and a fine art. The most that can be expected from the products of scholarship in such a situation is that they shall show painstaking effort to gather all available data, to disclose reality, and to reach tentative conclusions which stand some chance of survival in the light of facts as yet undisclosed. It is the author's hope that such expectations will prove to be justified with regard to this study.

Materials for the present work were gathered in Germany in the course of an eight months' sojourn during 1933. I went to Berlin with a research project originally formulated when the Weimar Constitution still survived and when the Nazi movement was declining and disintegrating. I journeyed toward a land I had already known and enjoyed as the home of music, philosophy, and *Gemütlichkeit* and as the birthplace of my Prussian and Hanoverian ancestors, now strangely transmuted into "Aryans" and "Nordics." Upon my arrival in April of the year of the Nazi seizure of power I found the Reich in process of violent, if orderly, transition from parliamentary democracy to Fascism.

The intellectual and emotional impact of developments which seemed at first utterly improbable in the absence of knowledge of their causes led me to devote most of my time to the study of Nationalsocialism through reading, interviews, and attendance at all the great political festivals and demonstrations. I spoke with hundreds of people of all ranks, confessions, opinions, and occupations. Several foreign correspondents then in Berlin were of invaluable assistance in my investigations. By the older German officials I was invariably received with courtesy and granted as much co-operation as was consistent with considerations of political and personal safety. By the newer Nazi administrators I was invariably received with evasions and complex circumlocutions or, as in the case of Hanfstängl, with gross and clownish discourtesy bred of psychic insecurity and conceit. Despite these obstacles I managed to carry through my inquiries to a point which seemed to justify publication.

My public acknowledgments are due in the first instance to the donors of the James-Rowe Fellowship of the American Academy of Political and Social Science, without whose aid I could not have spent the year 1933 abroad. My thanks are likewise due to the Social Science Research Committee of the University of Chicago for financial assistance in preliminary research and in the subsequent organization and writing of the book. I am also deeply grateful to Dr. Joseph Werlin, now of the University of Houston, for indispensable bibliographical and research work; to Mr. Richard Bauer of Lewis Institute, Chicago, for his counsels in Berlin; to Dr. Albert Lepawsky of Chicago for making available to me materials which he brought back from the Reich in 1934; to Gerhard Seger for first-hand information about his own illuminating experiences; to my esteemed and stimulating colleagues Professors Harold D. Lasswell, Melchior Palyi, Harold F. Gosnell, Quincy Wright, and Charles E. Merriam for their willingness to peruse certain portions of the manuscript and for their most helpful suggestions for its improvement; to Miss Brita Berglund, now of TVA, for highly efficient stenographic and secretarial assistance; and, not least, to my wife for useful comments on organization and style. I am likewise grateful to the editors of *The American Political Science Review* and of *The New Republic* for permission to reproduce here certain materials originally published in article form in their respective journals. None of these organizations or persons is responsible for errors of fact, for mistakes of interpretation, or for any of my opinions and conclusions.

All translations, including poems, are my own, save where English sources are cited. I have endeavoured to recapture the atmosphere of Nazi politics by means of a style of presentation not calculated to reduce a gigantic melodrama to a dry-as-dust academic compilation. I have sought to retain a sufficient amount of documentation to enable readers to consult the major primary and secondary sources of information if they are so minded. My objectives have been explanation, not condemnation; analysis, not indictment; description, not denunciation. Whether the pages which follow are to be regarded as "objective" or "impartial" is a question almost devoid of meaning in the present context. If objectivity means the analysis of social phenomena within a frame of reference broader than the phenomena themselves, then this study is objective. But the new dictators who "think with their blood" repudiate all objectivity and scientific detachment as evil products of liberalism and of "Jewish-Marxist materialism." Under these circumstances any effort at objectivity implies *per se* the adoption of an attitude evoking negative emotional responses from the patients under observation. Like every form of highly emotionalized and subjectivized mass mysticism, National-socialism demands acceptance or rejection. Objectivity is equivalent to rejection. But if this book contributes to a better understanding of the nature of Fascism it will have served its purpose.

FREDERICK L. SCHUMAN

The University of Chicago
February 11, 1935

CONTENTS

PROLOGUE

EPILOGUE

APPENDICES AND INDEX

PROLOGUE

CHAPTER I

THE REVOLT THAT FAILED

1. DEFEAT

ON NOVEMBER 11, 1918, a pale young man lay weeping on a sick-bed in the Lazarett at Pasewalk, a small Prussian town on the Ucker, northeast of Berlin. He was indistinguishable from hundreds of other war casualties lying on identical beds, save that he was of Austrian birth and had won an Iron Cross and the rank of corporal. Four years before, he had volunteered for service in Munich and had become a private in the Sixteenth Bavarian Infantry Regiment. The enthusiasm of those remote August days he always recalled with excitement and nostalgia. He had been twenty-five then: an intense, dissatisfied, neurotic youth, frustrated in all his ambitions—without parents, without wife or mistress, without friends, without hope, save the frustrated hopes of war-dreams and hero-fantasies nurtured from childhood and never outgrown.

Sarajevo, the spark of death for ten million men, had come to him as to most of the others as the spark of life and the herald of high adventure. Fantasy promised to become reality. Upon the news of the outbreak of war he had felt a great weight lifted from his chest. Here was release from the storm and stress of an unhappy young manhood. He had fallen on his knees, overcome with rejoicing and vivid anticipations, and out of the fullness of his heart had thanked Heaven for vouchsafing him the privilege of living in an age which was about to show, after years of humdrum dullness, that it, too, could be "heroic." [1]

"What man wills, that he hopes and believes." So wrote the pale young man ten years later about the inspiring fever of 1914 patriotism. *"Deutschland, Deutschland über alles!"* rang always in his ears as he

[1] Cf. Adolf Hitler: *Mein Kampf* (Munich: Verlag Franz Eher Nachfolger; 17 ed., 1933), pp. 177 f.

moved toward the front, fearful, he said later, lest the victory be won and the war be over before he saw battle. If other fears possessed him, they were conveniently forgotten later. This fear at least proved groundless, for he soon saw destruction and blood in Flanders. Like millions of others, he rejoiced and recoiled simultaneously, exalted by merging himself into a vast armed host engaged in grim and heroic deeds, but shocked no doubt by the hideous sights of death. He soon learned to enjoy death. Killing and escaping being killed were noble. Civilized men in arms, unlike barbarians and savages, cannot enjoy bestiality for its own sake. They must justify murder and arson and disguise their guilty joy in the slogans and symbols of patriotic sacrifice. The greater their joy and the greater their guilt at their joy, the more ardent their patriotism.

The pale young man was an ardently patriotic soldier who fought wisely and well. Months and years of slaughter on the western front became his life. He relished danger and became a dispatch-bearer. On October 7, 1916, during the British offensive on the Somme, he was wounded. He convalesced at Beelitz and later in Berlin. There he found time to denounce cowards and defeatists and, above all, the Jews and Marxists, who were to him the pests and parasites of the Fatherland. By March of 1917 he was again at the front. Glorious hopes of victory waxed strong as the year wore on. Then in the summer of 1918 they waned with the failure of the great drives and the inexorable pressure of French, British, American, and Belgian armies pushing the grey flood back toward the frontier. But the pale young man was undaunted till the end. In the autumn of the dark year he found himself again, for the third time since 1914, at Comines, in Flanders. On October 13 the British at Ypres launched a mustard-gas attack against his regiment. He fell choking, burned, and almost blinded—and eventually found himself in the Lazarett at Pasewalk with doctors and nurses uncertain as to whether he would recover his sight. At last he saw again, but his eyes opened on a world in dissolution.

One day rebellious sailors, perhaps from Stettin, came by the hospital, driving armoured cars and shouting: "Revolution!" They were led—so an embittered memory told him later—by a few Jews. Detestable swine! *They* had never been at the front. And now they waved red flags and cried: "Revolution!" Only a naval mutiny, the young man on the sick-bed reassured himself. That the Germans as a whole, *his* Germans, could yield to despair was inconceivable. But gradually he learned the appalling truth. On November 10 the hospital pastor announced the abdication of the Hohenzollerns to the sobbing and cursing veterans.

When, on the next day, the final news of the armistice came and he realized its import, he stumbled to his bed and wept—for the first time, he wrote later, since the death of his mother. All that he had worshipped, all that he had made the most cherished part of himself, was destroyed. Grief and misery at this catastrophe were soon transmuted into hate, as horror at the front had been transmuted into heroism. All that night his hate raged within him—hate against the authors of defeat. In his simple philosophy, all blacks and whites with no nuances of grey, the authors stood clearly revealed: Marxists, pacifists, democrats; above all, the pestiferous Jews. He laughed now at his dreams of becoming once more an architect. A great passion swept through him. He must destroy the authors of defeat as they had destroyed all that had meaning in his life. He must regenerate his countrymen, lead them back to the light, restore their will to what is warlike and heroic. He must, in short, enter politics and thereby fulfil his "mission."

Sixteen years later, on April 20, 1934, his forty-fifth birthday, the Bavarian barracks where he first served would be named after him. In Bavaria all mothers of sixty-five would be officially feasted in honour of the mother who gave Adolf Hitler to Germany. Her son, in the chancellery of the Reich, would receive hundreds of enormous birthday cakes from all parts of the nation. And he would receive thanks and congratulations, with comradely greetings, from his erstwhile commander, Paul von Beneckendorf und von Hindenburg.

In the dreary autumn of 1918 the pale young man returned to his regimental headquarters in Munich. His "mission" burned within him, but his immediate future was dark. To return to dull civilian life was unthinkable. No position awaited him. No family hearth would welcome him in his despair. No relatives or friends cared whether he lived or died, for he had always been lonely and apart. No Frau or Fräulein awaited his homecoming. He had no home. He had never experienced love, nor was he ever to know the exaltation and peace which it brought to other men. He returned—to his barracks. And in the general demobilization he managed to remain with his regiment. But even this was dull and dispiriting in the black winter which followed the armistice. He lived listlessly, seeking but not finding the opportunity for which he sought. Heroism was of the past once more—and perhaps of some dim, remote future. The present was drab and full of the antics of the cursed Jews, Marxists, labour leaders, liberals, a swinish lot whom he despised and detested with all his soul. They represented something broader than his little world of petty-bourgeois provincialism and something therefore alien and menacing. He withdrew into his memories and his anticipations.

His childhood and youth had been in no way remarkable. Indeed, they epitomized most perfectly the aspirations and frustrations of millions of little men throughout central Europe. He was born April 20, 1889, in the small border town of Braunau-am-Inn, near the Bavarian frontier. He was the only son by a third marriage of a petty Austrian customs official. The town later came to be for him a symbol of a mission: that of effacing the frontier, of uniting all Germans in a great German Reich. His early years were uneventful. His family was poor, though his father put on the airs appropriate to a *Beamter* and was apparently disliked by his neighbours, for Austrians did not worship authority and uniforms, as did Prussians. Frau Hitler (*née* Klara Ploetzl) was of uncertain ancestry, possibly Czechish. Herr Hitler had been christened Alois. His surname, a contraction of Hüttler, suggested the origins of the family in the small peasantry.

Adolf's relations with his parents were unhappy, even in his early childhood. He resented his father's authoritarian attitude, and his resentment was soon transferred to that which his father's uniform symbolized—the Austro-Hungarian monarchy. Neither the school nor the Catholic church which he attended broke down this transferred father-hatred. He hated his "Fatherland" with a childish hate and soon found reasons for his feelings. He pored over the cheap books in his father's small library, especially over a popular account of the Franco-Prussian War. He wondered why *all* Germans had not fought France. *He* was a German too, and like all boys he thrilled with vicarious joy at accounts of wars and of deeds soldierly and warlike. *His* motherland, he felt, was the Germany across the river, over there at Simbach and beyond. Only it wasn't the land of his mother. She spoke German with a Czechish accent. This was humiliating. As a German among the other Germans of the dual monarchy, he looked down upon the lesser alien peoples: Italians, South Slavs, Magyars, Poles, Czechs. But when his family went for a time to Passau, along the river on the German side, they were looked down upon as Austrians. And later, when the family went to Lambach, the Austrians treated them almost as foreigners. These subtle distinctions between in-group and out-group, and his own anomalous position in which he seemed to "belong" nowhere, deeply affected the boy. He disliked his father and was alienated from his mother. Like a small, rudderless boat without anchor or sail, he drifted through his too complex little world, bound for no certain destination save some mystic land of dreams.

After the turn of the century, when he attained to the dignity of twelve years, he decided that he would become an artist. He liked colour and form and romantic fantasy. The second opera which he witnessed, *Lohengrin* (*Wilhelm Tell* was the first), impressed him deeply and made him a devotee of Wagner. His father was horrified at his decision. "A painter—no, so long as I live, never!" He must become a respectable *Beamter* like his father. Painter, indeed! *His* son—to become a Bohemian, a metropolitan good-for-nothing! But Adolf was stubborn and his quarrel with his father became chronic. The boy's mother brought him little comfort, and he looked elsewhere for inspiration. He found it to some degree in the *Realschule* at Linz, where his history-teacher, Dr. Leopold Poetsch, made him a good German, aware at a tender age of the distinction between unworthy dynastic patriotism toward the Habsburgs and pan-German racial nationalism.

When he was thirteen his father died. His mother felt bound to carry out her husband's wishes and to make young Adolf a *Beamter*. But in the face of her insistence he fell ill, and, to his relief, the doctor diagnosed his malady as a lung trouble which would make office work highly inadvisable. His mother then agreed reluctantly to send him to the art academy in Vienna. But her intention was never carried out. After a lingering, painful illness, she followed her husband to the grave. Adolf was an orphan at fifteen. Relatives took him temporarily under their protection. They were poor and doubtless begrudged him his keep. None of them made any permanent impression on the unhappy boy.[1]

When he was seventeen he went to Vienna. He was poor and friendless but resolved to study painting. Full of confidence, he took

[1] *Mein Kampf*, pp. 1–17; Theodor Heuss: *Hitlers Weg* (Stuttgart: Union; 1932), pp. 15–18; Emil Lengyel: *Hitler* (London: Routledge; 1932), pp. 1–15.

the entrance examinations in the academy, only to fail and to be advised that his talents seemed to lie in architecture rather than painting. But entrance into the architectural school of the academy required preparatory work in the Bauschule der Technik and this in turn required the completion of a course in a *Mittelschule*. Adolf had never completed his secondary education, nor was he able to do so on his slender resources. Somehow he must earn a living. He did odd jobs. He borrowed a few schillings from his sister Paula. He painted picture postcards. All he could find in the way of a permanent post was a menial job as a building-trades helper. He carried bricks and mortar and mingled resentfully with common working men, his social inferiors. He lived in tenements and felt at home nowhere. Poverty, insecurity, and frustration did not lead him toward acquiescence in his lot. He rebelled and viewed the scene about him always through the small eyes of a half-peasant, half-bourgeois provincial who had known better days and who knew he was worthy of better things. Girls paid no heed to this surly, morose youth, and he ignored them. He hungered for beauty, but found none in this narrow, cramped life of the builders' scaffolding and the workers' quarters. His inner conflicts found expression in the development of the curiously warped social philosophy of an outcast. "In this period," he wrote long afterwards, "there was formed in me an outlook and a world philosophy which became for me the granite foundations of my behaviour at that time. I had to learn only a little in addition to that which I thus created in myself, to change it I had no need." [1]

This *Weltanschauung* (blessed word!) was, as he himself dimly recognized, the reflection of the resentments and fears of a petty-bourgeois youth at the prospect of being pushed down permanently into the ranks of the proletariat by the vast impersonal forces of a society of which he had little comprehension and no control. His fellow workers irritated him insufferably. They were Social Democrats. He sympathized with their hatred of the monarchy, but only because he desired the break-up of a State which was "Slavizing" its Germans. He hated Slavs—and yet he probably had no realization that he was here giving expression to his contempt for his mother and for something deep in himself. The workers urged him to join the union. He refused. They threatened him with violence. He hated them and perceived suddenly that Marxism and trade unionism con-

[1] *Mein Kampf*, p. 21.

stituted "a fearful instrument of terror against the security and independence of the national economy, the safety of the State, and the freedom of the individual." [1]

He studied this enemy of his "freedom" and finally found the "key" to all social problems. It was supplied by Karl Lueger, Mayor of the city, and by the bourgeois and aristocratic anti-Semitic groups which were so prominent a feature of pre-war Vienna life. "Only the knowledge of Jewry offers the key to the understanding of the inner and actual purpose of Social Democracy." [2] Before Vienna he had seen few Jews. They had been rare in Linz and these had been so "Europeanized" and "human" that he had mistaken them for Germans. In Vienna he had at first resented the anti-Semitism of a section of the press and of Dr. Karl Lueger's Christian-Social Party. But finally he saw the light. Once he met a Jew with long hair and a caftan and wondered at these sinister figures come out of the East. He began buying anti-Semitic pamphlets and learned that the Jews were a pestilential race, worse than the Black Death, poisoning all they touched. The completeness of the revelation was startling. Here was the road to self-righteous hatred of that world of cosmopolitan culture, of sophistication, of release from provincial inhibitions which he had tried in vain to enter. This was, after all, a world of literary filth, of artistic dross, of theatrical dirt—all produced by Jews! And his *"Weltpresse"* was run by Jews and was full of a thousand lies. Prostitution, the white-slave traffic, a hundred evils were devised by the Jews to debauch the people on whom they preyed. And the Social Democratic Party and its press were dominated by Jews. Lies, lies! "Gradually I began to hate them. . . . I was transformed from a weakly world-citizen [!] to a fanatic anti-Semite." [3]

This ferment continued to grow within the man during his five years in Vienna. By 1909 he was working independently, doing drawings and water-colours. He was even poorer than before, but at least his time was his own and he was free from distasteful contacts with grimy workers. Karl Lueger remained his guide to Jewish wickedness. His pan-Germanism found inspiration in Georg von Schönerer, leader of the Austrian pan-Germans. Later, in retrospect, he perceived that Schönerer was mistaken in building merely a parliamentary

[1] Ibid., p. 53.
[2] Ibid., p. 54.
[3] Ibid., pp. 67, 69.

party and in failing to win the masses to his cause by linking pan-Germanism and anti-Semitism with "social problems." Schönerer talked and negotiated, but failed to fight. He failed to develop a *Weltanschauung* championed by fighters and heroes. Here was needed force and fanaticism and Wagnerian mythology. Schönerer's end was good, but his means were inadequate. Lueger's means were excellent, but he had no clear goal He was, after all, only a sham anti-Semite. He fought the Jews only on religious grounds and failed to perceive the racial implications of his cause.

In 1912 Hitler went to Munich. Why he went is unclear. In February 1914 he returned to Linz to do his military service, only to be rejected as "too weak" and *"waffenunfähig."* About his two years in the Bavarian capital he says little in his autobiography, save that they were the happiest and most contented years of his life. His existence remained precarious, however. He worked at odd jobs as a carpenter and handy-man. He made drawings for newspapers. He painted a bit—unsuccessfully. He toyed with architecture, also unsuccessfully. His frustrations remained always with him. His fantasies remained unrealized and seemingly unrealizable. And then—with dramatic suddenness—war! He was accepted as a volunteer in the Bavarian army. Adventure! And the fierce, joyful years of slaughter, mud, and slime. And the trappings of a "heroism" in which his faith never wavered, even in the darkest hours of the final tragedy. Here was salvation and release from drabness. Here was glory and exaltation and victory—and then the bitter sting once more of defeat.

2. THE BIRTH OF A PARTY

THE soldier who returned to Munich in the winter of the year of disaster had learned nothing and forgotten nothing. Half-educated, he knew only such history and politics and economics as he perceived darkly through the glasses of pan-German romanticism and military hero-worship. His thwarted affection for a mother long dead had been transferred to a love for a motherland which was not his own. The symbols of its might, now tragically shattered, were the things dearest to him. These he loved more than he loved any human being, for, like all ardent patriots, he had identified himself with them and in worshipping them he worshipped himself. These were the devices which made him one with the vast, fearful, beloved, impersonal majesty of *Deutschtum*. And the gods of *Deutschtum* within him were jealous gods, brooking no rivals.

Only this mystic loyalty brought warmth to a heart otherwise closed by the heavy defences it had set up to conceal its own insecurities. The rich he hated because of his poverty. The poor he hated because of his frustrated ambitions. Jews he hated because they represented what he would have become and could not. Frenchmen he hated, not because he had fought them for four years, but because France too, and the faint breath of Paris which he had caught in pre-war Vienna, bespoke a polish, a sophistication, a cultural freedom, and a libertarian Bohemianism which was to him evil because he—narrow, uncouth, and provincial—was incapable of sharing it and finding it good. Slavs he hated because his mother's blood spoiled his own German purity. Since his life was empty, he romanticized it. Since war was a release from emptiness, he welcomed it. And since war was hideous, he romanticized it too— with a glorified *Heldentum* idealism as fanatic and tenacious as war itself was inglorious and foul.[1]

The defeat of German arms in the greatest of all wars was the ultimate frustration. It, too, was caused by the enemies of society upon whom he had long since fastened the hatreds generated by his earlier frustrations: Jews, Marxists, trade unionists, liberals, pacifists, internationalists. These were the foes of the new mother for whom he had fought and bled. These were the vipers from whom this mother must be rescued. In the rescuing he could vent his thwarted aggressions on these scapegoats and achieve self-realization and a release from his unbearable emotional tensions. This was now his mission. In its accomplishment his latent artistic and oratorical abilities were to come to the surface. In their exercise he was to know greater joy and self-satisfaction than he had ever known before. And he was to find what was sweetest to one obsessed with mother-rescue fantasies and with unconscious fears of impotence and castration: power.

This power came to him because he was able to capitalize upon his own value as a symbol of the mass frustrations and insecurities of the *Kleinbürgertum* from which he sprang. In finding an emotionally satisfying solution for his own problems, he was to afford a comparable solution for the problems of multitudes who suffered as he had suf-

[1] For interesting suggestions regarding Hitler's personality structure, see Fedor Vergin: *Das unbewusste Europa* (Vienna, Leipzig: Hess; 1931), 137–55; and H. D. Lasswell: "The Psychology of Hitlerism," *Political Quarterly,* Vol. IV, pp. 373–84.

fered. Because his own personality difficulties had counterparts by millions in the society in which he lived, he was to found a new political religion giving solace to its disciples. Because of his special talents as an actor, an orator, and a symbol-artist, he was to become the Messiah of this religion: Der Führer. Therewith began a cycle: from neuroses to fanaticism, from fanaticism to a following of fanatics, from a following to a party, from the party to a great mass movement, from the mass movement to revolution and to power beyond the dreams of despots.

The Munich to which Hitler returned seemed at first to offer few opportunities for the type of political activity upon which he desired to embark. The revolution had come here two days before it struck Berlin. On November 7, 1918, the two wings of Social Democracy, the Majority Socialists and the Independent Socialists, joined forces in a great labor demonstration for peace and for a republic. Kurt Eisner, the Independent Socialist leader (a Jewish lawyer of Berlin birth), addressed his followers with brave inflammatory words. The local garrison was won over to the proletarian cause. A Workers' and Soldiers' Council was created on the 8th, while the Wittelsbach dynasty came to an end with the flight of the King. Eisner became Minister-President of the new Bavarian "People's State." Labour had pushed over the old political order. Its leaders, who had preached social revolution for decades, directed the mass movement into safe channels. Monarchy gave way to republic, but the distribution of property and power remained as before. Proletarian radicals, inspired by the example of the workers of Russia, sought to engineer a genuine social revolution, but the conservative bureaucrats of the trade unions and of the Social Democratic Party held back.

But under the pressure of reaction the Independent Socialists and even the Majority Socialists of Munich drifted rapidly leftward, particularly after Eisner's assassination, on February 21, 1919. On March 21 a Communist *coup d'état* created a Soviet régime in Hungary. The Munich Workers'-Soldiers' Council effected a rapprochement with the Peasants' Union and began to play an important role. Early in April an agreement was reached between Majority Socialists, Independent Socialists, and Communists. On the 7th a Soviet Republic (*Räterepublik* or Council Republic) was proclaimed, resting, as in Russia and Hungary, upon the Councils of Workers, Soldiers, and Peasants.

The Soviet of Munich, like that of Budapest, was destined to be drowned in blood. The Spartacist movement in northern Germany had already been crushed. Berlin dispatched troops southward to "restore order." Before they arrived, General von Oven, with a patriotic volunteer corps, opened hostilities against the radical forces. The "Red army" of the Soviet was hastily organized. It was poorly equipped and no match for the troops sent against it. The patriot volunteers and the Reichswehr took few prisoners in their advance upon the city, resorting instead to the summary executions characteristic of violent class warfare. In reprisal the Soviet authorities executed ten hostages. On May 1, 1919, the Reichswehr marched into Munich. The local volunteers had already driven the Reds from the centres of power. In the course of the fighting, 38 government soldiers were killed and 547 Münccheners lost their lives, including 184 civilians "accidentally shot." A conservative government took power in Munich, and the city became a haven for disgruntled militarists, monarchists, soldier adventurers, and reactionary conspirators of all kinds.

This new atmosphere was most pleasing to the young Hitler and ultimately furnished him with opportunities for carrying out his resolution of the preceding autumn. At the end of November 1918, upon his return to the city, he discovered to his disgust that his regimental headquarters were in the hands of a Soldiers' Council. Rather than participate in the activities of such "Marxist traitors," he left with a comrade for the camp at Traunstein, where he stayed until the camp was dissolved. In March 1919 he returned to Munich. The Soviet régime, in his eyes, was simple "Jew-rule." He apparently played no part in the bloody events which followed, though on the morning of April 27 he narrowly escaped arrest as a suspect by the Soviet authorities. A few days after the "liberation" of Munich, he was appointed a member of an *Untersuchungskommission* of the Second Infantry Regiment to investigate the events of the revolution. A few weeks later he was entrusted with the task of giving a course in political education to his comrades, and so successful was he in instilling patriotism and hatred for the "November criminals" that he held the post for a considerable period.[1] He turned over various plans in his mind, but found no immediate field for action, despite the local proliferation of reactionary groups and of armed bands of political adventurers. In the Munich of 1920 he was but one of many

[1] *Mein Kampf*, pp. 226–7.

would-be *condottieri* leaders surrounded by reactionary conspirators, terrorists, and ambitious soldiers of all types, united only in their hatred of the Socialists and of the new republican order.[1]

Hitler, however, desired to organize a popular mass movement rather than to take part in military conspiracies. He conferred with some of his like-minded soldier colleagues. They must first of all find a name which would have popular appeal—perhaps "Social Revolutionary Party". . . ? But a name was only a beginning. Hitler attended political meetings. He was impressed with the flatness and dullness of the bourgeois party gatherings and with the superior propaganda technique of his enemies, the Marxists. Sound, colour, banners, slogans, parades—these were needed to appeal to the emotions of the masses. But what to do? By chance he happened, one June evening in 1919, to attend a small meeting in the Sterneckerbräu beer hall. It was sponsored by a group calling itself the *Deutsche Arbeiterpartei* (German Labour Party). Everyone was founding a new party. The speaker he had heard before: one Gottfried Feder, who had discovered the "key" to Germany's economic difficulties in the distinction between two kinds of capital—international, Jewish, exploitive loan-capital and national, purely German, productive capital. Hitler was much impressed with Feder's exposition, but was unmoved by the little audience of two dozen people. In the ensuing discussion a "professor" advocated the separation of Bavaria from Prussia and its union with Austria. Hitler rose indignantly to denounce him, with such effect, he wrote later, that the professor crawled out of the hall "like a wet poodle." As Hitler departed, an unknown man thrust into his hand a pamphlet which he took with him to his living-quarters: the barracks of the Second Infantry Regiment. The following morning, when he awakened at five—his usual hour for rising—he read it. It was entitled *My Political Awakening*. It described how the author had finally arrived at "national ideas" after passing through Marxist and trade-unionist confusion. Here Hitler saw an interesting recapitulation of the development of his own political emotions.

Less than a week later Hitler received a postcard informing him that he had been "admitted" to the "party" and inviting him to come to the next meeting, on Wednesday evening in the Alte Rosenbad

[1] Ernst Ottwalt: *Deutschland Erwache! (Geschichte des Nationalsozialismus)* (Vienna, Leipzig: Hess; 1932), pp. 133–143.

beer hall on Herrnstrasse. Uncertain as to whether to be angry or amused (he had wanted to found his *own* party), he went. He found four men sitting around a broken table under a gas lamp. One, Karl Harrer, was head of the *"Reichsorganisation"* of the German Labour Party, which had been established on January 5, 1919, by a somewhat muddle-headed young locksmith, Anton Drexler, who sought to achieve a synthesis of patriotism, trade unionism, socialism, and militarism.[1] Drexler read the notes of the last meeting, reported that the cash on hand totaled seven Reichsmarks, fifty pfennigs, and presented letters of sympathy from "supporters" in Berlin, Kiel, and Düsseldorf. The effect was ludicrous. Here was merely a name, a vague yearning, and four men under a lamp. Hitler's reason told him that the group was nothing and that it would be nonsensical for him to join it. But his intuition told him to join. And here, as often, he found emotion a better guide than reason. He joined.

"It was the most fateful decision of my life."[2]

He received a membership card. He was member No. 7 of the inner group. Every Wednesday the six or seven men met in the beer hall. Once a week they arranged a *Sprechabend* in some larger place. Almost no one came. Only a handful of people knew of the existence of this pitiable "party." It had no press, no funds, no organization, no leaders, almost no members. If only people would at least attack it or denounce it or in some way put it before the public eye. Hitler proposed a monthly mass meeting. He wrote out and typed invitations himself. Once he personally distributed eighty cards announcing a meeting. That evening only the same seven appeared. But next time eleven came. Then thirteen. Then seventeen, twenty-three, thirty-four. Still insignificant and apparently hopeless. But the little group persisted. Incredibly, it was to become a party, a great mass movement, and a *Weltanschauung,* destined to sweep all before it. But in the fall of 1919 it was nothing—the merest speck on a stormy horizon.

Funds were collected at these early meetings and an important and profitable precedent was thereby established. The funds at first were pathetically small, but, used wisely, they began to multiply. In a moment of happy inspiration Hitler published a notice of the next meeting in the *Münchener Beobachter,* then an independent sheet

1 Cf. Konrad Heiden: *A History of National Socialism* (New York: Knopf; 1935), pp. 3–8.

2 *Mein Kampf,* p. 244.

with superpatriotic and anti-Semitic leanings. The result was astonishing. One hundred and eleven persons came to the appointed place: one of the smaller rooms of the great Hofbräuhaus, largest of beer halls. A local professor opened the meeting. Hitler spoke second. It was his first public speech. Herr Harrer had given him only twenty minutes. He spoke thirty—and discovered that he was an orator of talent. *"Ich konnte reden!"* He dwelt on the sufferings of Germany, the injustices of the peace, the viciousness of the Allies, the wickedness of the Jews, the treachery of the Marxists. He was hypnotized and exalted by the emotional response of the audience, and the audience reciprocally felt joy and exaltation at the flowing phrases which afforded vicarious release for its own patriotic prejudices and resentments. Three hundred marks were contributed. The party had a treasury! Leaflets could now be printed.

Many of Hitler's war comrades joined the movement, and it became a movement of soldiers—patriotic, reactionary, disgruntled, unable to accept defeat and demobilization, unwilling to return to the inhibited humdrum of civilian life after years of emotional orgies and "heroism" in the army. Harrer and Drexler were not soldiers. The former was a petty journalist, too academic to become an effective swayer of crowds. The latter, leader of the München *Ortsgruppe,* lacked the requisite fire and fanaticism. Both were pushed more and more into the background as Hitler threw himself energetically into the tasks of speaking, organizing, and publicizing and assumed control of propaganda activities.

In October 1919 the second mass meeting was held in the Eberlbräukeller. Hitler, one of four speakers, harangued the crowd of 130 for an hour on the theme of "Brest-Litovsk and Versailles." The Marxists were arguing that the injustices of the conquerors' peace imposed on the Reich were perhaps, after all, no worse than the conqueror's peace which Germany had imposed on defeated Russia in March 1918. Such comparisons were disgusting. Hitler courageously took up the challenge. The audience went wild, for it heard what it wanted to believe. A few hecklers were suppressed by the guards and fled downstairs with broken heads. Two weeks later another meeting in the same place drew 170 people. Each time Hitler spoke, the audiences were larger, the contributions more generous, the new party members more numerous. He sought a larger hall and found one at the other end of the city, in the Deutschen Reich, on Dachauerstrasse.

But only 140 people came. The doubters were discouraged and advised fewer meetings. Hitler insisted and drew 200 to the next assembly—with an excellent collection. A fortnight later 270 came. Two weeks after this success, at the seventh mass meeting, over 400 crowded into the hall. Success begot greater success, and Hitler began to believe in his "mission."

He and his more fanatic war comrades gradually assumed a dominant role in the movement and crowded out the more timid and academic souls. Quarrels over names and tactics were frequent. Two adjectives were added to the party's title in April 1920, apparently at Hitler's suggestion: "National" and "Socialist." That Hitler was then familiar with Friedrich Naumann's pre-war Nationalsoziale Verein is unlikely, though he doubtless knew of the German National Socialist Party of Austria, with which his new party established contact in the summer. He probably adopted the name as one admirably designed to appeal to the deep-seated affection of the local populace for any cause calling itself "Socialist" and "National" simultaneously. The combination of a patriotic "socialism" purged of internationalism, pacifism, and Marxism, with a socially-minded "nationalism" was a masterpiece of political invention. Hitler had an intuitive feeling for mass reactions, for effective propaganda technique, for the art of identifying himself and his cause with clever combinations of symbols evoking favourable emotional responses in the community. And he was no less gifted in singling out as "enemies" of the movement those elements whose symbols had been discredited by the defeat, the revolution, and the Soviet dictatorship. Pacifists, Marxists, Jews, the "November criminals" were subjected to relentless and vicious attack—verbal at first, to evoke mass enthusiasm, physical later to intimidate the enemy and to afford psychically satisfying channels for the discharge of the animosities generated among the faithful. Husky soldiers were designated as guards at the meetings, and the speed and brutality with which they assaulted and ejected hecklers were most heartening. Those who deprecated violence and urged persuasion and spiritual weapons were soon a dwindling minority in the *Nationalsozialistische Deutsche Arbeiterpartei* (National Socialist German Workers' Party or NSDAP in the German abbreviation).

But Hitler, as an uneducated man, almost wholly illiterate in the fields of economics and politics, relied for guidance in phrase-making and program-formulation on others who appeared to him to be profound thinkers. One of his mentors was the somewhat mysterious figure of Dietrich Eckart, a former actor, would-be poet and dramatist who had seen better days. He had translated Ibsen's *Peer Gynt* into German and had written a play himself: *Lorenzaccio.* He was often seen in the beer halls and coffee shops of Munich, and when slightly inebriated, as he frequently was, he would exude a scintillating stream of witticisms, trivialities, and aphorisms which brought to his knees an adoring circle of listeners and disciples. How, when, and where Hitler first encountered him is uncertain. But the youth was fascinated by the old man's glib tongue and dramatic gestures. He perhaps learned from him some of the arts of acting and oratory. Eckart's rabid anti-Semitism only confirmed Hitler's admiration. So intimate and apparently sacred was this relationship between the elderly poet and the young soldier that Hitler made no mention of it in the autobiography which he wrote later to recount the events of these years. But the last sentence in the book was an expression of gratitude to Dietrich Eckart. Eckart's ultra-patriotic German mysticism was symbolized in a phrase which he used often: "*Deutschland erwache!* (Germany, awake!)." And this phrase Hitler adopted as the slogan of the NSDAP.

Hitler's other guide at this period, Gottfried Feder, stands out in contrast as a sharp, clear, small figure in post-war Munich. Born in Würzburg January 27, 1883, he was, like Hitler, the son of a *Beamter* and was destined to become a *Beamter* in turn. Unlike Hitler, he followed his father's wishes and became an engineer, subsequently engaging in construction projects in various parts of Germany, as well as in Italy, Bulgaria, and Russia. Lacking any formal economic training, he arrived by various processes of twisted reasoning, reflecting his petty-bourgeois resentment against "big business" and *Hoch Finanz,* at the conception of the two kinds of capital. The solution of all social problems was to be had through "breaking the bonds of interest slavery." Late in 1918 he published a *Manifest zur Brechung der Zinsknechtschaft,* and shortly afterwards he founded in Munich a *Kampfbund zur Brechung der Zinsknechtschaft,* into which he attracted Dietrich Eckart, Prince Löwenstein, Count Bothmer, Captain Mayr, and a motley assortment of malcontents and visionaries. He began publishing pamphlets and making speeches setting forth his panacea. Hitler listened and, in his simplicity and in his quest for simple catchwords to win the masses, was profoundly impressed. Feder's "economics" opened Hitler's eyes to new vistas, and they were soon close collaborators.[1]

3. BEER-MUGS AND BULLETS

EARLY in 1920 Hitler urged upon his party colleagues the necessity of a great mass meeting at which a formal party program should be announced. There was dissent and fear—lest the requisite audience should fail to materialize and lest the "Reds" should fill the hall and create disturbances. Hitler insisted. He was organizer of propaganda for the party. Drexler had replaced Harrer as party leader, though Hitler was already the real leader. Finally it was agreed: on the evening of February 24, 1920, all and sundry would be invited to the great *Festsaal* of the Hofbräuhaus. Hitler personally organized the preparations. Posters and leaflets were printed—a few simple points ceaselessly reiterated in accordance with Hitler's conception of the public mind—and on red paper, to emphasize the "socialist" character of the movement and to appeal to the proletariat. Guards were organized to deal with disturbers. Announcements were spread over the city. The police-president, Ernst Pöhner, and another police official, Wilhelm Frick, were sympathetic and even cordial.[2] Every mark and pfennig which could be gathered together were devoted to advertising the meeting. Its decisive character was clear to all the party members. If few came—or if many enemies came to throw the assembly into chaos with shouts and fists and beer-mugs and table legs—the movement would be set back by months. With desperate energy and many apprehensions Hitler and his colleagues prepared the meeting with meticulous care.

Success again attended these efforts. On the appointed evening the *Festsaal* was filled to overflowing with almost two thousand people. About a quarter of them seemed to be indifferent or hostile. Others were curious, expectant, amused, or serious. At seven thirty Hitler entered, unrecognized and unknown, for only a handful had heard him before. He took his seat beside the speaker's platform. The meeting opened. Dr. Johannes Dingfelder delivered the principal address,

[1] Cf. Edgar Schmidt-Pauli: *Die Männer um Hitler* (Berlin: Verlag für Kulturpolitik; 1932), pp. 134–41.
[2] *Mein Kampf,* pp. 403 f.

which evoked no enthusiasm. Then: Hitler. He pleaded, cajoled, and exhorted, his voice rising to hoarse and passionate crescendos. Hate—against Germany's enemies. Hate—against the "November criminals." Hate—against France and the Allies. *Deutschland erwache!* Germany must be freed. . . . Hecklers interrupted with cries and laughter. Canes clattered on tables and the heckling increased. But soon the guards intervened, ejecting a few, threatening the others, silencing the rest. The voice went on, more and more passionately. After the first half-hour bursts of applause began. They grew more enthusiastic under the hypnotic spell. Then the speaker began point by point to present and expound the new program.[1]

The document from which Hitler read had been prepared by Gottfried Feder, who was entrusted with the task of writing an interpretation, commentary, and defense. "Point One," shouted the voice: "We demand the union of all Germans to form a Great Germany on the basis of the right of self-determination enjoyed by nations. Who of you cannot support this point?" Applause and assent. "Point Two: We demand equality of rights for the German people in its dealings with other nations, and abrogation of the peace treaties of Versailles and Saint-Germain. Who of you cannot support *this* point?" Stormy applause and assent. "Point Three: We demand land and territory (colonies) for the nourishment of our people and for settling our superfluous population. Who of you . . . ?" Wild approbation. This initial display before the mob of popular and familiar demands, certain to evoke the responses of fervent patriotism, turned the trick. To stir hatred of the foreigner and to inflate vicariously the ego-symbols of patriotism was to appeal to the lowest common emotional denominator of the crowd. On the next level, and certain to evoke almost equal enthusiasm, was anti-Semitism. "Point Four: None but members of the nation may be citizens of the State. None but those of German blood, whatever their creed, may be members of the nation. No Jew, therefore, may be a member of the nation. Who . . . ?" Boisterous applause.

And so on through the twenty-five points of the program. Jews cannot be citizens. Only citizens may vote and hold office. Foreigners and non-citizens must be driven from the Reich if all cannot be nourished. All non-German immigrants must be expelled, including all non-Germans who entered the Reich since August 2, 1914. . . .

[1] For the text of the party program, see below, pp. 491–4.

And then the "socialistic" motifs: Abolition of incomes unearned by work. *Break the bonds of interest slavery!* All war profits must be confiscated. Trusts must be nationalized. The profits of wholesale trade must be shared. Old-age pensions. Municipalization of wholesale-business premises and department stores, and their lease at low rentals to small traders. Confiscation without compensation of land for communal purposes. Abolition of interest on land mortgages and prohibition of all speculation in land. Usurers, profiteers, etc., must be punished with death.

Then a melange of petty-bourgeois patriotism and morality: Roman law, serving the "materialistic world order," to be replaced by German law. The educational system to be reconstructed to give to every capable and industrious German the possibility of higher education. Development of the gifted children of poor parents at State expense. Health. Protection of mothers and children. No child labour. Sports and bodily development. A national army, not a paid army. A *national* press: all editors of German papers must be Germans. Non-German (Jewish) papers to be published in their own language and only with the special permission of the State. Non-Germans to be barred from owning or influencing German papers. Suppression and deportation. Prosecution of all tendencies in art and literature likely to disintegrate the national life. Liberty of religion. Positive Christianity. The party combats the Jewish-materialist spirit. *The common interest before self! (Gemeinnutz vor Eigennutz!)* A strong centralized State. Unquestioned authority of the politically centralized parliament, with chambers for classes and occupations. . . .

"The leaders of the party swear to go straight forward—if necessary to sacrifice their lives—in securing fulfilment of the foregoing points." Stormy applause. It is almost midnight. The crowd is unfatigued. All are impressed. Some are converted. A few are wildly excited. Dozens rush up to shake the speaker's hand, to congratulate him, to express their renewed hope for the Fatherland. "Who wishes to join the new party?" "Where can we reach you?" Pens and paper are produced. Names, occupations, addresses are written down. Almost a hundred new members are enrolled. The treasury is full with the gate receipts. The evening has been an enormous success, even though everybody, including Hitler's colleagues in the German Workers' Party, promptly forgets about the "program." Hitler has emerged as an orator of genius and as indisputable leader and spokesman for the resurgence of Deutschland. Forward! Onward and upward to the final victory! [1]

After the 24th of February 1920 the NSDAP decided to hold a great mass meeting once a week. Always there was anxiety among the timid. Always Hitler was optimistic. He was the principal speaker at every meeting. Week after week, in the *Festsaal* of the Hofbräuhaus, he preached, presenting his party as the bearer of salvation and himself as the Messiah and attacking ceaselessly all the groups which might be expected to evoke aversion and hatred in the audience. His simple message he drove home again and again with unceasing eloquence. Down with the Jews! Down with the Masons! Down with Marxists, pacifists, internationalists, capitalists! Two lectures in particular he went over repeatedly: "The True Causes of the World War" (presented as a Jewish-Masonic-Marxist-capitalist conspiracy) and "The Peace Treaties of Brest-Litovsk and Versailles."

The slight, pale man, talking simple German and sometimes bad German—earnestly, fanatically, hoarsely—became a familiar platform figure with his pleading hands, his burning eyes, his heavy black hair, parted on one side and falling over his perspiring brow, his sharp nose, his stubby smudge of black moustache above the lips that talked and shouted ceaselessly and hypnotically. He perfected his style, his gestures, his inflections, and became a polished actor on the beer-hall stage. He also issued pamphlets and leaflets, but he knew that the magic of oratory was far more effective. From the hated Marxists he had learned to appreciate and to practise the collective hypnosis of oral agitation and of mass demonstration. Only through demagoguery can the masses be won. "The German," he wrote later, "has not the slightest notion of how a people must be misled if the adherence of the masses is sought." [2] Great mass meetings give people courage and a sense of unity. Doubters are won by mass suggestion and by the collective *esprit de corps* created by the orator. Exultantly Hitler saw himself, through his ever growing audiences and through their ever greater enthusiasm, developing into a master demagogue.[3]

[1] *Mein Kampf,* pp. 400–6; Gottfried Feder: *Das Programm der N.S.D.A.P. und seine weltanschaulichen Grundgedanken* (Munich: Verlag Franz Eher Nachf.; 1st ed., 1927; 575th thousand, 1933); cf. article by Joseph Berchtold in *Völkischer Beobachter,* February 24, 1934, and T. Heuss, op. cit., pp. 19–22.

[2] This sentence, from *Mein Kampf,* was deleted from the 12th (1932) and all subsequent editions.

[3] For a summary of this period, with comments on the technique of political oratory, cf. *Mein Kampf,* pp. 518–38.

The frustrated artist now found scope for his talent for colour, design, and pageantry. Words alone he knew were not enough. Platforms were of little importance. The masses could be more easily conditioned to respond to visual symbols and to the external trappings of strength and discipline. Red placards and red cards continued to be used to draw workers to the meetings. The Marxist appellation "comrade" was useful. Audiences were never addressed as *"Damen und Herren,"* but as *"Volksgenossen und Volksgenossinnen* (Racial comrades or countrymen)" or as "*Parteigenossen* (Party comrades)." Friends and foes were welded together in a common fervor. The Marxist press now took notice. Sometimes it tried stony silence. More frequently it warned workers not to attend the Hitler meetings. Often it resorted to bitter attack, ridicule, and allegations of criminality and scandal. All in vain. More and more converts appeared. But hecklers and disturbers had always to be disposed of. Never did Hitler dream of relying on police protection, for he knew that police protection discredited any cause in the eyes of the masses. He dealt with disturbances by energetic leadership at the meetings and by the gradual organization of the ushers and "bouncers" into an *Ordnertruppe.* Iron discipline, savage attacks on enemies, immediate expulsion of disturbers were the techniques which brought results. In the summer of 1920 the *Ordnertruppe* was definitely organized, and by the end of the year it had hundreds of members: not venerable old men who would evoke respect, as at bourgeois party meetings, but young rowdies and ex-soldiers skilled in the arts of physical coercion.

The *Ordnertruppe* became the *"Sturm-Abteilung"* or Storm Division of the party on August 3, 1921. These husky S.A. men (Storm Troops) needed uniforms, salutes, and a flag—symbols to match the colourful spectacles of Socialist and Communist mass meetings. As symbol-maker Hitler was also a genius. Whether he studied and consciously copied the symbolism of Mussolini's Black Shirts in Italy in the 1920–3 period is uncertain. The only direct imitation was the Roman salute: right arm outstretched, with fingers together and hand open. Black shirts were transmuted (at the suggestion of Lieutenant Rossbach) into brown shirts for the members of the S.A., though black shirts and uniforms were later adopted for the smaller and more select armed guard of the *Schutzstaffel* (S.S.) the first unit of which was established in February 1921.

To the party flag Hitler devoted his most earnest thought. He thanked Heaven that his enemies, the democratic and Marxist parties, had adopted the detestable black, red, and gold republican banner of 1848 as the national flag. The sacred imperial black, white, and red was unsullied—the battle flag of Bismarck and Moltke and William II, the glorious flag of the German hosts in their conquest of Belgium, their invasion of France, their subjugation of Serbia and Rumania, their triumphs in Russia and Italy, in Flanders and on the high seas. It still evoked warm and powerful emotions and must in some form be used by the NSDAP. Much discussion among the party leaders took place on this point in the spring of 1920. Hitler rejected black and white as insufficiently striking and objected to white-black and white-blue on the ground that they were already state banners. The imperial black, white, and red must be used, but in some new and striking form.

The *Hakenkreuz* or swastika flag was the product of Hitler's cogitations on this problem. Where he first encountered the design of the swastika or hooked cross he has never recorded and has perhaps forgotten. The design itself is ancient and widely disseminated among the cultures of the world. Early in the nineteenth century the German archæologist Heinrich Schliemann, while conducting excavations at the site of ancient Troy, found hundreds of spindles marked with swastikas. In seeking their meaning Schliemann was told by the French archæologist, Emile Burnouf, perhaps facetiously, that they were used by the ancient "Aryans," who kindled their fires with bore-sticks. The swastika was the feminine counterpart of the bore-stick. Schliemann accepted this and wrote a commentary on the swastika as an "Aryan" symbol. But to the Chinese the emblem signified good luck, and to the Hindus it symbolized sexual ardour and fertility. In modern Europe it came to symbolize anti-Semitism. In the State Historical Museum at Kiev are black-and-white swastika flags used by the bandit leader Petlura in 1919, when he harried the Ukraine with fire and sword, slaughtering Jews wherever he went. Whatever his first contact with it, to Hitler it also signified anti-Semitism. He adopted the design and combined it with the imperial colours. A red flag: Socialism. On it a white circle: Nationalism. Within the circle a black *Hakenkreuz:* Anti-Semitism. The first flag was unfurled in midsummer 1920. It worked on youth like a charm and became a flaming torch of the movement. Swastika arm-bands were likewise devised for the storm troopers, and later came the "standards" of ancient Roman design, with the black metal swastika on top within a silver wreath surmounted by an eagle, "NSDAP" on a metal rectangle below, and below this, suspended by cords with fringe and tassels, a square *Hakenkreuz* flag with *"Deutschland erwache!"* blazoned upon it. Here was political artistry of the highest type. Its magic was as great as that of Hitler's oratory.

This colourful semi-military pageantry, combined with patriotic and socialistic slogans, with the old symbols of imperial glory and armed might, with the strange new symbols of a mysterious and glorious "Third Reich," with ceaseless denunciations of Jews, Marxists, foreigners, capitalists, Masons, pacifists, internationalists, and radicals, appealed powerfully to the imagination of the Bavarian *Kleinbürgertum*. The intolerable frustrations and resentments of these people were due to the cumulative effect of numerous dangers and disappointments: the defeat of 1918, the unwanted "revolution," the unwelcome republic, the Allied demands for reparations, the spectre of inflation, Spartacist uprisings and proletarian disorders, war profiteering, inflation profiteering, and the ever present dread of economic insecurity, social degradation, and psychic disintegration. Here, in the pale, passionate young man on the platform, in the flags and music and uniforms of determined soldiers, was a promise of solace and salvation. By the autumn of 1920 the party was holding two meetings a week and filling the largest beer halls with eager throngs. No other party save the Social Democrats could hold such impressive mass demonstrations. Even the Münchener-Kindl-Keller, holding five thousand persons, was often overcrowded. The party treasury grew constantly and in December 1920 Hitler was able to buy the *Münchener Beobachter* with money secured by Eckart from General von Epp. He changed its name to *Völkischer Beobachter* (Racial Observer) and, with the help of Hermann Esser, converted it into a strikingly effective propaganda sheet.

On February 1, 1921, Hitler demanded a decision from his colleagues on his earlier proposal to hold a gigantic mass meeting in the Circus Krone. This would be the most ambitious and expensive program yet undertaken. The skeptics were doubtful. Hitler insisted and arranged a meeting for Friday, February 3. A universally popular theme must be chosen to draw the crowds. He would protest against reparations. Only one day to advertise. Thursday morning it rained. But pamphlets were printed and they were distributed over the city throughout the day by storm troopers in two trucks painted red and decorated with the new flags. At seven o'clock Friday evening the huge circus was less than half full. By seven forty-five it was three-quarters full. At two minutes past eight Hitler came in. He was intoxicated by the spectacle. Fifty-six hundred tickets were sold. Unemployed and poor students were admitted free. In all, some 6,500 people were present. Hitler orated for two and a half hours on *"Zukunft oder Untergang."* The applause was never greater. At the end he received a tremendous ovation. The crowd sang the *Deutschland-Lied* as never before. For twenty minutes he watched enraptured as the inspired thousands poured forth from the hall. Power!

During 1921 and 1922 the NSDAP continued to grow rapidly and to develop its organization not only in Munich, but throughout Bavaria. The first *Ortsgruppen* outside of Munich were established at Landshut and Rosenheim in February 1921. Ambitious soldiers and political adventurers flocked into the movement. Various other reactionary and anti-republican groups with similar aims, such as Julius Streicher's Deutschsozialistische Partei in Nürnberg, merged with the NSDAP. By the close of 1920 there were three thousand members. Thousands more joined in the following year—some to save the Fatherland, some to recover the atmosphere of war for which they yearned, some to fish in troubled waters. Hitler became president of the party on July 29, 1921, and assumed dictatorial powers. Drexler faded from the picture. A few of the personalities who gathered around Der Führer were destined to have their ambitions fulfilled....

Hermann Göring was then a dashing blond young aviator, restless, ambitious, disgruntled with civilian dullness after the savage excitement of war in the air. He was born at Rosenheim, Bavaria, January 12, 1893, of Lutheran parents. His father was a high official, a Prussian army officer, and a colonial administrator in Africa. He sent his son into the army. He had influence. At nineteen young Hermann was a lieutenant in an infantry regiment at Mühlhausen. In October 1914 he became an aerial observer—and with the development of air combat he was presently a pilot (May 1915), a combat flyer (March 1916), and finally an "ace," shooting down enemy planes with enthusiasm, skill, and dispatch. In June 1918 he attained the highest of aviation honours: he was named Captain of the famous

Freiherr von Richthofen squadron, organized and led, until his death, by the greatest of all war aces.

After the war Göring, like Hitler, found a return to civil life intolerable. His fierce energies thirsted for action. He continued to be an aviator. He began taking morphine, first as an occasional stimulant and later in such quantities as to undermine his reason. In 1919 he was a pilot in Denmark. In 1920-1 he became an official in the Svenska Lufttrafik in Stockholm. When on one occasion he made a forced landing on the estate of a Swedish nobleman, Count Rosen, he met the beautiful Baroness Karin von Fock. The young aviator fell in love and subsequently married the frail girl, despite her attacks of epilepsy. The year 1922 brought Göring to Munich, where he undertook to study history and economics at the university. He lived with his wife in a near-by chalet high in the Bavarian mountains. The fanaticism and military fervour of the NSDAP soon proved a greater attraction than his studies. He joined, met Hitler, threw himself into organizing and disciplining the Storm Troops, and was appointed leader of the S.A. in December 1922, after he had made generous donations from his ample fortune. That his great hero, von Richthofen, had had Jewish blood in his veins did not deter Göring from embracing anti-Semitism. The movement promised action, conflict, and ultimately perhaps great prestige and power. This was enough for the inordinately vain and ambitious young flyer.[1]

Rudolf Hess—"the Egyptian"—was a soldier of a very different mien. Born April 26, 1896, in Alexandria, son of a German wholesale merchant and a Swiss mother, he spent the first fourteen years of his life in Egypt and then came to the Rhineland as a student. In 1914 he volunteered for war and served in the First Bavarian Infantry Regiment. On June 12, 1916, he was wounded before Verdun. Later he fought in the Rumanian campaign, and on August 7, 1917, was wounded again in the Carpathians. He served in Hitler's regiment on the western front and became one of his few friends. After the armistice he studied business in Munich, but he, too, could find no peace in peace. He became a vender of anti-Semitic pamphlets and barely escaped arrest by the Soviet authorities in April 1919. On May 1 he took part in the "liberation" of Munich and was wounded

[1] Cf. Edgar Schmidt-Pauli, op. cit., pp. 86–91, and sketches of Göring and other leaders in Curt Rosten: *Das A.B.C. des Nationalsozialismus* (Schmidt; 1933). pp. 257–76.

in the leg. In May 1921 he joined the NSDAP and became a storm trooper. In one of the many brawls in the Hofbräuhaus he received a deep gash on the head from a flying beer-mug. He was slim, dark, square-faced, thin-lipped, with beetling black brows in an unbroken line across his forehead, framing keen grey eyes. Quiet, unpretentious, retiring, and with a talent for secretarial work, he was perhaps closer to Hitler than anyone else.

Another soldier—one hundred per cent a soldier—was Ernst Röhm. His martial fervour made him a traitor to the pacific Weimar Republic. In 1928, in Munich, he published his autobiography under the title of *The History of a Traitor.* It begins: *"Am 23 Juli, 1906, werde ich soldat."* He was born November 28, 1887. His father was a railway official, and almost all his ancestors were Bavarian bureaucrats. But for him life began only when he became a soldier. He entered the Tenth Bavarian Infantry Regiment and in 1908 became an officer. He entered the war as a lieutenant and emerged as a captain. In September 1914 the upper half of his nose was shot away. In June 1916 he was seriously wounded in leading his company in an attack on Fort Thiaumont at Verdun. For a time he served in the Bavarian Ministry of War. May 1917 found him on the Rumanian front. April 1918 saw him on the western front again before Reims, where he came to know Ludendorff. In October 1918 he contracted grippe and was given up as lost by the physicians, but he recovered and joined his regiment in the retreat toward Brussels.

In 1919 Röhm joined Franz von Epp's illegal *Freicorps* and had to flee over the border to escape arrest. He marched under von Epp against Red Munich and became chief of staff of the municipal soldiery. In March 1920 he participated in the suppression of the Communist insurrection in the Ruhr. Wherever troops and fighting were to be found, there was Röhm. He was short, stocky, bull-necked, with a small moustache and small piggish eyes set in a hard, round, deeply scarred face. His participation in illegal terrorist bands jeopardized his official military position at times, but he continued to hold his post. He was one of the early members of the Deutsche Arbeiterpartei and later became an S.A. commander. His years spent in barracks and trenches, and again in barracks, had made him a homosexual—but this "defect" was (until many years later) an asset rather than a liability in the NSDAP.

There were many other soldiers in the movement—men wounded

in body and soul, men attuned by years of fear (and by over-compensation for their fear) to brutality and terror, men utterly unable to resume civilian life, frustrated men, embittered men, desperate men, violent men, thirsting for violence (and some of them doomed to die by violence), seeking a road back to the free camaraderie, the licence, the sacred death-danger of the trenches. There was Max Amann, a soldier in Hitler's regiment; Philip Bouhler, a war casualty and a worker on the staff of the *V.B.;* Wilhelm Brückner; Edmund Heines, destined to become a Feme murderer and to be murdered in turn by those whom he had served; Wilhelm Kube, who, in 1910, had founded the Deutschvölkischen Studentenbund under the sign of the *Hakenkreuz;* Hans Kerrl, war volunteer, lieutenant, jurist, party member in 1923 and district leader *(Kreisleiter)* in Peine. There was also Viktor Lutze, born September 28, 1890, in Bevergern, near Münster. He became a soldier in 1912 and lost his left eye in the war. He joined the party in 1922. And there was, not among the least, Gregor Strasser, born May 31, 1892, in Geisenfeld, Bavaria, a war volunteer promoted to lieutenant and decorated for his valour. In 1918 he became a druggist. In February 1921 he joined the party and later became leader of the S.A. in Lower Bavaria.

These men—and thousands of others like them—furnished the recruits and often the leadership of the innumerable "volunteer corps" which sprang up after the war. These bodies were in part an outgrowth of the pre-war "youth movement" and represented a middle class reaction against urban cosmopolitan life and against the inhibitions and regimentations of industrial society. In larger part they were associations of war veterans, ultra-patriotic, reactionary, and anti-republican. They found opportunities for action in the border disturbances and internal party and class conflicts of the early years of the new régime. The republican government repeatedly authorized army officers to organize *Freicorps* to protect the frontiers, to preserve "law and order," and to protect property against proletarian radicalism. Such officers often became anti-republican leaders, whose troops resisted attempts at dissolution, retained their arms, and became military secret societies of political terrorists. In 1922 some fifty such organizations were united in the Vereinigten Vaterländischen Verbände Deutschlands, comprising the Stahlhelm, Deutscher Reichskriegerbund Kyffhauser, Bund Oberland, Bund Bayern und Reich, Jungdeutscher Orden, Bund Viking, Grossdeutscher Baltikumverband, Werwolf, Deutscher Wehrverein, Reichsoffiziersbund, Nationalverband deutscher Offiziere, Reichskriegsflagge, Blücherbund, and many others.[1]

Nowhere did such groups of reactionary military adventurers flourish more abundantly than in Munich after 1919. The S.A. of the NSDAP was but another organization of a type already familiar. To it came many members of other organizations. In the relations between these groups of self-appointed and officially tolerated *condottieri* there was sometimes friction, sometimes collaboration, and always ultra-patriotic military mysticism, anti-Semitism, anti-republicanism, and an atmosphere of intrigue and conspiracy leading often to astonishing results. The soldier leaders who gathered around Hitler were men of this type,—violent, sincere, fanatic, ambitious, ready for any wild adventure which promised personal profit and prestige and a "liberation" of the Fatherland from the Marxists and Jews.[2]

While Hitler's movement was primarily a soldiers' movement, there was drawn into it a number of other figures without military experience but with other special talents which gave them prominence. Gottfried Feder has already been mentioned. His pamphlets against "interest slavery" were precursors of the party program which he wrote and interpreted. Wilhelm Frick (born in Kaiserlautern in the Pfalz, March 12, 1877), son of a teacher, was a jurist and police official. He did not become a party member at this period, but was an ardent sympathizer whose position in the Munich *Polizeidirektion* was invaluable to the NSDAP. Outstanding among the early civilian leaders was Alfred Rosenberg, the Russo-German with the Jewish name who later made amends for his name and his birthplace by becoming the most rabid anti-Semitic and anti-Russian leader of the party. He spent his childhood in Reval, where he had been born on January 12, 1893. In 1915 he moved to Moscow, along with the technical school in which he was studying. In 1917 he received his diploma as engineer architect and in February 1918 returned to Reval shortly before its occupation by the German army. As a good German, he volunteered for military service, but was refused because of his alien nationality. The remainder of the year he spent as a high-

[1] Cf. Ernst Ottwalt: *Deutschland Erwache!*, pp. 129–33.

[2] Cf. Ernst H. Posse: *Politische Kampfbunde Deutschlands* (Berlin: Junker and Dünnhaupt; 1931), pp. 3–19.

school teacher in his native city. In December 1918 he made his way to Munich, where he met Dietrich Eckart and became an anti-Semitic and anti-Bolshevist pamphleteer. On April 8, 1919, he delivered a twenty-minute oration in the Marktplatz, denouncing Jews and Marxists, and fled just in time to avoid arrest by the Soviet police. Later in the year he met Hitler and joined the new party. He collaborated with Dietrich Eckart on the *V.B.* and became its chief editor in July 1921. He was tall, blond, philosophical, and a prolific writer, championing "Nordic" purity and condemning with fanatical hate Jews, Slavs, Marxists, Masons, pacifists, liberals, et al. in hundreds of articles, brochures, and books. Here was the future philosopher of the movement and the man destined to become the party's unofficial foreign minister.

Such were the men with whom Hitler worked in building and expanding his movement. The party headquarters were at first located in a small dark room in the Sterneckerbräu, rented for fifty marks per month. Electric lighting was soon acquired, then a telephone, and finally some office furniture, including a safe. A soldier, Schüssler, was the first permanent secretary. He brought his own small typewriter with him and worked hard for the cause. In midsummer of 1921 Hitler persuaded his old comrade Max Amann to become business manager of the party, which by then had moved its headquarters to Corneliustrasse, where three rooms and a large office were rented and where the headquarters remained until November 1923. Amann administered his office ably, discouraged spoils appointments to party posts, and kept the organization out of debt despite the inflation. The *V.B.* became a widely read party organ as soon as its staff, consisting largely of former members of the Bavarian People's Party, was won over to the NSDAP. The paper, published at first twice a week, became a daily early in 1923 and in August of that year broke with Continental press traditions and adopted a large, sensational format with screaming headlines, comparable to "yellow journals" in the United States. By November 1923 the assets of the party, including the paper and its other properties, were worth 170,000 gold marks.[1]

The careful organization of the party and of its propaganda agencies was paralleled by an expansion of its storm-troop division. The S.A. was open not only to veterans, but to younger men. It was less

[1] *Mein Kampf,* pp. 662–9.

a military organization than a weapon of propaganda, of education, and, if need be, of disciplined force. It was not a secret political society, but a mass organization of fanatic fighters, wearing uniforms, emblems, and arm-bands. Their zeal in terrorizing and breaking up opposition meetings cost Hitler a month in jail in January 1922. In the late summer of 1922 the S.A. participated in a meeting in the Königsplatz of all the patriotic bands to protest against the dissolution order from Berlin, prompted by liberal indignation at the murder of Foreign Minister Rathenau. The S.A. created a great sensation with two bands and fifteen flags and beat off the attacks of republicans who tried to interfere with the march.

In October 1922 Hitler led 800 S.A. men and 1,400 party members to a "German Day" demonstration in Coburg, a hotbed of proletarian radicalism. When the flag-bedecked Sunday train entered the local station, the demonstrators were warned against marching through the streets with bands and banners. The warning was ignored and the march went forward. Infuriated workers called the brown-shirted storm troopers "bandits" and "criminals" and finally stoned them, thus precipitating a general riot. The disciplined S.A. men at length cleared the streets of the Red mob, which reassembled the next morning, however, to protest against the Nazi provocation. Hitler ordered his followers to march to the square designated for the meeting. A number of unarmed citizens were there beaten up by the storm troopers, who then proceeded to the railway station, gratified at having "suppressed the Red terror," restored "law and order," and demonstrated their ability to terrorize their proletarian enemies. The railway workers refused to transport them back to Munich, but finally yielded under threats of further violence. This "victory" encouraged Hitler to send his troopers to other towns to "clean up the Reds" and caused him to look forward optimistically to prospects of triumph over the "November criminals" and the whole republican régime.[1]

4. PUTSCH

THESE dreams of power on the part of a little group of obscure adventurers in Munich, led by an unknown Austrian fanatic, were ludicrous to outside observers. But the constantly deepening crisis of

[1] Ibid., pp. 579–620.

the Reich created a growing market for Hitler's panaceas and weakened the prestige of the republic sufficiently to offer hope of success for a well-planned revolt, with the collaboration of other reactionaries. Throughout the entire year of the Ruhr invasion and the disastrous inflation political tension between Right, Centre, and Left groups constantly increased, with rumours of putsches, conspiracies, and intrigues on every hand and no small amount of rioting, street battles, and general disorder.

Nazi demonstrations in Munich during the latter half of January precipitated bloody street clashes. On the "Party Day" of the NSDAP on January 27, 1923, six thousand men took part in flag ceremonies. Under the impetus of economic collapse and national humiliation the party membership grew to seventy thousand by autumn. General Erich von Ludendorff gave his sympathy and support to the movement—and his was still a name to conjure with, despite his political naïveté and his half-ludicrous, half-pathological reactionary fanaticism. Money was also forthcoming from those who hoped to use the party for their own advantage. Considerable sums were donated by Munich and Nürnberg industrialists, including one contribution of twenty thousand dollars. Dollars would buy millions of marks by midsummer, and Hitler even succeeded in banking some of the party's funds safely abroad.[1]

The party, however, would have been unable to continue its antirepublican activities and to make a bid for power had it not been for reactionary intrigue and treasonable conspirings in high places in the Bavarian government. Hitler found allies among conservatives and reactionaries with axes of their own to grind. Without their aid nothing could have been attempted. The drama of 1923 was to repeat itself on a larger stage in 1933. By then Hitler would have learned to use such allies to advantage, to trick them before they tricked him, and to betray his betrayers at the crucial moment. This hard lesson in Machiavellian politics he had not sufficiently learned in the year of the battle of the Ruhr. He was only dimly aware of the motives and purposes of those in high places who encouraged him. He could neither guess what they would do in a crisis, nor control their behaviour, nor yet outwit them by superior strategy. He could only use them (knowing vaguely that they were using him) and thus

[1] Tacitus Redivivus: *Die grosse Trommel. Leben, Kampf, und Traumlallen Adolf Hitlers* (Berlin, Zurich: Deutsch-Schweizer Verlag Anst.; 1930), pp. 83–4.

muddle and blunder to the threshold of power and there meet treason and defeat.

The intricacies of reactionary politics in the Bavaria of 1923 were not only beyond Hitler's full comprehension, but are difficult to unravel even in retrospect. Early in September, Hitler denounced the Reich government in a large gathering of the various *Kampfverbände* in Nürnberg. New Nazi slogans were now resounding through the land: "Up in arms against Red Berlin." "Never rest until the criminals of November 9, 1918, are overthrown!" "The pigsty in Berlin must be cleaned out!" Later in the month Gustav von Kahr became Generalstaatskommissar for Bavaria, with almost dictatorial powers. He was supported by the Catholic Bavarian People's Party and maintained close relations with Cardinal Faulhaber and the Vatican, as well as with numerous militarist and monarchist groups. His ambitions, in so far as they were formulated, tended in the direction of an independent Bavaria, possibly united with Austria under a Wittelsbach or Habsburg ruler. A "march on Red Berlin" was no part of his program. The Reich government was merely an obstacle to separatism and to a local monarchical restoration. The demagogue Hitler was useful only as a tool to secure mass support among the *Kleinbürgertum* and peasantry as a counterweight to the industrial proletariat, which was either loyal to the republic or interested in a general social revolution which would sweep away the existing ruling class, republican and monarchist alike.

By October 1 Kahr felt safe in announcing his monarchist sympathies. By the middle of the month Socialist-Communist coalition governments were set up in Saxony and Thuringia. The authorities in Berlin viewed this development with more alarm than the intrigues of the reactionaries and they defended the Bavarian government from Socialist allegations that it was conspiring with France to secede from the Reich. Kahr perceived correctly that he could proceed to great lengths in defying Berlin without provoking repressive measures. On October 18 he broke off diplomatic relations with the "Red" government of Saxony. On the 19th the Reichswehr Ministry, headed by General von Seekt, ordered the suppression of the *V.B.*, in which anti-republican agitation had reached fever pitch. General von Lossow, commander of the Reichswehr in Bavaria, refused to carry out the order, while Kahr sent the notorious freebooter and putschist, Captain Ehrhardt, to "defend" northern Bavaria, presumably against the Reich. In the face of this defiance Seekt ordered Lossow relieved of his command and appointed General von Kressenstein in his place. On the 20th the Reich government accused the Bavarian authorities of violating the Constitution. Seekt ordered the Seventh Division (in Bavaria) to obey his orders on penalty of being proceeded against for military insubordination, but Lossow calmly refused to give up his post. The removal order was set aside by the Bavarian Cabinet, with an appeal to Article 48 of the Reich Constitution. The Berlin authorities contented themselves with shooting Communist workmen in Hamburg and suppressing the radical governments of Saxony and Thuringia by force. The Bavarian reactionaries were immune.

In all of these events Hitler was an interested but not always an intelligent onlooker. The "march on Berlin" had become with him a fixed idea. He forgot that he was expected by his reactionary supporters to be only an agitator and demagogue and not a would-be dictator. Early in November Lieutenant von Seisser, Munich police chief, went to Berlin and returned to report to Kahr that Seekt was firmly supported and that the time was inopportune for a separatist *coup*. The Bavarian particularists and monarchists, moreover, were disorganized and mutually suspicious. At the same time the great industrialist Hugo Stinnes dropped his general director, Friedrich Minoux, who had been his liaison agent with various pan-German reactionaries and who apparently had had contacts with Hitler and Ludendorff as well. On November 6 Kahr told the leaders of the *Kampfverbände* that a march on Berlin would be dangerous and difficult. Hitler's representative at the meeting, Kriebel, received the impression that Kahr was personally willing to join in a revolt, but was hesitant and needed to be pushed into action. Hitler laid his plans accordingly. He had already decided, with his curious flair for superstition and symbolism, that the "national awakening" should be proclaimed precisely on November 9, the fifth anniversary of the detestable "Jewish-Marxist" revolution. He had armed forces at his disposal in the S.A. detachments. But they were inadequate for the task in hand, if they should be opposed by the armed forces of the State. He made no effort to mobilize them. He must make his revolution *with* the police and the Reichswehr, not against them. Seisser controlled the police. Lossow controlled the Reichswehr. Kahr controlled the government. If these three could be won over, all would be well. If not . . . ? But all doubts must be dismissed! His Destiny summoned him to duty and to glorious deeds.

On the evening of November 8, a great mass meeting of the *Kampfverbände* was held in the Bürgerbräu. Kahr, Seisser, and Lossow were present. Kahr spoke—in his usual inflammatory, anti-republican vein, though perhaps intending ultimately to urge moderation and delay. When he was only half finished, he was interrupted by shouting at the door. To his surprise, he saw Hitler appear, surrounded by uniformed and armed Nazi storm troopers. The treatrical Austrian had agreed to refrain from any unauthorized adventure. But he now jumped upon a table and fired two shots at the ceiling. With his revolver smoking, he leaped to the tribune and shouted to the audience: "The national revolution has broken out. The hall is covered by six hundred heavily armed men. No one may leave the hall. The Bavarian government is deposed. The Reich government is deposed. A provisional Reich government will be created. The barracks of the Reichswehr and the police are occupied. The Reichswehr and the police are united under the *Hakenkreuz* flag. . . ." This was untrue, but it produced the desired effect.

Hitler beckoned Kahr, Seisser, and Lossow to join him in a near-by room, where he pleaded with them to support the "revolution." He had the new Constitution and the personnel of the new government ready. Bavaria must prepare the national revolution. Bavaria must have a *Landesverweser*. Pöhner should be Bavarian Minister-President, with dictatorial powers. His Excellency Von Kahr should be *Landesverweser*. Hitler would head the national government, Ludendorff the national army, Lossow would be Reichswehr Minister. Seisser would be Minister of Police. . . . Please, please . . . you *must* fight on with me, to victory or death. . . . Hitler brandished his revolver and declared that he had four bullets left, one for each of his unwilling auditors and one for himself if they deserted him. He wept with excitement and ordered a stein of beer. Suddenly Ludendorff appeared in medals and uniform and urged them to accept. Kahr hesitated and finally said that as a monarchist he could accept the proffered post only as a *Statthalter* for the monarchy. Hitler assented. "Of course, Your Excellency." Kahr gave his two colleagues the wink. They assented. All four returned to the hall, where Göring had been haranguing the multitude.

Now for speeches. Hitler first: "The government of the November criminals in Berlin will be declared deposed. Ebert will be declared deposed. The new government will consist of. . . . Morning will find either a national government in Germany or us dead." Ludendorff was overcome with emotion: "This hour signifies a turning-point in our history. . . . If we do this work with pure hearts, German men, I shall have no doubts but that God's blessing will be with us. . . . The Lord God in heaven, when He sees that at last German men are again here, will be with us." Kahr: "In the Fatherland's deepest need I take over the destiny of Bavaria as *Statthalter* of the monarchy, destroyed five years ago by impious hands. . . ." Others spoke. Hitler was elated and trusted his "colleagues" with childlike faith. He left the hall with Kahr, Lossow and Seisser. He suggested that they proceed at once to the organization of the new government. Kahr complained that he was tired. *"Dazu ist morgen früh ja auch noch Zeit."* Hitler acquiesced. *"Ja wohl, Exzellenz, selbstverständlich."* They parted. Hitler remained in a daze in the Bürgerbräu. Kahr went home —presumably to bed. Everything would be arranged in the morning.

That night the tall Gothic spire of the Rathaus and the twin towers of the Frauenkirche looked down upon scenes of wild disorder. Armed Nazi storm troopers flooded the streets. They attempted to seize control of the main railway station and the telegraph office, but were thwarted by the police, who withheld their co-operation. They assaulted Jewish passers-by. The first Bürgermeister of the city, and the Social Democratic members of the City Council were imprisoned as hostages. The press establishments which printed currency were broken into and robbed by brown-shirted rowdies. The officers of an Entente mission were seized in their hotel in the middle of the night, and only the urgent warnings of the proprietor about the dangers of international complications prevented their immediate imprisonment. Trade-union headquarters were stoned and the offices of the *Münchener Post,* the local organ of Social Democracy, were plundered and destroyed. Hitler and his aides remained in the Bürgerbräu, waiting for they scarcely knew what.

Kahr was not in his bed. He conferred with Herr Matt, Minister of Education and a faithful son of the Church. Together they went to consult Archbishop Faulhaber, and from the latter's residence they telephoned the royal villa at Berchtesgaden and spoke to "His Highness" the Wittelsbach Crown Prince Rupprecht. He, as well as the Archbishop, repudiated the putsch. Kahr decided upon his course of action. Seisser and Lossow concurred. Hitler, though quite unaware of these events, was becoming nervous. He sent an agent to see Kahr. He was not at home. Seisser and Lossow were in the Reichswehr barracks. Hitler sent an agent to see them. The agent was arrested. A second, a third, was sent. None came back. The devil! Just before three a.m. the announcement came that the three conspirators had been compelled to support the putsch in the Bürgerbräu at the point of a gun and now repudiated Hitler and all his works. Two hours later the government announced: "Barracks and public buildings in our hands. Reichswehr and police reinforcements on march. City quiet."

This "treachery" was to cost the leader of the triumvirate his life, but Hitler's revenge was to strike eleven years in the future. What was to be done immediately? The dawn of November 9 found all strategic points in the city in the hands of the enemy. Hitler had no military force which could cope with this emergency. An alarm to the S.A. in Regensburg was intercepted by the Reichswehr. Gregor Strasser's S.A. unit from Landshut was not to arrive in Munich till afternoon. What to do? Speeches and a parade were all that Hitler could think of. He instructed his aides to make speeches and to win public opinion to the cause. A mass demonstration in the morning might yet save the day, even though Kahr proclaimed the dissolution of the NSDAP, as well as of the *Kampfverbände* Oberland and Reichsflagge. Reichswehr and police were everywhere, but they would not shoot. Röhm said that they would not dare to shed German blood. Ludendorff agreed.

"Wir marschieren!" The columns gathered near the Bürgerbräu in the morning, with flags and much hurrahing. A conflict must be avoided, since it meant certain defeat. The armed storm troopers were accordingly put in the rear of the procession. At the front were the flags and the leaders, including Hitler and Ludendorff. They marched through the beflagged streets amid ominous silence from the police and the Reichswehr. The Feldherrnhalle on Odeonplatz was their destination. As they approached it, they found their way barred by police and troops. It was high noon. They went forward.

A salvo of shots rang out. The first *Hakenkreuz* flag fell to the street. The firing continued. Men dropped to the right and left. Eighteen young men died before the guns, and as many more were wounded. The youngest of them was only nineteen—a student, Karl

La Force—ironically, of French descent. Ludendorff marched on. The troops parted and he passed through unharmed and disappeared. Hitler fell on his belly, dislocating his arm and fracturing a shoulder-blade. Whether he was pulled down by the man next to him, who was slain, Dr. von Scheubner-Richter, or whether he reverted automatically to the gesture which had repeatedly saved his life amid the machine-gun bullets and exploding shells on the western front is uncertain. In the confusion he was seized by his comrades, hustled into a car, and taken outside of the city to the town of Uffing, where he hid three days in the home of his wealthy friend Ernst Hanfstängl, before surrendering to the police. Göring was wounded and sought safety in flight. The other leaders scattered. The procession was smashed. The putsch was over. In the afternoon Kahr sent a polite telegram to Seekt, thanking him for his friendly offer of Reichswehr reinforcements and assuring him that they were unnecessary since the revolt was crushed and order had been restored. The storm troopers ran off in all directions and hastily divested themselves of their uniforms and arm-bands. "Germany's awakening" was not yet.[1]

5. LESSONS OF LANDSBERG AM LECH

On February 26, 1924, the memorable Hitler-Ludendorff trial began. The court was not a federal court, but one of the lower Bavarian tribunals—one which, incidentally, had assisted in the liquidation of the 1919 Soviet by imposing death sentences and long prison terms on surviving Socialist and Spartacist leaders. In this instance it was clear that there would be no vindictiveness, no judicial severity toward the accused. They had, to be sure, attempted to overthrow the state and national governments by force. And the German Penal Code (Article 81) declared: "Whoever attempts to alter by force the Constitution of the German Reich or of any German state shall be punished by lifelong imprisonment." But the letter of the law could be stretched to temper justice with mercy. The accused had acted from the highest "patriotic" motives. The primary purpose of the court

[1] Cf. Emil Lengyel: *Hitler,* pp. 80–8; Ernst Ottwalt: *Deutschland Erwache!,* pp. 196–211; Fritz Schwann: *Von Ebert bis Hindenburg* (Leipzig: Koch; 1928), pp. 249–57; Weigand von Miltenberg: *Adolf Hitler, William III* (Berlin: Rowohlt; 1931), pp. 41–8.

was to protect Kahr, Lossow, and Seisser from any suspicion of complicity. While there was no formal agreement to this effect, there was apparently an understanding that Hitler and his co-defendants would minimize the "betrayal" of November 9 in return for lenient sentences. Shortly before the trial opened, the Landesgerichtdirektor was promoted and replaced in the presidency of the court by Dr. Neidhardt, a prominent clerical who was evidently regarded as "safer" from the point of view of those in high public office.

While the NSDAP had been definitely outlawed on November 23, 1923, sympathy for the defendants among the Munich *Kleinbürgertum* had increased rather than diminished. Elaborate precautions were taken to prevent a possible Nazi demonstration. On the day before the trial opened, shots were fired, an alarm was sounded, and a military demonstration was staged as a warning. At the court itself, all witnesses and visitors, including the women, who came in large numbers, were searched for weapons. The proceedings were conducted in the dining-hall of the Infanterieschule. They assumed the form of a friendly discussion of the principles of National-socialism. The seminar atmosphere was at times superseded by the atmosphere of a political meeting. On one occasion Hitler was permitted to deliver a four-hour harangue to the audience and to "posterity." At the close of the hearings, as an appropriate climax, he was again permitted to appeal for the applause of the multitude. An outside observer would at times have had difficulty in ascertaining whether the government was prosecuting the conspirators or the conspirators were prosecuting the government.

There were ten defendants on trial for high treason: Ludendorff; Hitler; Pöhner; Frick; Wagner; Kriebel; Röhm, at this time both an S.A. commander and leader of one of the independent *Kampfbunde,* the "Reichskriegsflagge"; Brückner, Nazi leader of the München district; Weber, leader of the *Bundes Oberland;* and Pernet, Ludendorff's stepson, who had seized money for the Nazi storm troopers in two large business establishments on the morning of November 9. Kahr, Lossow, and Seisser were of course not prosecuted for their anti-republican activities or their dealings with Hitler. The only government official accused of complicity was Oberamtmann Dr. Wilhelm Frick, head of the political division of the Munich police administration. He testified that the police had protected and encouraged the NSDAP. "We held our protecting hand over Herr Hitler, because we saw therein the germ of Germany's regeneration. . . . Kahr tolerated the attitude of the police administration without complaint." But Kahr was immune.

Dr. Neidhardt questioned the defendants at length as to their past, their motives, their political beliefs. Ludendorff was red-faced, excited, nervous. For the Supreme War Lord of Imperial Germany to be subjected to such an indignity was too much. He asserted that he had nothing to do with planning the putsch. He had joined only because Lossow had joined. This was both untrue and dangerous, for the official triumvirate was, as far as possible, to be kept out of the proceedings. Pöhner was more diplomatic. Frick was frightened and plaintive. Hitler defended himself with his usual energy and eloquence—but, again most undiplomatically, asserted that his three betrayers had had the same objectives as himself. The defence attorneys, following this lead, sought to enlighten the court on the relationships between the triumvirate and the putschists. Weeks were spent "investigating" this problem, all to no effect. Kahr was glum and reluctant to answer questions. Lossow denounced Hitler as a hysteric and at the end, amid Hitler's closing address, rushed from the hall, slamming the door behind him. Both he and Seisser insisted that Hitler's claim that they had promised to aid the putsch was sheer "fantasy." The court itself had little interest in revealing the true facts.

Hitler's speeches, obviously intended for a wider audience than that assembled in the courtroom, were dramatic interludes. With a deft tongue he reiterated the old slogans which had proved so effective—minimizing (prophetically) the economic program of the party, saying nothing of national "socialism," but emphasizing his patriotism, his anti-Marxism, his supreme confidence in Germany's future awakening:

"The future of Germany means the annihilation of Marxism. Either this racial tuberculosis will grow strong, then Germany will die, or it will be cut out of the body of the people, then Germany will grow strong. . . . The Marxist question is the basic question of the German nation. Since the Marxist movement sets up mere numbers in the place of personality, the mass in the place of [individual] energy, it destroys the fundamentals of all human culture. Where this movement comes to power, human culture must go to pieces. . . . For us Germany will be saved on the day when the last Marxist is converted or destroyed. . . . Our movement was not founded to secure seats in parliament and stipends; our movement was founded to change destiny for Germany in the eleventh hour. . . . One does not die for business reasons, but only for the faith of serving the Fatherland! . . . When anyone believes that he is called to perform a mission, he must not permit himself to be influenced, he has the duty of doing that which he feels called upon to do. . . . Who is born to be a dictator will not be pressed, but must himself press forward. . . . Who feels himself called to rule a people has not the right to say: When you want me or send for me, I will come. He has the duty to do [what is necessary]. . . . I carry the responsibility all alone. I cannot concede that I am guilty, but I concede my deed."

When asked what post in the Third Reich he would take, Hitler answered proudly: "I wish to be nothing more than the drummer for the Third Reich!" On March 22, in his closing address, Hitler declared:

"What I saw before my eyes, *that* was from the first day a thousand times more than merely to become a minister. I wished to be the destroyer of Marxism. I shall solve this problem, and when it is solved, then the title of minister will be for me only an absurdity. . . . Not from arrogance did I wish to be drummer; that is the highest post, the other is a little thing . . . Declare us a thousand times guilty, the gods of eternal justice in history will laughingly tear apart the pleas of the prosecution and the judgment of the court: for they will find us innocent.

"We encounter punishment because the enterprise failed. The deed of November 8 did not fail. It would have failed if a mother had come and said: 'Herr Hitler, you have also my child on your conscience.' But, I may assure you, no mother has come. On the contrary. Thousands of others have come and placed themselves in our ranks. Of the young men who fell, it will some day be said: 'These, too, died for the liberation of the Fatherland.' . . . I believe that the hour will come when the masses which today stand with our flags on the streets will be joined with those who fired on us on November 9. I believe that blood will not always divide us. Some day the hour will come when the Reichswehr will stand on our side, officers and men. The army which we have built grows from day to day, from hour to hour more rapidly. . . ."

On April 1, 1924, the court handed down its decision. Ludendorff was held "not guilty" and released. Hitler, Weber, Kriebel, and Pöhner were fined two hundred marks each (or twenty days imprisonment in lieu thereof), plus five years' imprisonment with a recommendation of clemency for good behaviour and considerable praise in the sentence for Hitler's war record and his patriotism. The time already served was to be deducted from the terms. Frick, Röhm, Wagner, Pernet, and Brückner were sentenced to one year and three months. Wagner was at once paroled, and the others were paroled within six months. Hitler and Ludendorff were cheered by the crowds. On October 1, 1924, official steps were taken to secure Hitler's release. The state prosecutor objected. The highest Bavarian court overruled his objections. On December 20, 1924, he was freed. The others were the beneficiaries of a comparable leniency. By New Year's Day of 1925 they were all at large once more.[1]

During the interval Hitler and most of his colleagues remained in the prison fortress of Landsberg am lech. He had a large sunny room and many privileges. In all things the warden showed him special consideration, for here was no ordinary criminal, but a great patriotic leader of a patriotic cause which—who could say?—was perhaps not yet lost. Every evening Hitler could talk with his fellow inmates and friends. A month after his incarceration he was given permission to walk two hours a day outside the walls. The Bavarian spring was beautiful. But the prisoner of honour was morose and dejected. His brave optimistic words now sounded a little hollow. He wanted action, drama, artistry, excitement—the thrill and glory of rescuing his foster-mother Deutschland from her enemies. Instead he had got the insufferable boredom of prison routine. For a man without literary interests, incapable of enjoyable introspection, devoid of all subtlety in thought, and wholly the plaything of powerful prejudices and strong emotions, prison life was unendurable even among friends. There were devoted followers here, in addition to visitors and those sentenced with him. Other Nazi leaders had been incarcerated quietly after less spectacular trials. Brückner was particularly solicitous and encouraging. Rudolf Hess idolized him. So did young Ekkehard—to the point of jealousy of Hess. But Göring

[1] Cf. Karl Brammer: *Der Hitler-Ludendorff Prozess* (Berlin, 1924); Theodore Heuss: *Hitler's Weg*, pp. 5–15; Tacitus Redivivus: *Die Grosse Trommel*, pp. 93–101; Ernst Ottwalt: *Deutschland Erwache!* pp. 211–26; *Völkischer Beobachter*, March 27, 1934 and April 1, 1934.

was in exile. Feder was he knew not where. Dietrich Eckart had died shortly after the putsch—at Obersalzburg, near Berchtesgaden, on December 26, 1923. The dream of the Third Reich was a memory and a hope.

"What a man wills, that he hopes and believes." Hitler willed ultimate victory, therefore he hoped for ultimate victory and believed in it. But again he had encountered frustration. The artist in him had been frustrated. The architect had been frustrated. The soldier had been ultimately and bitterly frustrated. And now the politician was frustrated. Prison life was duller than his old poverty-stricken boredom in pre-war Vienna and Munich. That had been duller than barrack life. And barrack life had been dull compared to the fiery heroism of the trenches. He wanted action and struggle. Victory he wanted desperately. He had been cheated of it so often. It was self-fulfilment, self-realization, the end of struggle, the only thing to give meaning to the world he carried about within him. This world was strangely sealed from contact with outer reality. And yet it touched intimately the world of other frustrated and wounded spirits—so intimately that it symbolized a strange, fantastic life of delirium and dreams, born of the loneliness of man and the eternal doom of human aspiration. This life *must* be made true or else life had no meaning. But the imperative echoed dully against the walls of Landsberg.

Whether Hitler devoted much conscious thought to his mistakes of political strategy is doubtful. No hint of this appears in the pages which he wrote in prison. But these pages deliberately stopped short of the Bürgerbräu putsch. These mistakes he was never to repeat again. The wisdom of experience almost always assumed with him the form of feelings and intuitions rather than of generalized principles deduced from observation. After Landsberg he knew intuitively that certain things were too dangerous to be attempted and that certain other things were unwise. He knew that men of the reaction could be useful in crises, but that they would always use him for their own purposes and would discard him (or attempt to) when he no longer seemed to them useful. They were therefore not to be trusted beyond the point where safe retreat was still possible. He knew that his own converted party comrades were trustworthy. Only later was he to learn that in such a party as he had created this trust, too, could easily be misplaced. He knew that in a real test of power, oratory and parades were not substitutes for force. And he knew above all that such force as he could mobilize could never be adequate to overcome the troops and police of the State in open combat. Such combat must therefore be avoided at all costs.

As a soldier he had learned never to risk battle when the enemy's superiority is so great as to ensure defeat. As a politician he knew now that the same rule applied. Force as pageantry—uniforms, flags, music, parades—was good propaganda, and by propaganda one could win thousands and perhaps millions and thus immobilize the forces of the State and prevent them from being used against one's cause. Force against Marxists (out of public office) was good. But force as a weapon with which to attack the State openly was suicide. The masses must be won and power must be sought within the law, however oppressive the law might be. His democratic parliamentary enemies could be trusted always to leave him some field for effective action. Legality above all must be the watchword. And if power could be conquered by legal means, then the police forces and the army of the State would be at one's disposal to use as one saw fit. They served the State. One must therefore take the State not by storm, but by strategy and treachery and scheming. Having taken the State, having *become* the State, one could then use its forces in one's own cause. One would then have force to the utmost at one's disposal, as well as a claim to universal obedience, instrumentalities of propaganda more effective (in the right hands) than all others, and jobs, spoils, patronage, favours available for distribution among one's followers and friends.

These elementary lessons of politics sank deeply, albeit sometimes unconsciously, into the mind of the would-be dictator. And they brought hope and energy and determination. Landsberg, after all, was not St. Helena. Landsberg was not even Elba, for with wisdom and foresight the battle of the future might as well be Austerlitz as Waterloo. Brückner and Hess kept urging Hitler to write the story of his life instead of dawdling morosely with his gloomy thoughts. He finally yielded to their suggestions. To produce his autobiography at the age of thirty-five did not seem to him conceited or preposterous. He threw himself vigorously into the task and made the work at once an apologia, a confession of faith, a manual of politics, and a promise of future victory. A title? *Mein Kampf,* of course. My Struggle—for Deutschland's awakening. He wrote abominably, but no matter. Here was a new form of self-expression, the best to be had when all others were lacking—and it brought him joy. Hundreds of pages poured forth from his pen. Two volumes would be needed for such a "life." The second he completed later. Prudence dictated that nothing be said about November 1923 and its aftermath. His last pages were to close on a more popular note: preparation for the attack on France; the crime of the Ruhr; *"Notwehr als Recht"* for the last chapter; the restoration of the German fighting spirit—and then rearmament. "On the day that Marxism is smashed in Germany, her chains will in truth be broken for all time."[1] And, finally, homage to the eighteen hero dead who fell before the Feldherrnhalle—and thanks to Dietrich Eckart.

Five days before Christmas 1924 Hitler left Landsberg a free man. On one of his last days the warden paid him a courtesy call. He was most sympathetic—even admiring. He finally admitted his conversion: "Herr Hitler, I also am a Nationalsocialist."

[1] *Mein Kampf,* p. 775; cf. Lengyel: *Hitler,* pp. 99–107.

BOOK ONE

THE CONQUEST OF POWER

CHAPTER II

NSDAP: THE PARTY

1. RESURRECTION

THE party which was to destroy the Republic of Weimar in 1933 was, a decade earlier, in a state of complete disorganization. Following the Bürgerbräu debacle of November 8 and 9, 1923, the movement was dissolved, its funds and properties were confiscated, the S.A. was suppressed, and the *V.B.* was forbidden to continue publication. Hitler and other party leaders were sentenced to Landsberg on April 1, 1924. Those leaders who had escaped arrest were in exile or in hiding. The NSDAP was apparently dead—and its life had seemed no more than a somewhat sour comic-opera episode of the troubled years between Versailles and the Ruhr.

This popular impression was temporarily dispelled by the Reichstag election of May 4, 1924. During the fourteen months of Hitler's imprisonment the party was by no means inactive, despite its "suppression." Hitler himself apparently played no role as a leader during this period, though the privileges accorded to him at Landsberg might well have given him opportunities for doing so. He occupied himself with the writing of *Mein Kampf*. His representative outside was the druggist Gregor Strasser, formerly leader of the S.A. of Lower Bavaria. He too had been arrested in November, 1923, but was released in the following April. He busied himself with propaganda and reorganization activities. He was a soldier, a fighter, and a socialist—that is, a Nationalsocialist who took his "socialism" seriously. His creed was a melange of nationalism, collectivism, and *Kultur*. "Socialism in the old true sense, not in the international false sense, is: the spirit of collectivism plus the principle of achievement (*Gemeinschaftsgeist plus Leistungsprinzip*). Socialism—is the old officers' corps. Socialism—is the Cologne Cathedral. Socialism—is the wall of an old imperial city."[1] Gregor Strasser was above all devotedly loyal to Hitler and did everything in his power to keep the remnants of the movement together in Hitler's name.

This task was no easy one. There was much dissension within the ranks, with various leaders striving to unite the party under their own authority or endeavouring to take their followers with them into other political camps. Hermann Esser and Julius Streicher, the Nürnberg leader, sought to repudiate Hitler. Pöhner endeavoured to lead his supporters back into the ranks of the Nationalist Party, and in this he found support from Dr. Buttmann, leader of the Nazis in the Bavarian Landtag. The Bavarian People's Party also sought to enlist the Nazi rank and file among its own supporters. Ludendorff was at first indifferent. Kriebel and Röhm went their own way. Gregor Strasser, with the aid of Alfred Rosenberg, resisted clerical and reactionary blandishments and struggled to keep the Bavarian party organization intact. Strasser likewise attempted to extend the organization into north Germany. For this purpose he concluded an alliance with Herr Albrecht von Graefe of Mecklenburg, leader of another reactionary anti-Semitic group, the German Racial Freedom Party, which had Count Reventlow and Herr Wülle among its champions. It was this combination, under the name of the National Socialist German Freedom Movement, which nominated candidates for the Reichstag prior to the elections of May 4, 1924. To the astonishment of everyone, it secured almost two million votes and elected thirty-two representatives, including von Graefe, Wülle, Ludendorff, Röhm, Frick, Feder, Roth, Dolle, and Fritsch.

But this unexpected triumph was illusory and shortlived. It was due to the powerful appeal which the Nazi propaganda made to a middle class and a peasantry still impressed with the effects of the Ruhr invasion and of the inflation. The movement might have developed had middle-class insecurities continued or had the party established an effective central organization. Both of these conditions were lacking. The leaders quarrelled—in part because of friction between the Bavarian Catholic NSDAP and its Protestant Prussian allies in the north. By the end of the year, moreover, the *Kleinbürgertum* felt less disgruntled with the status quo. The Reichstag fac-

[1] Quoted in Edgar Schmidt-Pauli: *Die Männer um Hitler* (Berlin: Verlag für Kulturpolitik; 1932), p. 117.

tion devoted much energy to denouncing the Allies, the United States, and General Dawes. The Reichstag, however, adopted the Dawes Plan on August 30, 1924, over the opposition of the Nazi group, supported by its bitterest enemies, the Communists, and by some of its rivals among the Nationalists. In the Reichstag election of December 7, 1924, the party lost over half its supporters. It secured only 907,000 votes and retained only fourteen seats in parliament.[1]

Two weeks later Hitler left Landsberg. He was free to resume his political activities, save that the Social Democratic government of Prussia forbade him to engage in public speaking for three years —a ban which was a tribute to his oratorical prowess rather than a serious obstacle in the way of his efforts to reorganize the party. For six weeks he collected funds, conferred with leaders, loyal and disloyal, rallied his supporters, and prepared for a resumption of active work. On February 26, 1925, the *Völkischer Beobachter* resumed publication in Munich. It proclaimed the rebirth of the party, the revival of the S.A., and the renewal of the struggle against the most fearful enemies of the German people: Marxism and Jewry and their allies, the Centrum and the Democratic Party.

On the evening of February 27 Hitler again addressed the multitude in the first mass meeting of the new era. Again he harangued the mob in the Bürgerbräu, where he had so dramatically and hopefully proclaimed the "revolution" fifteen months before. Again huge crowds filled the hall long before the meeting was to begin. Herr Amann presided and introduced Hitler. Again the Austrian corporal, in the role of the Messiah, denounced the Allies, the Democrats, the Jews, and the Marxists. "Marxism can only be destroyed through a better idea and through the power of a great popular movement. The road to the heart of the people lies not in instruction and pleading, but only in ideas and power." The movement has nothing to do with religion. It is no sect, but a tool for the attainment of its single great end: the liberation of the German people. All the old Nazis must rally to the cause. Whoever cannot or will not come along, let him stay away. But let no one appeal to Hitler. *He* had founded the old party and he alone would dictate its goals and its methods. He alone would assume complete responsibility. "The

[1] On the developments of this period, see Ernst Ottwalt: *Deutschland Erwache!* pp. 248ff.; Emil Lengyel: *Hitler,* pp. 108ff.; René Laurent: *Le National-Socialisme. Vers le troisieme Reich* (Paris: Hachette; 1932), pp. 81–2.

hour will come in which the NSDAP will conquer. . . ." Buttmann and Esser agreed to dissolve their factions. Streicher, Feder, and Frick joined them in swearing fealty to Der Führer. The meeting was an unqualified success.[1]

But the road to party unity remained steep and stony. Hitler, Rosenberg, and Gregor Strasser worked against heavy obstacles. The fourteen Nazi members of the Reichstag were by no means united in acknowledging Hitler as leader. The party locals in north Germany were Protestant, radical, and genuinely socialistic. Gregor Strasser sympathized with their sentiments, though he himself was Catholic. His brother Otto was even more extreme. The German Racial Freedom Party was an awkward ally. Hitler decided to support Ludendorff as the party's candidate in the presidential election of March 29, 1925, but the northern allies supported Jarres, the Nationalist candidate. Ludendorff received fewer than 300,000 votes. In the second election of April 26 he withdrew and all reactionary groups, including the NSDAP, supported Hindenburg. Hitler, moreover, found it expedient to abandon his anti-clericalism and to "make his peace with Rome," much to the disgust of Count Reventlow. This cleavage made the northern alliance increasingly precarious.

The Weimar party convention (*Partei Tag*) of June 26, 1925, passed off without an open break, with ten thousand men participating in the ceremonies. In December 1925 another convention was held in Hanover. It was called by the Strasser brothers as an assembly of all the northern and western *Gauleiters* to build up a counterweight to the "unsocialist" Munich party leadership. Hitler sent Feder as his representative. Feder found the gathering predominantly anti-Hitler. "We will not be governed by the Munich Pope," was the cry. Otto Strasser attacked the rich, preached the socialization of wealth, and advocated a kind of anti-democratic, anti-Marxist Marxism. Feder dissociated Hitler's name from all such "disruptive" aims. But the meeting voted in favour of the confiscation of the property of the princes, a decision which Hitler subsequently denounced. Following this meeting, the alliance with the German Racial Freedom Party was definitely severed.

This rift between the "Left" and "Right" wings of the NSDAP was to become a permanent one. It was ultimately to lead to conflict,

[1] Cf. "*Der entscheidende Tag*" by Wilhelm Frick, *V. B.*, February 24, 1934.

revolt, suppression, expulsion, and at last to wholesale murder. The anti-Hitler group at the Hanover convention of 1925 represented substantially the same elements which were to constitute the Left opposition later. Hitler's original tactics of using red posters and socialistic slogans, his acceptance of "socialism" (national) and of Gottfried Feder's economic doctrines, his attacks upon "capitalism" and the "bourgeois" parties were to lead to the acquisition of a great mass following. But they were to bear bitter fruit. A movement led by demagogues who were all things to all men necessarily became a movement of incongruous elements divided against themselves. The socialistic radicals in the party, typified by Otto Strasser and to some degree by his brother Gregor, could never in the long run accept the domination of the party by a conservative leadership in the pay of property-owners and industrialists. In this cleavage were the germs of dissension and tragedy.

Hitler's own position was never in doubt. After Landsberg he was pledged to "legality." Revolutionary methods of achieving power must be eschewed. As for the purposes for which power would be used, as for the groups in the community who would be the beneficiaries of a seizure of power, convenient obscurity must be maintained. Labour and the more radical *Kleinbürgertum* were promised socialism. The peasantry was promised an end of "interest slavery" and the partition of the great estates. The mass of the *Kleinbürgertum* was promised dissolution of trusts, municipalization of department stores, and economic security. The upper bourgeoisie was promised salvation from Marxism and the destruction of trade unionism. Everybody was promised the elimination of the Jews, the rearmament of the Reich, and "national liberation." Such was the appeal of this "National," "Socialist," "German," "Labour" party. But Hitler knew, not by rational analysis, but by intuition, where the fountain-heads of power were to be found. Peasants, burghers, and workers could supply only the mass following. Power could be won only by converting the élite—or by causing it to support the movement for its own ends. Power lay with the industrialists, the financiers, the feudal military caste, and the aristocracy of money—the very groups most bitterly assailed by the Marxists and by the "socialists" of the NSDAP. In every crisis within the party ranks between the socialistic radicals and the conservatives Hitler was to side with the latter—out of preference, out of conviction, and out of long-run considerations of political expediency. Such a movement as he had created might win power and rule with the acquiescence and support of the ruling classes. It could never gain power and rule against them.

The conservatism of the Munich headquarters triumphed over the radicalism of the party locals at the Bamberg conference held in the spring of 1926. Gregor Strasser was prepared to expound his theory of a truly socialist Nazi State. He brought with him as his aide his new secretary, Dr. Paul Joseph Goebbels. Hitler's conservative followers, however, had a safe majority. The young Goebbels, who was far more astute and intelligent than his employer, took in the situation at a glance. He too was a "socialist." But advancement, he perceived, lay in a different direction. He deserted Strasser and aligned himself with Hitler. Munich triumphed over the radical north without an open break and without a vote. The NSDAP never reached decisions by debating and balloting, for these were devices of the despised parliamentary system. The party program of twenty-five points was declared unalterable on May 22, 1926—and therewith was an end to all discussion of whether it should be made more "socialistic" or less so. By the time of the great party convention at Weimar early in July, unity was restored and the authority of Hitler and of the Bavarian conservatives was recognized. The Left wing swallowed its fears and suspicions. Hitler at least talked socialism and sounded like a radical revolutionary. Perhaps all would yet be well.

Hitler's technique for the resolution of inner party conflicts was as simple as it was effective. He minimized those issues and proposals which created friction, and emphasized those upon which all party members were agreed. This involved persistent searching for the lowest possible emotional denominators of the incongruous elements within the movement. The results of this technique were clearly revealed in the great "Party Day" at Nürnberg, August 19–21, 1927. Delegates came in special trains from all parts of the Reich, and from Danzig, the Saar, Austria, Switzerland, and Czechoslovakia as well. The headquarters in the Deutscher Hof buzzed with activity. Hitler and his staff had already developed their peculiar skill in organizing and conducting great conventions. At eleven o'clock Saturday morning, August 20, the delegates assembled in the Kulturvereinshaus, not to deliberate or debate, but to listen to speeches and to applaud. Hitler wore a S.A. uniform. Julius Streicher opened the meeting by honouring the party dead and by denouncing the Jews. He gave praise to his native city for having driven out the Jews in the Middle Ages and for having hanged those who refused to leave. Gregor Strasser followed with further denunciations of Israel. Wilhelm Frick, a Nazi member of the Reichstag, then delivered an address on the evils of democracy and the virtues of the *Führerprinzip:*

"The contemporary democratic parliamentary system means the domination of those who are inferior, of those who are of the lower races, of money and of the Jews. . . . We Nationalsocialists in the Reichstag will hail the day when the well-known lieutenant with ten men puts a deserved and dishonoured end (by legal means, of course) to this whole devilish sham (*Teufelspuk*) and thereby frees the road for the deed of rescue, for the racial dictatorship. . . ."[1]

Dr. Buttmann concurred: the aim of the Nazis in the State legislatures was also the destruction of the System. He denounced the Dawes Plan and the League of Nations as devices to perpetuate German enslavement. Speeches and more speeches. Count Reventlow denounced Locarno, Stresemann, and Geneva. The Reich had disgraced itself by entering the League. It must withdraw. As for General Dawes, he was no "general," but merely the agent of Morgan and of Jewish *Hochfinanz* in New York. Gottfried Feder proved to the satisfaction of all that the Treaty of Versailles was the source of all of Germany's economic difficulties. Goebbels spoke on the art of propaganda: "Propaganda does not need to be rich in mental content, but it must be effective." . . . The anti-Semitic movement is a half-century old, but it needs a new propaganda technique. The party must rest not on intelligence, but on faith. Christ wrote no programs, said Goebbels, but preached a new world in the Sermon on the Mount: Love your neighbour as yourself. Rousseau and Marx wrote books. They remained idle books until thousands of agitators preached their gospel. This lesson was appreciated by the great propagandists of the past and present—Bebel, Lenin, Mussolini. . . .[2]

1 Alfred Rosenberg: *Der Reichsparteitag der N.S.D.A.P. Nürnberg, 19–21 August 1927* (Munich: Eher; 1927), p. 13.
2 Ibid., pp. 30f.

On Sunday Feder presided. Alfred Rosenberg spoke on *"Internationaler Weltstaat und nationale Raumpolitik."* He cited Hans Grimm's best seller, *Volk ohne Raum,* and commented:

"We are not only a people without room, but also in the opposite sense: the territory on which sixty-two million German-speaking peoples live is a room without a people. To place a people in this empty room is the internal political mission of Nationalsocialism; to create then the room for the coming hundred million Germans is the objective of Nationalsocialist foreign policy. . . ."

The worst of all crimes was the theft of German territory by the victors in the Great War. The world is ruled by internationalism and by the hegemony of the Banks and Bourse which began in Paris, where the Jews were first emancipated. Down with Rathenau and the House of Rothschild! Down with international Jewish capitalism! Down with the Strausses and with Bernard Baruch and Julius Klein, the Jew dictators of America! The first effective revolt against the Jewish international world State was Italian Fascism, which destroyed Freemasonry and Bolshevism. But the Jewish International is so powerful that only international action against it can be effective. The banks, the press, Freemasonry, Communism, the League of Nations, and Zionists are its tools.

"The Second and Third Internationals were and are only the tools of Finance for the destruction of racial defence. . . . Our obvious duty is to support all anti-Semitic movements in all States. . . . On the other hand, we must do everything to create an anti-Semitic movement in our own land to fight Jewish domination."

Down with Einstein and Lessing! Down with France, Poland, and the Little Entente! England and Italy must choose. Germany must endeavour to create an anti-French coalition. Russia is going to pieces.

"In the Ukraine a conscious nationalist movement is developing which we must follow with the closest attention. . . . Germany offers France coverage in the west for a free hand in the east. Germany offers England the protection of India on the Russo-Polish frontier (a conception of Bismarck's) and flank coverage against France. Germany offers Italy pressure on the south Slavs and coverage against France; the Ukraine, industry and coverage against Poland. *Das sind raumpolitische bündniswege!"* [1]

[1] Ibid., pp. 37–8.

This powerfully intoxicating infusion evoked an ovation. Hitler went up to shake Rosenberg's hand. Then Der Führer himself: War is coming. Power and more power are needed. Power consists of population (Germany's sixty-two millions are insufficient), territory (Germany's lands are pitifully small), and the inner strength of a people which rests upon capacity, self-reliance, and race-consciousness—

"If a people of today follows the theory of being able to find happiness in eternal peace and seeks to live according to this theory, it must some day go to ruin from this most primitive variety of cowardice. Pacifism is the most outspoken cowardice. . . . We have come into this political life as soldiers. . . . If I wish to bind our people together in unity, I must first create a new front which has a common enemy before it, so that everyone knows that we must be one since this enemy is the enemy of us all. . . . And when anyone says: you are imperialists, then ask him: Are you unwilling to be one? If not, then never dare to become a father, for if you beget a child you must provide its daily bread. And if you provide bread, then you are an imperialist! [Stormy applause.]" [1]

Hitler spoke further of honour and of the party's mission. Germany has no national flag. The party flag must become the national flag of the future by being identified with the national awakening. In closing, the Leader praised the delegates for paying their own fares, buying their own torches, and standing ready for new sacrifices for the cause. The convention resolved to set up a party school committee on educational questions; to establish party labour unions; to champion the constitutional rights of the *Beamtenschaft,* especially freedom of political opinion and freedom to change opinions; to eject all Jews from the Reich; and to establish a Nazi news service and a Nazi learned society. The parade and the consecration of the standards were most impressive. S.A. men, twenty thousand strong, marched with flaming torches, accompanied by S.S. detachments and a thousand Hitler Jugend. Hitler touched the standard of each delegation with the sacred flag of 1923 and re-presented it to its bearer. "Vienna: take this standard as a symbol of the indivisibility of our movement until the shame-treaties of Versailles and Saint-Germain are broken." "Bochum: bear this standard as you have borne the brunt of the struggle against the French in-

[1] Ibid., pp. 42–3.

vasion." "Essen: I give you this standard as representative of the old armoury-city of the German Reich." Etc. Thirty thousand men marched by to receive the salute of Der Führer. Here once more was pageantry and power—and the promise of greater glory to come.

2. DER FÜHRER AND HIS AIDES

THE Hitler of this period was by all odds the most unusual and extraordinary party leader in the Reich. He was still an alien Austrian and took no steps to acquire German citizenship. He could not therefore become a candidate for any public office. He was not interested in offices—not yet. He was a German neither in nationality nor in appearance nor in temperament nor in his mode of life. He had, to be sure, been a soldier; he liked dogs and Wagnerian music; and he was not averse to patting children on the head and beaming benignly at the populace. But in his posturing he accentuated precisely his un-German characteristics, for these strange traits somehow fascinated multitudes and contributed to the illusion of the Heaven-sent saviour of the Reich. He was thin, intense, fanatical. The German burghers to whom he appealed were, most of them, fat, stolid, phlegmatic. Because of gall-bladder trouble, he eschewed alcohol and drank only mineral water. His Germans were prodigious drinkers and consumed beer in amazing quantities. He avoided meat and professed himself a vegetarian. His Germans consumed mountains of sausages and *Sauerbraten* and *Wienerschnitzel*. He lived like an ascetic—or seemed to. His Germans were gourmands and addicted to the pleasures of the flesh. He avoided sports and popular recreation. His Germans preached and practised body culture and loved wine, women, and song—nowhere more so than in Bavaria. He was a bachelor and shunned women like the plague. His Germans were fathers and Hausfraus with many children. He was crude, ungrammatical, and contemptuous of intellect. His Germans were cultured and deferential toward Ph.D.'s and professors.

Here was the man who was to win the almost mystical adoration of the *Kleinbürgertum* and the peasantry. For he seemed the embodiment of those virtues to which millions of Germans aspired and to which few could attain: sobriety, chastity, asceticism, self-denial. Economic privation forbade self-indulgence, and resentment at this imposed self-denial was appropriately rationalized: flesh-pots (symbolized by profiteers, Jews, and the Marxian "materialists") were evil; sacrifice and flagellation were good. But the German bourgeoisie, having lived too long on the flesh-pots, could not embrace asceticism openly. It must enjoy self-denial vicariously. In Hitler it could indulge its asceticism to its heart's content.

Such was the saviour. His private life was a mystery, save to a few intimates. After the movement waxed strong and profitable, he lived comfortably in a nine-room house on Prinzregentenstrasse, Munich, with a married couple: his butler and his cook. He had three cars and often spent week-ends in his *Landhaus* on Starnbergersee, in the Bavarian Alps. He received visitors graciously in elegant and tasteful rooms. Before his aides and subordinates he posed—and often raged and shouted to inspire respect and fear and to galvanize his followers with his own dynamism. But the public saw only a smallish man with a lumpy, pasty face, a peasant head compounded of Teuton and Slav, heavy straight black hair falling boyishly over an unintellectual brow, an absurd smudge of Chaplin moustache beneath a thick, sharp nose, a sensitive mouth, an aggressive jaw bespeaking stubbornness and energy. At meetings and demonstrations he wore the S.A. brown-shirt uniform or, more frequently, the inconspicuous democratic garb of a drummer: soft fedora hat, black tie, white shirt, dark suit, and the inevitable tan raincoat.

When he spoke from the platform, he shouted and pleaded with his artist's hands and often brushed his forelock carelessly back from his perspiring brow. Fire glowed in soft mystic eyes that were otherwise dull and lifeless. The magic of his oratory baffled foreigners. Here was no subtlety, no brilliance, only a hoarse staccato of well-worn phrases, rising to screaming crescendos of passion. Here was an unpolished voice reiterating over and over again, with humourless gravity and terrible earnestness, what its audiences wanted to hear. But for Germans here was salvation. The importance of the message was judged not by its content, but by the emotionalism of its delivery. Shouting was confused with wisdom; delirium with sincerity; cloudy obscurities, shot through with Wagnerian thunder, with insight and inspiration. . . .[1]

[1] Cf. Walter Oehme and Kurt Caro, *Kommt "Das Dritte Reich"?* (Berlin: Rowohlt; 1931), pp. 105–9.

The men around Der Führer were as interesting and variegated a lot as had gathered around him in 1921–3. Some of the old stalwarts were again to be found in the party headquarters in Munich. Some new figures were there, later destined to enjoy power. Rudolf Hess was again Hitler's secretary and adjutant. After the putsch he had lived for six months in the mountains, evading the police. He was caught in 1924, arrested, and sent to Landsberg. After his release he became an assistant in the Deutsche Akademie through his friendship with Karl Haushofer, Professor of Geopolitik in the University of Munich. In the spring of 1925 he became Hitler's personal secretary and held this post for many years thereafter.[1]

Röhm had been arrested in November 1923 and put in Stadelheim Prison, where Dietrich Eckart was slowly dying. He, too, was soon released. In the election of May 1924 he was elected to the Reichstag as a Nazi representative. Later he founded another private military organization, the Frontbann, subsequently merged with the S.A. His loyalties were divided when Ludendorff and Hitler parted ways. He gave up his commissions in the S.A. and the Frontbann and returned to civil life. In 1928 he became military adviser of the Bolivian government in its perennial war with Paraguay. In October of 1930 Hitler called him back from South America to assume leadership of the S.A. He then became Chief of Staff and supreme commander of the storm troops immediately under Hitler.

Göring, wounded on November 9, had fled to Austria with his wife and thence to Italy, where he recovered his health. He spent several years in Italy and in Sweden. In 1925 he was again in Stockholm, working for an aircraft company. His frail wife was now afflicted with tuberculosis. The Swedish courts refused the couple control of the boy, Thomas Kantzow (his wife's son by her first husband), on the ground of the mother's epilepsy and the stepfather's addiction to morphia. On September 1, 1925, he was admitted to the Langbro Asylum for treatment, since his narcotic habits had rendered him unbalanced and irresponsible.[2] He recovered ultimately and resumed

[1] Edgar Schmidt-Pauli: *Die Männer um Hitler,* pp. 99–104.

[2] On page 133 of *The Brown Book of the Hitler Terror,* by the World Committee for the Victims of German Fascism (New York: Knopf; 1933), appear photographic facsimiles of Göring's registration card in the asylum and of Dr. A. R. Lundberg's statement as to the unfitness of the Görings to care for Thomas Kantzow. So far as the author has been able to determine, the authenticity of these documents has never been successfully disputed.

work. Under the amnesty of 1926 the former war-ace was able to return to Germany, where he resumed contact with Hitler and was elected to the Reichstag on the Nazi ticket in 1928. He became a member of the Reichsleitung of the party in 1930 and was re-elected to the Reichstag. In the spring of 1931 he visited Italy as a representative of the NSDAP and was received by Mussolini and also at the Vatican.

Göring's wife died in Stockholm, October 17, 1931. His bitterness at her death increased rather than diminished his restless energy and ambition. The one-time handsome aviator was corpulent now—a great, rotund man with a ruddy face, thin lips, and steely eyes. His *"Prunksucht,"* or passion for splendour and display, waxed with his vanity and his ambition. He lived in luxury and consorted with the Crown Prince and Fritz Thyssen. Exotic costumes and uniforms were his delight. He surrounded himself with ostentatious elegance, with ancient arms, with portraits of his heroes: Napoleon, Frederick the Great, Bismarck, and Mussolini—even of Balbo and Baron von Richthofen, though these were Jews. He was not a man to appeal to the multitude. But he was wealthy, polished, and aristocratic. And he was energetic, ruthless, and hard—a good organizer and a man capable of brutality, fit to execute daring and unscrupulous schemes. For this Hitler valued him.[1]

Alfred Rosenberg likewise resumed his old connection with the party. This Russian émigré had escaped arrest in the Munich putsch and later returned to the Reich to engage in journalism and other literary activities. He resumed his editorship of the *V.B.* and poured forth an endless stream of pamphlets and books, which became an important part of the literature of the movement: *The Protocols of the Elders of Zion and Jewish World Policy* (1923), *Bourse and Marxism—The Lord and the Slave* (1924), *International High Finance as the Ruler of the Labour Movement in All Countries* (1925), *Dietrich Eckart* (1927), *The Future Road of German Foreign Policy* (1927), *Houston Stewart Chamberlain as the Prophet and Founder of a German Future* (1927), *The World Conspirators' Congress at Basel* (1927), *Thirty November Heads* (1927), *Freemasonic World Policy in the Light of Critical Research* (1929), *The Swamp—A Sketch of the "Intellectual" Life of the November Democracy* (1930), etc., etc. His most erudite and ambitious work,

[1] Schmidt-Pauli, op. cit., 86–91.

almost seven hundred pages in length, was published in 1930 under the title of *The Myth of the Twentieth Century—An Evaluation of the Spiritual-Intellectual Value Conflict of Our Time* (Munich: Hoheneichen). In 1930 Rosenberg was elected to the Reichstag. As a member of the Reichsleitung of the NSDAP, he represented the party on the Foreign Affairs Committee of the Reichstag. In April 1931 he became chief editor of the *N.S. Monatshefte.* In December 1931 he was sent to London on a special political mission. Not only was he the chief writer and official philosopher of the movement, but he became its foreign-policy expert and was later made head of the *Aussenpolitische Amt der NSDAP,* the Foreign-Policy Bureau of the party. It was he who said on one occasion that when Hitler gained power every telegraph pole between Munich and Berlin would be decorated with the head of a prominent Jew.[1]

Among the most interesting and valuable of the new recruits was Dr. Paul Joseph Goebbels. This master propagandist was born on October 29, 1897, in the town of Rheydt in the Rhineland, near Düsseldorf. He was afflicted with a club-foot from birth. This, coupled with his extraordinarily Semitic features and a Jewish sharpness of tongue and mind, has at various times caused his enemies to whisper dark hints about his ancestry—the more so as the Nazi doctrine of race holds that hereditary physical defects are due to "blood-mixture." These allegations, however, would appear to be unfounded. His father, Fritz, was the son of Catholic peasant parents and was himself a farmer and the manager of a small business enterprise. His mother, Maria Oldenhausen, was the daughter of a blacksmith. Her mother had been the daughter of a labourer. The mother of the widow whom Paul Joseph was to marry, however, had herself married a Jew as her second husband—and after his death continued to bear his name until she saw the light and reverted to her first husband's name.[2] Paul began his studies in the Catholic *Volkschule* at Rheydt and then went to the *Gymnasium.* He was seventeen when the war broke out, but his infirmity made military service impossible. Aided by Catholic scholarships, he spent his next seven years studying history, literature, philology, and art in various universities: Bonn, Freiburg, Würzburg, Munich, Cologne, Berlin. In 1921 he

[1] Schmidt-Pauli, op. cit., pp. 170–6, and Kurt Rosten: *Das ABC des Nationalsozialismus* (Berlin: Schmidt; 1933), pp. 273–5.

[2] Cf. René Laurent: *Le National-Socialisme,* p. 121, and Rosten, op. cit., p. 263.

took his Ph. D. at Heidelberg, where he was much influenced by Professor Friedrich Gundolf, a liberal Jewish Shaksperian scholar.

Goebbels apparently learned of the NSDAP for the first time in Munich in 1922, when he attended one of its meetings. He was active in student politics, but did not then join the Nazi movement. He had literary ambitions and wrote poetry and plays, most of them bad. His efforts to get his drama *Der Wanderer* accepted by the Frankfurt Theatre in January 1924 were unsuccessful, though three years later it was played at the Nazi Volksbühne in Berlin. During the French occupation of the Ruhr he was active in organizing resistance and, under a pseudonym, even seems to have created Nazi units. On one occasion he alleged that he was whipped in a Belgian prison. It was in 1924 that he joined the party. He became editor of the *Völkische Freiheit* in Elberfeld and served as journalist, organizer, and agitator in the Ruhr. In collaboration with Gregor Strasser, he issued the *N.S. Briefe* in 1925, emphasizing the truly socialist character of the NSDAP. In the same year he became *Geschäftsführer* of the *Gau Rhein-Ruhr.*

Goebbels first won the attention of Hitler in 1926 when he deserted Strasser to support the Leader and the conservative wing of the party. His genius as propagandist and organizer, along with his reputation for radicalism, made him an ideal party leader for "Red Berlin," and he was named *Gauleiter* for the capital in October 1926, and later for the whole province of Brandenburg. Here he founded *Der Angriff* (The Attack), first as a bi-weekly, then as a daily paper. Under his direction it became the cleverest and most bitterly vitriolic of the Nazi propaganda sheets. He was extraordinarily skilful at invective against liberals, democrats, Marxists, Jews, and his competitors, the papers of the "Gutter Press" *(Asphaltpresse)*. He was elected to the Reichstag in 1928 and again in 1930. In 1929 he became Reich Propaganda Leader of the NSDAP. It was he who preached Nazi "socialism," organized the first Nazi shop-cells in 1931, and won part of the proletariat as well as the *Kleinbürgertum* of the capital to the cause.[1]

This small, subtle young man became the "brains" of the Nazi movement and entered the circle of Göring, Röhm, Rosenberg, Hess, and Frick immediately around Der Führer. Here was another twisted personality afflicted with terrific emotional overcompensa-

1 Schmidt-Pauli, op. cit., pp. 152–7; Oehme and Caro, op. cit., pp. 109–17.

tions for his physical infirmity and thereby driven furiously to action by boundless conceit and ambition. A flat brow with straight black hair brushed back and flanked by pointed, protruding ears. Piercing dark eyes in an angular, cadaverous face, deeply lined about the large, mobile mouth. Diminutive, emaciated, almost insignificant as he limped into meetings completely surrounded by S.A. or S.S. body-guards. But on the platform he was a wizard of demagoguery, with his resonant, penetrating voice, his keen, cynical intelligence, his satire and irony, his utter unscrupulousness in attack, and his restless hands with their fascinatingly delicate yet powerful gestures. In personal contact he was affable, smiling, almost shy. *"Der Junge ist richtig,"* the older party men were obliged to concede repeatedly. In *Der Angriff* he seethed volcanically and heaped scorn upon the System and all its works. He also wrote effective pamphlets full of catch-phrases: *Das Kleine ABC des Nationalsozialisten* (Griefswald, 1925), *Die zweite Revolution* (Zwickau, 1926), *Der Nazi-Sozi* (Munich, 1931), *Mjölnir—Die verfluchten Hakenkreuzler* (Munich, 1932), *Kampf um Berlin, Lenin oder Hitler,* etc.

Such were the aides of Der Führer. Between these men there was seldom harmony. Hitler had not grown up in vain in the Habsburg empire. *Divide et impera* was his motto within his own party, as within the Reich. By a nice balancing of conflicting ambitions and animosities he retained his own undisputed leadership. Amann and Rosenberg often quarrelled, as did Buttmann and Streicher. Göring detested the crippled intellectual, Goebbels. Goebbels scorned the grossness and crudity of Göring and Röhm. The Strasser brothers fell out—and the radical Otto, after his expulsion from the party in 1930, accused Gregor of remaining in the ranks only because of his financial dependence on the party. After Bamberg, Gregor Strasser and Goebbels were enemies and called one another *"Judenstämmlinge."* Between Rosenberg, Frick, Göring, and Goebbels no love was ever lost. These enmities among ambitious conspirators contained the germs of potential disintegration in so far as the leaders came to represent important rival groups within the party membership. But Hitler succeeded, with few exceptions, in holding the factions together during all the years of struggle and in welding them into a remarkably effective instrument for the conquest of the masses and the seizure of power.

3. THE MACHINE

The history of the Nazi party cannot be written until the voluminous records in the party archives are made available to scholars. This time is not yet in sight. Meanwhile reliance must be placed on such party materials as have been published, on newspaper and periodical sources, and on the circumstantial evidence of the course of events. The bulk of the literature published in Germany on the development of the party has been written as propaganda, either in praise of the movement or (prior to January 1933) in condemnation of it. Numerous phases of the party organization, to say nothing of the private lives of the leaders and their relationships with influential personalities of the German ruling classes, can be discussed only on the basis of conjecture. These difficulties always beset every effort in describing a revolutionary party. They are multiplied manyfold in the present instance by the circumstance that the NSDAP has been obliged, to a peculiar degree, to parade illusions before the German electorate and the world which are substantially at variance with the carefully concealed realities. Nevertheless, enough is known to make possible an analysis not merely of these illusions, but also to some extent of the stuff of which the dreams were made and of the dream-making machinery itself.

The dynamics of the party's growth may first be suggested in general terms. A political party aspiring to control the State—or to *become* the State—has at its disposal three fundamental techniques of power, which are not different in kind but only in degree from the techniques used by all States and by all ruling classes to evoke mass deference and obedience. These may be roughly characterized as force, propaganda, and the distribution of patronage and favours. Through the use of these techniques in various combinations, followers are won, supporters are unified, enemies are broken, submission is obtained—and a pattern of interrelationships is woven whereby power can be acquired, wielded, and preserved. A party in control of the State (that is, able to utilize the law-making and executive agencies of government for its own purposes, able to identify itself with the symbols of the State and thereby evoke the deference responses which these symbols elicit, able in a revolutionary situation to wipe out all competitors for popular favour) has violence, propaganda, and spoils at its disposal in infinitely greater quantity than has a party out of power. The NSDAP prior to 1933 was out of power and in the opposition. Before 1930 it had no opportunities, except on a small scale, to participate even in state or local government anywhere in Germany. Force and spoils were therefore available as instruments of growth and party discipline only to a slight extent. The armed forces of the State were in the hands of the enemy. Public posts and opportunities for winning, cajoling, or coercing various groups in the electorate through legislative and administrative measures were likewise not available.

Propaganda—that is, the systematic inculcation of emotional responses to collective symbols—had consequently to be the main reliance of the movement, both in gaining new converts and in keeping those already won. Violence, to be sure, could be used within narrow limits against dissidents and against political enemies and competitors outside of the ranks. But the exercise of this tool of power was sporadic and unsystematized prior to 1930. This was necessarily so in a party committed to "legality." As for spoils and patronage, there were hopes and promises of places on public payrolls, rather than actual posts available for distribution. But the party hierarchy itself, as it waxed large and prosperous, offered pelf and power to those favoured by Der Führer. Party speakers, editors of papers and periodicals, managers, organizers, and agitators were paid handsome stipends out of the party treasury. Prominent orators and journalists like Goebbels often got as much as 1,200 marks per month, the numerous secretaries in the central headquarters 400 marks, and subordinate clerks, organizers, messengers, etc., 150 to 300 marks monthly. The Reichsleitung of the party displayed great skill in distributing such jobs and used its power to enlarge and consolidate an extraordinarily effective political organization, paralleled (but not outmatched) only by the party machine of Social Democracy. But the organization itself was primarily a vast propaganda bureau. Even its militia, the S.A. and the S.S., were more effective as propaganda devices and as organization providing honours, titles, and incomes to deserving Nazis than as actual instruments of coercion.

Since available documentary records do not permit a detailed motion picture of the development of the party machine through its various phases, a static portrait of the organization as it had been perfected up to the 1930–3 period must suffice. The central agencies of the party were, in form, agencies of the N.S.D.A. Verein, established June 22, 1926, with its seat in Munich. But since the Verein was identical in leadership and organization with the NSDAP, this distinction had no practical significance. In the central Munich headquarters Hitler's frustrated ambitions as an architect found expression in the construction of an elaborate building, the famous Braunhaus at 45 Brienner Strasse, opposite the residence of Papal Nuncio. Completed at a cost of three-quarters of a million marks and paid for by a special assessment on the membership, this structure was a veritable palace. It was opened on July 5, 1930. In style it was simple, pleasing, and richly though tastefully decorated. Its square front, set back from the walk, faces on narrow fenced gardens and is broken by the main entrance in the centre, always guarded by uniformed S.A. men. Beyond the entrance is a large hall resembling a magnificent hotel lobby, with polished floors, swastika decorations on the ceiling, and a reception bureau to one side. Amid much coming and going of party officials and emissaries, there is always an atmosphere of order and military discipline. A wide staircase leads to the first floor (second floor by American reckoning). Here Hitler and his adjutant Hess have large suites of offices. In Hitler's simple study is a portrait of Frederick the Great and a bust of Mussolini. Near by is the *Senatorensaal,* which is the central unit of the whole structure. Before the door are two party standards surmounted by bronze eagles and two memorial tablets for the fallen heroes of the movement, decorated with large gilded evergreen wreaths. The *Saal* is decorated in red, with forty-two red leather chairs facing another row of chairs for the leaders. The upper floors contain other offices always humming with activity. Over the roof floats the *Hakenkreuz* flag. In the rear is a garden, and in the basement a wood-panelled restaurant and elaborate personnel records of the party membership.

The structure of the central party organization, most of the directors of which have offices in the Braunhaus, can best be suggested by the following outline, as of 1931–2.

THE REICH DIRECTORATE (REICHSLEITUNG)

A. Party and Highest S.A. Leader, President of the Nationalsocialist German Labor Society (*Partei-und-oberster S.A. Führer, Vorsitzender der NSDAV*)—Adolf Hitler

B. Personal Adjutants—Rudolf Hess and Wilhelm Brückner
C. Private Secretariat—Rudolf Hess and Albert Bormann
D. Chief of Staff—Ernst Röhm
Reich Youth Leader (*Reichsjugendführer*)—Baldur von Schirach
E. Reich Treasurer (*Reichschatzmeister*) and President of the Finance Committee—Franz Schwarz
Staff Director—Dr. Hans Stoch
1. Director of Central Bookkeeping (*Leiter der Hauptbuchhaltung*)—Fritz Haas
2. Director of the Review Division (*Leiter der Revisionsabteilung*)—Hans Gaupert
3. Central Audit (*Reichsrevisoren*)—Committee of Four Members
4. Director of the Aid Fund (*Leiter der Hilfskasse*)—Martin Bormann
5. Director of the Reich Armoury (*Leiter der Reichszeugmeisterei*)—Richard Büchner
6. House Inspector—Wilhelm Roeder

F. Reich Business Manager (*Reichsgeschäftsführer*)—Philipp Bouhler
Staff Director—Victor Brack
G. Secretary—Karl Fiehler
PRESIDIUM OF THE NSDAV: Hitler, Schwarz, and Fiehler
THE REICH DIRECTORATE: Presidium of the NSDAV plus all of the major officers above and the *Amstleiter* below

POLITICAL ORGANIZATION I (P.O.I)

Reich Organization Leader I—Gregor Strasser
Deputy—Paul Schulze
Adjutant—Rudolf Vollmuth
A. Foreign Division (*Auslandsabteilung*)—
Division Leader—Hans Nieland
B. Reich Press Office (*Reichspressestelle*)—
Division Leader—Otto Dietrich
C. Reich Shop-Cell Division (*Reichsbetriebszellenabteilung*)—
Division Leader—Walter Schuhmann

POLITICAL ORGANIZATION II (P.O.II)

Reich Organization Leader II—Constantin Hierl
Deputy—Paul Schulze
Adjutant—Capt. Dressler

A. Agrarian Division (*Abteilung Landwirtschaft*)—Division Leader
—Walter Darré

B. Economic Policy Division (*Wirtschaftspolitische Abt.*)—
Division Leader—Dr. Wagener
Public Economy—Gottfried Feder
Private Economy—Walter Funk

C. Race and Culture Division (*Abt. Rasse und Kultur*)—
Division Leader—R. Konopath

D. Internal Political Division (*Innerpolitische Abt.*)—
Division Leader—Dr. Nicolai

E. Legal Division (*Rechtsabteilung*)—
Division Leader—Dr. Hans Frank
Deputy—Dr. Ludwig Fischer

F. Engineering-Technical Division (*Ingenieur-Technische Abt.*)—
Division Leader—Gottfried Feder

G. Labour Service Division (*Abt. Für Arbeitsdienstpflicht*)—
Division Leader—Paul Schulze

REICH PROPAGANDA LEADER I
President of the Propaganda Committee—Paul Joseph Goebbels
Deputy—Heinz Franke

REICH PROPAGANDA LEADER II
Fritz Reinhardt

LEADER OF THE REICH INSPECTION I
Paul Schulze

LEADER OF THE REICH INSPECTION II
Robert Ley

THE INVESTIGATION AND ADJUSTMENT COMMITTEE
(Untersuchung-und-Schlichtungsausschuss or USCHLA)
President—Walter Buch
Deputy—Wilhelm Holzschuher
President of the First Chamber—Walter Buch
President of the Second Chamber—
President of the Third Chamber—Wilhelm Grimm

GYMNASTICS AND SPORTS COMMITTEE
President—Ernst Röhm

BUREAU LEADER FOR THE PRESS
(*Amtsleiter für die Presse*)
Max Amann

CENTRAL PARTY PRESS
(*Zentralparteiverlag*)
Publications Director—Max Amann

PERSONNEL BUREAU
(*Personalamt*)
Leader—Captain Loeper [1]

This scheme of organization was characterized by great fluidity and adaptability. Not only were individuals shifted from post to post as expediency dictated, but the number and arrangement of divisions were varied considerably with the needs of the hour, depending upon personal considerations, the orders of Der Führer, the resolutions of party conventions, and the like. Two outstanding party leaders had no official posts in the central offices and therefore do not appear in the table: Alfred Rosenberg and Hermann Göring. Both, however, were members of the Reichsleitung after 1930. The membership of this directorate has varied appreciably from time to time with the shifts in the relationships between Hitler and his chief aides.

The functions of most of the officials are suggested by their titles. As for the rest, the Aide Fund or *Hilfskasse* was a system of paying compensation to party members (or to their heirs) who were injured or killed in party service. After 1930, as the "conquest of the streets" proceeded apace and led to frequent street brawls with Communists and other enemies, this arrangement assumed the proportions of a vast contributory insurance organization. Between January 1 and July 31, 1932, the *Hilfskasse* considered no less than 8,300 cases involving personal "accidents," damages to motor vehicles and musical instruments, claims for damages to meeting-halls, etc.[2] The party "Armoury" (*Reichszeugmeisterei*) not only dispensed weapons but sold uniforms, arm-bands, emblems, flags, standards, etc., to the party members and the party locals through its eleven local branches.[3] The Reich Shop-Cell Division represented the Nationalsocialist

[1] *Nationalsozialistisches Jahrbuch, 1933* (Munich: Eher; 1932), pp. 134–6. Cf. Edgar Schmidt-Pauli: *Die Männer um Hitler*, pp. 56–8; René Laurent, *Le National-Socialisme*, pp. 132–6. The above outline is only one of several possible ways of presenting the interrelationships between the various central party agencies. The Arabic numerals and letters attached to the various divisions are not official party designations, but are employed here for clear schematization.

[2] *Nazi Jahrbuch, 1932*, pp. 160–79; ibid., *1933*, pp. 163–76.

[3] Ibid., *1933*, p. 162.

Shop-Cell Organization (*Nationalsocialistische Betriebszellen Organisation* or NSBO), which was designed to enlist wage-earners in Nazi trade unions or to penetrate the existing trade-union organization. The Legal Division furnished legal aid to party members arrested in the course of party work. The Labor Service Division dealt with the party's plans for instituting compulsory labour service. The famous USCHLA was the disciplinary agency of the party. Its local representatives investigated complaints against party members, settled disputes, and recommended the expulsion of disloyal comrades.

The largest unit in the local organization of the party membership was the *"Gau"* or district. The number of districts expanded with the growth of membership until by 1928 the Reich was divided into thirty-four *Gaue,* corresponding roughly in extent with the Reichstag electoral districts and each headed by a *Gauleiter.* There were also seven *Gaue* in Austria, one in Danzig, one in the Saar, and several in Czechoslovakia. The *Gauleiters* were appointed and removed by Hitler and, after the reorganization of 1932, worked under the direction of ten *Landesinspecteure,* nine in Germany and one in Austria. Each inspector was charged with the responsibility for carrying out party policy within the *Gaue* under his direction and with supervising the work of party representatives in state and provincial legislatures.[1] These officials, controlled by the central officers of the Reich inspection, constituted the liaison between the Reichsleitung and the *Gaue.* Each *Gau* was divided into a number of *Kreise* or "Circles," each headed by a *Kreisleiter* named by the *Gauleiter.* Each *Kreis* consisted of varying numbers of *Ortsgruppen* or Local Groups. These groups were headed by *Ortsgruppenleiter,* appointed by the *Gauleiter,* on the nomination of the *Kreisleiter.* Each was designed to be small enough so that its leader could be personally acquainted with all the members.

With the growth of party membership, the number of *Ortsgruppen* and *Kreise* increased within the framework of the *Gaue.* The *Ortsgruppen* were the smallest units in rural areas, but were subdivided in large metropolitan centres into Street-Cells and Blocks (*Zellen und Blöcke*). The Berlin *Gau* was divided into twenty geographical sections, comparable to the *Ortsgruppen* elsewhere. Each section

1 Engelbert Huber: *Das ist Nationalsozialismus* (Berlin: Union Deutsche Verlagsgesellschaft; 1933), p. 39.

was divided into Street-Cells of not more than five men each. The head of each Street-Cell, the *Obmann,* was appointed by his section chief, who was in turn named by the *Gauleiter,* Goebbels. After the summer of 1930 the Berlin *Gaubüro* occupied a large suite of rooms on the fourth floor of a house on Hedemannstrasse, which, ironically, had been used during the war to house various economic organizations headed by Walter Rathenau. From the former office of the murdered Foreign Minister, Goebbels directed the work of the party in the capital.[1]

As for the rank and file of the party members, accurate information regarding vocation, class and sex composition, economic status, recruitment, training, discipline, promotion, and expulsion is unavailable so long as the party records and archives remain closed to inspection. Members were ordinarily welcomed without too careful scrutiny, provided that they were Germans and "Aryans" (non-Jews), not members of Masonic lodges or similar secret societies, and willing to pay an initiation fee of one mark and minimum monthly dues of fifty pfennige, later raised to one mark. They were also expected whenever possible to make a single substantial contribution and to make additional monthly payments of optional amount. From time to time, as the membership expanded, national or local limitations of size were imposed and undesirable elements were eliminated by periodical "cleansings." On several occasions Hitler intimated that the maximum membership would be limited to one million, but this figure was greatly exceeded in 1932. The growth of membership, as shown by the number of dues-paying members at the end of each year, was as follows:

1925 —	27,000
1926 —	49,000
1927 —	72,000
1928 —	108,000
1929 —	178,000
1930 —	389,000
1931 —	862,000

[1] Huber, op. cit., pp. 35–42; *Nazi Jahrbuch,* 1933, pp. 136–42; Walter Oehme and Kurt Caro, *Kommt "Das Dritte Reich"?* (Berlin: Rowohlt; 1931), pp. 17–19; for charts, tables, and coloured reproductions of the uniforms and insignia of the S.A., S.S., Stahlhelm, etc., see *Die Uniformen und Abzeichen, Fahnen, Standarten und Wimpel der SA, SS, HJ, usw.* (Berlin: Kolk; 1933).

January	1932 —	920,000
June	1932 —	1,200,000

Closely related to and yet distinct from the party membership proper were the members of the *Sturmabteilung* and the *Schutzstaffel.* The brown-uniformed S.A. men or storm troopers were from the beginning organized on strictly military lines, copied even in detail from the Reichswehr. Since the membership of the S.A. has remained a carefully guarded secret, estimates of its size at various periods differ widely. By the close of 1931 it was generally believed that the storm troopers numbered almost half a million—or approximately half the size of the party membership. Since all S.A. men were required to be party members prior to 1933, this meant that one out of every two party members joined the S.A. and was thereby entitled to wear the brown uniform, with decorations appropriate to rank. Party members who were not storm troopers could wear only the party button, or at most a brown shirt. S.A. men who were employed paid special dues in addition to the party dues, and likewise paid for their own uniforms and equipment, while unemployed members (perhaps one-third of the total) received these things gratis, plus a small daily stipend not exceeding two marks. Unmarried storm troopers sometimes lived in small barracks housing twenty or thirty men each. In 1931–2 the "Brown Army" was divided into six major groupings, each corresponding to an army corps and commanded by an *Osaf* (*Ober S.A. Führer*). Each of these *Obergruppen* was divided into *Gruppen,* and each of these into a number of *Gausturme* or brigades. Each *Gausturm* consisted of three *"Standards"* or regiments. Each standard was composed of five *Sturmbanne* or battalions. Each battalion consisted of six to ten *Sturme* or Companies. Each company was composed of two or three *Truppe* or sections, and each *Trupp* of five or six *Scharen* or squads. This army possessed small weapons and had motor-car and motor-cycle corps at its disposal, as well as an aviation corps, the existence of which was suspected after 1930 and admitted early in 1932. In addition to the *N.S. Motorsturm,* the *N.S. Fliegersturm,* and the *Gasschutz* (Gas Defence) organization, the S.A. also possessed a "reserve" consisting of men over forty. In discipline, organization, and morale the S.A. was a military force. It was designed, however, not to fight foreign foes nor yet the police or the Reichswehr, but to combat other parties, especially the Communists, in mass demonstrations and street brawls. It likewise possessed an obvious value as a propaganda instrument to impress and terrorize the electorate and to afford honours, excitement, and glory to the party members.

The "General Staff" of the S.A. was almost as elaborately organized as the central headquarters of the party itself. Hitler was *Oberosaf.* Röhm was Chief of Staff and was assisted by an adjutant, a quartermaster, and various other subordinates. Under his direction were the *Gruppenführer,* a "General Inspector," the National Youth Leader, an Aviation Director, and bureaus for education, inspection of schools, motor transport, medicine, etc. On July 15, 1931, Hitler opened a *Reichsführerschule* for the training of S.A. leaders. In the autumn Röhm ordered each brigade to organize a *Führervorschule,* offering a two-weeks course for prospective officers. Closely connected with the staff of the S.A. was the *Wehrpolitische Amt der NSDAP,* headed by General Franz Ritter von Epp. This organization had five divisions in 1932—for external defence policy, internal defence policy, defence forces, popular defence potential, and the "defence movement." [1]

The black-uniformed S.S. or *Schutzstaffel* was a separate and smaller organization, also under the general command of Röhm. Originally the personal body-guard of Hitler, the S.S. became a small army of full-time mercenaries, carefully recruited, well equipped, and well paid for its services. Its original size was intended to be one-tenth that of the S.A., but this proportion was not observed after 1931. It expanded rapidly after January 1933, and by the late summer of the year of victory it had perhaps two hundred thousand members, all of them, of course, party members, as compared with about a million S.A. men. Some members of the S.A. became S.S. men, but transfers in general were discouraged, as was the recruitment of S.S. members from the ranks of the storm troopers. While the S.A. was the popular army of the movement, the S.S. was the picked Prætorian Guard. It was divided into five major groups, Southern, Western, Northern, Eastern, and Southeastern, with each of these hierarchically organized on military lines: *Abschnitte, Standarten, Sturmbanne, Stürme, Truppe,* and *Scharen.* It was in large part commanded by aristocratic army officers. Heinrich Himmler was Commander-in-Chief. The Crown Prince of Waldeck was

[1] *Nazi Jahrbuch, 1933,* pp. 155–7.

Stabsführer and Sigfrid Seidel-Dittmarsch was *Chef des Führungstabes.*[1]

A complete cataloguing of all of the subsidiary party organizations would require many pages. Particular attention was given to the conversion and mobilization of youth—and the members of "the lost generation" responded with enthusiasm to Nazi propaganda. The youth organizations were placed under the direction of Baldur von Schirach, who in turn was directly subordinate to Chief of Staff Röhm. The Hitler Jugend was established as an association of Nazi youths between fifteen and eighteen years of age. By 1932 it had twenty-two geographical sections throughout the Reich. It maintained a *"Reichsführerschule"* in Flechtdorf (Braunschweig) and published *"Der junge Nationalsozialist," "Jungvolk,"* and *"Die deutsche Zukunft"* as monthly periodicals and *"Der junge Sturmtrupp"* as a semi-monthly. Its central organization contained divisions on the press, culture, schools, propaganda, "defence sport" *(Wehrsport)*, etc. A junior organization, *Deutsches Jungvolk,* with Baldwin Geissler as *Bundesführer,* consisted of boys between ten and fifteen. The feminine auxiliary, the *Bund Deutscher Mädel,* led by Elizabeth Grieff-Walden, boasted forty-four *Gaue* by 1932. There was also the *Nationalsozialistischer Deutscher Studentenbund,* headed by Gerhardt Rühle, with ten geographical divisions. A Nazi Women's League (*Deutsche Frauenorden,* transformed in October 1931 into the *N.S. Frauenschaften*), a teachers' association, a German Physicians' Association, and Association of N.S. German Jurists, a *N.S. Kulturbund,* a *N.S. Beamtenabteilung* with branches in every *Gau,* the important NSBO, and numerous other national or local auxiliary organizations were designed to enlist people in all walks of life and with all possible human interests in the cause.[2]

Of major importance was the great press organization built up by the party. In 1930 there were 15 Nazi papers; in 1931, 45; and in 1932, 49 dailies, weeklies, or bi-weeklies, 40 periodicals, and 14 journals in frontier areas beyond the border. For 1932 the *Nazi Jahrbuch* listed 88 names and addresses of party newspaper and periodical offices throughout the Reich, publishing over a hundred daily or weekly sheets.[3] From a single local paper, the *Völkischer Beobachter*

[1] Ibid., pp. 158–9.
[2] Cf. Oehme and Caro, op. cit., pp. 27–31.
[3] *Nazi Jahrbuch, 1933,* pp. 142–54.

of Munich, the party press had grown to cover the nation. The *V.B.*, edited by Hitler and Rosenberg, was in format, if not in circulation, the largest German newspaper and appeared daily in two large editions, Munich and Berlin. Goebbels' *Der Angriff* was almost as well known. Scarcely a town of importance in the Reich was lacking a Nazi sheet by 1932. Most of the journals were owned by companies controlled by the local party leaders, who were also the editors. Hitler was sole owner of the *V.B.* and of the weekly *Illustrierter Beobachter*. Prior to 1931 *Der Angriff* was owned by a private company. It was then acquired by the Berlin *Gau* of the party.

Such party papers as *Der Angriff*, the *V.B.*, the *Diktateur* (Stettin), *Der Stürmer* (Nürnberg), *Der Flammenwerfer* (Munich), the *Hessen Hammer* (Darmstadt), etc., attained wide circulation and became sources of revenue rather than of expense to the party. Periodicals, pamphlets, and brochures likewise found a large market. About half of the party literature of this type was published at Munich, including the humorous weekly *Die Brennessel* (The Nettle) and the two series of brochures: the *N.S. Bibliothek*, begun in August 1927 under the editorship of Feder, and the *N.S. Monatsheft*, begun in April 1930 and edited by Rosenberg. While these publications were controlled by the central directorate of the party and were therefore completely orthodox, the editors of local papers and journals often deviated widely from the established party lines. In the interest of unity and consistency Hitler created a party press service, directed from the Munich headquarters, to supply news to editors and reporters and to set forth the official party view on all controversial matters. The Foreign Press Bureau of the party, headed by Ernst Hanfstängl, Harvard alumnus, performed a comparable service for newspapers abroad. This work expanded in various directions, and in January 1932 the *N.S. Korrespondenz* was begun as a syndicated news service.

Here, clearly, was no "party" in the ordinary sense of the term, but an intricately organized and skilfully contrived series of institutions admirably designed to disseminate a new *Weltanschauung* among all classes of the population. In politics as elsewhere, nothing succeeds like success, for the illusion of victory is the prerequisite of victory. As the party membership expanded, the party machine grew ever more complex and imposing. Enemies were frightened. Disinterested persons were impressed. Converts were inspired to energetic proselyting activity. Each party member found in the movement his heart's desire. His news of the world came to him through the party press, spiced with satire and denunciation and happily flavoured with phrases pleasing to the ear. There were also books, periodicals, pamphlets—serious, humorous, philosophical, popular—invented for every taste. Whatever the occupation of the *Parteigenosse,* the party organization was above all interested in *his* welfare, and some party organization was available in which he could share experiences with other converts in his own vocation. Whatever his hobbies and recreations, the party was on hand to serve them. His wife could join the N.S. Frauenorden. In the Hitler Jugend, the Jungvolk or the Hitler Mädel, his children could find wholesome, "clean" fun, coupled with moral earnestness and ardent patriotism. There were always meetings, parades, flags, and music. The members of every *Ortsgruppe* met at least once a month and usually oftener. There was hypnotic oratory, great drama, tremendous excitement and exaltation.

The vast machine which produced these pleasurable experiences was not only anti-democratic in its program, but profoundly anti-democratic in its inner structure. The Prussian army was its model: unlimited power at the top to send men, if need be, to death; unquestioning obedience at the bottom and joy in subservience and sacrifice. All power rested with Hitler. Terror could be broken only by terror. Mass organizations could be fought only by mass organizations. But, above all, iron discipline and complete responsibility of all leaders and members to Der Führer was of the essence. "The movement represents, in small things and in large, the fundamental principle of Germanic democracy: the election of the leader, but unlimited authority in his hands." [1] Hitler, however, was not elected to leadership. He carried a dog-whip. He had terminated the election of leaders in August 1921.[2] He named the members of the Reichsleitung and appointed the *Gauleiters.* The *Gauleiters* appointed the *Kreisleiters.* The *Kreisleiters* appointed the *Ortsgruppenleiters.* The rank and file were never consulted. Who grumbled or disobeyed was ejected. There was no discussion, no balloting at the party conventions. There was no formal procedure of consultation among the sub-leaders. Consultation there was, of course—and conciliation,

[1] Hitler, quoted in Oehme and Caro, op. cit., pp. 13–14.

[2] Cf. *Mein Kampf,* pp. 383–6, 659 f.

compromise, adjustment, for without these political leadership is impossible. But all consultation took place in secret. All must accept, in the last analysis, the decision of Der Führer.

This rigid regimentation was an enormous advantage in campaigning and manœuvring. It was, moreover, a necessity dictated by the latent conflicts within the ranks and by the exigencies of preserving unity among the incongruous elements. A hero-cult and a Messiah mythology were indispensable. The *Führerprinzip* was a danger, too, for suppressed tensions might explode disastrously at crucial moments. But the advantages of autocracy outweighed its perils during the struggle for power. An army must not debate. It must obey orders and fight.

The pattern was not new. In the fervour and enthusiasm of the Nazi crusaders were the emotions felt by millions in the early phases of every great religion. That the cult was political rather than ecclesiastical made its appeal the more enticing in a secular age in which the Church no longer afforded deep psychic satisfactions. The Fatherland was the new God. Hitler was the Saviour. Meeting-halls, gay with banners and filled with worshippers intoxicated with mystic words, were the temples of the faithful. Those of the inner shrine laboured with the devotion and fanaticism of Jesuits. The shades of the great prophets and politicians of the past haunted these secret conclaves. Mohammed was there—and Peter the Hermit, Machiavelli, Ignatius Loyola, Martin Luther, the great Frederick, Napoleon, and Bismarck. They had created myths and legends moving millions to joyous sacrifice for a vision of salvation. Their names were magic. Hitler's could be as potent. The Marxists, too, knew a little of the secret of winning the masses. Hitler learned from them, profited by their mistakes, and surpassed them. Lassalle, Bebel, Lenin were models to follow—and, above all, Mussolini. Thus the NSDAP became a great organized brotherhood of missionaries, comparable in the twentieth century only to the Communist Party of Red Russia or to the Fascist Party of the new Italy. Like them it was to win the multitudes, conquer power, and create a new heaven and a new earth.

4. PROPAGANDA

The American observer of Nazi propaganda cannot fail to be impressed with the circumstance that the methods employed bear a striking resemblance to certain other techniques widely employed for non-political purposes in the United States. Three distinct but converging sequences of skills are here combined. One is the skill of evoking a collective frenzy of emotional exaltation through the devices of "spellbinding." Here the voice from the platform, assisted perhaps by songs, images, banners and other appropriate paraphernalia, reaches out to its multitudes of auditors. By adept manipulation of word-symbols and of muscular and glandular reactions, it strips off acquired inhibitions, plays caressingly upon the naked and elemental id-drives with their aura of rationalizations and guilt-feelings, and evokes a spiritual orgasm leading to whatever type of violent mass behaviour the orator is seeking to produce. This is the technique of the religious "revivalist" who produces dramatic "conversions." It is the technique of certain Negro Baptist groups in the American South, of Holy Rollers, Shakers, and other orgiastic peasant sects, Christian and pagan. Billy Sunday, William Jennings Bryan, Alexander Dowie, Paul Rader, Wilbur Glenn Voliva, and Aimee Semple McPherson have been the best-known practitioners of the art. Numerous variants of the technique, applied to non-religious groups, come to mind at once. It is the technique of leaders of lynching mobs, of "blues singers," "Mammy singers," and "crooners" on stage, screen and radio, of "ballyhoo artists" in municipal politics, and, at times, of the managers of American presidential campaigns.

The second major source of Nazi propaganda technique is the "secret society." Here European precedents are as significant as American ones—for example, the Jesuits, the Masonic Order, the Carbonari, and sundry revolutionary and terrorist organizations in central and eastern Europe. Here again, however, the arts of the secret society have perhaps reached their highest development in the United States. Such groups achieve solidarity by familiar symbols of identification which are given mystic significance and evoke emotional affects highly gratifying to their members. In an atmosphere of mystery, noviciates are inducted into the sacred circle of those gifted with esoteric wisdom. The initiated enjoy ego-inflation by evoking deference through the use of the symbols with which they identify themselves. Such groups were numerous among many American Indian tribes. Masons, Odd Fellows, Knights of Columbus, Elks, Moose, Eagles, and members of other "lodges"—all exhibiting modern variants of fetishism and totemism—are to be seen parading with bands, uniforms, and standards in almost any modern American city. American "Greek-letter societies" and college fraternities and sororities are other obvious instances of the pattern.

In this connection it is worth recalling that the most perfect prototype of the NSDAP is the Ku Klux Klan—the southern Klan of the late sixties and seventies and the revived Klan of the 1920's and 1930's in the American "Bible Belt." In this remarkable organization are to be found parallels for almost all of the elements of Nazi symbolism. It is anti-Semitic, anti-Negro, anti-Catholic, anti-foreign. It employs strange names and honorary titles. The masked, hooded, and white-gowned night-riders, like the brown-shirted storm troopers, inspire awe and terror in the community. The "Knights of the Golden Circle" correspond to the S.S., the "Grand Kleagle" to the *Oberosaf,* the "Klaxons" to the *Gauleiters,* the fiery crosses to the flaming swastikas, and the "Invisible Empire" to the mysterious "Third Reich." Had Hitler studied the K.K.K. in detail, he could scarcely have imitated its organization and rituals more completely.

The third source of inspiration was the science of modern advertising, also carried to perfection in the United States. Here also primitive arts become highly conscious and sophisticated techniques for evoking collective responses. The tribal medicine-man and the wandering vender of herbs, roots, and patent medicines become in the twentieth century high-pressure salesmen and great advertising syndicates, utilizing the press, the radio, the screen, and all the graphic arts to enlarge shrinking markets for the vast output of modern machine industry. The major technique is that of constant and subtle suggestion, appealing to vanity, social prestige, mother-love, eroticism, fear of sickness, death, and economic insecurity, etc., *ad infinitum.* Goods of all kinds are named—and effective names are vested with magic properties. The names in turn are identified by words and pictures with health, beauty, riches, wisdom, distinction, security, adventure, and a dozen other enjoyable experiences. Thus is "sales resistance" broken down. Thus are chewing-gums, toothpastes, mineral oils, stocks and bonds, gasolines, sewing-machines, insurance policies, refrigerators, hotel accommodations, motor cars, and headache pills sold to the great public. Here the shades of P. T. Barnum and Lydia Pinkham are transfigured into Neon lights, billboards, the modern metropolitan press, and the Radio Corporation of America.

Nazi propaganda technique was (and is) nothing more nor less than an extraordinarily adroit combination of these three types of symbolism. It is not to be inferred that Hitler and his aides consciously copied American models. Religious revivals, secret societies, and modern advertising companies were to be found in Germany no less than in the United States. Above all, the highly perfected propaganda techniques of the belligerent governments in the Great War were available as models for the "drummer" of the Third Reich. The techniques of the Social Democrats and Communists were imitated to win proletarian converts. Many ingenious devices were worked out independently, stumbled upon accidentally, or created by sheer genius. And, what was most unusual, the Nazi propagandists were in general disposed to admit their opportunism and their unscrupulousness with perfect frankness. Instead of alienating followers, this frankness seemed only to evoke greater respect—from the intellectuals who "saw through" the propaganda but who admired cleverness, and from the masses who were willing and even anxious to be "taken in."

Hitler's personal contribution to the party's propaganda technique was of decisive importance. He supplied the "Bible" of the movement in his autobiography, the royalties from which gave him a comfortable independent income as soon as it became a best-seller. He invented the *Hakenkreuz* flag and much of the elaborate military insignia of the S.A. and S.S. He was the symbol artist *par excellence*. At the time of the Nürnberg convention of 1927 he spent three days in meditation and then emerged with the striking *Partei-Tag Plakate*. He was actor and stage director, as well as scene-painter, costumer, and property man. The pageantry of the great parades and mass meetings was his. The regimented, inspired storm troopers parading with flags and standards through flagged streets and down the aisles of bannered halls to the crash of martial music were his. The impressive *Fahnenweihe* ceremony was his. In its performance he walked down the ranked rows of S.A. standards and flags and touched each one solemnly and mysteriously with the sacred *Blutfahne* of 1923, the tattered banner stained with the blood of the martyrs who fell before the Feldherrnhalle.[1]

[1] Cf. Weigand von Miltenberg: *Adolf Hitler, William III*, pp. 26–9 and p. 49.

Der Führer excelled in flags, emblems, and ceremonies rather than in phrases. Slogans he borrowed freely from many sources. *"Gemeinnutz vor Eigennutz"* and *"Brechung der Zinsknechtschaft"* came from Gottfried Feder. *"Deutschland Erwache!"* came from the Pan-German League and from Dietrich Eckart. *"Freiheit und Brot!"* came from Gregor Strasser. Hitler had an intuitive feeling for what was effective in propaganda. But he wrote badly and was never at home in the world of written words. Visual symbols he could invent. Verbal symbols he got from his aides or purloined where he could. For him the spoken word was always to be preferred to writing. He was spellbinder, not journalist. But he had studied propaganda technique during the war and had learned what worked. The only sections of *Mein Kampf* which have scientific value are those dealing with propaganda technique. Allied propaganda, he perceived, was more effective than German propaganda because it was simpler, cruder, more striking. Propaganda should appeal to the heart (and the viscera), not to the mind. It should be a method of incitement, not of instruction. A few points should be reiterated ceaselessly. To inspire hate is better than to inspire ridicule, because hate implies fear, and fear, rather than laughter, produces energetic and heroic action. In political as in commercial advertising the products of competitors should never be conceded to possess any virtues. "Your weapon is attack, never defence! Never let the enemy rest a moment!" echoed Goebbels.

"Toward whom must propaganda be directed? Toward the scientific intelligentsia or toward the uneducated masses? It must always and exclusively be directed toward the masses. . . . Propaganda can no more be science in its content than a placard can be art. . . . The task of propaganda does not lie in the scientific instruction of individuals, but in the orientation of the mass toward specific facts, cases, needs, etc., whose importance should thereby be placed first in the eyes of the multitude. . . . The teachability of the great masses is very limited, their understanding small, and their memory short." (*Mein Kampf,* pp. 196–8.)

"Faith is more difficult to shake than knowledge, love undergoes fewer changes than respect. Hate is more permanent than antipathy, and the impetus to the most powerful revolutions in this world lies at all times less in scientific cognition dominating the masses than in the fanaticism inspiring them and sometimes in the hysteria driving them forward. Who wishes to win the broad mass must know the key which opens the door to its heart. It is not called 'objectivity,' i.e. weakness, but Will and Strength." (*Mein Kampf,* p. 371.)

"Every world-moving Idea has not only the right but the duty to avail itself of whatever means will make possible the realization of its purpose. The Result is the only earthly judge of the rightness or wrongness of such an undertaking." (*Mein Kampf,* p. 377.)

"A revolutionist must be able to do everything—to unchain volcanic passions, to arouse outbreaks of fury, to set masses of men on the march, to organize hate and suspicion with ice-cold calculation, so to speak with legal methods. . . ." (Goebbels in *Der Angriff,* February 18, 1929.)

Music and songs played a major role in evoking mass enthusiasm. Old folk-tunes and familiar military songs were used with striking new verses. The popular war song *Deutschland über Alles* was always on the lips of the storm troopers. Meetings and demonstrations were usually opened and closed with the singing of the *Horst Wessel Lied,* composed by one of the party's martyrs. Dietrich Eckart's *Deutschland Erwache!* was always effective:

GERMANY, AWAKE!

Storm, storm, storm, storm!
From tower to tower peal bells of alarm.
Peal out! Sparks fly as hammers strike.
Comes Judas forth to win the Reich.
Peal out! The bloody ropes hang red
Around our martyred hero dead.
Peal out—that thundering earth may know
Salvation's rage for honour's sake.
To people dreaming still comes woe.
Germany, awake! Awake!

There were also songs about "Jewish blood spurting under the knife," and love-songs about fallen heroes, and war-songs full of trumpets and revenge.

Rise Up in Arms!

Rise up in arms to battle, for to battle are we born.
Rise up in arms to battle now, to battle for the morn.
To Adolf Hitler, Leader, have we sworn our solemn oath,
To Adolf Hitler, Leader, hold we fast and true our troth.

O fearless, fear we never the Moscow legions bold,
We're fearless toward the Reichsbanner—black and red and gold.
Our enemies and foemen, may the Devil seize them all.
The grafters, crooks, and cowards, may each criminal hear his call.

We never fight, nay never, for the gold of millionaires.
To defy the Bourse and Capital our courage ever dares.
For national honour only do we all exert our might,
For the future bright of Germany, united all, we fight.

Our hero brave, Horst Wessel, falls martyr to Red plot,
Our Berlin's noblest victim of criminal, bestial shot.
But Freedom's will, invincible, they cannot slay nor burn,
For soon the page of Destiny relentlessly will turn.

God Who Makes His Iron Grow

God who makes His iron grow, He wishes now no slaves.
He gives to man in righteousness his spears and pikes and blades.
He gives to man his bravery, the anger of hot breath
Which man keeps keen in combat fierce, till bloody feud brings death.

Let sound what now can only sound: the drums' and cymbals' clash.
Today we stand, each man for man. The iron's bloody flash
With hangmen's blood, with Frenchmen's blood; our vengeance
now is sweet.
For Germans all, this is our goal. Hear drums and trumpets beat.

E. M. Arndt [1]

[1] Cf. German texts in the pamphlets of the *Nationalsozialistischer Liederschatz* (Berlin: Schmidt); the two typical songs given above are taken from *Band 6* of this series.

5. THE PURSE-STRINGS

THE great propaganda machine of the NSDAP rolled forward after 1929 like an intricate Juggernaut car, crushing out all opposition and conquering the emotions of the *Kleinbürgertum* by storm. Its chief enemies, the Social Democrats and the Communists, could offer no effective resistance, for they lacked both money and imagination. With money, imagination could be purchased. Without money nothing was possible. Whence came the millions of marks which the *Hitlerbewegung* dispensed so freely?

All questions of party finances are shrouded in mystery, rumour, and conjecture. Few political parties find it expedient to reveal all the sources of their revenue and all the purposes of their expenditures. In Germany, only the Social Democrats made full and regular reports on their finances, for a party supported by dues and small contributions from the pay-envelopes of wage-earners had little to conceal. It spent almost eleven million marks in 1928, eleven and a half million in 1929, and nearly fifteen million in 1930.[1] The Nationalists spent six to seven million marks annually, the German People's Party about three, the Centrum one and a half, the Democrats and the Communists perhaps one million each. German legislation required no publicity of party funds and no kind of public accounting. It imposed no limits on party contributions or expenditures, nor did it forbid corporations to contribute to campaign funds. The NSDAP has from the beginning kept all aspects of its finances a closely guarded secret. Its books are closed to inspection by all save the highest party leaders. From external evidence it is safe to assume that the party spent more on propaganda than any other party in the Reichstag election campaign of 1930. Its expenditures during 1931 and 1932 were also very large, but no accurate estimates of them can be made. Apart from campaigning, the overhead expense of maintaining the huge party bureaucracy was enormous.

The sources of party revenue were numerous and varied. All party members paid dues of one mark per month. By mid-year 1931 the party had half a million members. Six million marks a year was no inconsiderable sum by German standards. Each new member, more-

[1] Cf. Table in J. K. Pollock: *Money and Politics Abroad* (New York: Knopf; 1932), p. 214.

over, paid an initiation fee of varying amount, depending upon his economic status. He was likewise required to pay special assessments for particular purposes. At the close of 1929 Hitler ordered the party members to subscribe to a loan, at six and a half per cent interest, payable after January 1, 1931, with ten marks as a minimum subscription. Some eight hundred thousand marks were raised in this way. Party members also paid admission to meetings, subscribed to papers, bought books, emblems, flags, uniforms, etc. Non-party members and prospective converts were likewise induced to contribute. Following the example of the Social Democrats, the party sold tickets to its mass meetings. Unemployed might be admitted free. Others paid fifty pfennige, one mark, two marks, or even as much as ten marks, depending upon their means and the places they desired. Three big meetings in the Berlin Sportpalast in the campaign of 1930 yielded a total profit of thirty thousand marks. Thousands of meetings all over the Reich not only paid for themselves, but filled the party treasury. It is safe to estimate that each of the six and a half million voters who supported the party in September 1930 contributed, directly or indirectly, an average of at least three marks—or a total of 19,500,000 marks—during the course of the campaign. Many party papers and periodicals likewise made a profit, part of which found its way into the party coffers. Newspaper syndicates desiring interviews with the party leaders were charged all that the traffic would bear. The *Zeugmeisterei* made considerable profit from selling uniforms and paraphernalia. All party members contributed to the *Hilfskasse*.

In short, the party, like a church, was partially self-supporting. Unfortunately, there is no way of ascertaining the size of its annual budgets or the proportion of its revenues coming from the sources which have been mentioned. But it is clear that these internal resources could never by themselves have sufficed to pay the party's bills, even with the greatest economy and most scrupulous bookkeeping. Its propaganda expenditures were on far too lavish a scale. And its ordinary revenues were by no means all available for propaganda purposes. Regular salaries and honorariums had to be paid to the party's employees and officials. Unemployed party members often received financial assistance. Wounded S.A. men received insurance. Impoverished storm troopers could obtain small stipends. After 1930 half of the fees from new party members and half the profits of the *Zeugmeisterei* went to the *Sturmabteilung*.[1] Even then, with a membership of probably less than fifty thousand, the S.A. cost at least five million marks annually, less than half of which came from the storm troopers themselves. In the absence of evidence, guessing is dangerous, but it may be conservatively estimated that between one-third and one-half of the party's revenue came from sources other than dues, assessments, admission fees, and small individual contributions.

If the specific amounts of other donations to the party treasury cannot now be ascertained, the general sources admit of no debate. The NSDAP, like all political parties (other than those of the revolutionary proletariat), went for money to the people who had money —and who might be persuaded, for a *quid pro quo,* to part with some of it. The party went to the upper strata of the German wealth-and-income pyramid, to the already reactionary and anti-republican élite: to the bourgeois aristocracy of money, to the Junker aristocracy of land, to business men, employers, bankers, industrialists, landowners, and all others possessed of fortunes. These groups, in Germany as elsewhere, contributed to all parties save the Communists. Their donations went particularly to the German People's Party and to the Nationalists. They tended to view the NSDAP as a useful tool with which to win the masses to reaction. It could be used to crush not only Marxism and a pernicious democracy, but the entire German labour movement. As it grew and seemed likely to gain power, expediency dictated contributions as a matter of self-protection, even from people of wealth not otherwise sympathetic to the "socialism," national or otherwise, of a "workers'" party.

Out of the maze of rumour and allegation, the following facts seem fairly well established. In the 1920–23 period Hitler secured contributions from Herr Aust and Geheimrat Kuhlo, leaders of the Syndikus des Bayerschen Industriellenverbandes, who presumably transmitted funds donated by the industrialists comprising the organization. Money was also forthcoming from Duke Ludwig Wilhelm of Bavaria, the Duke of Coburg, Prince Henckel von Donnersmarck, and a few other nobles and large landowners.[2] Among the business leaders outside of Bavaria who contributed to the cause were Herr Mutschmann, a textile-manufacturer of Plauen; Herr von

[1] Cf. p. 139 below.

[2] Cf. the Berlin *Welt am Abend,* December 11, 1930.

Maffei, a Munich employer; August von Borsig of Berlin; Edwin Bechstein, the piano-manufacturer of Saxe; Herr Honnschuh of Külmbach; and apparently also for a time Hugo Stinnes and several other Ruhr industrialists.[1]

The list of industrialist and aristocratic contributors between 1925 and 1933 is much longer, especially after 1930. In the conflict of 1926 the Left wing of the party alleged that the Munich leaders had "sold out" to Big Business. Among the industrialists who were alleged to have contributed a hundred thousand marks or more apiece were Mutschmann, Bechstein, Schneider, Itzehoe, and Becker, all manufacturers. Hitler's agents made systematic collections among business men, apparently with a good deal of success. Borsig of Berlin and Emil Kirdorf and Krupp von Bohlen of the Ruhr contributed, although the latter supported Hindenburg against Hitler in the presidential election of 1932. The Lahusen brothers of Bremen, later tried for embezzling the funds of the Nordwolle concern which went bankrupt under their direction, also made offerings. Among the landed aristocrats, Baron von der Goltz and other east Prussian Junkers found it expedient to make contributions.[2] Among the defunct (but still wealthy) royalty, funds came from the Dukes of Coburg and Brunswick and the Grand Dukes of Oldenburg and Mecklenburg [3] and, among the Hohenzollerns, from the ex-Crown Princess Cecilie and from Prince August Wilhelm ("Auwi"), who joined the party.

Money also came from abroad, partly from deposits made by the party in foreign banks and partly from foreign sympathizers, though here the rumours are even more elusive. Funds from Austria and Czechoslovakia probably came from Nazi party locals rather than from large industrialists. There is some evidence, however, that two directors (von Arthaber and von Dutschnitz) of Skoda, the great Czech artillery firm at Pilsen, partly owned by the French Schneider-Creusot interests, contributed, for reasons which are obvious to those

[1] Cf. Richard Lewinsohn: *Das Geld in der Politik* (Berlin: Fischer; 1930). The extreme secrecy with which the party's finances are managed, coupled with *pro forma* denials of all such allegations, renders it obviously impossible to present any documentary evidence of the contributors to the party. The names given here have in one way or another leaked out. Doubtless many other wealthy contributors remain anonymous.

[2] Berlin *Vorwärts,* August 27, 1929.

[3] *Weltbühne,* April 30, 1932, cited in E. A. Mowrer, *Germany Puts the Clock Back,* p. 145.

familiar with the ways of armament-makers. Money came likewise from Switzerland and Holland and perhaps from Great Britain and the United States. Lord Rothermere was a wealthy British sympathizer who may have contributed. Sir Henri Deterding is alleged to have helped Hitler finance the presidential campaign of 1932 in the hope of securing a German oil monopoly. The Swedish match king, Ivar Kreuger, the American automobile king, Henry Ford, and the Italian Duce, Mussolini, are likewise reputed to have made donations.

The most important of Hitler's supporters among the German industrialists was the multimillionaire, Fritz Thyssen, the dry, hard-headed, academic and obstinate Ruhr magnate who was chairman of the Vereinigte Stahlwerke A.G., with its headquarters at Mühlheim. His firm, employing 170,000 workers in good years, was founded in 1871 by his father, August, who drank beer with his workers, walked to work rather than spend money on street-cars, and bought up Ruhr coal-fields, French and German iron ore in Lorraine, cement-factories, power-stations, shipping lines, and railways. In the Great War the Thyssens became large-scale manufacturers of ammunition, rivalled only by the Krupps. During the French occupation of the Ruhr they refused to comply with the invaders' orders and Fritz was sent to prison by a French court martial. Unlike his father, Fritz lived in a castle on a hill. He was bitterly anti-French, anti-republican, anti-pacifist. He joined the Nationalist Party and supported the Stahlhelm. In the crash of 1930–31 Thyssen was hard hit. He and his business allies, Flick and Voegler (successors of Stinnes), struggled desperately with their major competitor, the Otto Wolff-Deutsche Bank group, consisting of more liberal Catholic and Jewish industrialists and bankers. Thyssen knew Göring and became Hitler's personal friend. He introduced Der Führer to the Industrie Klub of Düsseldorf as the saviour of Germany and of German capitalism.[1] In 1930 he and Kirdorff contributed something like a million marks to the party. In 1932, prior to the presidential election, he donated three million marks. He likewise solicited contributions from his colleagues and subordinates and was, all in all, the most useful single supporter of the Nazis.[2]

[1] Cf. pp. 140–141 below.

[2] Cf. "August Thyssen" in Felix Pinner: *Deutsche Wirtschaftsführer,* pp. 66–74, and the sensational but undocumented allegations in Ernst Henri: *Hitler Over Europe* (New York: Simon and Schuster; 1934), "Thyssen's Plot," pp. 1–27.

All questions of motives are difficult. Glib formulations, according to which the industrialists "bought" Hitler to do their bidding, are too simple. Some industrialists contributed as patriots, sincerely believing in "Germany's awakening." Others, Thyssen among them, cherished far-reaching schemes of power and profit to be realized by the establishment of the Third Reich. Still others "played safe" by contributing to a party which seemed likely to achieve power. All were anti-Communist and anti-Social Democratic and therefore interested in any political movement promising the destruction of Marxism. All had an obvious interest in weakening or, if possible, destroying the collective bargaining power of German labour, to which they had been obliged to make many grudging concessions. For this they were prepared to pay a price: the price of subsidizing the NSDAP and the price of submitting to extensive governmental control in a Fascist State in which strikes would be forbidden, the proletariat would be impotent, and Marxism would be annihilated. Like the corresponding groups in Italy which backed Mussolini, they envisaged a Fascist State as one in which they would once more be secure, prosperous, and powerful. Hitler would take money wherever it was to be had and would use the support of the industrialists for his own ends. If these ends coincided with those of the moneyed aristocracy, well and good. He did not need to be "bribed" to oppose Marxism and trade unionism. These had long been the targets against which he discharged his personal resentments. "Socialistic" slogans and attacks on "capitalism" were necessary to win the masses. He at least regarded them as a means to power, not as a program, whatever the Strasser brothers might believe. On February 18, 1930, the Dresden *Gauleiter* wrote to the Weimar factory-manager Fritsche:

"Do not let yourself be continually confused by the text of our posters. . . . Of course, there are catchwords like 'Down with capitalism,' etc., but these are unquestionably necessary, for under the flag of 'German national' or 'national' alone, you must know, we should never reach our goal, we should have no future. We must talk the language of the embittered socialist workmen . . . or else they wouldn't feel at home with us. We don't come out with a direct program . . . for reasons of diplomacy." [1]

And on March 4, 1931, Hitler wrote to the Hessen *Gauleiter* giv-

[1] Quoted in Mowrer, op. cit., p. 150.

ing him a list of firms from which fifteen thousand marks must be collected in return for party work in the trade unions against the Communists.[1] Similar assurances were doubtless given to other industrialists. Thyssen, Kirdorf, and the aristocrats and princes did not believe that they were supporting a "Socialist," "Workers'" party. They were not. Insincerity and hyprocisy are words without meaning in Nazi mentality. They are inapplicable to the mental processes here involved. All means were permissible to win the masses and to gain power. Power once gained could be exercised *with* or *against* the ruling classes. Hitler and his aides had no ambitions or objectives requiring them to do battle with those of wealth and property. Such a conflict would be highly dangerous. Hitler, like Thyssen, believed in private property, individual initiative, profits, and the whole pattern of capitalistic economy. Those in public office who do not use the machinery of the State against the existing élite necessarily use it to the advantage of that élite. The perpetuation and defence of an existing social hierarchy perpetuate and defend the material and psychological benefits which those at its apex derive from it. And a movement which was determined, in the name of national unity, to crush class conflict, to destroy Marxism, and to demolish the trade unions could not but be advantageous to the German aristocracy and the upper bourgeoisie.

Thus financed, the propaganda machine did its work. Thousands upon thousands of great mass meetings echo with cheers of prospective victory as the tireless party chieftains dash about the Reich in swift motor cars or airplanes, preaching, beseeching, exhorting, denouncing.[2] A mass meeting of the NSDAP is no ordinary occasion. Converts, sympathizers, and even enemies pay gladly for the privilege of attending, for the spectacle is better than High Mass, Greek tragedy, and Wagnerian opera combined. Simple men, moreover, may here rub shoulders with generals, aristocrats, and millionaires and address them familiarly as "comrade." First there is doubt as to whether one can get in at all. The local branch of the party has hired the largest hall in town. It has left no stone unturned to pack it to the doors long before the meeting is scheduled to begin. Sus-

1 Quoted in Ernst Ottwalt: *Deutschland Erwache!* pp. 375–6.

2 See the description of a typical Nazi campaign meeting in Mowrer, op. cit., pp. 260–6.

pense adds zest to the occasion. People stand in line for half a day to hear Der Führer and for hours to hear Goebbels, Göring, Frick, the Strassers, or Rosenberg. In this there is no accident, nor is it mere chance that the meeting is scheduled for eight or nine o'clock in the evening. Hitler has written that people's resistance is lower in the evening than at any other time. A little added fatigue and suspense are good. The outside of the hall is gay with flags and banners. S.A. men sell papers, pamphlets, and song-books to the waiting throngs: heartening military songs full of hate for Frenchmen and Poles and most interesting pamphlets against the Jews, against the bankers, against Bolshevism. A company of S.A. men drill and sing in the street and perhaps stage a dramatic torch-light parade with bands and flags. *Herrlich!*

Within is an inspiring spectacle. Great *Hakenkreuz* flags are draped over the platform, decorated with pine bows and bunting. Around the balcony, more flags and huge white streamers with enormous black letters: "Germany, Awake!"—"Freedom and Bread!"—"Away with Reparations!"—"Down with Versailles!"—*"Gemeinnutz vor Eigennutz!"*—and *"Brechung der Zinsknechtschaft!"* Around the walls and on the stage stand sturdy ranks of storm troopers in uniform, with the light of crusaders on their faces. The doors are opened several hours before the meeting begins. The expectant audience waits patiently. A military band affords entertainment while people gossip and munch sandwiches.

Finally there is a stir among the packed thousands. Drums and trumpets crash at the door. A disciplined regiment of storm troopers marches in—slowly, solemnly, carrying bright standards and swastika flags with poles tipped with spear-points or bayonets. Scores of flags pass by in majestic procession to stirring martial music, or perhaps to the slow rhythm of "The Entry of the Gods into Valhalla." Then at the end a special body-guard—either in natty brown uniforms or in the striking black and silver of the *Schutzstaffel.* Within a hollow square of marching men are the party leaders, also uniformed. Then, the centre of all eyes, Der Führer—in his tan raincoat, hatless, smiling, and affably greeting those to right and left. A man of the people! Germany's Saviour! Trained party members in the audience raise their arms in salute and shout: *"Heil!"* Again *"Heil!"* Many join. Other arms shoot up. The third *"Heil!"*

swells into a great ovation, rushing upward like a mighty benediction from the sea of arms. Even surly and sour-faced critics feel their pulses beat faster. There are lumps in a thousand throats and thrills of ecstasy along a thousand spines.

The procession reaches the platform. The massed bands crash triumphantly and subside. The chairman speaks softly, confidentially, soothingly, like a good neighbour. He dwells on the misfortunes of his auditors. He shouts: "What is the cause of our suffering?" Mighty voices from the audience reply: "The System!" "Who is behind the System?" *"The Jews!"* "Who is Adolf Hitler?" *"A last hope—unser Führer!"* Hitler rises, comes forward, pauses—and speaks. Quietly, ingratiatingly at first. Then rough, hysterical climaxes. No reasoning, no persuasion, no analysis, no pleading. Only magnificent affirmation. Pity. Passion. Inspiration. Violence. The German people are the greatest of people. German *Kultur* is the highest culture. Germany is debauched, degraded, impoverished. Through no fault of Germans. The valiant, victorious German armies were stabbed in the back. By the Jews. By the Marxists. The Versailles shame-treaty is a plot of the French Negro-Jewish militarists, supported by English and American capitalists, bent on bleeding Germany white. Supported by the enemy within: the Jews, the pacifists, the democrats, the Red sub-humans, and the scheming Bourse capitalists who control these puppets. Our colonies! Our lost provinces! Food for our children! Honour and power! Of these things the System cheats us. The System must be smashed. The November criminals must be kicked out. Only Nationalsocialism can bring salvation. Only the party can cut the knot and lead the way to the glorious Third Reich. Liberation! Revenge! Victory!

The very air tingles with excitement. All eyes are on the speaker under the spotlights, thundering, waving his arms, sweeping back his hair from his perspiring brow. The banners and slogans, the flags and storm troopers, the audience, the hall itself fade into a blur. There is only a Man in a blaze of light, pulsating amid the all but perceptible beat of celestial wings. The audience sways, rocks, weeps, laughs, groans in delirium. *Richtig, sehr richtig!* At the end, in overwhelming chorus: *"Heil! Heil! Heil! Hitler!"* The bands blare and the multitude takes up the solemn, stirring chant of the *Horst Wessel Lied*:

Raise high the flags! Stand rank on rank together.
Storm troopers march with steady, quiet tread.
Our comrades brave, shot down by Red Front and Reaction,
In spirit march before the ranks they led.

Make free the streets for brown battalions marching!
Make free the streets! Storm troopers stride ahead.
Already millions gaze with hope upon our banner.
The day now dawns for Freedom and for Bread.

Once more the storm appeal calls all to combat.
We stand prepared. Our cause we shall defend.
Soon Hitler flags will fly o'er all the house-tops.
Our servitude will soon be at an end.

Raise high the flags! Stand rank on rank together. . . .

CHAPTER III

NSDAP: THE GOSPEL

1. NEUROSES OF THE KLEINBÜRGERTUM

THE *Weltanschauung* of Nationalsocialism has become one of the major mass ideologies of the twentieth century. As such, its origins and content deserve more systematic treatment than they have thus far received. The task of tracing each of the specific verbalizations of the NSDAP to its historical source will not be attempted here, but may be left to the historians of political theory. Suffice it merely to suggest at the outset that the student of political philosophy interested in the doctrinal progenitors of Nationalsocialism will find it profitable to peruse the literature of Italian Fascism, especially the writings of Giovanni Gentile and Alfredo Rocco, and to read among the German predecessors the works of Paul de Lagarde, Ferdinand Lassalle, Friedrich Naumann, Justizrat Class, Othmar Spann, and Oswald Spengler.

For him who would delve somewhat deeper, the books of Houston Stewart Chamberlain, Count Arthur de Gobineau, Friedrich Nietzsche, Fichte, Treitschke, and Hegel are to be recommended. The literature of the early nineteenth-century German Romanticist reaction against the French Revolution will also bear fruitful examination. Many leading Nazi ideas are to be found in the volumes of Ludwig von Haller [1] and of Adam Müller.[2] Along a slightly different genealogical line stand the works of Vilfredo Pareto, Wil-

[1] Cf. his *Restauration der Staats-Wissenschaft, oder Theorie des natürlich-geselligen Zustands der Chimäre des Künstlichbürgerlichen entgegengesetzt,* 6 vols., 1816–34.

[2] Cf. especially his *Elemente der Staatswissenschaft,* 1809. The writer is indebted to Professor Walter Dorn of Ohio State University for calling his attention to the remarkable parallelism between the ideology of Nationalsocialism and that of the German political Romantics of a century ago.

liam James, and Gustav Le Bon. In the background loom Edmund Burke, Thomas Hobbes, Bossuet, Bodin, and Machiavelli. Certain roots of the new creed are also to be found in the writings of Frederick the Great and Martin Luther, not to mention the *Gallic Wars* of Julius Cæsar and the *Germania* of Tacitus, where many interest-misconceptions regarding the peculiar virtues of the "German race" were presented to the Roman world. Beyond Tacitus it is perhaps scarcely worth while to go.

Such an analysis of the ideological origins of the Nazi gospel would be highly interesting, but not directly germane to the purposes of the present work.[1] Indeed, a general doubt may be raised as to whether such studies of political ideas are *per se* profitable to the student of social and political processes. The procedure usually employed may even be misleading, if it suggests that an identity or similarity of creeds necessarily indicates that a later ideology is based upon or copied from an earlier one. Nationalsocialism, Italian Fascism, French royalism, Japanese militarism, and early German political Romanticism all exhibit similarities of doctrine which are due less to direct cultural diffusion and imitation than to like causes producing, independently, like results. Historians of ideas, moreover, are prone to assume that man is rational and that ideas move the world. But the evolution of political and social word-symbols at the hands of the intelligentsia is merely a surface phenomenon of the evolution of social and political interrelationships. Political theories are socially significant only in so far as they reflect and influence mass emotions and collective public behaviour. The gospel of the NSDAP is intelligible not in terms of the history of political ideas, but only as a manifestation of widespread emotional maladjustments in post-war German society.

This circumstance suggests the desirability of beginning a presentation of the Nazi creed with an effort to ascertain what specific sources of tension gave rise to these maladjustments, how they were psychically resolved by the invention of a new political symbolism, and how this symbolism found a mass market. The intellectual techniques suggested by "economic determinism" and "psychoanaly-

[1] Cf. the author's article, "The Political Theory of German Fascism," *American Political Science Review*, April 1934, pp. 210–32, from which certain portions of the present chapter are taken.

sis" furnish useful approaches to such an effort.[1] The rulers and thinkers of Fascist Germany regard it not merely as bad taste, but as high treason to suggest that political ideas are products of economic interests or of neuroses. The Nazi *Weltanschauung* repudiates historical materialism and psychiatry with equal vehemence. Its Hegelianism is qualified, however, by the circumstance that it views political and social ideas not as the children of Reason, but as the offspring of obscure subjective impulses. These impulses are emphatically not to be explained by the pernicious doctrines of the Jew Karl Marx or of the Jew Sigmund Freud. They flow from *"Blut und Boden,"* from nation and race, from individual genius and from the esoteric depths of the German soul. But to the western observer who finds in this mysticism more a symptom than a diagnosis of the political mentality of contemporary Germany, German Fascism is comprehensible only in terms of the economic difficulties and the psychic disorders of the post-war *Kleinbürgertum.*

That Nationalsocialism was derived from lower middle class and peasant circles rather than from the feudal nobility, the upper bourgeoisie, or the proletariat will be disputed by few observers even among the Nazis themselves. Neither will many deny the intimate relationship between the economic "interests" of social groups and their political attitudes and behaviour, however debatable may be the precise fashion in which this relationship should be formulated. But an initial doubt may well be raised as to the propriety and utility of injecting psychopathological concepts into the discussion of a political program. The high priests of the Nazi cult, to be sure, have repeatedly proclaimed themselves to be not only non-rational but *anti*-rational. Anti-intellectualism and *Blut gegen Geist* (Spengler) are fundamental principles of Nationalsocialism. Hitler himself has always given feeling, emotion, fanaticism, and even hysteria precedence over calm ratiocination.[2] But the psychopathological ap-

1 For a typical Marxist approach to the problem, see F. David: *Ist die NSDAP eine Sozialistische Partei?* (Vienna: Int. Arbeiter Verlag; 1933); for a typical Freudian approach, see Fedor Vergin; *Das unbewusste Europa;* for an interesting synthesis of the two, see Ernst Ottwalt: *Deutschland Erwache!* Cf. also Wilhelm Reich: *Massenpsychologie des Fascismus* (Zurich, 1933).

2 Cf. Mussolini in his article, "The Political and Social Doctrine of Fascism," *Enciclopedia Italiano:* "My own doctrine . . . has always been a doctrine of action. . . . Fascism was not the nursling of a doctrine worked out beforehand with detailed elaboration; it was born of the need for action and was itself from the beginning practical rather than theoretical; it was not merely another political party but, even in the first

proach raises a general question which must at least be mentioned, even if it cannot be pursued here. Does the irrational character of Nationalsocialism mean that it differs in kind or only in degree from other political creeds and doctrines? Are other political attitudes and other patterns of political behaviour ever "rational"? Are not all political radicals "crazy"—and perhaps reactionaries, conservatives, and liberals as well? Are western bourgeois liberalism, with its worship of reason and reasonableness, and proletarian Marxism, with its claim to "scientific" objectivity and precision, any less products of the emotional tensions and maladjustments of social classes than Fascism? Is political behaviour in general ever sane, logical, and rational?

These questions can scarcely be answered here. They involve fundamental problems of human personality structure which cannot be precisely formulated until psychiatry and political psychology have made further advances. But it is at least arguable that Nationalsocialism merely exhibits in exaggerated and pathological form patterns of action which are inherent in all mass political behaviour. All collective human action is by definition emotionally motivated. All human societies are held together by shared emotions, by common glandular and muscular responses to collective symbols, not by cold abstract intellect. Any social group acts effectively to the degree to which it acts unitedly and enthusiastically. Unity and enthusiasm are functions of collective stimuli evoking intense and abiding collective reactions. Those political symbols and verbalizations are most effective which elicit the most satisfying emotional responses. Whether they bear any rational relationship to the "interests" of the group in question, objectively conceived, is irrelevant, at least in the short run. "Interests" are never the basis of collective action until they are dramatized and emotionalized into symbols playing a major role in the transfer of private motives onto public objects.[1] All mass political behaviour is therefore intelligible not in

---

two years, in opposition to all political parties and itself a living movement . . . [and] . . . a series of aphorisms, anticipations, and aspirations. . . . There was much discussion, but—what was more important and more sacred—men died. They knew how to die. Doctrine, beautifully defined and carefully elucidated, with headlines and paragraphs, might be lacking; but there was to take its place something more decisive—faith."

[1] Cf. H. D. Lasswell: *World Politics and Personal Insecurity* (New York: McGraw-Hill; 1935), *passim.*

terms of "reason," but only in terms of the mechanism of the conditioned reflex (Ivan Pavlov), of "kinesthetic substitutes" or "stereotypes" (Walter Lippmann), and of the processes of "non-logical inference" (Graham Wallas) or "non-logico-experimental" thinking (Vilfredo Pareto). All political behaviour is in this sense impulsive or "non-rational." The only rational politics, consequently, is the art of conditioning emotional responses in a designated direction and of manipulating the non-rational collective behaviour which results. An adequate science of politics must be a rationale of the non-rational. The clear and conscious realization of this fact, obvious but often forgotten by democrats, is no small part of the secret of success of the NSDAP.

There still remains a question, however, as to the applicability of the concepts and terminology of psychiatry, which deals with the organization and disorganization of individual personality structure, to the collective behaviour of social groups. Can a social class, no less than an individual, be said to undergo transformations of its collective personality in such a fashion as to justify describing the result in terms applicable to individual personality disorders? A collective neurosis is an aggregation of individual neuroses—which, however, are resolved in a fashion differing from that which would be employed in the absence of the widespread prevalence in the community of identical or similar emotional maladjustments. An individual is said to be afflicted with a neurosis (or with a psychosis, when the whole personality structure is involved) when he makes emotional adjustments to his environment of a type leading to irrational attitudes (as distinct from normal "impulsive" or "non-rational" reactions) or to behaviour socially unacceptable in the community. These adjustments may take the form of a "retreat from reality" into delusions and hallucinations. They often express themselves in overt behaviour annoying or injurious to others. Even in "normal" behaviour individuals necessarily react to their environment in terms of their own personality structures—that is, "objective" facts are meaningful only for their "subjective" significance. The community's criteria of rationality and acceptability are products of the whole cultural context. An individual is judged to be psychopathic on the basis of the accepted attitudes and norms of conduct. The "sane" people of the community incarcerate the "insane" in institutions or otherwise subject them to restraining or remedial measures.

But an emotionally unstable individual does not necessarily achieve an adjustment which is unique to himself and relevant exclusively to his own personality structure. If he lives in a community in which large numbers of his fellows suffer from comparable emotional maladjustments, a "solution" may take a collective form. The various individuals comprising the group may reintegrate their disordered personalities not through individual behaviour judged to be insane, but through collective behaviour judged to be quite sane by all others similarly afflicted. In this case, adjustment takes the form of identification with group symbols which evoke the requisite integrating emotional responses among large numbers of people, thereby promoting cohesion in the group as a whole and at the same time affording to each individual in the group an opportunity for the emotional reorientation demanded by his own psychic difficulties. Collective delusions and collective persecution of scapegoats play the role of uniquely individualized hallucinations. Here private personality disorders are expressed and in part resolved by the mechanism of public symbols. When such symbols are born of private neuroses many times multiplied in a given society and are utilized by manipulators to produce collective behaviour designed to influence the existing relationships of power, the result may not inaccurately be described as collective political insanity. If such a psychopathological mass movement gains power, the "insane" majority incarcerates or punishes the "sane" minority. But insanity does not become sanity by virtue of being universalized, except in the view of its victims. This process suggests in brief the social and psychological dynamics of Nationalsocialism—and also of many other political movements bred of collective emotional maladjustments.[1]

What, then, were the elements in the situation of the German post-war *Kleinbürgertum* which led to the emergence within it of the gospel of the NSDAP and predisposed its members in large numbers to organize themselves emotionally around the symbols and slogans of Nationalsocialism? It may be noted at the outset that this

[1] Cf. Caroline S. Playne: *The Neuroses of the Nations* (London, 1925); H. D. Lasswell, op. cit., and *Psychopathology and Politics* (Chicago, 1931); S. D. Schmalhausen: *The New Road to Progress* (New York, 1934). Cf. pp. 227–9 below on Communist and Social Democratic neuroses.

group has tended to grow in relative size in all twentieth-century industrial communities. The Marxist prediction of the reduction of the lower middle class to the economic level of wages-earners and its absorption into the proletariat has nowhere been fulfilled. On the contrary, technological improvements have tended to reduce the relative number of wage-earners as their individual productivity has been increased. The number of salaried employees, salesmen, advertisers, middlemen, retailers, engineers, professional people, small stockholders, etc. has tended to increase (in the proportion to the number of manual workers) in almost all lines of production, including agriculture. This tendency has been accelerated in recent decades as markets have shrunk and entrepreneurs have devoted proportionately more energy to distribution than to production. In Germany, even long before the war, the proportion of gainfully occupied persons in the ranks of the proletariat has slowly declined in relation to salaried employees, officials, salesmen, etc. By 1925 almost half of the total of the gainfully occupied persons consisted not of industrial wage-earners, but of small traders, professional people, salaried employees, officials, handicraft workers, and middle and small peasants. If employees and public officials alone be considered, they increased from one million in 1882 to more than five million in 1925—that is, from 6.4 per cent of the gainfully occupied to 16.5 per cent.[1] The number of salaried employees per thousand manual workers increased in Germany more rapidly than in any other industrial country: from 82 in 1907 to 154 in 1925 in industry; from 41 to 75 in mining and quarrying; and from 252 to 994 in transportation.[2]

What was the economic position in German society of this large, growing, and somewhat amorphous class in the post-war period as compared with the pre-war period? Even before the war its income and social position were declining (relatively) as it increased in numbers. It was becoming "proletarianized" and was casting about for

[1] Cf. F. David: *Ist die NSDAP eine sozialistische Partei?* p. 3: *Angestellte und Beamte in Deutschland,* 1882—1,077,000 (6.4 per cent *der Erwerbstätigen*); 1895—1,972,000 (10 per cent); 1907—3,157,000 (12.5 per cent); 1925—5,274,000 (16.5 per cent).

[2] These figures are taken from Hans Speier: "The Salaried Employee in Modern Society," *Social Research,* February 1934, pp. 111–33, where additional statistical data, coupled with a suggestive analysis, are to be found. For more detailed treatments of the status and psychology of the *Kleinbürgertum,* see Werner Sombart; *Der Bourgeois; zur Geistesgeschichte des modernen Wirtschaftsmenschen* (Munich: Duncker & Humblot; 1913); Theodore Geiger: *Die soziale Schichtung des deutschen Volkes* (Stuttgart: Enke; 1932); S. Kracauer: *Die Angestellten* (Frankfurt, 1930).

ways and means of maintaining its sense of superiority over manual workers. It probably suffered more heavily, psychologically and materially, from the post-war inflation than any other single group. The organized proletariat could—slowly and with difficulty, to be sure—force up wages to meet rising prices. At least there were jobs in the fevered, speculative "prosperity" which throve on the printing presses. And the proletariat, in any case, had less to lose than the *Kleinbürgertum*. Agrarian landowners, noble and peasant, profited from rising food prices and could pay off mortgages with cheap money. The upper bourgeoisie was in general able to protect itself by hedging operations and in some cases enriched itself enormously. A few small business men, shopkeepers, traders, and professional people indulged in masterly speculative ventures and became wealthy "inflation profiteers," climbing up over the mountains of paper marks into the upper bourgeoisie. But in general the *Kleinbürgertum* bore the brunt of loss and suffering. The salaries of unorganized employees tended to rise so slowly in proportion to prices that hundreds of thousands of middle-class families were reduced to poverty. Professional people, especially those in public service, suffered similarly, as did the millions of national, state, and local government employees. People living on pensions, annuities, rents, interest payments, etc., saw the purchasing power of their incomes approach the vanishing-point. By 1924 millions of petty-bourgeois families found themselves in a state of economic desperation.

Then came stabilization, an influx of foreign capital, a partial recovery of foreign markets, and five years of comparative prosperity. By 1928 the *Kleinbürgertum* was again well off, or at least hopeful as to its economic future. The distribution of the German national income in 1928, the year of maximum prosperity preceding the Great Depression, suggests the degree of prosperity to which the middle classes had attained. If receivers of income be grouped into three classes, the German income pyramid was as follows:

Distribution of German Monetary Income in 1928[1]

Annual Incomes	*No. of Recipients*	*Per Cent of All Recipients*	*Total Income*	*Per Cent of Total Income*
Under 1,200 RM	18,041,000	57.8	20,577,000,000 RM.	28.5
1,200–25,000	13,121,000	42.0	48,089,000,000	66.0
Over 25,000	59,000	.2	4,011,000,000	5.5
Totals	31,221,000	100.0	72,677,000,000 RM.	100.0

These income groups do not, of course, correspond with any degree of precision to class categories, since in German society there are numerous criteria of social status other than income. But the bulk of the *Kleinbürgertum* and of the more well-to-do rural landowners were certainly to be found in the middle income group. It likewise seems permissible to assume that the great majority of wage-earners—that is, the proletariat—were in the first group and that most of the aristocrats of land and of industry, commerce, and finance were in the third group. The individual members of the moneyed élite, defined as those with incomes of over 25,000 marks, had average incomes of 67,000 marks. Those of the poorest group each secured a little more than a thousand marks annually. The moderately well-to-do had average incomes of almost 3,700 marks. This group, moreover, was considerably better off than it was before the war and seemed in

[1] Compiled from figures in *Statistisches Jahrbuch für das Deutsche Reich, 1932,* p. 527. Comparisons with the pre-war distribution of income are difficult, because of the different bases of the statistics. In 1913, however, the distribution (ibid., p. 527) was as follows:

	No. of Recipients	*Per Cent of All Recipients*	*Total Income*	*Per Cent of Total Income*
Under 900 RM.	11,219,000	47.5	8,348,000,000 RM.	23
900–16,500	12,228,000	52.0	23,484,000,000	63
Over 16,500	103,000	.5	5,268,000,000	14
Totals	23,550,000	100.0	37,100,000,000 RM.	100

A comparison of the two tables possibly justifies the conclusions that between 1913 and 1928 the poor became more numerous, less poor in terms of money income, but actually poorer in terms of real income when higher price levels are taken into account; that the very rich became fewer and richer; and that the moderately well-to-do became slightly more numerous and were appreciably more prosperous. Cf. also J. W. Angell: *The Recovery of Germany* (New Haven: Yale University Press; 1929).

1928 to be advancing steadily toward greater material well-being and economic security.

The impact of the Great Depression abruptly changed this situation. By 1932 the national income had fallen to 48,067,000,000 marks, as compared with 72,677,000,000 in 1928.[1] Changes in the distribution of the total among the various income groups cannot be compiled from conveniently available data. But it is clear that in Germany, as elsewhere, the industrial proletariat suffered most from unemployment and wage reductions and that the very rich suffered least. In deflation as in inflation the *Kleinbürgertum* was the most defenceless group and therefore the hardest hit. Wage-earners had trade unions and public unemployment insurance to keep them from starvation and, having risen only a little way above the poverty line, fell back toward it acquiescently. The very wealthy could afford heavy losses without personal deprivation and could push off a large part of the burden of deflation onto other groups through the exercise of economic power and political influence. The *Kleinbürgertum,* however, was pinched between organized labour and corporate industry and paid the piper without calling the tune. Many of its members were to be found among the growing ranks of the unemployed, which swelled from 1,906,000 (monthly average) in 1929 to 4,565,000 (monthly average) in 1931, 6,042,000 in January 1932, and 6,014,000 in January 1933. The index of industrial production fell from 100.4 in 1929 to 58.5 (its low point) in August 1932. This meant declining profits and smaller dividends on corporate shares, which decreased sharply in value as the slump wore on. The decline in industrial production was less severe in Germany than in the United States, but more severe than in England and France. The German price index fell from 137.2 (1933=100) in 1929 to 100 in January 1932 and to 90.7 (the low point) in April 1933.[2]

The progressive economic deprivations of the *Kleinbürgertum* after 1929 constituted the decisive factor in creating a mass market for the brand of salvation peddled by the drummers of the NSDAP. There were many other considerations, to be noted presently, which predisposed the German middle classes and the peasantry to embrace

[1] *Statistisches Jahrbuch für das Deutsche Reich, 1933,* p. 494.

[2] The fall here was less severe than in the United States, Great Britain, or France. These and many other comparative indices of the depression are to be found in *Deutschlands Wirtschaftliche Entwicklung im ersten Halbjahr, 1933* (Berlin: Reichs-Kredit-Gesellschaft Akt.; 1933).

the new gospel, but these factors were not controlling. They had been present for a decade or more and were of diminishing rather than increasing importance after 1928. Loss of material income was more important for its social and psychological effects than for its actual economic consequences. People who are desperately impoverished do not ordinarily rebel or protest effectively. They are too demoralized and disintegrated, as individuals and as a group, to possess the capacity for collective action. The German *Kleinbürgertum* was not in this position. It probably suffered less economically than corresponding groups in Great Britain and the United States, but its consciousness of suffering induced by non-economic factors was greater. Its members were not as a group reduced to anything approaching starvation. Its consumption of beer, cigars, and *Konditorwaren* declined appreciably, but it is doubtful whether the ample waistline of the average burgher or the generous proportions of his wife shrank by very much. It is arguable that had the *Kleinbürgertum* been more impoverished or less impoverished, it would have acquiesced in its new status. But it was sufficiently impoverished to become acutely resentful and not sufficiently impoverished to prevent it from resisting and giving effective expression to its bitterness.

Material deprivation was less galling than the ubiquitous sense of social degradation. Millions of middle-class families felt themselves being pushed down to the level of the proletariat. A class occupying a middle position in the social hierarchy usually develops more resentments and aggressions as a result of being depressed to an inferior social status than a class which is already at the bottom of the social scale and is further impoverished by economic adversity. It is a general characteristic of the lower middle class in all modern industrial societies that it is an ill-defined group poised in a state of unstable equilibrium between the social strata above and below it. Its members identify themselves with the social élite of the upper bourgeoisie and the nobility and "look down upon" manual wage-earners and farmers. They aspire toward eventual entrance into the aristocracy of money—if not for themselves, then at least for their sons and daughters. "Progress" and "prosperity" are everywhere the shibboleths of this group. The "self-made man" who acquires wealth through business initiative and thrift is its idol. Its amorphousness, its anomalous social position, and its frequent cultural poverty are compensated for by a restless dynamism driving it toward business achievement.

"Security" in its established social position is less dear to it than the possibility of advancement and improvement in its status.[1] Nothing could be more appalling to enterprising burghers than the frustration of economic ambitions, the closing of avenues of opportunity, and the prospect of being degraded to a proletarian level of poverty from which there can be no escape. Emotional readjustment is rendered difficult by the circumstance that the new situation which must be accepted is, by definition, an unstable, "crisis" situation, the permanency of which cannot be assumed. Things must get either better or worse. When they fail to get better it is assumed that they must get worse. Given these conditions over a sufficiently long period of time, the result is the disorganization of innumerable personalities, the accumulation of explosive social tensions and aggressions, and the development of neuroses and psychoses which find collective expression in "abnormal" fads and fancies and strange creeds and cults.

Without anchor, rudder, or compass, the hopelessly insecure "solid citizens" of post-war Germany drifted perilously on troubled seas. The id-drives of the *Kleinbürgertum,* denied normal and satisfying expression by material and psychic impoverishment, expressed themselves in forbidden ways. The inhibitions of the *super-ego* were weakened. Sin became fashionable. But the puritan conscience of Lutheranism and Prussianism rebelled. Its unconscious protest against the violations of its imperatives was the stronger because its audible voice was stilled. These indulgences, therefore, brought no healthy animal satisfactions, no surcease from anxiety, no reintegration of personality on a new level of freedom, but only dark guilt-feelings engendering new anxieties and demanding punishment: masochistic self-punishment or sadistic punishment of others as scapegoats. And, as so frequently happens in neuroses, the psychic satisfactions derived from punishing sin became an unconscious motive for sinning. Moral offences had to be committed in order that they might be expiated by self-torture or by the torture of others. Devils had to be invented in order that they might be beaten. Only in this fashion could morality,

[1] For interesting presentations of petty-bourgeois psychology, see Thorstein Veblen: *The Theory of the Leisure Class;* Hans Fallada: *Little Man, What Now?* and Lion Feuchtwanger: *The Oppermanns* (on the German-Jewish middle class). Sinclair Lewis's *Babbitt* is an American counterpart. A more sympathetic treatment of certain aspects of business class values is to be found in *Rotary?* (University of Chicago Press, 1934).

self-righteousness, and *Kultur* be attained once more by the Tannhäusers and Parsivals of the new age of chaos.

The degradation of its symbols of patriotism likewise contributed powerfully to the pathological mentality of the German middle class. Where political unification has been belatedly attained, where national unity is menaced by survivals of particularism, bourgeois responses to patriotic symbols are likely to be peculiarly intense and insistent because of their very insecurity. When in such a community long-cherished national expectations are frustrated, the resultant castration phobia is likely to be peculiarly acute and to express itself in militant chauvinistic fanaticism—for example, post-war Italy, Japan, and Poland. These qualities could already be detected in pre-war German patriotism.[1] The war for "a place in the sun," the war of glorious victories, ended in defeat, the amputation by the enemy of various parts of the Fatherland, and the reduction of the Fatherland to impotence. The Weimar republic afforded no adequate channels for a discharge of the resulting resentments and no means for the recovery of national "honour." Man lives by faith rather than by bread. The most potent modern faith is patriotism. To attack it and to deprive its devotees of an opportunity to enjoy the emotional satisfactions which it affords is to sow seeds of fury. Here were new hates—the elemental hate for the enemy of home and hearth, the infantile hate for those injuring the motherland. The enforced repression of these hates engendered new guilt-feelings demanding expiation and suffering.

An additional deprivation was involved in the absence of a strong State authority which patriotic burghers could respect and obey. Deeply embedded in German culture were the habits of blind obedience and goose-stepping, the reverence for the drill sergeant, the Hegelian worship of the State. One could not worship, obey, or reverence the Weimar republic. It was born of defeat and grew up in disgrace. Its mother was the feeble daughter of domestic liberalism. Its father was Woodrow Wilson and the detested "democracy" in the name of which the hypocritical Allies had waged relentless war on the Reich. Weimar presented liberty to a people historically conditioned to desire despotism. Weimar presented democracy to a people conditioned to worship feudal absolutism. Weimar presented

[1] For a "mother-fixation" interpretation of nationalism, see Fedor Vergin: *Das unbewusste Europa,* pp. 121–9.

peace to a people which owed its very existence as a nation to militarism and war. Weimar offered to patriotic infantilism neither adequate mother-symbols nor adequate father-symbols. The motherland was in disgrace—unfruitful, unloved, and dishonoured. The Hohenzollern patriarch-kings were gone. The Hindenburg myth was a feeble substitute. To a patriotism which was impotent and castrated the phallic symbol of the bloody sword was necessarily an emblem of salvation and recovered strength. The *Kleinbürgertum* yearned for what was hard, well armoured, even brutal—to disguise and forget its own weakness. It received only admonitions to reasonableness—and impoverishment. It asked for a stone; it was not even given bread.

The deep hunger for militarist mysticism in the turgid depths of the German soul likewise contributed to the post-war neurosis. The war years left unhealed wounds. The millions who saw blood and death in the trenches did not return as pacifists. The forbidden but sanctified pleasures of mass murder were too keenly relished. Death-fears and guilt-feelings were transmuted into a highly enjoyable cult of "heroism" and admiration for that which had furnished opportunities for permissible sins and crimes. But guilt persisted and demanded blood absolution through violence and death. The unconscious terror of a generation of soldiers who had escaped destruction expressed itself in a cult of hero-mythology. The new post-war generation was nourished on war-dream fantasies. Its members aspired to the stature of the brave front-fighters who were fathers and brothers. Here was the psychological genesis of the *Freicorps,* the *Kampfbünde,* the Feme murderers, the military fanfare, and the hero-reverence of a nation deprived of an opportunity to be heroic.

This analysis might be carried much farther, but this will suffice to suggest the pattern of the psychological malady of which National-socialism became the chief symptom. The maladjustments of other classes were likewise important: the resentment of pious, thrifty, and debt-ridden peasants at urban creditors, bankers, atheists, and liberals; the disillusionment of proletarians with Marxist leaders whose promises of revolution, socialization, and salvation came to nothing; the disgust of bankrupt Junkers at a State in which aristocrats and soldiers were at the mercy of democratic politicians; the feelings of social and economic insecurity among the upper bourgeoisie. But fundamentally the disorder was a disease of the *Kleinbürgertum.*

This group suffered from acute paranoia, with all its typical delusions of persecution and systematic hallucinations of grandeur. In Hitler it found at last an articulate voice. In the *Weltanschauung* of the NSDAP it found solace for all its woes, forgiveness for all its sins, justification for all its hatreds, scapegoats for all its misfortunes, and a millennial vision for all its hopes.

2. "THE SOCIALISM OF FOOLS": JUDA VERRECKE!

ANTI-SEMITISM was genetically the foundation of the whole ideological superstructure of Nationalsocialism. It has long since become the cornerstone of the edifice of which the myth of Nordic supremacy is the crown and the cult of pan-German militarist megalomania is the banner flying over the roof. Long before Hitler was born, the Jew was the target of numerous resentments and animosities throughout central and eastern Europe. Religious anti-Semitism in Germany dates back to Martin Luther and to the Catholic Middle Ages. Modern racial anti-Semitism was from the outset the device whereby the antagonisms of an exploited and depressed *Kleinbürgertum* toward capitalism were deflected away from the ruling classes onto a defenceless scapegoat.

The emancipation of German Jewry, begun by Napoleon in the Rhineland, was not completed until after 1848. Politically organized anti-Semitism became active as soon as the lower middle classes began to be pinched economically between corporate business and organized labour.[1] Adolf Stöcker's Christlich-Soziale Arbeiterpartei flourished in Prussia in the eighties.[2] Religious, moral, and economic complaints against the Jews led eventually to the emergence of a racial myth reflected in the attitudes of the Deutschsoziale Partei and the Antisemitische Volkspartei, both established in 1889.[3] By 1893 there were sixteen anti-Semitic deputies in the Reichstag. Various anti-Semitic political groups have been continuously represented in the German parliament ever since.

[1] Cf. E. Ottwalt: *Deutschland Erwache!* pp. 42–72, and G. Winter: *Der Antisemitismus in Deutschland* (Magdeburg: Salinger; 1896).

[2] W. Frank: *Hofprediger Adolf Stöcker und die Christlich-Soziale Bewegung* (Berlin: Hobbing; 1928).

[3] Cf. Eugen Dühring: *Die Judenfrage als Frage des Rassencharakters* (Berlin: Reuther; 1892; reissued Leipzig: Reisland; 1930). Also Kurt Wawrzinek: *Die Entstehung der deutschen Antisemiten-Parteien* (Berlin: Ebering; 1927).

Hitler, it will be recalled, acquired his anti-Semitic fixation in pre-war Vienna without being at all familiar with these developments in northern Germany. The anti-Semitic motif was prominent in all of his speeches during the period between the establishment of the party and its temporary eclipse in 1923.[1] It also dominated the Deutsch-völkische Freiheitspartei of von Graefe, Wülle, and Hennig. Nazi appeals were addressed from the beginning to a *Kleinbürgertum* filled with resentment against Capital and Labour, the upper and nether millstones of an economic system which seemed to be grinding the German "forgotten man" into the dust. This resentment found voice in attacks upon "Capitalism" and upon "Marxism." Trusts and trade unions were both assailed as iniquitous and "unpatriotic." With consummate skill the Nazi leaders, in their quest on the one hand for funds from Big Business and on the other for converts from the middle classes, resolved the logical inconsistencies in this double resentment by deflecting it against the Jew. The nation, they asserted, was not menaced by a socially minded, patriotic *German* capitalism nor by a patriotic *German* socialism, but only by international Jewish *Hochfinanz* and by international, Jewish-Marxist socialism. Under Nazi persuasion the *Kleinbürgertum* perceived that all the things it had come to detest—pacifism, internationalism, Marxism, Freemasonry, Esperanto, nudism, reparations, democracy, inflation, liberalism, sexual immorality—were all but phases of a Jewish plot against the Fatherland. The integration of these divergent negative responses into a general assault upon the Weimar republic through their ideological unification in anti-Semitism is the most brilliant psychological achievement of Nazi propaganda.

This process was accompanied by the elaboration of a highly ingenious theory of a Jewish world conspiracy against the "white" race. The specific content of this theory varies somewhat with the Nazi sources which are consulted.[2] Many of the charges are based upon the *Protocols of the Elders of Zion*,[3] a mysterious document supposedly prepared as a campaign plan of Jewish world conquest. This curious publication apparently first appeared in Moscow in 1905

1 Cf. *Adolf Hitlers Reden* (Munich: Boepple; 1933), containing the Leader's speeches of this period.

2 Perhaps the most erudite exposition of this thesis is to be found in Alfred Rosenberg's *Der Mythos des 20. Jahrhunderts* (Munich: Hoheneichen; 1930).

3 Gottfried zur Beck (Hrsg.): *Die Geheimnisse der Weisen von Zion* (Munich: Eher; 15th ed., 1933).

as an appendix to a book by one Sergius Nilus, entitled *The Great in the Little or Antichrist as an Immediate Political Possibility.* It purported to be the minutes of a secret meeting of the leaders of Jewry in the autumn of 1897. They had met during the first Zionist congress in Basle to plot the eventual conquest of the world by the sons of Israel. The "minutes," it was shown later, had been in part copied almost verbatim from *A Dialogue in Hades between Machiavelli and Montesquieu,* an anti-Masonic and anti-Bonapartist pamphlet published in Paris in 1868 by Maurice Joly—with "Jews" substituted for "Masons" and "Bonapartists." The remainder was taken from a fanciful novel, *Biarritz,* also published in 1868 by one Goedsche (John Retcliff). It described how the princes of the twelve tribes of Israel met once a century in the Jewish cemetery in Prague to deliberate upon measures to establish Jewish world domination.

In Nazi literature the Jews are usually depicted as a hybrid Oriental-Negro stock which for thousands of years has practised incest (endogamy) to keep itself "pure" and has at the same time sought to poison the blood of superior races through miscegenation.[1] Since its expulsion from Palestine this race has lived as a parasite on other peoples, practising the ritual murder of Christian children, destroying the race purity of its victims, and seeking in every way to bring about the destruction of the host upon which it preys. In modern times its primary weapons have been prostitution and syphilis, the liberal press, intermarriage, Freemasonry, parliamentary democracy, international finance, and Bolshevism.[2] More specifically, the Jews, through their alleged control of the labour movement, the Bourse, the Socialist Party, etc., are held responsible for Germany's defeat in the Great War and for the establishment of the "Jew Republic" of the "November criminals" of 1918. All of Germany's woes since the armistice are likewise attributed to the Jews.[3] The

[1] Cf. Hitler: *Mein Kampf,* p. 357.

[2] In the Bavarian and Thuringian Diets legislative proposals were at one time introduced by Nazi deputies to have all unsolved murders treated as Jewish ritual murders. Cf. *Mein Kampf,* pp. 270–5, 386–7, 351 f., etc.; Anton Meister: *Die Presse als Machtmittel Judas* (N. S. Bibliothek, No. 18); Rudolf: *Nationalsozialismus und Rasse* (N. S. B. No. 31), p. 51; Alfred Rosenberg: *Das Verbrechen der Freimaurerei* (Munich: Hoheneichen; 1921); Friedrich Wichtl: *Weltfreimaurerei, Weltrevolution, Weltrepublik* (Munich: Lehmann; 1919); Gottfried Feder: *Die Juden* (N. S. B. No. 45); Dietrich Eckart: *Der Bolschewismus von Moses bis Lenin* (Munich, 1919).

[3] Alfred Rosenberg: *Die Entwicklung der deutschen Freiheitsbewegung* (Munich: Eher; 1933); Johann von Leers: *14 Jahre Judenrepublik* (2 vols.; Berlin: NS-Druck and Verlag; 1933).

ultimate objective of Judaism is the complete destruction of the German people through bastardization, pacificism, liberalism, and Communism.[1]

These hallucinations cannot be rendered intelligible by an analysis of the post-war position of the Jews in German society.[2] The fact that many Jews had attained prominence in business, banking, medicine, law, literature, journalism, and the theatre made them a more effective target of the Nazi attack, but had nothing to do with the genesis of the attack itself. This point cannot be too strongly emphasized, in view of the disposition of lay observers, unable to perceive that they are here dealing with psychopathic phenomena, to persist in believing that where there is so much smoke there must be some fire.[3] The fire is indeed there, but its sources are wholly divorced from the position or conduct of those being burned. Clever rationalizations of race prejudice, and persecution can never render these types of behaviour "rational." In the present instance, rationality and intellectualism have themselves been repeatedly condemned by the persecutors as fiendish devices of their victims and further evidences of Jewish wickedness.

Nazi anti-Semitism is precisely as rational—that is, as amenable to discussion within the framework of a scientific logic based upon observable and verifiable relationships of causation—as witch-burning, head-hunting, voodooism, or any other type of primitive magic and sadism. The victims are persecuted to appease the unconscious guilt-feelings of the persecutors and to afford a convenient discharge for aggressions in a direction relatively harmless to the established social order. This is not to say that the Jews of the Reich were uniformly virtuous, law-abiding, and socially desirable citizens. There were doubtless as many persons among the Jews addicted to antisocial types of behaviour as in any other group of the population. But the vices and crimes of the Jews, real or imaginary, had not a logical but a pathological relationship to the anti-Semitism of the NSDAP. Nazi Jew-baiting achieves an emotionally satisfying solution of individual personality difficulties and of the psychic disorders of the entire *Kleinbürgertum*. It likewise furnishes a device for the emo-

[1] Hitler, in *Mein Kampf*, pp. 310 ff., traces through in detail the consecutive steps of the Jewish world conspiracy, culminating in the Communist World Revolution.

[2] Cf. pp. 316–18 below.

[3] See, for example, E. Alexander Powell: *The Long Roll on the Rhine* (New York: Macmillan; 1934), pp. 85–109.

tional unification of the group infected with the anti-Semitic virus. The Jew merely happened to be the most convenient whipping-boy. In a slightly different context equally satisfying results could have been achieved by persecuting all people with red hair or with pug noses or with long (or round) skulls.

3. THE RACIAL MYTH: BLUT UND BODEN

THE first prerequisite to the protection of Germany from the Jewish menace is the awakening of "race consciousness" among her people. In the course of its development the Nazi doctrine of race, as a positive creed of German superiority, has passed through many vicissitudes. The program of 1920 did not employ the now universal term "Aryan," but spoke only of "German blood" and "*Volksgenossen.*" The same is true of Feder's *Der deutsche Staat,* which Hitler pronounced the "catechism" of the movement at the time of its publication in 1923. Hitler, in *Mein Kampf,* used the term "Aryan" repeatedly without giving it precise definition. Rosenberg is a champion of blond, blue-eyed Nordicism, but his doctrine was scarcely acceptable to such obvious brunets as Hitler and Goebbels.

The Aryan myth, with its corollary of Teutonic superiority, was first persuasively presented in 1852 by Comte Arthur de Gobineau in his *Essai sur l'inégalité des races humaines.* Richard Wagner became one of the most ardent proponents of Gobineau's theories in Germany. Wagner's friend Theodor Schemann founded the *Gobineauvereinigung* in 1890 for the publication in German of the Frenchman's works. In 1899 the Germanized Englishman Houston Stewart Chamberlain published *Die Grundlagen des neunzehnten Jahrhunderts,* which also affirmed the superiority of the Germans, but defined them by moral qualities rather than by physical characteristics. This method of definition led to the interesting discovery that Dante, Marco Polo, St. Francis, Giotto, Michelangelo, Bacon, Lavoisier, and Louis XIV were also Germans. These two works were points of departure for all later advocates of white superiority and Nordic supremacy. That a Frenchman and a Briton should first have demonstrated that the Germans are the cream of the race is regarded merely as another evidence of the correctness of the Nazi *Weltanschauung.*

Since 1930 the enormous Nazi literature dealing with race problems has exhibited a fair degree of uniformity, thanks to the work of Hans Gunther, appointed Professor of Social Anthropology at the University of Jena by Minister Frick. In the evolution of the Aryan myth Gunther is the successor of Gobineau and Chamberlain. In his voluminous writings,[1] he depicts the Germans as a blend of six "races": Nordic, Westic, Dinaric, Ostic, Baltic, and Falic. The Nordic element, constituting less than eight per cent of the population, has been decimated by war, emigration, and tuberculosis, but it is the most valuable biological strain in the nation. It is probable, according to Gunther, that all creative cultural endeavour in all ages was the work of a minority blessed with Nordic blood. This assumption leads to the interesting conclusion that the ancient Egyptians and Greeks, as well as the modern Japanese, must at one time or another have enjoyed an infiltration of Nordic blood. Every effort must be made, through race hygiene and eugenics, not only to protect the nation from the "Jewish ferment of decomposition," but to increase the proportion of Nordic stock in the population. Gunther's ideas have constituted a point of departure for a whole army of scholars who have propounded his gospel in a bewildering variety of works.[2]

The political implications of the new anthropology have furnished the ideological basis for many of the proposals of the NSDAP. The original party program called for the disfranchisement and expatriation of Jews (Points 4 and 5), the granting of official appointments only to citizens (Point 6), a ban on non-German immigration and the expulsion of all non-Germans who entered the Reich after August 2, 1914 (Point 8), and the expulsion of the Jews from journalism (Point 23). The Nazi State is conceived to be a "racial" State whose first care should be the racial purity of its citizens.[3] Walter Darré once proposed that all German women be divided into four classes: only the first, consisting of pure Nordics, would be permitted to marry the new noblemen of the Third Reich; those of the second class might be qualified to marry after a period of probation; third-class women might marry inferior men, but the husbands must be sterilized to prevent procreation; fourth-class women might neither

[1] *Der Nordische Gedanke unter den Deutschen; Rassenkunde Europas; Rassenkunde des deutschen Volkes; Rassenkunde des jüdischen Volkes; Adel und Rasse;* etc. (Munich: Lehmann; 1927 ff.)

[2] See the catalogue of Lehmanns Verlag, Munich.

[3] Cf. Rudolf Roebling: *"Staat und Volk,"* in *Hochschule für Politik der N.S.D.A.P.* J. Wagner and A. Beck, Hrsg., (Munich: Lehmann; 1933); cf. *Mein Kampf,* p. 445.

marry nor have children.[1] Darré is representative of that large school of Nazi theorists who perceive peculiar racial virtues in the peasantry, derived mysteriously from close contact with the soil. As in all primitive peasant fetishism, blood and soil are invested with magic qualities. "Blood-feeling" or the "instinct of blood" is the source of all virtue and wisdom. Alfred Rosenberg, in his *Mythos des 20. Jahrhunderts,* urged polygamy for the Nordic nobility, on eugenic grounds. He further essayed an elaborate racial interpretation of history.

The race myth plays the same role in the Nazi cult of racial nationalism as the class myth plays in the Marxian world outlook. The new Germany envisages world history as a conflict between races. The white or "Aryan" race is the source of all culture, the Negro is an inferior breed, and the Jew, as another representative of *Untermenschentum* or sub-humanity, is the source of all corruption. The Germans represent the highest point of Aryan development. Among the Germans the "Nordic" element is the most valuable. Germans must insist upon "honour," "freedom," and "equality of rights" with the victors of 1918.[2] The pan-German "racial State" of the future must include within its borders all German-speaking peoples of Europe. It must follow the heroic traditions of the Teutonic knights and win land in the east to ensure its future. This task demands the spiritual unification of the nation and the passionate devotion of all Germans to the new work of racial regeneration.

4. THE SOCIAL AND ECONOMIC PROGRAM: GEMEINNUTZ VOR EIGENNUTZ

In the literature and propaganda of the NSDAP, as much emphasis has been given to its "socialist" character as to its "national" aspirations. The Nazi use of the word "socialism," like the use of the terms "freedom," "race," "honour" and "equality of rights" is likely to

[1] Walter Darré: *Neuadel aus Blut und Boden* (Munich: Lehmann; 1930).

[2] The magic potency of the words *"Ehre"* and *"Gleichberechtigung"* among the Nationalsocialist *Kleinbürgertum* is not unrelated to the circumstance that most of the Nazi leaders and a great majority of their followers, as members of a social class suffering from lack of prestige, are afflicted with unconscious inferiority-feelings. These feelings have been transferred to the symbols of race and nation and find expression in discrimination against the Jews, in the prevalent national "persecution complex," and in chauvinistic braggadocio.

appear somewhat peculiar to western minds. "Socialism" is ordinarily understood to imply a greater degree of public ownership and operation of economic enterprises and a greater share in political power on the part of labour than prevail under "capitalism." This meaning of the term is to be found in much of the Nazi propaganda material. In practice, however, the Fascist revolution engineered by the NSDAP left private ownership of the means of production unchanged, and destroyed almost at once the economic and political organizations of the proletariat. Nazi "socialism" may therefore be regarded as having a peculiar character of its own which is deserving of special examination.

Successful politicians must always identify themselves with symbols evoking favourable responses in the community. In the United States the adjective "socialist" has long been a term of opprobrium. In Germany, on the contrary, "socialism" has long been a synonym for social progress. Thanks to decades of Social Democratic propaganda, even the term "social revolution" sounds attractive rather than repellent to the proletariat and the lesser *Kleinbürgertum*. Anti-Semitic and reactionary groups of superpatriots in post-war Munich adopted such labels as a matter of course in their efforts to win a popular following. The German Labour Party of Anton Drexler added the adjectives "National" and "Socialist" to its name shortly after Hitler became a member in 1919. Anti-Marxism was from the outset a corollary of anti-Semitism, but this did not deter Hitler from using red flags and posters and calling his enemies "bourgeois" in his efforts to attract supporters.

"Nationalsocialism," however, is more than a campaign catchword. Hitler, unlike Mussolini, was never himself a Marxian socialist. But his movement, like its Italian counterpart, has championed "socialism" vigorously—a purified, patriotic, non-Jewish, anti-Marxist "national" socialism. This conception of a purely national socialism, in opposition to Marxian internationalism, is, of course, not new. The old Prussian State of Frederick the Great is the historical prototype of the Nazi ideal.[1] Fichte advocated a comparable conception of the ideal State early in the nineteenth century. In the development of the German labour movement Ferdinand Lassalle's socialism was distinctively national in contrast to Marxism. Paul de Lagarde, Professor

[1] Oswald Spengler: *Preussentum und Sozialismus* (Munich: Beck; 1921).

of Theology in Göttingen, preached a similar doctrine of a pan-German authoritarian "social" State in the eighties, but without result. In 1896 Friedrich Naumann established the Nationalsoziale Verein, but he was also a prophet in the desert. In 1922 Moeller Van den Bruck published *Das Dritte Reich,* in which the idea of a German anti-Marxian, anti-liberal socialism was clearly set forth.[1] More recently a formerly distinguished economist, Werner Sombart, has discovered that there is a "German Socialism," which is not the socialism advocated by the German Marxists nor yet Nationalsocialism, but simply a "socialism for Germany which has application alone and exclusively to Germany . . . and fits like a dress." [2]

The precise political and economic implications of Nazi socialism, however, have been shrouded in considerable obscurity. The familiar slogans, *"Freiheit und Brot!"* and *"Gemeinnutz geht vor Eigennutz!"* throw little light on the problem. Hitler's economic ideas in the period prior to the formulation of the party program were largely moulded by Gottfried Feder, who preached social salvation through "breaking the bonds of interest slavery" *("Brechung der Zinsknechtschaft").* According to his doctrine, there are two kinds of capital: national, creative Aryan capital and international, exploitive Jewish capital (*Börsen- und Leihkapital*). This revelation showed Hitler that the real purpose of Marx and his followers in attacking the productive capital of national economy was to pave the way for the domination of Jewish international finance-capital. The Feder creed was incorporated in the program. The "Twenty-five Points" prescribed for all citizens the duty to work (Point 10), the abolition of incomes unearned by work (11), the ruthless confiscation of war profits, the nationalization of all businesses organized into trusts, profit-sharing in wholesale trade, old-age pensions, municipalization of department stores and their leasing out at low rates to small merchants, the death penalty for usurers, profiteers, "etc.," prevention of speculation in land, and confiscation of land for community purposes (12 to 18).[3] These proposals reflected a desire on the part of the Nazis to pander to demands for "cheap money" as a relief for debtors and to make political capital of the prevalent hostility among the peasantry and

[1] Hamburg: Hanseatischer Verlag: 1922; 3rd ed., 1931.

[2] *Deutscher Sozialismus* (Berlin: Buchholz and Weisswange; 1934), p. 121.

[3] Gottfried Feder: *Das Program der N.S.D.A.P. und seine weltanschaulichen Grundgedanken* (Munich: Eher; 575th thousand, 1933), pp. 19–22; on the last point mentioned, cf. pp. 134–36 below.

small bourgeoisie toward "Big Business," chain stores, mortgage-holders, and creditors generally. This hostility was in part deflected upon the Jews, but the political exigencies of the Nazi strategy never made possible the clear formulation of an intelligible economic program. Goebbels designated *"Kapitalismus"* as the chief enemy of freedom and asserted that Marxism was incapable of overcoming this enemy, because its leaders worked hand in hand with the representatives of *"Börsenkapital"* and were of the same Jewish race. But Nazi definitions of "socialism" have seldom been consistent or clear. Feder's efforts to distinguish between "loan-capital" and "productive-capital" have remained incomprehensible to uninitiated economists.[1] He, along with other Nazi leaders, proposed at various times the abolition of the gold standard, the repudiation of public debts, the abolition of taxes, and the financing of public works by certificates (the so-called *"Federgeld"*) secured by the workers themselves.

The Nazi coalition government in Thuringia in 1930 attempted to embark upon currency experiments. On February 4, 1931, the Nazi deputies introduced a resolution in a Reichstag committee demanding discontinuation of any further contraction of interest-bearing loans by Reich, states, or communes and the financing of public improvements through non-interest-bearing certificates.[2] But these efforts were not pursued. An organic economic doctrine of the party has never emerged. Inconsistency and incomprehensibility, however, are more often political assets than liabilities in winning the masses.

The whole social-economic program of the party was a masterpiece of practical political psychology. Proletarians were converted by the verbiage of a true German "socialism" and a patriotic "social revolution." Peasants were won by promises of cheap money, repudiation of mortgages, and special protection of their interests. Certain industrialists, no less than peasants, burghers, and workers, were hostile toward the banks and Bourse (cf. Henry Ford's attacks on "Wall Street") and were convinced of the utility of Nationalsocialism by its attacks on bankers and usurers. That the NSDAP, in its assault on "interest slavery," was charging against windmills made the attack

[1] Gottfried Feder: *Der Deutsche Staat,* pp. 135–42, and *Das Manifest zur Brechung der Zinsknechtschaft des Geldes* (Munich: Eher; 1919).

[2] Cf. Theodor Heuss: *Hitlers Weg,* p. 94; Ernst Ottwalt: *Deutschland Erwache!* pp. 321–41; Walther Scheunemann: *Der Nationalsozialismus* (Berlin: Neuer Geist Verlag; 1931), pp. 59–129.

all the more effective—for assaults on impersonal monsters and fiends, conjured up out of diseased imaginations, are invariably more exciting than actual violence against one's neighbours who happen to be bankers or mortgage-holders. In the end, the whole financial and credit structure of German society was to remain undisturbed after the party attained power. The only debts which were repudiated were foreign debts. The only "interest slavery" which was broken was the slavery to investors in other lands who had been so foolish as to purchase German securities. This repudiation was dictated by grim necessity, but apart from the necessity it would still have been good politics—at least as good as anti-Semitism. For here again popular expectations could be fulfilled and resentments could be discharged against scapegoats, while the moneyed élite and the propertied classes of the Reich were made more secure than ever.

In German, as in Italian, Fascism the new "socialism" meant only the destruction of Marxism and the suppression of the independent trade unions, along with the integration of professional and business associations into some semblance of a *"Ständestaat"* or "Corporative State." The real social and economic significance of Nationalsocialism lay in its widely heralded abolition of class conflict. In the name of national unity, the Marxist conception of the class war has been fought by the NSDAP since its establishment. Hitler's early Vienna experiences with labour unions led him to regard them as agencies of Jewish-Marxist treason against the State. The Nazi movement, while promoting the complete organization of labour for disciplinary purposes, insisted that unions should not be weapons of class struggle, but merely agencies to represent occupational interests. In the Fascist State, strikes are unnecessary and intolerable. Before 1933 the NSBO occasionally supported strikes for reasons of political expediency. But after March 5, 1933, there were to be no more strikes in Germany. With Marxism suppressed and the Reich saved from class conflict and Bolshevism, business would be able to lower production costs at the expense of labour, with no fear of resistance. This happy result was accurately anticipated by the industrialists and employers who donated funds so generously to the Nazi cause.

5. THE POLITICAL DOCTRINE: DAS FÜHRERPRINZIP

THE Nazi conception of the State is an outgrowth of the *Weltanschauung* which has already been suggested. This conception postulates the inequality of men, the subordination of individual liberty to national "freedom," and unlimited power over the nation, accompanied by unlimited responsibility to God and people on the part of a dictator. A political order based upon these postulates is regarded as the logical corollary of an economic and social order based upon private property, the profit system, individual initiative, and inequality of wealth and income. The liberal order of democratic parliamentarianism is viewed as a dangerous anachronism. The economic analogue of democracy is not capitalism but Communism. The political analogue of capitalism is not democracy but oligarchy and dictatorship. The organic, corporative, authoritarian State will at once revitalize capitalistic economy and unify the nation for the accomplishment of its mission through preventing class conflict, destroying Marxism, and suppressing pacifism and internationalism.[1]

From a genetic point of view, the Nazi theory of the State, like that of Italian Fascism, was a product of the party's war against parliamentary democracy. Just as the racial doctrine of Aryan supremacy emerged out of attacks upon the Jews, so the political doctrines of Nationalsocialism emerged out of assaults upon the "System." These doctrines, in their contemporary form, are nowhere expressly stated in the program of 1920. Here equality of rights and duties of citizens was championed (Point 9), Roman law was denounced as a tool of "the materialistic world order" (19), a national army was demanded (22), suppression of liberty of education and of the press was urged (20 and 23), religious liberty was upheld, and "the Jewish materialist spirit" was condemned (24).

Here, amid faint echoes of bourgeois liberalism, one finds no insistence on dictatorship. Neither is this demand voiced in Feder's original commentary on the program. But in the course of its campaign for popular support in competition with the Democratic and Marxist Parties, the NSDAP assailed the political ideology of the Weimar Constitution and gradually formulated its own anti-parlia-

[1] Cf. p. 141 below.

mentary political creed. This doctrine is presented somewhat tentatively in Moeller Van den Bruck's *Das Dritte Reich* (1922).[1] It can be seen taking more definite form in Feder's *Der Deutsche Staat* (1923). It receives even clearer expression in Hitler's *Mein Kampf* (1925–27), where there are bitter denunciations of such elements of liberalism as existed in the Hohenzollern empire and reiterated indictments of political democracy and majority rule. Democracy is presented as the forerunner of Marxism. As against the democratic State forms which emerged from the French Revolution, Hitler champions true "Germanic democracy," involving the free election of an omnipotent leader who will decide all questions without recourse to the majority principle.

The subsequent development of this doctrine was shaped by the exigencies of the Nazi fight for power. After the disaster of the Munich putsch the party renounced revolutionary violence and repeatedly insisted upon the "legality" of its tactics. Legality required the party to seek the support of a majority of the voters through the use of "democratic" campaign methods. The party itself, however, became anti-democratic in its structure as soon as Hitler assumed leadership. In the years that followed, the autocratic machine of the NSDAP, with Der Führer exacting unquestioning obedience from his subordinates, progressively conquered the emotions of the masses. Its dictatorial structure gave it unity and power in electoral contests and helped to create the illusion that Hitler was a Heaven-sent Messiah enjoying a monopoly of political wisdom. In Hitler's own view, the principle of the party structure was identical with the principle upon which the old Prussian army was organized: authority from the top down, responsibility from the bottom up.[2]

This principle became the basis of the entire political ideology of the movement. It is the antithesis of parliamentarianism, which prescribes that authority shall be conferred upon political leaders from below and that lines of responsibility shall run from those who wield power to those who have chosen them and conferred power upon them. "Responsible government" in the western democracies means either the responsibility of the executive to the legislature or the

[1] Cf. pp. 69–122. The mystic conception of an ideal "Third Reich" to succeed the Hohenstaufen empire of the Middle Ages and the modern empire of Bismarck and William I was not invented by the NSDAP, but was prevalent in all reactionary circles.
[2] *Mein Kampf,* p. 501.

responsibility of both to the electorate. In the new Germany the electorate and the party are responsible to Der Führer. Since men are unequally endowed, the conceptions of mass participation in government and of legislation through numerical majorities are deemed to be obviously absurd and contrary to "natural law." Constitutional forms are of no importance. What is important is the *Führerprinzip,* the role of personal leadership, the concentration of responsibility in the hands of the few, the exercise of power by a new élite.

This élite is answerable to the dictator. And the dictator is answerable only to God and to the people. His relationship to God remains as nebulous as was that of the divine-right monarchs. His relationship to the people has never been defined with complete clarity in Nazi theory or practice. In 1926 Goebbels could say: "The great leader will not be elected. He is there when he must be there!" [1] After the seizure of power Hitler repeatedly insisted that he held authority by a broad popular mandate. But these logical discrepancies offer no difficulty to the convinced Nationalsocialist. He accepts unreservedly Treitschke's "great man" theory of history. Italian Fascist doctrine asserts: "Mussolini is always right." The good citizen of the Third Reich subscribes to a similar principle: *"Hitler hat immer recht!"* [2] In the words of Göring:

"Just as the Roman Catholic considers the Pope infallible in all matters concerning religion and morals, so do we Nationalsocialists believe, with the same inner conviction, that for us the Leader is, in all political and other matters concerning the national and social interests of the people, simply infallible. Wherein lies the secret of this enormous influence which he has on his followers? . . . It is something mystical, inexpressible, almost incomprehensible, which this unique man possesses, and he who cannot feel it instinctively will not be able to grasp it at all. For we love Adolf Hitler, because we believe deeply and unswervingly that God has sent him to us to save Germany." [3]

But power in the new State was not to be exercised directly by Der Führer over the mass of the population. Only citizens would have the privilege of giving their approval to the dictatorship. Citizenship

[1] *Die zweite Revolution,* p. 5.

[2] M. A. Schlitter: *"Wirtschaftsbegriffe und ihre Problematik," Hochschule für Politik der NSDAP,* p. 132.

[3] Hermann Göring: *Germany Reborn* (London: Mathews & Marrot; 1934), pp. 79–80.

was ultimately to be restricted to male Aryans of German birth who had completed their patriotic education and military service and to Aryan German females not employed in industry or commerce and married to citizens.[1] The citizenry, moreover, would be organized into an integrated series of professional and economic associations, in accordance with the conception of the *Ständische* or corporative State.[2]

Above all, however, the citizenry must obey. Servile and unquestioning subordination to authority is the first duty of the liberated Aryan of the Third Reich. That an entire people could be propagandized into surrendering personal liberty and self-government—not reluctantly, but joyously in the name of "liberation" and "national awakening"—seemed incredible to western liberals insufficiently acquainted with the German past and with the pathological insecurity-feelings of the *Kleinbürgertum*. This miracle was nevertheless to be accomplished. Its accomplishment is explicable only in terms of the deep yearning of millions of Germans for an end of all thought, will, or action on their own part in the conduct of their public affairs. The *Führerprinzip* was (and is) merely a verbalization of the emotional satisfaction of having found at last in Hitler a symbol of absolute authority, a Great Father, a patriarch-ruler who can be worshipped as an all-wise Messiah, bringing solace and salvation to his sorely tried children. He relieves them of all responsibility for their own welfare, save that of implicit faith and blind subordination.

Here the pathological regression to infantilism of the *Kleinbürgertum*—and indeed of the entire German community—achieved its most complete expression. The citizens of the new Germany were to be safely nestled in the all-embracing arms of a deliverer. If the neurotic burgher could not quite return to the dark unconsciousness and the complete security of the unborn fœtus in the womb, he could at least become once more a little child. His whole life would be controlled for him by a stern but loving father,[3] solicitous for the safety, the health, the morals, the education, the work, and the play of all his adopted progeny. That this father should himself be an

[1] *Mein Kampf*, pp. 489–91; *Programm*, Point 4, 5, and 6; and Feder: *Der Deutsche Staat*, pp. 56–9.

[2] Cf. Max Frauendorfer: *Der Ständische Gedanke im Nationalsozialismus*, (N. S. Bibliothek No. 40); and Ernst Forsthof: *Der totale Staat* (Hamburg, 1933).

[3] For an interpretation of Hitler as a mother-symbol, see H. D. Lasswell, "The Psychology of Hitlerism," *Political Quarterly*, Vol. IV, pp. 373–84.

alien bachelor merely increased his affection for his millions of German children. That this king should be uncrowned and should himself have risen from the people made his title the more sacred and his despotism the more benevolent.

6. MARTIAL MAGIC: DEUTSCHLAND ERWACHE!

THE culminating mysticism of the Nazi *Weltanschauung* is an ethnocentric megalomania more ardent and fanatic than any that had before appeared in the Reich. Here the NSDAP found the final and most effective device for the hypnosis of the masses. That internal unity could be most easily achieved by dramatizing external threats and inculcating hysterical hatred of foreign foes was a lesson which Hitler learned early and applied always, with singular consistency and success. The propaganda of delirious chauvinism and swashbuckling militarism was carried on by all reactionaries. It was for the NSDAP to out-chauvinize the chauvinists, to out-militarize the militarists, to preach a passionate cult of patriotic hate and national conceit so extravagant and fantastic that it left all its competitors far behind. In this fashion the party became popularly identified with the purest and most fiery patriotism. Its enemies were stigmatized as less patriotic or unpatriotic, and its Leader became a symbol of national liberation from foreign oppressors. To the task of inculcating these attitudes the Nazi propagandists devoted themselves with the utmost energy and enthusiasm. And in the course of its accomplishment they made ultra-patriotic militaristic fanaticism the *Leitmotiv* of their whole philosophy.

Here, too, they built on the pre-war past and availed themselves of ancient and deep-seated responses to the symbols of national pride and power. The historian Heinrich von Treitschke had long since popularized military hero-worship. *"Männer machen die Geschichte!"* was his motto. Paul de Lagarde and Friedrich Naumann were here also the spiritual ancestors of the NSDAP. Nietzsche, with his flaming gospel of the "Blond Beast" and the "Superman," likewise contributed. In 1891, the year of Lagarde's death, the Pan-German League was established.[1] Its president, Justizrat Heinrich Class,

[1] Mildred Wertheimer: *The Pan-German League, 1890–1914* (New York: Columbia University Press; 1924).

advocated not economic imperialism for profits, but the German "mission" of conquest for power and glory. He began using the slogan *"Deutschland Erwache!"* in 1892. During the war he preached superimperialistic annexationism. Moeller Van den Bruck and a whole generation of post-war patriotic pamphleteers refurbished the dimmed splendors of Bismarck, Moltke, Frederick the Great, the Hohenstaufens, and the ancient pagan Germans and thereby paved the way for the acceptance by the masses of the most immoderate frenzy of patriotic bellivolency ever developed in modern Europe.

The psychic deprivations of the *Kleinbürgertum,* growing out of the defeat of 1918 and the aftermath of Versailles, have already been suggested. The degradation of national power was a personal affront to all patriots who identified themselves with the Fatherland. Emotional acceptance of defeat and of the burdens of the vanquished was impossible to a proud people conditioned to regard itself as militarily invincible. Acquiescence in the new order could scarcely be expected from patriots who had made tremendous sacrifices of blood and treasure during a conflict in which brilliant victories were numerous and in which ultimate triumph seemed inevitable, almost to the very end. The loss of European territories, of colonies, of army, navy, and air fleet, the forcible exaction of tribute, and the compulsory imposition of one-sided disarmament were hotly resented. The "war guilt" article of the Treaty (Article 231) added insult to injury and was instrumental in rendering the burdens of the peace psychologically intolerable. Patriots of all parties lauded the Foreign Office in its long struggle to prove German "innocence" and Allied guilt in 1914. Having demonstrated to its own satisfaction that the severity of the settlement was morally unjustifiable, the patriotic bourgeoisie found the task of fulfilment more onerous than ever.

For reasons of internal politics, these resentments and dissatisfactions were assiduously cultivated by Nationalist and Nazi propagandists. By virtue of the incessant dramatization of German woes and Allied wickedness, they were gradually developed to a point of pathological intensity. The resulting aggressions became the more explosive because they were repressed. Disarmed Germans could not fight Frenchmen and Poles armed to the teeth. Merely verbal xenophobia was unsatisfying. Hatred of the foreign enemy was perforce introverted and in part discharged against internal scapegoats. But the original Socialist and liberal efforts to cast the blame for the catastrophe on the old dynasts and the former ruling classes were never successful. The mass of patriots remained loyal to the old symbols for which millions had fought and died. The old ruling classes, moreover, were also the new ruling classes. And if "Germany" had been "innocent" in 1914, then obviously Wilhelm II and the feudal militarists were not to blame for her misfortunes. If it should be conceded that they were to blame, then all patriots were also blameworthy—or at least stupid—for having followed their leadership. Such an admission was psychologically impossible without a complete social revolution.

Other internal scapegoats must be found. Nationalists and Nazis supplied them: Germany was innocent; the old rulers were innocent; Germany was invincible; the grey armies had not been defeated; they had been "stabbed in the back" by Jews, Marxists, Masons, pacifists, and liberals; the revolution of 1918 was worse than senseless; it was a crime—and the same Jewish-Marxist "November criminals" who perpetrated it were constantly perpetrating new crimes which were responsible for the ever-deepening misery: "fulfilment," payment of tribute, acceptance of disarmament, and toleration of pacifism and internationalism. No matter that the Ruhr was freed in 1924, that Germany was given security at Locarno in 1925 and admitted to the League of Nations in 1926, that the Rhineland was evacuated in 1930, that reparations were scaled down and then abolished in 1932. These "victories" of republican diplomacy were too late—and too little.

Against this background the Nazi cult of militant nationalism evolved. Gradually the ultra-patriotism of the NSDAP took on a distinctive coloration of its own, nicely adapted to the psychic needs of the neurotic *Kleinbürgertum* and reflecting other elements in the new *Weltanschauung*. The racial myth made the "Nordic" or "Aryan" German burgher not merely a member of a nation struggling with other nations for a place in the sun, but a member of an ethnic group which was the salt of the earth. This group was the repository of all virtue, all wisdom, all power, for these were the fruits of its "superior blood." The rest of humanity was an inferior and degenerate *Untermenschentum*. The Slavs, in particular, were scum —and the most numerous of the Slavic people, the Russians, were debauched and doomed tools of those parasitic Orientals, the Jews, whose "world conspiracy" against the white race had culminated in the Marxist-Jewish *Weltpest,* Bolshevism. The French were bastardized by Jews and Negroes and addicted to liberalism, democracy, atheism, Freemasonry, and comparable vices. French "Negro-Jewish militarism" threatened the racial purity of all Europe. The Italians, though obviously not Nordic, were still on a high plane, for Mussolini's Fascists, too, were really anti-Semites. Not consciously perhaps, but they had crushed Marxism, the trade unions, and freedom of the press—and these were the prime weapons of the Elders of Zion. But the Germans alone had a great historic mission to perform. They must save Europe from Bolshevism and from the menacing Asiatic hordes. And they must build a mighty pan-German Fatherland, spacious enough to feed its millions of future warriors, powerful enough to destroy French hegemony, and sufficiently inspired, disciplined, and determined to remake the Continent after its own thinking and its own desire.[1]

More specifically, the "racial mission" of the Germans demanded first of all equality of rights (*Gleichberechtigung*) with the victors of 1918 and rearmament on land, sea, and air. It required next the recovery of the lost provinces and the union with Germany of all the Germanic peoples of Europe: the Austrians and the Germans in Czechoslovakia, Upper Silesia, the Polish Corridor, Danzig, Memel, Schleswig, Eupen, Malmédy, Alsace, and Lorraine. It demanded also the restoration of the overseas colonies, though the Nazi leaders in general are not colonialists. A mere return to the 1914 status quo was not enough. Germany's future lay not in Africa and not on the sea, but in the East. Germany must expand across Poland into the Ukraine, into barbarous Russia, and into the great Danube basin. And in the vivid imagination of Rosenberg, this Great Germany must eventually take unto its ample bosom the Danes, the Swedes, the Norwegians, the Finns, the Dutch, the Flemings, and the Swiss.[2] Such a program, however, could not be accomplished without foreign aid. France must be persuaded or coerced into giving the Reich a free hand in eastern Europe. Alliances must be concluded with England and Italy to checkmate the French bloc. This fixed idea of an

[1] Cf. p. 20 above, and *Mein Kampf,* pp. 689–705, 726–58; Gustav Sondermann: *Der Sinn der völkischen Sendung* (Munich: Lehmann; 1924); Heinrich Mass: *Deutsche Wehr* (N. S. Bibliothek No. 47); J. Goebbels: *"Nationalsozialismus als Staatspolitische Notwendigkeit"* in *Nationalsozialistisches Jahrbuch, 1933,* pp. 208–14.

[2] For a somewhat exaggerated treatment of this ambition, see Ernst Henri: *Hitler over Europe,* pp. 107 ff.

Anglo-German-Italian alliance has persisted tenaciously in Nazi thinking in the face of repeated rebuffs from London and Rome. For only by this means can French power be effectively broken and the road cleared for Germanic imperialism.

Hitler and his aides have never cherished the illusion that these dreams can be realized by pacific means. War will be necessary. And war is the prerequisite of racial virtue and national strength, offering values of self-sacrifice, co-operation, discipline, and heroism which make it good and desirable *per se,* regardless of the ends for which it is waged. Even successful war with honour is preferable to a dishonourable peace. "Better a terrible end than an endless terror." "Europe—the whole world—can go up in flames. We don't care! Germany must live and be free." [1] "Might is right!" is sound Nazi doctrine. Political power divorced from military force is regarded as a contradiction in terms. Hitler, in his autobiography, takes for granted the inevitability of war and the necessity of violence. So long as Germany remains disarmed among heavily armed neighbours, expediency dictates that sabre-rattling shall be figurative only and shall be accompanied by repeated assurances of peaceful intent. But woven into the warp and woof of the political doctrine of German Fascism are the heroic military traditions of the Prussian past, the *Heldentum* ideal of knights in armour and the deepest deference toward the vocation of the soldier. The Nazi leaders left to foreign observers the academic task of debating whether these values constituted "militarism." For their own part, they were content to spare no effort to awaken martial enthusiasm among their followers and prospective subjects.

"The Nordic race has a right to rule the world. We must make this right the guiding star of our foreign policy." (Hitler to Otto Strasser, May 21, 1930.)

"The measure of the strength of a people is always and exclusively its readiness for military conflict." (Alfred Rosenberg in *Völkischer Beobachter,* August 1, 1931.)

"Oppressed lands will not be led back into the bosom of the common Reich through flaming protests, but only through a mighty sword. To forge this sword is the task of the internal political leader-

[1] Ernst Röhm: *Geschichte eines Hochverräters,* p. 366.

ship of a people; to protect the forging and to seek allies in arms is the task of foreign policy." (Hitler: *Mein Kampf,* p. 689.)

"The only instrument with which one can conduct foreign policy is alone and exclusively the sword." (Goebbels, in *Der Angriff,* May 28, 1931.)

"One must be perfectly clear that the recovery of lost provinces is not achieved by solemn invocations of the Beloved Lord, nor through pious hopes in a League of Nations, but only through armed violence." (Hitler: *Mein Kampf,* p. 708.)

"The abandonment of a policy of acquiescence and the transition to a policy of resistance means nothing without further war. . . . The war of liberation is the end-point of the policy of resistance, but its immediate objective can only be that of gradually recovering the strength and power which are necessary to throw off our chains completely." (Konstantin Hierl: *Grundlagen einer deutschen Wehrpolitik.*)

"Once more we want weapons! Yea—and such a peace treaty [as Versailles] can serve even this end. In the infinity of its oppression, in the shamelessness of its demands, lies the greatest propaganda weapon for the reawakening of the slumbering life-will of the nation. Then everything, from children's primers to the latest paper, every theatre, every cinema, every bulletin board and every empty fence wall will be placed in the service of this single great mission, until the fear-prayers of our present pseudo-patriots: 'Lord make us free!' will be changed even in the brain of the smallest boy to the glowing appeal: 'Almighty God, bless our weapons for the future; be just as You have always been just: judge now whether we are worthy of freedom. Lord bless our struggle!' " (Hitler: *Mein Kampf,* p. 715.)

Here at last was an end of equivocation. Into the dark void of repression, degradation, anxiety, and hopelessness, into the black cavern of Fafner, came a message as bright as the flashing blade of Siegfried. Der Führer recognized his children in the role which they loved best: that of warriors. Blessed with magic blood, they were told over and over again that they were noble, heroic, invincible. Through no lack of wisdom or courage, through no mistakes of their own, had they suffered defeat, disgrace, and impoverishment. They had been betrayed and enslaved by the forces of evil. *Deutschland Er-*

wache! The hour of liberation is nigh. The traitors, the criminals, the Jews, the Marxists at home must be disposed of. And then to arms against the foreign foe—and to a victory glorious beyond all dreaming. Every fallen mother's son will be avenged. Blood will triumph, and land will be conquered for future generations. And the war of emancipation and expansion will be no slimy horror of mud, machine-guns, and mildewed corpses, but an adventure for the gods of old. Better death in battle than slavery in chains. Here castration phobias, sadism, masochism, and paranoia—morbid longings for murder and death, shot through with the illusions of despair and the hallucinations of grandeur—were subtly transmuted into a sacred mission. The faith of the new crusaders was as mad and glad and beautiful, as exciting and dramatic and heroic as any which has ever moved a generation of men to live and die for a cause beyond themselves.[1]

[1] Only the more important works in the enormous theoretical and doctrinal literature of Nationalsocialism have been indicated in the present chapter. Additional references are to be found in the writer's article: "The Political Theory of German Fascism," the *American Political Science Review,* April 1934, pp. 210–32; in the annotated bibliography in *Zwischenspiel Hitler* (Vienna: Reinhold; 1932), pp. 347–79; in the numerous brochures of the *N. S. Bibliothek;* and in the catalogues of the Franz Eher Verlag, Munich.

CHAPTER IV

TOWARD POWER

1. A HOUSE DIVIDED

Prior to the election of September 15, 1930, the NSDAP was regarded in the German and foreign press as an insignificant group of fanatics. The Nazi papers continued their persistent propagation of the new *Weltanschauung* and their insistent denunciation of the "System." The party congress in Nürnberg, August 3–4, 1929, was notable for the street brawling between Nazis and Social Democrats which characterized its conclusion. Conflicts between storm troopers and "Reds" became regular occurrences throughout the Reich and often led to fatal results. But relatively little attention was paid to them by the political leaders and journalists of other party groups. Nazi parades and mass meetings seemed to have no more significance than those of other "splinter" parties, save that a discerning observer might detect greater enthusiasm and a more effective application of the arts of pageantry, advertising, and demagoguery. The extent to which Nazi propaganda was permeating the lower middle class and peasantry was wholly unappreciated in the absence of any indication in election returns of the growing strength of the party. There were no national elections and few state elections between 1928 and 1930. In November 1929 the NSDAP made gains in various municipal elections, largely at the expense of the Nationalists. The party appeared for the first time in the Berlin City Council, with thirteen deputies. But these tiny straws in the wind were generally ignored.

In January 1930, however, the Hitler *Bewegung* availed itself of its first opportunity to acquire a ministerial post in a state government. The opportunity, strangely enough, came in Weimar, capital of Thuringia. It was not the result of a triumph at the polls. In the

Diet election of December 8, 1929, the Nazis made appreciable gains and elected 6 representatives. But there were also 6 deputies of the Communist Party, 6 of the Economic Party, 5 of the People's Party, 9 Agrarians, 3 Nationalists, 1 Democrat, and 18 Socialists. The Thuringian Cabinet, like the Reich Cabinet, was a coalition based upon the Socialists, the Democrats, and the German People's Party. Here, as elsewhere, the latter group, representing big business, chafed under the burden of co-operating with Marxists. Early in January its leaders in Weimar informed Hitler that they would accept a Nazi in the new coalition Cabinet. This invitation confronted Hitler with an important decision. He had repeatedly denounced the whole parliamentary system and had implied that the party would never play parliamentary politics. Many of his followers were committed, like the Communists, to non-co-operation with the "bourgeois" groups. But the temptation was too attractive to resist. Hitler accepted and designated Wilhelm Frick, leader of the Nazi faction in the Reichstag, as his man for the proffered post.

Frick took the solemn oath of office as Minister of the Interior, put aside his hopes of the "lieutenant and ten men" who would destroy the democratic régime, and embarked upon his duties of supervising police administration, education, and the fine arts. On the same day Hitler told a mass meeting in Weimar that this collaboration signified no abandonment of the program, but merely symbolized the party's iron determination to give reality to its ideas. Frick's first step was to discharge members of the police force suspected of Marxist views and to replace them by loyal Nazis. This action caused Karl Severing, Prussian Minister of the Interior and Social Democrat, to withhold that portion of the salaries of the Thuringian police paid by Prussia and precipitated an acrimonious controversy as to whether Frick was using his police force for anti-republican purposes. Frick soon appointed to a professorship at the University of Jena Hans Gunther, the racial specialist and chief contributor to the new "Nordic" anthropology. Adolf Bartels, anti-Semitic defamer of Heinrich Heine, became a lecturer on German literature. Professor Paul Schultze-Naumburg was made head of the State Art School and the State Collections. This gentleman was an outstanding proponent of "Nordic culture" and an apostle of a new Germanic religion which should be divorced from all notions of pity or humanity (*Mitleidsmoral*). While his wife fell in love with Frick, he proceeded to remove from the Schlossmuseum in Weimar the paintings of Picasso, Barlach, Klee, and other contemporary artists, on the ground that they were the works of "eastern sub-humans."

The Nazi Minister was tireless in his efforts to cleanse Thuringia of all traces of "Jewish intellectualism," pacifism, Marxism, and *"Kultur-Bolschewismus."* He increased his own salary, permitted house rents to be raised, and persecuted various workers' organizations. With the fury of a mediæval ascetic he assailed the *"Kunstbolschewistische Folterkammer im Weimarer Schlossmuseum,"* banned modern dancing and jazz music, and condemned the "niggerizing of German culture." Anti-republican and anti-foreign hate-prayers were made obligatory for all schoolchildren, though this policy was later held by the courts to be a violation of Article 148 of the Reich Constitution. On the anniversary of Goethe's death the Feme murderer Paul Schulze delivered a political oration in the National Theatre, where the Weimar Assembly had met. He denounced its members as traitors and criminals. These interesting goings-on continued until April 1931, when, in spite of Hitler's efforts, Frick was forced out of the Cabinet. His activities were looked upon with mild amusement in German liberal circles and regarded as a wholesome lesson certain to discredit the Nazi cause. But, on the contrary, they won new converts and brought joy to the hearts of a patriotic and pietistic *Kleinbürgertum* bent upon "purifying" art and education, no less than politics.[1]

The deepening of the economic depression brought new converts into the movement by thousands. Between January 1928 and January 1930 the party membership increased from 80,000 to 200,000. By January of 1931 there were 400,000 members. It was precisely during this period of rapid growth, however, that the incongruities and contradictions within the movement came once more to the surface. Many new members came from the peasantry and the backward petty bourgeoisie of Hanover, Mecklenburg, Silesia, and Pomerania. But a sufficient number of workers and of radicalized employees, shopkeepers, and small property-owners entered the movement to create dissatisfaction with the Munich headquarters. This unrest was largely due to Hitler's increasingly intimate contacts with large

[1] Edgar Schmidt-Pauli: *Die Männer um Hitler,* pp. 77–86; Ernst Ottwalt: *Deutschland Erwache!* pp. 265–74 and 315; E. A. Mowrer: *Germany Puts the Clock Back,* pp. 205–6.

industrialists and to his tactics of compromise and "legality." Participation in coalition governments was especially irksome to the more fanatic party members. In 1929 Hitler authorized Helmuth von Mücke, a prominent leader in Saxony, to enter into a coalition Cabinet in Dresden. This policy was opposed, however, by the textile industrialist Mutschmann, with the result that Hitler disavowed Mücke's efforts. Mücke then accused Hitler of being in Mutschmann's pay and under his domination. The charge of subjection to industrialists and of connections with Hugenberg and other reactionaries was frequently made by Otto Strasser and other party radicals. The Thuringian episode added to the ever growing discontent.

Long-smouldering friction developed into an open break in May of 1930. In Berlin, where Goebbels was talking social radicalism to win the proletariat, Otto Strasser, editor of the *N.S. Briefe,* established a *Kampfverlag* in co-operation with his brother Gregor. The publications of this press secured increasing attention in northern party circles. The Strassers championed social revolution, the expropriation of the owning classes, and the establishment of a socialized co-operative economy. Confiscation of war profits, appropriation of land for public use, municipalization of department stores, and nationalization of trusts had all been proposed in the original program. Otto Strasser's Nationalsocialism was genuinely socialist as well as national. It led him toward increasing criticism of Goebbels and of Hitler, whose "Fascist" and "capitalistic" tendencies he repeatedly attacked.

Der Führer, in his efforts to win financial support from business men, had already assured his industrialist and Junker friends that the economic program of the party implied no attack upon their interests. Point 17 of the program called for "confiscation without compensation of land for communal purposes." On April 13, 1928, Hitler issued the following statement:

"It is necessary to reply to the false interpretation on the part of our opponents of Point 17 of the NSDAP. Since the NSDAP admits the principle of private property, it is obvious that the expression 'confiscation without compensation' merely refers to possible legal powers to confiscate, if necessary, land illegally acquired or not administered in accordance with national welfare. It is directed in the first instance against the Jewish companies which speculate in land." [1]

[1] *Das Programm der N.S.D.A.P.*, p. 21.

The *Deutsche Tageszeitung* of January 25, 1930, addressed to the party a number of questions formulated by the Brandenburg Landbund. Gottfried Feder issued an extended reply, in which he said, among other things:

"Nationalsocialism recognizes private ownership as a principle and places it under State protection. It will seek to maintain a healthy combination of all businesses, small and great, in the economic life of the nation. The spirit of the whole program proves clearly that Nationalsocialism, being a convinced and consistent opponent of Marxism, utterly rejects its ruinous central doctrine of general confiscation, and considers a permanent agricultural class to be the best and surest foundation for the national State."

The party, declared Feder, recognizes inheritance as well as ownership of land and is prepared to "assist agriculture to the utmost" and to rescue the farmers from Jewish money-lenders. Interest on savings, mortgages or State loans would be unaffected by the "breaking of interest slavery." The party would not remove import duties on foodstuffs, but would favour them. "Profit-sharing" would have no application to agriculture. Old-age insurance benefits would not be raised by taxation, but by contributions.

"As an opposition party against a coalition government which has brought unhappiness to Germany, we naturally vote now and then, just like the Nationalists and the Christian National Peasants, with the Communists, although a whole world divides us from them. . . . We do not consider that 'social communication' with other parties is a proper method of freeing the German nation from the pest of Marxism and parliamentarianism—for it usually leads only to political horse-trading. Only dictatorial action and a ruthless will to power can pull Germany out of the swamp. The people do not want pretty speeches, but strength; not horse-trading, but determined work in the services of our poor, enslaved German people." [1]

Apparently deeming these reassurances insufficient, Hitler issued an official party Manifesto on Agriculture on March 6, 1930. It emphasized the necessity for agrarian self-sufficiency, limitation of imports of foodstuffs, and the protection of the rural population "as the bearer of the inheritance of health, the source of the nation's youth, and the backbone of its armed strength." Farmers would be aided by reduction of tax burdens, by protection from foreign competition,

[1] Ibid., pp. 12–15.

by reduction in the profits of wholesale middlemen, and by lower prices to the Jewish sellers of electric power and fertilizer. Land may be owned only by Germans and must be used "in the national interest." There must be no speculation in land, no unearned income from land, no private loans on land. "Farming on a large scale, however, has a very essential part to play, and if it preserves a healthy relation toward the smaller businesses, it is justifiable." Inheritance laws must prevent the subdivision of estates and the accumulation of debts upon them. Only land illegally acquired might be confiscated without compensation. Other land not cultivated by the owner might be appropriated with compensation for purposes of national defence. "Colonization of the eastern frontiers is of extreme importance. . . . It will be the duty of Germany's foreign policy to provide large spaces for the nourishment and settlement for the growing German population."[1] Thus were the Junkers promised that their rights would not be interfered with, while the peasantry was offered hope of economic salvation. Comparable reassurances with regard to industrial property and trusts were evidently not regarded as necessary, in view of the cordial relations already existing between the party leaders and many industrialists.

Such concessions to the propertied classes infuriated the Strassers and the northern "Jacobins," who redoubled their attacks on the Munich headquarters. Hitler acted against them with characteristic suddenness. At 12.45 p.m., May 21, 1930, Otto Strasser received a telephone call from Hess, inviting him to come to the Hotel Sans Souci in Berlin for a discussion of his differences with Hitler. He went. Before a small group of listeners, he was reprimanded by Der Führer for "deviating" from the party line. Hitler's purpose, however, was persuasion rather than coercion. "With us," he declared, "Leader and Idea are one, and every party member must obey the orders of the Leader, who incarnates the Idea and alone knows its final destination." A long debate followed, extending over into the next day. Strasser insisted vehemently on five points: a thorough revolution, opposition to bourgeois capitalism, real socialism, no coalitions, and no attacks on Soviet Russia. Hitler accused Strasser of advocating democracy and Bolshevism. "The working masses want only bread and circuses, they have no understanding for any kind of ideal and we cannot count upon winning the workers in

[1] Ibid., pp. 6–12.

large numbers." Strasser questioned the genuineness of Hitler's Socialism.

"But Socialism," explained the Leader, "does not mean that factories *must* be socialized, only that they *may* be when they act contrary to the interests of the nation. So long as they do not, it would simply be a crime to disturb business. . . . Just as the Fascists have already done, so in our Nationalsocialist State we will have employers and workers standing side by side with equal rights."

"What would you do with the Krupp A.G. if you came into power?"

"Why, nothing," was Hitler's reply. "Do you think I am so senseless as to upset business?"[1]

Hitler failed to convince his lieutenant either by threats or by tearful pleadings. Strasser was more certain than ever that his chief really was working hand in hand with the "Jewish Bourse" to uphold capitalism. For five weeks the issue hung fire. Then Hitler ordered Goebbels to "cleanse" the Berlin *Gau.* In a General Assembly on June 30 Strasser was bitterly attacked by Goebbels and ejected from the meeting. On July 1 he telegraphed Hitler in Munich, demanding an explanation within twenty-four hours. None came. Strasser, with two of his colleagues, Weigand von Miltenberg (Herbert Blank) and Major Buchrucker, then seceded from the party and established the *"Kampfgemeinschaft Revolutionäres Nationalsozialisten."* The issue was clear: Fascism or Socialism, cabinet posts or revolution. Strasser sought to keep control of his paper, *Der Nationale Sozialist,* and of the *N.S. Briefe.* He also sought to establish a Nazi Workers' and Peasants' Youth Movement. But the response among the party members was small. Otto's brother Gregor remained loyal to Munich. Otto presently abandoned his venture and later went into voluntary exile.[2]

But the sources of conflict were by no means removed. During the summer of 1930, great burdens were placed upon party leaders and members by the election campaign. Many storm troopers in "Red Berlin" were still under the influence of socialistic ideas. They found a spokesman in Osaf-Stellvertreter Ost, Captain Walter Stennes, and another in Osaf Pfeffer von Salomon. In August, Stennes sent

[1] Otto Strasser: *Ministersessel oder Revolution? Eine wahrheitsgemässe Darstellung meiner Trennung von der NSDAP* (Berlin, 1930).

[2] Cf. Walther Scheunemann: *Der Nationalsozialismus,* pp. 22–7; and Weigand von Miltenberg: *Adolf Hitler, William III,* pp. 1–75.

emissaries to Munich to plead for special compensation to the Berlin S.A. Parades, uniforms, posters, even bloody street brawls with Communists cost money as well as time—and many of the storm troopers were desperately poor. The emissaries were spurned by Hitler and came back empty-handed to the capital. On August 27 Stennes announced that the Berlin S.A. would refuse all further party duty. *"Nieder mit der Bonzokratie!"* was the cry of the rebels. These threats produced no results save condemnation from Goebbels. On Saturday night, August 31, a group of S.A. men stormed Goebbels's offices in Hedemannstrasse, demolished the windows and furniture in most of the thirty-two rooms, and smashed a near-by motor car belonging to one of Goebbels's friends. Soon afterwards the rebels scattered broadcast a leaflet:

"Deutsche Volksgenossen! Awakening Germany betrayed by Goebbels! The S.A. of Adolf Hitler, the storm troops for the German future, march no more. . . . For weeks we have been betrayed by our leaders, Goebbels, Wilke, etc. The young workers of brawn and brain in Hitler's S.A., who have freely offered their blood every day for Germany's future, who have led the election campaign for the NSDAP, should make no more sacrifices while our leaders enrich themselves. Our basic idea, *'Gemeinnutz geht vor Eigennutz'* is trampled underfoot by our leaders. The S.A. is expected not only to offer its blood, but to pay for its propaganda, its motor cars, its travelling expenses, because the party apparently has no money. Yet Herr Goebbels, at a time when our movement has no money, buys a new Mercedes car which costs at least 15,000–20,000 marks. Herr Goebbels has the party pay him for every speech. Herr Wilke, Gaugeschäftsführer, can buy himself a cigar business with his party profits. No worker, no S.A. man, is a candidate for the Reichstag. . . .

"We have a large number of party members who own factories. These members come to our demonstrations in their private cars, for they believe that we are going to protect their chests of gold. But these gentlemen are mistaken. The workers of brawn and brain will not permit themselves to be talked out of the socialist idea, which for Herr Goebbels is only a 'means to an end.' For us the goal is national socialism, liberation from capital at home and abroad. . . ." [1]

This was unendurable. Hitler decided to dissolve the entire S.A. of Berlin. But any such move would be disastrous two weeks before

[1] Ernst Ottwalt: *Deutschland Erwache!* pp. 301–2.

the election. Hitler flew to the capital, rushed to the S.A. headquarters, and there wept, pleaded, and threatened. In vain. Then he yielded. Certain Reichstag mandates were conceded to the storm troopers. On September 3, 1930, the *V.B.* published an order from Hitler:

"I order the raising of a special S.A. assessment of 20 pf. per party member, to be paid exclusively to the S.A. . . . I order the immediate raising of the entrance fee from 1 mark to 2 marks for every new member. One mark is to be paid directly by the *Ortsgruppen* to the S.A. The approval of the General Assembly of members will be secured later. I order the payment of 50 per cent of the campaign funds of the *Ortsgruppen* to the S.A. I order the payment of legal protection of arrested S.A. and S.S. men out of the *Gau* treasuries."[1]

These "orders" produced the desired effect. Osaf Pfeffer was dismissed, but Osaf Stennes and his storm troopers resumed their activities. But now a new difficulty arose. Hitler, who was being threatened with prosecution for high treason, insisted upon "legality" and complained of excessive violence, so much so that even Goebbels ridiculed his *"Legalitätspsychose."* The election was a brilliant victory, but the beatings and shootings of enemies continued. Between November and January the Berlin S.A. was involved in eight murders. The perpetrators were defended through the *Hilfsdienst,* but tension between Munich and Berlin continued to increase during the winter. On March 3, 1931, Hitler ordered all the S.A. divisions in Cassel disbanded for insubordination. On April 1, 1931, Hitler ordered his followers to obey Hindenburg's decree suspending constitutional guarantees and threatened to expel all violators from the party. Captain Stennes demurred. Hitler sent Röhm to Berlin to discharge Stennes from his post. The Feme murderers Paul Schulze and Edmund Heines were named the new S.A. leaders for Berlin. But Stennes defied Röhm and refused to be discharged. Confident that the S.A. of Berlin and of all north Germany would support him, he kept possession of his offices, seized the press of *Der Angriff,* and issued a proclamation accusing Hitler of liberal and bourgeois tendencies and of treason to the party. Hitler replied with an appeal in the *V.B.,* April 3, denouncing Stennes as a traitor. In the same issue Röhm summoned all S.A. leaders of the north and east to send to Munich before April 7 a written declaration of their unqualified

[1] Ernst Ottwalt: *Deutschland Erwache!* pp. 305–9; René Laurent: *Le National-Socialisme,* pp. 123–31; *Zwischenspiel Hitler* (Vienna: Reinhold; 1932), pp. 119–22.

loyalty to Hitler, on pain of expulsion from the S.A. and the party. The response was heartening.

Goebbels now undertook to cleanse the Berlin movement of dissidents. Stennes' hopes were disappointed. He surrendered his headquarters and the *Angriff* press, took an apartment near the Tiergarten, and assembled his followers. He denounced Hitler for building himself a palace in Munich while the storm troopers went in rags, but said that he had been pushed into revolt by sub-leaders who now abandoned him. Hitler meanwhile gave full authority to Göring to "restore discipline" in the eastern *Gaue*. In Berlin alone, Göring and Schulze discharged nine hundred party members. On April 10 Stennes published the first number of a paper, *Workers, Peasants, Soldiers*. He, like Otto Strasser, was a sincere revolutionist with proletarian sympathies. Like Strasser, he failed to shake the Munich leadership. The two men published *Die Schwarze Front* and issued "Fourteen Theses." But in the summer they quarrelled. Strasser likewise quarrelled with another rebel, Lieutenant Wendt. The "Left opposition," once outside of the party, was hopelessly divided and incapable of making headway against Der Führer.

Hitler meanwhile lost no opportunity to enlarge his profitable and promising contacts with Big Business. An NSDAP which was now the second largest party in the Reich was a force to be reckoned with by Junkers and industrialists alike—and a force to be used for such purposes as seemed good. Hitler spent much of his time in 1931 dashing about the Reich in his Mércedès car, meeting industrial magnates in secret, explaining, persuading, promising, and, above all, soliciting funds.[1] The economic crash of 1931 brought Fritz Thyssen to the brink of desperation. He now embraced the Nazi cause openly and undertook to "sell" Hitler to his fellow magnates in the Ruhr and the Rhineland. A movement which would smash Marxism and the trade unions could not but be welcomed by employers, if only they could perceive that its "socialistic" proposals were but devices to ensnare the masses. A movement that promised rearmament, imperialism, the war of liberation could not but be good business for the steel barons. Fritz peddled subscriptions to the Nazi treasury among his friends. Finally he brought Hitler to Düsseldorf to address the west German magnates in the Industry Club on the evening of January 27, 1932. Hitler drove up to the Park Hotel amid

[1] Otto Dietrich: *With Hitler on the Road to Power* (London: Lucas; 1934), pp. 12–14.

the booing of a Marxist mob. The "socialist" candidate for dictator addressed the wealth and power of German capitalism. The assembled magnates were cold and reserved, but under the spell of Der Führer's art they were fascinated and in large part "convinced." He spoke for two hours.

The economic crisis in Germany, he argued, was not due to the world's crisis, but to mistaken policies, to lack of political leadership, to the weakening of the national will, to democracy and internationalism. Germany must turn to the army for a model of government. The army is always and necessarily undemocratic, with authority from above and responsibility from below. Pacifism between nations and competition between industries are incompatible. The principle of democracy is battling the principle of authority. Germany must become a national State or a Bolshevist State. It cannot remain half and half, divided against itself. Russian Bolshevism menaces the white race. To achieve salvation Germany must have a spiritual regeneration and an army with at least eight million reserves. (Here, no doubt, mouths began to water in pleasurable anticipation. Orders for uniforms! Orders for guns! Orders for artillery, aircraft, tanks. . . .) A company composed half of soldiers and half of pacifists cannot fight in war. One or the other. Democracy must go. Pacifism must go. The party system must go.

"It is a contradiction to build economic life on the concept of accomplishment and the worth of personality, therewith practically on the principle of Authority, but to deny in politics this authority of personality and to set up in its place the law of the greatest number, Democracy. . . . The analogue of political democracy in the economic sphere is Communism. We find ourselves today in a period in which these two fundamental principles struggle with each other in all spheres and already penetrate business."

The NSDAP has already saved Germany from Communism. "Had we not been here, there would be today in Germany no bourgeoisie *(Sehr richtig!)*, the question: Bolshevism or no Bolshevism? would have long since been decided." The party's great task is to destroy the last roots of Marxism and to put an end to class conflict for all time.[1]

Loud applause. Congratulations. Donations. Der Führer was in-

[1] Adolf Hitler: *Vortrag Adolf Hitlers vor westdeutschen Wirtschaftlern im Industrie-Klub zu Düsseldorf am 27 Januar 1932* (Munich: Eher; 1932).

gratiating and persuasive. On the next day Hitler addressed the Krefeld silk magnates in Godesberg and later the National Club in Hamburg. This was the beginning of a firm alliance between the erstwhile building-trades labourer and the barons of industrial feudalism. For many years neither ally was to have cause to regret its support of the other.

2. BRÜNING AND THE BROWN BATTALIONS

Long before Hitler and the magnates broke bread in Düsseldorf, the last Socialist Chancellor of the Republic, Hermann Müller, had entered upon unhappy days. He presided over a coalition Cabinet of Social Democrats, Democrats, Centrists, and the German People's Party. The gradual drying-up of the streams of American and British capital was already becoming apparent in 1928. In 1929 the flow stopped, and with its stoppage the wheels of German industry began to turn ever more slowly. Unwittingly Müller was to lead his people into dark depression without the slightest conception of how to lead them out again. Müller resigned on March 27, 1930. He died March 20, 1931.

On March 28, 1930, President Hindenburg asked the new Centrist leader, Heinrich Brüning, to form a Cabinet. This clerical bachelor was suave, cool, honest, ascetic, eminently civilized and lacking somewhat in forcefulness. He was too catholic and sophisticated to believe that any political cause was worth violent excitement. He had succeeded Adam Stegerwald three months before as parliamentary chairman of the Centrum. His legislative support would be weak without the Social Democrats, but Hindenburg hinted that he might rule by emergency decrees under the ever convenient Article 48 of the Weimar Constitution and, if need be, dissolve the Reichstag. He created a "bourgeois coalition" Cabinet. The Social Democrats were out of the Cabinet once more—and for all time. Whether the Nationalists were in was doubtful. Hugenberg's leadership had split the party into factions. Treviranus and Count Westarp, who had quit the party in December, were unwilling to follow Hugenberg. The agrarian elements among Hugenberg's followers demanded support of Brüning, in view of his pledge to aid agriculture. Overruled by his own wavering followers, Hugenberg acquiesced reluctantly. On

April 3 the new Cabinet was approved by the Reichstag, 253 to 187. Of the Nationalist deputies, 53 out of 65 voted for the government, though the party reserved its freedom of action.

Brüning soon discovered that a Cabinet opposed by the Social Democrats and supported only half-heartedly by the Nationalists could not long retain a majority in the Reichstag elected in 1928. His program, like that of Hoover, MacDonald, and all conservative leaders in the early phases of the depression, was one of economy and stringent retrenchment. He accepted the agrarian protective tariffs, demanded by Schiele, Hugenberg, and the Junkers. The completion of the Allied evacuation of the Rhineland in June led to general rejoicing, though it was marred by reprisals against Separatist leaders. Brüning failed to secure a parliamentary majority for his taxation proposal and resorted to "emergency decrees" *(Notverordnungen)*. The Socialists took the initiative in assailing this "dictatorial" tendency of the Cabinet and introduced a resolution demanding the revocation of the decrees. The fifteen Nationalists who followed Hugenberg joined the Socialists and Communists in approving the resolution. The Cabinet was defeated on July 18 by a vote of 236 to 221. At Brüning's request, Hindenburg ordered the Reichstag dissolved and decreed new elections for September 14.

The NSDAP threw itself into the fray with unexampled enthusiasm. Hitler and Hugenberg reached an informal truce and directed their assaults on the republican and Marxist parties rather than on one another. Millions of marks were expended in winning new converts and arousing enthusiasm among the party members. No less than thirty-four thousand Nazi election meetings were held throughout the Reich. No hamlet was too small for a demonstration, with speeches and parades. Everywhere were flags, standards, pageantry, oratory, and the Austrian Messiah in the tan raincoat. Everywhere voters were cajoled, frightened, flattered, and promised everything. In many towns storm troopers sought to "conquer the streets" by forcibly assaulting their enemies. In Berlin, Communist posters were torn down by the Nazis as fast as they were put up. On "Constitution Day," August 11, storm troopers in motor trucks toured the capital, tearing down republican flags. Opposition meetings were repeatedly broken up by the Nazis by every device from armed violence to catcalls and stench bombs. On Saturday evening, September 13, Nazi provocateurs in trucks invaded the Berlin stronghold of the KPD,

Bülowplatz, and were fired upon by Communists on the roofs: one dead, twenty shot.

In this campaign, as in others, Der Führer was a human dynamo. It is doubtful whether any other political leader in the modern world has made so many speeches and addressed directly so many millions of people. Hitler was everywhere at once, dashing from town to town in his powerful Mércedès car or flying over the Reich in a chartered plane, preferably by night. Confident of the protection of Providence, he took great risks and permitted no storm, no threatened mishap, no personal discomfort to interfere with his arduous campaigning. The fury of his movements and the drama of his entrances and exits were political assets, no less than his glib tongue and his hypnotic eye. The Deliverer who travelled on gasoline, with roaring motors open, captivated more millions than ever. All observers anticipated substantial gains by the radicals of both the Left and Right. But the actual result was astounding.

REICHSTAG ELECTION, SEPTEMBER 14, 1930 [1]

Qualified Voters—42,972,851
Voted—35,224,464 or 82 per cent
Total deputies elected—577

	Seats	*Votes*
Communist Party	77	4,590,178
Social Democratic Party	143	8,575,343
State Party	20	1,322,039
Centrum	68	4,126,983
Bavarian People's Party	19	1,058,637
German Peasantry German Hanoverian Party Conservative People's Party	26	1,565,232
Economic Party	23	1,361,761
German People's Party	30	1,577,387
German National People's Party	41	2,457,680
NSDAP	107	6,406,397

In one incredible leap the NSDAP became the second largest party in the Reich. The "Twelve Apostles" elected on May 20, 1928,

[1] *Die Wahlen zum Reichstag am 14 Sept. 1930* (Berlin: Der Reichswahlleiter; 1930). The table shows the election returns for all parties receiving more than a million votes.

were now 107. The 810,000 voters had grown to 6,400,000 in twenty-eight months. The party's gains were greatest in the northern and eastern border areas, where patriotism was most intense; in the northeast, where Junkers and peasants constituted the electorate; and in scattered areas of small towns, small businesses, and small farms. In East Prussia the party secured 22.5 per cent of all votes cast; in Pomerania, 24.3 per cent; Silesia, 22.7 per cent; Schleswig-Holstein, 27.0; Braunschweig, 24.3; Pfalz, 22.8; Chemnitz-Zwickau, 23.8; Mecklenburg, 20.1. Much of the Nazi strength came from new voters. Over half of its supporters were salaried employees, officials, and other members of the *Kleinbürgertum*. One-sixth were farmers, another sixth workers, and the remainder indeterminate.[1] In the great industrial centres the party was weakest: Berlin, 12.8 per cent; Oppeln, 9.5; Westphalia, 13.0; Cologne-Aachen, 14.5; Leipzig, 14.0. And, curiously, in the south, where the movement was oldest, its followers were few: Upper Bavaria, 16.3 per cent; Lower Bavaria, 12.0; Württemberg, 9.4.

As for the other parties, only the Communists made spectacular gains—from 3,263,000 voters to 4,590,000, from 54 deputies to 77. These gains were made largely at the expense of the Social Democrats, who lost over half a million votes and ten deputies. "Red Berlin" was redder than ever. The KPD commanded 33 per cent of the voters, with the Social Democrats (28 per cent) a poor second. The Democrats (State Party) lost five deputies and the Economic Party two, while the Centrum gained seven. The most striking losses were suffered by the German People's Party, which lost over a million votes and fifteen deputies, and by Hugenberg's Nationalists, who lost almost two million votes and thirty-two deputies. These votes had obviously gone to the *Hitlerbewegung*.

The immediate aftermath of the election was a flight of capital from Germany and threats by the Reichswehr command to indict Hitler for treason. Before the Supreme Court at Leipzig, three officers were on trial for spreading Nazi propaganda in the army: Lieutenants Richard Scheringer, Hans Ludin, and Friedrich Wendt, retired. Hitler was subpœnaed as a witness. On September 25, in the course of his testimony, he declared:

"If our movement succeeds, we shall erect a people's tribunal

[1] Cf. Walther Scheunemann: *Der Nationalsozialismus,* pp. 11–16.

before which the November criminals of 1918 shall expiate their crime, and I frankly predict you shall then see their heads rolling in the sand. . . . Within ten years our movement has won a place as the second strongest political party in Germany. In three years it will be the strongest party, and in the future thirty-five million of the forty million voters will support us. That Germany which today hales us into court will some day be glad that our movement was begun. Nationalsocialism will convert this defeatist and pacifist State into a nation of iron strength and will." [1]

These predictions were strangely destined to be realized. In 1930 they were dismissed as another evidence of Hitler's fanaticism and colossal conceit, which the liberal press insisted would doom his movement to frustration. But the insistence savoured of whistling to keep up courage. Talk of "rolling heads" was not reassuring, even though Hitler professed his "legality." He was not indicted. Goebbels also managed to evade the innumerable libel suits which were filed against him. On October 4 the three officers were found guilty and sentenced to dismissal and to eighteen months' imprisonment in a fortress. The prisoners received an ovation from the crowd, while the *V.B.* raged over this fresh evidence of republican pacifism. Wendt later became a "Left wing" rebel, and Scheringer joined the Communist Party.

On October 13, 1930, the new Reichstag convened. All day long noisy Nazi throngs milled about in the Tiergarten near by, while brown-shirted rowdies scoured the streets of the capital, stoning Jewish shops and shouting: *"Juda verrecke!"* Disorders continued far into the night on Potsdamerplatz, as the weary police sought to arrest the elusive disturbers. At Wertheim's department store thirty-six plate-glass windows were smashed. Hitler expressed his disapproval and blamed the Communists and police. Under the command of Frick, the 107 Nazi deputies marched in military formation into the session chamber, wearing brown uniforms and swastika armbands and shouting: *"Heil!"* at frequent intervals. They introduced a motion of non-confidence. Frick was elected chairman of the Foreign Relations Committee, and his party colleague, Franz Stoehr, became first vice-president of the Reichstag. Paul Löbe, the venerable Socialist presiding officer, retained his post.

Brüning pleaded for support, peace, and economy. On the 17th,

[1] Emil Lengyel: *Hitler,* pp. 139–41.

amid a hubbub of catcalls, cheers, and curses, Gregor Strasser bellowed forth the Nazi demands: denunciation of the Treaty of Versailles; abrogation of the Young Plan; resort to war, if necessary, for "national liberation"; punishment as traitors for exporters of capital; restoration of universal military service; introduction of compulsory labour service; and the elimination of the Jews. He accused Reichswehr Minister Groener of treason. The Nationalist deputy Ernst Oberfohren likewise assailed the Young Plan. But the Socialists supported the government and, amid tumult and shouting, accompanied by street brawls outside, Brüning survived his first test on October 18, by a vote of 318 to 236. The Reichstag then voted to adjourn until December 3.

Political developments during the next few months remained confused. The Democratic Party finally dissolved and Hermann Dietrich, the Minister of Finance, became leader of its successor, the State Party. On November 25 the Economic Party, irked at Brüning's reliance on Socialist support, turned against the Cabinet. Its representative, Johann Bredt, Minister of Justice, resigned. In municipal elections in mid-November and early December the NSDAP continued to gain voters. On December 1 Hindenburg invoked Article 48 once more and decreed the enactment of a large number of financial measures sponsored by the Chancellor. On December 6, by a vote of 292 to 254, the Reichstag accepted Brüning's proposal over the opposition of the Communists, the Nationalists, and the Nazis. Parliament remained a scene of disorder, with Right and Left exchanging epithets and the Nazis shouting *"Heil Hitler!"* and "Heads will roll!"

On February 3, 1931, the Reichstag reassembled after the midwinter holidays. Nazi efforts to compel new elections and German withdrawal from the League of Nations were unsuccessful. Other Nazi legislative proposals also failed of adoption, including the death penalty for advocacy of disarmament and for military, political, economic, racial, or cultural "treason"; corporal punishment for insults to national heroes; high tariffs on foodstuffs; a fixed price for wheat, over double the prevailing world price; one-year compulsory labour service; and opposition to higher income taxes. The Nazis did secure the adoption of higher taxes on department stores, presumably for the benefit of small shopkeepers.[1] In general, how-

1 For an analysis of Nazi legislative proposals, see *Die Nazis im neuem Reichstag* (Ber-

ever, the NSDAP devoted itself to obstruction. To circumvent these efforts, the Reichstag adopted new rules to expedite its business. On February 10 the 107 Nazis, joined by the 41 Nationalists and a number of other reactionaries, dramatically marched out of the Reichstag in protest and expressed their intention of not returning. This gesture was apparently dictated by Hugenberg, with whom Hitler was willing to co-operate. It was of dubious efficacy. It lightened Brüning's task and caused the Reichstag, on March 23, to suspend the privileges of a number of Nazi deputies involved in litigation. The remaining deputies, with the exception of the Communists, supported the Cabinet, approved the budget, and on March 26 adjourned until October 13, thus giving the Chancellor a respite of five and a half months from legislative criticism.

On March 28, 1931, Hindenburg decreed serious curtailment of civil rights, again in the name of Article 48. Though the first result of this action was a Berlin police raid on the Communists, it was inspired by the increasing frequency of Nazi riots and anti-Semitic disturbances. Communists and Nazis were literally at one another's throats whenever opportunity offered, each accusing the other of being the aggressor. During 1930, 17 members of the NSDAP were killed and 2,506 wounded.[1] In the same year 26 non-Nazis were slain by storm troopers or other party members, with an untabulated number of wounded.[2] In 1931, 42 Nazis died under enemy fists, bludgeons, or bullets, and 6,307 were injured, while the party in retaliation apparently succeeded in killing only 35 of its enemies (to November 12). In 1932, 84 Nazis were dispatched and 9,715 wounded with an undetermined number of killed and wounded on the enemy side.[3] Murders, clubbings, and other acts of violence increased as the NSDAP expanded its membership and sought to "conquer the streets." The Hindenburg decree of March 28, 1931, was in part

---

lin: Verlag für Staats- und Wirtschafts-literatur; 1931) and Ernst Ottwalt: *Deutschland Erwache!*, pp. 281–8.

1 Adolf Ehrt: *Bewaffneter Aufstand!* (Berlin: Eckart-Verlag; 1933), p. 166, citing *Hilfskasse* statistics.

2 *Gewalttaten der Nationalsozialisten. Terror- und Mordfälle aus 2 Jahren* (Berlin. SDPD-Werbeabt., 1931).

3 Between January 1, 1923 and July 31, 1931, 457 Germans were killed and 1,164 seriously wounded in political conflicts. The police and Reichswehr had 14 dead and 53 wounded, republican organizations 34 dead and 110 wounded, the Right radical parties 86 dead and 251 wounded, and the Left radical groups 323 dead and 750 wounded. *Zwischenspiel Hitler* (Vienna: Reinhold; 1932), p. 319.

prompted by the fact that on March 16 Ernst Henning, a Communist member of the Hamburg City Council, had been slain late at night in a bus by three Nazi youths, who shot fifteen bullets into his body. Hitler, who had forbidden his followers to carry arms, expelled the murderers from the party, but appointed a lawyer to defend them. His insistence upon "legality" and obedience to the President's decrees, and his periodical reprimands to his more unruly followers, increased unrest among the irrepressible elements in the movement.

During the spring and summer of 1931 public attention was centred upon the depression and on questions of foreign policy. October brought a new crisis, leading to the formation of the famous "Harzburg Front." The resignation of Foreign Minister Curtius, following the failure of the Austro-German customs union project, led to the resignation of the whole Cabinet, in order to facilitate Brüning's efforts to bring about a more stable ministerial realignment. The Cabinet was reconstituted with few changes. Groener became Minister of the Interior as well as Reichswehr Minister and thus united in his own hands the control of the army and the police.

On October 10, 1931, Hindenburg consented for the first time to meet Hitler, who unfolded his plans to the President in a conversation lasting more than an hour. The result was inconclusive. Immediately afterwards Hitler motored to Bad Harzburg in Brunswick. Here, amid many speeches, much parading and military fanfare, were assembled various reactionary leaders, including Dr. Schacht, several Hohenzollern princes, and the leaders of the NSDAP, the Nationalists, and the Stahlhelm. Hitler and Hugenberg presided. Here was forged the "National Opposition"—a close alliance between the Nationalists, the Stahlhelm, the Landbund, and the Nazis to fight the Brüning government. Frick explained the alliance and left little doubt as to the ultimate fate of those shortsighted enough to co-operate with the NSDAP:

"We have been accused of mixing with wishy-washies. Let me state emphatically that we are willing to establish a united front with other nationalist movements only because we wish to seize political power. Mussolini, too, worked at first with coalitions. We claim to be the backbone of the Nationalist movement, and we must demand leadership." [1]

[1] Cf. René Laurent: *Le National-Socialisme,* pp. 225–8.

The industrialist-publicist-politician who here formed his alliance with Hitler paid no heed to such warnings. Alfred Hugenberg was destined to play a decisive role in the delivery of the Reich to Fascism. Son of a rich Hanoverian family, he had studied to be a jurist and had become a public official and an agricultural expert. His father-in-law and uncle (he married his cousin) made him head of a bank. From agrarian banking he went into industry and became a Krupp director and later a subordinate of Stinnes. He then went into politics and systematized the subventions of the Ruhr industrialists to politicians and journalists. Like Stinnes, he fought the Treaty of Versailles, the reparations settlement, the Dawes Plan, and the Locarno Treaties. In his political orientation he was more Prussian than the Prussians, more aristocratic than the aristocrats, more militaristic than the militarists. During the war he was a fanatic Nationalist and a pan-German annexationist. In 1916 he secured control of the Scherle-verlag, one of the three great newspaper trusts of Berlin (Ullstein and Mosse were the other two). After the war, with his inflation profits, he purchased the Ufa film trust (Universum Film Aktiengesellschaft) and acquired newspapers all over Germany. In his papers, in his news agency—the Telegraphen Union—in his movies, in his *Ufa Wochenschau* he preached revenge, counter-revolution, and the repudiation of pacifism, internationalism, socialism, and democracy. His was a power greater than Rothermere's or Beaverbrook's in England, greater than Scripps-Howard's or Hearst's in the United States. On October 21, 1928, this bitter, ambitious, and energetic little man with the walrus moustaches was elected sole chairman of the German National People's Party. He remained leader of the party until its destruction at the hands of its Nazi allies, with whom it co-operated in destroying the republic. Here was the industrialist preacher of reaction *par excellence,* who made money by preaching reaction and who sought to secure more profits and power by putting reaction in the control of the Reich.

In 1931 Hugenberg felt that he could play with the Nazi fire without being burned. On October 13 the Reichstag reconvened. Brüning demanded an end of party politics and threatened stern measures against opponents. Hitler, rather prematurely in view of the political situation, announced the readiness of the NSDAP to take over the government. On the 14th the Nazis and Nationalists returned to the chamber, but remained only long enough to hear their own speakers assail the Cabinet. The ostentatious entrances and exits of the Nazi deputies caused the parliamentary leader of the Communists, Ernst Torgler, to suggest ironically that an escalator should be installed for their convenience. Brüning's prestige with the middle parties was slightly enhanced by unmistakable evidences of Hindenburg's full support of the Chancellor. Again the Socialists saved the day for the Cabinet. Non-confidence motions were defeated 295 to 270, on October 16, and the Reichstag adjourned once more—to February 23. Parliamentary government in Germany was already dying. Legislation was enacted by "emergency decrees" of the Cabinet. The members of the Reichstag no longer deliberated or passed laws. Between mid-summer of 1930 and February of 1932, a period of eighteen months, the Reichstag had been in session less than ten weeks. If the Harzburg allies could not kill parliamentary government at a blow, they could slowly strangle it to death.

On October 18, 1931, 30,000 Nazis assembled in Brunswick. In the rioting which followed their invasion of the proletarian quarters, one man was killed. Hitler reviewed a five-hour parade of storm troopers while Nazi planes circled overhead. He expressed complete confidence: "The great hour when the disgrace of 1918 will be wiped out will surely come. Behind us today stand more than twelve million Germans, convinced that a solution of the German question can only come through the power of our united front. We have firm faith in our victory. Through the Nationalsocialist Party Germany will win freedom." On November 1 the NSDAP scored another electoral success in Mecklenburg-Schwerin and on November 8 still another in Bremerhaven. On November 15 the party doubled its September 1930 vote in Hesse, increased its representation in the Diet from 1 to 30, became the largest party in the state, and wiped out the majority of the Socialist-Centrist-Democratic coalition. Ten days later the Prussian Ministry of the Interior published alleged plans of the Nazi deputies in Hesse for a dictatorship and a reign of terror, but this démarche had little effect save to precipitate new police raids on the Munich Braunhaus and on the Nazi headquarters in Hamburg. No "incriminating" evidence was discovered. Undisturbed, Hitler warned his followers once more against violence: "Do not allow yourselves to be provoked, incited, or led astray. He who fails in the last testing days is unworthy of witnessing the victory." On December 1, while Nazis assaulted Jews in the Berlin ghetto, the

Braunhaus issued membership card No. 700,000 and Hitler announce that the party would be limited to a million members.

During December 1931 Der Führer irritated the Chancellor by sending Rosenberg to London, where he conferred with Lord Lloyd, leader of the high Tories, and by consulting informally in Berlin with foreign representatives—journalists, diplomats, and bankers. Hitler usually stayed in the luxurious Kaiserhof Hotel on Wilhelmplatz, close to the Ministry building. In interviews he assured the world that the Nazis, once in power, would recognize private debts, but would discontinue all reparation payments. In an Associated Press interview of December 6 he ridiculed all talk of a putsch or a "march on Berlin" and declared that the party would conquer by legal means. When questioned as to his economic program, he declared: "We do not propose to divulge our economic ideas until we are in control of the situation and can give effect to them." [1] In a syndicated and copyrighted article published in many foreign papers, he denounced the Treaty of Versailles, preached honesty, frugality, and discipline, predicted the early collapse of the Brüning régime, and asserted (falsely) that seventy-five per cent of his supporters were proletarians. "Spring is surely coming for our poor unhappy Germans, but we cherish no illusions that the beginnings of our régime will be easy. However, we are entering on this effort with a solemn determination to give Germany back to the Germans." [2]

Such tactics encouraged Hitler's followers, but did not facilitate that co-operation with the Centrum which some leaders on both sides believed possible. Negotiations looking toward such a combination were proceeding in Hesse, where the Nazi victory had destroyed every other possible basis for a coalition ministry. On December 8 new decrees cut rents and food prices ten per cent, reduced wages to the level of January 1, 1927, cut interest rates on mortgages, delayed foreclosures, and increased the turnover tax. Other decrees forbade the wearing of all political uniforms, prohibited political meetings and demonstrations until January 2, 1932, and provided jail sentences for defaming public officials. Coming out of his seclusion of many weeks, Brüning denounced Hitler in a broadcast and asserted: "The tendency to regard politics from the emotional viewpoint, however deeply rooted in the German soul, must never get the upper hand of

[1] *New York Times,* December 7, 1931.
[2] Ibid., December 8, 1931.

cool deliberation or there will be an end of Germany." Hitler endeavoured to reply to this statement, using the foreign press once more as his sounding-board. He was denied the use of radio facilities for a projected transatlantic broadcast, and Karl Severing hinted darkly that he might be deported from Prussia as an undesirable alien. Gregor Strasser, in an address at Stuttgart on December 11, poured oil on the flames:

"Let no one talk to us of mercy. No mercy has ever been shown to us. We shall be hard, ruthless, and brutal in cleaning up the trash of the past twelve years, and we shall not yield an inch—that would be admitting that we had been wrong. Nobody will be forced to cry '*Heil Hitler!*' but anyone daring to shout 'Hurrah for Moscow!' will be annihilated."

Two days later Hitler and his immediate subordinates hurriedly left the Kaiserhof Hotel and proceeded to Munich. It was reported that under the pressure of certain Ruhr industrialists Der Führer had decided to adopt a more moderate tone in order to facilitate a Nazi-Centrist agreement, but had been opposed by most of his aides. While the Reichsbanner, the Social Democrats, and the General Federation of Labour pledged anew their support of Brüning and their determination to fight Fascism to the death, Hitler published a long open letter to the Chancellor, assailing him once more for his emergency decrees and his reliance upon Socialist support. In his New Year's Day message Hitler emphasized again his "legality," insisted that the NSDAP was Germany's only salvation from Bolshevism, and appealed confidently to his supporters: "On to victory, without fear or blame, we will charge through hell, death, and damnation."

3. THE BETRAYAL OF WEIMAR

"I do not act from personal ambition, but from consciousness of my responsibility to Germany and my sense of duty. In consenting to have my name placed in nomination, I hope to be able with my last strength to serve what all my life I have held high and sacred: the Fatherland."

With these words Hindenburg, on February 16, 1932, accepted his renomination for the presidency of the Reich. Dr. Heinrich Salm, Mayor of Berlin, presented a petition signed by three million supporters to the old Field Marshal. Chancellor Brüning and the Social Democratic Party supported him for re-election in the name of saving the republic from Fascism and reaction. Brüning had endeavoured to avoid an election. Early in January he had proposed an indefinite extension of Hindenburg's term, which would expire in May. Such action, he believed, could be taken lawfully by two-thirds of the Reichstag. The Social Democrats were willing to co-operate. The Chancellor sought to secure Nazi acquiescence in a meeting with Hitler on January 8. But when Hitler and Hugenberg refused to consent, Brüning was obliged to drop this plan. In an elaborate memorandum Hitler argued that any such arrangement would be "unconstitutional." Hindenburg was accordingly renominated as a "non-party" candidate, assured of the support of all friends of the Weimar régime.

Paul Ludwig Hans Anton von Beneckendorff und von Hindenburg, who, more than any other single individual, was destined to be responsible for the delivery of the German republic to Fascism, was a typical member of the landed nobility. He accepted uncritically the values and ideals of his class and identified its interests with those of the Fatherland. These interests he served to the best of his ability all of his long life. Born October 2, 1847, in Posen, he was the heir of a line of feudal lords, long since impoverished. One of the Hindenburgs had been awarded an estate by Frederick the Great for losing a leg in the Silesian War. The Beneckendorffs were Teutonic Knights. Both families lived by the toil of their peasants and served the State as soldiers. The names were united with royal consent in 1789. Young Paul lived with soldiers constantly and was sent away to cadet school at the age of eleven. His parents gave him a faith in God, the Fatherland, and the Prussian kings which he never questioned. He admired the military brutality to which he was subjected and once boasted that since his days as a cadet he had never read a book which did not deal with military affairs. In 1866 he graduated and became a Prussian officer at Danzig and later at Potsdam. At Sadowa he was stunned by a bullet in leading a charge against the Austrian artillery and was decorated for his bravery. In the Franco-Prussian War he again distinguished himself and received the Iron Cross. Then for forty years he lived with garrisons, taught tactics, and drilled regiments, stolidly, thoroughly, without brilliance, rising step by step through seniority promotions to the rank of Lieutenant-General. In 1911 he retired from active service and prepared to spend his declining years in peace and quiet.

This obscure Junker General became a national hero overnight in 1914. Summoned from his retirement to assume command despite his sixty-seven years, he replaced General von Prittwitz as Commander-in-Chief of the Eighth Army, facing the Russian invaders of East Prussia. He accepted the suggestions of Ludendorff and adopted the plan of attack worked out and executed by General von François. Samsonoff's army of invasion was destroyed near Tannenberg, August 27–31, 1914. Hindenburg had signed the decisive orders and was hailed by the nation as a military genius and a saviour of the Fatherland. This fable [1] became the basis of a great myth which waxed steadily in grandeur and persisted unimpaired until the end of Hindenburg's life—and for a long time thereafter. His war career need not be reviewed here, except to notice that he became Chief of the General Staff in the autumn of 1916 and was used as a political tool by the extreme annexationists. With Ludendorff he planned the great offensive of 1918. On March 21, following the defeat of the British east of Amiens, he was awarded the "Iron Cross with Golden Rays" by the Kaiser, a symbol of final victory created for Blücher after Waterloo and never subsequently offered to anyone until 1918. But prospective triumph turned into defeat. Hindenburg and Ludendorff, needlessly panic-stricken at the military situation, insisted upon an armistice at the end of September. The "stab in the back" came not from the revolutionists at home, but from the General Staff, which realized too late, at the end of October, that its demands had compelled the civil authorities in Berlin to surrender and to commit the disastrous diplomatic blunder of the armistice. When revolution came, Ludendorff fled in disguise to Sweden. Hindenburg, however, remained at his post and supervised the execution of the armistice, thereby restoring the bright lustre of the legend which had gathered around his name.

In June 1919 he retired, presumably for the last time, though in March of 1920 he was not above asking the permission of the Kaiser at Doorn to accept a candidacy for the presidency of the Reich, should it be offered to him. The offer did not come. Hindenburg,

[1] For a critical evaluation of Hindenburg's military career, see Margaret L. Goldsmith and Frederick Voigt: *Hindenburg, The Man and the Legend* (London: Faber; 1930), pp. 68–188.

living in Hanover, devoted himself to hunting, collecting pictures of the Madonna, and writing his memoirs. Unlike Ludendorff, he remained aloof from politics and engaged in no anti-republican conspiracies. Only once did he appear in public—at a Nationalist parade in Königsberg in June 1922. In March 1925 he was prevailed upon to become a candidate for the presidency and to lend his magic name to the cause of reaction. In May the old monarchist became President of the republic. He betrayed his monarchist supporters and for seven years remained loyal to Weimar. In the summer of 1929 a three-mark coin was struck off to commemorate the tenth anniversary of the Weimar Constitution. On it appeared a bust of Hindenburg, an image of his hand raised in solemn oath, and the caption: "True to the Constitution." But it was he who was to betray his republican supporters in 1932 and to deliver the Reich into the hands of the aristocratic reactionaries. Then, in 1933, when these groups seemed no longer able or willing to regard the profits of the Junkers and the interests of the Hindenburg family as identical with the interests of the nation, the "Old Gentleman" was to deliver the Reich to Hitler.

In the political jockeying which followed Hindenburg's nomination to succeed himself, the "Harzburg Front" temporarily broke down. On December 5 Hitler had declared that under no circumstances would he be a candidate. When asked what his party proposed to do in the event of an election, he replied enigmatically: "That eventuality is already provided for." In fact nothing was provided for. On January 12, 1932, the executive committee of the Communist Party nominated as its candidate for the presidency its perennial leader, Ernst Thälmann, Hamburg transport worker.[1] He declared that Brüning was as much a Fascist as Hitler, with only a difference in tempo between them, and denounced the Social Democrats for supporting Hindenburg and thus playing into the hands of the enemy. He presented himself as "the candidate of the struggle against imperialist war." Late in January the Reichsverband der Industrie, the Kyffhäuserbund, the Stahlhelm, and the "Iron Front" of the trade unions, the Social Democrats, and the Reichsbanner all indicated that they would support Hindenburg. What Hitler and Hugenberg would do remained uncertain.

On February 5 Reichswehr Minister Groener announced that the ban on the entrance of members of the NSDAP into the army had

[1] Cf. Peter Maslowski: *Thälmann* (Leipzig: Kittler; 1932).

been lifted. Only Communists were henceforth to be barred. This decision was apparently a result of secret conferences between Hitler and various Reichswehr officers. His intermediary was General Kurt von Schleicher, an obscure and mysterious military bureaucrat in the Reichswehrministerium. This bland and smiling "office-General" encouraged the impression that he was a powerful "man behind the scenes" who had had a hand in the original appointment of the Brüning Cabinet.[1] That he was constantly engaged in hidden political intrigues is certain. Hitler perceived that he might be useful. Whether he was responsible for Groener's action of February 5 is uncertain. But on the same day Hanfstängl saw fit to declare that Hitler was not seeking the presidency, but desired to drive a wedge between Brüning and Hindenburg, in order that Groener might be made Chancellor, with Hitler as a member of the new Cabinet. This effort failed, as did Hitler's attempts to reach an understanding with Hugenberg. The Nationalist leader at length made an agreement with the Stahlhelm, whereby its leader, Theodor Duesterberg, would be their common candidate.

At this juncture, on February 22, Hitler announced his own candidacy. There was a legal difficulty to be overcome, however. Hitler was still an alien. He denied allegations that he had sought to acquire German citizenship by having Frick appoint him as a police commissioner in Thuringia. Dietrich Klagges, the Nazi Minister of the Interior in Brunswick, considered appointing him a professor in Brunswick Hochschule for this purpose. But on February 25 he was named attaché to the Berlin Legation of the State of Brunswick and *ipso facto* became a German citizen, eligible for the presidency. On February 23 the Reichstag met. Goebbels denounced the Social Democrats as "the party of deserters" and asserted that Hindenburg was supported by "superannuated excellencies of the Stone Age." He was excluded from the session for insulting the Reichspresident. The Reichstag fixed March 13 as the date of the election, with a second election on April 10 if no candidate received a majority. A non-confidence motion was defeated 289 to 264. Brüning hurled his defiance at the Nationalists and Nazis who walked out of the chamber. Parliament adjourned *sine die* on February 26.

The campaign was turbulent and hotly contested. Privately Hitler

[1] Rudolf Fischer: *Schleicher-Mythos und Wirklichkeit* (Hamburg: Hanseatischer Verlag; 1933).

probably had no hope of being elected. To run without the support of the Nationalists and the Stahlhelm against the legendary Hindenburg was dangerous. But to support Hindenburg as the candidate of Brüning and Social Democracy was impossible. In any case, Hitler would be the centre of attention. The Socialist leaders knew that their support of Hindenburg would alienate many of their followers. They therefore directed their campaign against Hitler, rather than for Hindenburg. With tremendous energy and efficiency the party machine of the NSDAP strove to roll up as large a vote for Der Führer as possible. No less than 120,000 Nazi meetings were held throughout the Reich—an average of 3,000 a day. A million Nazi posters were printed, as well as eight million pamphlets and twelve million extra editions of party papers. Hugenberg used UFA films to campaign for Duesterberg, who came out openly in favour of monarchical restoration. The Cabinet monopolized radio facilities for Hindenburg, a circumstance which caused Hitler later to contest the validity of the election. The President made only one speech, broadcast on March 10. He sought to refute critics and denied that he was a clerical-Socialist candidate.

"Had I refused, the danger would have arisen that, owing to serious party differences, owing especially to dissension among the Rightists, the radical Rightist candidate or one of the radical Lefts would be elected on the second ballot. Election of a party man, representing one-sided extremist views, who would consequently have the majority of the people against him, would expose the Fatherland to serious disturbances, whose outcome would be incalculable. Duty commanded me to prevent this. . . . If I am re-elected, I shall owe responsibility only to my God, my conscience, and my Fatherland. Thus I can take office as trustee for the nation. . . . Remember 1914! . . . The responsibility that made me hold out in the war until I brought my troops home, the responsibility that guided me as the President of the nation in the most difficult decisions, this responsibility impels me now to hold out again to serve the German nation in true faithfulness. To give my last remaining strength for this purpose I offer myself again. That is the meaning and aim of my candidacy." [1]

[1] *The New York Times,* March 11, 1932.

The balloting of March 13 resulted as follows:

PRESIDENTIAL ELECTION, MARCH 13, 1932 [1]

Qualified Voters	43,949,681	*Per cent*
Voted	37,890,451	86.2
Paul von Hindenburg	18,651,497	49.6
Adolf Hitler	11,339,446	30.1
Ernst Thälmann	4,983,341	13.2
Theodor Duesterberg	2,557,729	6.8
Adolf Winter	111,423	0.3

Hindenburg thus failed to secure the necessary majority by the narrow margin of less than half of one per cent. The Communists had gained almost four hundred thousand votes since September, 1930. Duesterberg's showing was disappointing. Hitler's vote, while insufficient to elect him, was nevertheless impressive, though it was generally interpreted (erroneously) to represent the high point of Nazi strength. The NSDAP had gained almost five million converts since September 1930. In none of the thirty-five electoral districts did Hitler secure a majority. He secured a larger vote than Hindenburg in three frontier districts, however: Pomerania, 37.4 per cent; Schleswig-Holstein, 42.7 per cent; and Chemnitz-Zwickau, 40.9 per cent.

On March 14 Hindenburg and Hitler both announced their candidacies for the second election.[2] Hugenberg declared that his followers were prepared to have Parliament validate the results of the first election, on condition that the Reichstag should be dissolved. His proposal was ignored. The Nationalist leader found himself isolated and decided to restore the "Harzburg Front." Duesterberg withdrew from the race, and the Nationalists swung over to Hitler. The Stahlhelm leaders, however, refused to co-operate and left their followers free to vote as they pleased. The Social Democrats claimed credit for Hindenburg's victory and redoubled their efforts to ensure his triumph in the second balloting. On March 17 Karl Severing, Socialist

[1] *Das Gesamtergebnis der Wahl des Reichspräsidenten am 13 März und 10 April, 1932* (Berlin: Statistisches Reichsamt; 1932).

[2] Cf. Joseph Goebbels: *Vom Kaiserhof zur Reichskanzlei* (Munich: Eher; 1934), pp. 61–4.

Minister of the Interior of Prussia, ordered his police to raid all Nazi headquarters. The homes of Nazi leaders were also broken into, and many files of documents confiscated. Severing announced the "discovery" of a plot whereby the S.A., then estimated to number five hundred thousand members, was to be mobilized for the revolutionary seizure of power by the code signal: "Grandmother dead." Hitler denied the allegation and sent Göring to Groener with new professions of "legality." Even the liberal press criticized Severing's stupidity. Hitler sued before the Supreme Court for an injunction against Severing, with the result that the Minister agreed to return the documents and records, on condition that the suit be dropped. The only effect of this stroke was that certain aspects of the military and espionage organization of the S.A. were revealed. It likewise appeared that the NSDAP had possibly planned to unleash the storm troopers against the Communists, in the event of Hitler's election. But Severing undoubtedly gained more voters for Der Führer than he frightened away.

The second campaign was almost as hard fought as the first, though there was little doubt of Hindenburg's election. Hitler spoke everywhere, championing autarchy, superpatriotism, family life, and morality. To women in the Lustgarten he promised husbands and homes, to burghers in Potsdam a revival of the military spirit, to wage-earners in the Rhineland a new workers' State, and to peasants in the eastern marches a restoration of their prosperity. Brüning campaigned actively for Hindenburg, as did the Social Democrats. Hitler's demand for radio facilities was refused. The Munich *V.B.* was suspended for a week for insulting the government. Two Hitler meetings in Munich were banned by the police, and Röhm was forbidden to mobilize the local storm troopers for election purposes. Despite these restrictions, Hitler increased his vote by more than two million:

PRESIDENTIAL ELECTION, APRIL 10, 1932 [1]

Qualified Voters	44,063,958	*Per cent*
Voted	36,771,787	83.5
Paul von Hindenburg	19,359,983	53.0
Adolf Hitler	13,418,547	36.8
Ernst Thälmann	3,706,759	10.2

[1] *Das Gesamtergebnis der Wahl des Reichspräsidenten am 13 März und 10 April, 1932.*

Hindenburg was thus elected by an absolute majority, while Thälmann lost over a million votes and most of Duesterberg's supporters went over to the Nazis. Undaunted, Hitler made preparations at once for the state elections scheduled for April 24. In apprehension, the Socialist Premier of Prussia, Otto Braun, demanded the dissolution of the S.A. He was ignored. Nevertheless, effective pressure was now brought to bear on Brüning and Hindenburg toward this end. The Social Democrats may have threatened to withdraw their continued support in the Reichstag. Severing's "documents" were not taken seriously. Possibly Brüning himself decided (much too late) that effective action should at last be taken against the Nazis. Or perhaps General von Schleicher had a hand in the situation. In the dense atmosphere of intrigue and conspiracy which now began to envelop the government of the Reich it became increasingly difficult to ascertain who was pulling which strings for what purposes. In any case, Hindenburg, on April 13, signed a decree, again under Article 48, dissolving the S.A. The Munich Braunhaus was once more occupied by the police. The Hitler Jugend was likewise banned. Throughout the nation police forces raided and padlocked the headquarters of the storm troopers, confiscating uniforms, arms, and other equipment.

This was the most serious blow ever struck at the NSDAP in the name of protecting the republic. But the Chancellor who acted was too "objective" and indecisive to scotch the Nazi hydra, and the President who signed the decree was on the point of betraying all who had elected him. Hitler urged his followers to work all the harder for the Diet elections and challenged the legality of the S.A. prohibition in the courts. The campaign now became bitter in the extreme. On April 23 Otto Wels, leader of Social Democracy, was assaulted and severely beaten by Nazis in Cologne. Twenty of the offenders were arrested. Two leaders were subsequently sentenced to jail: Herr Fuchs for five months and Robert Ley for three. The Diet elections of the 24th resulted in a Nazi landslide. In four of the five states where new legislatures were chosen, the NSDAP became the largest single party: Prussia, Württemberg, Hamburg, and Anhalt. In Bavaria the Nazi votes were barely exceeded by those cast for the Bavarian People's Party. In Prussia, where the last Landtag election had been held on May 20, 1928, the Hitlerites polled a million votes more than they had received on March 13. The Weimar Coalition was demolished. The Socialist deputies were reduced from 137 to 93, the Nationalists from 82 to 31, the Centrists from 71 to 67, the State Party from 21 to 2, the German People's Party from 40 to 7, and the Economic Party from 21 to 0. The Communists increased their deputies from 56 to 57 and the Nazis from 6 to 162.

This new Nazi victory further increased political tension. On May 4 the Communist free thinkers' societies were officially dissolved for promoting atheism. On May 9 the Reichstag reconvened. On the 11th the Nazi members launched a furious attack on Brüning and Groener. Goebbels, Frick, and Gregor Strasser bitterly denounced the Reichswehr Minister, whom they accused of suppressing the S.A. In the Reichstag restaurant several Nazi deputies, including Gregor Strasser, beat up a Socialist journalist. (Three of them were subsequently sentenced to three months in jail, though Strasser was acquitted.) The culprits, when expelled from the session, refused to leave. They were ejected by the police, amid scenes of disorder. Brüning, however, still retained a safe majority. A non-confidence motion was defeated 287 to 257. President Löbe then adjourned the Reichstag till June 6. On May 12 Groener resigned his post as Reichswehr Minister, retaining, however, his portfolio in the Ministry of the Interior. He denied that he was forced out as a result of an intrigue of generals. Schleicher in his office continued to smile in silence. On May 24, when the Prussian Landtag met, the deadlock created by the election remained unbroken, with all efforts to form a Nazi-Centrist coalition unsuccessful. When a Communist speaker on the 25th accused the Nazis of harbouring murderers in their ranks, he was assaulted by a hundred and fifty Nazi deputies. Fifty Communists rushed to his rescue, and in the ensuing battle the chamber was wrecked and the Communists were gradually driven from the hall by the superior numbers of the enemy. The Prussian Cabinet of Braun and Severing remained in office—without a majority.

Meanwhile the secret plottings which were to culminate in the dismissal of the Chancellor and the delivery of the republic into the hands of feudal reaction were already well under way. Precisely what occurred behind the scenes is still unclear. Hindenburg was prevailed upon to drop Brüning, to repudiate the Centrists and Social Democrats who had re-elected him to the presidency, and to make himself the tool of fantastic reactionary intrigues. Schleicher later boasted that he had "made" Brüning and broken him and had elevated

Groener to his post and then removed him. He likewise asserted that he engineered the construction of the Papen Cabinet even before the presidential election.[1] Whatever his precise role in influencing the President, there were other important elements in the situation. Schleicher was a friend of Dr. Otto Meissner, the Secretary of State to the President. He was also a friend of the President's son, Colonel Oskar von Hindenburg. And he was an intimate of Franz von Papen. Here were the strands of the Junker-militarist spider-web which was to ensnare Brüning and to draw the government of the Reich into a tangle of reactionary conspiracies.

In East Prussia, Hindenburg had many friends among his Junker neighbours. It was they who had raised funds from the industrialists by public subscription and presented the deed of the Gut Neudeck to the Field Marshal on his eightieth birthday, October 3, 1927. The estate was small, poor, and debt-ridden, but it had once been the ancestral home of the family, and the President deeply appreciated the gift. Herr von Oldenburg-Januschau had taken the initiative in this matter. He persuaded his neighbours that the offering would be an ideal means of ensuring Hindenburg's loyalty to the Junkers. In view of the President's advanced age, the gift was in form made to the President's son Oskar as a means of escaping the inheritance tax. To Neudeck Hindenburg habitually retired to rest and to meet his friends and neighbours. Most of them identified their own class interests as agrarian aristocrats with those of the nation. They wanted protective tariffs on foodstuffs, and subsidies from the public treasury with which to pay their debts and enlarge their estates. Any deviation from these policies they denounced as "agrarian Bolshevism." These interests were Hindenburg's interests —for was he not too, through his son, an estate-owner? If Neudeck cost Oskar fifty thousand dollars a year to maintain, so much the better. The impoverished Hindenburgs should know the "poverty" of all the Junkers. As militarists and monarchists, these blue-blooded nobles of the east were always prepared to tolerate any cabinet which

[1] *The Berlin Diaries, May 30, 1932–January 30, 1933;* Helmut Klotz, editor (New York: Morrow, 1934); pp. 27–40. This anonymous work is alleged to have been written in part by a general in the Ministry of Defence. Whether or not this is true, the author (or authors) had access to certain sources of information regarding the political intrigues of 1932 which were not available to outside observers. The allegations in the book must of course be used with caution in the absence of reliable evidence of their truth or falsity.

protected their interests and to do what they could to overthrow any cabinet which ignored them. Oskar was their agent. Dr. Meissner was their friend. Franz von Papen was an honoured guest. And it was upon these three that the "Old Gentleman" of Neudeck relied for advice.

Another source of pressure was the Herren Klub. This was one of a number of fashionable social clubs catering to the landed and moneyed élite. It had been founded in 1924. Its club-house was located in Berlin on Pariserplatz, between the Brandenburg Gate and Wilhelmstrasse, conveniently near the centres of power. Dr. Meissner was an influential member. Schleicher had entrée as a member of the executive committee of the National Clubs, a kind of loose federation of some seventy fashionable groups throughout Prussia. Here, in March 1930, the President of the Herren Klub, Count Bodo von Alvensleben, and his good friend Franz von Papen had called a meeting of influential reactionary gentlemen—Prince Löwenstein, Count Westarp, Count Keyserling, General von Schleicher, Baron Wilhelm von Gayl, and many others—to sponsor a semi-religious crusade against Bolshevism. They founded the Bund zum Schutze der Abendländischen Kultur, under the leadership of Werner von Alvensleben, brother of Bodo, and organized meetings against *"Kultur-Bolschewismus."* [1] In 1932 the Herren Klub president, Freiherr Heinrich von Gleichen, repeatedly assailed the Brüning Cabinet in his conservative weekly, *Der Ring*.

Here, evidently on Schleicher's initiative, the conspiracy to unseat Brüning was hatched by monocled aristocrats, business men, and generals, who perceived from the course of events that their hour of power had come. Many gentlemen of this type were not at all hostile to the Nazis. Werner von Alvensleben considered joining the party. Oldenburg-Januschau said, as early as February 1931: "If I were not Nationalist, I might be a Nazi!" And Prince August Wilhelm, in June of the same year, declared: "Where a Hitler leads, a Hohenzollern can follow." But for the present, politically minded Junkers and industrialists preferred to play Schleicher's game. The sly and unscrupulous General enjoyed intrigue for its own sake—and for the sake of the control of the Reichswehr, which he coveted.

[1] Walther Schotte: *Das Kabinett Papen, Schleicher, Gayl* (Leipzig: Kittler; 1932), pp. 1–15; Edgar Schmidt-Pauli: *Hitlers Kampf um die Macht* (Berlin: Stilke; 1933), pp. 8–12.

He revelled in the position of "king-maker." He decided to use as his tool Franz von Papen: wealthy, polished, a Catholic, a conservative, a diplomat, an army officer. Papen was a friend of Hindenburg's and could doubtless make a bargain with the Nazis which would ensure their support for the new order without enabling them to gain power. Their thunder would be stolen and they would be left helpless. Such was the calculation. Here in the Herren Klub a new Cabinet was prepared.

The exact time of the hatching of the plot is uncertain. There is reason to believe that Hindenburg was persuaded to dismiss Brüning immediately after the election of April 10. For the sake of appearances, he waited. Schleicher intimated to Hitler early in May that the Chancellor would soon be forced out.[1] Brüning has never revealed how much he knew of the intrigue against him. If he knew, he still felt safe. He, more than any other man, had re-elected Hindenburg. He still commanded a safe majority in the Reichstag. And he could not be dispensed with. After May 13 Hindenburg remained at Neudeck, "vacationing." On May 28, in an address on unemployment before the Foreign Press Association, Brüning outlined a new plan of a lottery loan, voluntary labour service, and the settlement of some of the jobless on the land through the division of certain of the large estates. New decrees were in prospect.

This was more than the Junkers could stand. On Sunday, May 29, 1932, the Nazis won a majority in the Diet election in Oldenburg. On the same day the President, again in Berlin, conferred for almost five hours with his Chancellor. Brüning desired support of his program and a free hand in reconstructing the Cabinet before his projected departure for the reparations conference at Lausanne. Hindenburg accused him of "agrarian Bolshevism" and finally made it clear that he expected him to resign. He offered him tentatively the post of Foreign Minister in a new cabinet. Brüning declined: "I also have honour and a name to protect."

Brüning departed coldly and called his Ministers together in the evening. It was apparently decided that the whole Cabinet should resign. Brüning perhaps hoped that this threat would move the Field Marshal to reconsider. On Monday morning, May 30, the Chancellor offered the President the formal resignation of the entire Cabinet. To the Chancellor's chagrin, Hindenburg accepted it at

[1] J. Goebbels: *Vom Kaiserhof zur Reichskanzlei,* pp. 90–4.

once. Brüning is reported to have said: "I give you herewith, Herr President, our formal resignation. It is exactly seven weeks since your re-election." Hindenburg made no reply. Brüning departed.[1]

The President went through the formality of summoning party leaders before announcing the new Cabinet. He conferred for an hour with Hitler. Der Führer was assured that the ban on the S.A. would be lifted and that the Reichstag would be dissolved if the Nazis would tolerate the new government. He agreed. Promises were easy. On Tuesday, May 31, Franz von Papen was named Chancellor, with Kurt von Schleicher as Reichswehr Minister. The other members of the "Barons' Cabinet" were the aristocrats of the Herren Klub. Everything was arranged within a few hours. Brüning could do nothing. He had campaigned for Hindenburg. Social Democracy was impotent. It had supported the President loyally and had spent three hundred thousand marks of trade-union campaign money, donated by the General Federation of Trade Unions, to ensure Hindenburg's re-election. Otto Braun went away for his health. No one knew what had happened, save that a Chancellor, with a safe majority in the Reichstag, was dismissed by the President for reasons not clearly specified and that a new Chancellor, who was a sworn enemy of Socialism, liberalism, and democracy, had been named in his place. But the German republic was here given its death-blow—not by Hitler, but by a President who had been re-elected to save it from Fascism, and by the militarists and aristocrats who used the President as their tool.[2]

1 Cf. Schmidt-Pauli, op. cit., pp. 13–20; and *Berlin Diaries*, pp. 51–4.

2 It seems scarcely relevant to discuss the "constitutionality" of Hindenburg's action. It was clearly the intention of the framers of the Constitution to create a chief executive who should act in accordance with the will of parliamentary majorities and who should appoint and dismiss his ministers not on the basis of his personal judgments, but on the basis of public opinion as expressed in election results and in party alignments in the Reichstag. In this sense Hindenburg certainly violated the Constitution in Brüning's dismissal. But all questions of "constitutionality" had already become irrelevant. The Weimar document was already a tattered garment worn so thin that it was scarcely useful any longer to conceal the naked realities of the struggle for power between anti-constitutional feudal reaction and anti-constitutional Nazi fanaticism. On the development of the presidential office in general, see H. J. Heneman: *The Growth of Executive Power in Germany* (Minneapolis: Voyageur Press; 1934).

CHAPTER FIVE

VICTORY BY DEFAULT

1. HERREN KLUB, HINDENBURG, AND HITLER

CHANCELLOR Franz von Papen, like his manager, Kurt von Schleicher, was an inveterate intriguer who enjoyed conspiracy as a pleasurable recreation. He had been an officer of the Uhlans. During the war he was a diplomat (by title, not by behaviour), a major, a battalion commander, and a divisional General Staff officer. In 1914–15 he served as military attaché in the German Embassy in Washington. In collaboration with Captain Boy-Ed, the German naval attaché, he concocted schemes for planting bombs in American cargo ships destined for Allied ports, for poisoning horse-fodder, and for blowing up bridges and canals between the United States and Canada. He was exposed when a female agent of the British secret service wormed her way into his affections and into his business. On December 28, 1915, he and Boy-Ed were expelled from the United States. In April of 1916 he was indicted for a plot to blow up the Welland Canal—this to ensure his arrest by Federal authorities should he ever attempt to return to America. After the war he became influential in Catholic circles and served as a Centrist deputy in the Prussian Landtag and in the Reichstag. But he was a renegade in his own party and usually voted with the Right reactionaries. An elegant, gracious, suave nonentity, clever to the point of stupidity, he was the ideal head of the new "Barons' Cabinet."

His colleagues came in part from the Herren Klub. Schleicher attained his immediate goal, the Reichswehrministerium. Baron Wilhelm von Gayl, jurist and agrarian, became Minister of the Interior. The Foreign Office went to Constantin von Neurath, former Ambassador to London. Lutz von Schwerin-Krosigk became Minister of Finance; Hermann Warmbold, Minister of Economics; Hugo Schäffer, Minister of Labour; Franz Gürtner, Minister of Justice; Paul von Eltz-Rübenach, Minister of Posts; and Baron von Braun, Minister of Agriculture and Food. They were all eminent feudal gentlemen, monarchists at heart, though pledged now to act "within the Constitution." Papen, Gayl, and Braun were members of the Herren Klub, where Schleicher and Krosigk were frequent visitors. None was a political leader. Such a Cabinet would obviously have no support in the Reichstag. Hindenburg accordingly dissolved the Reichstag on June 3, explaining that it no longer "represented the people."

On June 9 Gayl spoke before the Reichsrat, denying that the Cabinet was "reactionary." The Constitution would be respected, but must be "reformed." On the evening of the 10th, according to an apparently reliable account, Papen spoke privately at the Herren Klub before an audience including Göring, Goebbels, Röhm and Helldorf, as well as many prominent military figures. His theme was the necessity of a Franco-German coalition against Russia as a means of achieving German rearmament. The generals were skeptical, the Nazi leaders enthusiastic.[1] On the 11th the Chancellor delivered his first public address before the Agricultural Council: "The unprecedented spiritual and material situation of the German people demands the liberation of the government from the fetters of party politics and partisan doctrines and calls for the consolidation of all national forces for the rebirth of Germany. . . ." The "new" program would require sacrifices by "all" classes. On the 14th Hindenburg signed a new decree, cutting the appropriations for the unemployed five hundred million marks and reducing the dole by twenty per cent—to an average of about forty marks a month. Stipends to wounded veterans were also reduced and new taxes were imposed on consumers. What "sacrifices" the Junkers and industrialists were expected to make was not specified.

Hitler meanwhile was chafing over the delay in the promised legalization of the S.A. On June 13 he met Papen in Schleicher's presence and demanded the immediate repeal of the ban on the S.A. The Chancellor was encountering opposition on this score from the south German states, but he yielded to Der Führer. On June 15 Hindenburg signed the decree permitting the storm troop-

[1] Cf. *Berlin Diaries*, pp. 55–7.

ers to wear uniforms once more (all the tailors in Germany rejoiced), to parade, and to resume their terrorization of their enemies.

Protests at the resumption of S.A. activities came from Bavaria and Baden, but Papen ignored them. He was nursing plans for ousting the Social Democrats from the Prussian Cabinet. The deadlock in the Landtag remained unbroken. He promised Hitler that before the end of July the Prussian police would be brought under the control of someone friendly toward the NSDAP. On June 23 Goebbels, in the Berlin Sportpalast, attacked the Chancellor and declared that unless the police repressed the Reds, the S.A. would be obliged to clear the streets itself. Heines, in Breslau, was even more defiant: "If the police don't support us, we will drive them to the devil. In one month we'll be the police, and then no one else will march!" On the 24th Hitler handed an "ultimatum" to Gayl through Göring: Martial law must be proclaimed against the Reds. The KPD must be suppressed, and all Marxists must be expelled from the police forces. Papen and Schleicher were furious. Hitler was impossible. Schleicher found Gregor Strasser more tractable. Papen temporized and asked Hitler to restrain his storm troops, to lessen the likelihood of disturbances. Brawls and killings continued. The suppression for five days of the Socialist *Vorwärts* led for the first time to a joint Socialist-Communist demonstration on July 4. On Sunday, July 10, no fewer than 18 people were killed and 200 wounded in Nazi-Communist riots throughout the Reich. A week later a battle between storm troopers and Communists at Altona, near Hamburg, cost 12 lives, with 50 wounded. Schleicher had misgivings. But Papen was prepared to tolerate Nazi terrorism, in the hope of securing Hitler's support for the Cabinet after the Reichstag election scheduled for July 31.

The Nazi campaign, opened by Hitler in Tilsit on July 15, was soon in full swing.[1] Der Führer promised liberty, honour, and bread. Göring assailed Centrists and Marxists alike. Goebbels attacked everybody, including the Cabinet. Radio facilities were now available to all parties save the Communists, and the NSDAP made good use of them. Again its electoral tactics left all its competitors in outer darkness. Mass meetings, parades, pageantry, and oratory carried the gospel to every corner of the Reich. A gigantic climax was reached in the Grünewald Stadium in Berlin on July 27. Hitler

[1] Cf. Joseph Goebbels: *Vom Kaiserhof zur Reichskanzlei,* pp. 112–35.

drew an audience of over a hundred thousand which paid from one to eight marks per ticket. The gate receipts were four hundred thousand marks. The spectacle could only be compared to a world-championship prize-fight in the United States, save that it was far more colourful and dramatic. Twenty thousand storm troopers marched in a torchlight parade. Amid indescribable enthusiasm Hitler reiterated the old clichés and promised an end of the party system. The vast throng gazed in rapture at the tiny figure under the spotlights, waving his arms, pointing his finger heavenward, and shaking clenched fists before his pale, perspiring face. All listened enthralled to the voice of the Messiah, coming to them through microphones and amplifiers. At the finale, as the multitude took up the strains of *Deutschland über Alles,* fiery beacons appeared on the edges of the stadium, spreading until they joined one another and surrounded the whole arena with a ring of red flames. Amid echoes of the "Magic Fire Music," the new Wotan dedicated the sleeping goddess of German "liberation" to the great awakening of the days to come. . . .

Papen meanwhile had consummated "the rape of Prussia." At a secret meeting of notables at the Herren Klub on July 12, Papen disclosed his plan. He had convinced himself that the Reich government could "constitutionally" depose the government of a state. He would therefore depose the Socialist Cabinet of Prussia. But he must be certain of Reichswehr support. Schleicher was critical. The Socialists were still the largest party in the Reich. They controlled the sixty thousand police of Prussia. They could summon the trade unions, the Reichsbanner, the Communists, the underground "Red Front" to their aid. It might be a bloody and dangerous business. Papen pooh-poohed. Socialists would not fight. The matter was left in abeyance.[1] The Junkers demanded a clean sweep. The Socialists were "sabotaging" the *Ost-Hilfe* fund established by Brüning for agrarian relief; that is, they were withholding public money from the greedy and impoverished feudal estate-owners. More Bolshevism!

Papen made his plans. On the 15th he met the Cabinet. Some of the Ministers supported him. Others were dubious. Schleicher reiterated his objections. The scales were turned by Oskar, who declared that Papa demanded action: "The Reichspresident informs

[1] *Berlin Diaries,* pp. 92–7.

the Cabinet that he insists that final and decisive measures should be taken to save agriculture from being ruined by the Marxists. And that can only be achieved by a Cabinet of the Right in Prussia!" [1] Oskar, with Papen acquiescing, also told Schleicher that the proposed action was part of a bargain with Hitler. Schleicher reluctantly consented. The reins were already slipping from his hands. Two battalions of infantry were stationed at Döberitz in case of trouble. Hermann Diels, one of Severing's subordinates, apparently acted as Papen's *agent provocateur* in urging his chiefs to adopt courses of action which could be used as excuses for their elimination.

On July 20 Papen summoned to the chancellery Otto Klepper, the Democratic Minister of Finance in Prussia; Heinrich Hirtsiefer, Centrist Minister of Public Welfare; and Karl Severing, the Socialist Minister of the Interior. Otto Braun, Prussian Premier since 1920, was still away. Braun and Severing were good Social Democrats.[2] They knew what was impending, but had decided to wait. Papen told his auditors that Hindenburg had been worried about Prussia for some time. In the interest of "law and order" and for "reasons of State," Braun and Severing were to be removed from office. Papen would become Prussian Premier and Dr. Franz Bracht, Mayor of Essen, would be his Deputy Commissioner and Minister of the Interior. Severing replied that the Chancellor's action was a violation of the Constitution and that he would yield only to violence. Papen offered to supply the violence. The interview ended. Papen telephoned. A few moments later two decrees, already made out and signed by Hindenburg at Neudeck, were issued. The first, invoking the blessed Article 48, named Papen Federal Commissioner for Prussia and empowered him to remove ministers from office and to act as Prussian Premier. The second decree suspended seven articles of the Reich Constitution, guaranteeing personal liberty and freedom of speech, press, and assembly. Executive power and control of the police in Berlin and Brandenburg were transferred to the Reichswehr Minister and the army. Any disobedience would

[1] *Berlin Diaries,* p. 104. There is at the moment no way of proving that this statement was actually made, apart from this anonymous political narrative. There can be no doubt, however, but that it expressed the President's views.

[2] Cf. Erich Cuttner: *Otto Braun* (Leipzig: Kittler; 1932); Hans Menzel: *Karl Severing* (Berlin; Hist. Pol. Verl., 1932).

be punished by heavy penalties, with death for high treason, incendiarism, armed resistance, or inciting to riot.[1]

Severing returned to his Ministry on Unter den Linden—and waited. The Socialist Chief of Police, Albert Greszinsky, and his aides, Bernard Weiss and Lieutenant-Colonel Magnus Heimannsberg, were also to be ousted. They refused to obey the orders of General von Rundstedt, the local Reichswehr commander—and also waited. At noon a captain and two soldiers padlocked Premier Braun's offices. Later another captain and fifteen soldiers arrested Greszinsky, Weiss, and Heimannsberg. They were released in the evening when they consented to give up their posts. Bracht came alone to the Ministry of the Interior and invited Severing to depart. Severing refused. Bracht left and returned in the evening with two police officers. Severing yielded and went home.

This *coup d'état* was followed by no resistance. All observers, including Schleicher, were agreed that if Braun and Severing had arrested the Papen Cabinet for violating the Constitution, mobilized the Prussian police, made common cause with the Communists, called a general strike, and fought the *coup* to the death, their chances of success would have been excellent, even against the Reichswehr. Such tactics had defeated the Kapp putsch in 1920. But all fighting spirit had gone out of German Social Democracy. Severing feared to arm the German workers to fight reaction. The KPD would then have force at its disposal. By such tactics Kerensky in Russia had dug his own political grave. Severing explained that he yielded "to avoid bloodshed"—and appealed (in vain) to the Supreme Court to protect the Constitution. A Communist call for a general strike was denounced by the Social Democratic leaders as a Hitler ruse. When Severing, less than a year later, found himself in a Nazi concentration camp, his Communist fellow prisoners hung a placard around his neck: "On July 20, 1932, I failed to do my duty." After such a demonstration of cowardice and impotence Hitler knew that when his moment came he would have nothing to fear from the Social Democratic and trade-union bureaucracy. Papen was gleeful.[2]

[1] Texts in J. K. Pollock and H. J. Heneman: *The Hitler Decrees* (Ann Arbor, Michigan; Wahr; 1934), pp. 4, 5; also *The New York Times,* July 21, 1932.

[2] See E. A. Mowrer: *Germany Puts the Clock Back,* pp. 1–11; *Berlin Diaries,* pp. 92–122; Walther Schotte: *Das Kabinett Papen, Schleicher, Gayl,* pp. 71–8.

But the "Barons' Cabinet" needed more than this easy victory over the Socialists to keep itself in power. On the night of July 19–20, while Papen slept in his bed dreaming of his cleverness, Hitler in his private plane was lost in a storm over the Baltic sea coast. He did not arrive for a speaking-engagement in Stralsund until 2.30 a.m. But forty thousand people had waited in a pouring rain to hear him—and they listened enchanted to his message until the dawn of day.[1]

Papen did not dare to call off the elections and set up a naked military dictatorship. Such a move might precipitate proletarian resistance or, more probably, a Nazi insurrection. The Old Gentleman was not yet ready to go so far. The interests of the Junkers did not demand it. On the 27th Schleicher broadcast his program for reorganizing the army into a popular militia. Proposals from Röhm and Hitler for military training of the storm troops were evaded. In his last radio appeal to the electorate Papen denied any intention of establishing a dictatorship, denounced Communism and the Treaty of Versailles, and called for a reform of the Constitution. On the eve of the elections ten more people were killed in political riots and the Communist *Rote Fahne* was suppressed for ten days. Not a single Cabinet member was a candidate for the Reichstag. The only party which would support the Cabinet was Hugenberg's Nationalists, who by no stretch of the imagination could secure a majority. The election resulted as follows:

REICHSTAG ELECTION, JULY 31, 1932 [2]

Qualified Voters—44,226,835
Voted—37,162,072 or 84.0 per cent
Total Deputies Elected—608

	Seats Won	*Popular Votes*
Communist Party	89	5,282,626
Social Democrats	133	7,959,712
State Party	4	371,799
Centrum	75	4,589,335
Bavarian People's Party	22	1,192,684
Economic Party	2	146,876
German People's Party	7	436,012
German National People's Party	37	2,186,051
NSDAP	230	13,745,781

[1] Otto Dietrich: *With Hitler on the Road to Power*, pp 35–6.

[2] *Die Wahlen zum Reichstag am 31 Juli, 1932* (Berlin: Der Reichswahlleiter; 1932).

The NSDAP had more than doubled its strength since September 1930. It had won thirty-seven per cent of the electorate and was now by a wide margin the largest party in the Reich. In spite of the disappearance of the Right splinter parties, the Nationalists lost almost three hundred thousand votes. The Economic Party was wiped out. The State Party and the German People's Party were reduced to nullities. The Centrum and the Bavarian People's Party barely held their own. The Socialists lost over six hundred thousand votes, which the Communists gained. Less than five per cent of the new Reichstag supported the Cabinet. No workable majority, no conceivable coalition was in sight—unless Papen could strike a new bargain with the NSDAP.

Papen now declared that the Cabinet would remain in office, since no alternative Cabinet could command a majority in parliament. Brüning, who was again Centrist leader, toyed with the idea of a Black-Brown coalition, with Hitler as Chancellor and himself as Vice-Chancellor. Hitler suggested confidentially that Schleicher become Chancellor, with Nazi support assured for two years, on condition that three Nazis should be admitted to the Cabinet and Hindenburg should be permitted to retire in Hitler's favour. Schleicher contributed the following gem to a clarification of the issue:

"Germany's former error was a false optimism. Dr. Brüning told the people the truth, but after a while the masses always become unreceptive to asceticism, particularly when they are called upon to make sacrifices without understanding why. They will submit to the greatest privations, I think, if only one talks the language that touches their hearts. What says Hitler? He says: 'I will lead you to Italy's flowery plains.' Such a movement must be made use of. People, like individuals, need faith. Some people are so afraid of responsibility they can't sleep. I'm not. I don't suffer from insomnia either."[1]

Within two years Schleicher would sleep still better, thanks to the man with whom he was now willing to negotiate. He met Hitler on August 7. The Nazi leader demanded the chancellorship, if not the presidency. Schleicher offered him the vice-chancellorship. Hitler insisted that Papen and Gayl must go. Brüning would be Foreign Minister and Strasser Minister of Labour. But would Hitler's party

[1] *Zwölf Uhr Abendblatt*, Berlin, August 3, 1932.

colleagues agree—especially Goebbels? Hitler was uncertain. The Centrists refused to support any cabinet not including the Nazis. Hitler must be "MacDonaldized"—that is, tamed by being given some share of public responsibility. Rumours spread. Hitler Chancellor, Strasser Minister of the Interior, Göring Minister of Transport. . . . Goebbels insisted that Hitler must demand "all"—at least the chancellorship. Schleicher wondered whether Göring, a morphine addict and former asylum inmate, could really be admitted to the Cabinet. August 11 was "Constitution Day." Hindenburg came in from Neudeck for the celebration. Under no circumstances, he told Schleicher and Papen, would he permit Hitler to become Chancellor. He refused even to see Hitler—but finally consented, under pressure, only if Röhm, however, "that homosexual libertine," were not brought along. On the 11th Gayl and Papen addressed the Reichstag and condemned the Constitution. The republic was not mentioned. The delegates sang *Deutschland über Alles*. Not yet the *Horst Wessel Lied*.

Meanwhile Nazi terrorism was attaining unprecedented proportions. Shootings, bombings, and killings were especially numerous in East Prussia. On August 3 the Socialist headquarters in Königsberg were bombed, an oil station owned by a Socialist was fired, and a Communist leader was murdered. The Cabinet warned that disorders must cease within eighteen hours or special measures would be resorted to. The disorders continued. Hitler sought to quiet the S.A. leaders. Fifty Berlin policemen were welcomed to an S.A. rally by Count Helldorf. More bombings and shootings. On the 8th the local Reichsbanner leader in Lötzen was murdered by Nazis, who blamed the Communists. Killings in Silesia. The Cabinet hesitated. But on August 10 Hindenburg at last signed a decree approved by the Cabinet. It extended the "political truce" to the end of August, forbade all political demonstrations, provided the death penalty for political murder and arson, and set up special tribunals to try offenders. In the early morning hours of the same day five of Heines's storm troopers, after drinking heavily, forced their way into the house of a Communist workman in Potempa, one Pietrzuch, shot him in bed, and then kicked him to death in the presence of his mother, crushing his throat beneath their heavy boots. Reluctantly the local police arrested the "patriotic" culprits.

On August 13 Hitler was received by Hindenburg, thanks to the insistence of Schleicher and Papen and the intervention of Oskar. Hitler flew from Munich to Tempelhofer Feld in Berlin, where he was met by Röhm and Helldorf, who reported their discussion of August 12 with Papen. They brought a luncheon invitation from the Chancellor. In the morning Hitler saw Schleicher. He was then driven to Wilhelmstrasse while thousands cheered. At lunch with Papen he again demanded the chancellorship. Papen hedged and left the whole issue to the President. Der Führer was offered the vice-chancellorship if the NSDAP would support the Cabinet, but as for the chancellorship, Papen must really. . . . Hitler returned with Röhm and Frick at four in the afternoon and was received by Hindenburg in the presence of Meissner, Schleicher, and Papen.

According to Meissner,[1] Hitler attempted to bow, fumbled awkwardly with the doorknob, blushed, and stumbled over the rug. He began a public speech, but was silenced by Hindenburg. The President asked him whether he was willing to enter the Papen Cabinet. He refused and insisted on the chancellorship "with the same powers as Mussolini was given after his victorious march on Rome" (Hitler later denied using this phrase). Hindenburg asserted that, in view of Nazi terrorism, he could not deliver the State into the hands of the brown shirts. He reminded his guest of the pre-election promise to support the Papen Cabinet if the Marxists were ousted from the Prussian government. Had Hitler kept his promise? Silence. What would Hitler do now? "Opposition—to the last ditch," replied Der Führer. Hindenburg was furious: "You are to be then in opposition. I trust you will oppose in the way that will be chivalrous. And I enjoin you in your future course to keep always in mind your duty to the Fatherland and your responsibility to the German people."

The President left the room and went back to Neudeck. *"Ich will meine Ruhe haben,"* was a phrase which he now used frequently. Schleicher and Papen had failed to get the Nazis into the Cabinet. Hitler had failed to secure the chancellorship. He returned to Munich. The party at once launched a vigorous campaign against the government.[2]

[1] *Berlin Diaries,* pp. 159–61.

[2] J. Goebbels: *Vom Kaiserhof zur Reichskanzlei,* pp. 144–7.

2. DEADLOCK

AFTER August 13, 1932, the decisions before the Herren Klub Cabinet were more painful than ever. Should it endeavour to defy the Reichstag and rule as a "presidential" Cabinet? The Old Gentleman might object again. Should it dissolve the Reichstag? Should it hope for some bargain whereby the Nazis might after all be persuaded to tolerate it? Should it suppress Nazi terrorism and smash the Hitlerites by proceeding openly against them with the police and the army? It did none of these things, but waited hesitantly. The Nazi press raged against the Cabinet, but the radicals in the party were appeased by Der Führer's demand for all or nothing. Hitler sent the S.A. on a week's vacation. On August 16 Count Helldorf extended the leaves of the Berlin S.A. till August 28, two days before the Reichstag was to assemble. He told his storm troopers:

"The decision that we as men have been awaiting has been postponed for some time. I well understand that you who have waited impatiently will bear uneasily any further delay. . . . [But] nothing has changed with respect to the great revolutionary tasks you are to perform. There has only been a shift in point of time and I assume that within the next few weeks the political premises will have been achieved for the Nationalsocialists to take power. To any and all objections there is only one answer: We are soldiers of the Nationalsocialist Party and must obey our leader." [1]

Hitler declared that he would never sell his birthright for a mess of pottage. "Rather any fight or persecution than to become unfaithful to myself or the movement." [2] A company of storm troopers in Cologne was dissolved for mutiny. From his mountain retreat in Berchtesgaden, where his sister, Frau Raubal, kept house for him in the cozy cottage, Wachenfeld, Hitler asserted that there would be no "march on Berlin." He indulged in interesting mathematics: If a party with 51 per cent of the votes was entitled to 100 per cent of the Cabinet posts, then a party with 37 per cent of the votes ought to get 75 per cent of the posts. Negotiations for a Centrist-Nazi coalition in the Prussian Diet continued between Brüning and

[1] *The New York Times,* August 17, 1932.

[2] Interview in *Rheinisch-Westfälische Gazette,* the organ of the Ruhr industrialists, August 16, 1932.

Strasser—but without result, since here, too, the NSDAP demanded all.

A new storm broke when the special court at Beuthen sentenced the five Potempa murderers to death on August 22. The outcry against the judgment in the Nazi press was terrific. Heines excoriated the verdict. Frank protested to Papen and demanded a pardon. Hitler asserted: "My comrades, in the face of this frightful bloody sentence and from this instant on, your freedom becomes a point of our honour." Der Führer further declared:

"With this deed our course with respect to the Cabinet is definitely set. . . . In the face of this enormity, life can have but one meaning for us—fight and again fight! . . . Herr von Papen, your bloody objectivity does not exist for me. I want victory for national Germany and annihilation for the Marxists, who have corrupted and destroyed it." [1]

Röhm went to Beuthen and conferred with Schleicher. Goebbels screamed: "The Jews are guilty!" *Der Angriff* was suspended for a week for its vicious attacks on the Cabinet. At Beuthen the Nazis instigated anti-Socialist and anti-Semitic riots. The *V.B.* sent a special correspondent to interview the prisoners:

"Murderers? These magnificent fellows? Never! Straight, strong, every one of them faithful and unbowed. Joy and grief seize the visitor at the sight of these good men. Unconscious of any guilt, they are joyous like children when gifts are presented to them. They take the flowers, cigarettes, and tidbits offered to them in high spirits—until there comes some news that drives away hilarity. Burn the newspapers! Burn the papers of the Jewish *journaille!*" [2]

Papen and Schleicher, still hoping against hope for an understanding with the Nazis, did not dare to permit the sentence to be executed. On September 2 the Prussian Cabinet commuted it to life imprisonment. Hitler was still bitter and defiant and promised that the murderers would receive a full pardon when the Nazis gained power:

"The Jews and the feudal Herren Klub think they can save Germany. We won't let you keep power, not if you dissolve the Reichstag ten times. These old excellencies won't discourage us. . . . My great opponent is eighty-five years old and I am only forty-three. I am convinced that nothing will happen to me, because I believe Destiny has

[1] Quoted in *The New York Times,* August 24, 1932.
[2] *Völkischer Beobachter,* August 26, 1932.

assigned a task to me. And I say that Nationalsocialism will come into power through the Constitution."[1]

The Chancellor sought to pave the way for the Reichstag session. He must not only somehow win the Nazis, but please the Junkers and industrialists as well. The Federation of German Industries opposed new public works and urged compulsory labour service as a cure for unemployment. On August 25 Papen secretly conferred with Dr. Gustav Krupp von Bohlen, Dr. Karl von Siemens, Professor Bosch, and many other leading industrialists. In an address at Münster on the 28th Papen proposed to rescue the Reich through voluntary labour service and more public works. He lunched on the 29th with Hitler and Schleicher. The Black-Brown negotiations were still deadlocked and there seemed no hope of securing Nazi toleration for the Cabinet. In the afternoon Papen, Schleicher, Gayl, and Meissner repaired to Neudeck while industrialists and bankers expressed their approval of the Cabinet's plan to subsidize employers to hire additional workers. On August 29 the Cabinet presented a new demand to the Powers for arms equality. On August 31 new tariffs were announced, to become effective September 6. On many manufactured goods they were prohibitive. Food imports were subjected to quotas or to one hundred per cent increases in duties. Thus were Junkers and industrialists alike placated, with the consumers paying the bill. On September 3–4 the Stahlhelm, in the presence of Papen and other Cabinet members, held a great demonstration in the Sportpalast and on Tempelhofer Feld. At least the Stahlhelm could be relied upon! The Nazi press sneered. On September 6 *Der Angriff* and Ludendorff's *Volkswärte* attacked Duesterberg as a Jew. On the following day the erstwhile presidential candidate and Stahlhelm leader resigned his post. He had just "discovered" that his mother's father had indeed been an Israelite. Since it was obvious that no Jew could be a national patriot, he must retire. . . .

The Reichstag met on August 30. In accordance with custom, the oldest member took the chair as provisional president: Clara Zetkin, seventy-five-year-old Communist, who had come from Moscow for the occasion. Her appeal for the proletarian revolution was listened to in silence. The permanent president was then elected. The Socialist Paul Löbe, presiding officer for the past twelve years, got 135 votes and Ernst Torgler, Communist, 80 votes. Göring, nominated by a

[1] Address in Munich, September 7, 1932.

Centrist, got 367 votes and was thus elected. On August 31 the new Reichstag officers asked Hindenburg for an audience to plead for a continuation of the session, since they suspected that he had already signed a dissolution order. He refused to receive them at Neudeck. Obscure and futile negotiations continued. Hitler publicly attacked Papen, Hugenberg, and Hindenburg and privately asked Schleicher whether he would head a Nazi-Centrist Cabinet. The General declined. Papen asserted that he would dissolve the Reichstag unless it gave him a free hand for six months. Hindenburg supported him. Hitler and Göring rushed to the defence of democracy and parliamentary prerogatives against "dictatorship."

The crisis came dramatically on September 12. Papen entered the Reichstag with his speech in one pocket and the dissolution order in the other. Before he could talk, Torgler introduced a motion of non-confidence. Göring put the motion. It was unanimously adopted and thus became the first item on the order of business. Frick's proposal for a half-hour recess was likewise adopted. Hitler, in a near-by hotel, instructed his followers to vote against the government. When the deputies reassembled, Papen sought recognition from the chair. Göring ignored him and proceeded to the vote. Papen then deposited the dissolution order on the president's desk and marched out with his Ministers. The vote showed 32 deputies supporting the Cabinet and 513 against it. Papen asserted that the vote was meaningless, since the Reichstag had already been dissolved. Göring declared that the dissolution order was invalid, since the Cabinet had already been voted out of office. He threatened to reconvene the Reichstag on the next day. Papen threatened to prevent this by force. Each accused the other of violating the Constitution.

Göring yielded, however. The Reichstag, which had met in all for only six hours, did not reassemble. The Cabinet ignored the demand of its standing committee that it appear to explain its conduct. On the basis of a rumour that Communists had brought explosives into the building, the police searched it from roof to cellar in the face of Göring's impassioned protests. On September 15, as the Cabinet informed Arthur Henderson that the Reich would quit the Geneva Disarmament Conference unless it were granted equality, Göring filed suit against Papen for libel. Thus the former ace and would-be dictator became (temporarily) a champion of parliamentary democracy.

New elections were ordered for November 6. Hitler and the Nazi press now assailed Papen and the "reactionaries" in unmeasured terms. Goebbels went so far as to organize a boycott of Hugenberg's papers. Nationalist meetings were repeatedly broken up by Nazi rowdies, while street brawls and riots went on unchecked. The Berlin headquarters of the party were moved on October 1 from Hedemannstrasse to an "Adolf Hitler House" on Voss-Strasse, but this brought the NSDAP no nearer politically to Wilhelmstrasse. The government monopolized the radio for campaign purposes once more. Nothing was clear save that the NSDAP was at last losing followers and that the Nationalists and Communists were gaining. Nazi demands for the suppression of the KPD were ignored by Schleicher, who had no desire to serve the Nazi cause in this fashion. On November 2, Communists in Hamburg attacked the Nazis and shot ten. On November 4–5 a transit strike broke out in Berlin. The Socialist trade-union officials denounced it, and the police declared it illegal. But the Communists and Nazis vied with one another in their efforts to secure control of the strikers. The Nazi press asserted: "We will not permit the standard of living of German workmen to be lowered under the von Papen régime below the standard of Chinese coolies. We not only participate in this strike, but we take its leadership." Hitler told thirty-five thousand people in the Sportpalast that the Nazis would secure forty per cent of the vote.

The election results revealed a significant shift in opinion:

REICHSTAG ELECTION, NOVEMBER 6, 1932[1]

Qualified Voters—44,401,004
Voted—35,758,890—80.5 per cent
Total Deputies Elected—584

	Seats Won	*Popular Votes*
Communist Party	100	5,980,539
Social Democrats	121	7,251,749
State Party	2	338,613
Centrum	70	4,230,640
Bavarian People's Party	20	1,095,939
German People's Party	11	661,796
German National People's Party	52	3,019,099
NSDAP	196	11,737,386

[1] *Gesamtergebnis der Wahlen zum Reichstag am 6 Nov., 1932* (Berlin: Der Reichswahlleiter; 1932).

At last the Nazi tide was ebbing. The party had lost two million votes and thirty-four deputies since July 31. Instead of the forty per cent which Hitler predicted, the party's following fell to thirty-two per cent of the electorate. Trends of unemployment and industrial production subsequently compiled showed that the nadir of the depression had come in the summer of 1932. The slight economic recovery which took place in early fall had its effect in producing a sharp decline in Nazi strength. Greater recovery would doubtless have produced a greater diminution in the number of Hitler's followers by alleviating the insecurities which had bred the National-socialist neurosis. The apparent impossibility of the Nazis securing a majority of the electorate and the refusal of those in high office to entrust the NSDAP with power likewise contributed to discouragement. More intensive campaigning to counteract these obstacles was rendered difficult by lack of funds. Contributions from industrialists were no longer so generous as they had been after the first Nazi victories. The party treasury was described by Goebbels as being in a state of "financial calamity."[1]

Most of the million and a half voters who had gone to the polls on July 31 and stayed home on November 6 seemed to have been Nazis. The party leadership was already showing evidences of disintegration as a result of impending bankruptcy and hopelessness as to the future. On November 8 the party abandoned the Berlin strike as a failure. All the leaders were profoundly discouraged. Victory now seemed impossible. There is much reason to believe that, had continued intrigues among the Junkers and militarist reactionaries not brought Hitler his opportunity three months later, the NSDAP would have suffered a further sharp decline and would have gone to pieces as a result of internal dissension. But thanks to Hindenburg, Schleicher, Papen, and Hugenberg, this was not to be.

The Communists gained three-quarters of a million votes. The Socialists lost again—three-quarters of a million votes. The Catholic parties suffered small losses, the German People's Party gained heavily, and the State Party remained as insignificant as before. Hugenberg's Nationalists, however, gained almost a million followers and increased their representation from 37 to 52. This was the last election unaccompanied by governmental terrorization of the opposition. It was the last recording of public opinion in the German republic prior

[1] *Vom Kaiserhof zur Reichskanzlei,* pp. 167, 181, 192.

to its delivery into the hands of its destroyers. Its result may be taken to represent accurately an equilibrium of political forces which might have continued for a long period had it not been upset by secret intrigue and open violence. The five parties which were loyal to democracy and the Weimar Constitution (Centrum, Bavarian People's Party, Social Democrats, German People's Party, and State Party) controlled only 224 deputies out of 584. There was obviously no basis here for a Cabinet supported by a majority of the Reichstag. A Right coalition (Nazis, Nationalists, and German People's Party) could count upon only 259 deputies out of 584. The Nazi-Centrist coalition which had been proposed would have had a majority of one in the former Reichstag: 305 out of 608. In the new Reichstag it would not have a majority (226 out of 584) unless supported by the Nationalists, or by the Bavarian People's Party and the German People's Party.

A Left coalition was equally impossible, since the Communists would on principle enter no coalitions and would vote against any bourgeois cabinet, democratic or Fascist. The two Marxist parties controlled 221 deputies and together outnumbered the Nazis, though in the former Reichstag they had 222 deputies to the Nazis' 230. Here, if anywhere, was the only centre of effective opposition to the NSDAP. Numerically the two political extremes were almost evenly balanced. The difficulty lay in the fact that in the mathematics of power equal numbers are seldom equal. Collaboration between Communists and Social Democrats was unthinkable. Each accused the other of playing into the hands of the Fascists. Each was so hypnotized by its own ideology that it preferred to die separately rather than to live by co-operation. Social Democracy, with its still intact and apparently impressive machinery of party and trade-union organization, was a hollow shell. It could not fight because it would crumble to dust at the first blow. After July 20 Communist contempt for Social Democratic cowardice and treachery was unqualified. But neither could the KPD fight. It was not prepared for revolutionary action, nor did the existing balance of power, for all its instability, offer an opportunity for proletarian revolt. Moscow, moreover, vetoed revolution. The exigencies of the Five Year Plan and the need for peace forbade international conflict—and without Soviet military intervention no Communist revolution in Germany could succeed. Under these circumstances the representatives of the proletariat were helpless—helpless to preserve the Weimar democracy from its enemies by co-operating with its friends, helpless to rule themselves, and helpless even to avert their own destruction.

What next? Papen resumed futile negotiations for parliamentary support. He was everywhere rebuffed. Schleicher now demanded Papen's dismissal, but had troubles with the Old Gentleman, who continued to base his decisions on the interests of the Junkers. Gregor Strasser intimated that he and his supporters were disgusted with Hitler's megalomania and might support a Schleicher Cabinet. On November 17 the Cabinet resigned. Hitler, playing for Hindenburg's favour, urged measures to restore agrarian prosperity in preparation for the "war of liberation." He conferred with the President for an hour on November 19. He refused once more to enter any cabinet of which he was not the head, but asserted that with Centrist and Nationalist support the Nazis could build a parliamentary majority. Hindenburg was favourably impressed and authorized him to negotiate. For the second time Der Führer was offered a place in the Cabinet. This time he could have the chancellorship—if he would secure a majority and pledge himself to rule "constitutionally." Göring saw Kaas. Hitler saw Schacht. The latter sought to help in rebuilding the "Harzburg Front," but Hugenberg was not prepared for this—not yet. He and Papen pulled wires to frustrate Hitler's efforts. The Leader's negotiations failed. He then offered to head a "presidential cabinet" ruling by decree without parliamentary support. This offer Hindenburg refused on November 24:

"I fear that a presidential cabinet led by Herr Hitler would inevitably develop into a party dictatorship with the evil result of intensifying still more the dissensions within the German nation, and I cannot answer to my oath and my conscience for taking such a step." [1]

Hindenburg next asked the Centrist leader, Kaas, to try his hand, but with Hitler irreconcilable and Hugenberg in no mood to cooperate, nothing could be achieved. On November 26 Hindenburg asked Schleicher to make a new effort. Papen, Hugenberg, and the Junkers sought to frustrate Schleicher's attempt. The General conferred with the Social Democrats and with trade-union leaders. Hitler refused to see Schleicher and announced his opposition to any cabinet not headed by himself. Hindenburg toyed with the notion of retaining his friend Papen as Chancellor (he would be "safe" for the Junkers), but Papen's colleagues declined to co-operate.

[1] *Berlin Diaries,* p. 215; cf. Goebbels, op. cit., pp. 205–10.

The President disgustedly intimated that he felt like retiring from politics altogether, and would do so except for his anxiety over the state of (Junker) agriculture. On December 2 he asked Schleicher to accept the chancellorship, with or without a parliamentary majority. Schleicher consented. The personnel of the Herren Klub Cabinet was altered only slightly. Franz Bracht replaced Gayl as Minister of the Interior. Dr. Friedrich Syrup replaced Schäffer as Minister of Labour, after Hindenburg rejected the suggestion that Seldte, the Stahlhelm leader, should assume the post. Schleicher remained Reichswehr Minister. Dr. Gunther Gerecke was elevated to the new post of Employment early in January.

Schleicher sought to secure parliamentary acquiescence, if not support. The Reichstag was to meet on December 6. On the 4th Schleicher saw Göring, who agreed that the Reichstag should be adjourned at once until January. Schleicher sought to close the breach between the Left and the Right in an ingenious fashion. He aimed ultimately at a government of generals and trade unionists. The Stahlhelm of Seldte, the Catholic unions of Stegerwald and Brüning, the Social Democratic unions of Leipart, and the socialistic left wing of the Nazis led by Strasser would be united in a proletarian-militarist régime. By agreement with the Centrum, Strasser would become Prussian Premier. If he would enter the Cabinet, the Federal Commissioner for Prussia would be recalled. . . .

The trade-union leaders were agreeable. If Hitler created difficulties, Schleicher would threaten him with a dissolution of the Reichstag. Der Führer's depleted war chest, his campaign debts, and his electoral losses would make him hesitate. In local elections in Thuringia on December 4 the Nazi vote fell twenty per cent below the November 6 level. If Hugenberg made trouble, Schleicher would threaten the Junkers with an exposure of the *Ost-Hilfe* scandal, wherein millions of marks appropriated for agrarian relief found their way into the pockets of the Prussian gentry. The Reichstag, thought Schleicher, would acquiesce. The scheme was admirable and not without elements of genuine statesmanship. Schleicher planned on four years in office. Only such a régime could save the republic by enabling it to survive long enough for the Nazi losses to produce disintegration and reduce the movement to impotence. The only hitch was that Schleicher failed to reckon with his "friend" Papen and with Hindenburg.

On December 6 the deputies assembled in an atmosphere of calm. By right of seniority, the eighty-year-old Nazi, General Karl Litzmann, became provisional president and forestalled another Clara Zetkin "scandal." Göring was re-elected as permanent president. Hitler had "declared war" on the government and required the Nazi deputies to take a new oath of allegiance to him. Papen was intriguing as usual, Hugenberg was sulking, and Neurath was seeking to convince Hindenburg that the General-Chancellor would make a bad international impression. But Schleicher was optimistic. On December 7 a Nazi-Communist riot in the Reichstag compelled a one-hour suspension. Strasser offered Schleicher the support of half the Nazi deputies if he would agree not to dissolve the Reichstag and grant some vague *quid pro quo* to Strasser's followers. This savoured of treason to Der Führer. Still . . . ? Hitler, in the face of internal defection, agreed to an adjournment of the Reichstag to January 10. On December 9 the Reichstag adjourned, after passing a constitutional amendment to have the President of the Supreme Court, instead of the Chancellor, succeed to the presidency of the Reich in the event of Hindenburg's death.

Schleicher at least had a breathing-space. Better yet, Gregor Strasser now broke with Hitler completely. He resigned his party posts on December 8 and was replaced by Robert Ley, the frequently inebriated and disorderly deputy who was closely connected with chemical-manufacturers in the Rhineland. Hitler created a Central Political Commission of the party under Hess. Feder likewise asked for a three weeks' leave. The radicals had waited long enough for jobs. Schleicher considered inviting Strasser into the Cabinet. Deep depression reigned among the Nazi leaders. Hitler, in the Kaiserhof, walked up and down, up and down, tore his hair, and threatened to commit suicide if the party went to pieces.[1] On December 11 Schleicher won another victory: a Five Power declaration recognized "in principle" the right of Germany to equality in armaments. On the 15th the Chancellor broadcast his program. Five days later he proclaimed a general amnesty for political prisoners, with the exception of the Potempa murderers. He felt confident that his position was now secure. The Nazi ship was waterlogged and sinking under its burden of debts, while mutiny raged among the crew.

[1] Goebbels, op. cit., pp. 218–20.

3. DER FÜHRER, REICHSKANZLER

JANUARY 1933: Difficulties for Chancellor Kurt von Schleicher. Papen's wounded vanity led him to launch new secret conspiracies against the old friend who had made him Chancellor seven months before. He found an ally in Oldenburg-Januschau and the Junker Landbund, whose members suspected Schleicher, too, of "agrarian Bolshevism." Oskar and even the Old Gentleman listened to their complaints. Schleicher hesitated to launch a counter-offensive against this cabal lest he alienate the President. Oldenburg was collecting money again by subscription—450,000 marks, he hoped—to present to Hindenburg as a gift wherewith to renovate the bankrupt Neudeck estate. The Deutsche Bank was approached for 180,000 marks, but refused to contribute. On January 3 Schleicher urged Hindenburg to appoint Strasser Vice-Chancellor and Federal Commissioner for Prussia. The Landtag would then be dissolved and Hitler would be undone. Hindenburg refused. He criticized Schleicher's "land settlement" plans and opposed any action against the Nazis.

Thus encouraged, Count Eberhard von Kalkreuth, president of the Landbund, pressed his demands for new protective tariff duties on foodstuffs. These demands were resisted by Schleicher and by the Federation of German Industries. As a means of bringing pressure to bear on the Cabinet, the Landbund issued a denunciatory statement to the press on January 11:

"A deplorable situation in German agriculture, affecting particularly peasants and specialized farming, has under the present government assumed proportions not even conceivable under a purely Marxist government. The pillaging of agriculture for the all-powerful moneybag interests of the internationally minded export industry and its hirelings is continuing. Radio broadcasts and empty phrases are all agriculture is getting from the government."[1]

On the 12th Hindenburg received the Landbund leaders in Schleicher's presence and promised to do all in his power "to rouse agriculture to new life." Schleicher and Kalkreuth were cordial at the banquet which followed, until someone handed the Chancellor a newspaper containing the Landbund's blast against him. Schleicher

[1] *The New York Times*, January 12, 1933.

asked his neighbour for an explanation. Kalkreuth smiled. Schleicher left the room in high dudgeon and declared that the government would no longer receive the Landbund's representatives. The Junkers now attacked him furiously, and Hindenburg became more and more unsympathetic toward his Chancellor. A parliamentary commission was investigating the *Ost-Hilfe* scandal and playing with recommendations that owners of large estates should henceforth be barred from relief funds unless they were prepared to subdivide their holdings. If the commission reported, many titled names would be besmirched, including the Hindenburgs. What did Schleicher propose to do?

While Schleicher hesitated, Hitler found salvation. His situation seemed desperate enough: huge debts unpaid, no money available, Strasser in revolt, disaffection in the ranks. The Franconian division of the S.A., twelve thousand strong, had to be dissolved for insubordination. Other rifts were widening. The old year had closed in deep gloom for the party headquarters.[1] Then—Papen to the rescue!

On January 4 Hitler and Papen, on the latter's invitation, held a "love-feast" in Cologne at the home of the banker Baron von Schroeder, friend of Thyssen. The meeting was arranged in such secrecy that even Hitler's immediate companions did not know where he had been or with whom. But Schleicher's intelligence service was efficient. The fact of the meeting was announced in the press on the next day. Its import was a subject for conjecture. Rumours leaked out, however, and were confirmed by subsequent events.

Hitler needed money. Papen needed political strings for the web he was attempting to spin around Schleicher. He persuaded various Rhineland industrialists, including Thyssen and Springorum, to donate some four million marks to the Nazi treasury. They were more generous now that Hitler had broken with his socialistic colleagues, Strasser and Feder. The industrialists in general were supporting Schleicher in his stand against the Landbund, but Papen hinted that the Chancellor's days were numbered. Those who donated would fare well after Schleicher went. No intrigue, no treachery was too high a price to pay to assuage Papen's *amour propre*. The bargain was struck. Thyssen and Oskar gave their blessing.

When Schleicher, a few days later, reproached Papen for his al-

[1] Goebbels, op. cit., pp. 221–32.

leged pact with Hitler, his former colleague replied: "Kurt, in the name of our old friendship and on my word of honour as an officer and as a man, I swear to you that I will never undertake nor sanction any move whatever against you or against a government of which you are the head." Schleicher believed. Later he said of Papen: "He proved to be the kind of traitor beside whom Judas Iscariot is a saint." [1]

The next step in the anti-Schleicher conspiracy was the restoration of the "Harzburg Front." Hitler's political stock was rising again. Strasser was no longer being seriously considered as a Cabinet member. Already Göring and Goebbels had warned Hitler of Strasser's secret treachery, and with this news had intercepted Der Führer at Weimar on his way to Berlin for a conference with the Chancellor. The conference was never held. Hitler saw the light. If Röhm contemplated joining Strasser, he was deterred by the news from Cologne.

On Sunday, January 15, a Diet election took place in Lippe. Schleicher addressed the Kyffhäuser Bund and commemorated the establishment of the empire by urging rearmament and universal military service. Politically he seemed immobilized between his desires to placate Hindenburg and the Junkers and to effect a combination with the Socialists and trade unionists. In Lippe the Nazis waged a campaign of unprecedented intensity. Hitler concentrated all his heavy oratorical artillery in this little district. He himself spoke at eighteen meetings in halls, in town squares, and even in circus tents pitched in the fields. Every hamlet and farmhouse was visited by prominent party organizers. An impression must at all costs be made. In the result the NSDAP captured over forty per cent of the voters and made good its losses of November 6. With sufficient funds it could still recruit converts.

What was more important, Hugenberg conferred with Hitler during the campaign. He was alarmed at Schleicher's "socialism." Through Gerecke, the Chancellor was dickering with trade-union leaders. Against the advice of Ernst Oberfohren, parliamentary leader of the Nationalists, Hugenberg struck a secret bargain:

[1] From an interview of an English correspondent with Schleicher in March 1933: "Schleicher's Political Dream," *The New Statesman and Nation*, London, July 7, 1934, pp. 6–7.

Schleicher would be ousted. Hitler would be Chancellor. Papen would be Vice-Chancellor, and Hugenberg would be Minister of Economics. A majority of the new Cabinet would be non-Nazi (to restrain Hitler), but the Reichstag would be dissolved and a new election called. On this point Hugenberg was skeptical, but finally yielded. After mid-January Göring was in constant touch with Hugenberg, Papen, Meissner, and Seldte. How to unseat Schleicher? Simple—by playing upon the fears of "agrarian Bolshevism" entertained by the Old Gentleman of Neudeck. Papen and Hugenberg smiled. How clever they were! [1] Hitler smiled. Again he had deceived these clever gentlemen with what they took to be promises. He would deceive them again, and yet again—and then destroy them.

Schleicher waited. His negotiations with the trade unions and the Reichsbanner were inconclusive. Hindenburg received Hugenberg on the 15th and was more affable than usual. An East Prussian club of Nazi landowners now copied the technique of Oldenburg-Januschau to win over General Werner von Blomberg, divisional commander of the Reichswehr. They purchased an estate near Königsberg and presented it to the General, with the title to be held by one of his relatives. The Chancellor was furious, but could do nothing.[2] On January 18 Schleicher was obliged to consent to an emergency decree forbidding the forced sale of bankrupt estates east of the Elbe until October 31. Another victory of the Landbund and Hindenburg! Hugenberg's Nationalist press and Hitler's Nazi press now attacked Schleicher mercilessly. His retreat toward the Right was now cut off by the new Harzburg compact. Papen delicately suggested his retirement. On the 20th Hindenburg angrily protested to Schleicher over the parliamentary committee investigating the *Ost-Hilfe*. He must suppress the commission. The Chancellor said he could not legally do so. On January 21 the steering committee of the Reichstag accepted Frick's motion to defer the session from January 24 to January 31. Hitler needed delay.

Der Führer spoke the same evening in the Sportpalast and promised a speedy end of "the System of defeatism enforced since 1918."

[1] "The line between cleverness and silliness is sometimes vague"—Calvin B. Hoover: *Germany Enters the Third Reich* (New York: Macmillan; 1933), p. 87.

[2] *Berlin Diaries,* pp. 277–9.

Over Schleicher's protest, the storm troopers were permitted to provoke the Communists by marching past the Karl Liebknecht House in Bülowplatz on Sunday the 22nd. Large police forces with machine-guns and armoured cars preserved order by arresting eighty Communists and forbidding the local residents even to open their windows. In the square Hitler and Röhm reviewed the S.A. after unveiling a memorial tablet at the grave of Horst Wessel. In another huge meeting in the Sportpalast Hitler invoked divine aid: "We pray Almighty God to give us the same strength of spirit and self-sacrifice that characterizes our martyrs." On Monday the 23rd Hindenburg told Schleicher that he still possessed his confidence, but ought to rely more on Hugenberg and the Stahlhelm. Tentatively he assented to Schleicher's plan to dissolve the Reichstag and decree a state of emergency. Hugenberg, however, demanded the Chancellor's resignation. He had plans of his own. Perhaps he could outwit Papen and become the head of the next Cabinet himself. Papen waited. Perhaps he could outwit Hugenberg. Perhaps they could both outwit Hitler. Perhaps . . . ?

Press headlines: Nazi students riot at University of Breslau as Professor Ernst Cohn resumes his law courses. Police drive them out. January 25, Dresden police break up Communist meeting when speaker attacks NSDAP. Nine Communists killed, eleven wounded, all shot in back. Schleicher demands investigation. Schleicher demands political show-down. Hugenberg's efforts at Right Cabinet headed by Papen fail. Hitler bans Nazi participation in any cabinet not headed by himself. Schleicher will see Hindenburg. Schleicher reported unwilling to go before Reichstag without dissolution order. Papen reported ready to act. Centrists and Bavarian People's Party announce that they prefer a "parliamentary" cabinet headed by Hitler. Nazi students riot at Breslau.

On January 28 came the debacle. Early in the morning Hindenburg summoned his Chancellor and asked him whether he knew that the Reichstag committee had asked him to make a public statement before parliament on the *Ost-Hilfe* scandal. Schleicher replied in the affirmative. Would he make this statement? Schleicher saw no way of refusing—unless the Reichstag were dissolved.

Hindenburg rose. He is reported to have said:

"If you aren't strong enough to put a stop once and for all to these argumentations about the plain duty of the State toward agriculture, then I shall not empower you to dissolve the Reichstag, but ask you to resign instead. This pretence of governing has long ceased to have any point!" [1]

Schleicher blanched and announced that the whole Cabinet would resign. As he left by one door, Papen came in by another. Half an hour later Papen was entrusted with the task of forming a new government. Papen and Hitler conferred, each doubtless accusing the other of "double-crossing." Neurath objected. Bankers and business men voiced apprehension. Trade-union leaders warned the President against any new anti-labour cabinet. The *V.B.* declared war on Papen and asserted that Hitler must be Chancellor.

Papen's negotiations were possibly mere sham for the sake of appearances. The Papen-Hitler-Thyssen-Hugenberg-Landbund alliance had converted the Junker President. By the terms of the bargain (which Papen was perhaps attempting to evade), Hitler would be Chancellor of a cabinet including his new friends and the remnants of the Herren Klub.

What would Schleicher do? He had been Chancellor for fifty-seven days. Apparently he was cognizant of the conspiracy against him and appreciated his responsibility as the last defence against the Nazi revolution. He conferred in the afternoon with trade-union leaders and tentatively proposed a putsch, to be supported by the Reichswehr and by a general strike, as a means of keeping Hitler and Papen from power. The Catholic trade unions were agreeable. Theodor Leipart, leader of the Social Democratic unions, had scruples: the putsch would be "unconstitutional," all angles must be carefully considered, time was needed for deliberation. . . . Schleicher also conferred with certain Reichswehr commanders at Potsdam. They were willing to act. It seemed certain that the Socialist and Communist rank and file of the trade unions would overwhelmingly support Schleicher. But the leaders were "yellow." A putsch might mean civil war. The Reichswehr could then at last crush the NSDAP. There would be a Left military dictatorship supported by the proletariat. Still . . . ? Hindenburg would have to be ousted. Hitler, Papen, and Hugenberg would have to be arrested. Would the Reichswehr move against the President? Schleicher was unwell. He

[1] *Berlin Diaries,* p. 288.

hesitated irresolutely—until it was too late.

On Sunday the 29th, a hundred thousand workers met in the Lustgarten in a great anti-Fascist demonstration to oppose Hitler as Chancellor. But the liberal *Frankfurter Zeitung* opined that a Hitler cabinet might prove to be the only way of curbing the Nazis. Secret "negotiations" continued. For the last time a Centrist-Nazi coalition was discussed. Kaas asked guarantees that Hitler would abide by the Constitution and resign if defeated in the Reichstag. None was forthcoming. If any rumours of Schleicher's plans reached the conspirators, they served to hasten an agreement. But everything was kept secret to the end. Hitler did not see the President, but left all the bargaining to Papen.

At 11.00 a.m., Monday, January 30, 1933, Adolf Hitler was named Reichskanzler by Paul von Hindenburg. Two of his party colleagues entered the new Cabinet: Hermann Göring became Minister without portfolio, Federal Commissioner for Air Transport, and Prussian Minister of the Interior (on March 11 Göring became Premier of Prussia and on the 28th he became Reich Minister of Air); Wilhelm Frick became Reich Minister of the Interior. To the Nazi leaders who were unaware of the intrigue which had culminated in this wholly unexpected victory, the whole course of events was fantastic and incomprehensible—"like a dream," said Goebbels.[1] The other conspirators were rewarded. Franz von Papen became Vice-Chancellor. Alfred Hugenberg became Minister of Economics and of Food. His Stahlhelm ally Franz Seldte was named Minister of Labour. General Werner von Blomberg would be Minister of Defence. He was persuaded to join by Ludwig Mueller, divisional chaplain of the east Prussian Reichswehr. For the rest, the feudal gentry remained: Lutz von Schwerin-Krosigk, Minister of Finance; Dr. Franz Gürtner, Minister of Justice; Baron von Eltz-Rübenach, Minister of Posts and Transport; Dr. Günther Gerecke, Minister of Employment; Baron von Neurath, Minister of Foreign Affairs. It was all arranged within fifteen minutes. "And now, gentlemen," declared Hindenburg, "forward with God!"[2]

Three Nazis confronted nine non-Nazis. The NSDAP, to be sure, had the chancellorship and control of the police. But Hitler would

[1] *Vom Kaiserhof zur Reichskanzlei,* pp. 251–4.
[2] Hermann Göring: *Germany Reborn,* p. 114.

presumably be "tamed" by his colleagues. This fatuous supposition was scarcely encouraged by the Nazi proclamation which Hitler caused to be issued:

"After a thirteen-year struggle, the Nationalsocialist movement has succeeded in breaking through to the government; the struggle to win the German nation, however, is only beginning. The Nationalsocialist Party knows that the new government is no Nationalsocialist government, but it is conscious that it bears the name of its leader, Adolf Hitler. He has advanced with his shock troops and has placed himself at the head of the government to lead the German people to liberty. Not only is the entire authority of the State to be wielded, but in the background, prepared for action, is the Nationalsocialist movement of millions of followers united unto death with its leader. . . . In this historic hour we wish to thank President von Hindenburg, whose immortal fame as Field Marshal on the battlefields of the World War binds his name perpetually to that of young Germany, which is striving with burning heart to gain its liberty."[1]

Schleicher surrendered. A Communist call for a general strike was without result. The Socialist leaders said that Hitler had come into power "legally." They must wait for evidences of "illegality." It was intimated that the new government would go before the Reichstag on February 7. On Monday evening the Berlin and Brandenburg S.A., in collaboration with the Stahlhelm, staged a monster torchlight parade through the Brandenburg Gate and down Unter den Linden. No fewer than seven hundred thousand people marched through Wilhelmstrasse past the chancellery building. Hindenburg greeted the demonstrators from one window, Hitler and Göring from another. There were no disorders, save that a policeman and an S.A. man, Hans Maikowski, were shot to death, presumably by "Communists," as they returned later to their homes. During the ceremonies Göring addressed the radio audience:

"The 30th of January 1933 will be designated in German history as the day on which the Reich again found itself, created a new nation, and destroyed all the torment, insult and disgrace of the last fourteen years. Today will be the day on which we close in the book of German history the last year of want and shame and begin a new chapter, and in this chapter Freedom and Honour will stand as the foundation of the coming State. We thank today not only the Leader

[1] *The New York Times,* January 31, 1933.

of this great movement, but also the grey General Field Marshal von Hindenburg, who today has concluded an alliance with the young generation. . . . Bread and work for our countrymen, freedom and honour for the nation." [1]

On Tuesday the General Federation of Labour and the Christian Labour Federation issued a joint manifesto against the new régime. But since they proposed no action, their statement was pointless. Hitler conferred with the Centrist leaders, but would make no promises. The negotiations for Centrist toleration of the new Cabinet thus failed, and on Wednesday, February 1, Hindenburg dissolved the Reichstag and ordered new elections for March 5. Hugenberg apparently opposed an election. In vain. He asked for a joint government list of candidates. In vain. The NSDAP would stand alone. He formed a Black-White-Red Kampfbund with the Stahlhelm to support the Nationalist candidates. This too would ultimately be in vain. The government addressed the nation:

"More than fourteen years have passed since the unhallowed day when, dazzled by promises at home and abroad, the German people forgot the most precious heritage of our past—its honour and freedom—and thus lost all. Since that day of betrayal, the Lord has withheld His blessings from our people. Discord and hatred have entered among us. . . . One year of Bolshevism would destroy Germany. The section of the earth representing the richest and most beautiful culture in the world would be changed into chaos. Even the sufferings of the last fifteen years could not be compared to the sufferings of a Europe in whose heart the red flag of destruction was hoisted. . . .

"The national government sees as its first and highest task the restoration of the unity of mind and will of our people. It will shield and protect the foundations on which the strength of our nation rests. It will take under its firm guardianship Christianity as the basis of our entire morality, the family as the germ-cell of our people and our body politic. Despite vocations and classes, it will bring our people back to a consciousness of its racial and political unity and of the duties which flow therefrom. It will make respect for our great past, pride in our old traditions, the bases of the education of German youth. It will declare merciless war upon spiritual, political, and cultural nihilism. Germany must not and shall not sink into anarchism and Communism."

[1] W. Gehl: *Die nationalsozialistische Revolution* (Breslau: Hirt; 1933), pp. 69–70.

Hitler went on to describe his two "Four Year Plans" for the rescue of the peasantry and the unemployed. Within four years the work of ruination of the November parties would be undone. Through labour service and land settlement (*Arbeitsdienstspflicht und Siedlungspolitik*) agriculture would again be made prosperous and unemployment would be liquidated. In foreign policy, freedom and equality for the Reich would be attained. A free and equal Reich would work for peace and the welfare of Europe. To realize this program and to do its duty toward other nations, Germany must first conquer the Communist menace:

"The parties of Marxism and their followers have had fourteen years to demonstrate their abilities. The result is a heap of ruins. Now, German people, give us four years and then judge us! True to the command of the General Field Marshal, we wish to begin. May the Almighty God take our work in His grace, approve our purpose, bless our program, and favour us with the confidence of our people. For we wish to fight not for ourselves, but for Germany!" [1]

The line of campaign was clear. The new government would promise work, bread, and prosperity. It would identify itself with national unity, claim a monopoly of patriotism, and evoke support by appealing to popular ethnocentrism. At the same time it would hold up the bogy of Bolshevism before the electorate and make itself the beneficiary of the resulting insecurities by posing as the saviour of the Fatherland from Communist revolution. Other devices in the Nazi propaganda arsenal could be used later. At present they might antagonize the non-Nazis in the Cabinet—and these gentlemen were still useful.

On Thursday, February 2, the Cabinet forbade all Communist meetings throughout Germany and ordered police raids on the homes of Communist leaders. A projected meeting of the Social Democrats and the Anti-Fascist League, scheduled for Sunday in the Lustgarten, was banned by the police on the ground that it would interfere with the funeral of Hans Maikowski. Already Hitler was insisting on the suppression of the Communist Party. In this he was opposed by Papen and Hugenberg, who feared a Nazi majority in the new Reichstag. The Nazi minority in the Cabinet must be supported by a Nazi minority in parliament, in order that Hitler should

[1] Ibid., pp. 71–6. This manifesto was signed by all of the Cabinet members except Gerecke.

remain dependent upon the allies who had elevated him to the chancellorship. Papen and Hugenberg did not yet perceive the implications of what they had done. They continued to cherish illusions. During the weeks which followed, the issue between the Nazis and non-Nazis in the Cabinet tended to centre about the question of what should be done with the KPD. The Communist leaders themselves seemed to be paralysed. They perceived no means of offering effective resistance to Fascism. Their role was that of scapegoats and unwilling propaganda symbols wherewith the NSDAP could terrify the electorate and send it panic-stricken into the Nazi camp.

In preparation for the election Hindenburg decreed that every party must have 60,000 signatures on its petition in place of the usual 500. The "splinter parties" were thus destroyed. On February 3 *Vorwärts* was banned for three days for publishing a Socialist election appeal. On the 4th eight more Socialist papers and two Communist papers were suppressed. On Sunday, February 5, Hans Maikowski and the policeman who was slain with him were given a State funeral—an honour hitherto granted only to President Ebert and Chancellor Stresemann. Hitler, Göring, and the Crown Prince attended the ceremonies, in which twenty thousand storm troopers and a hundred and fifty thousand spectators took part. The affair was a complete success, except that the policeman's family and the Catholic Church objected to the Protestant ceremony. On February 6 another presidential decree forbade any press criticism of the Chancellor, despite the protests of the German Press Federation. Papen, acting as Premier of Prussia, dissolved the Landtag, which, on February 4, had rejected a Nazi dissolution motion by a vote of 214 to 196. New Prussian elections were ordered for March 5. Braun and Severing decided to ask the Supreme Court for another injunction.

Communists were now being shot with impunity throughout the Reich. While Göring called upon the civil service to co-operate in the national awakening, the Nazis in the Reichstag Committee on Parliamentary Rights denounced its chairman, Paul Löbe, as "Jewboy" and "swine" and made its further sessions impossible. Hitler asserted that "objective criticism" would be tolerated, but that "ten years from now there will be no more Marxism in Germany." In the Bavarian Diet the Nazis, with Socialist support, passed a resolution asking the government to nationalize the banks. It was ignored. On February 9 Göring rebuked the Swedish press for criticizing Hitler.

On the following evening Hitler spoke in the Sportpalast:

"Our program? . . . We will not lie and we will not swindle! The resurrection of the German nation is the question of the restoration of the inner strength and health of the German people. . . . We wish to work, but the people themselves must co-operate. . . . In us alone lies the future of the German people. . . . The laws of life are always the same, and we wish to undertake the rebuilding of the people not according to empty theories, conceived by some foreign brain, but according to the eternal laws which experience and history show us and which we know. . . .

"Worth of personality . . . rotten democracy . . . cleanliness in government, cleanliness in public life, cleanliness in culture . . . honour . . . freedom . . . art . . . music . . . tradition . . , respect for the past . . . our two million dead . . . the army. . . . If the German people should desert us, that will not restrain us. We will take the course that is necessary to save Germany from ruin. Therewith will this program be a program of national revival in all spheres of life, hard against everyone who sins against the nation, brother and friend of everyone who will fight with us for the resurrection of his people." [1]

On the next day a Nationalist-Stahlhelm rally was held in the Sportpalast. Hugenberg condemned Bolshevism and democracy and asserted that there would be no elections after March 5. Papen praised Hindenburg and declared that the national movement was not a coalition of parties, but a spiritual resurrection. Seldte asserted that the Stahlhelm had always fought for freedom. On the same day the Communist *Rote Fahne* was banned for two weeks. On Monday the 13th Göring ousted twenty-four Prussian provincial governors and police chiefs and replaced them by Nazis. On the 15th it was announced that all political meetings would be watched by armed "auxiliary police"—that is, Nazis and Stahlhelm men—and that all meetings at which the government was criticized would be at once dissolved. All Communist meetings were forbidden. Of the 11 Prussian provincial governors, 7 were already ousted; of the 33 district presidents, 15 were removed; and of the 35 police chiefs, 24 were replaced by Nazis. In Hanover the S.A. leader, Viktor Lutze, became police chief. The *Vorwärts* was again banned and the new Nazi Minister of Education in Prussia, Bernard Rust, took steps to expel

[1] Gehl, op. cit., pp. 76–80.

Professor Cohn from the University of Breslau.

On February 17 Leipart asserted that "the use of force against the working class can only portend a life-and-death struggle, the terrific possibilities of which ought to give the present rulers pause." But there was no struggle, only submission. On the next day more papers were suppressed, including *Germania,* the chief Centrist organ, which dared to print its party's election manifesto. On the 20th Göring ordered the police to shoot "Communist terrorists" on sight. They would be punished for "false consideration." "Failing to act is a graver fault than errors made in action." The police, moreover, must fraternize with the storm troopers and the Stahlhelm and must suppress all opponents of the government "with the greatest vigour."[1]

On the 20th also, Hitler met all the leading industrialists, including Krupp, Siemens, Flick, Bosch, Schacht, and others, in Göring's official residence. No statement was issued, but Big Business was apparently reassured as to its place in the Third Reich. On the 21st many Centrist meetings were broken up by Nazis. Stegerwald was assaulted at Krefeld. Brüning was obliged to seek police protection at a meeting in the Palatinate, where eleven Catholic ushers were wounded in an attack by S.A. men. Göring declared that the culprits were disguised Communists and demanded discipline in the S.A. On the 24th Göring cited the "growing excesses of the Left radicals" and formally authorized the arming of auxiliary police. The *Rote Fahne* was suspended for another six weeks (it was never permitted to reappear) and numerous Socialist meetings were suppressed.

These developments created grave misgivings among the allies of the NSDAP in the Cabinet. Who sups with the devil must use a long spoon. Papen, Hugenberg, and Seldte were beginning to wonder. Oberfohren had warned Hugenberg, but it was now too late. The Nationalist lion was to have swallowed the Nazi lamb. But what if they had been mistaken about the species? Suppressing the Marxists was all very well—but not as a means of giving the Nazis complete control of the State. Frick and Göring controlled the police. They were arming the storm troopers for the terrorization of their enemies. The Reichswehr was passive and Blomberg had been bought by the Nazis. The Old Gentleman dozed at Neudeck. He had played his part too well. The NSDAP was now waving the red flag of

[1] *The New York Times,* February 21, 1933.

Bolshevism before the masses and might frighten them into returning a Nazi majority on March 5. Between the 32 per cent of November 6 and 51 per cent there was still a wide gap, but this only made Hitler, Göring, and Goebbels all the more desperate and determined to win complete power. If they could outlaw the KPD in addition to bludgeoning all other opposition into silence, they might well make a clean sweep on March 5 and then dispense with their unwanted collaborators.

For these reasons the non-Nazi majority in the Cabinet apparently determined to prevent the complete suppression of the Communists. Goebbels was demanding that the police discover incriminating evidence of treason against the KPD in order that it might be banned in the name of the safety of the State. The Berlin police chief, Melcher, failed to discover any. Nazi pressure for his dismissal and replacement by Count Helldorf was resisted by Papen. Finally a compromise was effected. Melcher was displaced by Admiral von Levetzow. On February 24 the police broke into the Karl Liebknecht House, closed several weeks before by the authorities, and carted away large quantities of documents. On February 26 the government press service announced sensational disclosures of "catacombs," "underground vaults," "treasonable materials," and a secret illegal Communist organization in the basement. Papen, Hugenberg, and Seldte were doubtless indignant at the use of such cheap forgeries, but were helpless to intervene. For them to defend the KPD against the Nazis was unthinkable. They waited, hoping against hope for a way out of the cul-de-sac into which they had so blithely entered.[1]

From the point of view of the NSDAP, however, the election prospects were none too bright. The leaders considered a general mobilization of the S.A. around Berlin on March 5, but such a move would arouse grave suspicion and perhaps antagonize the Reichswehr. Even now, with the Nazis partially in control of the machinery of the State, any danger of an open conflict must be avoided. Papen and Hugenberg had trusted Hitler, but he had learned to trust nobody. What to do? If only the KPD would attempt armed resistance! But it did nothing. Some dramatic event, some sudden alarm was needed

[1] Cf. the Oberfohren Memorandum, *The New Republic,* August 23, 1933. This much debated document presents a version of the Reichstag fire which cannot be substantiated by the known facts. But there is no reason to suppose that its presentation of the latent conflict within the Hitler Cabinet is false.

to frighten the hesitant voters into acquiescence. How could it be provided?

4. THE SIGN FROM HEAVEN

ABOUT 8.40, Monday evening, February 27, 1933, a student of philosophy, Hans Flöter, left the University of Berlin and walked westward along Unter den Linden toward his lodgings. His route took him through the Brandenburg Gate and across the square beyond. Here Unter den Linden merges into Charlottenburger Chaussee, which runs through the Tiergarten. At right angles runs Friedrich Ebert Strasse, soon to be renamed Hermann Göring Strasse. It was dark and cold, with a thin crust of snow on the ground. Flöter turned right and skirted the black hulk of the Reichstag building. He was thinking of the supper that awaited him and perhaps of his work at school. He felt hungry and ill. He turned right again at the southwest corner of the building and cut diagonally across Königsplatz. When he was near the great statue of Bismarck, he heard a sound of breaking glass on his right. It was a few minutes after nine o'clock. He looked toward the darkened building. On the first-floor balcony outside of the large window to the right of the central portal, he perceived dimly the figure of a man waving a burning object in his hand. Flöter ran excitedly toward the northwest corner of the building, where he told a police officer what he had seen. The policeman, whose precise identity was never established, seemed unable to understand. Flöter gave him a thump on the back and explained more emphatically. The policeman then ran toward the central portal. Flöter was still hungry. A philosopher should not be concerned with the doings of night prowlers. He went home to supper.[1]

At the same time another passer-by had likewise seen the man on the balcony and had informed Police Sergeant Karl Buwert—about 9.05 p.m. Buwert and his informant ran to the central portal, where they saw flames behind the second window of the Reichstag restaurant occupying the first floor of the southwest corner. The sergeant asked his companion to go to the police station at the Brandenburg Gate and notify the guard. Buwert was joined by a third passer-by, Werner Thaler, a type-setter, who had also heard breaking glass and

[1] The following account is based upon the voluminous evidence presented at the trial. Cf. Douglas Reed: *The Burning of the Reichstag* (New York: Covici-Friede; 1934).

had seen someone—possibly two persons (the light was dim)—climbing through the northernmost window of the restaurant. Thaler had run back to the southwest corner, called the police, and then dashed up the carriageway to the central portal, where he found Buwert. He climbed the low parapet and saw flames on the farther side of the room through three of the restaurant windows. Then fire leaped up nearer to him around the broken pane. He told Buwert what he had seen. As they watched, a flickering light appeared behind the barred and frosted windows on the ground floor beneath the restaurant. They followed it from window to window, moving along the parapet toward the corner of the building. At the fourth window Thaler told Buwert to shoot, since beyond the fifth window was massive masonry which would protect the intruder. Buwert fired. The light vanished.

Buwert and Thaler waited a moment, irresolutely. Buwert then ran to seek help. He encountered a soldier, whom he sent to give the alarm at the Brandenburg Gate. He also encountered two policemen who had heard the shot and sent one of them to sound the fire-alarm in Moltkestrasse. Buwert then ran back up the carriageway and met Policeman Poeschel, whose beat covered the north and west sides of the building. Poeschel was sent to tell the porter, Wendt, at Portal 5, that the restaurant was on fire. (Only Portal 5 on the north side and Portal 2 on the south were in use that evening. The central portal on the west side, as well as the other portals, were locked.) At this point Police Lieutenant Lateit from the Brandenburg Gate arrived with a squad, told Buwert to watch the window and give the "grand alarm," and then ran round the corner. It was 9.17. Buwert waited two minutes until a fellow officer arrived to watch the window and then dashed off. At 9.21 the first fire-engine arrived. The Unter den Linden fire-station had received the first local alarm at 9.14, and the station in Alt Moabit at 9.15. The firemen climbed to the balcony, broke through the second window, and entered the burning restaurant. Curtains were ablaze, and a few pieces of furniture. The fire was small and easily extinguished, since the furnishings burned slowly or not at all. The firemen prepared to leave.

But meanwhile Lateit, accompanied by Officer Losigkeit, had entered Portal 5 after circling the building and vainly trying to enter Portals 2, 3, and 4. At portal 5 they met the porter Wendt, who already knew of the fire, and Scranowitz, the house inspector. They accompanied Scranowitz into the building, unlocking the inner doors with his keys. They dashed upstairs into the lobby and entered the great ante-room of the session hall. At 9.21 they entered the dark empty chamber where the Reich's legislators had deliberated for six decades. A curtain at the entrance was burning and flames were visible on the tribune opposite. But the benches were not afire and Lateit felt that this blaze, like the one in the restaurant, could be easily extinguished. He ran back to Portal 5, sent a fireman to the session chamber, hastened to the Brandenburg Gate, telephoned for reinforcements (9.25), and returned. Portal 2 was now open. He went in with six policemen, amid clouds of smoke. Inside he found broken glass panels and bits of burning cloth. In the lobby of Portal 2 he found a cap and tie. He then went back under orders to the Brandenburg Gate guard-room. During these events, Losigkeit and Scranowitz rushed through several rooms near the session chamber looking for incendiaries. Constable Poeschel had also entered the building and was searching for the culprits. He and Scranowitz went through the lobby around the session chamber. They looked in. The benches were now burning furiously. There were thirty or forty separate fires throughout the hall, with about four feet between them. This was at 9.22, scarcely a minute after Lieutenant Lateit had seen only two small fires. They finally reached Bismarck Hall, an ante-room northeast of the session chamber. Scranowitz stepped on a burning torch lying against a leather armchair.

Beyond, in the shadows, stood a man wearing only trousers and torn shoes. Tousled hair fell over his perspiring brow. He crouched, but made no effort to escape, responding at once to Poeschel's order: "Hands up!" Scranowitz excitedly gave him a blow with his fist. The constable arrested him and searched him: in his side pocket a small knife; in the hip pocket a handkerchief, a purse, and a Dutch passport bearing the name Marinus Van der Lubbe. Nothing else. It was 9.27. He was taken to the Brandenburg Gate station. When asked by Lieutenant Lateit whether he had fired the Reichstag, he said: "Yes." When asked his motive, he laughed like a lunatic, giggling and muttering incoherently in a mixture of Dutch and German. Two hours later, however, according to the unconvincing testimony of Detective Inspector Heisig, he was to give a detailed account of his act in excellent German. . . .

The session chamber was now a flaming furnace. Fire Captain

Waldemar Klotz of the Alt Moabit station had reached the Reichstag about 9.19, entered Portal 5, and opened the door of the session chamber at 9.24. A great blast of heat struck him. He saw only smoke and a glow of fire over the nearest seats through a thick gaseous haze. He expected a burst of flame momentarily. He ran back and ordered hoses brought in. By 9.26 water was playing on the chamber. Within a few minutes the two small fires seen by Lateit had enveloped the whole hall. Three fire experts, Professor Josse of the Berlin Technical Hochschule, Director Wagner, a senior fire-department official, and Dr. Schatz, the chemical expert of the Reich Supreme Court later testified that the fire had followed a course completely different from that of the restaurant fire and must have been carefully prepared.[1] Herr Gempp, head of the Berlin fire department, had observed a trail of gasoline in Bismarck Hall. Van der Lubbe had no gasoline, only fire-lighters and burning cloths, which could make little impression on the heavy woodwork and leather of the session chamber. Gempp was dismissed from his post shortly after the fire, presumably for having announced that a truckload of unburned incendiary materials had been carted away by the police after the conflagration. During the trial he indignantly denied having made any such statement. But inflammable liquid, probably self-igniting, had evidently been poured about in large quantities. According to the experts, incendiary materials had been piled in many places and connected by liquid fuel or celluloid strips. Van der Lubbe had perhaps lit the fire. But others had prepared it before his arrival.

At 9.27—the moment of the Dutchman's arrest in Bismarck Hall—the gases in the session chamber ignited. A slow muffled explosion shattered the glass in the central dome far above and gave the flames access to the outer air. Smoke and sparks poured out over the Königsplatz and the Tiergarten. Herr Gempp gave the general alarm at 9.42, but the fire was beyond control. The heavy brick walls of the Reichstag prevented it from spreading to other parts of the building. The chamber itself, however, was completely burned out. While the fire was at its height, at 10.00 o'clock, a Nazi deputy, Dr. Herbert Albrecht, rushed out of Portal 5 as if in flight—hatless, collarless, and breathless. He was hailed by the police, but upon identifying himself was allowed to go. He had been sleeping in his *pension* near by, he said later, when he learned of the fire. He had dressed hastily and

[1] Reed, op. cit., pp. 180 f.

rushed to the Reichstag to rescue some family papers from his locker. But the porter Wendt, on duty at Portal 5 since 8.00 o'clock, had not admitted him to the building. All the other portals had been locked. . . . ? [1]

What the Nazi leaders were doing while the fire raged and beforehand can only be conjectured on the basis of their own statements, supplemented by other evidence, still incomplete, given at the trial.[2] Hermann Göring, Prussian Minister of the Interior and President of the Reichstag, was working in his Ministry building on Unter den Linden when he first (?) heard the news. For weeks he had been planning the destruction of the Communist Party.[3] He would strike at the first word of the Communist "insurrection" which he professed confidently to expect. When he reached the Reichstag in his huge trench-coat and upturned fedora, he heard the word "arson" and knew at once, intuitively, "the Communist Party is guilty of this fire." It was the beacon (*Fanal*) of the proletarian revolution. Hitler had been dining with Goebbels in the latter's apartment on Reichskanzlerplatz. When Dr. Hanfstängl telephoned Goebbels that the Reichstag was on fire, Goebbels, according to his own account, hung up the receiver, taking the news for another clownish joke. Hanfstängl called again more insistently. Goebbels told Hitler and they drove together to the Reichstag. Here they met Göring, who said: "It is a Communist outrage. One man has already been arrested, a Dutch Communist, who is now being examined." Hitler declared that the fire was "a Sign from Heaven to show to what we should have come if these gentry had gained power . . . Now we can see where the danger lies. The German people can rest assured that I shall save it from this danger. . . . This is the end." [4]

Göring acted at once:

"I then took my measures against the Communists which Hitler approved. . . . I intended to hang Van der Lubbe at once, and nobody could have stopped me. I only refrained because I thought: 'We

[1] Ibid., p. 254.

[2] The version given in *The Brown Book of the Hitler Terror* (New York: Knopf; 1933), according to which Goebbels planned the fire and Göring executed the plan, using Heines, Schulze, and Helldorf as his aides, is no longer tenable and need not be discussed here. Cf. Reed, op. cit., pp. 166–8 and 232 f.

[3] Cf. his testimony, November 5, 1933, before the Reich Supreme Court.

[4] Göring: *Germany Reborn,* pp. 132–5; Goebbels: *Vom Kaiserhof zur Reichskanzlei,* pp. 269–70; Reed, op. cit., pp. 299, 244.

have one of them, but there must have been many. Perhaps we shall need him as a witness.' . . . I knew as by intuition that the Communists fired the Reichstag. The suspicion was enough to order the arrest of Torgler and Koenen. We put the whole police force and state apparatus in motion and, as it did not suffice, we also used the storm troops. I left Count Helldorf a free hand in details, but I gave him the clear order to use his storm troops and arrest every Communist leader, spy, and vagabond he could lay hands on. Without the praiseworthy help of the storm troops the colossal success of this night, during which 4,000 to 5,000 Communist leaders were brought behind lock and bar, would not have been possible. I am convinced that a number of people fired the Reichstag. . . . I will find the guilty and lead them to their punishment." [1]

Here at last, and at the correct psychological moment, was the golden opportunity to crush the KPD, to accuse it of arson and high treason, and to scare the whole non-Communist electorate into the arms of the NSDAP with the bogy of Bolshevist revolution. The leaders acted at once. Before midnight, while the Reichstag was still burning, orders went out for the wholesale arrest of leading Communists and Socialists. Lists had already been prepared and all plans had been laid for such a sudden blow. Count Helldorf, leader of the Berlin S.A., declared later that he had ordered the arrests "on my own initiative and without instructions from anybody. . . . In our view, criminal elements in the State are in general Marxists. There was for me no doubt that the criminals were to be found in Marxist ranks." [2] Göring issued an official statement accusing the Communists of burning the Reichstag as a signal for armed insurrection and alleging (falsely) that a Communist Party membership card had been found on Van der Lubbe.

On the next day President von Hindenburg was prevailed upon by Hitler to sign a decree "for the protection of the nation from the Communist Menace." [3] It suppressed all civil liberties and enabled the S.A., under the guise of legality, to continue wholesale arrests of suspects. Prisons were soon filled to overflowing and concentration camps were established for the surplus. On February 28 also, the Prussian Government Press Department issued a long statement

[1] Reed, op. cit., pp. 229–30.
[2] Ibid., pp. 166–7.
[3] *Reichsgesetzblatt* (hereinafter referred to as *R.G.B.*), 1933, No. 17, p. 83.

about the "documents" alleged to have been found by the police in their raid on the Karl Liebknecht House on the preceding Friday. The statement asserted:

"Government buildings, museums, mansions, and essential plants were to be burnt down. In disturbances and conflicts with the police, women and children were to be sent in front of the terrorist groups —where possible, the wives and children of police officials. The systematic carrying through of the Bolshevist revolution has been checked by the discovery of this material. In spite of this, the burning of the Reichstag was to be the signal for a bloody insurrection and civil war. Plans had been prepared for looting on a large scale in Berlin at 4.00 a.m. on Tuesday. It has been ascertained that today was to have seen throughout Germany terrorist acts against individual persons, against private property, and against the life and limb of the peaceful population, and also the beginning of general civil war." [1]

The documents in question, which would have constituted the only convincing proof of a "Communist conspiracy," have never been published. In all likelihood they never existed. The material presented to the press on September 12 by the "Union of German Anti-Communist Societies" purported to reveal details of a Communist "plot" involving the burning of the Reichstag, an insurrection in the Rhineland, and the assassination of Hitler and Hindenburg. These were no documents at all, but a summary of the product of Göring's vivid imagination, already revealed in a radio broadcast of early March. No precautions whatever had been taken by the authorities to suppress the alleged insurrection "discovered" three days before the fire and announced after it. According to his own testimony, Göring went unsuspecting to the Reichstag and only perceived the "truth" when others told him of the origins of the fire. Goebbels, like Hitler, professed to have been taken completely by surprise. "Civil war" was impending, but Goebbels said later that no defensive measures had been taken by the Reichswehr. The police and the S.A. would suffice.[2] Did Hitler, Goebbels, and Göring really believe in the genuineness of the "documents"? No matter. The nation would accept salvation from Communism at the hands of the NSDAP. Victory on March 5 was now assured. Nothing else was important.

[1] Reed, op. cit., p. 279.
[2] Cf. his testimony of November 8, 1933, summarized in Reed, op cit., p. 235.

Who burned the Reichstag? This mystery has not thus far been solved, in spite of ten thousand pages of evidence taken at the trial and volumes of accusation, counter-accusation, and endless debate. The psychopathic Dutchman, Marinus Van der Lubbe, confessed and insisted repeatedly that he had no accomplices. Born January 13, 1909, in Leyden, he had led the wandering life of a vagrant labourer. In 1927 a splash of lime had permanently injured his sight and entitled him to an incapacitation allowance. In September 1931, after being expelled from the Dutch Communist Party, he wandered through Austria, Jugoslavia, and Hungary. In 1932 he travelled again as a tramp through Germany, Austria, Hungary, and Poland and made an unsuccessful effort to enter Russia. He had arrived in Berlin February 18, 1933, and spent most of his time in Neukölln in the east end, where he talked loosely and wildly with local Communists. On the evening of Saturday, February 25, he had supplied himself with a box of matches and a few household fire-lighters and had attempted, with no success whatever, to burn the Neukölln Welfare Office, the Berlin town hall, and the former Imperial Palace. Sunday night, February 26, he had spent in a destitutes' shelter in Henningsdorf, a western suburb—"with the Nazis," he said on one occasion. But what this meant or what he did there was never made clear. On Monday morning he tramped back to Berlin, decided to burn the Reichstag, purchased more matches and fire-lighters, surveyed the outside of the building in the afternoon, and broke into the restaurant shortly after nine o'clock in the evening.

Did Van der Lubbe alone burn the Reichstag? This youth, who hung his head, drooled, giggled, and usually answered questions only in guttural monosyllables during his trial, would have had to accomplish miracles in order to have burned the building unaided. The police story was based on evidence taken by Detective Heissig and Dr. Vogt, the examining magistrates of the Supreme Court. Both insisted that the silent half-wit, who understood little German in the courtroom, had talked fluently and volubly during the original examination. According to their tale, he had clambered onto the balcony, lit some of his fire-lighters outside, kicked in the window-pane, climbed into the restaurant, ignited the curtain on the door opposite, returned to fire the curtain at the window and run out into the lobby and thence to the Kaiser Wilhelm Memorial Hall. Finding nothing inflammable there, he had taken off his upper garments, set fire to his shirt, run back through the restaurant into the waiters' room, unfolded a table cloth taken from a linen chest, and fired it with his burning shirt. He had then run down a narrow staircase, kicked in a glass door, climbed through into the kitchen, smashed another glass door with a plate, and passed through a number of rooms to a washroom (Buwert had shot at him during this flight), where he had set towels on fire and trailed them behind him back up the staircase to the Kaiser Hall.

All of this must have been accomplished, by a half-blind man in the dark, in two minutes five seconds, on the basis of the most careful reckoning which could subsequently be made. Van der Lubbe next set his jacket afire, ran into the lobby around the session chamber, fired a tablet and a wooden desk and ignited the curtains on the tribune in the chamber itself. After setting fire to another curtain and a leather sofa he had heard voices and run to the Bismarck Hall, where he was apprehended—unscratched and unburned. All of this, if the story be true, consumed not more than another nine minutes. At 9.12 Buwert had fired. At 9.21 Lateit saw the session chamber empty and already burning. Fire experts later failed in repeated efforts to burn heavy curtains, woodwork, and leather by means of fire-lighters and burning cloths. Five minutes after Van der Lubbe left the chamber, the whole room was a mass of flames and explosive gases. By a miracle the Dutchman might have done all this alone. But this explanation is the least probable of any. Van der Lubbe had no torch, no gasoline, no inflammable fluids. He had accomplices, whether known to him or not. Who were they?

The four other men who were arrested and tried were wholly innocent. Ernst Torgler, parliamentary leader of the Communist Party, had left the Reichstag about 8.15, accompanied by Deputy Koenen and a secretary, Fräulein Anna Rehme. They had proceeded slowly to one of the Aschinger restaurants near the Friedrichstrasse station, half a mile away. While dining here with a few colleagues, Torgler had learned that the Reichstag was burning. He made no change in his plans. With one Birkenhauer he had gone to Alexanderplatz, where he met Kuehne, the secretary of the KPD. With Koenen, Kühne, and two others he had played skat far into the night at Stawicki's café. Here, to his amazement, he had learned by phone from Walter Oehme that his name was being linked with the fire. He told Oehme that he would report to the police to clear himself.

He spent the rest of the night with Kühne, who was arrested by detectives early in the morning. At 9.30 Torgler phoned his wife at Karlshorst and learned that detectives had searched his dwelling. Later in the morning he went with a lawyer to police headquarters, where he was promptly arrested and charged with arson and high treason.

A week later a suspicious waiter in the Bayernhof restaurant on Potsdamerstrasse, one Helmer, told the police of a little group of "Bolshevist" foreigners who were in the habit of coming to dine there. He had seen Van der Lubbe's picture in the papers and "recalled" that the Dutchman had been with this group between May and October 1932. This was nonsense, but Helmer nevertheless informed the police on March 7. He was told to report when he saw the foreigners again. On March 9 they came. He phoned. Two detectives appeared and arrested three Bulgarians: Georgi Dimitroff, Blagoi Popoff, and Wassil Taneff. All were Communist exiles from their own country. On February 27 Dimitroff had been engaging in a flirtation on the Munich-Berlin express. Popoff, who knew little German, had been in Berlin a few months, and Taneff, who knew no German, had been in the city only three days. None of them knew either Van der Lubbe or Torgler, nor had these two ever seen one another before. No proof worthy of the name was ever offered to show that the Bulgarians had had any contacts with the German Communist Party, that the party or any of its members had anything to do with the fire, or that Van der Lubbe was in any sense a Communist at the time. Nevertheless, these five men were arrested, indicted, kept in chains for five months in prison, and at long last elaborately tried—with farcical results.[1]

Who burned the Reichstag? A few additional strands of evidence must at least be mentioned. Göring and the authors of the *Brown Book* were agreed on one thing: that those who prepared the fire escaped by means of a tunnel, a hundred and fifty yards long, connecting the Reichstag with the Speaker's residence and the engine-house behind it, both to the east of the Reichstag building across Hermann Göring Strasse. Paul Adermann, night porter in the Speaker's residence, was the only man who might have known what happened in the tunnel on the night of the fire. He swore that he had made his rounds as usual and seen no one. But many times previously

[1] Cf. pp. 330 f. below.

he had heard mysterious footsteps in the tunnel. He had glued paper strips on the two iron doors leading from the tunnel and six times had found his strips broken. Walter Weber, commander of the "Hermann Göring S.S. Body-guard," investigated the tunnel during the fire and testified that it was empty, with both doors locked. Were Adermann and Weber honest witnesses or perjurers, as were many others? The incendiaries, whoever they were, knew the Reichstag in detail and knew its routine. Between 8.25 p.m., when the lamplighter Scholz made his rounds, and 8.55, when the postman Otto appeared, they presumably planted their materials in the session chamber—to be ignited by Van der Lubbe or by the self-igniting liquid.[1] What did Van der Lubbe do in Hennigsdorf on February 26? Why did the Nazi Dr. Albrecht leave the Reichstag at ten o'clock "as if in flight"? Was Wendt telling the truth in saying that he had not admitted Albrecht? Who dropped the torch and the gasoline in Bismarck Hall? What were the noises which Adermann had heard in the tunnel? Why did Count Helldorf order the arrest of Communists on his own initiative? What was Van der Lubbe—half-wit, consummate actor, drug victim, pyromaniac, catatonic schizophrenic, manic-depressive . . . ?

On July 23, 1934, the London *Daily Herald* published a story of the "last surviving member of the Reichstag fire gang"—one E. Kruse, S.A. member No. 134,522. Kruse had been a personal servant of Röhm. According to this account, Röhm, Heines, and Karl Ernst, Berlin S.A. leader, recruited ten storm troopers on February 10, 1933, to burn the Reichstag. Van der Lubbe was employed by them as a dupe, with the promise that he would be arrested, sentenced, and then secretly pardoned and sent to America with a large fortune. The 10 men conducted two rehearsals in the tunnel. On February 27 they deposited their materials, connected with celluloid strips, in the

[1] The Oberfohren Memorandum, upon which the *Brown Book* was based, was written by the parliamentary leader of the Nationalist Party. It explained the fire in terms of the resistance of the Nationalists in the Cabinet to the Nazi demands for the dissolution of the KPD and for the appointment of Helldorf as Berlin police chief. According to this version, Goebbels and Göring planned the conflagration, which was executed by Heines and his S.A. men, with Van der Lubbe used as a dupe. Göring later asserted that Oberfohren had committed suicide when documents were discovered in his office showing that he had been plotting against Hugenberg (cf. *Berliner Tageblatt,* October 20, 1933). In his election speech in the Sportpalast Goebbels denied these allegations with unusual vehemence, denounced the *Brown Book,* and said: "Father, forgive them, for they know not what they do."

session chamber, where Ernst and Heines lit the blaze after Van der Lubbe had broken into the restaurant. The participants subsequently disappeared one by one. Röhm threatened to reveal the truth at the end of June, 1934, in the face of Hitler's threats to disband the S.A. On June 30 Röhm, Heines, and Ernst were killed.[1] Kruse escaped the "purge" by accident and fled to Switzerland.

This version would explain the noises in the tunnel, Van der Lubbe's contacts with the Nazis in Hennigsdorf, and his behaviour during the trial, but it still leaves many questions unanswered. If these were the perpetrators of the crime, they have been forever silenced. Three other men who were supposed to know have long since disappeared: Ernst Oberfohren was found shot to death in his home on May 7, 1933. George Bell, a Nazi renegade who joined the Centrum after the fire, was murdered on April 3, 1933, in the Tyrol by assailants who fled over the German frontier. Erik Hanussen, Nazi clairvoyant who "foretold" the fire on February 26, vanished. His body was found in a lonely wood on April 7, 1933. The mystery remains unsolved.[2]

5. THE LAST ELECTION

THE immediate effect of the Reichstag fire was to throw the entire German peasantry and bourgeoisie into a frenzy of fear. The Nationalists in the Cabinet still opposed the formal outlawry of the KPD, but were obliged to acquiesce in its practical suppression. All Communist papers in Germany and all Socialist papers in Prussia were suppressed. On March 1 hundreds of new arrests were made. In the evening Hitler, Papen, Hugenberg, Göring, and Seldte all

[1] *The New York Times,* July 23, 1934.

[2] *Le Journal* (Paris) for December 4, 1934, and *Socialistische Aktion* (Prague) for mid-December 1934, published the text of an alleged confession by Karl Ernst dated June 3, 1934, written and secretly sent abroad because of the author's fears for his life. According to this version, which is as plausible as Kruse's, though differing from his account at various points and making no mention of his name, Van der Lubbe was permitted to the end to believe that he acted alone. After Göring's original suggestion for a faked attempt to assassinate Hitler was rejected, Goebbels suggested the burning of the Reichstag. Göring approved. Röhm, Heines, Killinger, and Helldorf prepared the plans, which were made known to Hanfstängl and Sander and carried out by Ernst, Fiedler, and Mohrenschild. The three men entered the session chamber by way of the tunnel to Göring's residence at 8.45 and left by the same route at 9.05, having soaked the furnishings with gasoline and with a phosphorous compound which ignited spontaneously within thirty minutes. Röhm, Heines, Ernst, Fiedler, Mohrenschild, and Sander were all slain in the "purge" of June 30, 1934.

broadcast speeches against the "Red peril." Göring accused the KPD of plotting to poison food, burn granaries, and by the use of false orders provoke an occupation of Berlin by the S.A. and thus precipitate a conflict with the Reichswehr. On the evening of March 2 Hitler made another election speech in the Sportpalast, painting Russia's misery under Communism in vivid colours and denouncing Marxism and democracy.

The Nazi campaign culminated on Friday, March 3, with a great "Day of the Awakening Nation." Throughout the Reich, storm troopers and party members marched with torches. On all the hills along the Rhine, in the Bavarian Alps, in the Harz, and on the towers of ancient cities the fires of liberation flamed skyward. In all important squares in every town, loudspeakers were installed to broadcast Der Führer's final appeal from Königsberg:

"I live not for Socialism. I live not for Nationalism. I live not for democracy. I live not for pacifism. Everything must serve life. Either a thing is useful to life, then it is good; or it harms life, then it is bad. . . . We know that the highest Nationalism and the highest Socialism are the same: they are the highest service of the people, not for a group and not for a class. . . . Never forget the German peasant! All of us would not exist if he did not exist before us! He is the source out of which our people ever grow. . . . Peasant and worker, even the most primitive, are the healthiest and most eternally growing sources of the strength of the nation." [1]

The program ended with a prayer: "O Lord, make us free!" On the same day the small unheeded voice of Brüning declared that the Centrum would resist any overthrow of the Constitution. He demanded an investigation of the Reichstag fire and appealed to Hindenburg "to protect the suppressed against their oppressors." Neudeck was silent as thirty-five thousand S.A. men paraded through Berlin. On the eve of the election gigantic mass demonstrations against Marxism were held everywhere. On Sunday, March 5, the nation voted.

[1] Cf. Gehl, op. cit., pp. 87–8.

REICHSTAG ELECTION, MARCH 5, 1933 [1]

Qualified Voters—44,685,764
Voted—39,655,029—88.7 per cent
Total Deputies Elected—647

	Seats Won	*Popular Votes*	*Percentage of Total*
Communist Party	81	4,848,058	12.3
Social Democrats	120	7,181,629	18.3
State Party	5	334,242	0.8
Christian Social People's Service	4	383,999	1.0
Centrum	74 }	5,498,457	14.0
Bavarian People's Party	18 }		
German Peasant's Party	2	114,048	0.3
German People's Party	2	432,312	1.1
Black-White-Red Fighting Front (Nationalists and Stahlhelm)	52	3,136,760	8.0
NSDAP	288	17,277,180	43.9

Despite hysteria, coercion, and the most intensive campaigning, the NSDAP still failed to secure a clear majority. From 11,737,000 to 17,277,000, from 32 per cent to 44 per cent was an appreciable gain, but not as impressive a one as might have been expected in view of what had intervened. The new Nazi voters came from the four million who had stayed home on November 6—and also apparently from the ranks of the Communists.[2] In many peasant constituencies in the east and north the Nazis secured a majority: East Prussia, 56.5 per cent; Frankfurt-on-the-Oder, 55.2; Pomerania, 56.3; Breslau, 50.2; Liegnitz, 54.0; Schleswig-Holstein, 53.2; East Hanover, 54.3; Chemnitz-Zwickau, 50.0. The party fared badly, as usual, in the highly industrialized districts: Berlin, 31.3 per cent; North Westphalia, 34.9; South Westphalia, 33.8; Cologne-Aachen, 30.1, etc. The bludgeoned and discredited KPD lost only a million votes, and the other "Marxist" party, the Social Democrats, lost only 70,000 votes. The persecuted Centrum gained 200,000 votes and Hugenberg's Nationalists 117,000. The Nazis and Nationalists together had a 52 per cent majority. But the exclusion of the 81 Communist deputies

[1] *Statistisches Jahrbuch für das deutsche Reich, 1933,* pp. 539–41.

[2] The NSDAP gained 5,540,000 votes. The KPD lost 1,132,000 votes and 3,897,000 people who voted on March 5 had not voted on November 6. These two groups totalled 5,029,000.

would give the NSDAP alone a majority of 5 in the new Reichstag. Had the party been outlawed and barred from the ballot, its supporters might well have swelled the ranks of the other opposition parties and made a Nazi majority in the Reichstag impossible. As it was, the problem was simple. Communist deputies were excluded.

Hitler, with his obsession for "legality," and his intuitive grasp of the revolutionary logic of his movement, avoided any hasty action designed to eliminate the non-Nazi elements in the régime. Each step must be carefully prepared, psychologically and "constitutionally." Hugenberg, Papen & Company must not be struck down from above. They must be undermined from below and left suspended in mid-air. Meanwhile the forms of law must be observed and the nation must be subjected to an intensive process of emotional reorientation. The substitution of the symbols of the new order for those of the old was begun on March 12, when Hindenburg was prevailed upon to abolish the black, red, and gold republican flag and to give the Reich two new official flags: the old monarchist black, white, and red and the *Hakenkreuz* flag of the NSDAP. March 12 was also proclaimed a day of mourning for the war dead. Bernard Rust, Federal Commissioner for the Prussian Ministry of Science, Art, and Education (he was named Minister on April 21), addressed the schoolchildren by radio. He evoked heroic memories and appealed to the mothers and fathers, the widows and orphans of the fallen. Not in vain had they died. From their graves had come the German hero-spirit which would now once more unite all Germans into a powerful State after fourteen years of weakness and disgrace. On the 15th Hindenburg signed a decree establishing black, white, and red as the official colours of the army.

The new Reichstag was called together in the Garrison Church at Potsdam on March 21. "Germany has awakened!" declared Goebbels. "Beflag your houses. On the evening of March 21 torchlight parades of the national parties and organizations, of the students and schoolchildren, shall march through all the cities and villages of the entire Reich! On our German mountains and hills the fires of freedom shall flame up!" [1] On the great "Day of Potsdam" Hindenburg paid homage to the war dead and dedicated the Reich to the national resurrection. Religious services preceded the convocation of the deputies. Hitler took no part in the Catholic services, since the bishops

[1] Public appeal of March 18, 1933.

had barred all members of the NSDAP from the sacraments as traitors to the Church. He and Goebbels contented themselves with laying a wreath on the grave of dead comrades in a Berlin cemetery. In the little Baroque church in Potsdam, Hindenburg greeted the Reichstag, urging the Ministers and deputies to work together for Germany's liberation in the spirit of the old Prussia. The Social Democrats were excluded. Radios broadcast the ceremonies to all schools. Hitler likewise addressed the assembly:

"For years heavy sorrows have burdened our people. . . . In spite of industry and a will to work, despite ability and rich knowledge and experience, millions of Germans today seek in vain their daily bread. Business is devastated, finance is shattered, millions without work! . . . Always after exaltation follows a fall. The causes have always been the same. The German in himself disintegrated, disunited in spirit, divided in will and therewith impotent in deed, is powerless to preserve his own life. He dreams of justice in the stars and loses his land upon the earth. . . .

"Out of the madness of the theory of eternal victors and vanquished came the folly of reparations and in its wake the catastrophe of our world economy. . . . On March 5 the people decided to support us by its majority. In a unique uprising it restored the national honour within a few weeks and, thanks to your understanding, Herr Reichspresident, consummated the marriage between the symbols of ancient glory and young strength. . . . We wish to restore the unity of spirit and of will of the German nation. We wish to protect the eternal foundation of our lives: our people and the powers and virtues given to them. We wish to subject the organization and leadership of our State to those principles which in all periods have been the prerequisites of the greatness of the people and of the Reich. . . ."

Stability and authority must be restored, Der Führer continued. The "primacy of politics which is called to organize and to lead the life struggle of the nation" must be regained. A true German community must be rebuilt. "From peasants, burghers, and workers there must again emerge One German People." Faith, Culture, Honour, and Freedom must be recovered. The old Field Marshal whom Hitler had condemned as a useless anachronism only six months before he now praised to the skies.[1] Hindenburg beamed. The organ played Brahms. While the artillery outside fired salutes, the President laid

[1] Gehl, op. cit., pp. 100–4.

wreaths on the tombs of Frederick William I and Frederick the Great. He then reviewed a great parade of Reichswehr, police, storm troopers, Stahlhelmers, etc.

In the afternoon the Reichstag met in Berlin in the Kroll Opera, with the Social Democrats now permitted to participate. Göring, in opening the session, recalled that on the same day sixty-two years before, Bismarck had opened the first German Reichstag. Slowly the people had been divided and disrupted. Thanks to Hitler, unity would now again be restored. Fourteen years of want and shame lay behind. Now Weimar had been overcome and the spirit of Potsdam had triumphed. The new flags symbolized Honour, Freedom, Power, Faith, and Hope. . . . Far into the night, all over Germany, paraders marched, torches sputtered, beacon lights flared, bands played, huge multitudes chanted hymns, and all patriots experienced an exaltation reminiscent of 1914.

On March 23 Nazi and Nationalist deputies introduced into the Reichstag a *"Gesetz zur Behebung der Not von Volk und Reich."* This brief Enabling Act [1] was designed to give the Cabinet a free hand in its work of "national reconstruction":

"Article 1. National laws can be enacted by the national cabinet as well as in accordance with the procedure established in the constitution. This applies also to the laws referred to in Article 85, Paragraph 2, and in Article 87 of the constitution.

"Article 2. The national laws enacted by the national cabinet may deviate from the constitution in so far as they do not affect the position of the Reichstag and the Reichsrat. The powers of the President remain undisturbed.

"Article 3. The national laws enacted by the national cabinet are prepared by the chancellor and published in the *Reichsgesetzblatt.* They come into effect, unless otherwise specified, upon the day following their publication. Articles 68 to 77 of the constitution do not apply to the laws enacted by the national cabinet.

"Article 4. Treaties of the Reich with foreign states which concern matters of national legislation do not require the consent of the bodies participating in legislation. The national cabinet is empowered to issue the necessary provisions for the execution of these treaties.

"Article 5. This law becomes effective on the day of its publication. It becomes invalid on April 1, 1937; it further becomes invalid when the

[1] *R.G.B.,* 1933, No. 25, p. 141; translation from Pollock and Heneman: *The Hitler Decrees,* pp. 13, 14.

present national cabinet is replaced by another."

Articles 85 and 87 of the Weimar Constitution insured parliamentary control of the Reich budget. Articles 68 to 77 gave the Reichstag control of legislation and partial control of constitutional amendments. Henceforth the Cabinet could appropriate money and legislate without any responsibility to the Reichstag or any obligation to respect the Constitution. Here was no proposal to rule by decree because of the absence of parliamentary support. The new Cabinet possessed a majority in the Reichstag. The intention was rather to sweep away parliamentary government entirely.

Hitler delivered a long address demanding approval of the Enabling Act. He condemned the Marxist revolution of 1918 and the System of Weimar. The liberalism of the last century had logically developed into Communist chaos, robbery, arson, murder, and terrorism. "The setting on fire of the Reichstag, as an unsuccessful attempt forming part of a well-organized plan, is only a sample of what Europe had to expect from the victory of this infernal doctrine. When a certain section of the press, especially abroad, now attempts, in accordance with political untruth adopted as a principle by Communism, to identify the national renaissance in Germany with this outrage, this can only strengthen my determination to leave nothing undone in order to exact expiation for this crime by the public execution of the guilty incendiary and his accomplices. . . . It will be the highest task of the national government, not only in the interest of Germany, but in the interest of the rest of Europe, to conquer and eliminate this symptom in our land." (Stormy applause from the government parties.)

The German worker must be won to the national State. Unity must be created. Further reforms must grow out of living developments. "Its end must be the construction of a constitution which will join the will of the people with the authority of genuine leadership." Equality before the law would be extended only to supporters of the government. "The question of a monarchical restoration . . . is not now subject to discussion." (Applause from the Nazis, silence from the Nationalists.) A thorough moral cleansing of the people must be brought about. "Heroism raises itself as the coming creator and leader of political destiny. It is the function of art to give expression to this decisive *Zeitgeist*. Blood and race will again become the sources of artistic intuition. . . . Our jurisprudence must serve in the first instance the maintenance of the People's Community (*Volksgemeinschaft*). . . . Treason shall in the future be blotted out with barbaric ruthlessness." (Loud applause on the Right.)

In the economic sphere "the people do not live for business, and business does not exist for capital, but capital serves business, and business the people." There would be no resort to a government bureaucracy, but "the strongest support of private initiative and the recognition of property." (Applause from the Nationalists.) Taxes would be lightened and public expenditures reduced. There would be no currency experiments. Two great economic tasks are primary: "The rescue of the German peasant must under all circumstances be achieved. . . . The army of the unemployed must be restored to the productive process." The government must "protect and further the millions of German workers in their struggle for the right to live. As Chancellor and Nationalsocialist, I feel myself bound to them as companions of my youth." (Applause.) Autarchy is unthinkable for Germany: "It must always and again be emphasized that nothing lies farther from the government than hostility toward exports."

In closing, Hitler asked approval of the Enabling Act on the ground that the government in its work of recovery must not be expected to appeal to the Reichstag for approval of each specific measure.

"Authority and the fulfilment of the task would suffer if doubts should arise among the people regarding the stability of the new régime. The government regards as impossible a further session of the Reichstag in the present condition of profound excitement in the nation. There is scarcely a revolution of such great proportions which has run its course in so disciplined and bloodless a fashion as the uprising of the German people in these weeks. It is my will and my firmest intention to foster this peaceful development also in the future.

"All the more necessary is it that the national government shall be given every sovereign right which, in such a period, is necessary to prevent a different development. The government will only make use of these powers in so far as they are essential for carrying out the vitally necessary measures. Neither the existence of the Reichstag nor that of the Reichsrat is menaced. The position and rights of the President of the Reich remain unaffected. It will always be the foremost task of the government to act in harmony with his aims. The separate existence of the federal states will not be done away with. The rights of the churches will not be diminished and their relationship to the State will not be modified. The number of cases in which an internal necessity exists for having recourse to such a law is in itself a limited one. All the more, however, the government insists upon the passing of the law. It prefers a clear decision, in any case. It asks from the parties of the Reichstag the possibility of a peaceable development and the reconciliation which in the future will flow therefrom. The government, however, is equally resolved and prepared to accept the announcement of refusal and therewith the declaration of opposition. May you, *meine Herren,* now decide yourselves between peace or war." [1]

Here, despite promises of "barbaric ruthlessness" and the closing threat, was a masterpiece of moderation. The ears of Germany and of all the world were listening. Within the Reich all criticism had been silenced. But throughout Europe and America the new government had had a "bad press" from the outset. The NSDAP was under accusation of having burned the Reichstag and of contemplating the persecution of workers and Jews, the rearmament of the nation, and the adoption of a policy of internal despotism and external aggression. The Chancellor, well advised by Neurath and Goebbels, spoke softly. Everyone was reassured. The address achieved its purpose, at least within Germany. Foreign journalists remained skeptical, but cautious business men took heart, and labour leaders began to wonder whether the new régime was after all as black as the Communists had painted it. Der Führer had said that the Reichstag, the Reichsrat, the presidency, states rights, the churches, and the trade unions would remain undisturbed. Millions believed him. This atmosphere of reassurance and hesitation was essential to disintegrate in advance all possible resistance to that relentless seizure of complete power which the Nazi leaders were already planning. All Germany, and if possible all the world, must think that the fanaticism and dictatorial fantasies of the NSDAP had been sobered by the responsibilities of office and had given way to reason and toleration.

The Reichstag session did not end without melodrama. After a three-hour recess Otto Wels, the Social Democratic leader, took the

[1] Gehl, op. cit., pp. 110–21.

floor to affirm that his party had always been patriotic and solicitous of national honour. "The Chancellor spoke yesterday in Potsdam a sentence to which we subscribe. It reads: 'From the madness of the theory of eternal conquerors and conquered came the folly of reparations and in its wake the catastrophe of world economy.' This sentence applies to foreign policy. For internal politics it applies no less.. Here, too, the theory of eternal conquerors and conquered is a bit of madness." The Social Democratic Party could not vote for the Enabling Act. The Cabinet had a majority and had therefore the possibility and the duty of ruling according to the Constitution. Criticism is wholesome and necessary. Rights should be respected. If the gentlemen of the Nazi party desired to achieve socialistic deeds, they would need no Enabling Act. They would possess an overwhelming majority in the Reichstag. "We German Social Democrats pledge ourselves solemnly in this historic hour to the principles of humanity and justice, of freedom and socialism. No Enabling Act can give you the power to destroy ideas which are eternal and indestructible. . . ."

Hitler replied ironically and bitterly: "You come late, but yet you come! . . ." Where was your struggle against the war-guilt lie and against reparations when you were in power? Where was honour when you adopted an alien Constitution and foreign colours at the behest of foreign foes? Where were "equal rights" when you persecuted our supporters? Who loves Germany may criticize us. Who belongs to an International cannot criticize us. Read the lies about Germany in your Socialist papers abroad. "You say you are the only representatives of socialism in Germany? You are the representatives of a mysterious socialism which the German people could never perceive in actuality . . . By your fruits shall you also be known—and the fruits testify against you! . . . In everything, Herr Deputy, you come too late. . . . You are no longer needed. . . . The star of Germany will rise and yours will sink. . . . Whatever in the lives of people becomes rotten, old, and decrepit passes and does not come back. . . . I declare no eternal war. I give my hand to anyone who pledges himself to Germany, but I do not recognize an International in that offer. . . . I do not in the least want your votes. Germany shall be free, but not through you!" (Stormy applause.)[1]

Dr. Kaas for the Centrum, Ritter von Lex for the Bavarian Peo-

[1] Gehl, op. cit., pp. 121 f.

ple's Party, and Dr. Maier for the State Party all expressed reluctant and hesitant approval of the Enabling Act. Göring declared that the time for talking was past, the time for action had come. "Let the others lie, we shall work and our leader, the Chancellor of the Reich, may be certain that this faction also will talk no more, but will only work and will follow him in true obedience and in blind faith until the triumph of Germany!" While thousands of citizens and storm troopers outside the hall cheered and shouted for the Enabling Act, the vote was taken.

For: 441.

Against: 94.

Only the Social Democrats voted against the government. Göring adjourned the session. Within a week the NSDAP would begin to move, by propaganda and by terror, against friends and foes alike—toward the establishment of an undiluted Fascist dictatorship. The Nazi deputies sang lustily:

> Raise high the flags! Stand rank on rank together.
> Storm troopers march with steady quiet tread. . . .

CHAPTER VI

BUILDING THE FASCIST STATE

1. SMASHING THE PROLETARIAT

MONOPOLISTIC capitalism, aided by Junker militarism and nationalist reaction, placed Hitler in power in January 1933. The initial "victory" was but the prelude to the establishment of the single party dictatorship of the NSDAP. Der Führer had not studied the career of Mussolini in vain. Il Duce, in the months after October 1922, had not sufficiently employed the weapons of terrorism, collective hysteria, race prejudice, and national megalomania. He had therefore been obliged to proceed slowly and cautiously. Not until 1925 were all other political groups dissolved and outlawed by the Fascisti. What the Italian Dictator had done in three years Hitler was to do in three months. The specific tools of power employed by the NSDAP will be dealt with in the remainder of this volume, along with their results and limitations. It will suffice here merely to notice the major steps whereby all remnants of the old order were destroyed and the Nationalsocialist Party was enabled to achieve a monopoly of authority.

This process can best be considered in terms of the basic questions of all political analysis: Where are the focal points of power? What social groups in the community control the machinery of the State? These questions can never be answered adequately by simply taking cognizance of the political leaders and party groups which hold important public posts and constitute the "government." Even on this superficial level the situation in Germany in the spring of 1933 was confused enough, in view of the composition of the Hitler Cabinet. The problem, however, is a more fundamental one. What is the relationship between those wielding governmental authority and the equilibrium of power between groups and classes in the whole community? More specifically, what is the relationship between the class composition, the ideology, the "interests," and the overt behaviour of a revolutionary régime recently arrived in office and the existing distribution in society of power, wealth, income, and deference?

This question involves a consideration of the effect of the conquest of the State by the NSDAP on the existing structure of German society and on the whole socio-political process whereby that structure was maintained and modified. There was some initial doubt as to the precise class orientation of the new régime. Its spokesmen, to be sure, were avowed enemies of class consciousness, class conflict, trade unionism, democracy, and Marxism. They would therefore presumably proceed to reduce the proletariat to economic and political helplessness. And since power is relative and since in the distribution of a constant or declining national income the gain of one class is the loss of another, the proletariat (and to a lesser degree the *Kleinbürgertum* and the peasantry) was precisely the class at whose expense the élite must render itself more secure and more prosperous. The doubt lay in the circumstance that the NSDAP was by profession a "workers' " party, with a "socialistic" program. The program had long since been modified and rendered safe for propertied interests. And the party had its main sources of popular support in the peasantry and lower middle classes, who were more anti-proletarian than anti-capitalist. But there were still proletarian radicals in the party. The passivity of the workers in the face of the Nazi revolution was in no small measure due to the widespread belief among wage-earners that the NSDAP was not, after all, an anti-labour party, however anti-Marxist it might be. Would the party leadership act against the proletariat and thereby serve the purposes of the ruling classes? Could it safely do so without provoking dangerous opposition among its own Left-wing followers and among the workers in general, who still possessed the best-organized and most impressive trade-union organization in the western world?

The earlier attitudes of the Nazi leaders toward labour were reasonably clear. Hitler's anti-proletarian and anti-trade-union animus, like his anti-Semetism, was acquired in his years of penury in pre-war Vienna. Marxism and the Social Democratic unions he viewed as twin weapons of the Jewish world conspiracy. But at the same time he professed his solicitude for the interests of the working man and his enthusiasm for a new type of "national" unionism comparable in the economic sphere to Nationalsocialism in the political sphere.

"The Nationalsocialist union is no organ of class war, but an organ of vocational representation. The Nazi State knows no classes, but in a political sense only citizens (*Bürger*) with completely equal rights and also equal common duties, and next to them nationals (*Staatsangehörige*) who, however, in a political sense are entirely without rights [i.e., Jews]. . . . Not the union as such is directed toward class war, but Marxism has made of it an instrument for its class war. It uses the economic weapons which the international world-Jew utilizes for the ruination of the economic bases of free independent national States, for the annihilation of national industry and national trade, and therewith for the enslavement of free peoples in the service of supergovernmental Jewish world-finance." [1]

Hitler further argued that Nazi unions must never use the weapon of the strike to disturb national production, but only to correct conditions harmful to the general welfare. Workers and employers have common duties to society. State and Fatherland take precedence over all class interests. Strikes would have no justification after the creation of the Nazi State, for then vocational chambers and an economic parliament would settle all differences pacifically. The parties should not set up new unions, but work through the existing Marxist unions to destroy them.[2] This policy underwent many vicissitudes in the interest of winning proletarian converts. The Nürnberg party congress of 1929 resolved that all strike-breakers should be expelled from the party in disgrace. The *Reichs-Betriebszellenabteilung* of the party modified this position by declaring that members *might* be expelled who acted as scabs in strikes sanctioned by the NSBO. The NSBO, however, never became a genuine trade union, but remained an organization of Nazi "cells" within the existing unions. Its leaders talked of strikes, but conducted none.

Reinhold Muchow, founder and leader of the NSBO, wrote in *Arbeitertum,* August 1, 1931, that the NSBO would lead German Socalism to victory and would support strikes against wage reductions designed to help in the fulfilment of the Young Plan. Before the presidential election of 1932 a Nazi campaign leaflet: *Zehn*

[1] *Mein Kampf,* pp. 674–5.
[2] Ibid., pp. 677–82.

Fragen an Hitler, declared that the movement supported the existing system of collective bargaining and wage rates and recognized labour's right to strike "so long as the existing unethical capitalistic economic system remained in Germany." [1] The party, however, sponsored strike-breaking activities in a number of instances. But the NSBO was compelled, as a means of retaining its members, to support the Berlin metal-workers' strike in 1930 and the Berlin transport strike in 1932. This led to protests from industrialist supporters. On December 17, 1932, Hitler announced in the *V.B.* that all participation in strikes must henceforth be approved by the central party headquarters.

Reliable estimates as to the extent to which the NSBO penetrated the unions prior to 1933 are difficult to secure, but it seems safe to assert that the Nazi propaganda made little direct impression on the great majority of German trade unionists. The NSBO was organized into thirty-three geographical sections paralleling the party organization. As in the party, all leaders were appointed from above and members were pledged to uncritical discipline and obedience. During 1931–2 the party, in co-operation with the NSBO, waged a vigorous campaign under the slogan: *"Hinein in die Betriebe!"* (Into the factories!). The *HIB-Aktion* was intensively organized.[2] An order of the Reichsleitung of February 10, 1932, required every party member who was a worker or employee to join the NSBO. The NSBO also sought to induce non-party members to join, but with little success. None of the major unions was effectively penetrated. Approximately 4,500,000 German wage-earners in the "independent" unions and 700,000 in the Catholic trade unions remained loyal to their Marxist or Centrist leaders and refused to be cajoled or coerced by Nazi blandishments. The two political parties of the proletariat likewise remained intact, in form at least, until the end. In every national election save those of July 31, 1932, and March 5, 1933, the combined Socialist and Communist vote exceeded that of the NSDAP by a comfortable margin.[3]

[1] F. David: *Ist die NSDAP eine sozialistische Partei?* (Vienna: Int. Arbeiter Verlag; 1933), p. 33.

[2] Goebbels: *Vom Kaiserhof zur Reichskanzlei,* p. 19.

[3] Cf. F. David, op. cit., pp. 8–12; *Die Nazi-Schutzgarde der Ausbeuter und Profitjäger* (Berlin: Betrieb und Gewerkschaft; 1931), *passim;* Gerhard Starcke: *NSBO und Deutsche Arbeitsfront* (Berlin: Hobbing; 1934); P. Blankenburg and M. Dreyer: *Nationalsozialistischer Wirtschaftsaufbau und seine Grundlagen* (Berlin: Zentralverlag; 1934).

Why, then, did the strong and well-established organizations of the German proletariat collapse like a house of cards in the spring of 1933? An adequate answer to this question would require a detailed analysis and evaluation of the psychology and tactics of the unions and of the Socialist and Communist parties. For years the two great parties of the proletariat had fought one another more effectively and consistently than they fought their common enemy. The Communists made slow but steady electoral gains after 1928, largely at the expense of the Socialists. But the KPD never succeeded in gaining control of the trade unions. The "Red opposition" was in general helpless to control union policy. The union bureaucracy was closely integrated with the leadership of the Socialist Party and remained its great source of financial and political support. The Social Democratic leaders, however, had long since lost all disposition to resist Fascism by force. The party which drowned the proletarian revolution in blood in 1918–19 never made even a gesture toward forcible resistance of the NSDAP in 1930–3. The Social Democratic leaders were ideologically democrats rather than socialists and were committed to "legality" at all times. Through legality they had built up their vast organization in the bourgeois democratic era. The party and its unions worked not for social revolution nor even socialization, but for improvement in the economic status of labour within the framework of the democratic capitalistic State. Through its own organizations and through the Reichsbanner it fought (verbally) for the preservation of German democracy—and therewith for the maintenance of the bourgeois social and economic order of which parliamentary democracy was the traditional political expression. When the élite of this society repudiated democracy and embraced Fascism, the Social Democratic leaders were left stranded. And when Hitler, by "democratic," "legal," and "constitutional" means, won a mass following and secured power, the Socialists were helpless, for they could not oppose legality by illegal resistance and still remain true to their "principles."

This psychology of defeatism on the part of German Social Democracy made any united fighting front of the proletariat against Hitler impossible. The Social Democratic workers were quite as irrational and as much out of touch with reality as the Nazi *Kleinbürgertum* and peasantry. But the neurosis in the former case left its victims in a state of coma (collective catatonic schizophrenia), while in the latter case it expressed itself in dynamic delirious activism (paranoic schizophrenia). Hysteria in politics is always more effective than catalepsy. The KPD preached revolution and won increasing numbers of workers to its banner. But it could never act in a revolutionary fashion without the support of the Social Democratic Party and the unions. That support was never forthcoming, for the Socialist leaders alleged that the Communists desired to utilize a "united front" merely for their own partisan advantage. The allegation was often enough correct, but the logical correctness of the assumption rendered the non-co-operative policy based upon it no less fatal for both parties. Social Democracy preferred its own death at the hands of the Nazis to its absorption or "betrayal" by the KPD. It did not repeat the mistake of Kerensky. If compelled to choose between Fascism and Communism, the Socialists would choose Fascism.

In April 1932 the KPD and the Red trade-union opposition issued their first general appeal for a united front to combat wage reductions. The Socialist leaders refused. The second appeal was made on July 20, 1932 (after "the rape of Prussia"), directly to the executives of the Socialist Party and the General Trade-union Federation. The Communists proposed a general strike against the Papen Cabinet, to compel the repeal of the emergency decrees and the dissolution of the S.A. The Socialist leaders denounced the appeal as a "provocation" and declared that Fascism could be opposed only by the ballot. On January 30, 1933, the KPD made its third appeal. The Socialists replied that Hitler had secured power "legally" and should not be opposed. On March 1, 1933, after the Reichstag fire, the KPD made its last appeal. It was ignored. The Socialist and trade-union leaders were attempting to secure "toleration" in the Nazi régime.[1] Any

[1] R. Palme Dutt: *Fascism and Social Revolution* (New York: International Publishers; 1934), pp. 120–1. Even after its destruction and the imprisonment or flight of its leaders, the remnants of the SPD remained loyal to their "principles." In *Socialism's New Beginning—A Manifesto from Underground Germany,* by "Miles" (translation published by the League for Industrial Democracy, New York, 1934), the KPD is blamed for the triumph of Hitler because it drained away the radical elements from Social Democracy and thereby made it more conservative (pp. 103–4). Bourgeois democracy and a return to Weimar remain the objectives after the overthrow of Fascism. "We revolutionary Socialists know that the resumption of the Socialist struggle for emancipation in the form of a mass movement is impossible without the restoration of democracy. We know, therefore, that our immediate political objective is the overthrow of the Fascist State and its replacement by a democratic régime"—to be characterized, however (in what fashion is unspecified), by the "sole domination" of the Socialist Party (pp. 139–40).

general strike would abrogate the collective wage agreements which they valued so highly. Union funds, moreover, were at a low ebb. No chances could be taken.

The Communist leaders also, despite the essential correctness of their analysis of the situation, were paralyzed by curiously neurotic inhibitions. While "revolutionary," they were committed only to mass revolutionary action. The SPD made this impossible. The logical alternative was individual revolutionary action—that is, terrorism. But this weapon the KPD refused to use, Nazi allegations to the contrary notwithstanding. The Communist reply that such tactics would have alienated public opinion and led to the suppression of the party is unconvincing. This position was due in part to the policy of the Moscow Comintern and in part to the paralysis of the KPD itself. The party was to be suppressed in any case. And the largest and best-organized Communist movement in the bourgeois world was to be destroyed without lifting a finger in its own defence.

In this situation the Nazi leaders calculated correctly that they had nothing to fear from the Socialist Party and its trade unions, nor even from the KPD. Any disposition to fight on the part of the rank and file of the workers' organizations was destroyed by disgust and resentment at the cowardice of its leaders. The NSDAP could proceed to smash Marxism without encountering resistance. But the Left wing within the ranks must be placated and the masses of workers must, if possible, be won over to loyalty to the new order. The Nazi leaders therefore proceeded cautiously toward their goal. The mailed fist was hidden in a velvet glove of friendship. During March and April there was no organized attack upon the trade unions. Such acts of violence as took place were sporadic. The Nazi leaders continued to preach "true Socialism." [1] A master stroke of propaganda was achieved in the party's decision to convert May 1 into a great "Day of National Labour." The emotional fervour attached to the traditional holiday of the European revolutionary proletariat was thereby transferred to the new régime. The propensity of wage-earners to parade on May Day would be satisfied and the remnants of the SPD and the KPD would be deprived of all opportunity for demonstrating against Fascism. The result would be a test of the ability of the NSDAP and the NSBO to

[1] Cf. Göring's speech in the Sportpalast before delegates of the shop councils, *V.B.*, April 10, 1933.

regiment the working masses.

Elaborate plans were made with the meticulous care which was typical of the organizational activities of the party. Thousands of political prisoners were released in an amnesty, as a gesture of reconciliation. May 1 was proclaimed a national holiday, with wages to be paid by the employers. In every town and village in the Reich, all the arts of persuasion and coercion were utilized to induce all organized wage-earners to participate in the festivities. The result exceeded all expectations. For the first time in years there were no riots, no clashes between workers and police, no demonstrations against the government. On the contrary, the leaders of the General Federation of Labour supported the pageant and co-operated in making it a success. On the 1st of May the new flags flew everywhere, and great banners proclaimed the dignity of labour and the solidarity of the new régime with the working masses. Bands played, paraders marched, spectators cheered, vast proletarian multitudes listened—docilely or enthusiastically—to Nazi speeches.

The demonstration in Berlin was on so grandiose a scale that it exhausted all superlatives. It was accurately described as the most gigantic mass gathering ever staged in the modern world. Religious services were held in all churches on the preceding evening. In the morning a great assembly of youth came together in the Lustgarten. Goebbels proclaimed the end of class warfare: "Over the ruins of the liberal capitalistic State the idea of the social solidarity of the people raises itself." Hindenburg greeted the youth and led the cheering: "Germany, our beloved Fatherland, hurrah!" All day long, in the spring sunshine, contingents of paraders gathered in various parts of the capital and converged in enormous columns toward Tempelhofer Feld. Every trade, every craft, every factory was represented, as well as peasants, frontiersmen, and representatives of *"Deutschtum im Ausland,"* all with bands, banners, and colourful local costumes. While the Graf Zeppelin circled overhead, followed by dozens of planes, a million marchers entered the field, where a huge speakers' platform had been erected, surmounted by enormous swastika standards. Even the sanitary corps was organized to perfection. Strong men broke down in tears of joy. Women fainted. Even babies were born on the field. But there were no casualties. Planes from all parts of Germany brought almost a hundred labour representatives to the airdrome, where many other planes were gathered, including the enormous D-2500, recently christened "General Field Marshal von Hindenburg." The delegates were welcomed by Goebbels. At 6.30 they were received in the Chancellery by Hitler and Hindenburg. The Chancellor declared:

"You will see how untrue and unjust is the statement that the revolution is directed against the German workers. On the contrary, its deepest meaning and clearest aim is to unite our millions of German workers in the German Folk-Community."

In the evening, on the brightly lighted field, there were parades and manœuvres of Reichswehr, police, S.A., S.S., Stahlhelm, and NSBO. The party outdid itself in magnificent pageantry and, at the end, amused the masses with the most extraordinary fireworks display ever attempted in the Reich. The high point of the program was Hitler's speech, delivered on the field and broadcast over all stations:

"The nation is crumbling to pieces, and in this process of collapse all power and all vital energy are disappearing. The results of class warfare are to be seen all around us, and we wish to learn a lesson from them, for we have recognized one thing as necessary for the return to health of our nation: *The German people must learn to know each other again*. . . . What human madness once invented can be overcome by human wisdom. . . . We have made up our minds to lead the people of Germany to one another and, if necessary, to compel them.

"That is the meaning of the 1st of May, which day from now on shall be celebrated in Germany throughout the centuries, in order that on it all those who are taking part in our creative national work may come together and, once in the year, may give each other their hands, fully recognizing that nothing can be achieved if all are not ready to do their part in the great work. Therefore we have chosen as the motto of this day the following sentence: *Honour work and respect the worker!*

"The 1st of May must be the proof that we do not wish to destroy anything, but are concerned only with reconstruction. One cannot choose the loveliest spring day in the year as a symbol of strife, but only as one of constructive work. This day shall not stand for disintegration and collapse, but only for national unity and thus for rebirth. . . .

"Germans! You are not second-rate, even if the world wishes to have it so a thousand times. You are not second-class and inferior. Awake to a realization of your own importance. Remember your past and the achievements of your fathers, yes, and those of your own generation. Forget the fourteen years of decay, and think of the two thousand years of German history. . . . Germans! You are a strong nation, if you yourselves wish to be strong." [1]

On the following morning, Tuesday, May 2, 1933, the ax fell on the German trade unions.[2] Secret preparations for destroying the old German labour movement had been made long before. Hitler had resolved that the work of liquidation should follow soon upon May Day. Goebbels apparently knew on Monday evening what was to be done on the next day.[3] The actual initiative on Tuesday morning, however, seems to have been taken, without superior authorization, by the vain and ambitious Robert Ley, leader of the NSBO. "Action committees" of his organization, without police or S.A. co-operation, seized control of all the headquarters of the Social Democratic trade unions throughout the Reich, suppressed their newspapers, arrested their leaders, took possession of their funds, and decreed their dissolution—all without even a shadow of resistance. There was some violence (almost a year later the bodies of four trade-union officials of Duisberg were discovered in a lonely forest), but in general there was little disorder. The Catholic unions and other employees' organizations "placed themselves at the disposal" of the NSDAP on May 3 and 4. Theodore Leipart and Peter Grassmann, the chairmen of the General Trade-union Federation, had pledged themselves to co-operate with the new régime. They were arrested. Ley announced triumphantly, in the name of a "Committee for the Protection of German Labour":

"We have never destroyed anything which had any kind of value for our nation, nor shall we in the future. This is a fundamental principle of Nationalsocialism. This holds good particularly of the trade unions, which have been built up out of the pennies which the workers have earned with such bitter toil and starved themselves to give. No, workers, your institutions are sacred and inviolable to us Nationalsocialists. I myself am the son of a poor peasant, and I

[1] Pollock and Heneman, op. cit., pp. 73–4.

[2] Cf. Oskar Krueger: *Die Befreiung des deutschen Arbeiters—Die revolutionäre Aktion der NSBO gegen Gewerkschaften am 2. Mai 1933* (Munich: Eher; 1934).

[3] *Vom Kaiserhof zur Reichskanzlei,* p. 307.

know poverty: I myself was for seven years in one of the largest factories in Germany. . . .

"The NSBO journal, *Arbeitertum,* which deals with the theory and practice of the NSBO, becomes from today the official organ of the German General Trade-union Federation. . . .

"It is better that we should give Marxism a last shot to finish it off than that we should ever allow it to rise again. The Leiparts and the Grassmanns may hypocritically declare their devotion to Hitler as much as they like—but it is better that they should be in prison. Thereby we deprive the Marxist ruffians of their chief weapon and of the last possibility of strengthening themselves afresh. The diabolical doctrine of Marxism must perish miserably on the battlefield of the Nationalsocialist revolution." [1]

The work of destruction and "reorganization" was soon completed. The funds of the Socialist Party in Löbe's bank account in Munich were seized. Most of the union leaders were prosecuted for corruption and embezzlement. All properties, including newspaper plants, of the Socialist Party, of the Reichsbanner, of the labour banks, and of all subsidiary labour organizations were confiscated on May 10 to meet the "claims" of the unions. The German worker was thus "rescued" from his betrayers. On May 12 all the property of the unions and of the Consumers' Co-operative Societies was confiscated by Dr. Ley. On May 27 all properties of the KPD and its subsidiary organizations were confiscated by decree of the Cabinet. Meanwhile the "German Labour Front" was born. The organization meeting was held in Berlin on May 10. Hitler spoke:

"We do not regard any one class as being of paramount importance, such distinctions disappear during the course of centuries, they come and go. What remains is the substance, a substance of flesh and blood, our nation. That is what is permanent and to that alone should we feel ourselves responsible. . . . For fourteen or fifteen years I have continuously proclaimed to the German nation that I regard it as my task before posterity to destroy Marxism, and that is no empty phrase, but a solemn oath which I shall perform as long as I live. . . . Bismarck told us that liberalism was the pace-maker of Social Democracy. I need not say here that Social Democracy is the pace-maker of Communism. *And Communism is the forerunner of death, of national destruction and extinction.* We have

[1] Manifesto of May 2, 1933.

joined battle with it and shall fight it to the death. . . . We are taking the unions over . . . to save for the German working man all that he had put by in these organizations in the way of savings and furthermore, in order that the German worker might co-operate in the building of the new State, to enable him to do this on the basis of equality. We are not erecting a State against him; no, with him must the new State be built up.

"He must not have the feeling that he is something inferior and to be despised. No, on the contrary! We want to fill him from the very beginning, already in the earliest stages, with the feeling that he is a German with the same rights as any other. And in my eyes, equal rights have never been anything else than the cheerful undertaking of equal duties. One must not be always speaking of rights, but *one must also speak of duties.* The German worker must show the others that he no longer stands outside the German nation and its rebirth." [1]

The German Labour Front, under the leadership of Dr. Ley (his paper, *Der Deutsche,* became its organ), was so devised as to parallel the structure of the NSDAP itself. It is not, however, an organization of workers, and still less a trade union. Membership is open to corporate entities as well as to individual Aryan workers who pay about one and a half per cent of their monthly wages as dues. As in other Nazi organizations, there is no public control over the use of funds, no accounting for disbursements, no election of officers, and no discussion of policies. The groups comprising the Labour Front include the NSBO; NSHAGO (*Handels und Gewerbeorganisation*), representing salaried employees and displacing the "Fighting Organization of Middle-class Trade and Handicraft Workers" which was dissolved in July 1933; the *Reichsnährstand* or Food Estate, representing agriculture; the Reich Culture Chamber; the Association of N.S. German Jurists; the thirteen Trustees of Labour (*Treuhänder der Arbeit*), appointed by the Chancellor, June 15, 1933, and given arbitrary power to settle labour disputes within their geographical areas; the leaders of the twelve groups of the Reichstand der Industrie, the new organization of German industrialists created by the law of February 27, 1934; the *Gauleiters* of the party; and sundry others. On December 1, 1933, the Association of German Employers (a federation of over three thousand organiza-

[1] Pollock and Heneman, op. cit., pp. 75–6.

tions) dissolved itself. Its members joined the Labour Front as a "professional group." Capital and labour are here intricately synthesized into an organization whose function is the inculcation of Nationalsocialism and service to the State. The NSBO continues to carry on political work and ensures control of the proletariat by the NSDAP. Membership in these organizations is practically compulsory for all wage-earners.

Trade unionism in the old sense is non-existent in the Third Reich. As in Fascist Italy, there are no independent labour organizations, no collective bargaining, no collective wage agreements, and no right to strike. Employers and workers are now united in the service of the State. The lion and the lamb lie down together, with the lamb inside the lion. Ley, in speaking before representatives of office employees in Berlin on May 19, 1933, declared modestly: "We have done in a few hours and days what formerly would have taken years or decades. Sometimes I fear lest the gods become jealous at all the tremendous things now being done by one poor human." In an article on "Fundamental Ideas on the Corporate Organization and the German Labour Front," Ley asserted that limits must be imposed on human greed:

"Corporate organization will as its first work restore absolute leadership to the natural leader of a factory—that is, the employer—and will at the same time place full responsibility on him. The works council of a factory is composed of workers, employees, and employers. Nevertheless, it will have only a consultative voice. Only the employer can decide. Many employers have for years had to call for the 'master in the house.' Now they are once again to be the 'master in the house.'"[1]

In November blue uniforms and emblems were provided for all members of the *Arbeitsfront*—at their own expense. Ley declared, before the Congress of the NSBO and the Labour Front in Munich, that "the social question is no question of wage agreements, but a problem of education and schooling."[2] A week later a proclamation informed all German workers that employers and employees were now one. "According to the will of our leader, Adolf Hitler, the German Labour Front is not the place where the material questions of daily working life are decided. . . . The high aim of the

[1] *V.B.*, June 8, 1933.
[2] *Berliner Tageblatt,* November 21, 1933.

Labour Front is the education of all working Germans in National-socialism." [1]

2. LIQUIDATING THE PARTY SYSTEM

WITH the only possible threat to the Nazi dictatorship removed by the action of May 2, the leaders of the NSDAP next moved to wipe out all other political parties and thereby assure themselves of an undisputed monopoly of governmental authority. Papen and Hugenberg doubtless had misgivings regarding this possibility when they entered into their conspiracy with Hitler against Schleicher. They hoped, however, to keep the Nazi minority in the Cabinet under their control. The failure of the NSDAP to win a clear electoral majority on March 5 was reassuring. The Enabling Act was disturbing, but it specified that any change of government would render it void. Why Hugenberg and the feudal gentlemen of the Herren Klub, who never kept their own promises, should have supposed that Hitler would keep his is a little difficult to ascertain. But they did—and thereby placed their necks in the noose. Hitler had been outwitted by his reactionary allies in 1923. In 1933 his reactionary allies were to be outwitted by Hitler.

The drama unfolded slowly while the NSDAP seized control of the state governments and the police forces through the Reich and utilized the S.A. for its own purposes. Secrecy was maintained concerning the friction within the Cabinet between the non-Nazi members and Hitler, Göring, Frick, and Goebbels, who became Minister of Propaganda and People's Enlightenment on March 13. Whether the Nationalists agreed with the Chancellor or opposed him was immaterial. Their criticisms merely made the task of liquidation easier and more urgent. On March 10 the Nationalist leader, Winterfeldt, wrote a public letter to Hindenburg asking that steps be taken to curb rowdyism and restore "law and order." Papen remained Federal Commissioner for Prussia, while Göring was Prussian Minister of the Interior. The premiership was vacant save for the shadowy title still held by Otto Braun. Much would depend upon the outcome of the rivalry between Papen and Göring. On April 10 came the first suggestion of the dissolution of other parties. Dr. Otto Hugo, vice-chairman of the Reichstag, proposed that his

[1] Ibid., November 28, 1933.

group, the German People's Party, should dissolve and join the NSDAP. Whether he acted in response to hints from Nazi leaders is unclear. His suggestion was without immediate result.

On April 11 Göring was appointed Prussian Premier and Papen resigned as Federal Commissioner. Both of them were at the time in Rome. They denied that any rift had taken place, as did Hitler and Hindenburg. Having no alternative except resignation from the government, Papen accepted defeat. The NSDAP now proceeded to undermine the Nationalist Party by proceeding against the Stahlhelm. Hugenberg's friend and Hindenburg's campaign manager, Günther Gerecke, Minister of Employment, had been arrested for embezzlement on March 23. On March 29 the house of Ernst Oberfohren, parliamentary leader of the Nationalists, was searched by Göring's police, who discovered that he was "plotting" against Hugenberg. He was released on condition that he resign. Hugenberg acquiesced. He could no more defend embezzlers and plotters than he could defend the KPD a month previously. Sporadic S.A. action against the Stahlhelm had already taken place in various towns. Hitler and Seldte conferred on April 15 on the possibility of "co-ordinating" the Stahlhelm with the NSDAP. Hugenberg now perceived the direction of Nazi pressure and announced on April 22 that the Nationalists would not be eliminated from the Cabinet—and *could* not be under the terms of the Enabling Act.

But three days later the east Prussian Landbund asked that Hugenberg be displaced by a Nazi in the Ministries of Economics and Food. Whether this meant that the Junkers had decided that the Nazis would protect their interests more effectually than the Nationalists or that they had yielded to Nazi "advice" is unclear. On April 26 Duesterberg, who had opposed a fusion of the Stahlhelm with the NSDAP, was dismissed by Seldte from the posts which he still held. The Stahlhelm was now "co-ordinated." On the 27th Seldte formally joined the NSDAP, though it was specified that no other members of the Stahlhelm might belong to both organizations. At this, Hugenberg conferred hurriedly with Hitler. The Nationalists in the Reichstag asked Seldte to resign from the party. Hugenberg even hinted at his own resignation in the event of Göring's appointing a new Prussian Minister of Agriculture, but the issue was once more deferred.

In view of foreign denunciation of the Nazi régime, coupled with widespread apprehensions over German plans for rearmament and the "war of liberation," Hitler now decided that it would be expedient to issue a reassuring peace statement for consumption abroad. In order to create the impression that he spoke for a united nation, he assembled the Reichstag once more in the Kroll Opera for a three-hour session on May 17. There he presented his reply to Roosevelt's disarmament plan for the elimination of offensive weapons, made public the day before. Göring opened the session. The boxes were occupied by the diplomatic corps and by many notables, including the Crown Prince. Hitler, in an S.A. uniform, appeared shortly after 3.00 p.m. Amid faint denunciations of Versailles and reparations, he pleaded for peace and conciliation:

"No new European war would be able to place us or any other nation in a better situation, and it is the most ardent wish of the national government to prevent such an unpeaceful development. Even a decisive victory would only sow the germs of new conflicts and new wars. If such folly ever happened, it would be the ruination of the social order, endless chaos—Bolshevism. . . .

"In the course of the struggle of recent years against Communism, our storm troops have had 350 dead and 40,000 wounded. If today at Geneva these formations are counted as military units, then firemen, athletic clubs, and associations of night watchmen might as well be considered military. . . . Germany has disarmed. It has fulfilled the Treaty of Versailles beyond the limits of justice and reason. . . . The only nation that can fear invasion is the German nation. . . .

"Germany is prepared to dissolve its entire military organization, together with its supply of arms, without qualification, if the other countries—signatories to the Treaty of Versailles—are prepared to do likewise. If these countries are not willing to carry out the disarmament requirements of the Treaty, then Germany must insist at least on equality. . . ." [1]

The Chancellor further declared the willingness of his government to accept a five-year transitional period, to renounce all offensive weapons, to submit to international control of armaments, and to sign non-aggression pacts—always on condition of reciprocity and equality. At the close of his address the following resolution was introduced:

[1] *New York Herald* (Paris), May 18, 1933.

"The German Reichstag, as the representative of the German people, approves the declaration of the government and supports it on the decisive question in the life of the nation concerning the equality of rights of the German people."

The resolution was unanimously approved by acclamation. In this action those Social Democratic deputies who were neither in jail nor in exile voted "confidence" in the Hitler Cabinet, without a dissenting voice. A week before, all the property of the party had been confiscated. Two weeks before, the Socialist trade unions had been smashed. But apparently no humiliation was too great for the Socialist deputies, if they could only somehow retain a few jobs and preserve in some fashion the party organization which gave them a livelihood. They explained that after all they *did* approve that version of his foreign policy which Hitler had presented. Who could not? Otto Wels had resigned from the Second International on March 30 because it had criticized Hitler. On June 15 the party leaders repudiated their comrades abroad, and particularly the émigré party group in Prague, which was safely denouncing Hitler from a distance. But fawning and equivocation were fruitless. Hitler smiled at the thought. . . .

On May 18, over Socialist protests, the Prussian Landtag passed an Enabling Act transferring its legislative power to the Cabinet until April 1, 1937. The Nazi deputies demanded jobs for a hundred thousand unemployed party members before mid-July. Göring was inaugurated as Premier of Prussia on May 20. This enhancement of Nazi power stirred new apprehensions among the Nationalists. Winterfeldt opined that the boycott of the Jewish shops had hurt Germany more than the Jews. Various Hugenberg papers were now suppressed. A number of Stahlhelm leaders were arrested. Sundry Nationalist organizations and meetings were banned. On June 14 the police of Dortmund prohibited the Deutschnational Kampfring, a Nationalist military organization headed by Herbert von Bismarck and having perhaps ten thousand members throughout the Reich. The Kampfring was accused of harbouring Socialists and Communists among its members. The action of its leaders in excluding former Marxists was of no avail. Many local Stahlhelm groups were now dissolved. On the 20th a Nationalist meeting in Frankfurt-on-the-Oder, in celebration of Hugenberg's birthday, was disbanded by the police. When street fighting followed, the local

Kampfring was dissolved. Hugenberg pleaded in vain for mercy. Having no means at his disposal for resisting Der Führer, whom he had helped to elevate to the chancellorship, he was helpless.

The work of liquidation now moved forward rapidly. On June 21, 1933, the entire Kampfring was dissolved by action of the Cabinet. Whether the non-Nazi members offered objection made no difference. The weapons of power were in the hands of the NSDAP. The Stahlhelm was dissolved in the Rhineland, and elsewhere was completely *gleichgeschaltet* ("co-ordinated"), with its members forbidden to belong to any party other than the NSDAP. Hitler and Hugenberg conferred about the London Economic Conference, where on June 16 Hugenberg had been so indiscreet as to demand a restoration of the German colonies and a grant of authority to Germany by the Powers to use its "constructive and creative genius" to "reorganize" Russia. Litvinov observed: "It may be that the authors of Hugenberg's memorandum hoped to introduce an element of comedy into the heavy atmosphere created at the conference by the serious problems being dealt with." The bewhiskered Nationalist perhaps hoped that this gesture would please Hitler and Rosenberg, with their dreams of conquest in the east. But again he miscalculated. The German delegation in London repudiated his statement. On his hasty return to Berlin he received no comfort from the Chancellor. His threat to resign produced no change in Hitler's plans.

On June 22 a Cabinet decree dissolved the Social Democratic Party. It was accused of high treason by Minister Frick, who issued the order: "The SPD must be considered as subversive and inimical to the State and people and thus can claim no other treatment than that accorded to the Communist Party." Socialist leaders in Berlin, headed by Löbe, were accused of maintaining contacts with the émigrés in Paris and Prague, where the *Vorwärts* was being published by Otto Wels, though they had expressly repudiated these groups. All Socialist propaganda and all public or private gatherings of Socialists were forbidden. All civil servants were required to sever connections with the party. All Socialist mandates in the Reichstag, the Diets, and provincial and municipal councils were annulled. Simultaneously Ley ordered the seizure of all the offices still occupied by the Catholic unions and expelled their leaders from the *Arbeitsfront*. On the 23rd Paul Löbe and other Socialist leaders were arrested. No resistance was encountered anywhere. In some localities the Socialist Party functionaries even assisted the police in liquidating the organization and in listing its confiscated property. Thus perished ignominiously the oldest, largest, and best-organized Socialist Party of the world.

Hugenberg knew that the Nationalists were next. He apparently suggested his resignation to Hindenburg on June 24 and declared that it would void the Enabling Act, since it would change the composition of the government. The President deferred a decision. On the 26th the leaders and deputies of the Bavarian People's Party in the Reichstag and Diets were arrested. Hugenberg was scheduled to speak at a Nationalist meeting in the Kroll Opera. The meeting was prohibited by the police. Hitler went to Neudeck to report to the President. That Hindenburg opposed the dissolution of the party of the Junkers and reactionaries who had elevated him to the presidency in 1925 is more than probable.

On the 29th, however, Hugenberg's resignation was formally accepted, after considerable confusion as to his status. He had tendered it on the 27th as his final reply to Hitler's demand for the dissolution of his party. His aides had at once "voluntarily" dissolved the Nationalist Party and the "German National Front." On the 28th, a day of national mourning to commemorate the signature of the Treaty of Versailles, the State Party—pathetic remnant of German democracy—also dissolved itself voluntarily under Nazi pressure. Its liquidation began on the 29th. Goebbels predicted the end of the Centrum in an address in Stuttgart. He offered advice to its leaders: "Close up your shop, for there are no more customers coming your way." On June 29 the former Socialist Chancellor Gustav Bauer was arrested in Berlin in a spectacular police raid and charged with embezzlement. At the same time the question of Hugenberg's successor was resolved. Four officials in the economic division of the NSDAP were sent to a concentration camp for "conspiracy" to make Otto Wagener the heir of Hugenberg in the Ministry of Economics. This post was awarded to a conservative non-party business man, Dr. Kurt Schmitt, general director since 1921 of Germany's largest insurance company, the Allianz-Versicherungs A.G.; president since 1932 of the Federation of German Private Insurance Companies; vice-president of the Berlin Chamber of Commerce and Industry; and a member of the Central Committee of the Reichsbank. Premier Göring simultaneously appointed him Prussian Minister of Economics and Labour. Two sops were thrown to the Nazi radicals who were disgusted with this choice. Walter Darré was named Reich Minister of Food and Agriculture and Prussian Minister of Agriculture, Lands, and Forests. Gottfried Feder became Under-Secretary of the Reichswirtschaftsministerium through the ousting of the Nationalist Dr. Bang.

These developments completely altered the composition of the Cabinet. On January 30, there were three Nazis to nine non-Nazis among the Ministers. The addition of Goebbels made four, Seldte five, Darré six, Schmitt (who presently joined the NSDAP) seven, and Hitler's adjutant, Rudolf Hess, who began to sit informally in Cabinet meetings on June 29, made eight Nazis. The conversion of Seldte to the party and the ousting of Gerecke reduced the non-Nazis to seven, and the resignation of Hugenberg left only six (Papen, Neurath, Blomberg, Krosigk, Gürtner, and Eltz-Rübenach). The NSDAP now possessed a clear majority of the posts. The coalition of January 30 was demolished. Hugenberg was gone. Papen, the other prime mover in this too clever intrigue, remained. Hindenburg and Hitler, without intending irony, praised Hugenberg's "patriotic" work for the Fatherland. The Nationalist deputies in the Reichstag became "guests" of the NSDAP. To prevent a rush of newcomers into the ranks of the party, the Munich headquarters decreed a two-year probationary period for all new applicants, retroactive to January 30, while Hess urged simplicity and frugality on all party members.

Nothing now remained of the old party system save the Centrum and a few scattered splinters. While Papen in Rome negotiated with the Vatican for a Reich Concordat to replace the separate agreements with Prussia, Baden, and Bavaria, Nazi pressure was brought to bear on the Centrum. Brüning struggled hopelessly to preserve his party from destruction. On July 1 Göring suppressed all non-religious Catholic organizations in Prussia and confiscated their property: the Windhorst Union, the Catholic Peace League, the Young Men's Catholic Association, etc. On July 3 the Concordat was signed in Rome. The Vatican acquiesced in the suppression of the Centrum. The Holy See had made its peace with Mussolini under not dissimilar circumstances and had not regretted its decision. This victory restored some of Papen's waning prestige and deprived

Brüning of his last hope. On July 4 the dissolution of the Centrum and of the Bavarian People's Party was announced by their leaders. Their deputies were also invited to become "guests" of the NSDAP. Dingledey, for the German People's Party, and Arthur Mahraun, for the Jung Deutsche Orden, announced that their groups would also dissolve. On the 5th the dissolution of the Centrum was completed.

Darré and Schmitt took their oaths of office on July 7. On the same day the 121 Socialist Party seats and the 5 State Party seats in the Reichstag were abolished by decree. Brüning became an outcast in his own land, pursued from abode to abode by the secret police and threatened with imprisonment in a concentration camp. The erstwhile Chancellor who had paved the way for dictatorship by so blithely invoking Article 48 of the Constitution, and who had failed to crush the NSDAP when it might still have been crushed, was now a lonely prisoner on parole, in fear of his liberty if not of his life. In his obscurity he doubtless derived some comfort from the reflection that Schleicher, who had driven him from the chancellorship, was reduced to comparable insignificance, and that Papen and the gentlemen of the Herren Klub were helpless in Hitler's grasp.

The work of liquidation was completed by the Cabinet decrees of July 14, 1933:

"The NSDAP is the only political party in Germany. Whoever undertakes to maintain the organization of another political party, or to form a new political party, is to be punished with imprisonment in a penitentiary up to three years or with confinement in a jail from six months to three years, unless the act is punishable by a higher penalty under other provisions.

"The provisions of the law of May 26, 1933, concerning the confiscation of Communist property, are to be applied to the property and rights of the German Social Democratic Party and its auxiliary and collateral organizations, as well as to property and rights which are used or are intended to further Marxist or other movements which, according to determination by the Minister of the Interior, are hostile to the people and the State.

"The national Cabinet, by means of a referendum, may question the people as to whether or not it approves of a measure planned by the national Cabinet. . . . A referendum is decided by a majority of the valid votes cast. This also applies to a vote on a law containing provisions which would amend the Constitution."[1]

Thus all parties other than the NSDAP were destroyed and the organization of new parties was forbidden. The Stahlhelm, though "co-ordinated," retained its separate existence. The remaining monarchist organizations were dissolved on February 1, 1934.[2] All legislative as well as executive authority would be exercised by the Cabinet, in consultation, not with the Reichstag, but, at its discretion, with the electorate through popular referenda. And the Cabinet was in the control of the party of the dictatorship, possessing, like the Fascist Party in Italy and the Communist Party in the U.S.S.R., a "monopoly of legality." What this party had by this time become and what the orientation of its leadership was may be appropriately considered after a brief survey of the other steps toward the complete unification, in Nazi hands, of the whole German national community.

3. TOTALITARIANISM

THE measures of the Hitler government which have thus far been considered were negative in character. They destroyed the trade unions, the political parties, and other agencies and institutions inherited from the régime of Weimar. They were paralleled by other positive measures designed to facilitate the complete control of German public life by the NSDAP. These measures were for the most part enacted and administered in the name of *Gleichschaltung* or "co-ordination." They affected practically every organized activity of the citizens of the Reich in all walks of life, for the NSDAP enforced "the primacy of politics" with a vengeance. Many phases of this process will be dealt with in the following chapters. For the moment it will suffice to review the process up to the spring of 1934, as it affected the formal structure of "government" in the limited sense still familiar in the West.[3]

The final abolition of German federalism may first be considered.

[1] *Reichsgesetzblatt* (R.G.B.), 1933, Vol. I, No. 81, p. 479.

[2] *V.B.*, February 2, 1934.

[3] Perhaps the most useful and accurate brief presentation in English of these and related developments is to be found in Mildred Wertheimer's "The Nazi Revolution in Germany," in R. L. Buell (ed.): *New Government in Europe* (New York: Nelson; 1934), pp. 126–260.

The *Gleichschaltung* of the *Länder* was accompanied by the destruction of all remnants of local autonomy and democracy in all the political subdivisions of the Reich. This process was initiated in Prussia by Chancellor von Papen on July 20, 1932. It was greatly accelerated after March 5, 1933. On March 31 a "Provisional Law for the Unification of the States with the Reich" was enacted.[1] It empowered the state Cabinets to assume legislative authority and to ignore the state Constitutions. Treaties between states would no longer require legislative approval. The state legislatures, with the exception of the Prussian Landtag elected on March 5, were dissolved and reconstituted without new elections on the basis of the number of votes obtained within the states by each party in the Reichstag election of March 5. The seats of the KPD and its "appendages" were not apportioned. The size of the state legislatures was reduced. The seats were allotted on the basis of electoral lists filed by the parties before April 13, 1933—again with the Communist Party excluded. All the new legislatures were given terms of four years from March 5. "Earlier dissolution is not permissible," but "a dissolution of the Reichstag also causes the dissolution of the legislative bodies of the states" (Sections 8 and 11). All local law-making bodies were also dissolved and reconstituted in the same way.

A week later the Cabinet enacted a second unification law. This specified that in each of the states except Prussia the Reich President, on the nomination of the Reichskanzler, would appoint a *Reichsstatthalter* (Federal Governor or Regent) with power to appoint and remove the members of the state Cabinets, to dissolve the legislature and decree new elections, to prepare and publish state laws, to exercise the pardoning power, and "upon the proposal of the state Cabinet" to appoint and dismiss higher state officials and judges. The Statthalter, moreover, might preside over the sessions of the State Cabinet, but he could not be a member. For groups of smaller states with less than two million inhabitants apiece, a common Statthalter might be named. The Statthalters must be citizens of their states, but would

[1] *R.G.B.*, 1933, Vol. 1, No. 29, p. 153. For English translations of the texts of this and other decrees see J. K. Pollock and H. J. Heneman, *The Hitler Decrees.* Cf. also Mildred Wertheimer: "The Political Structure of the Third Reich" (*Foreign Policy Association Reports,* X, No. 8, June 20, 1934). Cf., for German texts, Werner Hoche: *Die Gesetzgebung des Kabinetts Hitler* (Berlin: Vahlen Verlag; 1933) and Georg Kaisenberg: *"Gleichschaltung der Länder mit dem Reich," Das Recht der nationalen Revolution* (Berlin: Heymanns; 1933).

be paid by the Reich and be subject to recall by the President on the proposal of the Reichskanzler. "Votes of no confidence by the state legislature against the head and members of the state Cabinet are not permissible." In Prussia the Reichskanzler would exercise the powers of Statthalter.[1]

Supplementary laws and decrees of April 25, May 26, June 1 and 18, and October 14, 1933 provided that the Chancellor might transfer his powers in Prussia to the Premier; that the Statthalters might transfer their powers to the state governments; and that they should receive official residences in designated cities, allowances for official expenses, and salaries comparable to those of members of the Reich Cabinet. The Chancellor's right of "recall" was interpreted to mean "removal." Hitler appointed Göring Premier of Prussia on April 11, 1933 and entrusted him with his powers as Statthalter. The other Statthalters appointed by Hitler, as of June 1933, were as follows:[2]

Bavaria: Franz Ritter von Epp, General
Württemberg: Wilhelm Murr, business man
Saxony: Martin Mutschmann, industrialist
Baden: Robert Wagner, army officer
Hesse-Nassau: Jacob Sprenger, postal official
Thuringia: Fritz Sauckel, sea-captain and official
Oldenburg and Bremen: Karl Röver, colonialist and official
Braunschweig and Anhalt: Wilhelm Loeper, army officer
Mecklenburg-Schwerin, Mecklenburg-Strelitz, and Lubeck: Friedrich Hildebrandt, farmer
Hamburg: Karl Kaufman, farmer, soldier, worker
Lippe and Schaumberg-Lippe: Alfred Meyer, army officer and jurist

All the Statthalters were members of the NSDAP, and all save Sauckel and Meyer were members of the Reichstag. Each one was given the powers of a dictator within his state, including the right to call out the Reichswehr to preserve public order. Each possesses legislative as well as executive power and dominates the state government as completely as Der Führer dominates the Reich government. The Statthalters, however, are completely answerable to the Chancellor and serve less as liaison officers between the states and the central government than as agents of the central government to

[1] *R.G.B.*, 1933, Vol I, No. 33 (April 7), p. 173.
[2] *Nationalsozialistisches Jahrbuch,* 1934, pp. 117–18.

control the states as administrative subdivisions of the Reich. State sovereignty and state autonomy therewith disappeared and Germany became for all practical purposes a rigidly unified and highly centralized State, autocratically administered as to local government by the arbitrary satraps of an arbitrary national despot in Berlin.

The subsequent developments in the *Gleichschaltung* of the states can be suggested by an examination of the course of events in Prussia, since the sequence here was followed, with minor local variations, in the smaller *Länder*. Premier Göring inaugurated the Prussian "reforms," which elsewhere were executed by the Statthalters. On July 10, 1933, the Prussian Cabinet, under his direction, enacted a law abolishing the old Council of State, the upper house of the Prussian legislature, which was elected by the provincial councils and had a suspensory veto in law-making. A new *Staatsrat* or Council of State was established to "advise" the Ministers. This body would be composed of "Prussian State Councillors" and would consist of not more than fifty persons appointed by the Premier, in addition to the Ministers and Premier as ex-officio members. The Councillors must be German citizens of Prussian domicile, at least twenty-five years old. They would be chosen from three groups: secretaries of state; the chiefs of the S.A. and S.S., the staff leaders of the PO, the Prussian *Gauleiters* of the NSDAP, and other party officials; and representatives of capital, labour, art, science, religion, and others deserving recognition for public service. Members of the third group would be appointed for life, and of the first two for the duration of their existing offices. All members were subject to removal by the Premier, who would preside over the Staatsrat.

"The Councillors express their opinions on proposals which come before the Council of State. Important laws shall be laid before the Council of State before their promulgation. If a Councillor of State decides that discussion of such a matter is desirable, he advises the Premier of this, with a declaration of his reasons; the Premier has the final decision whether the suggestion is to be complied with. The Council of State does not vote. The meetings of the Council of State are not published. The Chancellor may demand the summoning of the Council of State. He may appear before the Council at any time and be heard." [1]

On July 20 this law was supplemented by two others. One sought

[1] *Preussische Gesetzsammlung* (*P.G.S.*) 1933, No. 46, p. 241, Sections 10–12.

to put an end to the confusion and rivalries which had developed within the Prussian Cabinet by giving the Premier authority to regulate and define the departmental competence of the Ministers and by requiring consultation among the Ministers.[1] The other fixed the "allowance" of Councillors at one thousand marks per month, save for those residing in Berlin or Potsdam, who were to get five hundred marks.[2] The Councillors would continue to receive their regular salaries for other posts. A third law of August 7 amended the original act by omitting the limitation of its size to fifty members and by dropping secretaries of state as a group from which members might be chosen.[3]

These innovations of Premier Göring had several purposes. They were designed to give him patronage for distribution among deserving political friends and supporters. Göring's own power and his personal position in the government and in the NSDAP would thus be strengthened. The new Council, moreover, would be a highly dignified body which would lend prestige to Prussia and make less likely any abolition of Prussia as a separate political entity in the future reorganization of the Reich. Göring was not animated by particularistic loyalty to Prussia, since he was a Bavarian. But the Prussian state government was the basis of his own political influence. From a constitutional point of view the new Council was to be merely an ornament to a completely dictatorial régime. It could neither legislate nor vote, but merely "advise" in secret. The old lower house of the Prussian legislature had already surrendered its law-making authority on May 18. In Prussia, as in all the states and in the Reich, the executive would legislate as well as administer. And the executive would be controlled by leaders of the NSDAP sworn to blind obedience to Der Führer.

Göring appointed fifty-six members to the new Staatsrat. They included Ernst Röhm, commander of the S.A.; Karl Ernst, dashing young leader of the Berlin-Brandenburg storm troopers; Heinrich Himmler, commander of the S.S.; Fritz Thyssen; Dr. Ludwig Müller, the new Nazi Bishop of the Evangelical Church; Prince August Wilhelm; Wilhelm Furtwängler, the music director; Field Marshal August von Mackensen; Captain von Jagow, U-boat officer;

[1] Ibid., No. 49, p. 258.
[2] Ibid., No. 49, p. 265.
[3] Ibid., No. 52, p. 289.

General Litzmann; Admiral von Trotha; and many other notables. Here was represented the new political élite of the NSDAP, the old military élite of the war, and the élites of business, art, and religion. On September 15 the Staatsrat assembled in the University of Berlin, amid a great fanfare of trumpets and drums. What "advisory" functions it performed, then or later, has never been revealed. A double line of storm troops stood at attention along the entire length of Unter den Linden. S.A. men in brown steel helmets and S.S. men with rifles and black steel helmets paraded. Police and Reichswehr co-operated in giving the ceremonies an exclusively military character. Göring's address was broadcast:

"In the old parliament Authority and Responsibility were in reverse order. Responsibility went from top to bottom, and Authority went from bottom to top. That was a sin against natural law. . . . Here, however, the old principle holds good: Authority goes from top to bottom, but Responsibility always from bottom to top. Each is responsible to him who is called to stand next above him. Der Führer carries the final Responsibility and he carries it before his God and his people. . . . What Der Führer wants will be done. His will is law for us. . . . The goal is: Germany, and again Germany, and always Germany! And so has Prussia its mission. . . . The Prussian Staatsrat is opened, and it is opened with the cry: *To our leader, Adolf Hitler, the German Reichskanzler, a triple victory-cheer!*"[1]

District, local, and municipal government throughout the Reich was subjected to a similar transformation. In Prussia, by a law of July 20, 1933,[2] the twelve provincial Councils were changed from elected legislative bodies to appointive and honorary advisory bodies chosen by the Prussian Premier. The provincial Oberpräsidenten and the district Regierungspräsidenten were thus given a monopoly of all executive, administrative, and legislative power in local government. For the city of Berlin a commissioner was appointed by the Prussian Minister of the Interior (Göring), with powers of advice and supervision over the Mayor and the City Council.[3] In September the Berlin municipal council and the district councils

[1] *Berliner Tageblatt*, September 15, 1933.

[2] *P.G.S.*, 1933, No. 49, p. 254.

[3] Ibid., No. 37 (June 2), p. 196; cf. ibid., No. 78 (December 18, 1933), p. 427; ibid., 1934, No. 29 (June 30), p. 319.

were deprived of their authority, which was transferred to the municipal committee and the district boards—that is, to executive and administrative agencies.[1] All Prussian mayors were appointed by the Minister of the Interior. Municipal elections were abolished. Everywhere throughout the Reich local legislative bodies lost their powers and disappeared. By autumn the only elective legislature remaining in all Germany was the Reichstag—which had surrendered all its legislative powers and was "elective" only in a purely formal sense. Parliamentarianism and local self-government were by a few strokes of the pen completely blotted out.

Meanwhile the magnificently organized German civil service was likewise *"gleichgeschaltet,"* though with a minimum of disturbance to its organization and personnel. One of the earliest steps of the new government was to apply Nazi principles to the bureaucracy and to ensure its loyalty. The federal law of April 7, 1933 specified that various categories of citizens in all public and quasi-public employment might be discharged "for the restoration of a national civil service and for the simplification of the administration." Officials who entered the service after November 9, 1918 without the usual training or qualifications were to be discharged without pension rights, though with three months' salary after dismissal and with the possibility of obtaining an annuity equal to one-third of their former salaries.[2] Officials not of "Aryan" descent were to be discharged. Pension rights would be granted only to those who had completed ten years of service. Non-Aryans in service since August 1, 1914, and those who fought at the front for the Central Powers, or who had fathers or sons killed in the war, were exempted from discharge (Section 3).

"Officials who, because of their previous political activity, do not offer security that they will exert themselves for the national State without reservations may be discharged. For three months after dismissal they will be paid their former salary. From this time on they receive three-quarters of their pensions and corresponding annuities for their heirs" (Section 4).

Any official, at the discretion of the highest national or state authorities, might be transferred or pensioned without recourse to the courts. By a decree of April 11, 1933, "a non-Aryan is one who is

[1] Ibid., 1933, No. 61 (September 25), 356.

[2] *R.G.B.*, 1933, Vol. I, No. 34, p. 175, Section 2.

descended from non-Aryan, particularly Jewish, parents or grandparents. It suffices if either parent or either grandparent is non-Aryan. This is especially so if either parent or either grandparent has professed the Jewish religion." [1] On May 6, judges, policemen, teachers, and professors were included within the scope of this legislation, but the military forces were exempted. All officials who had ever participated in Communist activities, including the Nazi rebel group *Die Schwarze Front,* were to be discharged. Front fighters were defined as soldiers who had actually faced the enemy in battle. "Participation in the fighting in the Baltic States, in Upper Silesia, against Spartacists and Separatists, as well as against the enemies of the national revolution, is to be ranked as equal with participation in the fighting of the World War." [2]

This legislation was followed by dismissals from all branches of the pubic service of Jews, Communists, Socialists, liberals, pacifists, and others obnoxious to the NSDAP. But since the groups affected constituted only a small percentage of the bureaucracy, which the Socialists and Democrats after 1918 had left largely intact in the hands of reactionary officials, the volume of displacement was relatively small. The Nazi leaders were shrewd enough to perceive that a wholesale house-cleaning, followed by the introduction of the spoils system, would in the long run weaken their hold on the administrative machine rather than strengthen it. They accordingly preferred to weed out racially undesirable or politically unreliable elements, without disturbing the fundamentals of structure and personnel management which had made the German civil service the most efficient administrative machine in the modern world.

The weeding-out process was largely completed by summer. In order to carry it to a conclusion and to prevent the filling of vacant posts by incompetent political aspirants, a law of June 30, 1933 specified that "only such persons may be appointed as national officials who possess the prescribed education or customary training or who have special qualifications for the office about to be filled, and who guarantee that they will support the national State at all times without reservation." Women could secure permanent posts only after the age of thirty-five.

"Anyone of non-Aryan descent, or married to a person of non-

[1] Ibid., Vol. I, No. 37, p. 195.
[2] Ibid., Vol. I, No. 48, p. 245.

Aryan descent, may not be appointed a national official. National officials who marry persons of non-Aryan descent are to be discharged. The question of who is of non-Aryan descent is to be decided by regulations of the Minister of the Interior. . . . When the economic status of a female official appears to be permanently secured because of a family income, the officials . . . may decree her dismissal. The conditions for dismissal are always present when the husband is a permanent official not subject to dismissal." [1]

The same rules were made applicable to employees of state and local governments, of the Reichsbank, of the German State Railways, and of other quasi-public institutions. The new Aryan clause was reinterpreted on August 8, 1933,[2] to include illegitimate descent. Prospective national officials would be required to submit documentary proof of the Aryan descent of themselves and their wives. Officials desiring to marry were compelled to prove the Aryan descent of their prospective spouses. "If Aryan descent is doubtful, an opinion is to be obtained from the expert for racial investigation accredited to the Minister of the Interior." [3] In this fashion the "racial purity" as well as the political reliability of the civil service of the Third Reich was assured.

Further changes in the governmental structure of Germany were introduced after the "election" of November 12, 1933. By the end of summer the first tasks of the Fascist revolution had been completed. Marxism was destroyed. Trade unionism was smashed. All other political parties were outlawed. Federalism, democracy, representative government, civil rights, pacifism, internationalism, racial and religious toleration, "Jewish intellectualism"—all had perished in the Nazi flames. Not only had all opposition outside the party been destroyed, but the radical "Left opposition" within the ranks was silenced as well, at least temporarily. The next step was to paralyse all remaining critics and to impress a hostile world by offering visible evidence that the dictatorship was not maintained by terror, but rested upon the enthusiastic support of the populace. As master politicians and political psychologists, the Nazi leaders knew that the final steps toward the complete liquidation of the remnants of the Weimar régime should be taken after some overwhelming dem-

[1] Ibid., Vol. I, No. 74, p. 433.

[2] Ibid., Vol. I, No. 91, p. 575.

[3] Ibid., Vol. I, No. 85 (July 20), p. 518.

onstration of public confidence. Here, as always, propaganda was preferable to violence because it was more effective. Such a demonstration of confidence, moreover, would presumably strengthen the Reich's diplomatic position abroad, where émigrés were encouraging groundless hope of the early collapse of the Nazi State.

To what extent Hitler, Goebbels, and their colleagues indulged in careful calculations on the basis of these considerations it is difficult to ascertain. Perhaps sound political intuition continued to serve Der Führer better than sober reason. In any case, the internal and external factors in the position of the Nazi régime were combined with extraordinary skill to produce maximum results at home and abroad. How could the largest possible percentage of the electorate be induced to approve of the dictatorship? Obviously, by finding again the lowest possible emotional denominator of the masses and by identifying the government with the most basic emotional responses of the populace. Flattery of collective vanity and denunciation of national enemies were the techniques which must be used. But how? A new wave of anti-Semitism might serve the purpose. But since, in official theory, Hitler had already "saved" the Reich from the Jews in the spring, this would be difficult to dramatize. It would further stir up a new storm of protest abroad which might prove embarrassing. The symbols of intense nationalism would be more useful. If Hitler acted in a belligerent fashion toward foreign "enemies" and at the same time verbally championed "peace," he could retain the support of all his followers, win the approval of all patriots, and even, as he had learned on May 17, induce the spineless Social Democrats to give him their confidence. But Paris, Warsaw, Prague, London, and Washington must also be considered. Since German rearmament would require several more years of preparation, no risks of provoking sanctions or military action against the Reich could be taken. The necessary belligerent gesture must be of such a character that it would not involve this danger. And yet it must be so devised that the accompanying peace propaganda for consumption by foreigners and by peace-loving people at home would not create any doubts in the hearts of patriots as to the government's firm determination to restore Germany's might and protect Germany's honour. Stated thus in abstract terms, the problem seems impossible of solution. But the NSDAP was accustomed to achieving the impossible. It did so again in this instance, in a manner which must command the admiration of all students of the arts of politics and propaganda.

On October 14, 1933, the master stroke fell like a thunderbolt, leaving the nation and the world aghast. After a long, secret Cabinet session (in which, it may be surmised, Neurath, Krosigk, and possibly others were finally converted to the plan worked out by Nazi leaders) the government announced the withdrawal of Germany from the League of Nations and the Geneva Disarmament Conference, the dissolution of the Reichstag, a new Reichstag election on November 12, and a simultaneous popular referendum on the Cabinet's foreign policy. No hint of such action had previously been made. The immediate pretext was the refusal of Sir John Simon, the British Foreign Minister, to accept any agreement at Geneva which would permit German rearmament. The other Powers were on the point of concluding a limited disarmament convention which would allow Germany equality of status only after a four-year "trial period." For the government at Berlin to have repudiated Geneva earlier would have been a political error. For it to wait until the conclusion of the impending agreement would have been a psychological mistake. It acted at precisely the correct moment. Proclamations, speeches, slogans, and impassioned exhortations began to rain down from Wilhelmstrasse like autumn leaves in a storm. A government Manifesto to the nation was issued early on Saturday afternoon, October 14:[1]

"The German national Cabinet and the German people are united in the will to conduct a policy of peace, of reconciliation, and of understanding as the foundation of all decisions and of all actions.

"The national Cabinet and the German people, therefore, disavow violence as an unsuitable means for settling existing differences with the European community of States.

"The German national Cabinet and the German people renew the avowal to accede gladly to every actual disarming of the world, with the assurance of the willingness also to destroy the last German machine-gun and to discharge the last German soldier from the army, provided the other nations decide to do likewise.

"The German national Cabinet and the German people unite in the sincere desire to want to examine and solve without passion, and by

[1] The texts of this and other statements appeared in the *Berliner Tageblatt, V.B., New York Times,* and most other leading newspapers October 15, et seq., 1933.

means of negotiations, all existing questions with other nations, including all of our former opponents, in a spirit of overcoming the war psychosis and restoring finally a sincere relationship toward each other.

"The German national Cabinet and the German people therefore declare themselves willing, at any time, to assure the peace of Europe for all time and to serve its economic welfare through the conclusion of Continental pacts of non-aggression and participation in general cultural reconstruction.

"The national Cabinet and the German people are motivated by the same conception of honour which demands that the acceptance of equal treatment for Germany is the absolutely necessary moral and objective condition for every participation of our people and its government in international institutions and treaties.

"The German national Cabinet and the German people are therefore united in the decision to leave the Disarmament Conference and to quit the League of Nations until this actual equality of rights is no longer withheld from our nation.

"The national Cabinet and the German people have decided rather to undergo every difficulty, every persecution, and every distress than to subscribe in the future to treaties which for every man of honour and for every honourable nation must be unacceptable; and which would, in their consequences, lead only to the perpetuation of the unhappiness and misery caused by the Versailles Treaty and thereby to the collapse of the civilized community of nations.

"The German national Cabinet and the German people do not have the will to participate in any armament race with other nations. They only demand that measure of security which guarantees to the nation quiet and freedom for peaceful work. The German national Cabinet and the German people are determined to make certain, by means of negotiations and by treaties, these justifiable demands of the German nation.

"The national Cabinet puts the question to the German people:

"Does the German people agree to the policy of its national Cabinet here set forth and is it willing to declare the same to be the expression of its own opinion and its own will and to support it solemnly?"

Hitler at the same time issued a manifesto of his own:

" . . . As Chancellor of the German people and leader of the Nazi movement, I am convincd that the entire nation will back, as one man, this resolution, which originates as much from a love of our people and esteem of their honour as from the conviction that the definitive peace of the world, so necessary to all, can only be achieved if the ideas of victors and vanquished are replaced by a belief in equal rights for all."

The German delegates at Geneva hurriedly left the city. Rumours of sanctions, mobilizations, and appeals to the League Council or the Permanent Court failed to materialize, as did reports that the Reich would denounce the Treaty as a whole. At seven o'clock Saturday evening Hitler stepped before the microphone and broadcast an address to the nation and the world:

"Mein deutsches Volk! When the German people, trusting to the assurances given in President Wilson's Fourteen Points, laid down their arms in November 1918, an end was made of a fatal warfare for which perhaps individual statesmen, but certainly not the people themselves, can be held responsible. . . . It was the German people who suffered the deepest disappointment. . . .

"The German government is most profoundly convinced that its appeal to the whole German nation will prove to the world that the government's love of peace, and also its views on the subject of honour, represent the longing for peace and the code of honour of the entire nation. . . . May this great demonstration by our nation in favour of peace and honour be successful in providing the internal relations of the European States with that prerequisite necessary, not only for putting an end to the quarrels and disputes of centuries, but also for the building up afresh of a better community of nations; namely: *The recognition of a higher common duty arising out of common equal rights.*"

The election machinery began to move into action at once. Hindenburg dissolved the Reichstag and decreed new elections for November 12.[1] At the same time the President, with the consent of the Reichsrat, modified the election decree of March 14, 1924, by providing that the "ballots of all accepted district election lists must contain, together with the statement of the party, the names of the first ten candidates of each list." [2] On October 20, after several changes of form,[3] the text of the referendum ballot was announced. It was identical with the government Manifesto of October 14. At the end was posed the question, in the familiar *"Du"* form, instead of the formal *"Sie"*: "Do you German man and you German woman agree to this policy of your national Cabinet, and are you willing to declare it to be the expression of your own opinion and your own will and to

1 *R.G.B.*, 1933, Vol. I, No. 113 (October 14), p. 729.
2 Ibid., Vol. I, No. 116 (October 19), p. 746.
3 Ibid., Vol. I, No. 113 (October 14), p. 732, and No. 117 (October 20), p. 747.

espouse it solemnly?" This was followed, on the green ballot, by two squares containing circles and captioned by *"Ja"* and *"Nein."*

The white Reichstag ballot contained the single party heading: *Nationalsocialistische Deutsche Arbeiterpartei (Hitlerbewegung)* and under it ten names: Hitler, Hess, Frick, Göring, Goebbels, Röhm, Darré, Seldte, Papen—and, perhaps with intentional humour, Hugenberg. To the right of the names was a single circle in a rectangle. No provision was made whereby the voter could vote for any alternative list or even vote against the list presented. Blank ballots were to be held invalid.[1]

The ten names headed a Nazi list of 686 candidates, including the Nazis already in the Reichstag, some party members in the state Diets, many S.A. leaders, and all the Statthalters, the *Gauleiters,* and the Trustees of Labour. Certain Nationalist and Stahlhelm leaders in addition to Seldte and Hugenberg were given places on the list, including Dr. Bang and Justizrat Class. Two former deputies of the German People's Party were included: the colonial governor Schnee and the banker Dr. von Stauss. Dr. Hackelsberger and Count von Quadt, representing respectively the Centrum and the Bavarian People's Party, also received places. In addition there were a dozen industrialists, including Thyssen, Voegler, Springorum, and Dr. Grimm (all associated with Thyssen), some thirty bankers, and almost a hundred farmers, including many Junkers. The liberal professions were well represented. There were only twenty-five labourers and twenty-five office workers on the list. It was primarily a panel of the leading personalities of the NSDAP, with a few non-party members added for good measure. No women were nominated.

The propaganda machine of the NSDAP began working immediately at top speed. While figures on campaign expenditures are not available, it is probable that more money was spent than in any previous electoral contest—and this despite the fact that there was here no contest at all. Not only were there no opposition candidates, but no opposition activity or criticism of any kind was tolerated. The whole purpose of the campaign was to inculcate loyalty to the dictatorship and to roll up as large an affirmative vote as possible on November 12. *"Frieden und Gleichberichtigung"* (Peace and Equal

[1] For fascimiles of German ballots and an analysis of election procedure, see J. K. Pollock: *German Election and Administration* (New York: Columbia University Press; 1934).

Rights) was the slogan. Parades, mass meetings, and oratorical fireworks were the order of the day during the weeks preceding the election. The massed bands, the *Blutfahne,* the banners, the passionate pleas of the great spellbinders worked their ancient magic.

Goebbels spoke in the Sportpalast on October 20. The great hall was jammed hours before the meeting began. Storm troopers paraded in with 165 Nazi flags—with two small Stahlhelm banners buried in the mass. The Propaganda Minister aroused savage enthusiasm by denouncing the Jews, but these passages were deleted in the published versions of the speech. "We have saved Germany and Europe from Bolshevism. . . . Peace costs sacrifices, but we are of the opinion that it costs fewer sacrifices than a war. . . . The others should now disarm. . . . We shall endeavour to prevent war with all our means. . . . The old Reichstag is only a rump parliament. We want to have a new Reichstag. On November 12 the entire nation must approve Hitler and his policy. On November 12 no opposition worthy of the name can dare to exist. The whole world shall see that on this day the whole German people is united." On the 22nd Hitler in Kelheim: "We want nothing but our quiet and our peace, in order to work, and the world shall know that for this work the entire nation stands together."

At 8.00 p.m., October 24, Hitler appeared in the Sportpalast. Hundreds had waited in line for seats since early morning. Great placards proclaimed: "Hitler's Struggle is a Struggle for True World Peace!" "With Hitler for a Peace of Honour and Equality!" "Freedom and Bread in Honour and Peace!" "We Will Not be a People of Inferior Rights!" Ten great Nazi standards and 284 flags were carried in by storm troopers amid a sea of outstretched arms. Hitler was greeted wildly as he nodded and smiled along the aisle and accepted bouquets. Thousands cheered in sixty overflow meetings throughout Berlin. Der Führer, in a light brown uniform, wove his old spell. "Honour . . . Freedom . . . Equal Rights. . . . We have the will to peace, we see no possibility of conflict. . . . But we will not permit ourselves to be treated as inferior, nor will we ever sign anything that we dare not sign because it violates our honour. . . . Never will I do anything contrary to my honour and the honour of the nation. . . ."

No effort was spared to enlist everybody in the cause. On October 29 hundreds of organizations and associations unitedly pledged their support—butchers, bakers, candlestick-makers; dentists, doctors, teachers, lawyers; farmers, tennis-players, gardeners, Protestants; students, Catholics, veterans, poets; bicycle-riders, tobacconists, gymnasts, and others without end.[1] The climax came on Friday, November 10. Hitler appealed to the worker from the dynamo hall of the vast Siemens-Schuckert Electrical Works in Berlin. From a table under the glare of calcium lights Der Führer spoke to thousands of workers. Goebbels introduced him—and over all radios came, as an obbligato, the noise of great machines grinding to a halt. At 1.00 p.m. all over Germany there was a blare of whistles and a clang of bells, followed by one minute of silence, an honour hitherto reserved only for the war dead. Everywhere wheels stopped. Traffic ceased on all streets and roads from Kufstein to Heligoland, from Luxembourg to Memel. Passers-by stood still, hats off and hands raised in salute to the invisible Leader. He spoke perhaps to the largest audience in history. Thirty million workers in silenced factories listened for an hour (and worked an hour overtime later, to pay their employer's losses). Twenty million more people, in their homes or on the streets or in halls and theatres, heard the magic voice:

"*Deutsche Volksgenossen und Volksgenossinnen! Meine deutschen Arbeiter!* If I speak today to you and to millions of other workers, I do so with greater right than any other. I have myself come from your ranks. I have been among you for four and a half years in war, and I speak now to you to whom I belong. . . . I lead the struggle for the million-masses of our brave, industrious workers and our labouring people. . . . What is the difference between the theory of class war and the theory of international war? It is the same! The same nonsense to pretend that one class can profit because another class loses. . . . I must attempt first of all to give you again bread and work. . . . I need no title. My name, which I earned by my own strength, is my title. . . . Perhaps there are some among you who cannot forgive me for destroying the Marxist parties. I say: My friend, I have also destroyed the other parties. I have not conquered the representatives of the working class, no, I have conquered the representatives of all classes. . . . Our aim is that we shall all think together, with common efforts and common work, to create an endurable life for our countrymen, not for a class, but for all. . . . To the German burgher I must say: Do not think that it is in your interest

[1] *Deutsche Allgemeine Zeitung,* October 29, 1933.

when it goes badly with the worker. On the contrary, the more purchasing power he has, the better will it be for you. . . .

"They must not expect from me that I am so senseless as to want war. . . . I know war. . . . We want peace and understanding, nothing else. We want to give our hand to our former enemies! . . . They say I do not honestly mean it. I say: What, then, shall I do for you to believe us? My countrymen! I believe that in such times one must be very hard and before all must not concede a centimetre of his rights. . . . Honour means, in this case, equal rights, and equal rights mean the possibility of being able to represent one's own interests too before the others. If the world wishes to dictate, then without *my* signature! And if the world says: Yes, we are forced to do so because we can't trust you? How so? When has the German people ever broken its word? It has instead kept its word all too stubbornly and faithfully! . . . [No voice whispered: 'Belgium!'] We are not to be treated as shoe-shiners, as inferiors. No, either equal rights or the world will see us no more at any conference. . . . If the whole nation does its duty on the 12th of November, then it will be clear to the whole world, for the first time perhaps in German history, that it must now deal with us otherwise, that it can hope no more from our disunity and divisions, that it is confronted with that which is—the German people!" [1]

In a small town in northern Bavaria two factory managers looked out of the window during the broadcast and left five minutes before its conclusion. They were sent to a concentration camp for disrespect to Der Führer. Thinly veiled threats were breathed over the land against possible non-voters or "No" voters. After the election Duke Philip Albert of Württemberg was arrested for failing to vote. Many others, negligent in their civic duties, were branded as traitors and paraded through the streets in disgrace. There was no open pressure on voters. Subtler methods sufficed. Repeatedly the government announced that the election would be honestly conducted and that the secrecy of the ballot would be respected. Few believed these assurances. If one voted "No" and was discovered, one faced the loss of one's job, perhaps the loss of one's liberty, possibly the loss of one's life. People under suspicion had a habit of disappearing mysteriously. And, after all, who could oppose Peace, Honour, Freedom, Equal Rights? It was better to be safe. . . .

[1] *Deutsche Allgemeine Zeitung*, November 11, 1933.

On the last night, Saturday evening, November 11, Hindenburg added his voice to the chorus of Yea-sayers in a broadcast:

"German men and women! Let me also address to you a word of warning in this hour which concerns life questions of the German present and future. I and the government, united in the determination to lead Germany out of the divisions and the impotence of the post-war period, have called upon the German people to decide their destiny themselves tomorrow and to announce to the whole world whether they support our policy and make it their own. . . . For the first time in many years of dissension shall the German people go before the world tomorrow in firm unity, one in the announcement of its will to peace, one also in its demands for honour, equal rights, and the respect of others. . . . It is a lie and an insult when they attribute to us abroad warlike intentions. . . . With our whole hearts we want peace, but a peace of honour and equal rights. . . . Loudly and emphatically shall all Germans, united in one will, announce that Germany in the future may never more be dealt with as a second-class nation. . . . Show tomorrow your firm national unity and your solidarity with the government. Support with me and the Reichskanzler the principle of equal rights and of peace with honour, and show the world that we have recovered, and with the help of God will maintain, German unity!" [1]

Sunday was a bright autumn day. Germans voted everywhere—in concentration camps, on the high seas, in foreign lands. Hitler voted in the Siemens-Stadt, Hindenburg and Goebbels in an old Berlin inn where Bismarck once played cards. In the Oranienburg concentration camp, 330 out of the 377 persons who voted supported the government. In the Dachau camp, near Munich, 2,154 out of 2,242 expressed their support of the government which had imprisoned them. Every voter received, at his polling-place, a small tin button marked *"Ja"* in return for a small donation to the winter relief fund. Voters who were suspected of disloyalty by their neighbours often marked their ballots publicly, so that all should see that they too were for Hitler. So great was the rush to the ballot boxes that long lines gathered before each polling-place. Late in the afternoon storm troopers rounded up negligent voters who had not yet appeared. The result was all but unanimous.

[1] *Berliner Tageblatt,* November 12, 1933.

REICHSTAG ELECTION, NOVEMBER 12, 1933[1]
Qualified Voters—45,176,713
Voted—43,053,616—95.3 per cent
Deputies Elected—661

		Per cent
NSDAP	39,655,212 —	92.2
Invalid Ballots (unmarked)	3,398,404 —	7.8

REFERENDUM, NOVEMBER 12, 1933
Qualified Voters—45,176,713
Voted—43,491,575—96.3 per cent

		Per cent
"Yes"	40,632,628 —	95.1
"No"	2,101,191 —	4.9
Invalid	757,756	

This overwhelming result was wholly without parallel in any other national election or referendum anywhere in the modern world, save in Fascist Italy. It was not achieved by dishonest counting, nor yet by open threats or bribery of voters. It surprised only those observers who had not preceived the effect of subtle pressure on the electorate and those who underestimated the efficacy of Nazi propaganda. On Monday Hitler thanked his supporters for having justified his "faith in the inner worth of the German people." He also thanked the party.

The way was now clear for the completion of the process of governmental reorganization which had been begun in the spring. All of the state legislatures had been dissolved on October 14. No new state elections were held. On October 21 the permanent committee of the Prussian Landtag was suspended.[2] No new legislatures were to be organized. The Diets thus passed quietly out of existence. Amid rumours of the complete abolition of the states, the creation of fifteen administrative districts, the appointment of an all-Nazi Cabinet, and the promulgation of a new Constitution, Hitler remained silent as to his plans. On December 1 Rudolf Hess and Ernst Röhm were appointed Cabinet members without portfolio. The Cabinet now consisted of six non-Nazis and nine Nazis. At the same time legisla-

[1] *Deutscher Reichsanzeiger und Preussischer Anzeiger,* No. 279, November 29, 1933.
[2] *P.G.S.,* 1933, No. 66, p. 376.

tion empowered the authorities to compel certain classes of unemployed to enter workhouses. Other measures suggested the line which the NSDAP would now pursue: Several hundred suspected Marxists were arrested; the Prussian secret police was reorganized and published a list of enemies of the State; all bank deposits of the Reichsbanner and of German peace societies were confiscated; the oath of loyalty administered to members of the Reichswehr was modified to eliminate all references to the Constitution and the republic; and, perhaps most significant, a new law ensured the "Unity of the Party and State":

"1. After the victory of the Nationalsocialist revolution the NSDAP has become the carrier of the German government and is inseparably united with the State. It is a corporation of public law. Its constitution is determined by Der Führer.

"2. To secure the closest co-operation of the offices of the party and the S.A. with the public officials, the representative of the Leader (Hess) and the Chief of Staff of the S.A. (Röhm) are to be members of the Cabinet." [1]

This law further made party members and storm troopers, as well as members of other organizations at the discretion of Hitler, subject to special party and S.A. jurisdiction. The party leaders thus secured the right of arresting, imprisoning, or otherwise punishing party members guilty of insubordination or neglect of duty. These offences were so broadly defined as to give the leaders arbitrary power to proceed against dissidents within the ranks. Public authorities were required to assist party officials in apprehending offenders, who would be dealt with, not in the courts, but by special party agencies. Legal theorists might regard this piece of legislation with some astonishment, since the State here authorized a political party to exercise judicial and police functions over its own members. But in reality this "State within a State" was non-existent. Adolf Hitler, Reichskanzler, had merely authorized Adolf Hitler, Führer, to deal with his subordinates as he saw fit. All distinction between the NSDAP and the German State therewith disappeared, except in a purely administrative sense.

On December 11 the new Reichstag met in the Kroll Opera. Of the 661 members, 659 appeared in brown shirts. Only Papen wore civilian clothes. Hugenberg was excused from attending because of

[1] *R.G.B.*, 1933, Vol. I, No. 135 (December 1), p. 1016.

"illness." Hitler spent the day at Wilhelmshaven. There were no speeches and no legislation. Göring merely presented the names of the new officers. Hans Kerrl, Prussian Minister of Justice, Hermann Esser, Bavarian Nazi leader, and Dr. von Stauss, banker, were named vice-presidents. The list was accepted by acclamation. Göring called for three cheers for Hitler and the German people and adjourned the session, which lasted seven and a half minutes.

On December 15 Mecklenburg-Strelitz and Mecklenburg-Schwerin were united into a single state.[1] Six new laws effaced the remaining "liberalistic and democratic vestiges" in Prussia on December 18. All elective provincial, communal, and municipal legislative bodies were abolished and replaced by purely advisory appointive bodies composed of Nazi leaders and representatives of trades and professions. Since the party was known to be preparing a "Reich Reform Law," it was anticipated that the Prussian example would be extended throughout Germany. All plans were kept secret, however. On January 9 Dr. Ley, in his capacity as staff leader of the PO, announced that all party members who discussed the Reich Reform publicly in speech or writing would be heavily punished, by the order of Hess.[2]

On January 30, 1934, the first anniversary of Hitler's appointment as Chancellor, the Reichstag reassembled. Hitler and Hess entered together and were greeted with the Fascist salute. Göring opened the session: "Out of depression, out of the depths, out of black night, the German people have raised themselves anew and have again found Honour and Freedom. . . . With brutal fists we have repulsed the enemies of the State. We are ruthless against those who place their own interests above the interests of the nation. . . . The world must learn that as the people are united, so also is its leadership and its representation in the German Reichstag." Frick, as Nazi faction leader, placed a bill on the Reform of the Reich on the agenda. Hitler then stepped to the rostrum amid a storm of cheers and delivered a long address:

"Deputies! Men of the German Reichstag! If today, looking backward, we name the year 1933 as the Year of the Nationalsocialist Revolution, this characterization will be considered as justified in the history of our people through an objective evaluation of its experi-

[1] Ibid., Vol. I, No. 142, p. 1065.

[2] *V.B.*, January 9, 1934.

ences and its antecedents. . . . There could be only one question of the age after the ruthlessly propagated lesson of the Marxist idea of equality had at length overcome the last protection of business by bourgeois politics, in order to give a death-blow to the political and economic ideology of the bourgeois period. . . .

"For fourteen years Germany suffered a collapse which was unparalleled in history. It effected an overturn of all values. What was good became bad, what was bad, good. The hero was despised and the coward honoured. . . . This could only lead to Communist chaos! . . . Victoriously, in this year, the life power of our people raised itself over the ruins. . . . Formerly one built new governments, but in a year we have forged a new people. . . ." [1]

The Chancellor expressed his gratification at the recent agreement with Poland; denied any aggressive intentions toward Austria; spoke of the "traditional" friendship with Fascist Italy; reiterated his demand for equality of rights; and pleaded for reconciliation with France through a negotiated settlement of the Saar question, "the only territorial question between the two countries." He made no reference to the Reich Reform Bill. It was rushed through three readings in less than five minutes and adopted by acclamation. The Reichsrat, meeting simultaneously, performed its last official act by adopting the bill unanimously and without discussion. Frick expounded the law over the radio on the following day:

"The historical task of our times is the creation of a strong national unitary State to replace the former Federal State. . . . The state governments from today on are merely administrative bodies of the Reich. . . . According to the so-called Enabling Act, the Reich government was empowered to make certain constitutional changes, but was at the same time restricted to some extent. . . . The law concerning the new structure of the Reich does away with these restrictions and gives the Reich government complete power to undertake constitutional reconstruction." [2]

Though no new Constitution was promulgated, this important piece of legislation for the *Neuaufbau des Reichs* may well be regarded as the decisive step in the liquidation of federalism and democracy. It was signed by Hitler, Frick, Hess, Göring, Röhm, Goebbels, Darré, Seldte, Papen, and the Statthalters:

[1] Ibid., January 31, 1934.
[2] Ibid., February 2, 1934.

"The plebiscite and the Reichstag elections of November 12, 1933 have proved that the German people has been blended into an indissoluble unity which has done away with all inner political barriers and differences.

"The Reichstag has therefore unanimously accepted the following law, which, with the unanimous consent of the Reichsrat, is herewith proclaimed, after it has been established that the requirements for legislation changing the Constitution have been complied with:

"Article 1. The popular representations of the states are abolished.

"Article 2. (1) The sovereign rights of the states are transferred to the Reich. (2) The state governments are subordinate to the Reich government.

"Article 3. The Statthalters are subordinate to the Reich Minister of the Interior.

"Article 4. The Reich government may determine new constitutional law.

"Article 5. The Reich Minister of the Interior issues the orders and regulations necessary to carry out the law.

"Article 6. This law goes into force on the day of its proclamation." [1]

Thus at one blow the state legislatures, the rights of the states and the Reichsrat were all abolished and the Cabinet was authorized to promulgate a new Constitution if it so desired. On February 5 Frick issued a decree abolishing state citizenship and establishing a single Reich citizenship. A law of February 14 abolished the Reichsrat and the legations of the states in Berlin. Meanwhile, by a presidential decree of February 3, the Statthalters were deprived of such independence as they might have exercised, by being placed under the orders of the Minister of the Interior, and the state Cabinets were made mere agents of the central government.

Germany thus became, at long last, a purely unitary State as well as an unlimited autocracy. The old *Länder* survived as administrative areas, but had even less autonomy than the Departments of France. Early in January 1935 Frick announced that they would be entirely abolished and replaced by twenty administrative districts. The Statthalters, like the French Prefects, were now agents of the Ministry of the Interior. But whereas in France and in other democratic unitary States the central executive authorities are answerable

[1] *R.G.B.*, 1934, Vol. I, p. 75.

to an elective parliament with powers to enact laws, grant or withhold funds, and support or overthrow the Cabinet, the central executives of the Third Reich are answerable only to Der Führer, who is answerable only to God.

Like other absolutist rulers, notably Napoleon III, Der Führer has asserted his responsibility to the people and resorted to more or less farcical popular referenda, offering the electorate no genuine choice of any kind. In the long perspective of history it is probable that the "new" Fascist State, for all its elaborate paraphernalia of propaganda and "co-ordination," will be regarded merely as a reversion to the State-form of absolute and arbitrary divine-right monarchy, save that it possesses none of the continuity of a hereditary dynasty and none of the stability of a hereditary ruling class. Continuity must be supplied by Der Führer. Stability must be supplied by the organized brotherhood of the party, sworn to blind obedience and completely at the mercy of the Leader. The capacity of such a régime to survive social and economic crises comparable to those which swept away States, governments, and social systems in much of central Europe between 1917 and 1922 remains to be demonstrated in the aftermath of the next general European war.

4. THE DICTATORS

During the first year of the Hitler régime the internal organization of the NSDAP underwent certain significant modifications. In every dictatorial one-party State the competition of organized groups for power and the fruits thereof necessarily assumes the form of rivalry among factions in the party. In democratic States the political process revolves about the efforts of interest groups to secure control of the law-making and executive machinery of government through electoral and parliamentary majorities. In dictatorships in which one political group destroys all its competitors, there are two possibilities: (1) the pressures of divergent-interest groups lead to armed conflict between the dictators and their enemies, since there are no pacific procedures of criticism and compromise available; or (2) they may be expressed and resolved within the party, either by means which are democratic in theory and purpose, as in the Communist Party of the U.S.S.R., or by means which are undemocratic, as in the Fascist States.

Both German and Italian Fascist spokesmen insist on unity, leadership, discipline, and obedience. There cannot be and must not be any factions or divergencies of interests within the party or within the nation. But even the most brilliant propagandists and the most ruthless terrorists of Fascism are quite incapable of annihilating class distinctions and destroying the rich diversity of interest groupings which necessarily develops in modern industrial societies. They can only seek to suppress the political manifestations of social forces and pressures. If all opposition outside of the party is destroyed, an "opposition" arises within the party, and the political process is resumed on this level.

The basic cleavage between the "Left" proletarian radicals and the "Right" bourgeois conservatives within the Nazi movement has already been considered in the period prior to the seizure of power. Following the expulsion of revolutionary rebels in 1930 and 1931, the potential conflict between the two groups became quiescent. The exuberance of the socialistic radicals was in part drained off in the spring of 1933 by numerous opportunities for sadistic gratifications: terrorization of enemies, persecution of Jews, burning of books, etc. The expectation was prevalent that the second stage of the revolution or the "Second Revolution" would assume the form of the establishment of Nationalsocialism—that is, of a collectivist economy in which the agrarian and industrial propertied classes would be deprived of many of their privileges, to the advantage of the lower middle classes, the small peasantry, and the proletariat. These elements within the party found no leader—for those close to Der Führer knew at all times that advocacy of social radicalism meant demotion, dismissal, or expulsion.

Nevertheless, many local party and S.A. leaders leaned Leftward. They attempted to utilize their positions in the movement, and particularly in the NSBO and the Labour Front, to interfere with private business, to coerce employers, and to promote socialization of industrial and commercial enterprises. The Reichsverband der Industrie was rudely *"gleichgeschaltet."* The directors were dismissed on April 6, 1933. Thyssen remained president, but was "assisted" by two party commissars under the direction of Dr. Otto Wagener, chief of the economic department of the NSDAP and later Economic Commissar for the Reich. Other organizations of employers and business men were likewise "co-ordinated." On May 26 Wagener was obliged to dissolve the Kampfbund of Nazi workers in industrial establishments and to warn party members against "wild interference" with business. Count Reventlow, Stoehr, the trade unionist, and Muchow, leader of the NSBO, were also prominently identified with the Left wing. The incipient conflict over Hugenberg's successor, in which the radicals sought to secure Wagener's appointment as Minister of Economics, was symptomatic of unrest in the party ranks. Party commissars in business establishments became more active and gave voice to the growing agitation for "true German socialism." So widespread was this sentiment that many observers in June could speak of the NSDAP "going Bolshevik" and discuss seriously the proposed revolutionizing of capitalistic economy.[1]

This latent struggle for ascendency between radicals and conservatives within the NSDAP was temporarily resolved in the summer of 1933 without an open conflict. Hitler and his immediate subordinates had always been committed to the maintenance of private property and the profit system and regarded the new dictatorship simply as the political corollary of the basic power patterns of capitalistic economy.[2] Minor leaders in the party could not be permitted to misconstrue the meaning of the revolution. Meddling with business and loose talk of "socialization" and of a "workers' State" could not be tolerated. Hitler began emphasizing the necessity for "discipline" in mid-April. In his address of May 10 to the Labour Front, he warned dissenters that no one class could place its interests above those of the nation. Labour had "duties" rather than rights. It was not until after the suppression of the political parties, however, that Hitler moved vigorously against the advocates of the "Second Revolution." On July 2, at a meeting of S.A. and S.S. leaders at Bad Reichenthal, he declared:

"I will crush brutally and ruthlessly every attempt made by reactionary or other circles to overthrow the present order. I will turn equally ruthlessly against the so-called Second Revolution, because that can have only chaotic consequences. Whoever rises in opposition to the Nationalsocialist State will be hit hard, wherever he is."[3]

On July 7 Hitler addressed the Reichsstatthalters:

"The Nationalsocialist Party is the State. . . . Now we must de-

[1] Cf. Calvin B. Hoover: *Germany Enters the Third Reich* (July 1933), pp. 137–41 and pp. 185 f.

[2] Cf. pp. 135–42 above.

[3] *The New York Times,* July 3, 1933.

stroy the last vestiges of democracy, especially the methods of taking votes and reaching decisions by majorities, such as are still being used in the municipal governments, in business organizations, and in committees. The responsibility of the individual personality must everywhere be brought to a new importance. . . . Revolution is no permanent condition; it must not turn into an enduring situation. The liberated stream of revolution must be directed into the secure river of evolution. . . . Ability alone must decide in business.

"History will not base her judgment of us on how many business men we have deposed and locked up, but on whether we were able to provide work. Today we have all the power necessary to enforce our will, but we must be able to replace deposed business men by better ones. The business man must be judged first of all by his ability, and we must naturally put the business machinery in order. . . . Business is based on primitive laws that are anchored in human nature. . . . Our task is work, work, and once again work. . . .

"The ideas of the program oblige us not to act like fools and upset everything, but to realize our trains of thought wisely and carefully. In the long run our political power will be all the more secure, the more we succeed in underpinning it economically. The Reich Commissioners must therefore see to it and are responsible that no organizations or party offices assume the functions of government, dismiss individuals, and make appointments to offices, to do which the government of the Reich alone is competent and, with regard to business, the Reich Minister of Economics." [1]

On July 11 Der Führer told the party leaders emphatically that the revolution was over and that no "Second Revolution" would be tolerated. The Reichsverband der Industrie simultaneously ordered its members to drop all pending plans for the integration of industry into the "corporative State." On the 13th Hitler reiterated his warnings once more.

"I capitulate only before reason. We have conquered the land, now we must cultivate it in peace. Our influence on business must depend on training economic leaders. We must create a synthesis between the idealism of Nationalsocialism and the realities of business." [2]

Minister of Economics Schmitt declared:

"The problems facing German business can be solved only by

[1] Cf. Pollock and Heneman, op. cit., pp. 76–8; *The New York Times,* July 8, 1933.

[2] *The New York Times,* July 14, 1933.

business itself—that is, by responsible leaders who have grown out of it. The State shall administer and, with its economic policy, provide leadership for business, but it cannot do business itself. Every attempt to socialize business is doomed to failure because of the human factor."

Action against the radicals was not limited to warnings. The Ministry of Economics was now in safe hands. Darré's agrarian radicalism could be rendered innocuous despite his appointment to the Cabinet. Gottfried Feder was appeased by appointment as Under-Secretary in the Ministry of Economics, but was given no real authority. (Later, in April 1934, he was "promoted" to the leadership of the new Reich Commissariat for Land Settlement, but this agency was to deal only with garden homes for workers near urban centres and had no jurisdiction over the peasantry.) Hitler discharged the business commissars of the party on July 13 and sent Wagener into retirement. He appointed as his party plenipotentiary in economic affairs Wilhelm Keppler, a conservative engineer and friend of Ernst Tengelmann, Göring's special "economic adviser." Tengelmann's father and brothers were directors of various Thyssen enterprises. Hans Frank told the public prosecutor: "Whoever speaks of continuing the revolution or of a second revolution must realize that he rebels against the Leader and must therefore be treated accordingly."

Muchow was "accidentally" shot to death in the Rhineland. Stoehr was demoted. The "Fighting League of the Trading Middle Class" was dissolved in July. The S.A. "auxiliary police" was disbanded on August 8. Rebellious S.A. men were expelled. Thousands were secretly arrested and sent to concentration camps. Not a single trust was nationalized. Not a single department store was municipalized. Not a single Junker estate was divided. On the contrary, Fritz Thyssen was appointed to various honorary and advisory posts, was made a kind of economic dictator in Westphalia, and was assisted in extending and consolidating his monopolistic grip upon west German industry, commerce, and finance.

Thus the socialistic illusions of the more radical petty-bourgeois and proletarian elements were dispelled. The conflict was not yet ended. But for the present, unity was restored. The unanimous enthusiasm of the party members and their blind devotion to their leaders were appropriately celebrated by a gigantic demonstration in Nürnberg during the first days of September. This first *"Partei-Tag"* since the seizure of power was impressively staged on an unprecedented scale. As in all congresses of the NSDAP, there was no discussion of problems or policies, no criticisms, no voting, no decisions—only orders from above and obedience from below. But there were drama, pageantry, music, marching, and oratory on a gargantuan scale. On August 30 some half a million people descended upon the picturesque old city from all corners of the Reich: 60,000 Hitler Jugend, 160,000 party officials, 200,000 S.A. and S.S. officers and men, countless thousands of visitors and camp-followers. Amid enormous banners, reams of bunting, myriads of standards, mountains of sausages, oceans of beer, and solemn festivities without end, the brown and black armies drilled, manœuvred, saluted, listened to speeches, honoured the dead, consecrated ten thousand flags, and paraded a hundred thousand strong through the mediæval streets in celebration of the "Congress of Victory."

Hitler spoke three times. On the final day, September 3, he delivered a long address to the multitudes. Amid a torrent of words there was little new. The old phrases, their efficacy as yet undimmed by time, thundered out over the throng: *Kultur*. Destiny. Loyalty. Salvation from Bolshevism and the Jewish ferment of decomposition. Blood and soil. Race. Sub-humanity. Apes. The sacredness of private property and private initiative:

"Either men are all of equal capacity to govern a State, in which case the maintenance of private property is not only an injustice but simply a stupidity. Or men are not really capable of taking over collectively the collective material and cultural inheritance of a nation as common property in a common administration, in which case they are still less capable of ruling a State collectively!"

Obedience. Leadership. Sacrifice. Courage. Faith. Heroism. Mad applause followed and then, as always, the *Horst Wessel Lied*. All who participated were reborn anew and exalted in the service of a holy mission.[1]

Where were the centres of power in this party of the dictatorship? [2] The intricately articulated structure of the party organization, adapted

[1] Cf. *V.B.*, September 1, 2, 3, 4, 1933.

[2] Cf. the suggestive analysis in Ernst Henri: *Hitler Over Europe*, pp. 41–73, in terms of five major groupings: the triumvirate, Hitler-Göring-Goebbels; the S.S. and the secret police; the S.A. of Röhm, Heines, Killinger; the Right capitalists—Thyssen, Schmitt, Keppler, Funk, and Schacht; and the Left radicals—Wagener, Stoehr, Muchow, Brückner, and Reventlow.

as well to wielding power after January 1933 as it had been to conquering the tools of power before the victory, became more complex than before. Its local organization remained substantially unaltered. Its central agencies in the Reichsleitung expanded to fulfil the new tasks imposed upon them. Martin Bormann and Rudolf Reiner became the staff leaders of Hess in the party office of Der Führer. A *Verbindungstab* was created (55 Wilhelmstrasse, Berlin) to coordinate the work of the party and of the public authorities. A Political Central Commission was established under Hess, with subcommissions to supervise party work in the state and local governments, to guide the party press and to deal with economic questions. The Political Organizations I and II were united, with Robert Ley displacing Gregor Strasser as staff leader and Paul Schulze disappearing from the scene. Under the PO were grouped the *NSBO,* the *NSHAGO,* the *NS Frauenschaft,* the *NS Beamtenabteilung,* and the *NS Kriegsopferversorgung*. The two *Reichspropagandaleitung* sections under Goebbels and Reinhardt were retained. The Reich Inspections I and II were abolished. The Agrarian Policy Office and the Legal Division, formerly under PO II, became separate sections under the old leaders.

Otherwise the central party organization remained unchanged,[1] save than an Office for Defence against Lies (*Lügenabwehrzentralstelle*) was established[2] and another new office was created—the *Aussenpolitisches Amt* (APA), headed by Alfred Rosenberg. Rosenberg's APA ("Foreign Political Bureau") was located at 70 Wilhelmstrasse, near the Foreign Office, and was designed to engage in espionage and propaganda work abroad. Epp's WPA (Defence Policy Bureau) had its main headquarters in Munich and a branch at 70 Wilhelmstrasse.[3] It occupies the same anomalous position with regard to the Reichswehrministerium as the APA does with regard to the Foreign Office. On June 13, 1934, the APA moved to larger quarters in Margarethenstrasse.

All party activities continued to be directed from the great Munich Brown House, reconstructed and enlarged in the spring of 1934. Here or in near-by buildings were located most of the central party agencies. The staff of the Adjutant of Der Führer worked here under

[1] Cf. pp. 67–9 above and *NS Jahrbuch, 1934,* pp. 133–8.
[2] *V.B.,* March 24, 1934.
[3] Ibid., March 28, 1934.

the command of Hess and directed by Martin Bormann, with supervisory powers over the Verbindungstab in Berlin. In the offices of the Verbindungstab worked Dr. Otto Dietrich, Reich Press Chief of the NSDAP, and Ernst Hanfstängl, Chief of the Foreign Press Division.[1] The Munich Staff (*Stab des Stellvertreters des Führers*) contained sections on Race, Public Health, and Population Policy; the NS Physicians' Society; the Race Policy Bureau (*Rassenpolitisches Amt der NSDAP* or RPA, formerly called the "Propaganda Office for Population Policy and Race Hygiene"), with local branches and subsidiary organizations throughout the Reich; the Examination Commission for the Protection of NS Literature, created by Hess April 16, 1934, and directed by Bouhler, with contacts with the Propaganda Ministry and power to pass upon the orthodoxy of all Nazi writings; the Office of the Trustee for Economic Questions, A. Pietzsch; and sundry other bureaus.[2] Also in the Brown House were the headquarters of *Reichsschatzmeister* Schwarz, charged by Hitler on March 23, 1934 with jurisdiction over all matters of property and finances of the NSDAP and its allied organizations, and of the Financial and Administrative Organization of the party, with its thousands of local offices, its elaborate bookkeeping and auditing agencies, its complete records of the party membership, its *Hilfskasse,* its *Reichszeugmeisterei,* supplying arms and equipment to the S.S. and the S.A.[3] Here, too, laboured Dr. Hans Frank's *Rechtsabteilung,* controlling the organizations of lawyers and jurists,[4] and the important Political Organization of the party.

The PO is perhaps the most significant of the many central agencies established in Munich. Like most of the other bureaus, it has evolved from an administrative agency of the NSDAP to a vast organization of control and co-ordination. It centralizes and integrates the activities of the NSBO, the NSHAGO, the NS Women's Organization, the organizations of public officials, and the various *Fachschaft* professional groups within the civil service. Each of its branches is in turn an agency of central control for a bewildering variety of sub-organizations. The *Amt für Beamte,* for example, controls the *Reichsbund der Deutschen Beamten,* embracing no less than nine hundred distinct organizations of civil servants. The Staff Leader of the *Amt*

[1] Ibid., April 14, 1934.
[2] Ibid., April 17 and April 25, 1934.
[3] Ibid., March 28 and April 28, 1934.
[4] Ibid., May 5, 1934.

controls fourteen sub-bureaus, of which one, the *Fachschaften,* consists in turn of fourteen agencies supervising various professional groups of public officials.[1] Through its bureaus the *Amt* is represented throughout the Reich by corresponding subordinate organizations in the *Gaue,* the *Kreise,* and the *Ortsgruppen* of the party. Thus every local civil servant in Germany belongs to the local branch of his particular organization, which is federated with others in the Reichsbund and is supervised in localities, in districts, in the states, and in the Reich as a whole, by the corresponding agencies of the *Amt,* which in turn is a branch of the PO, which is a segment of the *Oberste Reichsleitung* (OR) of the party, which finally is under Hitler's personal direction.

The pattern of these interrelationships can be suggested by noting the following circumstances: The staff leader of the PO, Robert Ley, is also leader of the Labour Front and of the NSBO. The chief for the *Amt für Beamte* leads the *Reichsbund der Beamten.* The chief of the PO Office for War Victims leads the *Reichsbund der Kriegsopfer.* The chief of the PO Office for Communal Policy leads the *Deutscher Gemeindetag,*[2] etc. The personnel offices of these organizations, moreover, are divisions of the *Personal-Amt* of the PO. Their organization officials are agents of the *Organisationsamt* of the PO. Their publicity and propaganda bureaus are branches of the PO *Reichsschulungsamt.* The sixteen labour groups in the *Arbeitsfront* are divisions of the NSBO. Or, to take another example: on June 2, 1934 the Subcommission for Technology of the Political Central Commission (the Engineering-Technical Division of the former PO II) was converted by order of Hess into a Bureau for Technique, headed by Gottfried Feder and placed directly under the PO of the OR. The *Kampfbund der Architekten und Ingenieure* was dissolved and displaced by a *"NS Bund Deutscher Technik"* (NSBDT), with the same officers as the new *Amt* and also controlled by the PO. In the future, only party members may belong to the NSBDT—that is, architects and engineers not belonging to the party are practically excluded from a career. Feder's aide, Dr. Todt, took over the leadership of the *"Reichsarbeitsgemeinschaft der technischwissenschaftlichen Arbeit"* (RTA). A party commission was appointed to create a Reich Chamber of Technique.[3]

[1] Ibid., March 1, 1934.

[2] *R.G.B.,* 1933, Vol. I, No. 142, p. 1065; cf. Ley's order in *V.B.,* March 29, 1934.

[3] *V.B.,* June 2, 1934.

It would scarcely be an exaggeration to say that every man, woman, and child in Germany belongs to one or more organizations, vocational, political, ecclesiastical, educational, or recreational, which is directed and controlled by an intricate hierarchy of governing agencies, reaching down to the smallest of little men in the smallest of hamlets and controlled from above, in the last analysis, by Der Führer himself. No "un-co-ordinated" organizations are tolerated. And in all organizations the *Führerprinzip* prevails—no election of officers, no discussion of problems, no decisions by democratic agreement, but arbitrary authority from the top down and unlimited responsibility and obedience from the bottom up. In this sense, at least, the "Totalitarian State" is a reality. The principle that party and State are one means not merely that the NSDAP monopolizes public offices, but that it controls completely every manifestation of social life among the sixty-five million inhabitants of the Third Reich. The elaborate local, intermediate, and central machinery whereby this miracle is accomplished is so incredibly complex that it could not be presented adequately in even the most elaborate set of diagrams, nor could it be fully described in many hundreds of pages. But the principle is simple: every German, not only in his role as a citizen, but in every possible role which he plays as a human being from the cradle to the grave, is subject to the will of Der Führer.

The party itself is thus the framework within which and around which the Totalitarian State has been created. It is the instrumentality through which Hitler governs the Reich more autocratically than the most arbitrary of ancient Oriental despots. The membership, which had grown to over a million and a half by February 1933, expanded to almost two millions by autumn, with about two million additional applicants. Membership was then closed, reopened for one week prior to the election of November 12, and then closed again. Some 3,900,000 persons held party cards in January of 1934. The carefully recruited and well-drilled Prætorian Guard, the black-uniformed *Schutzstaffel* (S.S.), expanded to perhaps 200,000 members by the close of 1933, while the S.A. grew to a brown army of 2,500,000 men, including "reserves." Röhm announced on November 6, 1933 that in the future the S.A. would be the sole recruiting agency for the party. While formerly party members often became storm troopers, while some storm troopers never became party members at all, in the future all S.A. men would become party members and the party would secure new recruits from no other source.[1] Shortly afterwards Stahlhelm members over thirty-five years of age became members of the S.A. Reserve I and those over forty-five of the S.A. Reserve II. On September 24, 1933, in an impressive ceremony near Hanover, Röhm had "welcomed" the Stahlhelm members into the S.A. On March 27, 1934, following an agreement between Röhm and Seldte, the Stahlhelm was reorganized as the "NS German Front Fighters' League."[2]

The Stahlhelm, however, retained its separate identity, and friction between its members and the storm troopers continued. There were likewise rivalries and jealousies between the S.S. and the S.A. and between these and party officials who belonged to neither the black-shirt nor the brown-shirt armies. These rifts were repeatedly denied, but the denials themselves furnished the best evidence of continued disharmony.[3] In this potentially hostile alignment the rank and file of the S.A. represented the radicalized lower middle class and proletariat which had been disappointed by Der Führer's repudiation of the Second Revolution in July 1933. They looked with suspicion upon the S.S. mercenaries, who represented conservative bourgeois and aristocratic elements sworn to serve Hitler even, if need be, against the S.A. itself.

In the spring of 1934 the *Oberste Reichsleitung* of the NSDAP—Hitler's "party cabinet"—consisted of the following leaders:[4]

Rudolf Hess, Adjutant to Hitler, Minister without portfolio, Director of the *Stab des Stellvertreters des Führers,* and of the Political Central Commission.

Ernst Röhm, Chief of Staff of the S.A., Minister without portfolio.

Heinrich Himmler, Chief of Staff of the S.S. and (after April 20, 1934) Chief of the Secret Political Police.

Franz Schwarz, Reich Treasurer of the party.

Philip Bouhler, Reich Business Manager of the party.

Walter Buch, Chairman of *Uschla.*

Wilhelm Grimm, Chairman of the Second Chamber of *Uschla.*

Robert Ley, Staff Chief of the PO, leader of the German Labor Front and of the NSBO.

Walter Darré, Director of the Agrarian Policy Bureau, Minister of

1 *Berliner Tageblatt,* November 6, 1933.
2 Text of order, *V.B.,* March 29, 1934.
3 Cf. Rudolf Hess: *"S.A. und S.S.," NS Monatshefte,* January 1934.
4 Cf. pp. 67–70 above; *NS Jahrbuch,* 1934, p. 134.

Agriculture and Food.

Joseph Goebbels, Reich Propaganda Director and Minister of Propaganda and People's Enlightenment.

Hans Frank, Director of the *Rechtsabteilung* and Reich Commissioner of Justice.

Otto Dietrich, Reich Press Chief.

Max Amann, Director of the Press Bureau.

Alfred Rosenberg, Director of the APA and (after January 24, 1934) "Dictator of Philosophy and Education."

Franz Ritter von Epp, Director of the WPA and Statthalter for Bavaria.

Baldur von Schirach, Reich Youth Leader.

Karl Fiehler, Secretary of the *NS Deutsche Arbeiterverein.*

The OR thus included all the directors of the eleven major divisions of the central party apparatus, plus Himmler, Dietrich, Schirach, Fiehler, and Grimm. Only four of its members (Hess, Röhm, Goebbels, and Darré) were members of the Reich Cabinet. And the only old Nazi members of the Reich Cabinet who were not members of the OR were Göring and Frick, though Bernard Rust, appointed Minister of Science, Instruction, and People's Education, April 30, 1934; Hans Kerrl, named Minister without portfolio in June 1934; and Schmitt and Seldte, belated Nazi converts, were also not in the OR.

German high politics under the dictatorship centres about the relationships between these leading personalities and between the various groups in the NSDAP. Hitler continued to labour in lonely glory at the apex of the new hierarchy. The pomp of power brought no relaxation. At 78 Wilhelmstrasse are his Chancellor's offices, simply and tastefully decorated and breathing an atmosphere of quiet discipline and work in orderly progress. Here toil twoscore officials, a score of employees, and as many labourers and flunkies. Dr. Lammers is Secretary of State to the Chancellor and Chief of Administration in the Reichskanzlei. *Gruppenführer* Brückner, Adjutant to the Chancellor, *Oberführer* Schaub, Adjutant and private secretary, and Dr. Meerwalt, personal referendary, are Lammers' immediate subordinates. In the centre and over all sits Der Führer at his desk, below a huge portrait of Bismarck and next to the work-chair of the "Iron Chancellor." Here he labours for hours on end, receiving visitors and conferring with leaders from all parts of the Reich and from every capital of the globe.

When not occupied in the Chancellery, Hitler is usually busy elsewhere in Berlin, Munich, or Neudeck with travels, speaking-engagements, and sundry ceremonies throughout the Reich. He continues to live like an ascetic Messiah—no tobacco, no alcohol, little meat, no women, few recreations. Dictatorship has become his vocation, his avocation, his life, his love, his whole existence. For rest he retires to his mountain retreat in Berchtesgaden in the Bavarian Alps, or listens to Wagnerian opera (he has heard *Die Meistersinger* over a hundred times), or requests Ernst Hanfstängl, court jester and pianist, to play for him in seclusion. "Putzy" (Hanfstängl's nickname at Harvard) plays preferably Beethoven or Wagner. Isolde's *"Liebestod"* from *Tristan* is a favourite selection of Der Führer—suggesting to him, perhaps, the passion of a love which he has never known and symbolizing the frustrations of omnipotence.

Hitler is, above all, the liaison between the NSDAP and the old élite, the link between the party and the allies which he used so skilfully for his purposes. His "workers'" party is connected through him on the one hand with Thyssen, Krupp, Flick, Voegler, and the whole aristocracy of industrialists and financiers, and on the other with the agrarian-military aristocracy of the Junkers and the Reichswehr: Papen, Neurath, Blomberg, et al. And, prior to August 2, 1934, he was the link with Hindenburg. Campaign posters in November 1933 showed them together—"The Marshal and the Corporal." The Old Gentleman had qualms at times over the policies of the Nazis, but they had learned the way to his heart. On August 27, 1933, he received another "gift": five thousand tax-free acres adjoining Neudeck, donated by the Prussian government.[1] "I am thinking with reverence, fidelity, and gratitude," he said, "of my Kaiser, my King and Lord, in this hour when I am thinking also of my fallen comrades-in-arms and when I proceed to thank you for this gift." But his sentimental nostalgia for the Hohenzollerns was unnecessary. Hitler served the Junkers as well as William II. And Hitler lost no opportunity to praise and glorify Hindenburg. In his last New Year's Day greetings to Der Führer the Old Gentleman declared:

"In this hour when we look back into the old year and forward into the new, I feel a deep need for thanking you with all my heart for what you have done for the German people and the Fatherland,

[1] *R.G.B.*, 1933, Vol. I, 95, p. 595. This law exempted the president and his male heirs (Oskar) from all payment of Reich and Prussian taxes on the enlarged estate.

and also you gentlemen of the Cabinet and all others who have collaborated within and outside the government in the work of reconstruction.

"May 1934 lead us further upward from the firm foundation won through our having come together in a united nation! Let us start this year with firm confidence in the future of Germany, in divine aid, and in the unity of work for our beloved Fatherland." [1]

In dealing with his immediate subordinates in the party, Hitler retained their loyalty by applying the Habsburg maxim: "Divide and Rule." He played off Goebbels against Göring, Himmler against Röhm, Schmitt against Darré, Frick against Rosenberg, and each against all the others. By a nice distribution of posts, powers, and honours, he strives to satisfy all and to compose differences of interest and ambitions. Each aspirant to ascendancy in his counsels is allowed considerable latitude. Only three things are not to be tolerated—defiance of his wishes, insubordination and intrigue against him, and social radicalism directed against the Junkers and industrialists. He holds himself aloof and keeps always close to him the quiet figure of Rudolf Hess, who, like Hitler, is conservative in all social and economic matters and is impartially critical of monarchist reactionaries and socialistic radicals.

The most powerful and ambitious politician in Hitler's immediate entourage is undoubtedly Hermann Göring, Premier and Minister of the Interior of Prussia, President of the Reichstag, Reich Minister of Air, Commander of the Prussian Police, head of the Prussian Secret Political Police, commander of the S.A. "Auxiliary Police" of 1933, founder and president of the Reichsluftschutzbund, etc. This burly, blond giant—sadistic, bellowing, swaggering, vindictive—is an incarnation of that brutality which he has always regarded as a virtue. His vanity is a source of innumerable anecdotes. He has had a special police station built in the garden of his Berlin residence to protect him from harm. Dozens of medals and scores of uniforms, some of his own design, adorn his wardrobe. His conceit and theatricality have led him on occasion to receive visitors in a blue velvet dressing-gown trimmed with ermine and with a lion cub following at his heels. Rumour credits him with having a Jewish mistress. Whether he still takes morphine is doubtful. Jealous of such colleagues as Goebbels and Rosenberg, who write brilliantly, he too has published

[1] *The New York Times*, January 1, 1934.

his book—clumsy in style and naïve in content: *Aufbruch einer Nation.*[1] He has reached out in all directions for power and more power. With his military fantasies and Napoleonic dreams, he opposed the absorption of Prussia into the Reich and sought to enter the Reichswehr as well as to secure command of the police, the S.A., and the Secret Police. His "Flyers' Corps" is another source of pride and power. He apparently envisages the great air fleet which he is building as the decisive offensive arm in the coming "war of liberation."

Göring's ambitions have undoubtedly caused Hitler himself occasional anxiety. He has not been a member of the Oberste Reichsleitung since the seizure of power. During the summer of 1933 a noticeable coolness developed between the two men. The precise reasons are obscure. According to one version, Göring demanded the rank of a general in the Reichswehr. This was granted to him in the form of a secret commission from Hindenburg—perhaps in return for the new Neudeck donation—but on the understanding that the commission should become effective only if an international crisis over German rearmament should require that the police, the S.A., and the army be more closely articulated. The crisis failed to materialize, but Göring's vanity caused him to announce his appointment regardless. It was granted on August 29. He became an Infantry General and secured one more uniform to wear. This, coupled with his efforts to use the Prussian police for his own purposes and his clashes with Goebbels over control of theatres and other cultural tools of propaganda, irritated Der Führer considerably. The abolition of the Prussian Landtag weakened Göring's position, though he was allowed to retain his new Staatsrat. He remains outside of the OR and yet has powers far greater than anyone in it. The abolition of the S.A. auxiliary police on August 8, 1933, however, deprived him of one of his favourite weapons. On April 20, 1934, his subordinate, Diels, resigned as head of the Prussian Secret Political Police and was, at Hitler's orders, replaced by Himmler, chief of the S.S., who now consolidated control of all of the state political police in his own hands. This was doubtless a precaution on Hitler's part against Göring and Röhm. Göring's position was further weakened on April 30, when he resigned as Prussian Minister of the Interior and was succeeded by

[1] Berlin: Mittler; 1934; English version: *Germany Reborn* (London: Mathews and Marrot; 1934).

Frick. On May 11 he yielded control of the administrative and criminal police to Kurt Daluege, Berlin police chief, named head of the new police department of the Reich Ministry of the Interior. Since "Bloody Saturday"—June 30, 1934—Göring has again succeeded to some degree in regaining the favour of Der Führer.

The diminutive cripple, Goebbels, is sometimes spoken of as the third member of a triumvirate, though Röhm might once have claimed the honour. Far more intelligent and astute than either Hitler or Göring, Goebbels has been contemptuous at least of the latter. As a master propagandist and dramatist, he has been indispensable to the party and has been content to do this one job well. He entered the Cabinet as head of the new Ministry of People's Enlightenment and Propaganda on March 15, 1933. He has no force at his immediate disposal, save the overwhelming force of his own cleverness in hypnotizing the masses. Toward Göring, Rosenberg, and Röhm he has never been cordial.

The stocky S.A. commander, bent upon monopolizing the party and the State for his own storm troopers, was in his way as ambitious as Göring. But he was less adaptable and even less successful in worming his way into the Reichswehr. His addiction to pederasty made Goebbels and Göring feel virtuous and superior. Röhm was surrounded by equally unscrupulous and dissolute lieutenants, holding high S.A. posts: Edmund Heines, Breslau police chief and S.A. commander for Silesia and the East; Paul Schulze, also a Feme murderer; Karl Ernst, S.A. commander in Berlin; Killinger, Pfeffer, Schneidhuber, and others. Victor Lutze, S.A. commander for western Germany, was a somewhat more respectable functionary, though of no particular prominence. Franz Ritter von Epp was also an S.A. man. As Statthalter for Bavaria, a member of the OR and head of the WPA, he was more powerful than any other S.A. commander save Röhm himself. But he was sixty-five years old on October 16, 1933—and far removed from the radical young libertines who basked in the warmth of Röhm's affection.

Between the S.A. group and the S.S. group, which are the antipodes of intra-party politics, stand other leaders not definitely in either the radical or the conservative camp. Göring is a moderate in social and economic matters, but belligerent and aggressive in the diplomatic and military field. Goebbels favours caution and delay in foreign affairs and no longer talks social radicalism. Both are wise enough to know that they can shine only in reflected light from Hitler. The radical Feder and the extremist Gregor Strasser, of doubtful loyalty, remained political nonentities during 1933–4. The radical Wagener was retired; Darré was rendered innocuous, despite his occasional wild talk (for peasant consumption) about dividing the Junker estates. Schmitt, Rust, Frank, Kerrl, and Seldte are definitely conservative. Frick had once been a radical, but now was safely tamed. Robert Ley, while pushed toward radicalism by his *Arbeitsfront,* is also "safe," since his interest is primarily in drinking and in advancing the fortunes of Robert Ley. The latter interest can be served by following blindly the teetotaler, Hitler.

Alfred Rosenberg, philosopher and anti-Semite *par excellence,* is too concerned with racial mysticism, Nordic imperialism, the crusade against Bolshevism, and his beloved *Weltanschauung* to care very much whether social radicals or conservatives rule the Nazi roost. He remained editor of the *V.B.* and a member of the OR. On April 20, 1933, he was honoured by being made head of the new APA. Whatever ambitions he may have had toward the post of Minister of Foreign Affairs were doomed by his rabid anti-Sovietism and by the almost universal demonstration of popular disgust which he evoked in England during his mission of mid-May 1933. On January 24, 1934, he was appointed by Hitler "supervisor of the whole spiritual and *weltanschaulichen* schooling and education" of the party and all its subordinate organizations.[1]

On the extreme Right, close to Hitler and identified with Junker and industrialist interests, stands the mercenary army of the S.S., which has evolved out of Hitler's personal body-guard. This force was expanded rapidly in 1933–4 as a counterweight to the radical mass army of the S.A. Its leaders occupy many key positions. Its chief, Himmler, united his forces with the Secret Political Police in April 1934. Hess, Dietrich, Amann, Darré, and Daluege are also S.S. men. In the spring of 1934 this was the force held in reserve by Hitler for use, if necessary, against any possible recrudescence of socialistic radicalism and S.A. insubordination. If the cleavage between Left and Right should ever lead to a serious intra-party crisis, the S.S. could be relied upon to do its work swiftly and efficiently. It would ensure the continued domination of the NSDAP and of the Third Reich by the defenders of the social élite and of monopolistic capitalism.

[1] *V.B.,* February 2, 1934.

BOOK TWO

THE WEAPONS OF POWER

CHAPTER VII

THE USES OF VIOLENCE

1. POLITICAL SADISM

IT HAS long since become a truism to say that the history of human government, secular and ecclesiastical, is in large measure the history of man's inhumanity to man. The hands of rulers have almost invariably been red with the blood of their victims, for the killing of critics has ever been the simplest and most immediately efficacious way of disposing of opposition. So sweet are the fruits of power and so insistent are the imperatives of politics that in almost all cultures the assumption has been tacitly accepted that those who act in the name of the State may legitimately transgress all laws of God and man in their treatment of their enemies. The public administration of "justice," moreover, has ever sanctified the commission of acts which are banned by morality and prohibited by law in private interpersonal relations. As in war, the unrestrained expression of elemental id-drives becomes not only permissible but noble. Helpless victims are branded as public enemies. Prosecutors, judges, jail-keepers, and executioners become respected custodians of the public welfare. Unlike soldiers, hangmen are not quite of the stature of "heroes," but they are honoured and indispensable public servants. Frequently the public is treated to the vicarious sadistic and masochistic thrill of being permitted to view the last agonies of the condemned. In this fashion the psychic satisfactions derived by torturers and axmen from the practice of their profession are shared by the whole community. All onlookers are exalted by participating in solemn acts of justice—and frightened into submissiveness by direct knowledge of what awaits them should they, too, become law-breakers.

The use of terror and brutality by the dictatorship of the NSDAP does not distinguish it from other régimes. The form of the Nazi terror, however, differs in a number of important respects from other recent or contemporary counterparts. Generally speaking, mass terrorism has been resorted to by ruling classes in modern times only to safeguard a régime from imminent danger of destruction or to paralyze and wreak vengeance upon those who have temporarily succeeded in depriving an élite of its property and power. The "Reign of Terror" in the French Revolution began when foreign invasion and internal revolt, engineered by the former privileged classes, threatened to bring about the overthrow of the revolutionary régime. The slaughter of the Paris Communards of 1871 followed a bloody civil war in which an embittered and pitiless bourgeoisie triumphed over a rebellious and ruthless proletariat. In the Russian Revolution, the "Red Terror," as a procedure of systematic and indiscriminate massacre of the former propertied classes, was inaugurated only after Uritsky and Volodarsky had been assassinated, Lenin had been shot, and the Soviet had been assailed from all points of the compass by domestic insurrection and foreign invasion. The "White Terror" was the tool of the former ruling classes to punish their expropriators and regain their privileges. The savage mass persecution of Communists, Socialists, Jews, and workers by the Hungarian terrorists of Horthy in 1919 followed upon a temporarily successful Bolshevist revolution.

These extenuating circumstances, if they be such, have not been present in Germany, nor in any other Fascist dictatorship. The beatings and murders of Marxists in Italy in 1922–5 and the slaughter of Vienna workers in February 1934 were acts of frightened and sadistic ruling groups who were at no time seriously threatened by foreign war or by organized revolutionary opposition. The victims of terror in the Third Reich have not been members of menacing opposition groups. Liberals bent their necks to the Nazi yoke without a murmur. Social Democracy was putty before Hitler's knife. Communism was almost equally helpless. The NSDAP did not save Germany from an imminent Communist revolution, nor did it at any time encounter opposition from the KPD of such a character as to threaten its firm grip on the machinery of government. The allegation that Nazi ruthlessness prevented Communist revolt is unconvincing. Communism, like liberalism and Social Democracy, collapsed from forces within itself. The Nazi revolution, to the disgust of Spengler and of many of the storm troopers, was a victory won against enemies who could not or would not lift a finger in their own defence. There were no strikes, no street fighting, no barricades, no rebellions, no assassinations of public officials, no foreign war, no visible threat of any kind to the undisputed authority of the dictators. And yet there was a terror.

As a result of these circumstances the Nazi terror assumed a peculiar character all its own. The frequently boasted bloodlessness of the revolution was due to no lack of ruthlessness on the part of the leaders of the NSDAP, but only to the fact that no organized groups exposed themselves to danger. In no recorded instance did even a dozen Communists (or a thousand—courage is easier in crowds) take up arms or act concertedly against the Nazis. There were no mobs to shoot down and no victims for mass executions. This situation was a tribute not to Nazi mercy, but to the genius of the propagandists who had so completely demoralized the enemy and to the Nazi leaders who took such care that every conceivable agency of coercion should be in their hands. Hungry men in rags, who have had all fight taken out of them by the insidious pressure of mass suggestion and by betrayal at the hands of their own leaders, do not defy automatics and machine-guns in the hands of police, storm troopers, and soldiers.

The terror, therefore, was less a political weapon against foes than a channel for the discharge of the long-accumulated aggressions of the many botched and bungled personalities who had flocked to the swastika banner. These men and their highest leaders, unlike many terrorists (cf. Fouchet, Djerzhinsky, Noske, and even Horthy), had long extolled brutality and bloodshed as virtuous. Their psychic insecurities, their neurotic guilt-feelings, their intolerable sense of inferiority and oppression compelled them to worship "strength," to confound strength with symptoms of its absence, and to seek scapegoats for their woes. The sadism of many S.A. men sprang from the same sources as anti-Semitism, anti-pacifism, anti-rationalism—and the cult of war, heroism, and endless goose-stepping. These men had been punished—wounded, tormented, twisted, and warped by the unkind forces of defeat, depression, and collapse. Where there is punishment, there must be sin and guilt, for God, after all, is just. Guilt demands expiation. The pattern leads in two possible directions: to abject humiliation, masochistic asceticism, sackcloth and ashes to appease the wrath of the Almighty; or to the transfer of the guilt to others and the sadistic infliction of punishment on scapegoats. The liberals and Socialists of Weimar took the first road, the Nationalists and reactionaries the second.

Once "war guilt" was repudiated, reason suggested that the victors of 1918 and the makers of Versailles were the authors of Germany's ills. Rational behaviour would aim at a "war of liberation" in which the vanquished should become victors. This motif was ever present in the NSDAP, as in other nationalist circles. But the victors were too powerful to be attacked. Rage must vent itself irrationally elsewhere. Nazi terrorists tortured and killed literally for the sake of torturing and killing—that is, for the subjective satisfactions, the inner release of tensions which these activities afforded. Every terror tends to bring into positions of power men of this type. But the NSDAP was organized and led by such personalities. Terrorism was not a political necessity, but a psychological compulsion. The victims were but incidental instruments of self-gratification upon whose bodies inverted Nazi egoism could recover sanity and security.

This thesis can be abundantly supported by a consideration of the personality structures of many of the Nazi leaders. Der Führer and his aides did not personally indulge in torturing and killing. For them vicarious gratification sufficed—for the frustrated, embittered, and latently homosexual Hitler; for the brutalized drug victim, Göring; for the crippled and disappointed literary hack, Goebbels; for the pederast Röhm; for the émigré Rosenberg; for the half-blind Himmler; for the wounded Hess. These pathetic victims of the traumas of the trenches and of the physical and psychic lesions of post-war collapse became symbols of national frustration and neurosis. Their subordinates were often criminals and perverts for whom vicarious sadism was insufficient. Such men as Paul Schulze and Edmund Heines were confessed murderers. Count Helldorf and scores of other *Gauleiters* and *Gruppenführers* were social outcasts seeking revenge on a society which had denied their importance. Manfred von Killinger, later Nazi Premier of Saxony, boasted of how he had ordered a Communist agitator torn to pieces by a hand-grenade during the suppression of the Munich Soviet and how he had had a girl horsewhipped until she was bloody and unconscious.[1] The rabid Nürnberg fanatic Julius Streicher is equally in his glory when he can accuse rabbis of sucking blood from Aryan babies and can himself

[1] *Ernstes und Heiteres aus dem Putschleben,* pp. 13–15.

gratify his bestiality upon his victims:

"I went with several party members into Steinruck's cell [Dr. Steinruck, whom Streicher had taken into 'protective custody'] and took a look at the wretch. He began to talk with a weeping voice and acted like a schoolboy. He did not act like the man one expected after his big talk. Thereupon I gave him a good beating with my whip." [1]

Such attitudes and patterns of behaviour are by no means exceptional among the outstanding figures of the NSDAP, to say nothing of the rank and file of the S.A. and S.S. They manifested themselves in the spring of 1933 in a widespread campaign of sadism and terrorization. The terror was curiously secretive and underground, with apparently no particular plan and no publicity. To the superficial observer, life in German cities went on as before, serene and undisturbed in its smug complacency. There were no mass executions and no official admission at any time that any terror existed. Rumours whispered from mouth to mouth were more effective than proclamations. Actual killings were kept at a minimum, since a victim who was only tortured could live to be tortured again, whereas there was nothing to do with a corpse save bury it. Stories of mutilation and torment, moreover, instil more fear than tales of simple death.

Any effort here to detail the thousands of scattered episodes which constituted the terror would be pointless. The basic facts are well authenticated.[2] Only the general pattern need be suggested. Ordinarily the victim was arrested late at night by storm troopers who broke into his home; he was sometimes beaten at once in the presence of his family and sometimes dragged off immediately and not heard of for days or weeks. Amid curses and blows he was taken to some concealed basement dungeon, offering no evidence to passers-by of its function. He was here often obliged to run a gauntlet of S.A. men armed with whips or sticks. He was then questioned and compelled, if possible, to divulge the names and whereabouts of his "confederates" and made to pray, *"Heil Hitler!"* or sing the *Horst Wessel Lied*. Next followed, in many cases, his transfer to a near-by room, where, in a half-light, he beheld bruised and bleeding bodies thrown on straw, stinking of blood and sweat, and heard the groans of those who had preceded him. Sometimes he was told that he would be

1 Public address in Nürnberg, October 14, 1934, as reported in *The New York Times*, October 15, 1934.

2 See the hundreds of documented cases in *The Brown Book of the Hitler Terror* (New York: Knopf; 1933).

shot immediately or at dawn. More frequently the victim was stood up against a wall and fired upon by S.A. men, who took care, however, not to wound him too seriously. Then followed castor oil and prolonged pommelling on tables with fists, boots, clubs, or whips. When reduced to unconsciousness, the guest was revived with pails of cold water and beaten again.

The more delicate forms of torture, employing hot irons, racks, thumb-screws, and other mechanical devices, were usually eschewed in favour of those requiring violent physical exertion on the part of the administrators. Healthy exercise furnishes a more adequate release for tensions than mere passive contemplation, however enjoyable, of the torments of the condemned. At the end the victim might be thrown out into the street, sent to a jail or concentration camp, or transferred to a hospital or morgue, depending upon his condition and the fancy of his captors. Sometimes he came back to his family a broken wreck, sometimes he never reappeared.

Only in rare instances was any opposition encountered. To cite one, on June 21, 1933, S.A. men twice searched the house of the trade-union secretary Schmaus, in Köpenick (Berlin). During the night they came again, arrested Schmaus's son-in-law, and fired shots. Schmaus's son returned the fire and mortally wounded two storm troopers. The rest then shot the son-in-law, arrested the son and beat him to death, and so abused the mother that she died shortly afterwards. The father was found hanged a day later.[1] That night numerous Marxists were arrested in the neighbourhood, including Johannes Stelling, Socialist member of the Reichstag, Reichsbanner leader, and former Premier of Mecklenburg. All were beaten almost to insensibility. Stelling's mutilated body, sewn up in a sack, was later fished out of the Finow Canal. A dozen other men were done to death in similar fashion.[2]

This technique, or variants of it, was perfected by long practice.[3]

[1] *V.B.* and *Berliner Tageblatt,* June 22–3, 1933, with of course only a bare account of the shooting and "suicide."

[2] *The New York Times,* July 29, 1933.

[3] "It was a fascinating though fearful thing to observe the growth of this atmosphere of terror. The writer had previously had the experience of living in a land where terror was well established and a normal part of life. But here he was to see terror develop and to observe it lay its hand on men. Trotsky, the advocate of the theory of 'Permanent Revolution,' has said that revolutions destroy men. Never were truer words spoken, if one speaks of revolutions with a concomitant of terror. For terror does indeed consume the characters of men. One of the commonest of human reac-

It was followed by trials and by death sentences against numerous Communists. A study of recorded cases suggests that executions by judicial command got under way on an extensive scale in the summer and autumn, whereas sporadic beatings and murders were more numerous in the spring. In Prussia and in some other states beheading was substituted for hanging, on the ground that the broadax was the ancient German mode of inflicting the death penalty. The new skill was not always acquired immediately by the executioner:

"The *Mittagszeitung* (Vienna) publishes an alleged detail eyewitness account of the execution of six Communist workmen condemned for a murder in the courtyard of Klingelpeutz Prison in Cologne on November 30. The guillotine, the usual instrument of execution in the Rhineland, which owes most of its legal system to the Code Napoléon, has been abolished as un-German and has been replaced by the mediæval executioner with his ax. At dawn, according to the account, the six condemned men, with shaven heads, were led to a table beside the scaffold where the public prosecutor sat and he told them that His Excellency General Göring had refused a pardon. All the accused protested their innocence and said they were victims of perjury by Nazi witnesses at their trial. They declared it was not they but Nazis who had been the aggressors last February when the Nazi for whose death they had been sentenced was killed. The executioner beheaded each of the first three men with one blow of his ax. Then he appeared to lose his nerve. Three blows were necessary to decapitate the fourth, and two for the fifth. The last, however, was beheaded with one blow." [1]

These are but random episodes out of hundreds reported. Beheading was but one means of dispatching "enemies of the State." Another technique which was widely employed, even under the republic, was the simple murder of prisoners later reported to be "suicides" or "shot trying to escape." On March 12, 1933, at Felgeleben, near Magdeburg, the Socialist Councillor Kresse was arrested

---

tions to it is the attempt to save one's soul from the consciousness of submission to force by trying to identify oneself in some way with the power which exercises the terror. Thus the Nationalists were to attempt to build a bridge for conscience to National Socialism by saying to themselves that after all it was strongly nationalist. Socialists and even Communists tried to build the bridge for their conscience by telling themselves that after all it was socialist."—Calvin B. Hoover: *Germany Enters the Third Reich,* p. 119.

[1] *The New York Times,* December 9, 1933.

by the police and, after an altercation, shot through the head ("suicide") by S.A. men.[1] Another man, found burned to death in a barrel of tar, was also reported a "suicide."[2] On April 4, 1933, the Communist official Heinz Bäsler was arrested in Düsseldorf and killed "while seeking to escape."[3] On March 6, 1933, a working woman of Selbe, Bavaria, the mother of two children, was accosted in the street by an S.A. man and fatally shot through the throat. Her son and her husband were arrested. Otto Eggerstedt, war veteran, former police chief of Altona and Socialist member of the Reichstag, was shot to death on October 16, 1933, by frontier guards after fleeing the Kapendorf concentration camp. On February 1, 1934, four Communists, including John Scheer, deputy in the Prussian Landtag, were escorted by Secret Police from Berlin to Potsdam after Alfred Kattner, star witness of the prosecution against Ernst Thälmann, had been murdered by an unidentified assailant. All four were killed "while trying to escape."[4] On March 28, 1934, Dr. Ludwig Marum, Jewish-Socialist lawyer and former Minister of Justice in Baden, was found hanged in his cell. "A good job," commented Streicher's *Der Stürmer* (April 26, 1934).

There were, of course, many actual suicides in concentration camps, and a large number outside. On a single day, May 6, 1933, the following notables took their lives: Ernst Oberfohren; the Mayor of Leer; a democratic alderman of Stuttgart; Frau Nellie Neppach, woman tennis champion of Germany, who had brooded over the effects of the Aryan clause on her friends; Frau Katz (Scheidemann's daughter) and her husband. Hitler in his speeches has referred frequently to the large number of suicides under the republic, but has made no compilation of the number of persons driven to self-destruction by Nazi persecution. During the first quarter of 1934 suicides in large cities increased 7.1 per cent over the corresponding period of 1933, and in towns of less than fifty thousand inhabitants they increased 14.5 per cent. In March 1934 the American National Committee to Aid Victims of German Fascism published figures compiled by a Paris group presided over by André Gide. According to this estimate, 67 political prisoners were officially executed between January 1 and October 1, 1933; 3,000 more were murdered, 119,000

[1] TU Dispatch, March 14.
[2] *V.B.*, April 25, 1933.
[3] *Der Angriff*, April 5, 1933; cf. *Brown Book*, pp. 313–16.
[4] *Börsen Zeitung*, February 2, 1934.

were wounded and 174,000 were jailed. These estimates were declared in Germany to be so "senseless" and obviously "hateful" that no reply to them was necessary.[1]

That scores of thousands have been arrested admits of no doubt. Some have been tried and sentenced to jail. Others, without trials and often without charges, have been incarcerated in concentration camps. The victims ranged from simple workmen and peasants to former chancellors of the republic. On June 29, 1933, Gustav Bauer, Chancellor in 1919–20, was arrested for "emblezzlement." Five of Scheidemann's relatives were imprisoned about the same time, in retaliation for articles which he had written abroad. Again, random samples from thousands of cases are illuminating. On September 8, 1933, Johannes Gommert, a labourer, was sentenced to five years in prison for making disparaging remarks about the Nürnberg convention. On September 18, 25 Communists were arrested in Wanne-Eickel and 76 in Lauterberg and vicinity. In Harburg-Wilhelmsburg two thousand houses were searched by the police, and many "Communists" arrested. In mid-November an instructor at the University of Giessen, who had joined the S.A., was sent to a concentration camp for making critical remarks; two Jewish merchants of Beueren were incarcerated "for their own protection from threatening villagers"; and two travellers who expressed a desire to go to Russia, "where things are better," were sent to a camp. On January 16, 1934, Ludwig Renn, author, was sentenced by the Supreme Court to thirty months' imprisonment for "preparing high treason." In February Lieutenant Richard Scheringer, former Nazi and later a Communist, was arrested in Munich and sent to jail. A Saxon court early in March sentenced 39 Socialists to jail for from six months to two years for circulating copies of the new *Vorwärts,* published in Prague. At the same time the wife and nineteen-month-old daughter of Gerhart Seger, Socialist Reichstag member who escaped to Czechoslovakia from the Oranienburg concentration camp, were sent to a camp near Dessau pending the surrender of the fugitive. They were later released under pressure from members of the British Parliament.

The "concentration camps" have from the beginning been a conspicuous feature of the Nazi penal system. In June 1933, perhaps forty thousand out of a possible total of sixty thousand political

[1] *V.B.,* March 27, 1934.

prisoners were held in camps in "protective custody." There were some forty-five such camps in the summer of 1933, or perhaps as many as a hundred, according to some estimates. Prisoners were ordinarily divided into categories of "harmless," "convertible," and "inconvertible." The first two groups, while obliged to live in primitive barracks and to engage in hard labour and military drill on scant rations, are usually not maltreated. The remainder are often victims of sadistic S.A. guards. Most prisoners are sent to camps for an indefinite term and released when they have been "converted" or are regarded as no longer dangerous. There is good reason to believe that in the autumn of 1933 and again in the summer of 1934 a large proportion of the prisoners in many camps were insubordinate storm troopers.

Official statements regarding the camps have been contradictory and unreliable. In reply to a report that a hundred thousand political prisoners were under restraint in Germany, the Prussian government announced in July 1933 that there were 18,000 prisoners in the entire Reich, of whom 12,000 had been arrested by the Prussian State Secret Police. In October it was asserted that 22,000 offenders were being held. On March 1, 1934, the Secret Police announced that the number had been reduced to 7,500. On March 9, 1934, Rudolf Diels told the Foreign Press Association that some 30,000 persons had passed through the camps, of whom 9,000 remained, including 200 women. He declared that at first most of the prisoners were Socialists and Communists, but that more recently monarchists were appearing in greater numbers. The work of "conversion" had progressed favourably. "We had intended maintaining the camps for ten years. Now I believe we shall be able to liquidate them in two years." On April 21 Göring declared that the number of political prisoners was 6,000 or 7,000. Thus, within seven weeks, official estimates of the number of inmates ranged from 6,000 to 9,000. A thirty per cent margin of error is too great to admit of any of these figures being trustworthy.

In any case, the tempo of terrorism was gradually relaxed between June 1933 and June 1934. On August 15 the S.A. auxiliary police, which had been largely responsible for the more brutal forms of violence, was disbanded. Many prisoners in concentration camps were freed in the autumn. The number of camps was sharply reduced—in Berlin from fourteen in June to two in October: Oranienburg and Sonnenburg. Some 5,000 prisoners, including Paul Löbe, were released early in December. Karl Severing and Fritz Ebert, Jr., not only were released, but had their pension rights restored. In March 1934 the Sonnenburg camp was "closed," and it was announced that only 2,800 prisoners remained in the Prussian camps, though Göring gave a figure for political offenders almost twice as high a month later, suggesting that many individuals in camps had been transferred to prisons. In April the mistreatment of prisoners was forbidden and certain guards were even punished for their sadistic proclivities. On September 1, 1934, Göring released 742 prisoners in Prussia and "abolished" the Oranienburg concentration camp. In the future, it was said, political prisoners would be tried by the regular civil courts, though "exceptionally dangerous" individuals might still be placed in "protective custody." It appears improbable that the types of repression characteristic of the early months of the dictatorship will again be resorted to. In future crises more drastic measures not involving torture and imprisonment are likely to be taken. The Oranienburg and Sonnenburg camps, however, are still functioning as S.S. camps. In October 1934 the Prussian Ministry of Justice announced that the total number of prison inmates had increased from 32,525 in 1931 to 56,928 in 1933. The average daily number of prisoners in camps during 1933 was set at 18,000.

While enemies were being punished, friends were rewarded. All imprisoned Nazis, save those under sentence for "private" crimes, were released in the spring of 1933. Even the vicious Potempa murderers were pardoned by Hitler on March 19. The assassins of Erzberger were pardoned on April 10, since the new *Weltanschauung* made the murder of republican leaders a virtue. The slayers of Rathenau, unfortunately, were dead. But they were nevertheless honoured. On July 17, 1933, at Saalek Castle in Thuringia, where they had committed suicide, a memorial tablet was dedicated: "Here died, fighting for Germany, July 17, 1922, our comrades, Naval Lieutenant Erwin Kern and Lieutenant Hermann Fischer of the Ehrhart Brigade."

Captain Ehrhart himself unveiled the tablet, amid impressive ceremonies attended by throngs of S.A. and S.S. men, as well as by many civilian patriots. Röhm praised the "glorious deed" of the assassins, and Himmler asserted: "Without the deed of these two, Germany today would be living under a Bolshevist régime. Let it be realized that, irrespective of civil law, neither one's own nor other's blood must be spared when the Fatherland's fate is at stake." [1] Of other's blood the S.S. leader had never been sparing. He was to be even less so in the future.

2. THE TOOLS OF TERROR

WHILE much of the terrorism of 1933 represented the sporadic and unsystematized activities of storm troopers, the German passion for *Ordnung* and Hitler's passion for "legality" required that measures of repression be dignified with the forms of law and that governmental agencies be expressly authorized to act against "enemies of the State." Nazi legislation directed against political offenders is far too large in sheer bulk to be reviewed here. But it may be noted that the more important federal decrees began by authorizing the Minister of the Interior to prohibit political meetings and to impose fines and prison sentences for parading or wearing uniforms other than S.A., S.S., and Stahlhelm. The suppression and confiscation of printed matter was also authorized.[2] The memorable Article 48 was invoked after the Reichstag fire to justify the suppression of all personal liberties and the substitution of the death penalty, with confiscation of property, for life imprisonment.[3] On March 21 penalties were provided for the unauthorized wearing of uniforms and for the circulation of statements harmful to the régime.[4] On October 13 life imprisonment was provided for incitements or attempts to kill officials, judges, jurors, soldiers, sailors, policemen, members of the S.A., S.S., Stahlhelm, and the Luftsportverband, and also for the circulation abroad or introduction into the Reich of treasonable printed matter.[5] Other laws authorized the confiscation of property

[1] *The New York Times,* July 18, 1933.

[2] *R.G.B.,* 1933, Vol. I, No. 8 (February 4), p. 35.

[3] Ibid., Vol. I, No. 17 (February 28), p. 83: "Restrictions of personal liberty, of the right of free expression of opinion, including freedom of the press, of association, and of assembly, interference with letters, mail, telegraph and telephone secrets, orders to search houses and to confiscate as well as restrict property beyond existing legal limits are permissible. . . . The crimes which under the Criminal Code are punishable with penitentiary for life are to be punished by death, i.e., high treason, poisoning, arson, explosions, floods, damage to railroad properties, and general poisoning." Death, life imprisonment, or incarceration for fifteen years was also provided for attempts on the life of public officials, for rioting or disturbing the public peace with arms, and for political kidnapping.

[4] *R.G.B.,* 1933, Vol. I, No. 24, p. 135.

[5] Ibid., Vol. I, No. 112, p. 723.

of public enemies, first of Communists [1] and later of Socialists and others.[2]

Repressive legislation was enforcible by the regular police and the ordinary courts. But the traditions of German police authorities and judges were not such as to ensure the desired degree of terror. Emergency courts were established in March 1933. Göring strove mightily to instil severity into his Prussian police. He expelled all Socialists and liberals from the force and supplemented it with the auxiliary S.A. police. He made energetic efforts to ensure that "barbaric ruthlessness" promised by Der Führer. On March 10, at a meeting in Essen, he said: "I would rather shoot a few times too short or too wide, but at any rate I would shoot." For all shootings he assumed full responsibility. "If you call that murder, then I am a murderer. Everything has been ordered by me. . . . It was only natural that in the beginning excesses were committed. It was natural that here and there beatings took place; there were some cases of brutality." [3]

But since the regular police were not sufficiently addicted to "naturalness" and brutality, and since even the purged IA (political) police division was still useless for his purposes, Göring created on April 27 a new "State Secret Police" (*Geheime Staatspolizei* or *Gestapo*). The new agency was placed directly under Göring's control, with its headquarters in Berlin.[4] Rudolf Diels, though not a Nazi, became head of the *Gestapo*. He was vice-president of the Berlin police department and under Severing had specialized in rooting out Communist activities. The *Gestapo* functioned efficiently throughout the spring and summer and became one of the pillars of Göring's personal power. On December 1, 1933, it was made an independent branch of the Prussian administration. Göring henceforth supervised it in his capacity of Prussian Premier, not as Prussian Minister of the Interior. Diels became "Inspector" of the *Gestapo* and head of the new office. All local police were made subject to his orders.[5] In April 1934 Diels tendered his resignation—because of "ill health," though

[1] Ibid., Vol. I, No. 55 (May 26), p. 293.

[2] Ibid., Vol. I, No. 81 (July 14), p. 479. Translations of these decrees are to be found in J. K. Pollock and H. J. Heneman: *The Hitler Decrees.*

[3] Hermann Göring: *Germany Reborn,* pp. 125 and 129.

[4] *P.G.S.,* 1933, No. 29, p. 122.

[5] Ibid., No. 74, p. 413: "To the sphere of activities of the State Secret Police belongs all business of the political police which was taken care of by the officials of the general and internal administration. The particular functions to be taken over by the State Secret Police are left to the decision of the Premier."

possibly because of friction with dissident S.A. leaders whom he was called upon to watch for evidences of treasonable activities.[1] He became head of the government of Cologne.

On April 20, 1934, the *Gestapo* was co-ordinated with the S.S. by the appointment of Heinrich Himmler as leader of all the Prussian political police. At the same time Göring united all the political police forces of the various states under Himmler's direction.[2] The new chief had been a soldier, a freebooter, a member of the Reichskriegsflagge, and a participant in the putsch of 1923. He declared that the members of his force must regard themselves as soldiers. "There are still thousands and tens of thousands who remain enemies, even though they raise their arms and are *gleichgeschaltet*. . . . Our task is heavy, but in confidence of our victory we shall proceed with our work in faith and comradeship. Be assured, Herr Ministerpräsident, that we shall do our duty to the end." [3]

In spite of the general disposition of German courts to serve the political purposes of the dictatorship, there was increasing dissatisfaction among party leaders with the administration of justice. Vestiges of impartiality apparently remained. The decision of the Supreme Court in the Reichstag fire trial was denounced in the Nazi press as a gross miscarriage of justice. Since all of the defendants were Communists, they should obviously have been beheaded on general principles. Even more serious was the action of the court on March 2, 1934. For technical reasons, it overruled the death sentences passed by a criminal court in Dessau on the ten Communists who had witnessed the murder of a storm trooper.

Disgust at such evidences of liberalism prompted the creation, on April 24, of a new "People's Court" (*Volksgerichtshof*) to deal with treason cases. Under the new law a tribunal of five members, not bound by legal technicalities, would be appointed by the Chancellor. Only the presiding officer and one judge would be regular judicial officials. The other three might be chosen from among persons "with special experience in fighting off attacks directed against the State." The announcement of the law on May 2 followed a small fire in Augsburg and the arrest of seventy-three persons as alleged incendiaries. The death penalty was provided for the betrayal of mili-

[1] *The New York Times*, April 16, 1934.
[2] *V.B.*, April 21, 1934.
[3] *V.B.*, April 21, 1934.

tary or other State secrets, for efforts to detach any part of the Reich or deliver it to a foreign power, for hampering the army or police, and for conspiring with foreign governments to cause war or an application of force against the Reich. Sentences at hard labour were provided for "atrocity mongers."[1] The new tribunal was subsequently enlarged to twelve professional and twenty lay judges, including five S.A. leaders, and was sworn in by Gürtner on July 14, 1934. It was given exclusive jurisdiction over treason and sedition cases. It was anticipated that rebellious S.A. men, as well as leading Marxists still in custody, such as Thälmann and Torgler, would be tried here. The court announced the imposition of a number of death sentences in October, but the proceedings and the identity of the victims were kept secret.

The first step in the evolution of the judicial system of the Third Reich was the identification of the NSDAP with the State and the punishment of offences against the party as crimes against the State. If the regular courts are remiss here, the People's Court will act. The second step has been to make the party greater than the State and to punish offences against the State as offences against the NSDAP. The spirit of the new jurisprudence was adequately stated by Göring in an address of July 12, 1934, before the prosecutors of Prussia, in which he explained the bloody events of June 30:

"The action of the State leadership in those days was the highest realization of the legal consciousness of the people. Now that this action, which was legal in itself, has also been formally legalized, no authority can claim the right to probe into it. . . .

"We do not recognize the exaggerated dictum that the law must prevail, even if everything collapses. We consider as a primary thing not the law, but the people. First come the people, and the people created for themselves both the law and the State. We are therefore free of all formalistic overestimation of the law. . . .

"Der Führer has expressly emphasized that he considers every attack and every undermining of the State as an attack and an undermining of Nationalsocialism. Thus it becomes your task, as guardians of the law, to defend the State with all means and consider every attack against it as an attack against Der Führer. The insecurity that existed temporarily until Der Führer acted has been ended.

[1] *V.B.* and *The New York Times,* May 3, 1934; *R.G.B.,* 1934, Vol. I, No. 47 (April 24), p. 341.

Now it is the task of the judiciary to contribute its share to the security of the State. . . .

"I have clearly said to you that the rule of the law must be assured. There can be only one concept of the law: namely, the one laid down by Der Führer. . . . The law and the will of Der Führer are one." [1]

3. CONSENT THROUGH FEAR

ANOTHER familiar device of dictatorships is censorship and control of the press. In its extreme form, as exemplified in the U.S.S.R., this technique involves the complete suppression of all newspapers and periodicals save those issued by the government, the party, or affiliated organizations. In the Third Reich this end-point has not yet been reached. All Marxist papers, as well as some Centrist organs, were suppressed in the spring of 1933. But in general the great metropolitan dailies were rigidly censored and "co-ordinated" rather than abolished.

This agreeable task was entrusted to Dr. Goebbels, who had already had extensive experience in reviling the "gutter press" in his own journal, *Der Angriff*. The editorial and news staffs of all papers were vigorously *gleichgeschaltet* by the discharge of Jews and Marxists and by the appointment of Nazis to responsible supervisory positions. As a further precaution, local censors were appointed in each office, subject to control and veto by the central censor. The entire contents of every paper must be approved before it can go to press. If the local censor makes an error, in the judgment of the Propagandaministerium, the edition in question is suppressed. The morning edition of the *Berliner Tageblatt* of September 13, 1933, for example, contained headlines noting that in the Evangelical Church synod the Nazi supporters of Reichsbishop Müller had threatened the opposition with concentration camps. The local censor approved, but Goebbels decided that the sensibilities of the public in such a delicate matter must be protected. The edition in question was confiscated and the local censor discharged. For Goebbels the joys of purifying the press and protecting the public are doubtless comparable to the gratifications which less subtle souls derive from torture and murder.[2]

[1] *The New York Times,* July 13, 1934.

[2] On the psychology of censorship, see Fedor Vergin: *Das Unbewusste Europa,* pp. 39–51.

For the purpose of completing the co-ordination of the press and systematizing the mass of regulations already issued, a general Reich Press Law was promulgated on October 4, 1933.[1] This statute made journalism a "public vocation," regulated by law. It covered newspapers and political periodicals, with the definition of the adjective in doubtful cases to be made by the Minister of Propaganda. Seven qualifications were laid down for editors: German citizenship; full possession of civic and political rights; Aryan descent and, if wedded, marriage to an Aryan; twenty-one years of age; "competence"; professional training; and the "qualifications required for the intellectual influencing of public opinion." Thus no alien, no Jew, no German married to a Jew, and no persons judged incompetent or disqualified by Goebbels may become an editor. Admission to the vocation is by licensed registration, with the state organizations of the press subject to the supervision and veto of the Propaganda Minister and to such exceptions as he may make. Rejected petitioners may appeal to the court for the settlement of vocational disputes. Editors are forbidden to publish anything which "confuses selfish with common interests in a manner misleading to the public"; weakens "the strength of the German nation nationally or internationally, the will toward unity of the German nation, German defensive ability, German culture, or German business, or that injures the religious feelings of others"; anything "offensive to the honour and dignity of a German, illegally injuring the honour or the well-being of another person, hurting his reputation, or making him ridiculous or despicable"; and anything that "is for other reasons indecent." [2] It is interesting to note that if these provisions had been in force in the pre-Hitler epoch, *Der Angriff,* the *Völkischer Beobachter,* and almost the entire Nazi press would have been suppressed on all grounds specified.

The law further declared that all editors must join the National Association of the German Press. Its director is appointed by the Propaganda Minister and draws up rules subject to his approval. The association is divided into state associations. It maintains vocational courts for the press, district press courts, and an appellate Supreme Court of the Press in Berlin, for the purpose of settling disputes between editors. It provides for their training and welfare.

[1] *R.G.B.,* 1933, Vol. I, No. 111, p. 713.
[2] Part III, Section 14, of the Reich Press Law.

It assesses membership dues, which are collected like taxes. The chairmen of the courts and their assistants, consisting of publishers and editors in equal number, are appointed by Goebbels. All persons engaging in editorial activities while not registered or while temporarily forbidden to work are fined or imprisoned up to one year. Publishers employing banned persons are fined or jailed up to three months. Fines, jail sentences, and other penalties are provided for "bribery" or "coercion" of the press, both broadly defined.

Goebbels appointed Otto Dietrich, leader of the Press Division of the NSDAP, as head of the National Association (*Reichsverband der deutschen Presse*). In an address of October 4 to the Association, Goebbels declared:

"Liberty of intellect must be limited when opinion conflicts with the interests of the nation. The present government is perhaps not always right, but no better government is conceivable. If the journalists say that our press is too uniform, it is not our fault. I cannot be responsible if newspapers which once were opposed to us are now more papal than the Pope. . . .

"The concept of the absolute freedom of the press is definitely liberalistic and proceeds not from the people in its entirety, but from the individual. . . . The more freedom of opinion that is conceded to an individual, the more it can harm the interests of an entire people. The conception of freedom of opinion, in its absolute overestimate, has been badly shaken throughout the world. The German press hereafter must be single-minded in will and many-sided in expressing its will." [1]

Other regulations have followed from time to time. On November 1, 1933, all papers were required to publish their circulation figures daily. All new papers and periodicals carrying advertising were required to secure a special government permit. The Wolff Telegraph Agency and the Telegraphen Union, owned by Hugenberg, were both subjected to rigid control and censorship. Their revenues were sharply reduced by the censorship on all news and by the monotonous uniformity of the resulting product. On December 13 the Reich Press Chamber, a division of the Reich Culture Chamber, forbade the establishment of new papers and periodicals until March 31, 1934. Its head, Max Amann, appealed for greater variety and deplored "the present far-reaching uniformity of the press, which is

[1] *Berliner Tageblatt,* October 5, 1933.

not a product of government measures and does not conform to the will of the government." [1]

All Marxists and all Jews, save front-line war veterans, were barred from journalistic activity after January 1, 1934, though workers on Jewish papers, editors married to Jewesses prior to October 4, and Jewish printers, advertising men, and scientific and technical workers were exempted from this ban.[2] On New Year's Eve, Wilhelm Weiss, president of the National Association of Journalists, hailed the new freedom:

"The life of the nation shall no longer be allowed, as formerly, to be the object of the sensational journalism of shrewd business men.

"The journalist in the new Reich has accepted his work in the sense of a spiritual call that gives him justice, but also places upon him deep responsibilities. . . . Let us enter our work in full gratitude for the new State and its Nazi leadership, which gave the German journalist the freedom of his inner consciousness—the first to give him this gift and make him the richest and most distinguished journalist in the world." [3]

The new dispensation produced interesting results. As early as April 9, 1933, Hans Lackmann-Mosse, owner of the *Berliner Tageblatt,* was forced to resign and surrender his interest in this once world-famous liberal journal to a committee appointed by Goebbels. The house of Ullstein, founded in 1877—likewise Jewish and, along with Mosse and Scherle (Hugenberg), one of the three greatest newspaper concerns in Germany—was also forced to relinquish control early in November. It published four papers in Berlin: the *Morgenpost,* the *Berliner Allgemeine Zeitung,* the *Berliner Zeitung am Mittag,* and the *Vossische Zeitung,* as well as the weeklies: *Grüne Post* and *Berliner Illustrierte Zeitung,* each with a circulation of over a million. It also maintained an independent news service covering all central Europe, a travel bureau, and a large book-publishing plant, which issued, among other works, the memoirs of Bülow and Stresemann and *All Quiet on the Western Front,* translated into twenty-eight languages and a best-seller throughout the world. All "non-Aryan" subordinate executives and editors were forced out in the spring and summer of 1933 by a Nazi strike. After November 2

[1] *The New York Times,* December 14, 1933.

[2] Decree of the Ministries of Propaganda, Interior, and Justice, December 20, 1933.

[3] *The New York Times,* December 31, 1933.

two sons, Franz and Karl, remained in executive positions, but the family was compelled to relinquish its majority stock. On June 9, 1934, it was forced to surrender all its stock as a result of pressure from the Eher firm, of which Max Amann is a director, and from other Nazi journalists. This final surrender was insisted upon as a condition for the reappearance of the *Grüne Post,* suppressed on May 2. Control of the Ullstein enterprises was taken over by a group of banks headed by the Deutsche Bank.[1] All non-Aryan owners of the *Frankfurter Zeitung* were forced out in May 1934.[2]

Meanwhile many non-Nazi papers were forced into bankruptcy and compelled to suspend publication. In October 1933 the Berlin *Täglische Rundschau* disappeared and the *Vossische Zeitung* reduced its three daily editions to one. At the same time the *V.B.* attained a circulation of 500,000 and *Der Angriff* of 100,000. On December 31 the *Börsen Courier* ceased publication. The *Vossische Zeitung,* founded in 1704, with Frederick the Great, Lessing, Walter Rathenau, and Georg Bernard among its contributors, was discontinued on April 1, 1934. The *Frankfurter Nachrichten* also closed up in April. The lost readers of these and other papers, however, did not become subscribers to the Nazi press. The deadly monotony of all German newspapers led to a great increase in the circulation of such foreign papers, especially Austrian and Swiss, as were permitted to enter the Reich. The circulation of the *V.B.,* chief organ of a party with almost four million members and over forty million supporters, fell to 325,000 by March. *Der Angriff* declined to 94,200 in December, 68,600 in February, and 60,000 in March. Non-Nazi papers suffered even more severely. The *Morgenpost,* which once had 800,000 readers, had only 340,000 in February 1934. The *Berliner Tageblatt,* which once had 200,000, fell to 70,000. Between December and April 1933–4 the total circulation of all Berlin papers declined by more than 75,000.

This disconcerting development led Dr. Goebbels to plead repeatedly for greater interest and variety in the press. The deadening hand of the censorship, however, made these pleas futile. Ehm Welke, editor of the *Grüne Post,* took Dr. Goebbels too literally. In a published appeal to the Propaganda Minister he pointed out, under the pseudonym of "Thomas Trimm," that Nazi periodicals were copying

1 *The New York Times,* June 10, 1934.
2 Ibid., May 31, 1934.

the features of the *Grüne Post* and thus contributing to press uniformity, and that wit and irony at the expense of the government were now forbidden. He also justified publishing the letter rather than appealing directly to Goebbels, on the ground that the Minister "lived in a large house with a thousand rooms, in which sit a thousand men and which also contains a thousand waiting-rooms, wherein probably ten thousand men are already waiting." Goebbels at once denounced Welke's article as "one continuous and irresponsible slander on the intentions of the Propaganda Ministry" and accused him of ridiculing Nazi ideas, "which today are sacred to every German peasant." The *Grüne Post* was promptly suspended for three months. Welke was dismissed and sent to a concentration camp. He was also guilty of having married a Jewess and of cherishing democratic ideas.[1]

To Goebbels' chagrin, this procedure did not lead to any display of greater independence and initiative on the part of editors. On May 8, 1934, he therefore ordered the press to be "free"—"as far as necessities of State permit." He insisted on free and individualized commentaries, decreed the abolition of discriminatory exclusion of journalists at public events, and declared that official texts of speeches need no longer be printed. Hitler at the same time delivered a long lecture to the Nazi press leaders, urging them to show more initiative and a greater sense of responsibility.[2] But still the results were disappointing. In May and June Goebbels conducted a nation-wide campaign of denunciation against critics and grumblers. After June 30, 1934, numerous arrests were made for "spreading rumours" and criticizing the government.[3] Goebbels warned the press on July 24 that only the Propaganda Ministry had the right to influence opinion. Under these circumstances, the German press has continued to languish. Point 23 of the party program has been fulfilled. But increasing numbers of Germans have stopped reading papers.

This situation suggests one of the obstacles inevitably encountered by every régime employing force and fear to silence criticism. Resistance on the part of individuals subjected to arrest, incarceration, and torture is usually ineffective, though in exceptional circumstances it

[1] *The New York Times,* May 2, 3, and 6, 1934.
[2] *V.B.,* May 8, 1934.
[3] Cf. list of instances compiled by AP, *The New York Times,* July 22, 1934.

may produce surprising and dramatic results.[1] Active mass resistance is impossible when all the machine-guns are in the hands of loyal henchmen of the dictatorship. But collective passive resistance can often paralyse even the most ruthless tyranny.[2]

The dictatorship of the NSDAP has effectively destroyed all organized parties and movements of opposition through the murder, execution, bludgeoning, or imprisonment of leaders, through the confiscation of funds and property,[3] through the public ridicule of critics,[4] through the suppression of all liberty of political expression and activity, and through the maintenance of an elaborate machinery of espionage and repression. At the same time the incessant and extraordinarily effective propaganda of the Nazi régime has silenced or converted millions of potential opponents. Such tactics necessarily fail, however, in dealing with the more subtle and intangible forms of sabotage.

People cannot in the mass be compelled to buy newspapers. Strong-arm tactics were used in 1933 to increase subscriptions to various Nazi journals and then abandoned. In general the German intelligentsia has accepted "co-ordination" without a murmur, and no instances of significant student opposition have come to the writer's attention. But a little handful of rebels has accepted martyrdom in the name of academic freedom—and the ultimate effect of their gesture is not wholly negligible. In ecclesiastical circles other rebels resist the politicalization of the Church. Clubs and guns are dangerous weapons to use against churchmen. People cannot be prevented from passing sly remarks and coining jokes at the expense of the régime:

[1] Cf. the case of Dimitroff, pp. 333 f. below.

[2] Cf. "The Poverty of Power," in C. E. Merriam: *Political Power: Its Composition and Incidence* (New York; McGraw-Hill; 1934).

[3] On December 1, 1933, the *Gestapo* announced the confiscation of the possessions of Emil Ludwig, Heinrich Mann, Rudolf Breitscheid, Wilhelm Münzenberg, Johannes Werthauer, Leopold Schwarzschild, Max Sievert, the German Peace Society, the League of Free Thinkers, the League for the Protection of Motherhood, the Executive Committee of the Socialist Party, the Reichsbanner, and dozens of other individuals and organizations. All the property of Bernhard Weiss, former vice-president of the Berlin police, was confiscated on December 8. Thousands of Jews, liberals, and other critics of the régime have suffered a similar fate.

[4] For example (one among hundreds), a Dr. Engeland of Salzuelen was overheard making a remark derogatory to Hitler and was paraded through the streets with a placard around his neck: "I am a scoundrel; I have insulted Der Führer." AP dispatch, April 27, 1934.

Under Schleicher and von Papen
We had meat, like good "Rostbraten."
Under Hitler, Goebbels, Göring
We scarcely even get a herring.

Oranienburg, Oranienburg,
How brown you have become!
Once only Marxists lingered there,
Now it's become a storm-troop lair.

"Hitler, Göring, Goebbels, and Röhm walked down Unter den Linden together yesterday, and no one recognized them."

"How's that?"

"Hitler had his hair combed, Göring had on civilian clothes, Goebbels had his mouth shut, and Röhm was with a woman."

"Papa, who burned the Reichstag?" asked the little boy at table.

"Sh-sh," says Papa. *"Ess, ess!* (Eat, eat!)"

"But, Papa, who burned the Reichstag?"

"Sh, S.S.!"

A vaudeville comedian declares: "Yesterday I saw a Mércedès car, and, just think, there wasn't a Nazi in it!" He is repróved for disloyalty and compelled to apologize. He says: "Yesterday I saw a Mércedès car, but it was all right—there was a Nazi in it."

Why is Hitler now a widow? Röhm is dead.

Why is Göring so fat? He wears all his uniforms at once.

A passer-by plunges into the Spree and rescues a drowning man. He discovers that it is Hitler. Der Führer offers him any reward he may ask. "But my name is Cohen," says the rescuer. "No matter, you may still have anything you ask for." "Ach, Herr Hitler, I have only one request." "And what is that?" "Please don't tell anybody who rescued you."

Such tales, passed from mouth to mouth behind closed doors, are infinite in number and spiciness. They are, of course, of little political significance and are often relished by Nazis themselves, though men and women have lost their jobs and been sent to concentration camps for less. The actual extent of organized "underground" opposition cannot be estimated with any degree of accuracy. The Communist Party still lives. It still eschews individual terrorism. But its agents work ceaselessly in a fantastic atmosphere of espionage and counter-espionage reminiscent of Tsarist Russia. Their purpose is to keep the organization alive and to circulate forbidden Marxist literature. The famous "Groups of Five" consist of Communist cells in factories. They hold no meetings and keep no records. Only one man in each group knows members of other groups. He is the link to others and to the secret district committees. He works to establish new groups and to circulate copies (secretly multigraphed or printed in miniature or in disguise, between the covers of theatre programs, novels, or advertisements) of the *Rote Fahne,* the *Brown Book,* and other publications attacking or exposing the NSDAP. Occasionally "lightning demonstrations" will be staged in back streets. A crowd of workers will appear suddenly, shout in chorus: "Down with Hitler! Hail the proletarian revolution!" and then vanish as by magic into buildings, alleyways, and side streets before the police arrive. Police spies and stool-pigeons worm their way into the *Fünfegruppen,* where they betray their "friends" to the authorities. They are sometimes discovered and secretly beaten up or murdered by unknown persons. The Socialist exiles abroad likewise claim to be in contact with secret Socialist organizations in Germany, some of which, in certain districts, are apparently larger and better organized than those of the KPD. Such nuclei of opposition are of no importance in the short run, so long as the dictators are united, the masses are quiescent, and the Reich is at peace. What their significance might be in a grave nation-wide political crisis can scarcely be predicted.

Despite these minor symptoms of unrest, there can be no doubt but that Nazi terrorism, coupled with propaganda, has served its double purpose: that of furnishing a channel for the discharge of the sadistic propensities of party members and that of destroying all opposition and frightening critics into silence. It has often been said that terror is a necessary weapon of dictatorship. It is equally true that dictatorship is the corollary of terrorism. Indeed, it might well be argued that the dictatorial or non-dictatorial character of a régime is a function of the degree to which it persecutes those who oppose its policies. The totalitarian Fascist State is a jealous State which brooks no gods but Hitler. All criticism must be liquidated, not because the régime is imperilled, but on principle—because of the *Führerprinzip,* which exacts blind obedience and gives citizens only duties, not rights. Those who cannot be liquidated by propaganda must be liquidated by force. Terror thus becomes a permanent instrument of power. Once the pattern is established, terror begets more terror. It becomes the normal means of dealing with differences of opinions, interests, and ambitions, even though the very existence of terrorism may be denied.

CHAPTER VIII

THE PERSECUTION OF SCAPEGOATS

1. PERISH THE JEW!

If the tools of political power be ranked from the simple to the complex, from the brutal to the subtle, the persecution of minorities deserves to be regarded as the most ancient, most direct, and most immediately efficacious device which can be used by a ruling class, next to the outright imprisonment, torture, or execution of opponents. This weapon possesses numerous advantages over simple terrorization of disturbers of the status quo. Terrorism, even on a mass scale, affords a channel for the discharge of aggressions for only a few members of the whole community. The remainder is merely frightened or left unmoved. In neither case is loyalty to the régime promoted. In the persecution of minorities, however, the entire community (excepting only the victims) can participate in one way or another. Fear of government is transmuted into detestation of those branded by government as public enemies. Where the device is used successfully, resentments against the beneficiaries of the political and social status quo are transferred to scapegoats, whose persecution affords emotionally satisfying channels for the release of social tensions. The élite is enabled to identify its critics with those labelled as foes of the whole society. It evokes deference and loyalty by undertaking the praiseworthy mission of rescuing the community from corruption and exploitation.

The creation of pariah caste, singled out for discrimination and contempt, serves another function useful to every ruling class. It affords to those disgruntled strata near the bottom of the social hierarchy the emotional satisfaction of being able to "look down upon" a group which is still lower in the social scale. Impoverished workers and poor peasants, infused with collective consciousness of the "superiority" of their race, language, or religion, are distracted from their misery and enabled to share in the psychic satisfactions which the élite derives from its position at the apex of the social pyramid. This pattern explains in large degree the extraordinary stability of the Indian caste system and the imperviousness of white wage-earners in the American South to appeals for trade-union organization and "class consciousness." In the former case, each segment in the hierarchy can give thanks for the opportunity which it enjoys to despise the next lowest segment, down through the social scale to the "untouchables" at the bottom. In the latter case, the prospective joys of class solidarity and union activity, with employers as targets of aggressions, are derived from despising the Negro, "keeping him in his place," and occasionally beating, torturing, and lynching members of the "inferior" race.

Anti-Semitism in the modern world has frequently played this role. It is the lightning-rod by means of which unrest in the lower social strata is deflected away from aristocratic or bourgeois élites and onto a helpless minority which is ideally adapted for use as a scapegoat, by virtue of its relatively small numbers and its wide dispersion throughout the western world. Even in the Middle Ages and the early modern period, when European Jews were segregated and discriminated against as a religious group rather than as a racial minority, anti-Judaism served the interests of political and ecclesiastical rulers. The hatred of Christian for Jew had its obvious uses for princes and nobles, bishops and priests. Protestant Christianity, no less than Catholicism, was anti-Jewish. Luther attacked the Jews as savagely as he did his deluded peasant followers who were so sinful as to rebel against their landlords and priests. In 1570, thirty-four Jews were burned to death in Berlin for the alleged "ritual murder" of a Christian child. The gradual establishment of religious toleration diminished Jew-baiting on religious grounds. Not until the French Revolution, however, did the emancipation of European Jewry from its disabilities and its ghettos begin. And not until 1847 did the Prussian government, with many exceptions, grant Jews equal legal rights with Christians. Bismarck then opposed this measure, but in 1869 he pushed through a law in the North German Confederation for the complete emancipation of German Jewry.

Scarcely had the last vestiges of religious anti-Judaism disappeared from the statute books, when modern racial anti-Semitism emerged. It was, and is, a product of the insecurities of a peasantry and *Kleinbürgertum* increasingly exploited and oppressed between corporate industry and finance on the one hand and the organized proletariat on the other. Modern anti-Semitism was born in Germany during the business depression after 1873. The term was apparently coined by Wilhelm Marr in 1879.[1] In 1880 Bismarck told the Jewish merchant Bleichroeder that he tolerated anti-Semitism only because it provided a safe discharge for the anti-capitalistic leanings of the *Kleinbürgertum*. The development of the movement paralleled the growth of the "Aryan" and "Nordic" myths.[2] The Jews were now denounced, not as followers of Judaism, but as members of an alien "race." The terms "Aryan" (Indo-European) and "Semitic," familiar to scholars as names of groups of languages, came to be applied to biological stocks. Hebrew, like Arabic, is a Semitic language. Yiddish, like German, is an Aryan language. No such entities as an Aryan "race" or a Semitic "race" have ever existed. But the scientific conclusions of philology and anthropology were here of no consequence. Racial "Aryanism" and anti-Semitism became the vogue in petty-bourgeois circles. The first International Anti-Semitic Congress was held in Dresden in 1883. Anti-Semitic parties had deputies in the Reichstag continuously after 1890. Stöcker, Ahlwardt, Eugen Dühring, and Liebermann von Sonnenberg were the founders of the new faith, no less than Gobineau, Chamberlain, Marr, and Wagner. It waxed and waned in the pre-war period, depending in part on the state of the business cycle. In 1913 "Daniel Frymann," in a popular book: *Wenn ich der Kaiser Wär* (published in Munich, where Hitler was then living), urged that all Jews should be deprived of citizenship, of political rights, and of the right to own land and lend money, and should be barred from parliament, the public service, the army and navy, the legal profession, banking, theatres, and journalism. Anti-Semitism was reborn and flourished after 1919.

The sources and content of Nazi anti-Semitism, which subsequently absorbed all other brands, have already been dealt with.[3]

[1] Cf. his *Der Sieg des Judentums über das Germanentum;* see also the references in Benjamin Ginzburg: "Anti-Semitism," *Encyclopaedia of the Social Sciences.*

[2] Cf. pp. 113f. above, and Wickham Steed: *Hitler, Whence and Whither?* (London: Nisbet; 1934), pp. 3–40, on "The Nordic Legend."

[3] Cf. pp. 109–13 above.

All the party leaders continually denounced Judas and made anti-Semitism the basis of their entire *Weltanschauung:*

"Is the Jew also a human being? Of course, and no one of us has denied it. We merely deny that he is a respectable human being. A human being, in any case—but what kind of a one!

" 'Anti-Semitism is unchristian.' To be Christian means: Love thy neighbour as thyself. My neighbour is my racial comrade. If I love him, then I must hate his enemies. *Who thinks German must despise the Jews.* The one implies the other." [1]

After January 1933, anti-Semitic pamphlets flooded German streets. Such books as Johann von Leers: *Juden sehen Dich an* (Berlin: NS Verlag; 1933) and *14 Jahre Judenrepublik* (2 vols.; Berlin: NS Verlag; 1933) became best-sellers. Goebbels declared: "Our hatred of Jews is no passing fancy, but rather the logical consequence of our love for the German people. The Jews brought international capitalism, which recklessly threw chains of slavery around Germany, and they also brought Marxism. Germans have a gigantic fight against Marxism, and especially against Communism." [2] At the Nürnberg "Congress of Victory" Hitler quoted Mommsen to prove that the Jews were "a ferment of decomposition." Hans Frank asserted in October 1933:

"Anti-Semites we are, and have been from the beginning. We are so, however, and this we must emphasize, not out of hatred for the Jew, but out of love for the German people. We are of the opinion that the blood substance of the Germanic race constitutes so preeminent and unique an asset of the world as a whole that we should be justified in counting it the duty of the entire human race, in gratitude, to safeguard this basic Germanic element, for we know that from this racial substance have issued the highest achievement of man." [3]

Once in control of the State, the NSDAP found that anti-Semitism not only could serve the role already suggested, but could serve other political purposes as well. The blame for all tales of terror and atrocities, all foreign criticism of the régime, all denunciations and boycotts abroad was laid on the Jews. A tremendous anti-Semitic literature blossomed forth. Accusations against the Jews have ranged all

[1] P. J. Goebbels: *Mjölnir* (Munich: Eher; 1931).
[2] *Der Angriff,* March 6, 1933.
[3] Quoted in the London *Times,* October 10, 1933.

the way from allegations that Jews are sloppy housekeepers [1] to insistence that the Jews burned Nordics in the Inquisition,[2] invented democracy and Marxism, caused the Great War, brought about Germany's collapse, poisoned German race-purity, raped Aryan women, imported French Negroes into the Rhineland, and drank the blood of Christian children.

While the role of the Jews in German society has only an accidental connection with their persecution, brief attention must be given to it because of Nazi efforts to prove the contention that the Jews dominated German life.[3] German census figures of religious confessions indicate that in 1925 there were 564,379 "Israelites" in the Reich, as compared with 20,193,334 Catholics and 40,014,677 Protestants. Between 1910 and 1925 the number of Protestants per thousand decreased from 659 to 641, of Catholics from 326 to 323, and of Jews from 9.3 to 9.0, while the number of free thinkers and pagans increased from 3 to 24.[4] Professing Judaists thus constituted, in 1925, 0.9 per cent of the total population of 62,410,619. This figure does not include those Jews who had adopted Christianity, those with no admitted religious faith, and those who by ancestry were only partly Jewish.

The German-Jewish community had lived in Germany since the early mediæval period (if not since Roman times) and had perhaps, despite its disabilities, become more thoroughly assimilated than any other Jewish group elsewhere. The very language of world Jewry, Yiddish, is a variant of German. Intermarriage between Jews and Gentiles was forbidden by law until the middle of the nineteenth century, but thereafter became fairly common. The number of Jews in the Reich was slowly decreasing before the war, owing in part to a lower birth-rate. The total German birth-rate fell from 41.05 per thousand in 1880 to 33.05 in 1910, while the Jewish birth-rate declined from 32.26 to 16.55. In Hamburg the Jews declined from 4.5 per cent of the population in 1866 to 1.7 per cent in 1925; in Berlin from 5.5

1 Cf. *V.B.*, January 5, 1934, with photographs.

2 *Journal of the Aryosophs*, October 8, 1933.

3 Cf., for example, the works of Leers cited above and the English leaflets issued by the Fichte-Bund, Hamburg, under the caption: "Help to Kill the Lie!" especially No. 642: "The Truth about the Jews in Germany," containing numerous falsifications and misrepresentations of statistics.

4 *Statistisches Jahrbuch für das deutsche Reich, 1933*, p. 18.

per cent in 1871 to 4.3 in 1925.[1] On the other hand, the number of Jews in Prussia increased by 37,093 between 1910 and 1925. In the latter year there were 601,779 aliens in Prussia, of whom 76,387 were Jewish. This, then, is the total of that much advertised "flood" of *Ostjudentum* which the Nazis insist poured into Germany after the war. In this connection it is worth recalling that during the war Ludendorff invited Polish Jews to enjoy German "freedom" and that during the German military occupation thousands of Polish and Russian Jews were deported as labourers to Germany, where they were obliged to remain.

The accusation that the Jews dominated German public life and controlled certain professions is likewise a product of Nazi imaginations. Nazi anti-Semitism has notoriously been most rabid in peasant districts, where the Jews were fewest and poorest: in Bavaria, where the Jews in 1925 numbered 6.7 per thousand of the population; in East Prussia (5.0); in Pomerania (4.1); in Upper Silesia (7.3); in Prussian Saxony (2.4); in Schleswig-Holstein (2.7); in Thuringia (2.2); and in Braunschweig (3.5). These were long the strongholds of the NSDAP. Where the Jews were more numerous and prosperous, anti-Semitism and Nationalsocialism were weakest: Berlin (43.0 Jews per thousand population in 1925); Hesse-Nassau (21.7); Baden (10.4); Hessen (15.2); Hamburg (17.3); etc.[2] The denunciation of scapegoats is always most effective where the scapegoats are not one's neighbours and can be painted in hideous colours because of the lack of inter-personal contact with them.

The Jewish contribution to Germany during the war was impressive, though Jews were largely barred from the old army. Of the total Jewish population, 96,327 or 17.3 per cent served in the army and navy, as compared with 18.7 per cent for the whole German population. Of these 12,000 were killed, 78 per cent were at the front, and 12 per cent were volunteers.[3] Manfred von Richthofen, "Red

[1] Cf. Heinrich Silbergleit: *Die Bevölkerungs- und Berufs-Verhältnisse der Juden im deutschen Reich* (Berlin: Akademie Verlag; 1930); and Mildred Wertheimer: "The Jews in the Third Reich," *Foreign Policy Association Reports,* Vol. 9, No. 16, October 11, 1933.

[2] *Statistisches Jahrbuch für das deutsche Reich, 1933,* p. 18.

[3] Cf. Jakob Segall: *Die deutschen Juden als Soldaten im Kriege 1914–1918* (Berlin: Philo; 1922); compare *Der Stürmer,* January 1934: "If the Jew-lover remonstrates that there have been courageous Jews as soldiers in the Great War, some of whom even won decorations, then point out to him that they were bastards of the second or third

Knight of Germany," greatest of war aces and Göring's commander, was of Jewish extraction. And it is no exaggeration to say that without the genius of two Jews the Reich could never have withstood its enemies for four years: Walter Rathenau, who organized the German war industries; and Fritz Haber, who invented the process of fixing nitrogen from the air and thus made Germany independent of foreign supplies of nitrates for explosives. As for the "Weimar Jew Republic," Hugo Preuss, framer of the Constitution, was indeed a Jew. But of the 250 Ministers in the republican Cabinets between 1918 and 1933, only two were Jews and only four of Jewish descent. Of the 608 members elected to the Reichstag in July 1932, there was only one Jew, and only fourteen were of Jewish extraction.[1]

The proportion of Jews in the learned professions was high, owing perhaps to special Jewish aptitudes and to the century-long exclusion of Jews from agriculture, the army, the public service, and many other vocations. In Prussia in 1925, where the Jews numbered 1.5 per cent of the population, only 0.7 per cent of gainfully employed Jews were in public administration, as compared with 2.3 per cent of gainfully employed non-Jews. Of the occupied Jews, 71.7 per cent were in commerce and industry, as compared with 51.7 per cent of non-Jews, and 10 per cent were in the professions, as compared with 6.8 per cent for non-Jews. The Jews, however, numbered only 3.4 per cent of all persons in commerce and industry, 2.3 in the professions, and 0.3 in the public service.[2] In Prussia Jews numbered 7 per cent of all independent druggists, 18 per cent of doctors, 5 of artists, 27 of lawyers, and 15 of dentists. For Berlin the corresponding figures were 32, 48, 7, 50, and 9.[3] In the theatre, music, cinema, journalism, university teaching, and the stock exchange the Jews were also numerous. That "Aryan" doctors, lawyers, dentists, actors, and musicians should in some cases have embraced National-socialism as a means of disposing of their competitors is understandable. That the Jews, by deliberate choice and design, sought to "dominate" these professions is an allegation wholly without basis in fact.

---

generation, who had to sacrifice themselves in the interests of World-Jewry. . . . The first thing one has to do with a fellow who speaks like that is to bash his teeth in."

[1] Computation of Wickham Steed, op. cit., p. 140.

[2] Cf. table on p. 178 of Wertheimer, loc. cit.

[3] Cf. tables in Leers: *14 Jahre Judenrepublik*, pp. 151–8.

2. ANTI-SEMITISM IN ACTION

One of the first steps of the Nazi régime was to exclude Jews from the public service. The Civil Service Law of April 4, 1933,[1] with its supplementary decrees, bars all Jews from public service, including railways, courts, schools, and universities. Jewish teachers and professors were likewise ousted from their posts. Scores of prominent scholars were compelled to quit academic seats because of their unwisdom in the choice of grandparents or wives. They included five Nobel Prize winners: Albert Einstein and James Franck, noted physicists; Gustav Hertz and Otto Meyerhoff, famous physiologists; and Fritz Haber, chemist, who was found dead in a Swiss hotel on January 29, 1934. Emil Lederer, economist, was discharged from the University of Berlin. Max Liebermann and Karl Hofer, noted painters; Bruno Walter, Otto Klemperer, and Fritz Zweig, conductors; Lotte Schöne, soprano; Max Reinhardt, theatrical director; Kurt Glaser, historian of art; Hans Kelsen, perhaps the most noted contemporary political philosopher of the Continent; and hundreds of other scientists, teachers, artists, musicians, and writers have been driven to retirement, exile, or suicide.[2] Many non-Jewish liberals or radicals have suffered a similar fate. The hatred of the Nazis has pursued some of these men beyond the frontier. Professor Theodor Lessing, pacifist, was expelled from the Hanover Technical Institute in 1932. He went to Marienbad, Czechoslovakia, where he was murdered on August 31, 1933.

Jewish students have also been discriminated against. The "Law against the overcrowding of German schools and Universities"[3] specified that in all non-obligatory schools and in all universities, the number of students must be limited to the requirements of the professions. The state Cabinets determine how many new students may be admitted each year. New non-Aryan students must not number more than 1.5 per cent of the total student body. Exceptions are permitted, however, and students whose fathers fought at the front, those whose parents married before 1933, and those with one Aryan parent or two Aryan grandparents are exempted (Section 4). These exceptions make the law chiefly significant for the future,

[1] Cf. pp. 250f. above.
[2] Cf. partial list in *The New York Times,* March 5, 1934.
[3] *R.G.B.,* 1933, Vol. I, No. 43 (April 25), p. 225.

though where non-Aryan students exceed five per cent of the student body they may be expelled. Jewish medical and dental students already enrolled and not falling within excepted categories can secure degrees only by giving up their German citizenship and, therewith, their right to practise in Germany. In the lower schools non-Aryan Christian children are barred from common religious services. Aryan pupils are often encouraged to revile and persecute their Jewish playmates. These practices have perhaps embittered German non-Aryans more than any other single feature of Nazi anti-Semitism.

The legal profession has likewise been "cleansed." Almost all Jewish judges, court officials, and prosecuting attorneys were dismissed under the Civil Service Law. Provision was likewise made for the disbarment of non-Aryan lawyers and for the non-admission of Jews to the bar after September 30, 1933. Jewish doctors, dentists, actors, musicians, and stage directors have also been deprived of their livelihoods.

In commerce and industry, where the first Nazi attacks against Jews were concentrated, there has been less persecution than in other fields. It was precisely here, however, that the anti-Semitic aggressions of the *Kleinbürgertum* and the peasantry were most intense. To drive Jewish shopkeepers out of business, to municipalize Jewish department stores, to expropriate Jewish bankers, to "break the bonds of interest slavery" were the professed objectives of the NSDAP. After the appointment of Hitler as Chancellor, there were high hopes in certain S.A. quarters that "the night of the long knives" was near—that is, a pogrom. Non-Aryan shopkeepers and business men would undoubtedly have been the first victims. The pogrom failed to materialize, however. Hitler demanded discipline and legality. Göring, to be sure, declared on March 10 that the police would not be used to protect Jewish stores. There were numerous instances of Jews being robbed, beaten, or murdered by storm troopers. But the hoped-for massacre and general expropriation was not authorized by the party leaders.

This situation created another dilemma for the directors of the NSDAP, which they resolved with their usual skill. On the one hand, the foreign press was denouncing the régime for persecuting the Jews. On the other hand, many party members and S.A. men were denouncing their leaders for not persecuting the Jews. The legitimate expectation of loyal Nazis had somehow to be satisfied, particularly as anti-Semitic activity would distract attention from the convenient amnesia of the party leaders with regard to their "socialistic" promises. But any action which would multiply the "atrocity stories" circulating abroad and intensify anti-Nazi feelings in foreign capitals must be avoided for diplomatic reasons. What to do? Hitler and Goebbels were equal to the occasion. The solution: blame the Jews for the "atrocity propaganda"; organize an official boycott against all Jewish businesses in Germany; hold the German Jews as "hostages" and threaten them with complete ruin unless foreign attacks on the Nazi régime were discontinued. Thus the exuberant anti-Semites in the party would have their energies directed into relatively safe channels, many German Jews would be coerced into denying the "atrocity tales," and enemies of the NSDAP abroad would be frightened into silence, out of fear of subjecting the Jews in Germany to still worse treatment.

This product of political genius was apparently the brain-child of Hitler himself. On March 26, 1933, Der Führer disclosed his plan to Goebbels at Berchtesgaden. Goebbels was enthusiastic and approved the appointment of Julius Streicher, the Nürnberg fanatic, as director of the boycott. On the 27th it was announced that the "Nationalsocialist movement will now take the most drastic legal counter-measures against the intellectual authors and exploiters of this treasonable agitation which is mainly conducted abroad by Jews formerly resident in Germany." It was likewise announced that "Committees of Action" would organize the boycott.[1] The Manifesto of the NSDAP on March 28 proclaimed a national boycott of Jewish business and professional men to begin on Saturday, April 1. It laid down eleven detailed rules to be followed in the organization and execution of the boycott and declared:

"Communist and Marxist criminals and their Jewish-intellectual instigators, who managed in good time to escape abroad with their money, are now conducting a conscienceless treasonable propaganda against the German people . . . from the capitals of the former Entente countries." [2]

The boycott machinery was hastily but efficiently organized. Great mass meetings were held and all papers were compelled to print the

[1] *Frankfurter Zeitung,* March 28, 1933.

[2] For text of Manifesto, see Mildred Wertheimer: "The Jews in the Third Reich," *Foreign Policy Association Reports,* October 11, 1933, pp. 175–6.

party Manifesto. Many prominent Jews repudiated the "atrocity stories." The *Berliner Tageblatt* appealed frantically for a cessation of the "atrocity propaganda." [1] Goebbels, on March 28:

"I telephone the Leader. The boycott proclamation will be published today. Panic among the Jews! . . . In the evening I telephone the Leader and report the effects of the boycott proclamation. It has cleared the atmosphere like a thunder-storm." [2]

But still there were difficulties. The Foreign Office and the non-Nazi Cabinet members were in as much a panic as the Jews. Private protests poured in from industrial, financial, and shipping circles. Papen was dubious. Neurath threatened to resign. "Many hang their heads and see ghosts," wrote Goebbels on the 31st. "They think the boycott would lead to war. But if we defend ourselves we can only win esteem." [3] The Cabinet refused to approve, however, unless the boycott were limited to one day. Reluctantly Hitler and Goebbels yielded. They also repudiated the demand of the NSBO and the Committees of Action that all Jewish employers be compelled to discharge their Jewish workers and to pay two months' advance salary to their Aryan employees. The boycott was limited to Saturday, with a threat of renewal on the following Wednesday if the foreign press had not mended its ways. Proclamations went up on all kiosks:

"The Jews have time to reflect until Saturday morning at ten o'clock. Then the fight begins. The Jews of the whole world are planning to destroy Germany. German people, defend yourselves! Don't buy from the Jews!"

Banners and placards were prepared all over the Reich, under the direction of Streicher and Goebbels: "The Jews are our bane!" "In defence against the Jewish atrocity and boycott campaign!" "Don't buy from Jewish stores!"

At 10.00 a.m., Saturday, April 1, 1933, the boycott began. Everywhere Jewish stores and all Jewish establishments save banks and newspapers were picketed by S.A. men, who posted placards, scribbled insulting epithets on windows, and warned customers away. Jewish lawyers, judges, teachers, doctors, and dentists were frequently prevented from entering their places of work by storm troopers. Most of the Jewish shops closed up business for the day. There was

[1] Cf. *"Es ist nicht wahr,"* March 28, 1933.
[2] *Vom Kaiserhof zur Reichskanzlei*, p. 289.
[3] Goebbels, op. cit., p. 290.

no violence, but only disciplined hatred and enthusiasm.[1] In the afternoon a hundred and fifty thousand Berliners demonstrated against the Jews in the Lustgarten, and in the evening a hundred thousand Hitler Youths paraded. "The boycott," said Goebbels, "is a great moral victory for Germany. . . . The Leader has again hit on the right thing. . . . At midnight the boycott is broken off by our own will. We await the echo in the foreign press." [2] On April 1 Hitler named Alfred Rosenberg head of the new APA, one of the functions of which would be to justify anti-Semitism to the world and to manufacture anti-Semitic sentiment in other countries. On Tuesday the Cabinet approved the new Civil Service Law, with its Aryan clause. It was decided not to resume the boycott. An official announcement declared that the world was "learning some sense." Since the tone of the foreign press had improved (the exact opposite was the case), it would be unnecessary to resume the boycott. It persisted, however, in some smaller centres, and Jewish business men have everywhere suffered since from prejudice and discrimination.

Despite this inauspicious beginning, it may be said that the Jewish business community in Germany has suffered less than the professional and intellectual classes. In their determination to prevent the party radicals from "disturbing business," the Nazi leaders have to some extent protected non-Aryan as well as Aryan entrepreneurs. On September 27, 1933, Minister Schmitt condemned discrimination against Jewish firms, on the ground that it "must disturb the work of economic reconstruction and unfavourably affect the labour market, since the boycotted firms are being compelled to reduce their staffs." Despite this plea, many Jews were expelled from the Berlin Stock Exchange and fifty-one Jewish traders were excluded from the Berlin Produce Exchange early in November. On November 24 Minister Seldte, in an order not made public till January, forbade the NSBO to coerce employers into dismissing Jewish workers. On January 6, 1934, Frick and Göring declared that the molestation of Jews in business must cease. The Aryan clause must not be applied to private business. All government officials were instructed to enforce these orders.

The "cold pogrom" has affected every human relationship in the

[1] For circumstantial accounts see C. B. Hoover: *Germany Enters the Third Reich*, pp. 122–8, and Lion Feuchtwanger: *The Oppermanns*.

[2] Op. cit., p. 291.

Reich. Apart from public legislation, numerous private organizations have adopted the "Aryan clause" under Nazi pressure or in patriotic imitation of the totalitarian State. Non-Aryans are thus barred not only from the public service and the professions, but from tennis clubs, chess clubs, sport organizations, singing societies, church socials, and numerous other activities. In September 1934, Jewish youth groups were forbidden to wear insignia, hold parades, conduct field sports, live together, or issue publications.[1] Storm troopers are required to prove the purity of their Aryan ancestry beyond 1800. On August 30, and again on the 31st, 1934, Hess denied that he had ordered S.A. men not to talk to or mingle with Jews: "There has been no such order; there is no such order; there will be no such order—in fact I haven't yet even thought of such an order." [2] But on September 14 the German press published an order from Hess, dated August 16, forbidding all party members to assist Jews in the courts, to accept Jewish contributions, and to associate with Jews in public. The order declared:

"The party has had to make immense sacrifices in its struggle against the domination of the destructive Jewish spirit, and it must be regarded as shamelessness for party members to stand up for those who have brought so much ill fortune to Germany." [3]

At the same time Wilhelm Kube, Governor of Brandenburg, declared:

"The Jews betrayed us in 1918. The Jews brought Field Marshal von Hindenburg before the humiliating forum of the criminal Reichstag of the Jewish Weimar régime. The Jews caused the inflation. The Jews remain enemies of the German people." [4]

The Jews of Germany are thus outcasts in their own land to an even greater degree than the Negroes of the United States—reviled, insulted, discriminated against, condemned to impoverishment, and held up to ridicule and hatred before the rising generation. The pain of persecution is felt all the more keenly since the overwhelming majority of Germans of Jewish origin have for centuries regarded themselves as an integral part of the German community. They have shared the trials and triumphs of the Fatherland and have contributed abundantly to its common life. To the enrichment of German *Kultur*

[1] *The New York Times,* September 16 and 22, 1934.
[2] AP dispatch, August 31, 1934.
[3] *The New York Times,* September 15, 1934.
[4] *The New York Times,* September 15, 1934.

they have given Heine, Mendelssohn, Liebermann, Reinhardt, Feuchtwanger, Preuss, Rathenau, Richthofen, Haber, Einstein, and hundreds of lesser figures. Now, however, they are treated as enemy aliens and as the source of all that is evil in the Reich.

The question of whether the tempo of anti-Semitism has been retarded or accelerated since the close of the first year of the dictatorship admits of no easy answer. As early as October 1930 Hitler said: "I have nothing against respectable Jews, so long as they do not identify themselves with Bolshevism." [1] But in the Nazi view, no Jew can be "respectable" and all Jewish activity is *"Kultur-Bolschewismus."* Even the fanatic Streicher, however, disclaims any desire to slaughter the Jews and hopes only for international action to break "Jewish hegemony." [2] In response to pressure from the Foreign Office and from various sources abroad, a special issue of *Der Stürmer* (May 3, 1934, *"Ritualmord-Nummer"*), accusing the Jews of plotting to murder Hitler, was suppressed after it had been generally distributed, on the ground that it "attacked the Christian communion of the Lord's Supper." It depicted rabbis sucking blood from Aryan babies and "disclosed," in words and pictures, Jewish ritual murders from 169 B.C. to 1932 A.D. While this number was only slightly more extreme than other issues of Streicher's paper, it was nevertheless suppressed. There have been instances of Nazis punished for extorting money from Jews. On March 23, 1934, Hans Frank warned "150 per cent anti-Semites" to desist from their grumbling over the fact that Jews were still alive.

To balance these evidences of moderation, other instances of continued or intensified anti-Semitic activity may be cited. On February 28, 1934, Dr. Benno Walter, vice-president of B'nai B'rith, was arrested by the Berlin Secret Police for no announced reason. In a speech in the Sportpalast on March 23, Johannes Engel, labour Trustee, declared that Jews must be forbidden to give the Nazi salute—though anyone in Germany failing to give it on ceremonial occasions is in danger of assault, as many foreigners discovered during 1933. On May 1 Dr. Jakob Wassermann of the Commerz- und Privatbank was arrested by the *Gestapo* for criticizing Goebbels "with cynical freshness." It was indicated that he would have ample opportunity, in the Oranienburg concentration camp, to learn how one should

[1] London *Times* interview, October 15, 1930.
[2] *The New York Times,* May 7 and 17, 1934.

conduct oneself "as a guest of the German people." [1]

In an address in the Sportpalast on May 11, Goebbels warned the world that if foreign boycotts of German goods continued, "the hatred, rage, and despair of the German people will first of all vent itself on those Jews who can be grabbed in the homeland. . . . We have spared the Jews, but if they think they can therefore reappear on the stage and in the editorial office, if they imagine they can again stroll along the Kurfürstendamm as if nothing at all had happened, let them take my words as a last warning. . . . German Jews will be left alone by us if they will quietly and modestly retire within their four walls and if they will refrain from putting forth a claim to equal worth and equal rights with Germans. If they do not, they will have themselves to blame for the consequences." [2]

Der Angriff of May 11, 1934 declared:

"The brazen fashion in which many Jews have begun once again to behave themselves has attracted general attention in the last few months. . . . We expect every reader, party member, storm trooper, and worker to report to us every case of Jewish shamelessness in the last weeks and months, so that we can publish it in *Der Angriff*."

The future fate of the German Jews can only be discussed intelligently in terms of the role of the Jew as scapegoat and whipping-boy in the Third Reich. When economic conditions improve and the acquiescence of the masses can be secured through propaganda, anti-foreign agitation, and bread and circuses, the Jews will enjoy relative peace within the inferior status to which they have been reduced. When impoverishment is acute, when stifled criticism breaks through the censorship, when intra-party friction is serious (as in July 1933, May and June 1934, and again in October and November 1934), efforts will necessarily be made by the Nazi leaders to distract attention by playing upon anti-Semitic prejudices. If this fails, naked terrorism is the last resort—not against the Jews, but against those whose position is such that they might conceivably jeopardize the régime. After "Bloody Saturday" the anti-Semitic motif in the Nazi press was noticeably modulated. If, however, some embittered Jewish youth should ever assassinate a prominent personality in the régime, as happened on occasion in Tsarist Russia, a general pogrom of German Jews is by no means outside the realm of possibility. Anti-

[1] *V.B.*, May 13, 1934.
[2] *The New York Times*, May 12, 1934.

Semitic tirades in the Nazi press, accompanied by denunciation of "Peroxide Aryans," began to increase again during the winter of 1934–5. Meanwhile the Jews will carry on, since they have been accustomed for centuries to survive even the most savage persecution. All things considered, it is probable that the Jews can dispense with Germany more easily than Germany can dispense with the Jews. The ultimate fate of the anti-Semitic despotisms of the past does not lend support to the prediction that Nationalsocialism will ever conquer or outlast Judaism.

3. LIBERALS AND MARXISTS

NUMEROUS groups in the Reich other than the Jews have likewise served the dictatorship as scapegoats. Marxists, liberals, pacifists, Freemasons, nudists, internationalists, feminists, modernists in music and art, and advocates of birth-control have all, in greater or lesser degree, been suppressed and browbeaten. The persecution of these groups, like that of the Jews, has furnished a convenient means of discharging sadistic tensions and has served in part to distract public attention from economic problems. All of them, in Nazi ideology, are but tools of the Israelite world conspiracy. If the values for which they stood were not regarded as obnoxious on their own account, they would be none the less damned because of their alleged relationship to Judas and Bolshevism.

Only a few phases of this process need be touched upon here. Nazi insistence upon the intimate connection between Marxism and liberalism has been vehement from the beginning. While the KPD served as the great bogy from which Hitler saved the Reich in March 1933, the SPD and the bourgeois State Party were crushed in June. Nationalist and Centrist deputies were permitted to become "guests" of the NSDAP, but all avowed Marxists and liberals were deprived of their seats, and many of them arrested. Einstein was deprived of his property and citizenship, less because he was a Jew than because he was a liberal and a pacifist. On August 23 the government issued a list of thirty-three "outcasts" doomed to similar treatment. It included the pacifists Alfred Kerr, Otto Lehmann-Russbildt, Friedrich Foerster, Kurt Grossmann, and Hellmuth von Gerlach, as well as such avowed Communists as Wilhelm Münzenburg, Hans Neumann, Max Hoelz, and Ernst Toller. It likewise included such liberals as Georg Bernard and Leopold Schwarzschild, along with the Social Democrats: Philip Scheidemann, Otto Wels, Friedrich Stampfer, Albert Grzesinski, Bernhard Weiss, and Rudolf Weissmann.

Not only were the bank accounts and other properties of such exiles confiscated, but they were branded as traitors and even deprived of their academic degrees. On March 29, 1934, the Ministry of the Interior published a list of thirty-seven other "enemies of the State," who were deprived of their property and citizenship: Albert Einstein, Otto Friedländer, Arthur Gross, Helmut Klotz, Kurt Rosenfeld, Mrs. Max Hoelz, et al.[1] Many republican officials who remained, including Heinrich Hirtsiefer and Karl Stingle, were prosecuted and imprisoned for "embezzlement." The periodical arrests and prosecutions of Communists for alleged crimes committed prior to January 1933 have been noted in the preceding chapter. Raids and arrests of this kind, like anti-Semitic activities, have become frequent whenever social unrest and intra-party friction have been acute. When, on May 1, 1934, a fire burned down the Augsburg Sängerhalle, seventy-three alleged Marxists were arrested, on the ground that this was "another Bolshevist conflagration." [2]

Freemasons and Jews were denounced as "arch-enemies of the German peasantry" by Walter Darré, in an address to fifty thousand farmers at Hamm on December 3, 1933. On January 16, 1934, Göring invited the Masonic lodges of Prussia to dissolve themselves voluntarily, under threat of forcible suppression.[3] A week later the *V.B.* announced that the German defeat at the first battle of the Marne, hitherto attributed to the Jews, was probably the result of a Masonic conspiracy. One Steiner, an anthroposophist, was alleged to have delivered an address to army officers in the general headquarters in Coblenz at the end of August 1914, thereby presumably distracting their attention from the campaign. The Mason, Lieutenant Hentsch, alleged to be the son of a French banker, then gave the orders to retreat. The Reichswehrministerium offered documentary proof that Steiner never gave the address in question and that Hentsch had given no orders, was not a Mason, and was the son of German Aryan parents. The *V.B.* nevertheless entitled its account: "The

[1] *V.B.*, March 31, 1934.
[2] *The New York Times*, May 2, 1934.
[3] *V.B.*, January 17, 1934.

Battle of the Marne—A Masonic Betrayal?" [1] While a few Masonic lodges apparently survive in the Reich, the entire organization has been repeatedly denounced and subjected to official pressure and local dissolution under charges of having initiated the French Revolution, betrayed Germany in 1918, and made itself a tool of democracy, liberalism, and the "Jewish world conspiracy."

Pacifism has been ruthlessly exterminated. All known pacifists have been dismissed from their posts in journalism, teaching, and other professions. Their books have been burned or banned and they have been driven into exile, imprisoned, or deprived of their citizenship and property. On April 16, 1934, a Berlin labour court upheld the right of an employer to discharge a worker who had boasted of having sold his Iron Cross when taken prisoner during the war:

"Such disparagement of military decorations assails grievously the spirit of defence and the patriotism of the new Germany. The court is convinced that the appellant was actuated in his utterances by a pacifist and defeatist disposition and the intent to ridicule war medals and to strike at the military spirit." [2]

Many organizations which were in no sense pacifist, but which merely sponsored the amicable settlement of international disputes, have been dissolved, among them the German Society of International Law. The peace weekly *Das andere Deutschland* was suppressed on March 3, 1933, and its editor, Friedrich Küster, imprisoned. *Die deutsche Zukunft* was suppressed on March 1, 1933. Its editor, Herr Riechert, and his son were imprisoned. In June S.A. men took them from jail, fastened a placard about the son's neck: "I am a traitor," affixed another about the father's neck: "And my family also," and paraded them in a wagon through the streets of Heide. Other liberal periodicals which were suppressed, with the jailing of their editors, were: *Die neue Generation* (Helene Stöcker); *Die neue Erziehung* (Paul Oestreich); *Die Frau im Staate* (Lida Heymann); *Die Menschenrechte; Der Friedenskampfer* (organ of the Friedensbund Deutscher Katholiken, dissolved on July 1, 1933). Captain Georg Lichey, editor of the *Chronik der Menschheit,* sought to establish a "national" peace society to support the "peace policy" of the government. In July 1933 he was sent to a concentration camp for his pains, and his paper suppressed. When *Die Friedens-Warte,* founded by Alfred

[1] *V.B.,* January 25, 1934.
[2] *The New York Times,* April 17, 1934.

Fried in 1889 and edited by the distinguished jurists Walter Schücking and Hans Wehberg, was compelled to move to Geneva, the last peace periodical printed in Germany disappeared.[1]

Even the ultra-patriotic monarchists have been repeatedly denounced by the NSDAP. In September 1933, police raided a castle near Heidenheim and announced the discovery of a "plot" of aristocrats and intellectuals against the régime. "Brazen reaction" was vigorously denounced by Goebbels during the spring of 1934. *Der Deutsche,* in January 1934, went so far as to condemn the Crown Prince for refusing to permit the cultivation of a moor belonging to his Silesian estate and reserved for hunting.[2] On the seventy-fifth birthday of the Kaiser, Darré and other Nazi leaders criticized the former Emperor and persuaded the Stahlhelm *Kreuz-Zeitung* ("Forward with God for King and Fatherland") to temper its praises.[3] All remaining monarchist organizations were dissolved in February. While the Junkers have been left undisturbed with their estates and privileges, and even subsidized by the Nazi régime in the style to which they were accustomed, all political activity looking toward a monarchical restoration has been suppressed.

Meanwhile Marxist heads have "rolled in the sand." The most spectacular prosecution of "Marxist criminals" was the Reichstag fire trial.[4] As the most extraordinary and politically important judicial proceedings in the history of post-war Germany, it was the centre of world-wide attention. Upon its issue hinged the answer to many questions: Had the Reichstag been burned by Communists? Did the NSDAP save Germany from an impending Communist insurrection? Had the Nazis fired the Reichstag, as many of their enemies alleged? The KPD was on trial, with all the machinery of the German State organized to prove its guilt. The NSDAP was on trial, with the same machinery organized to defend it from the accusations of the *Brown Book*. Here was to be Hitler's great *auto-da-fé,* with public beheadings of the culprits promised. The German public must be convinced of the truth of the myth which delivered the panic-stricken electorate to the Nazis on March 5.

When the trial opened, and thereafter for many months, the salva-

[1] For details of these developments, cf. *Die Friedens-Warte,* April–May 1934, pp. 79–81.

[2] *The New York Times,* January 18, 1934.

[3] Ibid., January 21, 1934.

[4] For an account of the fire, cf. pp. 201f. above.

tion of Germany from Bolshevism was a constant theme of the press. An anti-Communist "Revolutionary Museum" was opened in Berlin. In September, to the tune of much trumpeting, appeared a book published by the Union of German Anti-Communist Societies: Adolf Ehrt's *Bewaffneter Aufstand! Enthüllungen über den kommunistischen Umsturzversuch am Vorabend der nationalen Revolution* (Berlin: Eckart; 1933), subsequently translated into English under the title: *Communism in Germany*. On its front cover appeared the burning Reichstag—and amid the flames two armed Spartacists and the figure of Van der Lubbe holding a membership card of the KPD. On the back cover was the grotesquely tattooed torso of the murderer of Horst Wessel, the *Rot Front* emblem, and the bloody head of a dead hero. Within was a sensational history of the KPD, with numerous ghastly photographs of S.A. men shot, stabbed, beaten, or otherwise maltreated by Red ruffians. Pictures of Horst Wessel and other martyrs were to be found within, as well as caricatures of Communist leaders. But none of the "documents" proving the existence of a Communist conspiracy in February 1933 were here. Few readers would notice this, however. The "proof" of Communist criminality was sufficient. The great trial would offer more proof.

There were obstacles, however, in the way of making the trial serve its intended purpose. These obstacles led to much muddling and finally caused the whole proceeding to fail in its major aim: that of convicting the five defendants of having burned the Reichstag on behalf of the KPD, as a signal for a Red uprising. First of all, there was "world opinion" to consider. Though the Nazi leaders were contemptuous of foreign critics, they could ill afford to convict the defendants on perjured evidence and rush them to their death. Four of them were foreigners, though subjects of small, weak States whose governments could not or would not protect them. All eyes were focused on Leipzig. The trial would be a test of "justice" in the Third Reich. Some pretense of judicial impartiality must therefore be maintained. This necessity imposed obvious limits upon the degree of political coercion which could be exercised against the court and the extent to which perjury could be resorted to. By the time the trial opened, moreover, it seemed more important to prove that the Nazis did not burn the Reichstag than to prove that the Communists did. For this purpose, too, the rituals of the law must be observed, for otherwise there would be no popular confidence in the court nor respect for its verdict. The *Brown Book* must be refuted and the "parallel trial" held in London by an international committee of jurists must be discredited. And if, as is probable, the conflagration was the work of Nazis, it was of the most vital importance that no hint of the truth should leak out at the trial.

Dr. Karl Werner, Chief Public Prosecutor of the Reich, and Dr. Parisius, his assistant, spent almost seven months in preparing the case. Herr Heissig had conducted the initial examination of Van der Lubbe and had gone to Leyden to gather more evidence. For five months the defendants were kept in chains day and night, a barbarity "justified" only by the fact that Dimitroff had once "threatened" Dr. Vogt, the examining magistrate of the Reich Supreme Court, and that Taneff had attempted suicide. The tactics which the prosecution was to follow were indicated early. On March 22, 1933, Dr. Vogt issued a statement containing one allegation which was never verified—namely, that Van der Lubbe had been in touch with German Communists—and three statements which were later shown to be false—namely, that Van der Lubbe was a Dutch Communist, that he had communicated with foreign Communists, and that these included the culprits in the Sofia cathedral explosion of 1925. The lengthy indictment was never published in full. The defendants were accused of "actions preparatory to high treason, with the object of changing by violence the Constitution of the German Reich." They were tried under *ex post facto* laws. The retroactive decree of February 28 and the acts of March 24 and 29 provided the death penalty or long terms of imprisonment for crimes against public security and arson from political motives.

The trial opened September 21, 1933, before the Fourth Penal Chamber of the Reich Supreme Court in Leipzig—the same body before which Hitler had declared, three years previously, that "heads would roll" when he came into power. Dr. Bünger was presiding judge. His four associates were Doctors Coenders, Rusch, Lersch, and Fröhlich. The prosecution was conducted by Werner and Parisius. Only Torgler was defended by a lawyer of his own choice: Dr. Alfonse Sack, a Nazi attorney and an old friend of his client. Van der Lubbe rejected the services of a defender, but the court named Dr. Seuffert as his attorney. It likewise assigned Dr. Teichert to defend the Bulgarians, who were denied the right to employ foreign counsel. From September 21 to October 7 the court met in Leipzig. From

October 10 to November 18 it met in Berlin, in the Budget Committee Room of the Reichstag building, where the session chamber was still in process of repair. From November 23 to December 23 it met again in Leipzig, sitting in all for fifty-seven days. Ten stenographers filled ten thousand pages with testimony. Excerpts were recorded on seven thousand wax disks for broadcasting. Over a hundred witnesses were called from all parts of Europe.

Van der Lubbe, led in with chains about his waist and wrists, sat through the proceedings in a stupor—eyes dull, tousled head between his knees, mucus dripping from his mouth and nose. He answered questions by "Yes," "No," or "Can't say." He admitted his own guilt, refused to talk or to implicate his co-defendants, and occasionally mumbled incoherently. "Communist tactics," said the prosecution. "Imbecility," said foreign observers. Only twice was he aroused from his coma. When on October 20 Count Helldorf suddenly barked at him: *"Mensch, mach doch den Kopf hoch! Los!"* Van der Lubbe slowly raised his head. "His master's voice," said unkind foreign reporters who suspected Helldorf of being one of the incendiaries. But the Dutchman denied knowing the Count. Then again on November 23 Van der Lubbe roused himself and talked ramblingly and childishly: He could not agree with the way in which the trial was conducted; he had fired the Reichstag "for personal reasons" and had no accomplices; he wanted to be sentenced; he was tired of his cell, of chains, of too many meals, of "all this symbolism." He heard voices. . . . The subsequent interrogation revealed nothing. The experts said that he was sane and responsible. Others were skeptical. During the final plea of the prosecutor for his death, he fell asleep.

The "hero" of the trial was Dimitroff.[1] Popoff and Taneff remained passive. Torgler defended himself ably—and was conscientiously represented by Dr. Sack. He was thoroughly honest, intelligent, unbroken, and unafraid, but lacking in daring. Dimitroff was a lion—a true professional revolutionary, a Communist ready to die for his faith, a scholar, a gentleman, a linguist, a master of irony, a veritable *enfant terrible*. No threats could silence him. He made speeches, cross-questioned witnesses, trapped perjurers in contradictions, expressed his contempt for the court, sent the audience into gales of laughter with apt phrases, and dared to taunt even Göring and Goebbels. Five times he was excluded from the court-room. Five times

[1] Cf. Stelle Blagoyeva: *Dimitrov* (New York: International Publishers; 1934).

he came back and resumed his effective attacks on the prosecution. Even the stolid and testy Dr. Bünger came at last to respect him. In February 1933 he was unknown. By December he had won the admiration of half the world.

Only the strategy of the prosecution need be reviewed here, and this only in part. Most of the prosecution witnesses were perjurers, stool-pigeons, criminals, or otherwise untrustworthy persons. The prosecution had no consistent plan. Its witnesses repeatedly contradicted themselves and one another, forgot things they had once remembered, remembered things they had once forgot, and tangled themselves up in a hopeless maze of lies and inconsistencies. A partial roll-call is illuminating: Ernst Panknin, labourer under arrest, averred confusedly that he had heard Van der Lubbe discuss arson with Neukölln "Communists." Paul Bogun, engineer, "identified" Popoff as a man whom he thought he saw run from Portal 2 at nine o'clock. Leon Organistka, tramp, testified that he had met Van der Lubbe near Lake Constance in October 1932 (when Van der Lubbe was in Holland) and had heard him make threats against the Reichstag. Willi Hintze, convicted swindler, had "heard" Van der Lubbe plotting terror. Frau Helene Pretzsch, housewife and gossip, had seen Torgler carrying brief-cases, probably filled with "incendiary materials," on the morning of February 27. Wilhelm Hornemann, day porter at Portal 5, "remembered," after eight months' silent reflection, that he had seen Dimitroff leave the Reichstag on the afternoon of February 27 (when Dimitroff was in Munich) and had heard him say: "The Reichstag may go up in the air in fifteen or twenty minutes." He had also seen Koenen acting "suspiciously" and had smelled gasoline.

Berthold Karwahne, ex-Communist, and Kurt Frey, both Nazi members of the Reichstag, as well as Stefan Kroyer, a Nazi fugitive from Austria, swore solemnly that they had seen Torgler in the Reichstag talking with Van der Lubbe and Popoff. Major Hans Weberstedt, head of the Nazi Parliamentary Press Department, swore that he had smelled gasoline near the Communist Party room on February 27 and had seen Van der Lubbe and Taneff near by together. "A German officer does not lie!" he said pompously. Dr. Ernst Dröschel, who had identified Dimitroff as one of the men who blew up the Sofia cathedral in 1925 (Dimitroff left Bulgaria in 1923), saw Torgler and Dimitroff in the Reichstag "from two to five days before the fire." When confronted with other men resembling the defendants, the Nazi witnesses declared it "quite impossible" that they could have been mistaken. All of which was sheer nonsense and invention. The five Nazis were never punished for perjury, though the poor defence witness Sönke was jailed for telling petty lies to shield himself.

The other prosecution witnesses were, if possible, even more dubious. Fräulein Willa Hartmann, an employee of the Prussian Diet, had seen Koenen in an elevator on the afternoon of February 21, giving "a funny look" to a man "resembling" Van der Lubbe. August Lebermann, thief and convict, asserted that Torgler offered him sixteen thousand marks in January 1932 to burn the Reichstag. Gerhard Hoeft, Nazi restaurateur, testified that Torgler was suspiciously unexcited when he heard the news of the fire at Aschinger's. Emil Stawicki testified that Torgler was suspiciously overexcited in his café later in the evening. Herr Zimmermann, journalist, swore that Torgler had told him on a train a few days before the fire: "When the beacon blazes up, the Nazis will creep into their holes." The miner, rapist, and ex-convict Otto Kunzack had been released from jail in order to "ferret out terrorist groups through their female associates." He had seen Van der Lubbe at a Communist meeting in Düsseldorf in 1925 and had observed Torgler in 1930 experimenting with explosives in a forest near Berlin. He first met Torgler in his offices in the Karl Liebknecht House and heard him speak in the New World Gardens in Neukölln in 1930. (Torgler had no offices in the Karl Liebknecht House and spoke only once, in 1925, in the New World Gardens.)

Other witnesses likewise "identified" various of the defendants in places where they had never been or at times when they were elsewhere. Popoff was seen with Communists in an apartment on Zechlinerstrasse, when he was in Russia. Frau Schreiber, charlady where Dimitroff once lived in 1931, had seen him with German Communists—and had incidentally ransacked his papers and accused him of trying to ravish her! Otto Groethe, labourer, related how he had been told that the firing of the Reichstag was plotted by Thälmann in the Karl Liebknecht House, and that all the defendants had met in the Tiergarten on the afternoon of February 27 to plan the conflagration. His "informants," when summoned, expressed doubts of his sanity. There followed a convict, an inmate of a concentration camp, a police official, several detectives, a Ph.D. who read a paper on Communist theory, several arrested Communists, a lunatic, and at the end several more Communists from scattered villages, one of whom said he had signed a confession under threats of being beaten by S.A. men.

Several prominent personalities of the NSDAP lent colour to the proceedings. Count Helldorf denied the charges in the *Brown Book*. Lieutenant Schultze, Feme murderer, proved that he was in Bavaria in February 1933. Edmund Heines asserted on November 6: "I should like to say quite openly that we S.A. comrades hardly understand the forbearance with which the accused in this trial are being treated." He had not led any incendiaries through the tunnel on February 27. He had been making a speech in Gleiwitz. Goebbels appeared on November 8—also to refute the *Brown Book*. Göring on November 5 told of his fight against Communism. Dimitroff boldly accused Göring of lies and misrepresentations. The corpulent Minister grew red with anger. He shouted: "You behave yourself brazenly. You come here, burn the Reichstag, and then behave yourself impudently in the face of the German people. Your place is on the gallows!" "Are you afraid of these questions?" asked Dimitroff, while judge Bünger bawled: "Out with him!" Dimitroff retorted: "I am satisfied," as policemen dragged him from the chamber. Göring screamed at the top of his voice: "I am not afraid of you, you scoundrel. I am not here to be questioned by you. . . . You crook, you belong on the gallows! You will be sorry yet, if I catch you when you come out of prison!"

The prosecution had failed miserably to prove its case. Its witnesses who were reliable incriminated nobody save Van der Lubbe. The others lied so clumsily that even the judges were embarrassed. While the *Brown Book* version of the fire was in part refuted, the possibility of Nazi complicity was by no means excluded by the evidence. All that was proved was that the State had no case against four of the defendants, nor against the KPD, and that a Dutch half-wit had burned some curtains and furniture. But Dr. Werner, in his ten-hour closing plea on December 13–14, asked the death of Van der Lubbe for high treason and arson, the execution of Torgler for high treason, and the acquittal of the Bulgarians for lack of proof. The evidence upon which Torgler was accused was exactly comparable to the evidence against the Bulgarians. But Werner insisted that Torgler was implicated "in some sort of fashion." Dr. Teichert for the defence concurred in asking the acquittal of the Bulgarians. Dr. Seuffert argued that Van der Lubbe's connections with Communists had not been demonstrated and that he was guilty of arson, but not of treason; a heavy prison sentence should suffice. Dr. Sack defended himself from criticism and assailed the attack upon Torgler. The prosecution had proved nothing and Torgler should be acquitted. Dimitroff delivered himself of a concluding philippic on December 16, attacking Fascism, defending Communism, and asking compensation "for his wasted time." Turning to Van der Lubbe bitterly, he declared:

"There sits this stupid dupe, the shabby Faust, but Mephistopheles is absent. The alliance was struck in Hennigsdorf between political madness and political provocation. Van der Lubbe is no Communist; he is not even an anarchist; he is a rebellious ragamuffin." [1]

On December 23, 1933, the court delivered its verdict:

"The accused Torgler, Dimitroff, Popoff, and Taneff, are acquitted. The accused Van der Lubbe is condemned, for high treason in the overt act of insurrectionary arson and for attempted arson, to death and the permanent loss of civic rights." [2]

In reading the grounds for the judgment, Dr. Bünger defended the Nazis and said strangely that it had been proved that the fire was the work of Communists and "that the German people, early in 1933, was in peril of delivery to Communism and thus had stood on the verge of the abyss from which it had been saved in the last moment." In the court's opinion, Van der Lubbe had not fired the Reichtag alone. He acted "in deliberate co-operation with others." But the others were unknown. The various "identifications" were doubtful.

"All things considered, it must be affirmed that the deed was an act of high treason undertaken by the KPD. Torgler, Dimitroff, Popoff, and Taneff cannot be regarded as convicted of complicity in the overt act. On the other hand, Van der Lubbe fired the Reichstag in conscious co-operation with unknown accomplices. . . . In doing so he pursued the treasonable aims of the KPD, which were to bring about a violent upheaval leading to the erection of the proletarian

[1] Douglas Reed: *The Burning of the Reichstag*, p. 328.
[2] Ibid., p. 330.

dictatorship by inflaming the masses and provoking a general strike." [1]

The verdict was hailed in the foreign press as a "triumph of justice" and in the Nazi press as a "travesty on justice." [2] The public beheading of Van der Lubbe never took place. He sat apathetically in his cell, giving no evidence of activity in his dark and befuddled brain. On December 27 the Dutch government protested against the death penalty, on the ground that it was based on an *ex post facto* law. The protest was unavailing. In great secrecy the Fourth Penal Chamber met for the last time on the morning of January 10, 1934, in the yard of the Leipzig Provincial Court. Doctors Werner and Parisius were there, as well as the prison chaplain (whose services Van der Lubbe rejected), the prison governor, two doctors, twelve citizens, and a gentleman in a top hat, evening dress, and white gloves: the executioner. Van der Lubbe was led out. His twenty-fourth birthday was three days away. He had killed no one and injured no one. Ten years before, another young building-trades labourer had engaged in open treason and had brought death to eighteen young men. For this he had served fourteen months in jail. He was now Chancellor of the Reich. But Van der Lubbe must die. He shambled listlessly, his head down and saliva dripping from his gaping mouth. There was no ax, but a guillotine. Van der Lubbe obediently laid his tousled head on the board. He made no motion as he was fastened in. A momentary pause, the swift fall of the heavy blade, a thud in the bloody sawdust. Van der Lubbe's family requested the removal of the body to Holland. The request was refused —perhaps out of fear that some strange discovery might be made. The remains were interred at Leipzig on the 15th.

Torgler remained in jail. Thälmann and other Communist leaders have also been in jail since March 1933. They are presumably to be tried before the new "People's Court." As for the three Bulgarians, Göring's violent threats remained unfulfilled. On February 15, 1934, the government of the U.S.S.R. made them Soviet citizens and at once demanded that they be released to Russia. Whether the Hitler Cabinet welcomed this opportunity of getting rid of the prisoners or resisted the demand is uncertain. If, as reported, Göring and Hitler

[1] Ibid., p. 335–6.

[2] *V.B.*, December 24, 1933, *"Das Fehlurteil von Leipzig,"* with interesting criticisms of the "formal juristic grounds" of the judgment and of "foreign liberal ideas," accompanied by a plea for judicial reform and "true German justice."

quarrelled over the issue, the will of Der Führer prevailed. On February 27 the Bulgarians were placed aboard a plane bound for the Soviet capital. Dimitroff, defiant to the last, said that if he ever returned, it would be to a German Soviet republic. The refugees were received as heroes in Moscow.

CHAPTER IX

THE DRAMATIZATION OF EXTERNAL THREATS

1. "LUFTSCHUTZ TUT NOT!"

On June 24, 1933 the *V.B.*—and, on official command, all other German papers—carried the following news item, prominently featured on the front page:

> FOREIGN AIRPLANES THROW MARXIST LEAFLETS OVER BERLIN
>
> The Catastrophic Results of the Ban on Police Planes for Germany
>
> Away with the Unendurable Chains of the Versailles Treaty!
>
> This afternoon airplanes of a type unknown in Germany appeared over Berlin and threw down, over the government quarters and over the east of Berlin, leaflets with a text attacking the Reich government. Since the air police had no planes of its own at its disposal and the sport planes summoned from the air-field could not achieve the speed of the foreign planes, they remain unidentified.
>
> This event illustrates vividly the intolerable situation in which Germany today finds herself. Airplanes of a type hitherto unseen in Germany can appear without hindrance over the government buildings and throw down leaflets with unheard-of insults to the German Reich.

The next day thousands of posters throughout the nation screamed:

"This time *Hetz-blätter!* Next time bombs!? Germany must have planes! *Luftschutz tut Not!"* When foreign correspondents inquired about the details of the "raid," which no one had observed at the time, they were told that three "enemy" planes of unprecedented speed had flown over the city at a height of nine thousand feet—invisible to most Berliners because of a light fog. No one could produce a sample of the leaflets. It was officially explained that they had fallen only in Wilhelmstrasse and that their contents were such that they could not be divulged. Millions of Germans were impressed with the defencelessness of the Reich. The foreign correspondents were impressed only with Göring's ingenuity—and with his naïveté.

The Reichsluftschutzbund (RLB) was founded on April 28, 1933, by Göring. Lieutenant-General Grimm and Major Waldschmitt headed its präsidium. It was organized into fifteen *Landesgruppen,* with each of these divided into *Ortsgruppen.* Local police stations are everywhere used as recruiting offices. The work of the Air Defence League is supported by manufacturers of gas-masks, chemicals, and building-materials, who advertise their wares in its two periodicals, *Der Reichsluftschutz* and *Deutsche Flugillustrierte.* It carries its message daily to the entire public by lectures, films, posters, pictures, pamphlets, books, magazines, training schools, demonstrations, and incessant advertising. A typical meeting proceeds as follows:

Time: 11.30 any Sunday morning. Place: Any large cinema theatre in Berlin—or any other large German city. Occasion: *Luftschutz-appel!* Posters are plastered all over the neighbourhood billboards: "Nine Thousand Enemy Airplanes Menace Germany!" Outside on the walk an S.A. band, smartly attired in brown uniforms, plays military music. The Berliner burghers are present *en masse,* fat, well dressed, and seemingly unfatigued by the church services from which many of them have just come. The crowd overflows the lobby and there are hundreds in the street who will be unable to obtain seats. Inside, there is a stir of suppressed excitement and anticipatory appreciation of promised thrills. The interior of the theatre has been decorated with flags. The S.A. band retires to the stage. As the curtains part, the air vibrates with the martial rhythm of bugles, trumpets, and drums. After each number the conductor clicks his heels and responds to the applause with the Fascist salute.

At length a smallish S.A. man appears behind the improvised pulpit, decorated with swastikas. He is a district leader of the brown army. He salutes, repeats with solemn emphasis the current slogans of the Reichsluftschutzbund ("Air Protection is Self-Protection!" "Air Protection is the Need of the Hour!" "Air Protection is a National Duty!" etc.), and introduces the lecturer. The latter is a war veteran, an S.A. major, an oldish thundering man with thin lips, grey hair, a belted paunch, and bowed legs in leather knee-boots. A collection of military decorations glitters on his natty brown uniform. He clicks his heels, salutes, and bellows: *"Heil Hitler!"* The audience responds as one man with a salute and an answering *"Heil!"* He begins:

Volkesgenossen und Volkesgenossinnen! The next war will be won in the air and on the home front. Let us not forget that the last war was not lost on the battlefield. The civilians lost their nerve, and the army was stabbed in the back by the Jewish-Marxist traitors. If we had held out only two months more, we should have had a very different peace. In the next war civilian morale will be even more decisive. The enemy will seek to paralyse the home front by means of air-raids. Treaties? Does anyone expect treaties to be observed in war? League of Nations? The Geneva Disarmament comedy? (The major snorts and chortles. The audience titters.) We shall soon make an end of all that! Protection against air-raids is not to be improvised on short notice. The need is for action *now*. The need is for action by *civilians,* by the whole population, by everybody —especially by women, for women's services are particularly important in air defence. The best defence against bombers is attack—by pursuit planes and by anti-aircraft guns. But these are forbidden to Germany by the damnable Treaty of Versailles. Civilian self-help is the only refuge of a defenceless people.

What is the danger which we face? France had 4,500 military planes, Belgium 400, Czechoslovakia 950, Poland 1,000. Within two hours enemy bombers can reach *any city in the Reich* from the frontiers! (The Major becomes terrifying. His hearers grow tense.) There are no more border cities. Berlin is a border city. Planes from Posen or Prague can reach Berlin in an hour! Germany's strategic situation is appalling. We are menaced from all sides. *Luftschutz tut Not!* But let no one believe wild tales. Berlin can *not* be destroyed overnight. All its inhabitants can *not* be gassed by enemy squadrons. Such stories are nonsense—or treason. There are not enough explosives, not enough gas, not enough planes in the world to accomplish this. The real danger is sufficiently terrible. No one can guarantee one hundred per cent protection. But adequate defence measures will be effective—*if* the population is awakened, educated, and, above all, strictly disciplined. (Applause.)

What is to be done? First, against explosive bombs: These are highly destructive only to upper storeys of buildings and to people in crowds. When the alarm is given, all market-places, streets, tramways, schools, theatres, factories, etc., must be evacuated promptly. The populace must take refuge in bomb-proof basements. Huge mine-bombs, weighing a thousand kilograms or more, can of course destroy whole buildings, cellars included. But (the Major is reassuring) these are much too expensive for general bombing operations against civilians. . . . Second, gas-bombs: The refuge cellars must be gas-proof. Sanitary and hospital corps, the police and fire brigades will be equipped with gas-masks. Everyone should, if possible, secure a gas-mask. Mustard gas is most dangerous, as it attacks both skin and lungs. But sanitary precautions and prompt treatment are effective. Third: incendiary bombs. These are most difficult to combat, for they are small and each plane can carry several hundred. Forty per cent of such bombs thrown out over a city will land on roofs and generate an intense heat within a few seconds. No fire department can cope with this menace. Only civilian self-help will suffice.

The necessary work is already under way. All attics are being cleared of inflammable rubbish. In one raid in Schöneberg fifteen old featherbeds were discovered in an attic (laughter). Such negligence is criminal! It may endanger hundreds of lives. All attics must be cleared, and every attic floor must be covered with bricks, cement, or at least several inches of dry sand. There must be several water-pails and a sand-barrel. Only dry sand will quench fire-bombs. Basements are already being cleared out and equipped with reinforced ceilings and first-aid stations. Every house must have a roof-watcher who will be responsible for attic service when the alarm is given. At least ten per cent of the population must be enlisted if *Luftschutz* is to be effective. The goal of the RLB in greater Berlin is a membership of four hundred thousand.

This task (the Major concludes with patriotic flourishes) is a peculiar responsibility of the Nationalsocialist movement. It is "national" because it concerns the defence of the Fatherland. It is "social" because it concerns the entire community: bombs will fall with complete impartiality on rich and poor, employers and workers, Aryans and—yes, even on Jews! All must help! Save the Fatherland! Join the *Luftschutzbund!*[1]

The RLB has carried on its work with great vigour and efficiency. Göring's public appeal for police planes after the "raid" of June 23 brought no response from foreign capitals. The *Bund* therefore issued an appeal on July 12 for the co-operation of the whole people in preparing to resist air-attacks.[2] Neurath, in an interview with the foreign press on September 21, professed the pacific aims of German foreign policy, but demanded protection against air-raids.[3] Striking coloured posters, showing Berlin in flames under the attack of dozens of huge enemy bombers, called the citizenry to action: "Save Yourselves in the RLB!" A decree of the Ministry of Finance of October 10 specified that all expenditures for *Luftschutz*—that is, the construction of shelters, reinforcement of walls and roofs, purchase of fire-pumps, extinguishers, alarm signals, etc.—might be deducted in making out income-tax returns, provided that the expenditures were made in the course of a single year.[4] In November the first great *Luftschutz* exposition in Berlin was opened on Alexanderplatz. Staatssekretär Milch announced that the *Bund* had 1,400 *Ortsgruppen* and over 750,000 members throughout the Reich.[5] "Every German must become a flyer!" was the slogan.[6] For the first time in the demilitarized Rhineland, a mock air-raid on Cologne was elaborately staged on April 18, 1934. The Berlin municipal authorities appropriated 8,652,000 marks for *Luftschutz* in the same month and announced a loan of 7,000,000 marks for the construction of bombproof shelters.

At the end of April 1934 the *Bund* had 2,000 *Ortsgruppen* and 2,500,000 members. By January 1, 1935, it had 5,000,000 members, including 1,800,000 officers. Exhibits and meetings are arranged in every city in the Reich. On many street intersections terrifying models of enormous bombs have been erected. The RLB works in co-operation with the building and chemical industries, the Luftsportver-

[1] This description is taken from the writer's article, written in Berlin: "Germany Prepares Fear," *New Republic,* February 7, 1934.

[2] *Berliner Tageblatt,* July 12, 1933.

[3] *V.B.,* September 22, 1933.

[4] *Berliner Tageblatt,* October 19 and November 5, 1933.

[5] Ibid., November 25, 1933.

[6] Cf. the regular *V.B.* supplement on *"Luftschutz"* and *"Die Luftrustungen der Anderen."*

band (an association of private pilots and sportsmen), and Göring's Aviation Corps, a uniformed and disciplined body of aviators employed by the Luft Hansa. "German Air-Sports Week" was inaugurated in June 1934. "The German people shall become a nation of flyers," declared Göring.[1] Lectures, radio talks, films, plays, exhibits, and torch-light parades were organized everywhere. Flyers collected funds in all cities for the cause. On October 22 the RLB, the Commissar for Berlin, the Chief of Police, and the Association of Berlin House- and Real-estate-Owners announced that "heavily armed foreign powers force the Germans to take immediate steps to protect women and children against air-attacks." All house-owners were called upon to construct a bomb-proof shelter in every dwelling and to contribute five marks each to a fund to assist less prosperous owners to construct safety cellars at once.[2] By the close of the year over seven thousand air-raid cellars had been constructed throughout the Reich.

Such activities, apart from their obvious strategic utility in the coming "war of liberation," are of primary significance as a means of manufacturing national unity and evoking mass consent to the dictatorship. Fear of the concentration camp and the ax is always a less effective device for the mobilization of acquiescence than the systematic inculcation of fear of foreign "enemies." Hatred of the out-group creates unity of the in-group. Ethnocentrism and xenophobia are opposite facets of the same coin. The bonds of unity which are thus created render more secure the position of the élite. The feudal nobility ruled by force and magic. The ascendant bourgeoisie of the democratic era ruled by nationalism. The decadent bourgeoisie and its Fascist spokesmen of the post-war epoch rule by the inculcation of mass paranoia and megalomania.

In order that the already established responses of aversion toward Frenchmen, Poles, Czechs, et al., might be transformed into fear and hatred, it was necessary for the NSDAP to undermine the most basic security-feelings of the German populace. Even depictions of the horrors of war, usually regarded as good pacifist propaganda, may be used to evoke feelings of insecurity, fear, and hatred, the fountainheads of militarism, rather than a love of peace. They are so used in the Third Reich. When the populace has been reduced to

[1] Cf. Wilhelm II: "Our future lies upon the sea."
[2] *The New York Times,* October 23, 1934.

a state of terror, when aversion has been transmuted into panic and rage, when thousands are prepared to adopt any measures which offer promise of safety, the political élite steps forth as the great defender of women, children, widows, orphans, farms, factories, and homesteads from the cruelty, pillage, and rapine threatened by the outer barbarians. It calls upon all to save themselves by common efforts. The régime thus becomes the beneficiary of the insecurities which it has created, since loyalty to leaders is the first law of self-defence.

This technique, familiar to all ruling classes and utilized effectively by diplomats, superpatriots, and armament-manufacturers everywhere, has been perfected and applied with extraordinary results in the Third Reich. One of its most interesting collateral aspects is to be found in the use of foreign "atrocity stories" to stir up patriotic resentment. Far from seeking to prevent the German masses from learning what is said about their government in the foreign press, Goebbels and his subordinates have consistently dramatized the more unfavourable foreign comments. They have in effect said: "See how we are lied about abroad. Germany wants peace and work. All is quiet and happy in the Reich. But abroad they say we are lawless, barbarous, and disorderly. Germans! Protect yourselves from such lies. Rally to the defence of your honour and your Fatherland!" The formula works like magic. Dozens of former liberals or radicals, originally hostile to the NSDAP, informed the writer during 1933 that, while they did not approve of the dictatorship, they were shocked at the "lies about Germany" printed abroad, and, as good Germans, would at least support their government in repudiating such shameless atrocity stories.

2. IMPERIALIST FANTASIES

"We must no longer have a pacific conception of peace. In the Middle Ages it was otherwise. The existence of the individual had no exaggerated importance. Pacifist literature depicts death on the field of battle as an unnatural death because it does not understand the ancient Germanic horror of death on a bed, and arteriosclerosis appears to it more virile than a bullet. Pacifists dwell on the horrors of the war dead as if a peace corpse were more æsthetic. The representatives of the national revolution are men and soldiers who are physically and morally warriors."

Thus Vice-Chancellor von Papen, who carefully kept out of the trenches during the Great War and who is now safely beyond military age, characterized the values and ideals of the Third Reich in a speech to a Stahlhelm gathering at Münster on May 13, 1933. In October 1933 Baldur von Schirach, Nazi youth leader, declared at the unveiling of a war memorial in Westphalia, consisting of a statue of the (Aryan?) Archangel Michael:

"Here we will not speak the warm words of peace, the words 'home' and 'Fatherland.' Our words are spoken in the face of the awful summons of war. Youths, your hands are now raised in an oath before this monument which is erected to the sublimity of bloodshed—and Michael is the Angel of Death—and you are swearing that your lives belong to the Reich, and your blood to Der Führer."[1]

The pan-German nationalism and the *Heldentum* militarism of the NSDAP, as well as the psychological and political exigencies which gave rise to these attitudes, have been discussed above.[2] The history of Nazi foreign policy is outside the scope of the present volume.[3]

It will nevertheless be necessary to review the conceptions of national interest and foreign policy which prevail in the Third Reich, if the implications of the particular political weapons here under consideration are to be appreciated. In the cult of militarism the good citizen of the new Germany preceives nothing incongruous or pathological. He has long since learned to relish, with Teutonic earnestness and enthusiasm, many things which to outsiders seem perverse or tragic or indubitably mad. Every day in every German city he cheers endless parades of troops—S.A., S.S., Stahlhelm, Reichswehr, police—and, by scores and by hundreds, he follows each parade through the streets for the sheer joy of goose-stepping, head high, chest out, and a strange light in his eyes. He goes in thousands to the Deutsche Koloniale Austellung on Potsdamerstrasse, for he sees nothing queer in a country without colonies having a colonial exposition. Over the door he reads, in flaming letters:

[1] London *Times,* October 31, 1933.

[2] Cf. pp. 124f. above.

[3] Cf. F. L. Schuman: "Nazi Dreams of World Power," *Current History,* February 1934; "The Third Reich's Road to War," *Annals of the American Academy,* September 1934; "The Conduct of German Foreign Affairs," *Annals,* November 1934.

" 'Never forget that the most holy right in this world is the right to land, and that the most hallowed of sacrifices is the blood which one sheds for this land'—Adolf Hitler." (Hitler is an anti-colonialist and his words refer to territories in eastern Europe which the new Germany is to conquer, but this is a minor incongruity.) Crowds of Berliners daily throng the war show *Die Front,* on Unter den Linden. "As it really was!" the signs announce. There are no horrors within, only heroism, victories, and graphic appeals for German rearmament. Lecturers lead crowds of schoolboys through the exhibits and fire their hearts with hero-tales. Their eyes glow with envy and admiration . . . and with hope.

The old militarism involved domination of civil authorities by the imperial army. The new militarism involves almost universal civilian warrior-worship, sponsored not by the Reichswehr but by the "civil" Nazi authorities. For reasons of internal policy and diplomatic expediency the Nazi leaders rejected the theory of the next war held by the Reichswehr High Command—that is, that it will be a contest between small, professional, highly mechanized field armies. They preach incessantly the more heroic doctrine of a war between whole peoples—or at least did so until "Bloody Saturday" removed some of the apostles of the "nation-in-arms." Their task was set for them years ago by Der Führer:

"The question of a restoration of German power is not a question of how to fabricate arms, but a question of how to create the spirit which makes a people capable of bearing arms. If this spirit dominates a people, the will finds a thousand ways to secure weapons." (*Mein Kampf,* p. 365.)

To the creation of this spirit the present German leaders are devoting all their genius as propagandists and all that profound knowledge of German mob psychology which enabled them to secure power. "War-mindedness," like "race-mindedness," is stimulated by high-pressure advertising and collective suggestion. Despite the prevalence of this ideology (or, in another sense, because of it), the leaders of the NSDAP have never ceased to profess their undying devotion to peace. Their various peace pronouncements would fill a large volume.

These pacifistic verbalizations on the part of the leaders of a dictatorship in which all pacifism is ruthlessly suppressed would deserve to be taken at their face value only if they bore some demonstrable relationship to the obvious determinants of German foreign policy. Their only relevance to these determinants is that they reflect the necessity of gaining time—time to rearm, time to find allies, time to set the stage for a "war of liberation" that may be fought with some prospect of success.

This judgment assumes that the foreign policies of Great Powers are not created in a vacuum, but are a product of forces and pressures largely independent of any particular group of individuals. The underlying presuppositions behind this evaluation are these: the State is an institutionalization of power relationships between social groups; the State, in its contacts with other States, is an embodiment of power and an expression of the will-to-power of its élite; all international politics is a competition, by diplomacy or by arms, for power, for the means of power, for the fruits of power, and for the components thereof—population, territory, colonies, markets, armaments, shipping, raw materials, etc.; each élite and each ruling group within an élite defines the stakes of diplomacy (that is, the content of its power interests) in terms of its own values and ideology. But the broad direction of this striving, and its orientation toward the existing distribution of power between States, are determined by geographical position and by the outcome of the last armed contest. Victorious "satiated" States seek to preserve the status quo of which they are the beneficiaries; they therefore champion "peace" and "security." Defeated "unsatiated" States seek to modify the status quo of which they are the victims; they therefore champion "justice" and "equality." In the absence of an international constitutional consensus in terms of which conflicts for power can be pacifically reconciled, the ultimate method of maintaining or modifying a given status quo is armed coercion. Dominant States accordingly insist upon preserving military superiority over potential disturbers of the peace. Oppressed States strive equally for a restoration of a balance of power which may some day be upset to their own advantage.

When two such groups of States crystallize into coalitions competing with one another as power blocs, each controversy between foreign offices tends to become a major "diplomatic crisis" involving danger of armed conflict between the two groups. Unsatiated States, striving for a brighter place in the sun, often appear to be "aggressors," since they must take the initiative if the status quo is to be modified. Satiated States, defending their gains, often appear to be victims of aggression, since passive maintenance of the existing distribution of power best serves their interests. In the long run, the behaviour of the Powers follows this pattern, modified at times by institutions of co-operation and of pacific settlement and by symbols, ideologies, and principles of law which transcend national frontiers. In particular crises clever diplomats may be able to create the illusion of a reversal of the roles. Germany, unsatiated and ascending in the power scale, was "attacked" by France in 1870. Serbia, unsatiated and irredentist, was "attacked" by Austria-Hungary after Sarajevo. The unsatiated Entente was "attacked" by the Central Powers in August 1914. It is the task of the diplomat to pave the way for the defeat of the enemy and to make the enemy appear the aggressor when the time is ripe for a test of force.[1]

An application of this formulation to the Reich suggests the permanent determinants of its international behaviour and leads to a solution of the paradox presented by militaristic superpatriots professing peace. As a State defeated, humiliated, partitioned, and disarmed, Germany's orientation toward the distribution of power incorporated in the Treaty of Versailles admits of not the slightest doubt. Germany, like Hungary, Italy, and, in a somewhat different sense, Japan, is an unsatiated "revisionist" Power. The most elementary considerations of diplomacy and strategy demand that those entrusted with the formulation of a German foreign policy strive to recover equality of status, freedom of action, an equilibrium of armaments, and a restoration of a balance of power between the victors and the vanquished of 1918. These have been the consistent aims of every Chancellor and Foreign Minister since June 28, 1919. In the Weimar republic, as in the Third Reich, diplomatic and military impotence dictated professions of peace and conciliatory policies. The liberal ideology of the republican Foreign Ministers—for example, Rathenau, Stresemann, Brüning—perhaps dignified these professions and policies into "principles" rather than mere opportunistic expedients. The ultimate goal, in any case, was a recovery of equality and freedom to act. The means adopted achieved no territorial changes and no grant of actual equality in armaments.

[1] For a more extended presentation of this thesis, see the writer's *War and Diplomacy in the French Republic* (New York: McGraw-Hill; 1931), pp. 401–22, and *International Politics* (New York: McGraw-Hill; 1933), pp. 491–532.

But they achieved a rapprochement with Russia in 1922, the evacuation of the Ruhr, the fixing of reparations on a more reasonable basis in the Dawes Plan of 1924, the Locarno Pacts of 1925, the admission of Germany to the League in 1926, the evacuation of the Rhineland in 1930, the virtual termination of reparations in 1932, and a pledge of arms equality "in principle."

These accomplishments could be persuasively presented as "defeats" by Nazi spokesmen, since patriotic expectations and diplomatic possibilities were at all times far apart. The general objectives, as determined by geography and by Versailles, were not changed through the seizure of power by the NSDAP. Specific means to ends were in part modified by the Nazi *Weltanschauung*. The ultimate goals were clarified and reformulated. The repudiation of reparations and the emancipation of the Rhineland from alien military occupation were already achieved. For the rest, the foreign policy of Hitler, Rosenberg, Göring, and Thyssen reflects the interests and values of monopolistic capital seeking markets, of Junkers seeking land and glory, and of an ultra-patriotic peasantry and *Kleinbürgertum* seeking honour, the illusions of might, and the psychic gratifications of a collective Napoleonism.

The *Realpolitik* program of Nazi imperialism has been stated so clearly and so frequently that it admits of no debate. The Continental territories lost in 1919 must be recovered. A pan-German State, embracing all of the eighty million German-speaking peoples of Europe, must be created—with the Swiss, the Dutch, the Flemings, and the Scandinavians as appendages. Overseas colonies and naval power are unimportant. Territories and markets in the Danube basin and in eastern Europe are indispensable. The Reich must therefore secure a free hand in the east in order to invade, conquer, and partition the Ukraine and Russia. This ambition was stated in the *V.B.* as early as January 1921, and was made part of the Nazi program by the potash magnate, Arnold Rechburg, and by Alfred Rosenberg. For this purpose *Anschluss* with Austria, the dissolution of the Little Entente, the termination of the Franco-Polish alliance, and the breaking of French hegemony are prerequisites. The status-quo bloc will thus be disintegrated.

The ultimate goals cannot be attained without war. Victory in war requires at least equality of armaments with the prospective enemy. If possible, British and Italian aid against France must be secured.

If this is impossible, then temporary bargains with Hungary and Poland must be sought, and perhaps with the Baltic States and Jugoslavia. Thus, arms and allies may be secured and the final reckoning may be scheduled for such a date as will coincide with the low ebb of French power and the high tide of Germanic ascendancy. German "self-respect" will thus be recovered. The tradition of Teutonic invincibility will be restored. France will be crushed and the *"Drang nach Osten"* will be resumed.

3. TOWARD WAR

THE program outlined above is a product of the Nazi *Weltanschauung*. This in turn has been shaped by the traumas and frustrations of patriotic soldiers who have come to glorify and idealize the very experience—namely, war—which has wounded them, broken them, and converted them into physical, spiritual, and mental wrecks. As the dictators of the Third Reich, these casualties of the trenches must evoke consent by the dramatization of national dangers, by the inculcation of military heroism, by the incessant preaching of war and revenge. Only thus can they identify themselves with bourgeois-peasant patriotism and distract the attention of the proletariat from its poverty. Militarism is indispensable for the amusement of the masses. It is equally indispensable for the satisfaction of the classes whose interests the NSDAP has always served. For Junkers it means military careers, glory, and lands in the east. For industrialists it means orders for guns, planes, tanks, and artillery, as well as new sources of raw material, new markets for goods, new fields for lucrative investment, all to be won by the sword. These are the permanent values and interests which must be served by Nazi foreign policy. All else is a temporary expedient.

The program has thus far been pursued with that singular obtuseness toward the psychological imponderables which has frequently characterized German diplomacy. Foreign opinion has been alienated by clumsy anti-Semitic and pro-Nazi propaganda disseminated by the APA, the Auslands Organisation of the party, the Deutsche Auslands Institut, the foreign branches of the NSDAP, the Fichte-Bund, the various agencies championing *"Deutschtum im Ausland,"* and, with regard to the United States, by the Steuben Society, the German headquarters of the Carl Schurz Association, the Amerika

Institut, and the "Friends of New Germany." These activities have been designed to enlist sympathy and support by fostering anti-Semitic and anti-Marxist sentiment. In America and England they have provoked official investigation, unofficial anti-German boycotts, and widespread popular hostility toward the Third Reich. The late Ivy Lee, "public-relations adviser" to numerous American corporations, was paid twenty-five thousand dollars by the German Dye Trust to manufacture American friendship for Germany.[1] Nazi propaganda in the United States reached such proportions in 1933 that it led to exposures, indictments, and the appointment of a Congressional investigating committee headed by Representative Dickstein of New York.[2] In Rumania comparable activities produced rioting by the Fascist "Iron Guard" and the assassination of Premier Duca in December 1933. Nazi propaganda in Czechoslovakia and Jugoslavia have bred resentment and suspicion. To add insult to injury, the Nazi leaders have repeatedly denied that they conduct any propaganda abroad.[3] But Goebbels alone spent millions of marks for such purposes, until Schacht, in September 1934, indicated that such wholly unprofitable expenditures must be reduced.[4]

Italy, comrade-in-Fascism and hoped-for ally, has been similarly alienated by persistent Nazi efforts to dominate Austria and to erect a Germany of seventy million people at the Brenner Pass, certain to press southward toward Bolzano and Trieste. Instead of capitalizing on Franco-Italian rivalry in the Mediterranean, Nazi policy in Austria has thrown Rome and Paris into more intimate and friendly contact than has existed at any time since 1919. Austrian independence was indeed terminated, but Austria became an Italian dependency, not a German province. Austria was indeed driven to Fascism in 1933, but to the anti-German, anti-Nazi, pro-Italian Fascism of Dollfuss and the Heimwehr. On February 17, 1934, following the slaughter of the Socialist workers of Vienna and the conversion of the Austrian government into a kind of branch of the Italian Foreign Office, the British, French, and Italian governments, acting jointly against Berlin for the first time in many years, issued a warning that Austrian "independence" must be respected. When sporadic terror-

1 *The New York Times,* July 12, 1934.

2 Cf. *Today* (Raymond Moley, ed.), March 31, April 7, April 14, 1934.

3 Cf. *The New York Times,* December 10, 1933 and August 15, 1934 (Hanfstängl), and *V.B.,* November 1, 1933 (Hitler).

4 *The New York Times,* September 5, 1934.

ism, economic pressure, and mass revolution all failed to produce the desired result, Hitler met Mussolini in Venice in mid-June 1934 and gave "assurances" that there would be no more German interference in Austrian affairs. On July 25 an unsuccessful Nazi putsch led to the assassination of Dollfuss, the mobilization of Italian troops on the Austrian border, and the bloody repression of the Austrian Nazis. More "disclaimers" and "assurances" followed, with the clever Papen sent to Vienna to restore "friendly relations." Even Jugoslavia, Italy's traditional enemy across the Adriatic, has not been brought into the German orbit. The trade treaty of May 1934 has not been followed by a political entente, thanks to Serbian doubts as to the desirability of a Nazified Austria.

To the east, Poland has been in part conciliated, but the U.S.S.R. has been completely alienated. Vague Hitlerite schemes of partitioning the Ukraine or the Baltic States or both with Pilsudski, coupled with Polish aspirations toward diplomatic independence and the stature of a Great Power, have led to various understandings between Berlin and Warsaw: a ten-year non-aggression pact signed January 26, 1934, whereby Germany surrendered all designs on the Corridor and Upper Silesia; an agreement of February 26, 1934, whereby both governments contracted to control public opinion in the interests of friendly relations, and Germany renounced the privilege of indulging in official anti-Polish polemics; a trade agreement of March 7, 1934, whereby a nine-year tariff war was terminated by German concessions; and agreements of August 1934 between Poland and the Nazi government of Danzig for a restoration of more advantageous trade relations. These surrenders to Warsaw on the part of Wilhelmstrasse have infuriated the Nazi radicals and aroused grave suspicions in France, Russia, and the Baltic States. But they have apparently not led to any actual political entente between Poland and the Reich. Poland has gained everything and yielded nothing. Germany has yielded everything and gained nothing—save a slight breach in the encircling wall of enmity.

Nazi ambitions to conquer and "colonize" eastern Europe have produced a complete revolution in Soviet foreign policy. Veiled threats of aggression and obscure conspirings between Rosenberg and Ukrainian separatists have been accompanied by innumerable pin-pricks. In the summer of 1933, and again a year later, the Nazi press carried horrendous tales, illumined with "authentic" photographs, of the great "famine" in Russia—all to show the happy citizens of the Third Reich that Hitler had saved them from the hunger-hell of Bolshevism.[1] Funds were collected in Germany for Russian "famine relief," until the Soviet authorities, in the summer of 1934, refused to tolerate such activities.[2] For a time, in the autumn of 1933, a counter-revolutionary group of Russian émigrés in Berlin was encouraged to found a Russian Nazi movement.[3] After appeals for Soviet "friendship" Rosenberg could still say, in January 1934, that a German understanding with France must not cut off the Reich from all "economic possibilities" in the east.[4]

Under these circumstances, Moscow embraced the least dangerous of its "bourgeois enemies" and initiated an intimate rapprochement with France. The Quai d'Orsay and the Narkomindel both expressed unalterable opposition to German rearmament. Litvinov nevertheless attempted, in pursuit of the Soviet Union's peace policy, to conclude a non-aggression pact with the Third Reich. He was repeatedly rebuffed. Both a bilateral pact and a general regional pact were rejected at Berlin. Barthou and Litvinov met British objections to a new Franco-Russian alliance by concocting the "Eastern Locarno" project of June 1934. Wilhelmstrasse rejected this likewise. The Soviet Union then joined the League of Nations and proceeded to tighten its diplomatic and military ties with France and the Little Entente. If Poland has been to some degree alienated from the French bloc, Italy and Russia have been thrown into the arms of Paris by the blunders of Nazi diplomacy. French hegemony is more assured than ever, and the united front of Paris, Rome, Moscow, Prague, Belgrade, and Bucharest makes it impossible for the Reich to dream of challenging her neighbours in arms. The only notable diplomatic "victory" thus far achieved by the Third Reich was the Saar plebiscite of January 13, 1935. The Reich of 1930–2 was on the point of gaining some of its major diplomatic objectives. The Reich of 1935 is encircled by heavily armed and uniformly hostile States, determined to block the realization of Nazi ambitions.

To conduct foreign policy with the sword, one must first have swords—and some sense of the subtleties which are the prerequisites

[1] *V.B.*, August 18, 1933.
[2] *The New York Times*, August 12, 1934.
[3] Cf. the weekly periodical *Russlands Erwachen, Organ der Russischen N.S. Bewegung*, printed in Berlin and embellished with swastikas and with the Romanov double eagle.
[4] Interview with Paris *Midi*, *V.B.*, January 3, 1934.

to success in war. If Nazi efforts in the diplomatic field have produced only negative results, Nazi efforts in the direction of rearmament are undoubtedly creating a finely forged instrument of imperialistic aggression for use when the time is ripe. Although no international agreement on armaments has been reached, although the Geneva conference is dead but unburied, although both France and Great Britain have refused to grant Germany a legal right to rearm in contravention of Part V of the Treaty of Versailles, the NSDAP has nevertheless evaded the treaty, remilitarized the Reich, and built up armed forces of considerable size. The secrecy of these preparations makes accurate estimates of the results impossible. But the federal budget for 1934–35, decreed on March 22, 1934, provided 210,187,650 marks for the Air Ministry, compared to 78,348,450 marks in 1933 and nothing in 1932. The army and navy were allotted 894,-143,850 marks, compared to 671,114,150 marks in 1933. These expenditures were only 43.3 per cent less than the total cost of the imperial army and navy in 1913. German naval and air forces now consume 17.1 per cent of the national budget, as compared with 16.4 per cent in Great Britain, 17.9 in the United States, 20.8 in Italy, 22.3 in France, and 43.7 in Japan. This calculation does not include the 250,000,000 marks devoted to the S.A. and the Labour Service, making a total of 1,354,331,500 marks for military or semi-military expenditures, as compared with 1,947,700,000 marks in 1913–14.[1]

The Reichswehr is now being expanded into an army of 300,000, though it is limited to 100,000 by the Treaty. The third "pocket battleship" was launched in June 1934. Submarine and airplane parts have been constructed in Holland and Sweden.[2] German youth is again receiving systematic military training, either in the S.A., the S.S., the Reichswehr, or in the labour camps. Schoolboys are trained in handling rifles and hurling grenades. The profits of militarism are already apparent. The Rheinmetall A. G. is again paying dividends. The stocks of the Berlin-Karlsruhe Industrie Werke fluctuated between 16 and 58 in 1932, but in 1933 they reached 95. The stocks of the Bayerische Motoren Werke (aircraft motors and trench mortars) rose from a low of 28 in 1932 to a high of 140 in 1933. The I. G.

[1] Cf. *The New York Times,* March 28, 1934; and William T. Stone and David H. Popper: "The Increasing Burden of Armaments," *FPA Reports,* October 24, 1934.

[2] Cf. documented testimony before U.S. Senate Committee investigating munitions, *The New York Times,* September 7, 1934.

Chemical Combine was listed in 1932 at 81 at its low point. In 1933 it reached 148. By October 1934 German steel-production had reached a rate of output equal to 13,500,000 tons per year, compared with 5,600,000 tons in 1932.

It is clear to German military experts, however, that with the odds in man-power and resources heavily against the Reich, victory must be won by new strategic plans and by new weapons of offence which can break through or circumvent the Franco-Belgian border wall of steel and concrete. New explosives, new poison gases, new types of artillery and anti-aircraft guns, new plans of bacteriological warfare, and new types of tanks, mortars, and ray devices are in process of fabrication. In 1914 German heavy artillery smashed the "impregnable" fortress of Liége, Namur, and Antwerp. Later in the war, German submarines destroyed millions of tons of shipping, German planes and dirigibles bombed foreign capitals, and German cannon shelled Paris from a distance of seventy miles. Similar surprises are doubtless in store for 1940 or 1945, even though there are no more Habers, Richthofens, or Rathenaus to aid. There is discussion of the "new Schlieffen plan," whereby Belgium is to be invaded through Dutch Limburg. There is discussion of attacking France through Switzerland by means of a powerful thrust down the Rhone valley through Geneva, paralysing Lyons and the French steel centres and cutting down toward the Mediterranean.

But, above all, there is the feverish preparation of a gigantic air fleet which is to be the spear-point of attack. With the largest heavy commercial air squadrons in Europe, with thousands of pilots receiving training, with motors being imported from Great Britain and the United States, and with German plants being equipped to turn out military planes by the hundreds, Germany will in all probability have the most efficient fighting air force in the world by 1936, despite British determination to maintain a fleet second to none and to defend England, if necessary, on the Rhine. Germany's planes are not to be used for defence. The RLB will take care of this function. They will be concentrated on a few strategic points, and with heavy explosives and gas will blast a way through for the infantry and artillery. The "war of movement" must at all costs be re-established in order that a quick decision may be reached. Even with autarchy and economic self-sufficiency achieved at tremendous cost, another war of attrition is unthinkable. The flying terror of the skies will, it is hoped, turn the trick. Such, at least, is Göring's Napoleonic dream.[1]

These calculations are contingent upon diplomatic developments not yet in sight. Germany alone cannot fight Europe. All risks must be avoided until the game of war can be played with at least a gambler's chance of winning. Since French passivity cannot be counted upon while Germany moves eastward, France must first be smashed. For this, Polish and British neutrality is essential and Italian support is almost a prerequisite. If the *Anschluss* is abandoned or if a bargain with Rome can be struck in Vienna, an alliance of the two Fascist States is not inconceivable, with Hungary, Austria, Albania, and Bulgaria as satellites. Or if this is impossible, Jugoslavia might be detached from the Little Entente and joined with Hungary, Austria, and Bulgaria in an anti-French and anti-Italian coalition, though the Jugoslav-Hungarian quarrel following the assassination of King Alexander renders this improbable. Russia might conceivably be immobilized by an understanding with Tokyo. If Japan strikes at Siberia while Germany moves against France, the Reich's rear will be protected. A grand German-Italian-Japanese alliance against France, the Little Entente, and the Soviet Union is within the realm of the possible. Out of the troubled waters of Austrian, Jugoslav, Hungarian, Polish, and Baltic politics clever Nazi diplomats may fish up undreamed-of combinations in the years ahead. The devious and dangerous diplomacy of Rome and Warsaw offer hope to Berlin.

When a balance of power is thus restored, war may safely be risked. After France and Czechoslovakia are crushed, the conquest of Rumania and the Ukraine can proceed. The supposition that dictators dare not arm their subjects is of dubious validity. History's only lesson is that history teaches no lessons. William II learned nothing from the example of the two Napoleons, and these nothing from Louis XIV. There is no reason to suppose that Hitler and Göring

1 *The New York Times,* May 11, 1934, and Ernst Henri: *Hitler Over Europe,* pp. 206–268. Between January 1 and August 31, 1934, foreign sales of United Aircraft (U.S.) totalled $1,753,646. Of this total, $1,445,913 represented sales to Germany (*The New York Times,* September 18, 1934). The Armstrong-Siddeley Works (British) likewise sell motors to the Reich with the approval of the British Foreign Minister. Secretary of State Hull expressed his "grave disapproval" of the export of military planes from the United States to Germany. So vigorous has the new German arms industry become that it exported sub-machine-guns to the United States in 1934 (*New York Times,* September 19, 1934).

will profit by the example of William II. They have in fact no alternative, since they are driven toward imperialism by the exigencies of monopolistic capitalism in a state of strangulation and by the dynamics of the hero-cult which they have propagated. On March 16, 1935 the Hitler Cabinet openly repudiated the disarmament clauses of the Treaty of Versailles by decreeing the inauguration of universal military service and announcing the enlargement of the Reichswehr to thirty-six divisions. Forward to *Der Tag!* Meanwhile—talk peace and use militarism and the threat of war as tools to ensure the loyalty of the masses. Such is the program in foreign affairs of the NSDAP.

CHAPTER X

THE INCULCATION OF THE GOSPEL

1. SYMBOLS AND CIRCUSES

EVERY absolutistic political order which does not rest alone on naked violence must rest on a myth. Every political community—even the most libertarian and pluralistic—can exist only so long as its members are bound together by common loyalties. In the western bourgeois democracies the general dissemination of the symbols of nationalism and of democratic and equalitarian values ensures the maintenance of a constitutional consensus usually adequate to keep the peace and to permit the preservation of a relatively free market for competing values, symbols, and ideologies. But wherever a political élite claims omniscience and omnipotence, destroys all its competitors, and monopolizes all power and all access to power, it must create consent by manufacturing its own mythology. It must elevate that mythology, moreover, into a dogma which reveals all truth and is a guide to all life. Otherwise the only weapons of tyranny, aside from the distribution of jobs and favours, are terrorism against enemies, the focusing of resentment against scapegoats, and the building of unity on fear of foreign foes.

These weapons by themselves have seldom sufficed to mobilize acquiescence for any considerable period of time. Force is futile save against small, dissident minorities or against groups without the will to resist—and against these it is unnecessary. Resentment and fear undirected by some *Weltanschauung* are dangerous double-edged tools. Mass consent and collective enthusiasm can only be evoked through magic, mysticism, and the systematic inculcation of some "philosophy" capable at once of winning the respect of a portion of the intellectual élite and of catching the imagination of the multitudes. The "credenda" and "miranda" of power are indispensable to the rulers of a totalitarian State.[1]

The origins and ideational content of the Nazi *Weltanschauung* have already been suggested.[2] Here an effort will be made to describe the techniques whereby the German masses have been indoctrinated with the new creed. The Nazi leaders from the beginning have appreciated the urgency of this task and have recognized that their power could endure only if it rested on general acceptance of their own world-outlook. Thus Hitler:

"We have the power. No one today can resist us. But now we must educate the German people to this State. . . . The German people must place itself one hundred per cent in the service of our Idea. . . . We are the greatest organization that ever existed in Germany. But not only that: we are today the only organization. . . . We must accomplish the great task, for beyond us there is no one who can do so." [3]

This task has been the work of the entire NSDAP, with all its agencies and subsidiary organizations. But specifically its fulfilment has been entrusted to the new Ministry of People's Enlightenment and Propaganda. During the Great War the creation of such an agency was proposed by Erzberger, but no action was taken. In mid-February 1933 the proposal to establish a Propaganda Office was publicly discussed, but was officially denied. On February 16 Goebbels was named "Reich Commissar for Radio and Propaganda." On March 8 there was talk of a "Ministerium für Staatskultur." On March 10 it was announced that Goebbels would become "Propaganda Minister." Two days later the present name of the Ministry was announced, and on the 13th Goebbels was officially appointed by Hitler and confirmed by presidential decree.[4] The initial organization of the Ministry was completed by April 1. It moved into an old palace on Wilhelmplatz. Its first great achievement was the organization of the "Day of National Labour" on May 1. On July 5, 1933, its duties were clarified in another decree.

"The Minister for People's Enlightenment and Propaganda is competent to deal with all measures for the mental influencing of the

[1] Cf. C. E. Merriam: *Political Power* (New York: McGraw-Hill; 1934), Chapter 4.

[2] Cf. pp. 95f. above.

[3] Speech to the S.A. of Dortmund, *Berliner Tageblatt,* July 10, 1933.

[4] *R.G.B.,* 1933, Vol. I, No. 21, p. 104.

nation, the publicity of State culture and business, the instruction of the public, inside and outside of the nation, concerning the above, and the administration of all agencies which serve these purposes."[1]

To facilitate this work the Foreign Office yielded to Goebbels its jurisdiction over propaganda, art, films, and sports abroad. The Ministry of the Interior transferred to Goebbels its control over domestic publicity, the Hochschule für Politik, national holidays and State celebrations, press, radio, art, music, theatres, and the enforcement of legislation against obscenity. From the Ministries of Commerce and Agriculture Goebbels took over the advertising of expositions and fairs, and from the Ministries of Posts and Communication all control of travel publicity and the non-technical aspects of radio. By midsummer of 1933 Goebbels had established thirteen local offices, which had grown to thirty-one a year later. Walter Funk became his chief aide. The Ministry was originally divided into seven major *Abteilungen:* Administration, Propaganda, Radio, Press, Film, Theatre, and Popular Education. It was subsequently reorganized into divisions of Administration and Law; Propaganda; Radio; Press; Film; Theatre, Music and Art; and Defence against Lies. During 1933–4 the Ministry spent 14,257,500 marks, and during 1934–5, 28,148,300 marks.[2] It collected in radio receipts sums more than sufficient to cover these expenditures. These receipts, however, do not appear in full in its budget. Their disposition appears to be a "State secret." Among its more notable achievements have been the creation of the Reich Culture Chamber, the Law for the Protection of National Symbols (May 19, 1933), the Press Law of October 4, 1933, the Cinema Law of February 16, 1934, and the great campaign against critics and grumblers in the spring of 1934.[3]

Any full account of the highly ingenious and variegated activities of the Propagandaministerium would require a volume by itself. Every agency and organization of the party has its own propaganda bureau, working usually in co-operation with Goebbels. Only the more significant and striking aspects of this work need be dealt with in the present chapter.[4]

The NSDAP was from the beginning an army with banners,

[1] *R.G.B.*, 1933, Vol. I, No. 75 (June 30), p. 449.

[2] *The New York Times*, March 28, 1934.

[3] Cf. *V.B.*, March 11, 1934.

[4] Cf. Eugen Hadamovsky: *Propaganda und Nationale Macht* (Oldenburg: Stalling; 1933).

marching forth to battle to the tunes of martial music. The Third Reich is a nation marching in uniform and carrying flags. The old familiar costumes of the S.A., S.S., Stahlhelm, and Reichswehr have been supplemented by dozens of others. The Prussian police have in part discarded their blue coats and visored hats for light green uniforms and grey steel helmets embellished with white swastikas. Göring's air corps boasts handsome blue-grey outfits. All the millions of members of the *Arbeitsfront,* male and female, are expected to have simple blue uniforms for ceremonial occasions. The five million boys and girls of the Hitler Youth are also in military garb. The labour-service army wears denim. The Third Reich is a veritable paradise for tailors.

Each organization, moreover, has its emblem or button. Many have medals and insignia of rank. Some have flags of their own. Hundreds of different emblems and medals are to be seen on breasts and coat lapels throughout the Reich, as well as "Daggers of Honour," epaulets, service stripes, and other decorations. In July 1934, orders were given by the Cabinet for the issuance of bronze or iron crosses to all war veterans and their widows, including Jews. The Nazi colours are everywhere, even on post-boxes and postal wagons, which once were Prussian blue. All the old black-red-and-gold flags have disappeared. Their display is forbidden and most of the statues and other symbols of republican leaders have been destroyed. After the death of Hindenburg it was reported that the old monarchist banner would likewise be suppressed.

The Fascist salute is equally ubiquitous. The "German greeting" —borrowed from Mussolini, who borrowed it from the Roman legions—is compulsory in innumerable situations. Nazi flags, uniforms, and leaders must always be saluted. Göring made the upraised arm obligatory for the Prussian police in September 1933. In December a decree of Frick required the salute in all school and university classes, on the ground that "the highest task of the school is the education of youth to the service of people and State in a Nationalsocialist spirit." At the beginning and end of each school term the entire faculty and student body must honour the flag and sing the *Deutschland Lied* and the *Horst Wessel Lied.* At the beginning and end of every class the teacher salutes and shouts: *"Heil Hitler!"* and the students respond in chorus. For non-Aryan students the salute is optional. Scholars who neglect to participate are subject to expulsion. Disloyal teachers who fail to perform—or who enter classes with books under both arms as means of evading the salute—may be disciplined.[1] Sundry uniforms, flags, and emblems must be saluted on all occasions.[2] In contacts between passers-by, the "German greeting" has replaced handshaking. Telephone conversations and private letters are often initiated and terminated with *"Heil Hitler!"* Recently, however, efforts have been made to restrict these practices on the ground that a too common use of the greeting may diminish its emotional efficacy. But in general all citizens of the Third Reich salute and *"Heil Hitler!"* at least half a dozen times a day.

The new symbols may not be cheapened, however, by improper use. Under the Law for the Protection of National Symbols,[3] the Propaganda Ministry forbade the following activities: the manufacture of mattresses with swastika design; the production of cookies and sausages in the shape of the *Hakenkreuz;* and the use of the *Hakenkreuz* as a trade mark on cigarettes and other goods. Firms indulging in such practices would in future be denounced by name in the *Reichsanzeiger.*[4] Dancing to the *Horst Wessel Lied* is also forbidden on pain of arrest. The use of the national symbols in advertising and in the manufacture of toys, tobacco, and candy is banned.[5] In this fashion the requisite degree of sacredness for the new devices is maintained.

Hero-worship is likewise an integral part of the new cult. First among heroes stands Der Führer. His busts and pictures are everywhere, since he has long since abandoned the tactics of 1920–1, when he sought to add a mysterious glamour to his personality by forbidding the publication of his likeness. Pamphlets, brochures, and books without end on his life, character, ancestry, horoscope, bright sayings, and personal habits are on display in every book-store and news-stall. Literature on Hitler which is purely imaginative, "untrue," or in any way derogatory is subject to confiscation.[6] In March 1934 Frick decreed that the name *"Führer"* must be restricted to Hitler, with *"Leiter"* applied to other Nazi officials. It is doubtful whether there is a single town in the Reich which does not have its Adolf

1 *V.B.*, December 21, 1933.
2 Ibid., February 14, 1934.
3 *R.G.B.*, 1933, Vol. I, No. 52 (May 19), p. 285.
4 TU dispatch, September 16, 1933.
5 *V.B.*, February 17, 1934.
6 Order of Brückner, *V.B.*, May 16, 1934.

Hitler Strasse or its Adolf Hitler Platz. In the official *Weltanschauung* Hitler is a demigod, omniscient, omnipotent, infallible.

"Hitler is always right." (Albert Schlitter, in *Hochschule für Politik der NSDAP,* p. 132.)

"If Adolf Hitler had arisen in the Middle Ages, we should have been today the foremost nation in the world, the master of the inhabited earth." (Richard Suchenwirth; *Von Ersten bis zum Dritten Reich.*)

"Whoever heard Der Führer at Nürnberg make his speech, so full of meaning, about German culture and German art, felt the same thing: there spoke in him the revelation of a Higher One." (Wilhelm Kube.)

"Hitler and Luther belong together; they are of the same German stamp and substance." (Bernard Rust.)

"In this newly begun chapter of history the German people have elected Adolf Hitler as their champion before God." [1] (Hans Frank.)

"Hitler is lonely. So is God. Hitler is like God." (Hans Frank.)

The lesser Nazi leaders are almost equally in the public eye. Streets and parks everywhere have been named for Göring, Goebbels, Hess, Frick, Rosenberg. Here, too, any unflattering observations are rigidly suppressed. When Frick, on his fifty-seventh birthday, in March 1934, married the divorced wife of Professor Paul Schultze-Naumberg, after divorcing his own wife, with whom he had enjoyed thirty-three years of matrimony, no German newspaper published any notice of the wedding. Goebbels' club-foot and Göring's idiosyncrasies are also banned as subjects of comment, as well as the pederastic proclivities of some of their colleagues and subordinates. Great events in the history of the party are likewise used as names for streets and public buildings, though this practice is less prevalent than in Paris, Rome, Leningrad, and Moscow. In Munich a street has been renamed "The Street of November 9."

Dead heroes and martyrs, as well as those still living, are likewise honoured. The traditional panel of German heroes has been considerably modified. Charlemagne (Karl der Grosse) is no longer in favour. His pagan enemy, Widukind, who fought against the Christianization of the Saxons, has replaced him in the hall of fame. Arminius (Hermann), who annihilated the legions of Varus, A.D. 9, is likewise a hero. Frederick the Great is more popular than

[1] Cf. compilation of John Gunther, *Chicago Daily News,* November 2, 1933.

ever. On October 7, 1933, an actor dressed as Frederick addressed the storm troopers at Beuthen. Frederick and Bismarck rank as only slightly inferior to Hitler himself. Since his death Hindenburg has remained as much of a legend as before. The Nazis have excelled, however, in elevating obscure and unknown patriots to the rank of heroes. Hans Maikowski and dozens of other S.A. victims of the "Red terror" are everywhere revered in solemn ceremonies. On November 8, 1934, Hitler ordered five hundred thousand marks distributed annually among the immediate relatives of the 248 Nazi "martyrs." The two great figures here, however, are Albert Leo Schlageter and Horst Wessel.

The former, designated as "the last soldier of the Great War and the first soldier of the Third Reich," was an adventurer who organized a band of guerrillas to fight the French occupation of the Ruhr. He blew up coal-trains and railway tracks. When he dynamited a railway bridge between Duisberg and Düsseldorf, he was caught, court-martialed, and shot on May 28, 1923. On the tenth anniversary of his death a gigantic demonstration was staged on the site of the execution near Düsseldorf. Göring talked at the tomb, where a huge cross was erected. A thousand massed flags saluted the martyr. Golzheim Heath was declared holy ground. Around the new Golgotha stood 260,000 S.A. and S.S. men and 250,000 spectators, overwhelmed by awe, reverence, sorrow, and lust for revenge. Here was indeed a hero! Plays, films, books, and songs about Schlageter had been produced in such quantity that his name is as famous as that of Frederick, Bismarck, or Hitler.[1]

Horst Wessel was born in 1907. His father was a Lutheran pastor who became an army chaplain. After the war the son became successively a Reichswehr volunteer, a student at the University of Berlin, a Nazi, and, after May 1, 1929, an S.A. leader. For the purpose of combating Communism more effectively, he moved to Berlin's east end, where he rented a room from one Frau Salm and lived with one "Lucy of Alexanderplatz." Here he secured the inspiration which led him to write the *Horst Wessel Lied*. Lucy was a lady of easy virtue. Whether Horst lived on the rewards of her prostitution or lived with her to "reform" her is debatable. Whether his landlady disliked him because he was behind in his rent, or because he was a procurer, or because she was a Communist is equally unclear. He has

[1] Cf. Hans Johst: *Schlageter;* Rolf Brandt: *Albert Leo Schlageter;* etc.

also been accused of having homosexual relations with prominent party leaders. Truth is doubly difficult to unearth about figures that have become legends. On January 14, 1930, a group of alleged "Communists" led by one Albrecht (Ali) Hoehler—a rival customer and lover of Lucy, say the Communists—invaded the apartment at 62 Grosse Frankfurterstrasse and shot the S.A. leader. He died in a hospital on February 23. He was young, handsome despite a weak chin, and an obvious martyr in a sacred cause. His song became the battle hymn of the NSDAP. His life, appropriately edited, became an inspiration to all young storm troopers. Pictures and books about Horst Wessel are even more numerous than those dealing with Schlageter.[1]

The murderer Ali was sentenced to six years in jail (the court found extenuating circumstances), along with seven accomplices. Ali died in prison, whether from violence or natural causes has never been revealed. In December 1933 it was announced that new culprits would be tried for the murder. In May 1934 the trial was opened of Peter Stoll, tailor; Hans Ziegler, barber; and Solly Epstein, a Jewish painter. All three had been under arrest since August 1933. These specimens of "Red sub-humanity" were finally found guilty of some kind of connection with the murder.[2] Epstein and Ziegler were beheaded on April 10, 1935.

The martyred composer of the Nazi anthem has become one of the major saints of the NSDAP. The hospital in which he died has been named after him. Bülowplatz, the former Communist stronghold, is now "Horst Wessel Platz." The Karl Liebknecht House was renamed the "Horst Wessel House." On his birthday, October 9, 1933, Goebbels spoke in the hospital and led a torch-light parade to his grave, where impressive ceremonies were staged. An elaborate anti-Communist propaganda film based on his life, with incidental music by Hanfstängl, was to have had its first showing at the same time. It was suppressed by Goebbels at the last moment, on the ground that it was not up to the requisite artistic standard and was not a faithful portrayal of the hero. A number of Jews had been compelled to act offensively in the anti-Semitic scenes. Some of these were cut out and the film was finally permitted to appear under the name

[1] Erwin Reitmann: *Horst Wessel. Leben und Sterben* (Berlin: Steuben; 1933); Hans Ewers: *Horst Wessel* (Berlin: Cotta'sche; 1933).

[2] *V.B.*, December 23, 1933; May 4, June 14, 1934.

of *Hans Westmar*. The prevalent attitude toward the martyr was well stated by *Der Brünnen* (Düsseldorf) on January 2, 1934:

"How high Horst Wessel towers over that Jesus of Nazareth—that Jesus who pleaded that the bitter cup should be taken from him! How unattainably high all Horst Wessels stand above this Jesus!"

Since its seizure of power, as before, the NSDAP has excelled in mass pageantry, creating by collective suggestion an atmosphere of almost delirious enthusiasm which is perhaps without parallel in modern politics. Local patriotic assemblies are of weekly and sometimes daily occurrence in every town and hamlet in the Reich. About once a month some colossal demonstration is arranged—always with that consummate skill and that fine sense of dramatic values characteristic of Hitler and Goebbels. The Nazi régime was initiated with the celebrations of January 30, 1933, the "Day of Potsdam," the "Day of National Awakening," and the "Day of National Labour." Lesser festivities followed in the summer, culminating once more in the gigantic Nürnberg *Partei-Tag* of September 1–3, the opening of the Prussian Staatsrat on September 15, and the *Erntedank-Tag* of October 1. In this harvest festival there were speeches, concerts, parades, and picnics everywhere throughout Germany. Five hundred thousand peasants gathered at the Bückeberg, near Hameln, where they were entertained by music, parades, and military manœuvres. Here Hitler spoke, praising the peasantry to the skies as the source of all racial strength and wisdom.[1]

On November 9, 1933, came the solemn festivities in Munich celebrating the tenth anniversary of the beer-hall putsch. Christmas itself was converted into a great patriotic, cultural, racial, and pagan holiday, as well as a Christian festival. New Year's Day brought more speeches, proclamations, parties, and parades. On February 24, 1934, the fourteenth anniversary of the promulgation of the party program, a great festival was staged in Munich. Here and elsewhere throughout the country a solemn oath—"I swear unswerving loyalty to Adolf Hitler and unconditional obedience to him and to the leaders designated by him"—was administered to 1,017,000 political chieftains, including 373,000 party leaders, 205,000 youth leaders, 120,000 officials of the NSBO, 68,000 officers of the N.S. Welfare Organization, 57,000 from the NSHAGO, 53,000 from the N.S. Frauenschaft, 34,000 of the Amt für Beamte, 14,000 propaganda

[1] Cf. *Berliner Tageblatt* and *V.B.*, September 16 and October 2, 1933.

officials. Hitler spoke to the "Old Guard" in the Hofbräuhaus. He pledged himself to appeal to the people for the judgment of his régime at least once a year. Hess declared in his address: "Adolf Hitler is Germany, and Germany is Adolf Hitler."

On February 25 the entire nation honoured its war dead in heroic demonstrations. On March 21, anniversary of the "Day of Potsdam," more awe-inspiring ceremonies were staged. "Work, work, and more work!" was Der Führer's appeal. The Labour Day festival of May 1, 1934 was double the size of the one the year before. The Nürnberg *Partei-Tag* of September 1, 1934 outshone all its predecessors. In true American style, each ceremonial was made bigger, better, more elaborate, more stupendous, colossal, and gigantic than ever before. Whether this constant crescendo could be continued indefinitely was becoming doubtful by the end of 1934.[1]

The magicians of the NSDAP have achieved almost miraculous results with this technique. Only a wholly inanimate being can resist the infectious exaltation of these throbbing, heart-stirring rituals. In the spring of 1934 the party systematized the mass ceremonials to some degree by reviving the ancient Germanic "Thing" or tribal assembly, with open-air folk-plays and dances, huge choruses, and group singing. The second "Nordic Thing" was held in Bremen on May 17, 1934, and was embellished by an address on ancient clocks by Hanfstängl. The Nazi leaders know full well that inspiring emotions shared with tens of thousands of *Volksgenossen* are the surest means of binding the masses to the dictatorship. These ceremonies reawaken deep strains of communal life and æsthetic appreciation long lost in the modern age. They are not "democratic." One does not see here "The People" in all its tumult and diversity, but only vast, regimented throngs singing, saluting, parading like a single dynamic organism in which all individual life disappears in the collectivity. Here is a pagan mass, a mediæval immolation, an orgy of personal effacement and group hysteria conjuring up memories of ancient Asia. Here, in the chants, the *"Heils!"* and the seas of outstretched arms, is the visible living expression of discipline, militarism, totalitarianism, the *Führerprinzip*. And for decades to come, long after the NSDAP has passed into the tomb of tyrannies, there will be simple souls left behind who will tell their children and

[1] For detailed descriptions of these demonstrations, with photographs and texts of speeches, see *V.B.* for the days following the dates given above.

grandchildren, with pride and joy, of the great mass festivals of 1933 and 1934, where a transfigured *Deutschtum* lost its mind and found its soul.

2. THE SCHOOLING OF YOUTH

THE entire educational system of the Reich, from kindergartens to professional schools, is now in the service of the totalitarian State.

"The racial State must build up its entire educational work in the first instance not on the pumping in of empty knowledge, but on the development of healthy bodies. Only in the second place comes the training of mental faculties. Here, however, comes first again the development of character, especially the promotion of Will and Decisiveness, united with education toward joy and responsibility, and only last, scientific schooling." (*Mein Kampf,* p. 452.)

"The soldier should learn to be silent, not only when he is dealt with justly, but he should also learn when necessary to endure injustice in silence." (Ibid., p. 459.)

"It is especially the task of a racial State to see to it that a world history should at last be written in which the race question shall be raised to a dominant position." (Ibid., p. 468.)

"The epoch of 'pure reason,' of 'objective' and 'free' science is ended." (Ernst Krieck: *Nationalpolitische Erziehung;* Leipzig: Armanen; 1933; p. 1.)

"Absolute academic freedom in universities is absolute nonsense. . . . The university is itself an organ of the whole and therefore has its being, like every other organ, directly in the name of and by the right of the whole. Consequently, the whole, represented in the State, must see to it that no self-governing member separates itself from the totality, from the sworn goal of racial unity and *Weltanschauung.*" (Ibid., p. 173.)

"All education must today be political education, in order to safeguard the life of the community and therewith the life of the individual. And all learning must fulfil the unqualified goal of education in co-operation with the political function." (F. A. Beck, in *Hochschule für Politik,* pp. 36–7.)

"Education in the last half-century became a magic means of trickery, unbiological and contrary to all inner laws of race and people. . . . German education will not be formal and æsthetic, it will not strive for an abstract training of reason, but it will be in the first instance an education of character. . . . This cleansing of spirit and instinct, the recovery of the emancipation of the blood, is perhaps the greatest task which the Nationalsocialist movement now has before it." (Alfred Rosenberg, in *V.B.,* March 15, 1934.)

The negative aspects of this task have already been suggested. Thousands of teachers and students who were Jewish, Marxist, liberal, pacifist, or otherwise obnoxious have been driven from their posts. Those who remain have repeatedly been warned that academic freedom is at an end and that they must embrace and inculcate the Nazi philosophy. Summer encampments for teachers, where they receive intensive political drilling, have already been provided. Discipline, obedience, and the martial virtues are the new ideals for students and faculties alike.

The *Gleichschaltung* of academic groups proceeded apace throughout 1933. Student bodies in scientific colleges were organized for the purpose of enabling students to "fulfil their duties toward people, State, and university." [1] In October, Frick named Dr. Oskar Staebel, leader of the N.S. Deutschen Studentenbund, head of the Deutsche Studentenschaft.[2] On October 30 the Prussian Minister of Education abolished faculty meetings in Prussian universitics and decreed that all presidents and deans would henceforth be appointed by the Minister instead of elected by the faculty. Under the law of April 25 against the overcrowding of German schools,[3] the number of new students to be admitted to higher educational institutions was limited to 15,000 for 1934, with only ten per cent women, as compared with 24,700 in 1932 and 29,000 in 1931. Special consideration is given to applicants who are members of the S.S., S.A., or Hitler Jugend. All new students are required to spend half a year in "labour service." On February 7, 1934, Frick ordered the amalgamation of the Deutsche Studentenschaft and the Deutsche Fachschulschaft into the Reichschaft der Studierenden, under an arbitrary Reichsführer.[4]

These and other innovations have in general met with the approval of the German university students, who were among the first to embrace the Nazi cult of "anti-intellectualism." The once colorful Stu-

1 *R.G.B.,* 1933, Vol. I, No. 40 (April 22), p. 215.
2 *Berliner Tageblatt,* October 11, 1933.
3 *R.G.B.,* 1933, Vol. I, No. 43, p. 225.
4 For the constitution of this body, see *V.B.,* February 8, 1934.

dent Corps have declined, though duelling is again encouraged. Groups of twenty to forty students now live in disciplined "fellowships" in a highly military atmosphere. Regimentation and the "levelling mania" have encountered some opposition. On July 16, 1934, Nazi students and members of the old Student Corps at Göttingen engaged in a riot, followed by arrests. Three days later, Oskar Staebel and Ernst Zaeringer, leaders of the new Nazi Studenthood, retired and were displaced by Andreas Feikert, by order of Minister Rust. But there has been thus far no general student rebellion against the new order. During the summer of 1934 there were only 95,667 students in the higher schools, compared to 115,722 in 1933. The number of male students declined 15 per cent and of female students 26.5 per cent.[1] In the autumn only 4,000 men and 700 women were admitted to the universities and technical colleges as new students.

As for children, Hitler declared in an address at Erfurt on June 18, 1933: "If the older generation cannot get accustomed to us, we shall take their children away from them and rear them as needful for the Fatherland." Despite this threat, no sweeping administrative changes have been introduced in the lower schools, save instruction in race science, race history, and military sports. The new literature used in primary and secondary schools is indicative of the purposes of the new education. A few typical titles follow: Georg Hanke: *World War, Collapse and Resurrection of the German Nation; The War-Guilt Question in the German School;* Peter Jugwerfen: *How We Stormed Kemmel;* Karl Westerhausen: *Between Courland and Galicia; My Last Year in the West;* Gustav Engelkes: *World War Burns in Young Hearts;* Ernst Weber: *From the World War to To-day;* Friedrich Hiller: *The Dictate of Versailles;* Paul Felstan: *The National Uprising of 1933;* Ernst Weber: *People and Race;* Fritz Kern: *National Biology and Eugenics;* Heinrich Benser: *The Fight against Smut; Bleeding Frontiers*—a series of brochures on the Saar, Upper Silesia, the Corridor, etc.; and sundry biographies of Horst Wessel, Schlageter, Hitler, Hindenburg, Bismarck, Stein, Luther, Andreas Hofer, and other heroes.[2] In November 1934 Minister Rust ordered the introduction into the schools of Hitler's *Mein Kampf,* Rosenberg's *Myth of the Twentieth Century,* Theodore Fritsch's *Handbook of the Jewish Question,* Gunther's *Race Science of the*

[1] *The New York Times,* November 4, 1934.

[2] Berlin: Beltz, 1933; titles translated by author.

German People, and the *Protocols of the Elders of Zion.*[1]

The conversion of youth is necessarily a prime task of all totalitarian dictatorships. No effort has been spared by the NSDAP to enlist German youth in the sacred cause. Unity, discipline, obedience, fanaticism in the service of the State are the new ideals.[2] Special "political schools" for youth, and in some cases for adults, have been established throughout the Reich.[3] The Nazi Hochschule für Politik has established a special seminar for Hitler Youth leaders.[4] Parades, demonstrations, and festivals of youth are everywhere prominent features of political pageantry.

The regimentation of German youth has been achieved through a complex hierarchy of co-ordinated organizations. The *Reichs-Jugend-Führung* is headed by Baldur von Schirach, who is a member of the OR of the party. His staff consists of thirteen *Abteilungen,* including divisions for organizations; hygiene and labour service; sanitation; propaganda; German youth abroad; aviation training, in liaison with the Reich Preparatory School for Flyers; leadership school, in liaison with the Reichsführerschule der H.J.; N.S. Jugend B.O., in liaison with the youth office of the Labour Front; students, in liaison with the Reichsschaft der deutschen Studierenden; etc. These agencies supervise the corresponding activities of the four great organizations of German youth. The German Young People (*Deutsche Jungvolk*) are divided into geographical *Jungbanne,* these into *Stämme,* these into *Fähnlein,* these into *Jungzüge,* and these into *Jungenschaften.* Each *Jungenschaft* consists of 15 boys; each *Jungzug* of 50 (3 *Jungschaften*); each *Fähnlein* of 150 (3 *Jungzüge*); each *Stamm* of 600 (4 *Fähnlein*); and each *Jungbann* of 3,000 (5 *Stämme*). The Hitler Youth is similarly divided into *Obergebiete* (375,000 youths or 5 *Gebiete*); *Gebiete* (75,000 or 5 *Oberbanne*); *Oberbanne* (15,000 or 5 *Banne*); *Banne* (3,000 or 5 *Unterbanne*); *Unterbanne* (600 or 4 *Gefolgschaften*); *Gefolgschaften* (150 or 3 *Scharen*); *Scharen* (50 or 3 *Kameradschaften*); and *Kameradschaften* of 15 young men each. Girls and young women are similarly organized. The Young Girls (*Jungmädel*) consist of a hierarchy of *Untergaue, Ringe, Gruppen, Scharen,* and *Jungmädelschaften* of 15

[1] *The New York Times,* November 9, 1934.
[2] Cf. interview with Baldur von Schirach, *V.B.,* April 26, 1934.
[3] Cf. *V.B.,* November 15, 1933; April 4, 1934.
[4] *V.B.,* May 4, 1934.

members each. The *Bund Deutscher Mädel* for older girls comprises *Gauverbände, Obergaue, Gaue, Untergaue, Mädelringe, Gruppen, Scharen,* and *Mädelschaften.*[1]

Here, as in all other phases of German life, the application of the *Führerprinzip* has meant that youth is drilled and disciplined like an army preparing for war and is commanded by leaders appointed from above and ultimately answerable to Hitler. So fanatical has become the militarism of German adolescents that protests have been made over the daily preoccupation of boys in their teens with saluting, shouting orders, and reviewing their troops. There has been some friction between the HJ and such remnants of the Catholic youth organizations as survive. The HJ has been accused of being anti-religious. Schirach views neo-paganism sympathetically and insists that iron unity and discipline forbid any Catholic-Protestant differentiation. But youth is in its glory, playing at war and revelling in race science, political romanticism, and half-heathen mysticism. Parents seem proud to see their sons transformed into young soldiers, carrying daggers, securing practice in throwing grenades, and preparing assiduously for *"Der Tag."* Youth has been won to the NSDAP. Only a major national catastrophe can break the spell and lead to new quests for truth, beauty, and goodness in other directions.

3. NAZI *KULTUR*

In May 1933, strange ceremonies took place in most German cities, the like of which had not been seen in the western world since the late Middle Ages and the period of the wars of religion. On May 6, Berlin student groups staged a raid on the Institute for Sexual Science, conducted by Magnus Hirschfeld. The director was away. He was four times damned as a Jew, a liberal, a pornographist, and a scientific student of sex phenomena. In his Institute he had gathered together perhaps the most complete collection of sex literature in the world—scientific, erotic, diverting, and serious. At 9.30 Saturday morning the students brought several trucks to the Institute, decorated with banners: "German Students March against the Un-German Spirit," "Down with Un-German Trash and Smut!" At a trumpet signal, they invaded the library and dragged out thousands of books, pamphlets, and pictures, which they dumped into the trucks while

[1] Cf. diagrams in *V.B.,* June 29, 1933 and February 6, 1934.

the band played. There were speeches, cheers, and the *Horst Wessel Lied*. In the afternoon, storm troopers came and completed the work of demolition. The premises were wrecked and much personal and foreign property, including library and research materials of the World League for Sexual Reform, was destroyed or seized for subsequent burning. Other students descended upon various book-stores in Berlin and elsewhere. At the same hour Rust, Prussian Minister of Education, was speaking at the University:

"Freedom of research and national philosophic unity are the pillars upon which the university of the future must be built. In the spirit of Adolf Hitler and in the name of the great German folk-community, I call to you: German students and professors, unite! *Heil!*"[1]

On the following Wednesday evening, May 10, forty thousand students and spectators gathered in a drizzling rain in the great square beside the Staatsopera on Unter den Linden, opposite the University of Berlin. Thousands of students, parading in colourful uniforms, reached the square at midnight. The torches of the marchers ignited a huge funeral pyre, twelve feet square and five feet high. As the flames mounted, armful after armful of books were tossed into the fire by willing and enthusiastic students. In Berlin 20,000 volumes were burned, in Kiel 2,000, in Breslau 5,000 pounds of books and pamphlets, in Frankfurt—to the tunes of Chopin's Funeral March—several thousand more tomes. Among foreign authors whose books were consigned to the flames were Lenin, Stalin, Freud, Ben Lindsey, Morris Hillquit, Jack London, Upton Sinclair, Margaret Sanger, H. G. Wells, Havelock Ellis, Count Coudenhove-Kalergi, Arthur Schnitzler, Helen Keller, André Gide, Émile Zola, and Marcel Proust. Among German authors represented were Hugo Preuss, Walter Rathenau, Albert Einstein, Bertha von Suttner, Karl Marx, Friedrich Engels, August Bebel, Karl Liebknecht, Emil Ludwig, Erich Remarque, Lion Feuchtwanger, Thomas and Heinrich Mann, Alfred Kerr, Georg Bernard, Theodore Wolff, Arnold Zweig, and Jacob Wassermann. The burnt offerings included, in the words of one of the student appeals, "anything that works subversely on family life, married life, or love, or the ethics of our youth, or our future, or strikes at the root of German thought, the German home, and the driving forces of our people; any works of those who would subor-

[1] The entire press of Berlin, May 6 and 7, 1933.

dinate the soul to the material; anything that serves the purposes of lies." A bust of Dr. Hirschfeld was also tossed into the fire.

At the end of the ceremonies, after the volumes had been reduced to ashes and before the singing of the *Horst Wessel Lied,* Goebbels spoke:

"Jewish intellectualism is dead. Nationalsocialism has hewn the way. The German folk-soul can again express itself. These flames do not only illuminate the final end of an old era, they also light up the new. . . ."

Near by, across Unter den Linden, stands the great Preussische Staatsbibliothek. Its director patiently explains to foreign visitors that the book-burning was purely "symbolic" and that the library retains copies of all books destroyed. But these books and thousands of others are *"sekretiert"* and kept under lock and key. They may be used only by special permission—and then only for "scientific"—that is, pro-Nazi—research. Even foreigners have difficulty in securing access to them. On the first anniversary of the *auto-da-fé,* "The German Library of Burned Books" was opened in Paris under the presidency of Heinrich Mann.

The cleansing of German literature has been carried forward relentlessly. The Prussian Academy of Poets was purified by the ejection of Thomas and Heinrich Mann, Jacob Wassermann, Bernhard Kellermann, Alfred Dölin, Franz Werfel, and Ludwig Fulda. The new Nazi members include Hans Grimm, author of *Volk ohne Raum,* and Hans Johst, author of a Schlageter play. Hans Ewers, biographer of Horst Wessel, became head of the Association of German Authors. In October 1933 the Thuringian Minister of Education announced that German book-stores must carry the works only of those wedded to *Blut und Boden* and *Heldentum* idealism. Jewish works, bourgeois-decadent "subjectivist" literature, metropolitan literature divorced from the land, Marxist, pacifist, internationalist, anti-religious, and foreign literature which is un-German or un-Nordic are all barred. Among scientific works, the ban was placed on anti-militarist works, liberal-democratic works, popular presentations of Darwinism, and materialistic interpretations of the Great War.[1]

At the same time, strenuous efforts have been made to promote the development of an orthodox literature expounding and inculcating

[1] *Berliner Tageblatt,* October 18, 1933.

the Nazi philosophy. "Out of the past *Weltanschauung* grew the political System and the so-called humanistic culture. We denounce this today as a frightful falsification. . . . We wish to found a new epoch. In the life process of a people we do not see eternal peace, but eternal conflict. August 1914 is the beginning of the German revolution." [1] The writers of the past who are sufficiently "heroic" are still acceptable. Spengler, having for all practical purposes embraced the new cult, is generally praised, though his *The Hour of Decision* [2] was assailed for its veiled ridicule of certain Nazi values and its rejection of the Nazi doctrine of race.

In the interests of orthodoxy, Rosenberg was named dictator of the educational and spiritual work of the party on January 24, 1934. On April 17 Hess established a new censorship of Nazi publications. All manuscripts purporting to be "Nationalsocialist" must first be submitted to the Propagandaministerium and then approved by Philip Bouhler in the Brown House. A fee is charged for examination. Only those approved may appear in the new *Catalog of Nationalsocialist Literature* and be published with the blessing of the "Examining Board for the Protection of Nationalsocialist Literature." Such manuscripts must first be offered to publishing houses owned by the party. Goebbels, Rosenberg, and Bouhler supervise the work of the board. On May 1, 1934, public prizes were awarded by Goebbels, at a session of the Reich Culture Chamber, to the best literary and artistic work done during the first year of the dictatorship. A medal and a purse of twelve thousand marks (the "Stefan George prize") went to Richard Euringer, unknown author of *The German Passion of 1933*. A second prize was awarded for the winning film, *Fugitives,* depicting the flight of Germans from the Bolshevist terror. The star actor, Hans Albers, was not mentioned because of his insistence on marrying a Jewess. Goebbels declared that "the decade of Germany's regeneration has not yet reached its final artistic expression." [3] Because of declining book-sales Goebbels inaugurated a "National Book Week" early in November 1934, to stimulate the buying of Nazi literature.

As in all totalitarian dictatorships, culture is deliberately used as

[1] Alfred Rosenberg, *V.B.*, April 29, 1934; cf. his address in the Kroll Opera, *V.B.*, February 24, 1934.

[2] New York: Knopf; 1934.

[3] *The New York Times,* May 2, 1934.

a weapon of politics.[1] The values of the old culture, moreover, must be discredited and a new culture, or at least the illusion thereof, must be established. In this fashion the new political élite identifies itself with new æsthetic values and makes itself the beneficiary of the enthusiasm invariably evoked by the announcement that a new day has dawned in all the arts. The "new" cultural dispensation in the Third Reich, like the new socialism, the new politics, the new morality, and the new religion, is thinly disguised reaction—that is, a repudiation of modernism in all its manifestations and a reversion to values and standards of centuries long dead. At the Nürnberg convention of 1933, Hans Sachs, Peter Vischer, and Albrecht Dürer were depicted as the forerunners of Nationalsocialism. Modern metropolitan culture is denounced as "experiment, foolery, or bluff." "Bloodless dilettantism" is rejected. Culture is to be revived by a restoration of the soil which nourishes it. *"Blut und boden,"* "soldierly rhythm," "heroism," "a steeled Romanticism" are the new watchwords.[2] Rust, speaking before the Nordic Society of Lübeck in June 1934, even went so far as to forecast the conquest of western civilization by Nazi *Kultur*.[3] In general, however, the new culture is looked upon as a unique and sacred flower of German blood and soil, not only superior to all other cultures, but incapable of being transmitted to inferior races.

In the autumn of 1933 a Reich Culture Chamber was established in Berlin under the supervision of the Ministry of People's Enlightenment and Propaganda. It consists of the seven "corporations" into which all cultural activity has been *gleichgeschaltet*—namely, the chambers of literature, the press, radio, film, theatre, music, and painting and sculpture.[4] Goebbels and Göring clashed in their efforts to control the Prussian theatre, but finally composed their differences and co-ordinated their activities.[5] In the spring of 1934 Göring was obliged to surrender his post as Prussian Minister of the Interior in favour of Frick. At the same time the Prussian Minister of Science, Art, and Education, Bernard Rust, while retaining this

1 Richard Bie and Alfred Muhr: *Die Kulturwaffen des Neuen Reiches* (Jena: Diederichs; 1933).
2 Cf. Goebbels's address opening the Culture Chamber, *Berliner Tageblatt,* November 15, 1933.
3 *The New York Times,* June 3, 1934.
4 *R.G.B.,* 1933, Vol. I, No. 105 (September 22), p. 661.
5 *V.B.,* December 23, 1933.

post, was elevated to the new Reich Ministry of Science, Education, and People's Schooling (*Wissenschaft, Erziehung und Volksbildung*), to which certain functions were transferred from the Ministry of the Interior.[1] Rust, *Gauleiter* in Hanover and a friend of Hitler since December 1924, had distinguished himself in the Prussian Ministry, where he had laboured since February 1933, by "liquidating the school as an institute of intellectual acrobatics," restoring bodily training and character-building, and filling the youth with warlike ardour.[2] In his new post he was given jurisdiction over school affairs, youth organizations, adult education, scientific institutes, and scientific relations with foreign countries.[3] The "co-ordination" of culture was completed by the union of the Kampfbund für Deutsche Kultur and the Reichsverband Deutsche Bühne into a N.S. Kulturgemeinde, supervised by Rosenberg and made a part of the *"Kraft durch Freude"* organization of the Labour Front.[4]

A detailed consideration of æsthetics in the Third Reich is beyond the scope of the present study. Only a few general tendencies can be suggested. Art is "national," "Germanic," anti-Semitic, and anti-cosmopolitan.[5] Art and life are reunited.[6] Art flows from race and blood.[7] Music is emancipated from Jewish, foreign, and "European" influences and made again truly German. Mendelssohn is repudiated. Wagner is restored to full pre-eminence, with his exile from Germany as a revolutionist conveniently forgotten. The Bayreuth Festival is heavily subsidized by the Reich. Toscanini may refuse to conduct, Paderewski, Hubermann, and other artists may spurn Furtwängler's pleas for "reconciliation," but Teutonic, "Aryan" music must go its way. Furtwängler himself, director of the Berlin Philharmonic Orchestra and of the Staatsopera, was compelled to resign early in December 1934, because of his interest in "modern" and "Jewish" music.

The theatre serves "the people."[8] Musicians, actors, singers, and

1 *R.G.B.*, 1934, Vol. I, No. 51 (May 14), p. 375; cf. exchanges of letters between Hitler and Göring, March 17 and May 1, *V.B.*, May 1, 1934.

2 *V.B.*, May 1, 1934.

3 Order of Hitler, May 11, 1934, *V.B.*, May 15, 1934.

4 Cf. Rosenberg's order of June 6 and exchange of letters between Rosenberg and Ley, *V.B.*, June 14, 1934.

5 Cf. Hitler's address on art at Nürnberg, September 1, 1933.

6 Cf. Rosenberg's address in *V.B.*, May 8, 1934.

7 Cf. Frick in *Berliner Tageblatt*, October 20, 1933.

8 Cf. Göring in *Berliner Tageblatt*, September 13, 1933.

vaudeville and circus performers are all "co-ordinated." Max Reinhardt is in exile, practising his incomparable stage art abroad, but the German stage is "pure," even if puerile. Under the new film code Goebbels is dictator of the cinema. "Jewish" films, "immoral" films, everything "un-German" or anti-Nazi is barred. Darré went so far as to denounce a Nazi propaganda picture produced by UFA, *Blut und Scholle,* because the chief character resembled Van der Lubbe.[1] Film critics in the press who complain of propaganda, or who even suggest that excessive romanticism in the cinema may diminish its æsthetic value, are promptly squelched by the Propaganda Minister. The radio likewise serves the revolution. Military marches and political speeches fill the programs. Listeners who tune in on Soviet stations are punished and those who boycott the new programs by discontinuing their monthly taxes and disconnecting their sets are denounced.

Most outside observers are agreed that the new culture has created nothing noteworthy in any field of æsthetic activity save popular pageantry and political circuses. If new painters, sculptors, composers, architects, and writers are being developed, they have not yet become productive. The themes of war, heroism, mediævalism, and racial mysticism offer no lack of subject-matter for great art. But the art has not emerged. Such new dramas as *Schlageter, U-Boat 116, Land in Twilight* (Friedrich Blunck), *All against One* (Forster-Burggraf), and *The Hour of Sacrifice* (Hellmuth Unger) have often bored even Nazi audiences. Some of the propaganda films, notably *S.A. Man Brand, Hitlerjunge Quex,* and *Schuss an die Grenze,* have artistic merit, but the German revolution shows no promise of giving birth to a new art of the cinema. Modernistic or "functional" architecture is shunned for weak copies of baroque or neo-classical models. Nazi architecture has thus far been limited to the erection of Brown Houses and the construction of war memorials and bomb-proof *Luftschutz* cellars. The new fiction and verse appear barren. The "art of escape" has re-emerged in new forms: light musical comedies, sentimental ballads, and sugar-coated novels and plays.

The apparent sterility of Nazi art, like that of Italian Fascist art, is probably not to be explained by the familiar formula which holds that art and propaganda are incompatible. The greatest æsthetic achievements of western culture in architecture and painting were

[1] Ibid., November 3, 1933.

propaganda for Church or State in the French Middle Ages and the Italian Renaissance. In the Soviet Union, where propaganda and art are also indistinguishable, notable new styles have developed in music, the theatre, the cinema, and the dance. The explanation perhaps is that Nazi *Kultur* strives to re-create and repopularize the values and forms of epochs long dead, without being able to re-create the social, economic, and cultural soil out of which the old art originally sprang. Race and blood can probably not be made to nourish great art, even at the command of a totalitarian dictatorship, in a land of monopolistic capitalism and urbanized industry.

The sciences have been *gleichgeschaltet* to a comparable degree, not only by the dismissal of all Jewish scientists and professors and the regimentation of the survivors into organizations under the complete control of the party, but also by the repudiation of all notions of scientific "detachment" or "impartiality." The social studies have undergone most radical transformations. "It is not true," says Rosenberg, "that there is such a thing as an objective view of history." [1] All history is in process of being rewritten from the Nazi viewpoint, with emphasis on race. Anthropology is little more than the glorification of Nordic superiority. Political science is the *Führerprinzip*. Economics must serve the cause of autarchy. Sociology is national megalomania. Some German social scientists, as a means of survival, have abandoned all generalizing and, taking their cue doubtless from the United States, have devoted themselves to weighing, measuring, and tabulating—all relatively innocuous occupations. But in general social science, as it is understood in the West, is nonexistent in the Third Reich.

Geography, physics, and chemistry are useful only as they serve military purposes: "*Wehrwissenschaft*." Astronomy is overshadowed by the popular cult of astrology. Even medicine is under suspicion. "Nature-healers" are favoured by the régime.[2] The tender solicitude of the Nazi leaders for non-human organisms has led to rigid restrictions on vivisection, with deplorable results for medical research.[3] The storm trooper who tortures or murders "enemies of the State" is idolized, but the citizen who chastises his horse or the bacteriologist or physiologist who performs operations on dogs without special

[1] Speech at Münster, September 16, 1934.
[2] Cf. address by Hess, *Berliner Tageblatt*, November 27, 1933.
[3] *Berliner Tageblatt*, November 25, 1933.

authorization is subject to heavy fines and jail sentences.[1] More than one operation on a single animal is unqualifiedly *verboten*. The cause of kindness to animals is thereby presumably furthered, but science is again placed in mediæval shackles.

Above all, science must serve the cause of race purification. Under the Sterilization Law a series of "Hereditary Health Courts" *(Erbgesundheitsgerichte)* were established throughout the Reich, with Appellate Courts and a Supreme Hereditary Health Court with power to deliver final judgments. Before these bodies all persons suspected of hereditary disease are obliged to appear and show cause why they should not be rendered sterile through a surgical operation. It was originally estimated that 400,000 persons would be affected, comprising nine categories: feeble-mindedness, 200,000; schizophrenia, 80,000; epilepsy, 60,000; manic-depressive insanity, 20,000; physical deformity, 20,000; deaf-mutism, 18,000; chronic alcoholism, 10,000; St. Vitus's dance, 6,000; and blindness, 4,000. These categories are obviously unscientific and would necessarily include many instances of disabilities which are in no sense hereditary. Should Goebbels be sterilized for his club-foot, Ley for alcoholism, and Streicher for schizophrenia, the Reich might obviously be deprived of gifted children. But it may be presumed that the tribunals, supplied with competent medical advice, will avoid such miscarriages of justice.

The Sterilization Law went into effect on January 1, 1934.[2] Some of the tribunals were apparently embarrassed at the outset by an influx of healthy young men and women desiring to be sterilized for reasons best known to themselves. Voluntary operations were not performed, however, unless hereditary defects could be shown. The Berlin court, during the first ten weeks of its activity, ordered 325 operations. In July it held that aliens, resident or transient, were also subject to the law. By midsummer 200 persons had been sterilized in Düsseldorf, 761 in Hamburg, 572 in Baden, etc. Complete privacy is observed and some states have provided penalties for those ridiculing the subjects of such operations. The estimated total of 400,000 will evidently not be reached for many years.

If defectives are thus prevented from reproducing their kind, healthy Aryans, particularly "Nordics," are officially encouraged to marry and raise large families in accordance with the dictates of the

[1] *R.G.B.*, 1933, Vol. 1, No. 132 (November 24), p. 987.

[2] *R.G.B.*, 1933, Vol. I, No. 86 (July 14), p. 529; No. 138 (December 5), p. 1021.

new "race science." Leaders of the Hitler Jugend and the Hitler Mädel sign pledges to perform their racial duty: to keep their bodies healthy; to refrain from marriage if afflicted with hereditary diseases; if untainted, to find a healthy Aryan mate; to protect the Fatherland from a declining birth-rate; and to strive for all that is healthy, strong, and heroic.[1]

Women in the Third Reich are relegated to the traditional *Kinder, Küche, Kirche* (children, kitchen, and church). According to the Reichsreferentin of the Bund Deutscher Mädel, Trude Mohr, two-thirds of the work of the *Bund* is to be devoted to bodily development. For the rest, German girls must mould their lives according to the new *Weltanschauung* and fulfil their duties to family, race and State.[2] Co-education is discouraged and is eventually to be abolished. Some ten thousand women have been placed in small camps where they are trained to grow crops and to love the soil.[3] Hitler has condemned women's rights as "a product of decadent Jewish intellectualism":

"Liberalism has a large number of points for women's equality. The Nazi program for women has but one: this is the child. While man makes his supreme sacrifice on the field of battle, woman fights her supreme battle for her nation when she gives life to a child." [4]

A similar conception is to be found in the recommendations of *Das Wissen der Nation* (August 1933), a Nazi periodical:

"Every Aryan hero should marry only a blonde Aryan woman with blue, wide-open eyes, a long, oval face, a pink and white skin, a narrow nose, a small mouth, and under all circumstances virginal. A blond blue-eyed man must marry no brunette, no Mediterranean-type woman with short legs, black hair, hooked nose, full lips, a large mouth, and an inclination to plumpness. A blond, blue-eyed Aryan hero must marry no Negroid type of woman with the well-known Negroid head and thinish body. The Aryan hero must marry only his equal Aryan woman, but not one who goes out too much or likes theatres, entertainment, or sport, or who cares to be seen outside her house."

Woman suffrage is eventually to be abolished. Illegitimacy is to

[1] Text of pledges in *V.B.*, April 15, 1934.

[2] *V.B.*, June 14, 1934; see also regular *V.B.* supplement, *"Rasse, Volk, und Staat."*

[3] *The New York Times*, April 18, 1934.

[4] Address at Nürnberg party convention, September 8, 1934.

be heavily penalized. Another ideal is the prohibition of divorce for parents with children and the facilitation of divorce for childless couples. Frick, divorced and re-wed to a divorcee at the age of fifty-seven, grows lyrical over the beauties of family life and the necessity of German women giving birth to three hundred thousand more children each year. "It is of the utmost importance to educate our girls to become virtuous German housewives and mothers. . . . The German woman who is bred in a true Nationalsocialist sense to be a German mother will secure from German youth the respect which is due her."[1]

Marriage, the family, and children are objects of particular Nazi solicitude. Single men (Hitler always excepted) are encouraged to marry young and beget a large progeny. In November 1933 the Mayor of Frankfurt am Main ordered fifteen hundred unmarried municipal officials to find wives or lose their jobs. Numerous agencies have been created to encourage matrimony and reproduction among those who are "racially pure." In March 1934 a membership campaign was launched to support the N.S. Welfare Organization (*N.S. Volkswohlfahrt* or NSV). As in the "winter relief" campaign, special donations were called for and an *Eintopfgericht* Sunday was decreed for March 4 to aid the work of the NSV on behalf of mothers and children, comprising vacations, recreation homes, and "honorary godparenthoods."[2] In May 1934 Hindenburg, Hitler, and Papen became godfathers to male triplets born in Langenberg.

Various measures have been taken to increase the birth-rate. Government loans of a thousand marks are available to newly married couples, with a quarter of the loan cancelled for each child. In October of 1933 a fifteen per cent income-tax reduction was announced for each of the first four children in the family, with a thirty per cent reduction for each child born thereafter.[3] School fees have been reduced for large families.[4] Comparable reductions have been made for medicinal services in the *Krankenkassen*. During 1933 there were 621,000 marriages throughout the Reich, an increase of 24 per cent over 1932. In July 1934 the Prussian Statistical Bureau calculated that in thirty-six cities the number of marriages during the first quarter

[1] *V.B.*, June 12, 1934.
[2] Ibid., March 3, 1934.
[3] *Berliner Tageblatt*, October 19, 1933.
[4] *V.B.*, January 6, and March 3, 1934.

of 1934 was 52 per cent greater than in 1933, and the number of births 23 per cent greater.[1]

Nazi strategists view with alarm the decline of the excess of German births over deaths from 504,000 in 1912 to 292,000 in 1932. They have calculated that if past tendencies continue, the annual increment to the German population will be less than 300,000 by 1952, scarcely larger than in France, Poland, or Italy. In 1936, however, Germany will increase her population by 281,000, as compared with 105,000 for France. This will represent the low point caused by the Great War. But the Reich will not be ready for the next war by 1936. Consequently, no efforts must be spared to give Germany a teeming population of prospective cannon-fodder by the mid-century.[2]

The *Gleichschaltung* of religion and the transformation of the churches into propaganda agencies for the inculcation of National-socialism were also inevitable corollaries of the dictatorship. And precisely here, in the clash of two totalitarian *Weltanschauungen,* the NSDAP has encountered the most vigorous and articulate resistance to its policy. While the confused and stormy course of the new struggle between Church and State is beyond the scope of the present volume,[3] it may be noted that in the Church, and in the Church alone, the Nazi dictatorship has found an insuperable obstacle to its absolutistic pretensions. Every other German institution has been *gleichgeschaltet* and converted into an agency for the propagation of the Nazi gospel. The power of the Catholic Church was such that, in fundamentals at least, it won its fight for independence without a battle. Nazi efforts to control the Evangelical Church through Reichsbishop Ludwig Müller have split the organization and introduced endless conflict and confusion among clergy and laity. But they have not conquered Lutheranism nor converted German Protestants into such enthusiastic Nazis that they are willing to give the State precedence over the Church in all things or to acknowledge paganism or Nordic Christianity as their faith. The religious struggle

[1] *The New York Times,* July 20, 1934.

[2] Cf. population table in *V.B.,* February 6, 1934.

[3] Cf. Charles S. MacFarland: *The New Church and the New Germany* (New York: Macmillan; 1934); Erdmann Schott: *Die N.S. Revolution als theologisches Problem* (Tübingen: Mohr; 1934); H. M. Mueller, *Der innere Weg der deutschen Kirche* (ibid., 1934); Cardinal Michael von Faulhaber: *Judaism, Christianity, Germany* (New York: Macmillan; 1934); Wilhelm Gerdemann: *Christenkreuz oder Hakenkreuz* (Cologne, 1931); Jacob Noetges: *Nationalsocialismus und Katholismus* (Cologne, 1932); etc.

has not as yet seriously undermined the political domination of the NSDAP. Like most other modern peoples, Germans are patriots first and Christians second. Whether the Third Reich can still be described as being in any sense a Christian State is debatable in view of its values and practices. But its citizens, however loyal to Hitler, still regard themselves in overwhelming numbers as Christians and have successfully resisted the destruction of the Christian Church.

The explanation of this phenomenon is doubtless to be found in the circumstance that the Nazi *Weltanschauung* has here come into conflict with another *Weltanschauung* far older, more stable, more secure, and more consistent than its own.[1] Each is absolutistic and universal in its pretensions. The irresistible force meeting the immovable body has proved to be not so irresistible as its champions believed. The organization and integration of emotional life and social activities about the symbols of liberalism and Marxism could be smashed. Christianity—and, be it noted, Judaism as well—have survived the assault. Dogmas, creeds, and ways of life as ancient as Moses and the apostles of the Carpenter of Nazareth, and as deeply rooted in the soil of successive western cultures as Jerusalem and Rome, have not yielded to a new dogma which only fifteen years ago was merely hot air in Munich beer halls. A new set of values, like Communism in Russia, which actually fills all the emotional wants formerly satisfied by organized religion, can conceivably supersede older faiths. But a set of values which is in its essence a product of temporary neuroses, of mass paranoia and megalomania, cannot weather away the great structures reared by ancient faith.

[1] Cf. the highly suggestive article by Paul Tillich: "The Totalitarian State and the Claims of the Church," *Social Research,* November 1934; pp. 405–33.

CHAPTER XI

LOAVES AND FISHES

1. THE PROFITS OF POWER

THE ultimate technique of politics is the apportionment of material benefits among the major strata of the social hierarchy in such a fashion as to ensure acquiescence in the status quo and loyalty to those wielding governmental power. This technique is "ultimate" in the sense that the whole political process may be regarded as a product of competition and conflict among social groups for material and psychic satisfactions. Property and money are but two means toward satisfactions, but since they command all others, the competition for possession of them is not only the focal point of economic motivations and activities, but is likewise the most basic incentive to political behaviour. Save for the Soviet Union, all known civilized societies and all cultures have conformed to this pattern. Material wealth in such societies is the key to social position, prestige, and power. Status, deference, and influence in turn are often sought after because of the opportunities which they afford for the acquisition of additional property and money. Since the human animal, however, habitually makes ends of his means, these opportunities are frequently striven for as things good in themselves, affording psychic satisfactions not to be measured by the current medium of exchange.

Control of the State is an end normally sought after as a means of influencing the distribution of satisfactions in a fashion advantageous to each group of aspirants for power and pelf. It is likewise an end in itself and an immediate channel to jobs and perquisites for professional politicians. But no group of politicians can secure or retain power unless it serves not only its own interests but those of decisive interest-aggregations in the community as a whole. In the expanding and prosperous economies of the western world in the nineteenth century, the role of the State in the distributive process was first reduced to a minimum and then, in appearance at least, transformed into that of a service agency for the entire population. Where goods and services are increasingly abundant, the competition among groups for a larger share of the total is less keen, less embittered, less significant for politics than in societies afflicted with famine and impoverishment. In the contracting and impecunious economies of the post-war world this competition has frequently been intensified to the point of open conflict. The State must arbitrate, intervene, and regulate the agencies and procedures of distribution which were once "private" and uncontrolled. Ruling classes and revolutionists must again protect and promote their interests by "political" means in the narrower sense. The dictatorial, totalitarian "corporative" State is the end-point of this development in the increasingly monopolistic economies of the twentieth-century imperialisms. The State is again the decisive distributive agency. Control of the State becomes indispensable to those groups which would secure for themselves the largest share of a shrinking income.

The Fascist State is the creation of a political movement reflecting the neuroses of a lower middle class and a peasantry reduced to desperation by social insecurity and impoverishment. It is also the product of the determination of business and agrarian élites to safeguard their social positions by destroying the power of other groups who challenge or undermine their privileges. The NSDAP grew out of the social and spiritual sickness of the *Kleinbürgertum*. It became the tool of the established ruling classes against their enemies. As soon as its leaders rejected social revolution and identified themselves with the rural aristocracy and the urban plutocracy, they were obliged to protect the classes against the masses and to use their power in a way advantageous to the élites which they served. Any alternative policy would alienate the classes where ultimate political and economic power reside, and disintegrate the social bases of the dictatorship. This inner contradiction of a "socialistic" mass party serving the interests of Property and Profits is the secret of the economic and social program of the rulers of the Third Reich. It explains the political techniques employed by the NSDAP and the role of the new State in the whole distributive process.

The weapons of power thus far reviewed are products of political exigencies inherent in the paradox already suggested. The composition of the party and of the S.A., no less than the content of a new *Weltanschauung* born of petty-bourgeois frustrations, rendered any open and avowed championship of Junkerdom and monopolistic capitalism impossible. Hitler and his aides were compelled to talk "socialism" and to glorify small business men, peasants, and wage-earners as a means of retaining their mass following. They were also compelled to appease aristocrats and industrialists or face destruction. This apparently impossible task was simplified by the neurotic and irrational character of mass expectations. Political sadism, the persecution of scapegoats, the glorification of war, the encouragement of racial megalomania, and the systematic inculcation of the new faith have afforded substantial psychic satisfactions to a populace whose sickness of the soul has progressed so far that it makes a virtue of poverty and abnegation, idealizes armed conflict and death, prefers mythology to nutrition, demands swords instead of beefsteaks, and gives precedence to goose-stepping over the pleasures of digestion. Circuses have in part taken the place of bread.

It may be assumed, however, that ultimately the ancient and eternal question will pose itself imperatively: "When do we eat?" For the leaders of the NSDAP and for many of their party followers, this question had already been answered. While no authoritative information is available as to the detailed distribution of wealth and income among the political élite of the party, it is clear that places on public pay-rolls, royalties from publications, receipts from collections, and innumerable opportunities for legal or extra-legal profit have enriched thousands of leaders. The process of making the party pay large dividends to its organizers began long before it secured power.[1] Once in complete control of the machinery of the State, opportunities for profit were greatly multiplied. Hitler, who generously gave up his salary as Chancellor, was believed, in 1932, to have an annual income of more than 400,000 marks, derived from royalties on *Mein Kampf,* the profits of the party press, lecture fees, donations, party posts, and sundry invisible sources. Since January 30, 1933, he has probably received more than 500,000 marks per year as a net income. Göring, already wealthy, perhaps collects 100,000 marks a year in his various salaries and fees. Goebbels is probably not less fortunate. The Statthalters receive 33,000 marks annually as basic salaries. Almost all of the higher party leaders occupy one or more

[1] Cf. pp. 85f. above.

important governmental posts, and most of them receive rent-free homes, travelling expenses, and living allowances from the State.

These incomes compare favourably with those of people in the lower brackets of the industrial and financial élite. Ostentatious display and conspicuous waste, however, are discouraged. Hitler, as an ascetic Messiah, creates the public impression of living simply and modestly. He and Hess have repeatedly urged simplicity and frugality upon their subordinates, at least in their public roles. Göring's extravagant foibles are an exception to the rule among party leaders. Privately the dictators are free to gratify their every whim. Those who fall from Der Führer's favour and are condemned to liquidation are accused of luxury and vice.[1] But since the accusation is certain to be made in any case as a means of discrediting victims of Hitler's wrath among the populace, the joys of extravagance and sinning may as well be tasted while they last. Those who remain among the faithful are free to indulge themselves in private, so long as they do not thereby create envy and resentment among their less fortunate followers.

Apart from salaries, the party leaders have access to funds from the innumerable "voluntary" assessments and donations levied upon party members and upon the public at large. While the bulk of such funds doubtless goes to the causes for which they are nominally collected, it is probable that a considerable portion finds its way into the private pockets of the collectors—not usually the S.A. men or Hitler Youth, with their tin cups and subscription blanks, but rather the higher party and S.A. leaders who direct the collections. Many contributions are gladly given, even by those of moderate means. Others are extracted from business men and property-owners by methods not far removed from blackmail. Following the revelations of graft and corruption in high places after "Bloody Saturday," the voluntary donations manifested a tendency to decline. In July 1934 *Der Angriff* began publishing detailed reports on wealthy west-end contributors, hoping in this fashion to flatter the generous and stigmatize the stingy. Withholding donations or grumbling about collections may be followed by highly unpleasant consequences. Millions of marks can therefore be extracted with little difficulty from individuals and corporations. There has never been any public accounting made of the use of such funds, nor any effort other than

[1] Cf. p. 447 below.

exhortation to ensure honesty in their administration.

As for the rank and file of the party, all members of the S.S. are well paid (salaries of this kind are kept secret) and many S.S. leaders hold other lucrative posts. While many of the higher S.A. leaders have enhanced their incomes from party or State posts, the majority of storm troopers with regular jobs have been obliged to contribute rather than to share in the distribution of the profits of power. S.A. men receive no stipends for their services unless they are unemployed. Their poverty has bred unrest and led to successive crises within the movement. Through dues and assessments, as well as through exhortations, other party members are likewise assured that it is holier to give than to receive. There can be no doubt but that the great majority of the four million party members and applicants have derived only psychic satisfactions from their creed. Efforts have been made, however, to find jobs first for unemployed *Partei-genossen*. Party members receive preferential treatment in the administration of employment offices. By June of 1934, ninety per cent of the "old fighters" in Berlin had received jobs, and all party members throughout the Reich with cards from No. 1 to No. 100,000 had been provided for.[1] During 1933 many party members secured jobs as "protectors" of Jews and non-Nazis: lawyers, deputies, guards, etc. On the other hand, storm troopers and party members are subject to special party discipline, are discouraged from belonging to organizations without military or political aims, and are forbidden to take time off from their regular employment for party service.[2] It may nevertheless be said that, with the exception of certain groups of S.A. men who are habitually under suspicion, the distribution of jobs, favours, and honours among the members of the NSDAP has been such as to ensure their loyalty for motives not exclusively philosophical or altruistic.

2. CAPITAL

How has the business élite fared under the dictatorship, which was so generously subsidized and called into being by influential business men? Such initial fears of "socialism" as employers and entrepreneurs entertained in the spring of 1933 have been largely dispelled. The

[1] *V.B.*, June 8, 1934.

[2] *Berliner Tageblatt*, November 22, 1933; *The New York Times*, March 30, 1934.

early efforts of the Nazi radicals to create a "Workers' State" and to regiment private business initiative in the name of the new socialism were promptly squelched by Der Führer. All hope of a "Second Revolution" was crushed by Hitler in July 1933.[1] On July 11 Frick issued a decree to the Statthalters ordering them to prevent all meddling with business by self-appointed party commissions and to dissolve such groups by October 1. The business commissars were dismissed. Unauthorized interference by party members in the management of enterprises was forbidden. With Muchow dead, Feder relegated to an innocuous role, Wagener discharged, and Schmitt and Keppler appointed to important posts, no question remained as to the determination of the party leaders to protect private property and private profits.

The *Gleichschaltung* of business within the framework of private capitalism nevertheless continued. The new capitalism differed from the old in that free competition in a free market was largely displaced by governmentally protected monopolies subjected to State regulation of prices, wages, and marketing. The illusory National Economic Council, created in 1919, was abolished on March 24, 1934.[2] On September 20, 1933, however, a new General Economic Council (*Generalrat der Wirtschaft*) held its first session in the presence of Schmitt and Hitler. This body was designed to assist the government in preparing its economic measures in consultation with representatives of business. Among its members were Fritz Thyssen and Dr. Voegler of Mülheim; Karl Bosch and Krupp von Bohlen und Halbach of Essen; Karl von Siemens of Berlin; Banker-Baron von Schroeder of Cologne; bankers Fink, Otto Fischer, Friedrich Reinhart, and Hjalmar Schacht; factory managers Boehringer, Diehn, and Hackelsberger; many other financiers and industrialists, and—Dr. Robert Ley.[3] Hitler declared that economic recovery depended upon private initiative. Critics would be repressed. "The power of the State is always the pathfinder of business." Local and national public finances would be put in order through a sharp reduction of welfare expenditures. The labour-creation program would be pushed forward, but taxes on business and agriculture would be lightened

[1] Cf. pp. 267f. above.

[2] *R.G.B.*, 1934, Vol. I, No. 15, p. 115.

[3] *V.B.*, September 19, 1933.

and the capital market would be left undisturbed.[1]

The provisions of the Nazi program calling for nationalization of trusts and municipalization of department stores were conveniently forgotten. Interest rates were reduced, but the credit structure remained unchanged and the "bonds of interest slavery" continued to bind. The captains of industry and the much maligned barons of the Bourse were encouraged to reaffirm the sacredness of property and profits. Krupp, president of the Reichsstand der deutschen Industrie (successor to the Reichsverband der Industrie), declared in October 1933 that private initiative would remain the basis of the State's economic policy. Employers would carry out their practical mission and would eschew "theories" and experimentation, confident of the support of the government to which they acknowledged allegiance. "On September 20 I thanked Hitler for the confidence he had shown to men of practical business by summoning them into the General Economic Council. I promised him the unqualified support of all branches and organizations of business." [2] Keppler asserted that production was the central problem of economic life. Trade serves production by distributing goods. In commerce responsibility must be restored to the individual merchant—and great merchants are as necessary as small ones.[3] On November 7, 1933, in a great demonstration in Berlin, Voegler, Krupp, Fischer, Schacht, and other industrialists expressed their complete accord with Hitler's "peace" policy.[4]

Even the more radical party leaders followed this line:

"Our socialism . . . is the legacy of the Prussian army. . . . It is that kind of socialism which enabled Frederick the Great to carry on a war for seven years." (Goebbels in *Berliner Börsen Zeitung,* December 15, 1933.)

"Nationalsocialism sees precisely in creative personalities the prerequisite of the co-operation of State and Business. . . . Nationalsocialism achieves a synthesis of State and Business. . . . The State should lead business, not conduct business." (Gottfried Feder, *V.B.,* January 4, 1934.)

[1] *Berliner Nachtausgabe,* September 21, 1933.

[2] *Berliner Tageblatt,* October 18, 1933.

[3] *V.B.,* October 21, 1933.

[4] *Berliner Tageblatt,* November 8, 1933.

"Feder has found a most happy formulation in the phrase: 'nationalizing the banks.' By this, of course, he does not mean nationalization or socialization of the banks." (*Deutsche Bergwerks Zeitung*, December 1, 1933.)

Business was further liberated from radical pressure and at the same time further co-ordinated in the spring and summer of 1934. On March 13 Schmitt, acting under the "Law for the Organic Upbuilding of German Economy," [1] which authorized him to simplify and unify the various organizations of German business men, announced to the General Economic Council that German business would henceforth be organized in twelve great groups, each with its "leader": mining and metallurgy (Krupp); shipping, engineering, electro-technical, optical, and other fine mechanical industries (Blohm); iron, tin, and metal products (Hartkopf); stone, earth, lumber, glass, ceramics, and building (Voegler); chemicals, oils, fats, and paper (Pietzsch); leather, textiles, and clothing (Dierig); foodstuffs (Schüler); handiwork; commerce; banks and credits; insurance; and transportation. The first seven groups were united in the Reichsstand der Industrie, still headed by Krupp. The remainder were united on December 3, 1934 into a "Reich Chamber of Business," headed by Ewald Hecker, a Harz steel magnate. Schmitt became industrial dictator, aided by Philip Kessler, chairman of the board of the Verzmann Electric Company of Berlin, and by Count Ruediger von der Goltz as Kessler's deputy. These officials were given supervisory powers over the twelve industrial groups, with authority to enforce their regulations by punishing offenders. German business is regulated by State decrees enforceable in the courts, rather than by more or less voluntary codes, as in the United States under the NRA. Schmitt indicated that fixed prices and production quotas would be exceptional rather than general. Competition would be regulated and made "fair and honest" by regulations enforced in the "Courts of Honour." [2]

The basic principle of the new economy is the ultimate authority and responsibility of the individual entrepreneur.[3] The new State represents "True Lordship," in the opinion of Papen: "A difference in human talents demands a division into leaders and led. Whether

[1] *R.G.B.*, 1934, Vol. I, February 27, p. 185.
[2] *The New York Times*, March 14 and 15, 1934.
[3] Cf. Kessler in *V.B.*, April 25, 1934.

the national wealth takes the form of individual ownership or common ownership, there will always remain the fact that only a few heads dispose of it and only a few hands guide the reins." [1] At the Second Labour Congress on May 16, 1934, Hitler ridiculed the Soviet planned economy and asserted that natural selection and the survival of the fittest must rule in business.[2] Ley declared: "Here in Germany we mean to breed masterful men in all strata of the population, men imbued with pride founded on their capabilities and performances." [3]

Friction between Schmitt and Kessler and certain conflicts of views among industrialists over the reorganization of industry led to Kessler's abrupt dismissal from his post as Reich Economic Leader on July 11, 1934. He was replaced by Count von der Goltz. The new leader was not entirely welcome to some business groups because of his criticism of cartels. His appointment was interpreted in some circles as a victory of Thyssen, Krupp, and the iron and steel interests over electrical interests favouring extensive State control of monopolies.[4] The conservative Wilhelm Keppler remained confidential economic adviser to Hitler.

In practice, however, the Minister of Economics has assumed more and more control over German business life. Under the law of July 15, 1933 [5] he was empowered to form compulsory cartels or price-fixing agreements, to regulate the rights and duties of their members, to dissolve existing business combinations, and to forbid the establishment of new firms or the extension of existing ones in any branch of industry. Up to March 1934 compulsory cartels had been formed in thirteen industries, and by July twenty industries had been forbidden to expand plants or build new ones.[6] The whole system of price-fixing through cartels, which had been falling into decay, was revived by Hitler and made an integral part of the Fascist economy. An emergency decree of July 3, 1934 [7] empowered the Minister of Economics, up to September 30, "to take all measures necessary to promote German commerce as well as to protect and

[1] Quoted in *The New York Times,* April 26, 1934.
[2] *V.B.,* May 17, 1934.
[3] Quoted in *The New York Times,* May 17, 1934.
[4] *The New York Times,* July 19, 1934.
[5] *R.G.B.,* 1933, Vol. I, No. 82, p. 488.
[6] Cf. J. W. F. Thelwall: *Economic Conditions in Germany* (London: Department of Overseas Trade; 1934); and Mildred Wertheimer: "The Economic Structure of the Third Reich," *FPA Reports,* September 26, 1934.
[7] *R.G.B.,* 1934, Vol. I, No. 74, p. 565.

improve economic conditions." Such measures might deviate from existing law. The Minister was further authorized to punish violations of his orders by imprisonment or unlimited fines.

Following the retirement of Kurt Schmitt because of illness, Hjalmar Schacht was appointed by Hitler as Minister of Economics for a period of six months beginning August 2, 1934. He continued to hold his post as president of the Reichsbank, in which capacity he exercised extensive powers over the German banking system. As Minister of Economics he assumed authority to appoint and remove all chairmen and all members of the advisory committees of all chambers of industry and commerce throughout the Reich. The new business dictator is even more completely free from all suspicion of social radicalism than was his predecessor. He long ago dropped his two baptismal names: Horace Greeley. A bank director at the age of twenty-six, he became financial administrator of occupied Belgium during the war, president of the Darmstädter National Bank thereafter, and stabilizer of the mark in 1923. He remained a Democrat as long as it paid him to do so, and then became a Nazi. In 1919 he delivered socialistic harangues in Wittenbergplatz in Berlin. Jewish and liberal friends, including Georg Bernard of the *Vossische Zeitung,* helped him to secure his first appointment as president of the Reichsbank. He was appointed by Hilferding Socialist Minister of Finance, to ensure "liberal" and "democratic" control of the institution. Hitler appointed him to this post once more on March 16, 1933, in the face of considerable Nazi opposition. He had played an important, though still somewhat obscure, role in the Thyssen-Papen-Schroeder-Hugenberg-Landbund conspiracy which elevated Hitler to the chancellorship. The evidences of embezzlement in Belgium, for which he had almost been jailed during the war, were expunged from the Reichsbank reports. This economic Napoleon of the Third Reich is unscrupulous, eccentric, and ambitious and is at all times the staunch protector of German capitalism. He has changed his politics as readily as he changed from soft collars to the high, stiff halters which he now affects.

The NSDAP has thus kept the faith with the captains of industry and finance. Hitler is unshakably loyal to Thyssen, Krupp, Schroeder, et al. The new German capitalism—monopolistic, cartelized, and regimented—is safe in the hands of capitalist Schacht, who, more than any other, defends property and profits, scoffs at socialization, champions a Spenglerian imperialism, and makes certain that the burdens of the new era rest lightly on the backs of his fellow industrialists and financiers.

3. LABOUR

The smashing of the German trade unions has been discussed above.[1] There remain for consideration the position of labour in the second year of the Third Reich and the fruits of toil vouchsafed to the toilers by the Nazi dictatorship. The Labour Front and the NSBO remain the two great organizations of German workers, though the former includes employers as well. By May 1934 the Labour Front had twenty-three million members—that is, practically the entire gainfully occupied population of the country save those in agriculture.[2] The organization has never been envisaged as a trade union or an agency for the protection of workers against employers. The two are now one in the Nazi view. In the words of Ley:

"I went myself to the worker, gave him my hand, and spoke as man to man. . . . Not one asked me if I had in my pockets higher wages or new wage agreements. I recognized the justice of the words that the love of the child for the mother does not depend on whether she is rich or poor, but only on whether she cares for the child. . . . The struggle of the workers is not for pennies, but for honour and respect." [3]

The work of the *Arbeitsfront* has been largely confined to the fields of propaganda, circuses, and conversion. To fulfil its task it has extended its activities to cover the whole life of German workers. It has its own youth organization. Late in 1933 Ley decided to copy the Italian *Dopolavoro* organization established by Mussolini in May 1925. This was designed to control and regiment the use of leisure time by wage-earners and to provide recreation to keep them from "dangerous thoughts." The German counterpart was at first christened *"Nach der Arbeit"* (After Work) and then definitely named *"Kraft durch Freude"* (Strength through Joy). Ley indicated that the rationalization of industry, with resultant shorter hours of work, must not cause workers to waste their idle time in trade-union activity or in political discussion. All recreational associations in the

[1] Cf. pp. 223f.
[2] *V.B.*, May 16, 1934.
[3] Ibid., March 2, 1934.

Reich were brought into the new organization, which has offices for culture, sport, travel, vacations, education, and the honour and duty of labour. "I am convinced," declared Goebbels, "that we have actually begun a work which will last for centuries. I am further convinced that this work will develop into an unending blessing for millions of people in Germany, now and in the future."

Kraft durch Freude began operations at the end of December 1933. It provides entertainments, concerts, lectures, and outings. Those workers who are sullen or uninterested are encouraged to participate by gentle hints and by the example of their happy fellow workers, now liberated from union domination, political activity, and revolutionary fantasies. Twelve thousand workers were sent to winter sport resorts. A resort proprietor who refused to entertain workers was put to digging ditches in a labour service camp "to show him what Nationalsocialism means." [1] During the summer of 1934 thousands of workers were given special prizes, in the form of vacation cruises on ocean liners in the North and Baltic Seas. Naval manœuvres contributed to the festivities. The goal is a vacation for every worker. Employers who are recalcitrant are to be disciplined.[2] The purpose of this program, like that of Bismarck's social legislation, is to win the loyalty of the proletariat to the established social and political order. While Bismarck apparently failed in the short run, the behaviour of German labour in 1914, 1919, and 1933 showed that his policies had indeed succeeded in reducing the revolutionary sentiments of German labour to harmlessness. Given favourable economic conditions, *Kraft durch Freude* might succeed as well—if its propaganda were accompanied by material benefits and enhanced economic security for the worker, as it is not.

Meanwhile, the adjustment of disputes over employment, dismissals, wages, and conditions of work was entrusted to thirteen Trustees of Labour, appointed under the law of May 19, 1933.[3] These political officials, most of whom were not labour leaders, but *Beamters* or retired army officers, were given full power to settle disputes through co-operation with employers and with factory councils named by the leaders of the *Arbeitsfront*. This tentative arrangement was not entirely satisfactory, since the councils tended to act as

1 *The New York Times*, March 27, 1934.

2 Cf. statement of Dr. Daeschner, Brandenburg Labour Trustee, ibid., September 4, 1934.

3 *R.G.B.*, 1933, Vol. I, No. 52, p. 285.

spokesmen for the interests of wage-earners.[1] This difficulty was gradually remedied, however, and labour was finally given a "new social constitution" in the form of the law of January 20, 1934. On Sunday, January 14, before its terms were announced, two hundred thousand workers were assembled in the Berlin Lustgarten, with comparable throngs in other cities, to celebrate the new freedom. Goebbels declared:

"We are no troops to guard the moneybags of capitalism. We have come to give labour its bread, and the nation its honour. Ours was a socialist revolution, a revolution of the labour movement. It was made not by the rich, but by the poor. It was a revolution not only against Marxism, but against reaction." [2]

The new labour code—the "Law for the Organization of National Labour" [3]—abolished trade unionism, collective bargaining, the right to strike, and the freedom of workers to organize for their own protection. It abrogated eleven republican laws designed to protect the rights of labour. It asserted the principle of "leadership in business." Each employer was designated as a "leader" in his enterprise. Workers are "followers." "The leader decides all questions relating to the undertaking. He must care for the welfare of his followers. These must accord him the loyalty demanded by the shop community" (Paragraph 2). The employer is chairman of his Shop Council, which is charged with discussing working conditions and with "deepening the common consciousness of trust within the factory community." The council members are elected by the workers from among "nationally reliable employees" at least twenty-five years of age and one year in the plant. The employer makes all decisions, fixes wages, and draws up his own shop code within the terms of existing legislation, but the council, by a majority vote, may appeal to the local Labour Trustees. The trustee, a political appointee with a one-year term and supervised by the Minister of Labour, may regulate minimum wage rates. He hears all disputes and may impose fines and prison terms. Lock-outs, like strikes, are forbidden. Mass

[1] *Deutsche Bergwerks Zeitung,* December 10, 1933: "Unfortunately the Shop Councils have until now often represented only the one-sided interests of the workers, contrary to the regulations of the law concerning Shop Councils. This was because only the workers and the office employees were represented in them. In the future the employer, who bears the economic risk, will be the deciding factor in the Shop Councils, in accordance with the leadership principle."

[2] *V.B.,* January 16, 1934; *The New York Times,* January 15, 1934.

[3] *R.G.B.,* 1934, Vol. I, pp. 45f.

dismissals must be preceded by four weeks' notice. An individual worker who is discharged may apply to a labour court for redress. He may be reinstated with compensation if his dismissal appears unjustly harsh or if it is "not warranted by the condition of the plant."

The law further establishes "Courts of Social Honour" (*Ehrengerichte*), one in each district of the Labour Trustees. They consist of a judge as chairman, appointed jointly by the Ministers of Labour and Justice, one "leader," and one "follower" who is a member of a Shop Council. The latter two are appointed by the judge from lists prepared by the Labour Front. These courts are designed to ensure the fulfilment of responsibilities by both employers and workers. Suits may be initiated only on the application of the Labour Trustee. An appellate Reich Court of Honour was also established. The courts may impose fines up to ten thousand marks, issue warning, and order the dismissal of "followers" or of "leaders." Employers may be tried who "maliciously exploit the labour of their followers or insult their honour." Workers may be tried who "through malicious agitation endanger labour peace within the shop, deliberately interfere with the management, or make frivolous complaints to the Labour Trustee." "The conflict of interests," declared Minister of Labour Seldte, "is to be abolished. Both sides will have but one common interest, that of keeping on with the work in hand, which is a matter of social honour." [1]

These arrangements are almost adequate to satisfy the most ardent advocate of the "open shop" in the National Manufacturers Association of the United States. Strikes are outlawed. Lock-outs or shutdowns are permissible if notice is given. Each employer himself fixes wages, hours, and conditions of work within the limits of national law. He may rid himself of agitators by application to the trustee. Labour has no voice in management. Exploitation is permissible, so long as it is not "malicious" or "insulting." The trustees and the courts are "safe," from the employer's point of view. The code went into effect on May 1, 1934. Most existing wage scales were continued and wage increases were declared impossible as long as unemployment prevailed. Many Jewish employers appointed Aryan deputies as "leaders." The conservative William Green, president of the American Federation of Labor, declared that the code completed the

[1] AP dispatch, January 16, 1934; cf. Seldte in *The New York Times,* March 8, 1934.

reduction of German workers to servitude and asserted that the Federation would continue its boycott on German goods as a means of protest.[1]

Sufficient time has not yet elapsed to allow a definitive judgment of the new system. Where labour is deprived of the right to organize and strike, the eventual result is almost invariably a lowering of wages, a worsening of working conditions, and a progressive exploitation of the proletariat comparable to that which existed prior to the rise of modern trade unionism. In Fascist Italy, where an identical system has prevailed for over a decade, monetary and real wages have steadily declined until, by 1933, the average hourly wage was slightly more than 1.5 lire, less than in any other important industrial country. In Germany no general reductions of money wages have been publicly admitted, though rising costs of living have reduced real wages. When further reductions of costs become necessary to compete in ever shrinking markets, it may be surmised that labour will pay the bill. Practical political and military considerations, no less than the new race mysticism, serve to check exploitation to some degree. The NSDAP has not yet swept away the elaborate social insurance systems built up under the empire and the republic, though it has curtailed them and shifted a portion of the burden from the public treasury to the workers themselves. It has definitely limited the freedom of employers to discharge workers arbitrarily.

But labour in any case is a ward of the State. If it fares well, it will be because its masters and its rulers are both prosperous and benevolent. If it fares ill, it has no means of defence. The transfer to the Labour Front of the property of the former employers' associations, as well as of the old trade unions, in October 1934, and the admission of Labour Front officials to the "arbitration" of disputes before they are submitted to the trustees were regarded as victories for those of Ley's subordinates who wished to convert the *Arbeitsfront* into a genuine union.[2] The labour code, moreover, deviates from the *Führerprinzip* in that elections of Shop Councils are permitted. It was rumoured that in the summer of 1934 many members were elected who were not regarded as "nationally reliable" by the Nazi leaders. But in general, German labour is at the mercy of its employers. These employers are highly regimented, restricted, and con-

[1] *The New York Times,* January 18, 1934.

[2] *The New York Times,* October 29, 1934.

trolled by the State. They are often blackmailed and exploited by Nazi politicians. The State, however, is in the exclusive power of a party which grew out of the anti-proletarian prejudices of the *Kleinbürgertum* and peasantry and is committed to the service of large industrialists and financiers. To the degree to which Ley and his aides yield to mass pressure to protect workers' interests at the expense of employers, they are in danger of dismissal by the party leaders.

The proudest boast of the NSDAP is that it has conquered unemployment. The number of registered jobless reached a high point of 6,016,000 in February 1933. This figure declined rapidly as the year wore on and then increased slightly, in accordance with the usual seasonal fluctuations, to 4,058,000 on December 31, 1933. By March 1, 1934 the total had again fallen to 3,374,000, or 2,630,000 less than the year before. On March 21, 1934, Hitler opened his second great drive against unemployment, with much trumpeting and a goal of two million more jobs.[1] In June it was announced that the remaining total of unemployed was 2,525,000, as compared with 5,039,000 a year before. The figure fell to 2,426,000 in August and 2,398,000 in September. If taken at their face value, these figures represent the largest decrease in unemployment in any major industrial country during the same period.

This achievement, however, is an appearance rather than a reality. The "battle against unemployment" was from the beginning a symbolic test of the Nazi régime. No efforts were spared to reduce the unemployment figures sharply. There are approximately 20,000,000 German adults normally employed in industry and commerce.[2] The *Krankenkassen* statistics, which include practically all employed persons in the Reich, listed 14,336,000 regularly employed (monthly average) in 1931, or 69.1 per cent of the total number of potential workers, and 11,983,000 (63.5 per cent) in December 1932. At the end of 1933, when Hitler claimed to have found work for almost two million jobless, the number of regularly employed persons had risen to 13,300,000—only 1,300,000 more than the year before. Many other contradictions can be found in the official statistics. Thousands who

[1] *V.B.*, March 22, 1934.

[2] The *Statistisches Jahrbuch für das deutsche Reich, 1933,* p. 19, gives a total of 32,009,000 gainfully occupied persons in 1925, of whom 13,239,000 were in industry and hand work, 5,274,000 in trade and transport, and 1,643,000 in domestic service. Cf. also p. 290.

lost their positions as the result of anti-Jewish and anti-Marxist legislation are not registered as unemployed entitled to relief. Hundreds of thousands have been stricken from the relief rolls on other grounds. The "invisible" unemployed—that is, those still jobless, but not registered as such—have increased enormously. The Institut für Konjunkturforschung estimated that there were 2,000,000 invisible unemployed in March 1934.[1] Substitute employment, part-time work shared with those already employed, emergency work, and labour service account for most of the apparent decline of unemployment. The displacement of women workers and of unmarried men by heads of families accounts for the remainder. Of those restored to work between January 1933 and March 1934, only 12.8 per cent were women.

Compulsory labour service has been one of the favourite panaceas of the régime. After much experimentation and delay, caused in part by foreign protests against what was regarded as thinly veiled military conscription, steps were taken in the summer of 1934 to introduce universal and obligatory labour service. There were already 200,000 men in voluntary labour camps under Brüning—probably a larger figure than in 1933. In the Third Reich the camps were militarized. All university students, aspirants to certain professions, and many unmarried unemployed have been obliged to take work of this kind. Universal compulsory labour service for all males between seventeen and twenty-five years of age was decreed locally in a number of districts in June 1934. On July 12 it was announced that 300,000 young men would be compelled to enter camps by the end of the year. Party leaders in Saxony called upon all young workers to quit their jobs and enter the labour camps. At Nürnberg in September 1934 Hitler reviewed 52,000 youths bearing shovels. While no national system of compulsory labour service has yet been announced, at least a quarter of a million young workers were "voluntarily" in camps in the autumn of 1934. In this fashion youth is kept out of the labour market, jobs are created for older workers, and unemployment is reduced. The camp inmates drill, build roads, clear land, construct canals, or in some cases carry dirt from place to place more or less aimlessly. Living and working conditions in some of the camps were such as to cause insubordination and rioting in November 1934, followed by arrests.

[1] *The New York Times,* March 10, 1934.

Public works and business recovery have also absorbed many of the unemployed. A "work-creation program" was initiated on an extensive scale by Brüning and Papen and was financed by tax certificates and short-term borrowing. Since 1932, 5,400,000,000 marks have been allotted to this purpose, including Hitler's motor-roads program announced in June 1933. By June 1934 some two billion marks had been expended in this way. Many unemployed are obliged to accept jobs of this kind, under threats of being stricken from the relief rolls, and are paid less than they received in unemployment stipends. Perhaps half a million workers have been given jobs on public roads. The general business recovery which began in the summer of 1932 has continued, with minor recessions, and has absorbed over a million unemployed into industry and agriculture, though many of these are employed part time or have been placed in positions where they are not actually needed for purposes of production. At the end of July 1934 German industry was producing 46 per cent more than in 1932 and only 10 per cent less than in 1928. By September 1934 it was estimated that 63 per cent of the loss of production during the depression had been recovered.[1] Some fifteen million people were employed, as compared with almost nineteen million in June 1929.

This improvement has been due entirely to domestic factors, since the Reich's foreign trade has continued to decline rapidly. While it is in part attributable to the government's program, it parallels developments in other industrial countries. And in Germany, as elsewhere, it is already clear that a complete restoration of productivity to pre-depression levels will not by any means absorb the number of workers employed in 1929. In April 1934 Hitler conceded that a million unemployed could be regarded as "normal," though this figure is not yet in sight. It appears likely that in the autumn of 1934 there were still well over five million persons, "visible" and "invisible," able and willing to work and without regular jobs.[2]

What is of greater significance to the German proletariat, however, is the fact that the reduction of unemployment has been accompanied by a progressive decline in wages and living-standards. A majority

[1] Cf. John C. De Wilde: "Germany's Trend toward Economic Isolation," *FPA Reports,* November 7, 1934.

[2] Cf. R. L. Baker: "Is Germany Facing Bankruptcy?" *Current History,* July 1934, pp. 425–30.

of the new unemployed are now drawing no public relief. The remainder have had their stipends sharply reduced. Social service expenditures were cut during 1933 by 450,000,000 marks. The average dole per family was twelve marks a week in the summer of 1934. The average wage of employed workers was twenty-six marks for a forty-eight-hour week. From this numerous "dues" and "voluntary" donations to various Nazi organizations must be deducted. During the first quarter of 1934 the total national pay-roll was 6,100,000,000 marks, about ten per cent below that for the first quarter of 1932, though millions of more workers were presumably employed. During 1933 average money wages were said to have fallen one per cent, though this figure is probably an underestimate and apparently does not include the hundreds of thousands of low-paid emergency, substitute, and part-time workers.[1] While hourly wage contracts have in most cases been kept intact for workers already employed, the newly employed jobless have been given posts for a pittance, and many old workers receive employment only three or four days a week. Many large concerns greatly reduced their total pay-rolls while they increased the number of their workers. The average hourly wages of skilled men workers were 78 pfennigs in July 1934, as compared with 80 in January 1933, 85 in January 1932, and 102 in January 1931. Corresponding figures for skilled women workers were 51, 52, 53, and 64 pfennigs.[2]

Meanwhile, according to the *Frankfurter Zeitung* Index, retail prices rose 9.6 per cent in the last quarter of 1933 and an additional 5.6 per cent in the first quarter of 1934. Between January and July 1934 the general cost of living rose 5.5 per cent, while food costs were 6.8 per cent greater during the first third of the year than in 1933.[3] By the summer of 1934 the cost-of-living index had risen from 116 to 121. Rents have been kept down in part by the flight of Jews. The food index rose from 106 to 114, the clothing index from 110 to 115.[4] New wage taxes begin to take toll of monthly incomes of 80 marks. The income tax now hits all incomes over 500 marks a year, beginning at 2 per cent and running up to almost 50 per cent for incomes

[1] *The New York Times,* March 3, 1934.

[2] *Statistisches Jahrbuch, 1933,* p. 273; *The New York Times,* July 16, 1934; cf. E. Henri: "The Transformation of the Working Class into a Sub-human Race," *Hitler over Europe,* pp. 73–103.

[3] *Vierteljahrhelfte zur Konjunkturforschung,* Ninth Year, Vol. II, B, p. 146.

[4] *The New York Times,* July 16, 1934.

over 50,000 marks. Unmarried workers pay more in wage and income taxes than ever before. Only poor fathers of large families pay small taxes. Compulsory dues to the Labour Front amounted in the summer of 1934 to 12 marks per month on wages of 185 marks.

In short, German labour is already experiencing that decline of living-standards, even in the face of business "recovery," which Italian labour has been suffering ever since 1922. Money wages are falling and may be expected to fall further as the rates for the old employed workers and the new re-employed workers tend to be equalized. Prices, taxes, and party collections are rising. The extent of the decline of real wages is difficult to estimate, but has been at least fifteen per cent. The mass consumption of food, clothing, and household goods, however, has apparently not declined. In 1928, 4,333,000,000 marks' worth of foodstuffs were imported into the Reich. In 1933, 1,113,000,000 marks in foodstuffs were imported, and in the first half of 1934 only 494,000,000 marks. This progressive disappearance of foreign food products on the German market has not been compensated for by any comparable increase in German supplies. On the contrary, the drought of 1934 led to a thirty per cent decline in the German grain harvest. But indices of consumption exhibit a mixed picture of declines in some lines and increases in others, due in part to panic buying and hoarding.[1] Increased consumption has seemingly come out of the accumulated savings of the middle classes, not out of increased earnings. It is therefore not a symptom of prosperity, but of progressive economic decay.

The impoverishment of the masses has caused the Nazi leaders to resort to various ingenious expedients to prevent actual starvation and to distract attention from empty stomachs. The cut in welfare expenditures and reduction of the dole have meant that the prevailing rates of public relief are often quite inadequate to provide bare nutrition, to say nothing of clothing and housing. A restoration of adequate relief standards would require increased taxes and a further enlargement of the public debt. To tax capital for the benefit of labour in this "unproductive" fashion is not to be contemplated by the leaders of the "Socialist" "Workers' " party which now serves the interests of the German plutocracy. Funds for recovery and relief must be wrung not from business, but from the working class and from Germany's foreign creditors. These funds must not go to feed

[1] Cf. reports of the Institut für Konjunkturforschung for 1934.

unemployed, but to subsidize business and to put the jobless to work. For patriotic and psychological reasons it is better that a man be set to digging ditches at twelve marks a week than that he remain idle and receive a dole of the same amount. For military reasons it is better that the unemployed march, build roads, and clear land than that they do nothing at public expense, even though, in Germany as elsewhere, work relief is more expensive than a simple dole. But many of those not provided for in this way face starvation. And starvation must at least be minimized and concealed and to some degree relieved—but again not at the expense of business.

The Nazi solution is to revert to "private" relief—that is, to relief activities not involving any burden on the public treasury. The N.S. Welfare Organization does work of this kind from funds collected in dues and donations. The great "winter relief campaigns" are a notable feature of the system. In both cases, many contributions are voluntary in name only. The procedure is such that the poor are fed and clothed by money collected from others scarcely less poor. On September 13, 1933, Goebbels and Hitler announced a great propaganda campaign for winter relief, in the name of "true socialism." It was insisted that all must participate. Donations would be appreciated only if they signified a genuine sacrifice.[1] On September 22 Goebbels officially opened the campaign by an address in the Sportpalast:

"No German must hunger or freeze during the coming winter. . . . It is only in appearance that we have placed ourselves against the masses. In reality we have won the masses. . . . It is nonsense to suppose that a people wants to rule itself; it always comes to such ideas only when it is badly ruled. At the moment when the people sees that it is well ruled, it gladly permits itself to be ruled. . . . We must strengthen the party, for the party is the backbone of our State. . . . We must watch jealously and spy around everywhere where a saboteur sits, in order to destroy him. . . . For us the service of the people must be a service of honour." [2]

On the first Sunday in each month, beginning October 1, all Germans were required to eat, instead of a dinner, an *"Eintopfgericht"* costing not more than fifty pfennigs. The balance of what a dinner would have cost was turned over to the relief fund by householders

[1] *Berliner Tageblatt,* September 13, 1933.
[2] *Berliner Tageblatt,* September 23, 1933.

and restaurant-proprietors. Street-corner and house-to-house collections were made by storm troopers and Hitler Youths, who listed those who refused to donate and distributed buttons, flowers, placards, and other insignia to the generous. In theatres and cinemas effective propaganda films appealing to bourgeois fears of Communism were used to stimulate contributions to the uniformed boys and girls who passed through the aisles with rattling tin boxes. Over a hundred and fifty thousand speeches for winter relief were delivered throughout the Reich. All the propaganda facilities of the régime were used to stimulate donations.

The results were highly gratifying. After a final intensive collection campaign in March, special recognition was given in Berlin to the most efficient collectors: to "Auwi," who gathered 2,300 marks on the first day, to Karl Ernst, who collected 600 marks, and to others. On March 31, 1934, the campaign ended. Goebbels announced that the huge sum of 320,000,000 marks had been collected, of which 140,000,000 were spent on food, 60,000,000 on clothing, 85,000,000 on coal and wood, and the balance on other goods and credits.[1] Seventeen million people were alleged to have received relief. This estimate would mean that, on the average, each individual assisted received only eighteen marks apiece during the whole winter—*if* all the funds collected went for relief. But overhead costs were substantial and it was later admitted that some funds found their way into the pockets of party officials. No detailed accounting was ever made of these funds, nor was any indication given of the amounts donated by corporations and business men, as compared with those given by people of smaller means. Hitler asserted that it was no sacrifice when a millionaire gave five marks, but that a worker earning a hundred marks a month was doing his duty when he gave fifty pfennigs.[2] He later declared that it was shameful that more money had come from poor districts than from fashionable residential sections.[3] The 1934–5 winter relief campaign began with a goal of four hundred million marks to be collected and eighteen million people to be aided. On December 8, 1934, "National Solidarity Day," Nazi notables collected relief funds personally throughout the Reich. Schacht made a record haul of 32,000 marks on the Berlin Bourse.

[1] *V.B.*, April 19, 1934.
[2] Ibid., April 18, 1934.
[3] *The New York Times*, October 14, 1934.

Bread must be accompanied by circuses. Before May 1, 1934, the most elaborate preparations were made for the most colossal and stupendous national holiday ever held in the Reich. In Tempelhofer Feld in Berlin a maypole was set up, 144 feet high, made from a Black Forest pine 160 years old and weighing nine tons. A wall of the Anhalter Bahnhof had to be removed to permit it to pass into the city. Swastika banners 33 feet wide and 150 feet high were erected on steel towers weighing forty-three tons apiece and set in thirteen feet of concrete. A large general staff planned the demonstration to the last detail.[1] A million Berlin workers gathered at nineteen points on the morning of May Day and converged in thirteen enormous columns. Even university professors were compelled to march. All marchers received tickets to be turned in on the field as evidence of their participation. Another million spectators were present. Sausage- and sandwich-venders to the number of 5,000, 410 physicians, an ambulance corps of 6,500, and a guard of 65,000 storm troopers were mobilized. Employers were obliged to pay full wages for the day, totalling fifty million marks. Their compensation was the new labour code, which went into effect on May 1. Bands, aircraft, and military manœuvres added to the delights of the occasion. Police gave strict orders that no babies were to be born on the field. Hitler spoke in the late afternoon through 142 loudspeakers. The gay throngs cheered and applauded in wild enthusiasm.[2] Der Führer reiterated the old clichés and proclaimed labour's "new deal":

"Many employers and industrialists may not understand why we proclaim May Day as a labour holiday for which they must pay. But formerly German economy lost hundreds of millions of national wealth in labour struggles, strikes and lock-outs which the Nazi State has abolished. A day's wages is only a small sacrifice. . . . We raise labour to the noblest level. Through our labour-service army we want to try to force Germans in positions that carry no physical labour to learn what such labour is. We want to kill the haughtiness of intellectuals who look down upon manual labour. . . .

"Let us, however, my German countrymen and countrywomen, all those in the tens of thousands of cities, towns, and villages who are celebrating with us today—let us not forget also to give humble thanks to Him who has blessed our work for a whole year and pray

[1] *V.B.*, April 28, 1934.
[2] Ibid., May 1 and 2, 1934.

to Him not to withhold His Blessings from our nation in time to come. . . ."[1]

Thunderous cheering greeted the Chancellor. As the sinking sun glowed over the endless multitudes, the shouting of millions of voices dissolved into a stirring chant intoned by the greatest of all choruses. The *Horst Wessel Lied* and the *Deutschland Lied* rang out over the field as Der Führer departed. In the evening the weary but singing crowds dispersed homeward—overcome once more by the magic that never fails. For such exaltation perhaps no price is too high to pay. And the cost to the business élite of the Reich is far less than the cost of any alternative and more nutritious mode of allaying proletarian dissatisfaction.

4. PEASANTS AND JUNKERS

THE salvation of the German peasantry has from the beginning been a major mission of the NSDAP. The peasantry is envisaged in the Nazi *Weltanschauung* as a new nobility, the life source of the Nordic race, the fountainhead of Aryan purity, the repository of sturdy German virtues, and the basis of national strength. It must be saved from the Jews, the Marxists, the middlemen, the mortgage-holders, the Junkers, and other exploiters. It must be elevated to a new dignity and a new prosperity. Its fecundity makes it the focal point of Nazi population policy. *Blut und Boden* will furnish food, warriors, economic self-sufficiency, and a solution for unemployment. "Save the peasantry!" and "Back to the land!" were the Nazi battle-cries. Walter Darré and other Nazi leaders carried this cheering message to the farmers of the Reich in the years of struggle and won extensive support for the party. The great agrarian border districts were long the centres of Nazi electoral strength. The Nazi gospel itself is not only a product of petty-bourgeois neuroses, but also of peasant resentments—against capitalism, urbanism, liberalism, socialism, atheism, and all the other major features of modern metropolitan civilization.

Darré became Minister of Food and Agriculture in June 1933, following Hugenberg's dismissal. He had long demanded division of the Junker estates, the settling of impoverished farmers on better lands, and the transfer of the unemployed to the soil. Point 17 of

[1] Quoted in *The New York Times,* May 2, 1934.

the program demanded "land reform," "confiscation, without compensation, of land for communal purposes, abolition of interest on land loans, and prevention of all speculation on land." Save for the last phrase, none of these proposals had been carried out, even in part, during the first two years of the Nazi régime. There have been peasant pageants, glorification of agriculture, idealization of the German farmer for his industry, his honesty, his religiosity, and his fertility. There have been exhortations to Junkers to divide their estates, and exhortations to workers to go back to the land. But of concrete measures to achieve these results there have been none on any scale sufficient to warrant discussion. Indeed, Darré, as early as July 1933, could say:

"Land settlement as practised by the Nationalsocialists has nothing in common with the Marxist methods of proletarianizing the country population. In full unanimity with the Chancellor, no estate will be touched, no matter how big, if it is economically healthy and able to maintain itself from its own resources. But even indebted big estates will not be touched. If they do not voluntarily offer themselves for peasant settlement, they will be left alone in full recognition of the principle of private enterprise." [1]

The explanation of this paradox is not dissimilar to that of the disappearance of "socialism" in the program of the NSDAP. Part of the proletariat and the radicalized *Kleinbürgertum* were converted to the cause by talk of socialization. Much of the peasantry was converted by talk of dividing the Junker estates. But the party leaders who made these promises were in the pay of large employers and large landowners, of the plutocracy and the aristocracy. Long before victory was in sight, Hitler reinterpreted the program in such a fashion as to ensure the support of his movement by the moneyed and landed élites.[2] He came into power not only through the machinations of Papen, Schroeder, Thyssen, Schacht, and Hugenberg, but more immediately through the action of the Junkers of the Landbund and the favour of Hindenburg. He has kept his pledges to these groups, not from gratitude, but from a realistic perception of where real power lies in the German social hierarchy. Big Business controls the centres of power in industry and commerce. The Junkers control the centres of power in agriculture and in the Reichs-

1 *Vossische Zeitung,* July 19, 1933.

2 Cf. pp. 131f. above.

wehr. Nazi leaders propose, but capitalists and aristocrats dispose. That they could find means of disposing of Hitler should he ever cross them in fundamentals has been clearer to no one than to Der Führer himself.

Nazi agrarian policy is intelligible only in the light of these relationships. The NSDAP has striven first to wipe out class cleavages between peasants and nobles, as well as between workers and employers, and to serve the common interests of both. This goal has been more possible of realization in agriculture than in industry. German peasants were only slightly imbued with class consciousness. The class consciousness of the Junkers did not preclude a betterment of the lot of independent farmers so long as it was not achieved at the Junkers' expense. Both could profit from government subsidies and protective tariffs on foodstuffs assuring lucrative prices in the home market for products of the soil. The pre-war import duties on cereals were restored in 1925 and steadily raised thereafter. Subsidies to bankrupt estates and to mortgaged farms were regularly granted under the republic. Both peasants and Junkers benefited. A large section of the peasantry, perceiving that its interests lay with the aristocracy, voted Nationalist or Nazi through all the later years of Weimar. Public assistance to agriculture in the name of race, blood, soil, and agrarian autarchy has been extended in the Third Reich to a point at which the rural classes are being systematically protected and enriched through higher food-prices and lower living-standards for the proletariat and the *Kleinbürgertum*.

Under the law of September 13, 1933, creating the "Food Estate" (*Reichsnährstand*),[1] agriculture includes forestry, horticulture, fishing, hunting, wine-making, and bee-keeping as well as farming. The Minister of Agriculture has incorporated into the Food Estate all wholesale and retail agricultural co-operatives, all trade organizations dealing in farm products, all industries utilizing farm products, and all the innumerable chambers of agriculture and other agrarian associations. The Food Estate is authorized, either directly or through its component branches, to regulate the production, marketing conditions, and prices of all rural products. It may effect such organizational changes as may be necessary and punish severely any infractions of its laws and regulations.

The Reichsbauernführer, who is leader of the Food Estate, is the

[1] *R.G.B.*, 1933, Vol. I, No. 99, p. 626.

Minister of Agriculture, Walter Darré. The chief function of his organization is to ensure stable and profitable prices for farm products. In September 1933 Darré forbade all trading in futures in wheat and rye and fixed the price supplements of wheat between 1 mark per ton for November 1933 and 13 marks per ton in June 1934, as increments to basic fixed prices ranging from 175 marks per ton to 193 marks per ton in eleven designated price areas. Rye prices were fixed at 140 marks per ton in the lowest-price districts up to 158 marks per ton in the highest-price districts, with a permissible fluctuation, as a supplement to these prices, from 1 mark in November 1933 to 18 marks in June 1934.[1] Farmers were required to reduce their grain acreage to provide more barley, fodder, fibres, oils, fruits, wool, and fat. Mills were compelled to buy certain quantities of grain at fixed prices. The determination of the major agricultural prices through free competition was terminated.

This removal of agriculture from the orbit of the free market was accompanied by the fixing of prices at a level ensuring prosperity for farmers at the expense of urban consumers. This policy has been frequently rationalized in terms of basic Nazi formulas. Darré has often denounced free trade in foodstuffs, based on supply and demand, as ruinous to farmers and consumers alike. Here at least capitalism is conquered and the *"Brechung der Zinsknechtschaft"* is attained. The mediæval conception of production for needs at fixed prices must take the place of the Jewish conception of the profit motive in a free market. Speaking before thousands of peasant leaders at the closing session of the second national convention of the Food Estate, Darré declared, on November 18, 1934:

"The economic conception of two diametrically opposed races is struggling for the supremacy of our people. The fundamental error of the liberal or Jewish theory of economics is the claim that economics is something governed by its own laws, independent of such supereconomic conceptions as blood, race, nation, and Fatherland.

"A further fundamental error is its contention that personal advantage is the motive power for all economic undertaking. Against this we pose the Aryan or Germanic conception of the primacy of blood in all questions of life, including economics. . . . We assert that the ethical conception of labour for the common weal must constitute the motive power for all our actions. . . .

1 Ibid., No. 110 (September 29), p. 701.

"Europe also will introduce a similar order, which alone can guarantee European peace. Since our Führer is the guarantor of this new conception of economics, his person also is in the last analysis the guarantee for Europe's peace. . . .

"History shows that the Jew never created values, but always injected himself where he could earn without working." [1]

The drought and the food shortage of 1934 led to the new grain law of June 27.[2] Under its provision Darré is empowered to require farmers, co-operatives, and other distributors to deliver fixed amounts of wheat, rye, and fodder, at fixed prices, to State-controlled agencies, to regulate the amount of cereals the mills are permitted to grind in accordance with the demand for bread, and to regulate the quantity and prices of all bakery products. Heavy penalties may be imposed on those who violate the orders of the Minister of Agriculture. The purpose of this arrangement, which is strikingly similar to that enforced by the Communist Party of the U.S.S.R., was to provide adequate amounts of grain at prices profitable to producers. Shortage was not permitted to result in higher prices, as would occur in a free capitalistic economy, nor were higher prices permitted to stimulate increased production with a resultant surplus later. A decree of July 16 fixed prices for oats and barley and required the maintenance of a stable price for bread, despite increases in grain prices. The farmer would secure more for his grain, but the consumer would pay the same, and the difference would come out of the profits of middlemen, millers, and bakers.[3]

The decree further established a central association of nineteen grain organizations to regulate the production and sale of grain from all farms larger than twelve acres—that is, all farms producing a surplus for the market. All such farms were required, between July 16 and November 1, to deliver rye to the amount of 30 per cent and wheat to the amount of 25 per cent of what was marketed in 1933. In July 1934 wheat in Berlin cost 193 marks per ton, as compared with 82 marks in Chicago. Rye cost 160 marks in Berlin and 55 in Chicago. The German farmer is perhaps more prosperous than the American farmer, though the small increases of grain prices do not compensate for reduced crops, and leave him in most cases with a

[1] AP dispatch, November 18, 1934.

[2] Cf. *V.B.*, July 2, and *Frankfurter Zeitung*, July 1, 4, 17, 1934.

[3] *V.B.*, July 27, 1934.

net loss of income. But German bakers, millers, middlemen, and urban consumers are exploited and impoverished. This is the cost of rural prosperity and agrarian self-sufficiency. In 1933 German agriculture supplied about 90 per cent of domestic food requirements. The shortage of 1934 indicated a necessity of supplying 20 per cent of the domestic demand from imports—at the expense of the imports of raw materials for industry.

Another notable feature of Nazi farm policy, also reminiscent of early Soviet agrarian measures, is the Hereditary Farm Law (*Reichserbhofgesetz*) of September 29, 1933.[1] By its provisions all estates up to 125 hectares (308 acres) which are capable of providing a living for a family are converted into hereditary farms. Upon the death of the owner the estate must pass undivided to the eldest son or the nearest male relative, who must provide a living and an education to younger brothers and sisters until they reach their majority. The farm cannot be sold, mortgaged, or attached for debts. The owner, who alone may be called *"Bauer"* or peasant, must be a German citizen of Aryan descent, able to prove that none of his ancestors since January 1, 1800 were Jewish or coloured. It was anticipated that a million such farms would be established, comprising sixty per cent of the total arable land in Germany. The German middle peasantry is thus attached to the land, as were the serfs of the feudal system, save that the peasant himself is "owner." But his ownership gives him the obligation of paying taxes, delivering grain to the State at fixed prices, and supporting his disinherited relatives. He cannot sell or divide his estate. So unwelcome were these restrictions that peasants in certain districts were reported to be searching frantically for Jewish ancestors as a means of escaping the application of the law.

The rural proletariat has likewise been deprived of almost all freedom of movement and has been subjected to the competition of unemployed urban workers. In the summer of 1933 some thousands of jobless were compelled, under threat of losing their dole, to hire themselves out to farmers in East Prussia at nominal wages. On May 15, 1934, a new law gave the president of the Institute for Employment authority to prohibit the hiring in urban districts of workers not locally resident.[2] Workers who have laboured on the land

[1] *R.G.B.*, 1933, Vol. I, No. 108, p. 685.

[2] Ibid., 1934, Vol. I, p. 381.

during the past three years may be employed only for agricultural work. Factory employers may be required to dismiss workers earning less than 3,600 marks per year who have done agricultural work during the past three years, "in order to supply the demand for farm labour." A decree of May 17 forbade the hiring in specified industries of workers who had previously worked on the land. Rural workers going to the cities to seek employment are thus forced back to the farm. The younger sons, disinherited by the Hereditary Farm Law, are compelled to become farm labourers. Dr. Friedrich Syrup on May 16 ordered the Berlin district closed to rural emigrants seeking employment. Urban employers were thus deprived of a free labour market and subjected to heavy penalties for infractions of the rule. This measure guarantees to independent farmers directly, and Junker estate-owners indirectly, a plentiful supply of cheap agricultural labor, though in some cases farmers are compelled to hire labourers at fixed wages, whether they need them or not.

The only agrarian group which has had no cause for profound dissatisfaction is the landed nobility. The loudly proclaimed Nazi promises of dividing up the Junker estates have dissolved into rhetoric. A few landed proprietors have been persuaded to give up portions of their holdings for peasant settlement.[1] Darré periodically denounces the Junkers before peasant audiences. For example:

"The large land holdings across the Elbe have long ago lost all economic reasons for being, and their titled owners should take note of this. The Nationalsocialist government will no longer evaluate this or that noble family one-sidedly by the criterion of how much blood it has shed in Prussian history. Nationalsocialism will want to know also whether it has taken an understanding attitude toward the tillers of the soil and the needs of the country as a whole. The sooner the large landowners east of the Elbe realize the actualities of the present, the sooner will they get out of their present monetary difficulties. . . . There are not going to be any more subsidies for estates that are not on a paying basis." [2]

In practice, however, the Junkers have remained in full possession of their ancestral estates and privileges. During 1933 less than 4,000 new peasant holdings were established, as compared with 8,877 in

1 Cf. the strange case of the three Hanoverian nobles, *The New York Times*, May 8, 1934.

2 *The New York Times* and *V.B.*, May 11, 1934.

1932—and these not on lands taken from the Junkers, but on cleared or reclaimed areas. This figure was expected to be doubled in 1934, but again not at the expense of the Junkers. Brüning and Schleicher both were undone because of their efforts to restrict the privileges of the landed aristocrats. Hitler has left them in peace, even since the death of their great champion, Hindenburg. The *Osthilfe* subsidies have apparently come to an end, but the Junkers are again fairly prosperous, with cheap rural labour and high grain prices. They still dominate the high command of the Reichswehr. General Blomberg, Minister of Defence, was paradoxically won to the Nazi cause by being given an estate. The Junkers would perhaps be helpless in the face of a determined effort of the NSDAP to break up their holdings, with inevitably enthusiastic support from the small peasantry and the urban workers. But Der Führer appreciates that the landed aristocracy has means at its disposal for getting rid even of a Hitler. Thus far the agrarian élite has been as secure in its honours and its properties as the industrialists and financiers.

The economic dilemma of Fascist Germany is not fundamentally different from that of western capitalism in general in the epoch of monopoly and imperialism, save that it is intensified by Nazi policies and is rendered more desperate by the paucity of the Reich's resources. The dilemma can be stated quite simply. Capitalistic production tends to outrun mass consumption because of the profit incentive to productive efficiency and because of the meagre participation of the masses, relatively to the classes, in the fruits of industry. The glutting of the market makes competition destructive and leads to combinations, cartels, and trusts to restrict competition. It also leads to the accumulation of vast surpluses of goods and capital for which there is no profitable home market. Temporary relief is available so long as populations grow, wages rise, and the state of the market permits a continued expansion of production. Foreign markets, however, soon become indispensable, as does the protection of the domestic market from foreign competition. Free trade gives way to protective tariffs, and economic self-sufficiency to commercial and financial expansion. Imperialism, protectionism, high-pressure advertising, and instalment purchasing are all aspects of the quest for the vanishing market. Free competition and laissez-faire are displaced by monopolies, State intervention, and "economic planning." The exploitation of the labour and raw materials of backward areas poor in capital affords a temporary relief—until the clash of competing imperialisms leads to the first world war of the machine age. The Great Depression, the most recent and most disastrous collapse of markets in post-war capitalism, is but another manifestation of the incurable disease of the acquisitive societies born of the industrial revolution.

Fascism is an aggravating symptom rather than a cure of the malady. In their quest for social and economic security, the business and agrarian élites support a dictatorial State form in which free speech, free press, and representative government disappear with free trade, free competition, and a free market. Political totalitarianism goes hand in hand with monopoly, price-fixing, and governmental regimentation of economic activity. But where Fascism has been longest in power it has afforded no guarantee of stability or security. The vaunted "Corporative State" was not finally inaugurated in Italy until November 1934, when the Council of Corporations was established. The monopolistic centralization and State regimentation of German industry had already progressed far before the creation of the *"Ständische Staat"* of the Third Reich. The profits, interests, and rents of the propertied classes are at first protected at the expense of peasants and workers. The resulting decline in mass purchasing power, however, leads finally to new crises and to a disappearance of profits as well. Home markets vanish more rapidly than they do where labour can still protect its living-standards. Social democracy resting upon trade unionism is destroyed as the last bulwark of competitive capitalism—that is, as the last guarantee that the working masses will be able to buy enough of the output of industry to make private enterprise lucrative.

The Fascist solution of fixing wages, prices, production quotas, and even profits by dictatorial decree solves nothing. If all prices are fixed, the margin between costs of production and receipts from sales tends to disappear—and therewith vanish the profits of the entrepreneurial class which the Fascist State serves. Unless some fluidity and flexibility of prices is preserved, an economy resting upon private property and private profit becomes static and sterile. But if some prices remain flexible, those monopolistic segments of the economy which are removed from the sphere of competition are enabled to profit only at the expense of the other segments in which prices are still somewhat elastic. German agriculture profits at the cost of lower profits for middlemen and lower living-standards for consumers. German heavy industry profits at the cost of light industry, of labour, and of the taxpayers who provide the government orders and subsidies. The most vulnerable element in the economic process—namely, the proletariat—is exploited and buys less and less of the output of farms and factories. This process of stealing from Peter to pay Paul can only be defended as a "temporary" or "emergency" device pending a restoration of markets and a resultant general participation in an increased total income. But if a restoration of markets and of general prosperity were possible, Fascism would be unnecessary. It flows precisely from the disappearance of markets. By no conceivable magic can it recover them so long as private property and profits remain the basis of the economic order. On the contrary, it destroys them the more rapidly and begins to devour itself.

Out of this situation there will probably emerge a new era of imperialistic war. Autarchy spells extinction for such a State as Germany. Only temporary relief can be afforded by *Grossraumwirtschaft,* debt repudiation, currency depreciation, and tariff bargaining between "planned economies" on the basis of barter. To restore free trade and free competition is as difficult as to make time stand still or to reverse its direction. New markets must somehow be conquered. If they cannot be secured through increased efficiency and lowered costs—which breed an unending cycle of technological unemployment and impoverishment—then they must be won by the sword. Rosenberg's visions and Hitler's dreaming about a new *Mittel Europa* and the partition of Russia are not mere fantasies of a neurotic *Kleinbürgertum* worshipping violence and bloodshed because of its own insecurity. Imperialism is an economic necessity for Thyssen, Krupp, Siemens, Schacht, and the remainder of the German business élite. General world recovery, accompanied by a partial restoration of foreign markets and international trade, may afford relief and postpone the day of reckoning until the next major economic crisis. But *Der Tag* must come. Cartels, *Gleichschaltung,* price-fixing, and exchange manipulation as means toward the recovery of markets will then give way to marching armies, poison gas, heavy artillery, and bombing-planes. For such is Fascism's "salvation" for the ruling classes of a social order sick beyond hope of recovery.

EPILOGUE

CHAPTER XII

GÖTTERDÄMMERUNG

1. CRITICISM

FRIDAY, May 11, 1934: In the late Berlin afternoon, already warm with the promise of summer, throngs of people are gathered outside the Sportpalast. The memory of May Day is still fresh. A new demonstration, a new campaign is about to begin. There is a bit of weariness with so many parades, so much oratory, so much excitement. But the multitudes are nevertheless assembled. Party members and S.A. men must go as a duty. Others have been supplied with tickets. It is not wise to be counted among those absent. The crowd swells. Thousands stand patiently in the muddy courtyard within the entrance gates on Potsdamerstrasse. At 5.30 the doors are opened and the mob pours into the great hall, each anxious to secure seats near the front on the main floor or in the first row of the balconies.

As always, great *Hakenkreuz* banners decorate the interior and bold placards scream their message from the walls and galleries. The messages this time are more strident than usual—and vaguely menacing: "Against Kill-joys and Critics! (*Gegen die Miesmacher und Kritikaster!*)" "Against Grumblers, Know-It-Alls, and Church Agitators! (*Gegen Nörgler, Besserwisser, und Konfessionshetzer!*)" "Not Grumbling, but Work! (*Nicht meckern—sondern arbeiten!*)" "Deeds are Silent! (*Die Tat ist stumm!*)" "First Achievement, Then Criticism! (*Erst Leistung, dann Kritik!*)" At 6.30 a band begins to play martial tunes. By 7.00 the hall is almost full. The massed thousands gossip, read papers, munch sandwiches, order beer, and wait patiently and expectantly. Shortly after 8.00 storm troopers march in to the crash of trumpets and drums. The usual procession of flags and banners comes down the centre of the hall. S.A. men line the aisle from entrance to platform. All is excitement now. "Goebbels is coming!"

The little Propaganda Minister, his limp concealed within a square of storm troopers and his head barely visible behind the tall S.A. men, hobbles forward boldly between the rows of brown shirts and visored caps, flanked by seas of upraised arms. There is cheering and stormy applause. Children throw bouquets. Goebbels smiles indulgently, half concealing a hint of sternness and anxiety in his sharp face. The *Deutschland Lied* thunders over the multitudes. Goebbels reaches the platform and takes his seat. The adjutant of the *Gauleiter,* Görlitzer, opens the meeting. He gives homage to the eighty-six victims of a mine disaster in Buggingen: "heroes of labour." All arms shoot up in salute. "With this demonstration," he says, "begins an enormous wave of meetings against grumblers and critics. This wave flows out from the Berlin Sportpalast, from the Berlin battleground!" Goebbels steps to the microphone.

The voice commences. "Formerly they complained about the parties. Now they complain because there are no parties!" The little man is as eloquent and persuasive as ever, though his message is solely one of denunciation and warning. No promises now. Work and more work! Down with all grumblers! The mouth opens, closes, opens between the large ears. The larynx oscillates above the soft collar and the large, bright-hued tie. Delicate hands vibrate around the dark, shiny alpaca suit—now resting lightly on hips, now grasping the standard of the microphone, now reaching out and up, pleading, pointing, threatening. An atmosphere of combat reminiscent of the years of struggle exudes from the stage, with its swastikas and its flowers. The recapture of the old fighting spirit is welcome and yet disturbing. A shadow hangs over the arena. . . . "Even if all problems are not solved, they *will* be solved! . . ." The heat is stifling in the upper gallery. A woman faints. Words, cheers, more words, and at last the chant:

> Raise high the flags! Stand rank and rank together.
> Storm troopers march with steady, quiet tread. . . .

The battle is joined. The Propagandaministerium has decided shortly after May Day to launch a great campaign against grumblers.[1] For weeks there are demonstrations, meetings, parades, lec-

[1] Cf. *V.B.,* May 5, 8, and 12, 1934.

tures. "Anyone may grumble who is not afraid to go to a concentration camp! . . . Formerly they took offence at the gentleman with the monocle; now they take offence at the party comrade who can afford a motor car. Formerly they complained about shady business men; now they find that members of the Hitler Youth are ill-behaved." [1] Let them be silent! People who grumble are arrested. A woman in Mainz who is heard to say: "It will never get any better," is sentenced to appear daily at the Mayor's office and repeat "Every day is better already and will get still better and better!" Speeches are given everywhere, and by everyone save Hitler, who is preoccupied. Frick speaks in Dresden on May 31, Goebbels in Gleiwitz on June 7. Flags, parades, assemblies in all corners of the Reich. But after mid-June the critics of the critics are on the defensive. And at the end of June the campaign fades out into failure.

Eloquence and circuses do not suffice when the eloquence rings hollow and the circuses are without bread. The weapons of power are failing. There is dissatisfaction, friction, vague unrest—more menacing because ill-defined and scarcely articulate. Prices are rising. Wages are falling. Bright promises become hot air over ashes. The NSDAP, caught in its own contradictions and in the dilemma of an economy whose maladies have been aggravated by its incantations, has failed to distribute loaves and fishes sufficiently widely and wisely to still the voices of protest. This ultimate weapon having failed, the next lowest in the scale must be tried: propaganda and more propaganda.

Goebbels, who secured power through eloquence and magic, believes that power can be retained through eloquence and magic. If this fails, then one must beat the tomtoms and create unity at home by attacking "enemies" abroad. If this fails, further persecution of the Jews may suffice to deflect resentments away from the dictators. But these more primitive devices cannot be fully tested. Der Führer has preached peace for consumption by the foreign press. Peace has been made with Poland. Austria is a powder-keg. Mussolini is threatening. Barthou is suspicious. International conciliation has itself bred unrest among the S.A. and created a need for more trumpeting. But diplomatic adventures or new polemics against foreign sub-humanity are scarcely possible for the isolated Reich. And as for the Jews, new persecutions will lead to equally unfortu-

[1] *Der Angriff,* May 18, 1934.

nate diplomatic results. Propaganda must be used to the utmost. If it fails, there is still, as a last resort: terror. The slow sadism of 1933, however, cannot be resumed. There are real enemies now, or ghosts of enemies even more terrifying. Perhaps nothing will suffice save . . . ?

Some of the sources of unrest in the dictatorship's second spring have already been suggested—the betrayal of the *Kleinbürgertum,* the impoverishment of the proletariat, the enslavement of the peasantry. There were still those in the party who recalled promises of national Socialism. The Left radicals had not been wholly liquidated by the expulsion of Otto Strasser in '30, the ousting of Stennes in '31, the demotion of Gregor Strasser in '32, and the suppression of the "Second Revolution" in the summer of '33. But the issue in May and June of '34 was no clear-cut issue between Right and Left. There was grumbling also on the Right—from industrialists, landowners, business men, Junkers, Catholic leaders, and others. And there were obscure personal rivalries in the higher ranks of the party, as well as military friction between the S.A. on the one hand and the S.S., the Stahlhelm, and the Reichswehr on the other. Hess had long since demanded "discipline." But the storm troopers regarded themselves as the crusaders and victors of the revolution. In their ranks lingered not only remnants of social radicalism, but frustrated hopes for jobs and honours and unfulfilled military ambitions.

Ernst Röhm, Chief of Staff of the S.A., became the focus of these tensions. Personally ambitious and solicitous in his crude way for the interests of his subordinates, he had dreamed of making the S.A. Germany's great people's army for the war to come. In this he had been thwarted by the Junker command of the Reichswehr, which welcomed an expansion of the national army from 100,000 to 300,000, but adhered to the view that the war of liberation would be fought not between mass armies, but between small, mechanized professional forces. For blue-blooded Prussian officers to admit the upstart Röhm to their ranks was impossible. Göring they had accepted under protest. For them to regard the brown-shirted rowdies of Röhm's "army" as soldiers, capable of being absorbed into the Reichswehr, was still more impossible. Röhm, along with Hess, had secured a Cabinet post on December 1, 1933. Beyond this he could not go, for he was blocked by the Reichswehr command, by Hindenburg, by

Hitler, by Göring and Goebbels, by Hess and Himmler, and by the S.S.

On December 27, 1933, General Kurt von Hammerstein-Equord, intimate friend of Schleicher, announced his resignation as chief of the Reichswehr, a post which he had held since October 1930. Here, if ever, was the opportunity for Röhm and the S.A. Röhm was talked of as a new Minister of Defence who might put the best of his storm troopers into the regular army. His relations with Hitler were as cordial as ever. Der Führer sent him New Year's greetings with warm thanks for his "unforgettable services." But the opportunity was lost. Blomberg remained Minister of Defence. On January 3 Hindenburg, with Hitler's approval, appointed another aristocrat as chief of the Reichswehr: General Werner Baron von Fritsch.

Behind the Reichswehr generals stood the Junkers, and near to them conservative industrialists and bankers. These groups would resist, at all costs, any radicalization of the party or any infiltration of the S.A. into the army. If Hitler played Röhm's game, so much the worse for Hitler. Even he could be liquidated if an open showdown became necessary. The wholly intact Reichswehr and the partly intact Stahlhelm were on the side of the higher gods. Monarchists and other reactionaries in lofty places were not above new intrigues. Against them, as against the radicals, Goebbels directed his shafts. But Hitler was loyal to his aristocratic and plutocratic friends. To defy Röhm and the S.A. was dangerous. But to defy the ruling classes of land and money was still more dangerous. Göring and Goebbels, Himmler and Hess, Frick and Rosenberg, Rust and Ley also knew on which side their bread was buttered. Only Röhm, a few of his subordinates, and a motley group of radicals seemed uncertain as to what interests the dictatorship must serve.

The full story of friction and jealousy in the spring of 1934 may never be told, since dead men are silent. Surface eddies in the stream of events, however, suggests the direction of the current and the hidden rocks below. In April fulsome laudations of the S.A. on the part of the Nazi press and Nazi leaders suggested that all was not in harmony between Der Führer and the storm-troop high command.[1] On April 18 Röhm delivered a long address to the diplomatic corps and the foreign press in Berlin. Amid old clichés, bombastically reiter-

[1] Cf. *V.B.*, April 11, 1934.

ated, was a note of pride and protest, a glorification of the S.A., an identification of the storm troopers with the revolution. But still: "Loyalty to the death to Osaf Adolf Hitler! Goods and blood, life and limb, all for Germany!"[1] Three days later, however, Röhm ordered a general furlough for all S.A. men for the month of July—as "an opportunity for relaxation," the official announcement declared. That Röhm gave this order voluntarily is doubtful. It was probably insisted upon by Hitler. And Hitler perhaps was driven to his insistence by Fritsch, Blomberg, Hindenburg, Seldte, Himmler, Hess, and possibly by Thyssen and Krupp as well.

Friction ensued between the S.A. and the Stahlhelm (N.S. Front Fighters' League), which seemed reluctant to amalgamate itself with the storm troopers. Röhm complained on May 14 that Stahlhelm men seemed hesitant to join S.A. Reserve I and that some who had joined were seeking to resign. The older members of the Kyffhäuser Bund in S.A. Reserve II were displaying proper comradely sentiments, but the Stahlhelm seemed hostile. Still, Röhm would order no individual action by storm troopers. A warning should suffice.[2] Sporadic arrests of Stahlhelm leaders nevertheless followed. At Frankfurt and Dortmund the organization was publicly banned. Brawls took place between its members and S.A. men. In Stettin the *Gestapo* arrested Stahlhelm leaders for reactionary treason. Other arrests were made elsewhere.[3] Seldte was reported to have offered his resignation from the Cabinet. An alleged "monarchist plot" or "great Guelph conspiracy" in Hanover caused Goebbels to redouble his attacks on "reactionaries." This label was attached to all critics, carpers, and kill-joys. Feder struck new anti-Semitic notes as a distraction, but Dietrich Klagges explained apologetically that Nationalsocialism could not really exterminate all the Jews.[4]

Röhm and other S.A. leaders now made a bid for new popular support through a series of well-staged public appearances. In a great demonstration and review Röhm was named an honorary citizen of Stettin on May 26. The handsome, dashing Karl Ernst became leader of *Obergruppe III* of the S.A., with the elevation of the *Gruppe* Berlin-Brandenburg to an *Obergruppe*. He had assumed command of the Berlin S.A. on March 21, 1933. That he should be

[1] Text in *V.B.*, April 19, 1934.
[2] Ibid., May 15, 1934.
[3] Ibid., May 24 and 26, 1934.
[4] Quoted in *The New York Times*, May 26, 1934.

thus honoured was natural, in view of his cordial relations with Röhm and Hitler. At his wedding Der Führer had presented him with a portrait in a gold frame, with the words: "Through Blood and Faith Forever United!" On May 28 Ernst proudly reviewed his troops and addressed them in Oranienburg, assuring them that their destiny and that of the Nationalsocialist revolution were one. At the same time Röhm made a triumphal march through Pomerania, cheering and greeting his men and addressing the multitudes.[1]

But on June 7 it was announced that Röhm had been obliged by his physician to take a leave of several weeks because of illness. To remove all "misunderstandings," Röhm asserted that he would resume his full duties as soon as his health permitted and that the S.A. would be strengthened and would resume all of its activities after the July vacation.[2] He explained further that a painful nervous disorder had obliged him to take the cure. He urged all S.A. leaders to take their vacations in June before the rank and file went on leave. On August 1 the S.A. would again resume work. "If the enemies of the S.A. hope that the S.A. will not be recalled or will be recalled only in part after its leave, we may permit them to enjoy this brief hope. They will receive their answer at such time and in such form as appears necessary. The S.A. is and remains the destiny of Germany.[3]

Here was clear evidence of dissension. The enemies of the S.A. were not the men of the Stahlhelm, even though Seldte and his staff officers were booed and stoned by storm troopers and Hitler Youths near Magdeburg. It was intimated that the Stahlhelm would be completely amalgamated with the S.A. This conflict, however, was but a symptom of the determination of conservatives in the government, in the Reichswehr, and in business to keep the radical storm troopers in check. The "leaves" and Röhm's "illness" were doubtless insisted upon by Hitler—with the only result of making Röhm and his friends more determined than ever to protect their interests. The admission to the Cabinet on June 16 of Hans Kerrl, Prussian Minister of Justice, as Reich Minister without portfolio was apparently unrelated to the rising tide of dissatisfaction, except that it co-ordinated further the administration of justice and thereby rendered easier court action

[1] Cf. *V.B.*, May 15, 27, and 29, 1934.

[2] Ibid., June 8, 1934.

[3] Statement from Munich, June 8, in *V.B.*, June 9, 1934.

against dissidents, should it become necessary.

At this juncture Vice-Chancellor von Papen added fuel to the flames by an address at the University Union of Marburg on June 17. He said in part:

"This place is dedicated to science; therefore it appears to me particularly appropriate for testifying to the truth before the German people. Voices demanding that I take a clear position toward contemporary events in Germany . . . multiply and are becoming more urgent. . . . My inward obligation to Chancellor Hitler and his work is so great—and so intimately am I attached to the renewal of Germany now on the way—that from both a human and a political standpoint it would be a mortal sin not to say what, in this decisive period of the German revolution, must be said. . . .

"We have experienced this reunion of minds in the intoxication of thousands, in the manifestations of the flags and festivals of a nation rediscovering itself. But now, when the enthusiasm is lessened and our labour is demanding its rights, it is manifest that a catharsis of such historical dimensions necessarily produces a slag from which it must purify itself. . . .

"Open manly discussions would be of more service to the German people than, for instance, the present state of the German press, of which the Reich Minister of Enlightenment and Propaganda asserted: 'It has no longer any physiognomy.' This defect is beyond doubt. . . . When, however, the proper organs of public opinion do not clear up sufficiently the mysterious obscurity which at present seems to overspread German popular opinion, the statesman himself must intervene, to call a spade a spade. Such action should prove that the government is strong enough to stand decent criticism—that it is mindful of the old maxim: 'Only weaklings suffer no criticism.'"

These observations were unprecedented. Papen was pleading for open criticism and for an airing of tensions which were festering in darkness. After some delving into historical speculation and religious metaphysics, he denounced working-class emancipation and pleaded in scarcely veiled terms for monarchical restoration and an end of the one-party dictatorship. Following reproofs to the advocates of neo-paganism and of permanent, limitless dictatorship, Papen assailed the party radicals who were still speaking of a "Second Revolution" and of collectivization.

"Mental revolutions cry for an aristocratic conception of nature. A social overturn, however, is exposed to the danger of being influenced, in a measure, by the dynamics exhibited by Marxism.

"Such a conjecture confronts leadership with a gigantic task, the solution of which demands the utmost decisiveness from a statesman. A similar historical situation was described by Conrad Ferdinand Meyer in his masterly story: *The Temptation of Pescara,* which he characterized by quoting Luther on the peasant wars: 'A man making history has two tasks. He has what his time demands, but beyond that—and that is his most difficult task—he stands up like a giant against the upspurting froth of his century and hurls to the rear excited fools and knaves who would take a hand, exaggerating and degrading his work.'

"It is realized that this enormous task, which at all times is imposed upon a revolution, has yet to be performed in Germany. Leadership will have to watch out lest a new class struggle revive under new colours. . . .

"It is a wholly reprehensible notion that a people could be united through terrorism. The government will counter any endeavour in such a direction, realizing that terrorism is a sign of bad conscience and that it is the worst counsel to any leadership. . . .

"I have outlined the problems of the German revolution in my attitude to it so sharply because there is no end of talk of a second wave which is to complete the revolution. Whoever irresponsibly toys with such ideas should not hide from himself that a second wave might be followed by a third, and that he who threatens the guillotine might soonest fall its victim.

"Nor is it clear where such a second wave should lead. There is much talk of the coming socialization. Have we gone through an anti-Marxist revolution in order to carry out a Marxist program? For every attempt to solve the social problem by collectivization of property is Marxism."

These words might imply not only that Papen was aware of the frustrated expectations of the party's "socialists," but that he had knowledge of some terrorist conspiracy on the Left. There is no reason to suppose, however, that Röhm or any of his supporters were thinking in such terms. Apart from occasional wild talk against reactionaries, they were making no plans to terrorize or expropriate the propertied classes, and still less to resist Der Führer. The Vice-

Chancellor closed with an admission of the abuses of the régime, another veiled attack on Goebbels, and a plea for confidence through reform and open discussion:

"The government is well informed of how self-seeking, characterlessness, untruthfulness, unchivalrousness, and presumption are trying to expand on the troubles of the German revolution. Nor is the government shutting its eyes to the recognition that its great treasure in the German people's confidence is imperiled. If one desires closeness and unity with the people, one must not underestimate the people's sagacity. One must reciprocate its confidence and one must not everlastingly keep it in leading-strings. The German people realizes the gravity of its situation, its economic distress, and discerns clearly the defects of many laws born of emergency. It has a delicate sensibility for coercion and injustice and mocks at clumsy attempts to deceive it with whitewash.

"No organization, no propaganda, however excellent, would be able by themselves to maintain confidence in the long run. I, therefore, all along held a different opinion of the propaganda movement against so-called critics. Not by incitement, especially of youth, not by threats against the helpless part of the nation—only by a confidential talking-it-over with people can confidence and devotion be raised.

"The people is aware that heavy sacrifices are demanded of it. It will follow the Leader in unshakable loyalty if it is permitted to cooperate in counsel and deed, if every critical word is not interpreted as malevolence, and if despairing patriots are not branded as enemies of the State. . . .

"People treated as morons, however, have no confidence to give away. It is time for joining together in fraternal love and respect for all fellow countrymen, so as not to disturb the labours of serious men and to silence doctrinal fanatics. . . . History is waiting for us—but only if we show ourselves worthy of it." [1]

This remarkable address is difficult to evaluate on the basis of what is now known about the whole political situation in mid-June. Papen's past suggests that he probably had obscure motivations of a purely personal nature for expressing himself as he did. As the outstanding figure among the non-Nazis in the Cabinet, he doubtless felt called upon to defend this group from the assaults of both Goeb-

[1] Official translation of text, *The New York Times,* June 24, 1934.

bels and Röhm, who condemned it as reactionary. Talk of liquidating reactionaries necessarily made Papen nervous. Property, titles, rank, and privileges were to him sacred and divinely ordained. But he was not too clear as to the direction from which these values were being menaced—or, if clear, not clever in making distinctions. He made no mention of Röhm. But he seemed to be talking against him none the less, as a symbol of the "Second Revolution." At no time had Röhm ever displayed any interest in social radicalism. Röhm, like other commanders of *condottieri,* was interested in his own advancement and in the strength of the soldiery upon which his own power rested. If his S.A. men, especially the new recruits, were permeated with radicalism and dreams of socialization, it might be expedient for him to pander to these fantasies, as Hitler had once done. But there is little evidence that he did even this. He was seeking greater military prestige—by securing control of the Reichswehr, if possible; by enlarging his storm-troop army; by assailing whoever seemed to stand in his way. This crude, burly homosexual could at no time be accused of social idealism. Never had the cause of radical National-socialism had a more unlikely leader. Ley of the Labour Front was closer to the sources of proletarian pressure against the landed and moneyed élite. But Ley, even more than Röhm, knew how his own interests could best be served. Other erstwhile radicals were nowhere in the public eye. Feder was harmless. Darré exhausted his energies in idle rhetoric against the Junkers. Gregor Strasser had been in retirement since December 1932. Goebbels was never a radical, but only a phrase-maker.

In any case, the Marburg speech, like other acts of Papen, was a bit of courageous stupidity. Courageous, because it was certain to bring wrath on his head from various Nazi quarters. He had apparently consulted with none of the party leaders before delivering it. His friend Edgar Jung was in part responsible for the content. Stupid, because it irritated too many people in high places unnecessarily. There were kind words for Hitler, Rosenberg, and Rust. But Goebbels was openly condemned and identified with the apostles of the "Second Revolution," even though Papen may merely have wished to express dissent from Goebbels's methods. Röhm was almost insulted and other party groups, both radical and conservative, could easily take offence at the phraseology employed. People with guilty consciences take offence easily. If Papen wished to denounce the party radicals, he should have conciliated the conservatives and recognized that Goebbels was inseparable from them.

The Propaganda Minister acted at once against the Vice-Chancellor and thereby precipitated a mild political crisis quite incidental and irrelevant to the major issue. Goebbels spoke in Gera, Thuringia, on the same day. "Let it be said once and for all," he declared, "that we Nationalsocialists alone have the right to speak in defence of Der Führer." When he learned of Papen's address, he immediately suppressed its publication in the German press on Sunday, June 17, and forbade its repetition over the radio. On Tuesday the two men clashed in a Cabinet meeting. Papen was reported to have threatened his resignation. Hitler sought to keep the peace and assured Papen that he still possessed his confidence. The Vice-Chancellor finally agreed that while the address was appropriately given to a university audience, it was not suitable for general publication. Göring had also failed to secure publicity for certain of his recent addresses and perhaps sided with Papen. On Thursday, June 21, Hitler conferred with Hindenburg at Neudeck, ostensibly about his Venice conversations with Mussolini. It was rumoured that Hindenburg had "summoned" his Chancellor and asked him to curb the party radicals. Papen had evidently supplied the President with an advance copy of his Marburg address. Hindenburg sent a telegram of congratulation to him as Vice-Chancellor and "best comrade." Papen received many other congratulatory messages, particularly from industrialists. He began to think he had been clever again. And again he had been much too clever. Once his cleverness had cost a nation its liberties. Now it was almost to cost him his life.

Reverberations continued to echo. Rosenberg, in the *V.B.* of June 19, took issue with Papen's contention that the Nazis and the conservatives were seeking the same end. Göring, on the other hand, in an address to the Prussian State Council on Wednesday evening, agreed that the new radicalism could accomplish nothing. "If Der Führer wishes a second revolution, then we will be on the streets tomorrow. If he does not wish it, then we will crush everybody who tries to make such a revolution against his will." Goebbels remained hostile, though on Thursday afternoon he and Papen somewhat ostentatiously permitted themselves to be seen at tea together in the Propaganda Ministry. On Thursday evening Goebbels spoke in the proletarian suburb of Neukölln and aroused great enthusiasm by denouncing government by divine right, the "reactionary clique," and "gentlemen in club chairs." "The Nationalsocialist government would have done better to place all these fine gentlemen behind locks and bars."

On Sunday Goebbels spoke in Essen. He asserted that the peaceful character of the revolution had "spoiled" both the party and the nation. "It might have befallen differently. . . . If for the present we do not disturb our enemies in their mouse-holes, it is only for getting them out into the open. . . . Only members of the Nationalsocialist Party have the right to criticize. . . . We have annihilated Marxism, but we still tolerate reaction in our midst. If, however, our Führer were to come forward and say: 'Comrades, let us show them,' there would be nothing left of the reactionaries within twenty-four hours." On the same day Hess, in Mülheim, urged silence and moderation upon Youth leaders. Schirach, in Oldenburg, denounced the reactionaries for resorting to methods of the "ill-famed Jewish newspapers."

During the last week of June the course of events suggested increasing tension, but no immediate danger of an explosion. On Friday the 22nd, it was reported that 150 of Göring's special bodyguards had been sent to a concentration camp for insubordination. He had recently punished two guards for maltreating prisoners in a camp near Stettin. On the 23rd the "mutiny" was denied and the body-guard was incorporated into the Field Hunters Corps. On Monday the 25th, *Der Angriff* printed a cartoon of a German soldier being stabbed in the back by a Socialist, and next to it a storm trooper kicking an aristocrat (with Papen's features) who was similarly endeavouring to stab him in the back. On the same day Hess broadcast an address in which he condemned both "eternal yesterdayers" among the reactionaries and "visionaries with blinders" who would inaugurate a second revolution: "Woe to him who breaks faith and belief to serve the revolution through rebellion! Woe to him who clumsily tramples Der Führer's strategic plans, in the hope of quicker results! Some indulge in revolutionary talk, but the achievement of those who, in quiet work and at poor pay, give visible expression to the revolutionary aims of Nationalsocialism is far greater." Simultaneously Göring and Streicher denounced the Jews in a meeting in Franconia, and Edmund Heines, S.A. commander of Silesia and police chief of Breslau, reviewed his troops:

"Keep a stiff upper lip and be ready for all emergencies. The German people, in their true German way, have been far too kind to their enemies. The Jews are more insolent than ever. The virus of Judaism is a plague infecting the whole world. . . . Germany will be eternal because the storm-troop organization is eternal." [1]

Following the news of a stabbing affray in the Pomeranian village of Quetzin, the S.A. headquarters announced that the continued existence of the Stahlhelm was intolerable. Röhm was "absent on a rest trip." His officers announced that after the July leave the drills and parades of the storm troopers would be greatly curtailed. Karl Ernst in Berlin banned entirely the wearing of brown shirts during July, ostensibly in the name of removing causes of complaint over excessive service on the part of wives and employers. He went ahead with his plans for a vacation with his wife in the Balearic Islands. On Wednesday, June 27, Hitler, after conferring with Seldte, ordered Röhm and the S.A. to cease their attacks on the Stahlhelm, the dissolution of which, he declared, could not be contemplated. He conferred at length with Papen in the afternoon. Word leaked out that Edgar Jung, the Catholic author of Munich who had aided in the preparation of the Marburg speech, had been arrested. Before leaving his apartment with his captors, he had scribbled "Secret Police" on the bathroom wall. Papen protested, but his efforts to effect Jung's release were without result. Rumours circulated that the S.A. might be dissolved or at least greatly reduced. Goebbels announced that the campaign against grumblers would end on June 30. All party speakers would be given a vacation during July, when there would be no speeches, meetings, parades, or even uniforms. Herr Görlitzer declared on June 26 that the party would soon be purged of undesirable elements and that "organizational changes" would follow. This was interpreted to mean another of the periodical cleansings in which inactive or insubordinate members are expelled.

Thursday, June 28, 1934: Hitler and Göring flew to Essen to attend the wedding of a local leader; Papen reasserted his loyalty to Hitler in an address; Blomberg, in the *V.B.,* affirmed the loyalty of the Reichswehr to the régime; Kurt Schmitt fainted in the midst of a speech and went into retirement to recover his health; rumours spread that Hitler was angry with Röhm and the S.A. leaders. The

[1] *New York Times,* June 26, 1934.

storm troopers were ordered to be silent about the Stahlhelm, but it was denied that Der Führer contemplated any punishment. The *Reichsbote* called for the quiet elimination of inefficient sub-leaders in the party. . . .

What was taking place behind the scenes is by no means so clear. An atmosphere of highly charged nervous tension brooded over the places of power. The public was apparently quiet, even if somewhat apprehensive. But party leaders, industrialists, S.A. commanders, aristocrats, storm troopers were suspicious, each of the other and of one another. Conservatives feared that Hitler might yield to the S.A. radicals. The radicals suspected that the régime had thrown in its lot definitely with reactionaries and betrayed the rank and file of the party. Business men and Junkers, while confident of Hitler's support, feared a possible putsch by the S.A. Papen's speech was reassuring, but Goebbels's denunciations and Jung's arrest were not. Some storm-troop leaders feared a military *coup* by reactionaries supported by the Stahlhelm and the Reichswehr. Friction between the party leaders and the Catholic Church was at a high point. "Vacations," "truces," "leaves of absence" promised peace—but who would be victor was uncertain. It was not even clear where the lines of conflict were being drawn, or whether there was any conflict, save for the S.A.-Stahlhelm imbroglio. Censorship, propaganda, mysticism covered everything with a dense fog of rumours and alarms. Something had happened. Something would happen. No one knew what, how, or why.

What passed in Hitler's mind can only be conjectured. As the focal point of all tensions, he was subjected to a terrific strain. Strong nerves, clear vision, sound judgment were needed. He had none of these qualities. Pale, distraught, at times almost hysterical, he vacillated. His reproof to Röhm and his championship of the Stahlhelm constituted his first and only public pronouncement since the Marburg speech. He suspected Papen and the "reactionaries" as much as he suspected the S.A. radicals. He had learned never to trust "gentlemen," even though they must be relied upon and favoured, since they controlled the real sources of power. He could handle his enemies. It was friends who were dangerous. Who could have real friends at the dizzy and lonely heights which Hitler occupied?

It is certain that Der Führer conferred secretly with Röhm some time—perhaps several times—during these hectic weeks. He was suspicious. Röhm was suspicious. The old comrades-in-arms could no longer trust each other. The S.A. chief, frustrated in his most cherished ambition, had been forced to bow to the will of the Leader, whom he suspected of harbouring designs against the storm troops. Hitler suspected his aide of insubordination or worse. There were doubtless heated words and guarded threats. Obedience or . . . ? *Ja wohl, aber . . . ?* The S.A. was restive. Was Ribbentrop in Paris promising its dissolution? Röhm could not guarantee its behaviour if Hitler insisted on tolerating reaction. Deadlock. But Röhm seemingly yielded and made no plans for resistance. Hitler waited.

From this was to come as mad an outbreak of insane savagery as has ever occurred in a modern State—a reversion to barbaric fury comparable only to the blood orgies of Oriental despotisms or of Imperial Rome at the lowest ebb of its degeneration. The responsibility was Hitler's. His nerves broke down in what he imagined to be a grave crisis threatening his power. But beyond question the voice at his ear was Göring's. Bully, fool, sadist, or Mephistopheles, he it was who whispered poison to Der Führer. Perhaps he advised alone. Perhaps he conferred with Himmler, chief of the S.S. and the *Gestapo*. Possibly others proposed a proscription of their best-hated enemies. The flight to Essen on Thursday was decisive. Göring hinted that a "plot" was under way—menacing and immediate. Hitler, already suspicious, believed. Who? Enemies to both right and left. Men in high places. Names and fictitious details: a foreign diplomat, a former Chancellor, a Cabinet member, S.A. commanders, Catholic leaders, aristocratic reactionaries, erstwhile radicals, a hodge-podge of incongruities. Hitler believed.

Swiftly, suddenly, Der Führer must strike to left and right. The culprits must be disgraced and discredited by being linked with the worst enemies of their friends and supporters. No chances must be taken. Perhaps even Röhm? Hitler believed. Röhm had not accepted defeat gracefully. Perhaps even Papen? Perhaps Goebbels? Hitler recoiled. Murder requires strong nerves. Not these, not these. Why, without Papen and Goebbels he would never have become Chancellor. Nor without Röhm—but no matter. The poison worked its way. Der Führer sank into a kind of frenzy. Göring would take care of things in Berlin. Hitler must go to Munich without arousing suspicion. And there. . . . Motors droned to silence as the plane descended at Essen.

Hitler visited the Krupp works. He conferred with Krupp and with other industrialists—not breathing a word of the anticipatory guilt already hanging on his conscience. That they gave names or suggested means is improbable. But at least they were loyal and would welcome action. . . . Some kind of action . . . what should he do . . . Göring said obedience why faithlessness horrible but for the fatherland forward with god why had his father forbidden him to be an artist murder was ghastly unless heroic his mother had a czech accent suicide was yesterday on a building scaffold when christ and the virgin on painted postcards in the burgerbrau blessing men dying on odeonplatz were corpses of sister paula in berchtesgaden on barbedwireriddledby machinegunsbecause. . . . Fear and misery bred madness in Hitler's unstable brain.

2. MASSACRE

GÖRING returned to the capital. Hitler remained in the Rhineland, visiting labour camps. Secret orders went out to S.S. and *Gestapo* leaders, and to a few party officials in Berlin, Munich, and elsewhere. Der Führer's loneliness was terrifying. He summoned Goebbels from Baden. He was needed. He must see. He *must* be true. As master of rhetoric, Goebbels must reassure his Leader and must present the painful events to come in a good light. Late Friday night Hitler stood with Goebbels on the terrace of the Rhine Hotel in Godesberg, near Bonn, gazing moodily at the crowd below and at the Labour Service band playing music, more music, and at last the *Horst Wessel Lied*. Midnight struck. Dispatches arrived. There were consultations. Göring phoned from Berlin, with new alarms about an S.A. "revolt" scheduled for the next day. There was no time to lose.

Hitler and Goebbels proceeded to the flying-field near Bonn and boarded a three-motored Junkers plane. At 2.00 a.m. Saturday morning, June 30, the plane roared away southward and eastward into the black fog. Der Führer had known many night flights in the course of innumerable campaigns, but never a flight on such a mission of death as this. At four o'clock the plane landed near Munich in the grey of the early summer dawn. A full report was ready at the field, detailing the location of the victims and telling of "sedition" during the night on the part of the local S.A. Hitler and Goebbels proceeded at once to the Bavarian Ministry of the Interior, where Minister

Adolf Wagner had already arrested and assembled a number of sleepy and perplexed S.A. leaders. Der Führer, tense and pale, accosted them, denounced them, tore insignia from their uniforms . . . and ordered them shot.

Did Goebbels believe in the myth of the "revolt"? Had he learned of the plan before going to Godesberg? There is as yet no means of knowing. He who rides a tiger dare not dismount. He who flies with a homicidal maniac must humour his host. Desperately Goebbels clung to his chief, never daring to leave his side an instant. It was decided to proceed to Röhm's villa in Bad Wiessee, the "nest of plotters." A small fleet of motor cars was filled with S.S. guards who obeyed all commands. Hitler, Goebbels, Lutze, Brückner, Schaub, Schreck, Dietrich, and Buch of the *Uschla* were driven at tremendous speed over the empty roads. The countryside lay sleeping in the cool of sunrise. No one was awake at Wiessee.

At seven o'clock Röhm's villa was invaded. None of the "conspirators"—Röhm's friends visiting him for the week-end—had yet arisen. There had been a party. These men who were alleged to be plotting to ruin the Reich had been enjoying Bavarian *Gemütlichkeit,* embellished by special diversions peculiar to many Nazi leaders. Empty bottles and unwashed dishes, containing remains of a feast, stood about. Röhm and his friends dozed in soft beds, some of them in the embrace of male lovers. A few had brought men prostitutes from Berlin. Edmund Heines slept affectionately with a young lad of his heart's desire. In this there was nothing remarkable, for those in Röhm's entourage often spent week-ends in this fashion.

Awakened by the intruders, the bleary-eyed guests could not quite comprehend. Shouting with rage to conceal his own fears, Hitler accused them of treason and ordered them arrested by the S.S. guards. Röhm's day guard from Munich arrived soon afterwards and was sent back, unresisting, to the city. Röhm denied all guilt when he was arrested and deposed from his offices. He spurned an invitation to shoot himself. He was dragged off by his captors. According to one account, Heines was shot dead in the villa when he made a threatening gesture. Hitler motored back to Munich, meeting S.A. leaders along the way who had been summoned for a conference. He greeted some and ordered the arrest of others. In the city he joined Wagner and Epp and issued a decree deposing Röhm and appointing Viktor Lutze as S.A. Chief of Staff. From Munich he flew to Berlin, always with Goebbels at his side. They arrived in the capital at 10.00 p.m.

The Munich captives were taken to Stadelheim Prison. There was little pretence of any trial. S.S. men guarded the prisoners and S.S. squads executed them. Röhm was shot Sunday night when he persisted in his refusal to take his own life. August Schneidhuber, district S.A. commander and police superintendent of Munich, was reported to have said: "Well, boys, I don't know what this is all about, but anyhow shoot straight!" How many died at Stadelheim may never be known. Executions continued all through Monday and Tuesday. Most of the dead were presumably on the proscription lists which Göring, Hitler, and Himmler had prepared. Others were slain by unknown S.S. men or secret police out of revenge or spite—some in their homes, some against prison walls, some in lonely woods. The mutilated body of Kahr was found in a swamp. Lossow and Seisser escaped. The death of the former Bavarian Premier was not admitted until July 5—"heart attack." Others murdered informally were Karl Steutzel, former Bavarian Minister of the Interior; Richard Scheringer; Herr Sempner, proprietor of an inn frequented by Röhm; and Dr. Otto Ballerstedt, a critic of the NSDAP in 1923. Hour after hour the volleys rang out against the walls of Stadelheim. Hour after hour S.A. leaders fell to earth, bullet-riddled and choked with blood.

Göring and Himmler in Berlin had meanwhile acted no less ruthlessly. They struck high. Papen was assaulted, ejected from his office, closely questioned by S.S. guards, and at last saved from death only by the intervention of Hindenburg and the Reichswehr. He was subjected to "house arrest" for his protection. His offices were occupied and searched by the S.S. and he was forbidden to leave his home. His friend Edgar Jung, already in custody, was shot to death. His aide Herbert von Bose, chief of the Vice-Chancellery staff, was slain. His comrade Werner von Alvensleben, was likewise reported to have died before the guns of the S.S. (though his brother reported him alive in a concentration camp on August 8), and perhaps also Gottfried Treviranus. Other aides of Papen were arrested, but later released: Fritz von Tschirsky, Karl von Savigny, and Margarete von Stockzingen.

At 1.30 p.m., June 30, half a dozen secret police called on Gregor Strasser as he was about to sit down to dine with his family at the board where Hitler, Göring, and Goebbels had often enjoyed his hospitality. He was arrested, turned over to the S.S., and, according to his brother, beaten and trampled to death in Grünewald. At four o'clock in the afternoon an open car with six men in plain clothes drove up to the suburban home of General Kurt von Schleicher in Neubabelsberg, between Potsdam and Wannsee. Here the former Chancellor lived alone with his wife. One man alighted and rang the doorbell, while the car was backed into the drive with its motor kept running. The summoner climbed back into the car. When the General and Frau Schleicher appeared at the portico, perhaps expecting guests, they were cut down by a hail of bullets. The car sped toward Berlin. Schleicher was killed instantly. His wife expired in a hospital two hours later. Rumour alleged that the General was slain because he had documents in his possession, from the Reichswehrministerium, proving that Hitler had never been awarded an Iron Cross. . . .

Karl Ernst, Berlin S.A. leader, was apprehended by S.S. men in his car between Bremen and Bremerhaven, where he was about to catch a boat for the Mediterranean. His wife and chauffeur were wounded. He was knocked unconscious and taken back to Berlin by plane. S.S. guards brought other prisoners, by plane or motor, from all parts of the Reich. Ernst's staff leader, Sander, concluded that Göring had become demented and flew to Munich, where he hoped to see Hitler. He was arrested, taken back to Berlin, and shot. Ernst's adjutants, Captain Gerth and Captain Mohrenschild, were also sentenced to death. Gerth was a *Pour le mérite* officer. At the last moment he was rescued from the firing squad and offered an opportunity to commit suicide by Hitler. When he refused, protesting his innocence, he was taken back to Lichterfelde prison and shot, as he saluted his executioners with: "Comrades, aim well!" Here, at the outskirts of Berlin, military tribunals sat, supervised by Daluege, Fritsch, Göring, and Himmler. The "proceedings" were swift. Every few minutes a new death sentence was passed. In the barren courtyard floodlights glared at the red brick wall before which stood the S.S. firing squads. Ernst collapsed. He could not, even at the end, comprehend what was happening. To him it seemed that Hitler's enemies had overthrown him and were killing the most faithful friends of Der Führer. A moment before the rifles drilled him with lead, he cried out: "I am innocent! *Heil Hitler! Heil Deutschland!"*

All day Saturday, all day Sunday, all day Monday the volleys rang out, half muffled by the roll of drums. Others were shot in Breslau and elsewhere, but most of the formal executions, apart from sporadic murders, took place in Lichterfelde and Stadelheim. Erich Klausener, head of the Catholic Action group, was slain in his office by S.S. men. Captain Fischer of the Berlin *Gestapo;* Colonel von Marlow; General von Bredow; retired General Otto von Ossow; Bollwitz, head of the S.A. press department; S.A. commander von Heydebreck of Pomerania; S.A. commander Hayn of Saxony; Berlin S.A. leaders Sander, Engels, Konze, and Hoffmann; Klaus Heim, leader of Holstein farmers; Adelbert Probst, leader of Catholic Youth; Dr. Heimsoth, friend of Röhm; Fritz Beck, brilliant Nazi educator of Munich and head of the German Academic Foreign Bureau; and possibly Captain Ehrhardt, Captain Rossbach, and Dr. Held were among the victims. Scores of other S.A. men of lesser prominence were dispatched, as well as many former radicals, friends of Ernst, Röhm, or Strasser, men and women (including Frau Ernst) who might know who had burned the Reichstag, men who were inconvenient, men who were disliked, men who were potentially dangerous. Thousands more were arrested and later released or sent to concentration camps. These included Killinger, Duesterberg, Alphonse Sacks, Papen's surviving aides, the Vice-Chancellor himself, with his son ("house arrest"), and no less a personage than "Auwi," whom Göring released on the ground that he was too stupid to have had a hand in the "conspiracy." The roll of the dead has not yet been called. First official reports spoke of seven, and then of not more than fifty. Initial accounts declared that Röhm was a suicide and that other victims, later admitted to have been slain by firing squads, had taken their own lives or had been shot while seeking to escape, or, like Schleicher, had been "shot resisting arrest." Most observers agreed that several hundred people perished. From confidential but probably reliable sources the writer has received an estimate of 1,186 persons murdered on "Bloody Saturday" and during the week which followed.

The disposition of the dead was scarcely less gruesome than the manner of their slaughter. All bodies were at once cremated, without a funeral or benefit of clergy. Schleicher's burial was scheduled for Wednesday, July 4. The ceremony was forbidden by the police, who seized the bodies of the General and his wife, burned them, and returned the ashes to the relatives. On Saturday they were interred in a nameless grave, with only eight mourners permitted to attend. In many cases the ashes were filed by number in cigar-boxes or crude urns and delivered to the widows or parents by mail, or at special offices where they could be called for by numbered checks. Hoffmann's ashes bore number 238. Only strictly private funerals were permitted. The cremation of the Catholic leaders infuriated the Roman clergy. Klausener's widow shrieked: "Assassin!" at Hitler. When Gerth's aged mother received the ashes of her son, she screamed out that he had been murdered by Göring. When the remains of a certain Dr. Willi Schmitt of Munich, music critic and journalist, were delivered to his widow, a police official called to apologize: another Dr. Schmitt had been on the list; the victim had been shot by mistake; the authorities were very sorry; it would never happen again.[1]

3. APOLOGIA

THESE events were presented to an incredulous world in the form of news communiqués, explanatory proclamations, and orders reorganizing the S.A. The first proclamation of June 30 from the Munich party headquarters declared:

"For many months individual elements have been trying to drive a wedge and produce conflicts between the storm troops and the party, as well as between the storm troops and the State. Suspicions of this became more and more confirmed, but it was also plain that these endeavours were to be charged to a limited clique of certain leanings.

"Chief of Staff Röhm, in whom the Leader placed an exceptional amount of confidence, not only did not oppose these endeavours, but undoubtedly sponsored them. His well-known unfortunate characteristics gradually led to intolerable burdens which drove the Leader of

[1] Cf. *V.B., Der Angriff, The New York Times,* London *Times,* Budapest *Pester Lloyd,* Vienna *Neue Freie Presse,* Vienna *Telegraf am Mittag,* July 1–6, 1934; cf. Gerhart Seger: *Hitlers Weg Bergab* (Zurich: Oprecht; 1934), and the émigré *Weissbuch über die Erschiessungen des 30 Juni* (Paris; Carrefour; 1934).

the movement and the Highest Leader of the S.A. into most serious conflicts of conscience.

"Chief of Staff Röhm established contacts with General von Schleicher without the knowledge of Der Führer. His go-betweens were another S.A. leader and an obscure person well known in Berlin to whom Der Führer had always strongly objected.

"Since these negotiations also led—of course without the knowledge of Der Führer—finally to contacts with a foreign Power, or rather its representative, it was not possible to avoid intervention, both from the standpoint of the party and the State.

"Provocative incidents brought about according to the plan, caused Der Führer to fly from Bonn to Munich at two o'clock this morning, after visiting labour camps in Westphalia, in order to remove and arrest the more seriously compromised group of leaders. Der Führer himself went with only a few companions to Wiessee in order to still any attempts at resistance.

"The execution of the arrests revealed such immorality that any trace of pity was impossible. Some of these storm-troop leaders had taken male prostitutes along with them. One of them was even disturbed in a most ugly situation and was arrested.

"Der Führer gave orders for this plague to be done away with ruthlessly. In the future he will not permit millions of decent people to be compromised by a few such sick men. Der Führer instructed Premier Göring of Prussia to take similar action in Berlin and especially to arrest the reactionary accomplices of this political plot.

"At noon today Der Führer spoke to assembled Hitler storm-troop leaders and stressed his unshakable bond to the storm troops, at the same time declaring he intended from now on to remove and destroy without mercy all undisciplined and disobedient persons, as well as unsocial and sickly elements.

"He pointed out that service in the storm troops was a service of honour, for which tens of thousands of brave storm-troop men had made the greatest sacrifices. He expected, he said, from the leader of each unit proof that he was worthy of such sacrifice and that he would be an example to his troops.

"Der Führer pointed out furthermore that for years he had protected Chief of Staff Röhm against attacks, but that developments obliged him to place above all personal feelings the welfare of the movement and the State. He had to suppress at the root attempts in ambitious circles to propagate a new revolution." [1]

Hitler at the same time issued orders expelling Röhm from the S.A. and the party, appointing Lutze, and threatening arrest for any S.A. or S.S. men disobeying the new leader. In a letter to Lutze—"the same true and ideal S.A. leader through many years"—Hitler spoke of Röhm's "most serious ill deeds." Lutze addressed a communication to his new subordinates, asking of them the virtues which he claimed for himself: "Unconditional faithfulness! Severest discipline! Self-sacrificing devotion!" Seldte ordered the Stahlhelm to refrain from wearing uniforms and to display "dignity, calm, and discipline." Göring issued the following statement:

"All of Prussia is firm in my hands. The special guards and my police have everywhere taken charge of party headquarters. The storm troops have not offered any resistance. They were merely misled. I have naturally also taken measures against those circles that in any way endangered the existence of the State and have turned against the reactionaries, whether Left or Right.

"The S.A. is brave and we must show to it in what way it has been misused. There is no cause for any uneasiness. Some S.A. leaders, overwhelmed and despondent upon realizing what they had done, have committed suicide. Some have had to be shot when they offered resistance. They, however, constitute only a small part."

Göring also met the foreign press and told its representatives that "for weeks and months we have observed that a certain clique of S.A. leaders tried to misuse loyal storm troopers to precipitate a so-called second revolution, in order to overthrow the State and establish their own ridiculous régime." He accused these leaders of brutality and of trying to exert pressure on Der Führer. He and Hitler had struck "with lightning speed to suppress any resistance, without respect for persons." Schleicher he described as the "principal go-between" for the S.A. leaders and the reactionaries who had "tried to establish a connection between Röhm and a foreign Power." Schleicher lost his life because "he attempted to make a lightning attack on the people who were to arrest him." "A mutiny had been planned by only a small part of the S.A. Law and order has been preserved throughout the country. Today or tomorrow Der Führer

[1] Text of this and subsequent proclamations from translations in *The New York Times.*

will explain the whole action to the country in a speech over the radio."

Also on "Bloody Saturday," Hitler addressed eleven puritanical injunctions to Lutze and the S.A.: (1) "Blind obedience and unquestioning discipline"; (2) behaviour which would set an example to followers; (3) expulsion of leaders who publicly disgrace themselves; (4) the simple life sans costly dinners; "I prohibit the use of S.A. or party funds for festivals and the like. It is shameless to stage debauches with the pennies of our poorest citizens. The luxurious headquarters in Berlin, in which it has now been discovered that some thirty thousand marks monthly were spent for banquets, is to be done away with immediately. I prohibit for all party groups banquets or dinners paid for with any variety of public funds. I forbid all party and S.A. leaders to partake of such banquets." (5) No business trips in expensive limousines at public expense; (6) expulsion of leaders who become publicly intoxicated; (7) co-operation in preserving the S.A. as a "clean and upright institution" and the instant dismissal of all guilty of homosexual crimes; "I desire men in the party, not absurd apes." (8) Loyalty for loyalty and no greater demands on subordinates for courage and sacrifice than leaders are willing to display; (9) gratitude to the old guards, no expensive and unnecessary staffs, and promotions on the basis of leadership, not abstract knowledge; (10) physical and intellectual training of all S.A. men as thorough Nationalsocialists; (11) loyalty, fellowship, "respect for the law and obedience to my commands."

On Sunday, July 1, while troops, police, and S.S. guards retained control of all principal streets and public buildings in Berlin, Göring issued special orders to the Berlin-Brandenburg S.A., threatening severe and relentless punishment for any criticism or discussion of the executions. The furlough would be carried through. The wearing of uniforms during July was forbidden, and the carrying of "daggers of honour" was banned until further notice. All S.A. leaders and men must keep to their houses. Anyone calling them together to "enlighten" them would be called to account. Only the press and the radio would be used for enlightenment, and only by Hitler and his agents. The provisional command of the Berlin S.A. was entrusted to Kurt Daluege, S.S. leader and Chief of Police. It was officially admitted in other quarters that Bose and Klausener were not suicides and that Schleicher "was not seriously involved." Papen was kept in strict confinement under guard. Goebbels issued a highly coloured description of his night drive with Der Führer, who was heroic, serious, meditative, grieved, stern, merciless, brisk, indignant, contemptuous, determined, bitter, kind, harsh, and a Real Man. The victims of the purge he described as disloyal, disgusting, incorrigible, puffed-up, revolutionary, dissipated, immoral, extravagant, sexually abnormal, narrow-minded, short-sighted, and traitorous. "The boil has been lanced. Morality, decency, and purity have been restored. The whole nation breathes easily again, as if freed from a horrible nightmare. Peace, order, and public security are again assured. The Reich is there and, above all, our Führer."

On July 1 the *Westdeutsche Beobachter* carried the following editorial, which was typical of the comments of the Nazi press:

"A parallel case is not to be found in the whole of history! Never before has a leader submerged his personal feelings so completely, never before has there been a statesman so utterly concerned for the welfare of the nation, as Der Führer. Neither Alexander the Great nor any other emperor or king in ancient history, neither Bonaparte nor Frederick the Great, has done anything like it. Superhuman leadership such as we have just witnessed will surely never be equalled. One needs to have followed Der Führer for years, as we have done, have felt the spirit of the movement pulsate through one's veins, in order to appreciate the immensity of his sacrifice; to understand what it meant to him to order so many of his old friends, many of them men with splendid pasts, to be shot. We stand in awe of this man and his unexampled self-sacrifice. In this solemn and tense moment we swear that we also will forgo all human weaknesses and errors. The blood that was shed yesterday will purify all of us; it is the sacrifice, which we dedicate to fate, necessary to keep our magnificent movement pure."

Hindenburg lay ill at Neudeck. Rumour asserted that his "political will" named Papen as his successor. The Vice-Chancellor remained under arrest. On Monday the President was informed of what had happened by the press chief of the Propaganda Ministry. He issued telegrams at once, congratulating Hitler for crushing "traitorous machinations" through "resolute energy and courageous personal action" and "rescuing the German people from great danger." He thanked Göring for his "energetic and successful action" in suppressing high treason. These messages were broadcast, in the hope of reinvigorating all party and government officials who were so paralysed with fear that they hesitated to make any decisions or even continue with their work. Frick, however, warned all that Hitler's will was law and that death awaited all mutineers. Berliners stayed home or cautiously discussed the weather on the streets, while police kept the crowds moving. Official statements ridiculed foreign reports that hundreds had been killed. After Göring visited the Vice-Chancellor, Papen and "Auwi" were released from house arrest, though Papen's retirement was forecast. The press department of the S.A. was abolished. Goebbels praised the German press for its "loyalty" and "straightforwardness," while Ley berated Röhm, and Darré renounced the luxury and corruption of the "plotters."

On Tuesday, July 3, Papen was permitted under guard to see the Chancellor. He appeared pale, red-eyed, and weary. He tendered his resignation. Hitler flew to Neudeck to consult Hindenburg. The Chancellor declared officially that only fifty had been executed and that remaining prisoners would be turned over to the ordinary courts. With Papen excused from attending, the Cabinet met and passed a law declaring: "The measures taken on June 30 and on July 1 and 2, 1934, for the suppression of acts of treason are legalized as necessary measures for the defence of the State." [1] It was announced that a compromise had been reached with the Catholic Bishops on the preceding Friday, whereby the suppression of Catholic youth and workers' societies would be deferred for a year. The press published long accounts of colossal graft and corruption in the S.A., while storm troopers were forbidden to solicit funds publicly in the future. It was rumoured that only twenty per cent of the S.A. would be recalled to service at the end of July. Göring assumed two new titles and two new uniforms: Reich Forest Master and Reich Master of the Hunt.

On Wednesday, July 4, Hindenburg refused to accept Papen's resignation. Lutze forbade S.A. men to wear uniforms, assemble, or engage in activity during July. Brown uniforms disappeared throughout the Reich. Black-uniformed S.S. men everywhere swarmed in the streets. Party leaders assembled in Flensberg, near the Danish border, to plan a reorganization under the chairmanship of Hess. Addresses were delivered on unemployment, health, and philosophy.

[1] *R.G.B.*, 1934, Vol. I, No. 71, p. 529.

The German press published reports naming France as the "Foreign Power" implicated in the "conspiracy" and accused Schleicher of dealing with Barthou for Hitler's overthrow. Ambassador André François-Poncet declared this "an absurd fable." Lutze officially announced on Thursday that the S.A. would be reorganized. Its headquarters were moved from Munich to the building adjoining the Chancellery in Berlin, where Papen had formerly had his offices and where Bose had been shot. Röhm had made the S.A. a recruiting agency for the party. Lutze intimated that in future all S.A. men must be party members. At the close of the Flensberg conference, however, Hess declared that the S.A. would not be allowed to fall to a secondary place.

By the end of the week it was clear that the orgy of bloodshed was over and that it would be followed by no immediate consequences unfavourable to Der Führer. The bitterness of the storm troopers was repressed. Cries of "Revenge!" were stifled. No organized resistance to Lutze developed anywhere. The same amazing fear of authority, reverence for power, and paralysing psychic impotence which had caused the SPD and the KPD to accept destruction without a blow in self-defence now reappeared in the S.A. Old crimes and betrayals were forgotten and new promises were believed. Resentment in Catholic circles was acute, though the German Christians and the neo-pagans blessed Hitler for his "heroism."

Industrialists were content. Qualms of conscience at connivance in murder were overcome by the reflection that all danger of the dreaded second revolution was now over and that all remnants of socialism in the NSDAP were liquidated. The Junkers and the aristocratic officers of the Reichswehr were less pleased. They welcomed the elimination of Röhm and Strasser, of the S.A. and the party radicals. But they had not reckoned on the indiscriminate killing of their own friends by the butchers of the S.S. whom Hitler had unleashed. They had no alternative, however, save to continue their support of the régime. The terror had achieved its purpose. Hitler was now secure, with the loyal support of the S.S. mercenaries. The landed and industrial ruling classes were now dominant in the Reich beyond all question, supported by the reliable Schutzstaffel instead of by the unruly and radical Sturmabteilung. Nothing remained but to lend greater plausibility to the "conspiracy" myth and to complete the S.A.'s liquidation.

Hitler called for peace and quiet on July 7 and retired to rest at Berchtesgaden. On Sunday the 8th, Hess delivered an address at Königsberg. He offered no new facts nor any proof of the "plot," but eulogized Hitler and stirred the old enthusiasms. "The Leader has punished the guilty. Our relation to the S.A. is just as it was of old." Der Führer had saved the nation by acting with soldierly swiftness and severity. And now the nation must have peace. "Let no one dare attack us, let no one invade the new Germany. We would fight as bravely as any people have ever fought for freedom." The brave French veterans, too, recalled the horrors of war. All soldiers are comrades. Barthou also admired Wagner. Given equality of rights, Germany desired nothing more than peace. . . . On Monday Lutze announced that the S.A. would be reduced from 2,500,000 to 800,000. The balance would be put in labour camps or in a temporary reserve. The Stahlhelm was given a vacation until August 18.

On July 10 Göring summoned the Reichstag to meet in the Kroll Opera on Friday evening, July 13, to hear Hitler's final version of "Bloody Saturday." There were rumours that a "White Book" of documentary proofs would be issued by the Ministry of Justice, along with a full list of the "traitors." Neither has ever appeared. On the 12th Alfred Frauenfeld, successor in Munich to Theodore Habicht as Nazi leader in Austria, accused Chancellor Dollfuss of complicity in the "plot." Extensive broadcasts of Hitler's address were arranged. He conferred all day with S.S. and *Gestapo* leaders, and himself wrote his apologia. He appeared in the Kroll Opera at 8.00 p.m. and for an hour and a half spoke furiously, with clenched fists. Hugenberg, a lonely, pathetic figure, sat silently in a front seat, refraining from applause. Der Führer read from his manuscript, hoarsely at first and then with growing animation as the old spell of words fell upon his hearers and himself. His defence was unanimously acclaimed by the deputies, to the tune, at the end, of the *Horst Wessel Lied*.

"I shall be ruthlessly frank. I shall only observe such restrictions as are imposed for reasons of State interests and, on the other hand, by feelings of shame."

Hitler reviewed the achievements of his régime since January 30, 1933 in winning the loyalty of the masses. Certain "negative" groups had not been won over and were potential dangers: the Communists; the old political leaders who could not accept defeat; the professional agitators who desired "permanent revolution"; and the drones, gossips, and mischief-makers who chatter of intrigue and a new upset. "Only three months ago the party leadership was convinced that it was a case only of irresponsible chatter of political reactionaries, Marxists, anarchists, and all possible sorts of loafers, for which all documentary evidence was lacking." In mid-March Der Führer had ordered a new propaganda wave. But "it was revealed that in the ranks of several high S.A. leaders tendencies had become evident that must give rise to the most serious apprehension. At first there were only general evidences whose inner connections were not apparent at first sight."

Against Hitler's orders and Röhm's promises, the S.A. had been filled with elements bound to endanger its homogeneity. In the upper ranks the Nazi *Weltanschauung* was being forgotten. The relations between the S.A. and the party were beginning to loosen. Promotions were based on knowledge and intellectual ability, instead of on faith and veteran service. New men got high posts. Old fighters were pushed down. The appearance and attitude of new leaders were "un-Nazi-like and revolting." Hitler had called Röhm's attention to these abuses, without result. In April and May complaints multiplied and Hitler received reports, "supplemented by documentary evidence," about conferences "which could be labelled nothing else than gross insubordination. For the first [?] time it was unmistakably proved in several cases that references were made to the necessity for a new revolution and that leaders had received orders to prepare for such a new revolution spiritually and materially." Röhm tried to deny the reality of these happenings and declared them to be veiled attacks upon the storm troops. Witnesses were maltreated. All efforts at reform were in vain. Röhm ignored his promises. Some were arrested, for S.A. and party leaders who indulge in "bad conduct, drunken excesses, and interference with decent, peaceable folk" are "detestable" and must be held to higher standards than other citizens.

In all of this, it may be noted parenthetically, there was nothing new and nothing which could justify what followed. These vague general charges could have been made against the S.A. for many years past. The "second revolution" had been widely talked of more than a year before—as soon as Hitler had betrayed the *Kleinbürgertum* to the industrialists and Junkers. Insubordination—some of it far more "gross" than anything attempted in 1934—had been manifested constantly during the past four years. The Left elements, converted by promises of socialism, had protested and grumbled continuously at Hitler's alliance with Thyssen and big business. As for moral delinquencies, they permeated the Nazi ranks from the beginning. Homosexuality, drunkenness, luxury, and arrogance were not confined to Röhm and his entourage. Hitler's defence must therefore be judged not on these general charges, but on the specific evidence presented of an actual "conspiracy" against him.

"These differences led to a very earnest conversation between the Chief of Staff and myself, in the course of which, for the first time, doubts arose in my mind concerning the loyalty of this man. After I had rejected every such thought for many months and after I had previously for years protected this man with my person in unshakable faithful comradeship, warnings now began gradually to fill me with apprehension which, with the best of will, I was unable to rid myself of. These warnings were especially uttered by my deputy in the party leadership, Rudolf Hess.

"Since May there could no longer be any doubt that Chief of Staff Röhm had engaged in ambitious plans which, if carried into effect, could only lead to the most serious convulsions."

Der Führer presented no evidence here save "warnings." He declared that he hesitated to act because he could not believe that Röhm's loyalty was a "delusion" and because he hoped for a settlement without an open clash. He reverted again, at this point, to general charges. A "terrible realization" came to him that homosexuals were being promoted—only terrible, apparently, when Röhm resorted to it, not terrible when Hitler had resorted to it repeatedly in earlier years. This "sect" constituted a "nucleus for plotting." Orders were disregarded. Three S.A. groups developed: "elements held together by common abnormality and blindly in the hands of Röhm"—for example, Ernst, Heines, Hayn, and Heydebreck (Ernst was not a homosexual, and Hayn and Heydebreck were doubtful)—a second group which felt bound in duty to obey Röhm; and a third group repelled by the first and therefore demoted or ignored—for example, Lutze and Himmler (Lutze had always been a nobody, and Himmler belonged to the S.S., of which he was Reichsführer, not to the S.A.). Then:

"Without ever informing me, and without my even so much as having an inkling of it, Chief of Staff Röhm entered into relations with General von Schleicher through the mediations of a thoroughly corrupt mountebank, Herr von A—. General von Schleicher was the man who gave outward expression to the innermost wish of Chief of Staff Röhm. It was he who concretely put into language and defended the conception, first, that the present German régime was untenable; secondly, that, above all, the Reichswehr and all patriotic societies must be concentrated in one hand; thirdly, that the only man destined for this task could be none other than Chief of Staff Röhm; fourthly, that Herr von Papen must be removed and he (Schleicher) would be ready to take the position of Vice-Chancellor, and beyond that, several essential changes must be made in the Reich Cabinet.

"As always happens in such cases, they now began a search for men for a new government, always under the assumption that I myself would at least for the immediate future be retained in my position.

"Fulfilment of these proposals by General von Schleicher had necessarily to meet opposition on my part, which could never be overcome as regards Point 2. It would never have been possible for me, either factually or humanly, to give consent to a change in the Reichswehr ministry and to fill the post with Chief of Staff Röhm."

Here in comment it may be said that Röhm and Schleicher probably had contacts, in view of Schleicher's tentative plan of January 29, 1933, for a Left military dictatorship based on the army and the trade unions, and in view of Röhm's ambitions to secure control of the Reichswehr. Whether Alvensleben was the go-between is dubious. Why Hitler should conceal his name and call him "a thoroughly corrupt mountebank" is unclear. For Röhm to discuss possible Cabinet changes was not treason by any reasonable definition of the term. Hitler here sought to indicate why he could not permit control of the army by any party leader: His policy was to keep the army and the party separate; Röhm's character made him unthinkable as Minister of Defence; Hitler had promised Hindenburg "to keep the army as a non-political instrument"; he trusted Blomberg. "There are obligations of loyalty which one may not and should not violate." Here Der Führer was concealing his real reason for blocking Röhm's military ambitions: his intimate alliance with the East Prussian Junkers who dominated the Reichswehr.

Next Hitler came to the "plot." Röhm was uncertain of Hitler's reception of his overtures. He therefore made "large-scale preparations" to create systematically psychological conditions for the outbreak of a second revolution by spreading reports that the Reichswehr planned the dissolution of the S.A. and that Hitler had agreed to this plan. "A grievous and infamous lie!" (That the Reichswehr high command desired the reduction of the S.A. to a negligible quantity and that Hitler, if forced to choose between the army and the S.A., would yield to the former is not open to debate.) Second, the S.A. plotted to remove reactionary elements and seize supreme power in the State. Third, financial preparations were made. "Chief of Staff Röhm succeeded in diverting amounts running into millions through camouflaging—that is, by putting out the lie, among other things, that he wished to carry out social relief measures for the storm troopers. Twelve million marks were collected for this purpose." (No proof of this was offered.) Fourthly, terror groups or "staff guards" were formed of paid mercenaries with criminal records. (Again no proof; most S.A. leaders were paid mercenaries with criminal records.) At conferences and on vacation trips leaders were brought together.

"That means that while leaders of the inner set were carefully preparing the real action, the second circle of S.A. leaders only received information in general terms to the effect that the second revolution was before the door, that this revolution had no other aim than restoring freedom of action to me, and that therefore the new, and in this case bloody, uprising—'the night of the long knives,' as it was gruesomely described—was in accordance with my own wishes."

Of this likewise no proof was offered, only simple affirmation. "Foreign political preparations for this action were placed in the hands of Herr von Detten. General von Schleicher partly conducted the foreign political game personally and partly he had his courier, General von Bredow, translate it into practical politics. Gregor Strasser was invited in." No proof whatever was produced to support these statements. The charge against the mysterious "foreign Power" was withdrawn.

"In the beginning of June I made a last attempt, by inviting Chief of Staff Röhm to come to me once more, for a conference of nearly five hours, which dragged on until midnight. I informed him that I had the impression from countless rumours and numerous attestations and declarations of old faithful party members and S.A. leaders that conscienceless elements were preparing a national Bolshevist action that could bring nothing but untold misfortune to Germany. I told him further that rumours had come to my ears concerning an intention to include the army within the circle of these plans.

"I assured Chief of Staff Röhm that the claim that the S.A. organization was to the dissolved was a filthy lie; that I could not even express myself concerning the lie that I myself had in mind to undertake measures against the storm troops, but that I would personally and immediately thwart every attempt to have chaos come upon Germany and that anybody who attacked the State must count me among his enemies.

"I adjured him for the last time voluntarily to abandon this madness and instead lend his authority to prevent a development that, in any eventuality, could only end in disaster. Again I raised the severest objection against the accumulation of impossible excesses and demanded that these elements be completely eradicated. . . .

"Röhm left me with the assurance that these rumours were partly untrue, partly exaggerated, and that he would do everything possible to put things right. The result of our conversation, however, turned out to be that Röhm, realizing he in no circumstances could count on me for his scheme, now started preparations to eliminate me personally.

"For this purpose the larger circle of S.A. leaders who had been drawn upon was informed that I myself was quite agreeable to the undertaking envisaged by them, but that I personally must not know anything about it or that I had a wish to be taken into custody twenty-four or forty-eight hours at the outbreak of the uprising, in order to be relieved by the accomplished fact of unpleasant embarrassment that would result for me from the foreign political point of view, in case this did not happen to me.

"This declaration finds its last illustration in the fact that meanwhile, as a precautionary measure, the man had been hired who was to carry out my later removal: standard-bearer Uhl confessed only a few hours before his death his unwillingness to carry out such an order."

Again no proof was given. Julius Uhl was a member of Röhm's personal staff. To what had he confessed? This was the only reference in the whole situation to any "confession." None was ever published. All of the victims of the purge professed their innocence, though a few, under torture or in the hope of escaping death, may have made the kind of statements desired by their captors.

Hitler next referred to the S.A. vacation as part of the plot. During the leave "tumult of undefinable extent was to break out," compelling Hitler to entrust Röhm with supreme power to restore order. (There is not the slightest shred of evidence to support this allegation. On the contrary, Röhm resisted the "vacation" order.) There was to be a "sudden surprise attack on government buildings" in Berlin. Hitler was to be arrested and further action taken in his name. "Röhm, Ernst, Heines, Hayn, and others have stated before witnesses that they planned a bloody fight, lasting several days, with those against them. The question of who would pay for it all was waved aside with crazy recklessness and the suggestion that bloody terror would furnish the means somehow or other."

No witnesses were named. No statements were reproduced. That Röhm had any such naïve scheme in mind is most improbable. In any case, declared Hitler, Röhm had lost all right to speak for "pure Nationalsocialism" because his life had become "miserable." Bredow, as foreign political agent of Schleicher, spread the impression, in the foreign press, that a new revolution was imminent. This completed the marshalling of the "evidence" of a conspiracy.

"I therefore determined, at the end of June, to put a stop to this impossible development, and that, too, before the blood of tens of thousands of innocents was to seal the catastrophe. As the danger and tension upon all was fast becoming unbearable, and as certain party centres and State offices had to take defensive measures, as was their duty, the peculiar lengthening of the service before the stormtroop vacation seemed a questionable proceeding to me and I therefore decided, on Saturday, June 30, to dismiss the Chief of Staff from his office, take him for the time being into custody, and arrest a number of S.A. leaders whose crimes were clearly proved.

"As it was doubtful whether Röhm, in view of the acute situation, would come to Berlin or elsewhere, I decided to proceed myself to the leaders' conference at Bad Wiessee. Building upon the authority of my person and my power of determined action, which has never deserted me in case of need, I intended to dismiss the Chief of Staff at noon, arrest the chief culprits among the S.A. leaders, and recall the others to their duty by an urgent appeal."

This plan was modified by "threatening news" received on June 29.

"At 1.00 a.m. I received two alarming news reports of the most urgent kind from Berlin and Munich: First, that a state of alarm had been ordered for Berlin for 4.00 p.m., that for the transportation of the real shock formations a requisition of motor lorries had been ordered and was already in progress, and that at 5.00 p.m. action was to begin by the seizure of government buildings. Group Leader Ernst had for this reason not gone to Bad Wiessee, but had remained behind in order personally to conduct the action in Berlin. Secondly, the alarming of the S.A. in Munich had already been ordered for 9.00 p.m. The S.A. formations were not permitted to go home, but were sent to their alarm quarters. That was mutiny, for the commander of the S.A. is myself and nobody else."

Here Der Führer, knowingly or unknowingly, indulged in patent misrepresentation. The "alarming reports" came, of course, from Göring, possibly aided by Hess and Himmler of the S.S., who perceived an opportunity to make the liquidation of the S.A. the means to their own supremacy. No evidence whatever, save Hitler's allegations, supports this story about "motor lorries" or the "Munich alarm order." Röhm was asleep after a party on the eve of the "great revolt." Karl Ernst was *not* invited to Bad Wiessee and did *not* remain behind in Berlin. He was indisputably in Bremen, about to depart on his vacation. Here Hitler either lied deliberately or believed Göring's lies without investigating them.

"Under these circumstances there could be but one resolve for me. If disaster was to be averted, action had to be taken with lightning-like rapidity. Only a merciless bloody stroke could perhaps smother the spreading revolt. Better that a hundred mutineers, conspirators, and plotters should perish than that ten thousand harmless S.A. men and ten thousand equally harmless citizens on the other side should pour out their blood. For if the criminal Ernst's action had been allowed to start in Berlin, the consequences would have been unthinkable.

"How the play with my name worked was shown by the alarming fact that these mutineers succeeded in Berlin, by using my name, in obtaining from unsuspecting police officers four armoured cars, and Heines and Hayn had made police officers of Saxony and Silesia waver by calling on them to decide between S.A. and anti-Hitlerites in the coming crash. Thus it became clear to me that only one man could and should face the Chief of Staff. He broke his faith with me, and I alone could call him to account.

"At 1.00 a.m. I received the last alarming dispatches. At 2.00 a.m. I flew to Munich. Premier Göring had meanwhile already received orders from me in advance. In the event of action for purification, his part was to take analogous measures in Berlin and Prussia. With an iron fist he beat back the attack upon the Nationalsocialist State before it fairly got started. . . .

"In this hour I was responsible for the fate of the German nation; thereby the supreme court of the German people, during these twenty-four hours, consisted of myself."

With Hitler as the court, this tale was plausible. Before any other court it could not possibly stand. Der Führer repeated the lie about Ernst. The news of the "mutiny" had come at the last minute. But, by Hitler's own admission, he had given orders to Göring "in advance." He concluded with further excuses and details. He, too, pitied the widows and orphans, but German womanhood in general must be protected. A "foreign diplomat" averred that his meeting with Schleicher and Röhm was harmless. "I do not have to discuss that with anybody. Opinion as to what is harmless and what is not will never agree in the realm of politics. If, however, three traitors in Germany agree to meet a foreign statesman and carry this agreement out, and themselves designate it as 'service,' and if they keep the servants away and give strictest orders to keep the meeting secret as far as I am concerned, then I let such men be killed, even if it should be true that in the course of a conference that was thus kept from me the participants allegedly spoke about nothing other than the weather, old coins, or similar things."

Who was killed? According to Hitler: 19 higher S.A. leaders; 31 S.A. leaders and members; 3 S.S. leaders; 13 S.A. leaders and civilians who "resisted arrest"; 3 suicides; 5 party members; and 3 S.S. men who maltreated prisoners. Total—77. There was no mention of names, no reference to those shot "by accident," to the Catholic leaders, to Papen aides, to the victims of personal revenge, to the hundreds of others who were wiped out in the purge. "Normal conditions were restored on the night of July 1. A number of deeds of violence that were not in any way connected with this action will be turned to the normal courts for trial." Der Führer assailed the foreign press for its lies, declared that the mutineers planned to murder Papen and Seldte, who were in no way connected with the revolt, denied that he had had a nervous collapse, and reasserted his confidence in the storm troopers.

"I am ready before history to take the responsibility for twenty-four hours of the bitterest decision of my life, during which fate has again taught me, in anxious worry, to cling with every thought of mine to the dearest thing we possess in this world: the German people and the German Reich." [1]

Such was Hitler's case. It bears a striking resemblance to the Reichstag fire charges against the KPD, save that the mistakes there made were not repeated. On the 14th it was announced that no "White Book," no list of names, no further details would be issued —to save the families of the victims from disgrace, said Göring. The incident was closed. The co-ordinated German press waxed lyrical over Hitler's "stupendous speech" and over his masterly vindication. No documentary evidence of any of Hitler's allegations had appeared by the end of the year. There was none. To invent some was too dangerous. There were no public trials of anyone involved. That too would be dangerous. Hitler's own apologia was a tissue of insinuations, misrepresentations, and lies. There had been no conspiracy. Göring had simply disposed of his rivals. The S.S. leaders had climbed to ascendancy over the corpses of the S.A. leaders. Hitler, in a state of hysterical apprehension, had been used by these ambitious adventurers to serve their own purposes.

For the rest, the secret "reorganization" of the S.A. proceeded apace. Some groups were dissolved, many surviving leaders were dismissed, and many special administrative and control agencies of the S.A. were suppressed. A special party court martial, dominated by the S.S., continued to sit in Munich and to expel S.A. members. Hess issued new warnings. Those denouncing S.A. men anonymously for personal revenge were reproved. On July 29 Lutze appointed Dietrich von Jagow as Ernst's successor in Berlin, thus relieving Daluege of his temporary duties. No official figures have been issued as to the extent of the reduction in S.A. membership. On July 20, in an address at Halle, Göring declared:

"Always Der Führer is the strongest. For that reason the people love him. The people know that he is just and charitable, but also has an iron hand. For that reason the people trust Der Führer. This

[1] Translation of text as given by AP, July 14, 1934.

trust is the bond that holds Germany together.

"Der Führer accomplishes great deeds out of the greatness of his heart, the passion of his will, and the goodness of his soul. Trust in him is alone the basis for our life. When anyone dares to touch our faith in him, then he must be destroyed. Such a one has ceased to be a German.

"Storm trooper or Minister, we are all the creations of Der Führer. Only one thing matters—that Der Führer has faith in us. His faith makes us the most powerful of men. If he removes his confidence, we are nothing, we are plunged into darkness and lost to the memory of man, for Germany is Adolf Hitler."

4. OMNIPOTENCE

On August 2, 1934, Hindenburg died. He had been failing in health all summer. On July 31—the day of the hanging of Otto Planetta, the Austrian Nazi who murdered Chancellor Dollfuss in the ill-fated putsch of July 25—the physicians at Neudeck warned the German public that it might fear the worst. The eighty-six-year-old President, long afflicted with atrophy of the prostate gland, suffered an apoplectic stroke during the night. Hitler summoned the Cabinet members to Berlin. Lutze ended the S.A. vacation and summoned the storm troopers back to service, with all restrictions removed. Discussion of the succession was discouraged. Under the constitutional amendment of December 1932, which had been sponsored by the NSDAP, the President of the Supreme Court (Erwin Bumke), rather than the Chancellor, would temporarily succeed the Reichspresident in the event of his death. This law remained unchanged. Rumours had long been current as to the Old Gentleman's plans for his successor. As early as September 1933 it was reported that Hindenburg favoured the abolition of the presidency and the creation of a *Reichsführer,* for which post he apparently preferred some Hohenzollern prince or perhaps Franz von Papen. On August 1 Hindenburg lapsed into unconsciousness. The Cabinet met in emergency session at 9.30 p.m. No statement was issued, but it was believed that Hitler would himself take over the presidency. He called at Neudeck during the night. At 9.25 the following morning Hindenburg expired without reawakening. It was announced that at the Cabinet session a law had been promulgated combining the functions of the Chancellor and the President into a *Reichsführerschaft*.[1] In a letter to Frick, Hitler declared:

"The necessity for regulating the question of the chief of State, caused by the national misfortune that has overtaken our people, leads me to issue the following order:

"First—the greatness of the deceased has given to the title of Reich President unique and non-recurring significance, according to the feeling of all of us, and, in what it meant to us, this title is indissolubly bound up with the name of the great deceased. I therefore request that care be taken, in official and unofficial communications, to address me just as heretofore, as Führer and Reich Chancellor only. This stipulation is to be observed in the future also.

"Second—I desire that the vesting in my person, and thereby in the Reich Chancellor's office as such, of the functions of the former Reich presidency, decided upon by the Cabinet and constitutionally valid, shall receive the expressed sanction of the German people.

"Steeped in the conviction that all authority of the State must proceed from the people and by them be ratified in a free, secret election, I request you immediately to lay the decision of the Cabinet, with possible necessary additions, before the German people for a free plebiscite."[2]

With the approval of the Cabinet, the plebiscite date was fixed for August 19. The ballot contained the text of the new law, with the question: "Do you, German man, and you, German woman, approve of the arrangement made in this law?" Two circles followed, headed by "*Ja*" and "*Nein*." The plebiscite was announced by Hitler twelve hours after the issuing of the decree conferring upon him the President's powers. All members of the army were at once required to take a new oath of obedience to Adolf Hitler as Commander-in-Chief. Thus, within a month after Röhm had been killed—among other reasons for desiring to subject the Reichswehr to Nazi party control—Hitler took full charge of the war establishment. The S.S.

[1] "1. The office of Reich President is herewith united with that of Reich Chancellor. In consequence, the authority of the Reich President is herewith transferred to Der Führer and Reich Chancellor, Adolf Hitler. He designates his deputy. 2. This law becomes effective from the moment of the death of Reich President von Hindenburg." (*The New York Times*, August 3, 1934.)

[2] Translation from AP dispatch, August 2, 1934.

leaders also took a new secret oath to the Reichsführer. Hitler told the Cabinet that he had lost a "fatherly friend" and sent condolences to Oskar. At the same time Schacht succeeded Schmitt as Minister of Economics, and Papen, though technically retaining the vice-chancellorship, was provided with a graceful exit from the political scene: he was sent as "special envoy" to restore "friendly relations" with Austria, whose Chancellor had just been murdered by the NSDAP. Papen was permitted to see Hindenburg in death, though all his efforts to visit him during July for the purpose of tendering his resignation had been blocked.

Hindenburg's funeral was made the occasion for another grandiose display of pageantry. The family agreed to his burial in the great war memorial at Tannenberg, which was elaborately decorated for the occasion. On Monday, August 6, Hitler addressed the Reichstag in the Kroll Opera, amid flowers, dimmed lights, and music. He eulogized Hindenburg, "the symbolic expression of the indestructible and ever nascent vitality of our people," whom "Almighty God had taken under His protection" for almost eighty-seven years. Without this man Hitler would never have become Chancellor. But this he did not say. Instead:

"We bow humbly before the Inscrutable Will which, with things that appear to be accidental or even inconsequential, serves in moulding life in a manner that the investigative mind of man only afterwards sees and recognizes in the entire wonderful necessity of their interrelationship."

He reviewed Hindenburg's life in terms of the events of 1847 and the development of Europe in the nineteenth century.

"Here I fulfil no duty by making the truthful assertion when, before the German people and deeply moved with gratitude, I refer to the immeasurable service which the Field Marshal General rendered historically by reconciling in his name the debt in Germany's past with the passionately yearned-for better German future. From the hour that I, as Chancellor of the Reich, was privileged to swear the oath into his venerable hand, I felt in ever increasing measure what a bountiful fate it was that gave us this fatherly, kindly patron.

"Like a mystic arch of light, this figure stands from the confused revolution of 1848 over an incredibly long way to the national resurgence of the year 1933. The German people can only be happy over the disposition of fate that placed its most German resurgence under the protection and patronage of its most venerable nobleman and soldier. . . .

"Let the strong realization enter our hearts: the Herr Reich President Field Marshal General von Hindenburg is not dead. He is living. For in dying he now wanders above us, amidst the immortals of our people, surrounded by the great spirits of the past, as an eternal patron and protector of the German Reich and the German nation." [1]

In the evening the funeral cortège moved out of Neudeck toward Tannenberg, sixty-five miles away. Six black horses slowly drew the gun-carriage bearing the flag-draped coffin through lines of torch-bearers until it was transferred to a motor carriage accompanied by infantry and artillery. Torches lighted the way all along the route. On Tuesday the impressive final ceremonies took place in the courtyard of the war memorial at Tannenberg, where the Hindenburg legend was born. All leading notables were present, save only Ludendorff—as well as thousands of worshipping pilgrims. Following an address by a chaplain, emphasizing Hindenburg's loyalty to Kaiser and Reich, to people, to Fatherland, and to God, Hitler delivered the funeral oration:

"It was due to the miraculous move of a mysteriously wise Providence that under President von Hindenburg preparations for the national uprising could be initiated and that finally he himself could still live to open the gates to Germany's rejuvenation. In his name was forged the tie that united the vigorous strength of the uprising with the best talent of the past. As Reich President the Field Marshal became protector of the Nationalsocialist revolution, and therewith of the regeneration of our people. . . .

"Departed General, enter now into Valhalla!"

To the music of the *Horst Wessel Lied,* the Field Marshal, who had served his Junkers so well and who had delivered Germany to Fascism, was laid to his final rest. His wife's body was subsequently moved from Hanover to the Tannenberg Monument. Oskar resigned from the army on September 24 and retired from public life. On November 30 Professor Leisegang of Jena was sentenced to six months' imprisonment for referring to Hitler's address as an "election speech."

Ten hours after the burial the ingenious Goebbels broadcast from

[1] Translation from AP dispatch, August 6, 1934.

records Hindenburg's appeal of November 1933 for electoral support of Hitler. It was the opening gun of the referendum campaign. Two days later Hitler decreed an amnesty for all minor political and criminal offenders. The campaign opened officially on Monday, August 15. It was brief but intensive. Unanimity was again demanded to convince the world that the régime had the overwhelming support of the people. Goebbels's address of Monday evening in Neukölln was a condemnation of the foreign press and a personal eulogy of the Chancellor, who, he said, did not begin the day by asking what the Bourse or the bankers say, but who compelled the Bourse to ask: "What does Hitler say?" Göring, Hess, and Frick spoke elsewhere.

On August 15 it was announced that Papen had delivered Hindenburg's "political will" to Hitler before departing for Vienna. The will was dated May 11, 1934. Almost half of it consisted of a "will" which Hindenburg had written to the German people in 1919. "We were finished. Just as Siegfried fell under the treacherous spear of the evil Hagen, so our wearied front broke down. . . . [But] the blood of all those who have fallen, believing in Germany's greatness, has not been shed in vain. In this faith I lay down my pen and put my whole confidence in you—the youth of Germany." The balance of the will was a defence of his policies as President and a eulogy of the Reichswehr. The document closed:

"My Chancellor, Adolf Hitler, and his movement have taken a decisive stride of historical importance toward a great goal of leading the Germany people to inner unity, regardless of differences of rank and class. I know much remains yet to be done, and from the bottom of my heart I wish that the act of the national regeneration and unification may be followed by an act of reconciliation to embrace the whole German Fatherland.

"I part from my German people in the firm hope that what I wished for in 1919 and led in gradual process to January 30, 1933, will ripen to full fruition and the completion of the historical mission of our people." [1]

This final paragraph was received with skepticism in London and Paris, though Papen insisted upon its authenticity. It was alleged in certain quarters that the original will had named the Kaiser as Hindenburg's successor and had named Papen as Chancellor. These

[1] Translation from AP dispatch, August 15, 1934.

provisions, it was said, were deleted and the final paragraphs rewritten by Goebbels. But most of the German electorate accepted the will as another endorsement of Hitler by Hindenburg. The Reichsführer spoke in Hamburg on August 17, in a conciliatory vein, making all possible pleas for a unanimous acclamation of himself in the referendum. He averred that the hostility of the world toward the Third Reich had compelled him to assume the President's powers at once.

"Even my most vicious maligners will admit I never wavered or faltered in this fifteen-year fight. Whether at liberty or in jail, I stuck to my colours, which today are the flag of the Reich. Nor can they prove that I committed or omitted a single political act for reason of personal gain, and they must finally admit that this battle has not been without success; out of a movement of humble origin there has emerged a victorious revolution, one that has brought the German people a new and better standing, both at home and abroad.

"I gladly assume responsibility for such mistakes as may be charged to me. They fall within the scope of human frailty. But I have never committed a deed or an act which I was convinced would not rebound to the benefit of the German people. Ever since I first stood in the thick of this political battle, I have been actuated by only one motive—so help me God—only one thought: Germany!"

On the eve of the election the press declared that only scoundrels and traitors would dare to vote "No." The result was as follows:

REFERENDUM OF AUGUST 19, 1934 [1]

Eligible voters —	45,474,157
Total votes cast —	43,530,232
"Yes" —	38,368,195
"No" —	4,294,727
Invalid —	872,310

The endorsement was overwhelming, but less overwhelming than the year before. The spoiled "invalid" ballots were for the most part gestures of protest, since the ballot was extremely simple and the percentage of spoiled ballots was unusually high. Combined with

[1] *Wirtschaft und Statistik*, XIV, p. 552.

the "No" votes, they gave a total of 5,167,037 voters who dared to express disapproval—12 per cent of the electorate. The "No" vote alone was 10.1 per cent of the total, as compared with 5.0 per cent on November 12, 1933. In Berlin the "No" vote was heavier in the bourgeois than in the proletarian quarters. The rural vote was almost solidly affirmative. Cologne led the country in its opposition vote, with only 78.7 per cent of the electors voting "Yes." Hamburg was next, with 79.5 per cent, and Berlin third, with 81.5 per cent. The negative vote was impressive throughout the Rhineland. *Der Angriff* asked tartly: "What is the matter with the 'No' voters? Why did they leave the wide highway of the nation and take to the bush?" Hitler promised to win "every remaining citizen to Nationalsocialist ideals and doctrines." But all in all, with nearly 90 per cent of the electorate still disposed to support him, whether through conviction, fear, or despair, Hitler had little cause for apprehension.

A week later Goebbels foreshadowed the winter relief campaign by glorifying sacrifice, suffering, and generosity. Two weeks later the party's great annual congress at Nürnberg opened. Again lack of bread must be compensated for by circuses. Elaborate preparations on a greater scale than ever were made for a gigantic, colossal, stupendous demonstration. Again over half a million party members—770,000 visitors in all—converged on the old city. This Sixth Congress was christened the "Congress of the United Nation." The Reichswehr was prominently featured in the festivities. S.A. was overshadowed by S.S. On September 4, 1934, Hitler opened the sessions in the festival hall of the Rathaus. Otto Dietrich announced to the foreign press that the party had abolished class war and saved the nation: 169 labour organizations, with 7,000,000 members, had been abolished and replaced by the Labour Front, with 29,000,000 members; strikes and lock-outs were unknown in the Third Reich; unemployment was conquered; new building was under way; workers and mothers had vacations; agriculture was prosperous; industry was booming; the national income had risen; crime had decreased; and marriages had increased.

Hitler, on September 5, in an elaborate proclamation read by Minister Wagner, also emphasized the great achievements of the Third Reich ("the German miracle") and declared that it was eternal. Permanent revolution was impossible. Nationalsocialism is a *Weltanschauung*. "The will of the Nationalsocialist government is imperturbable and immovable. The government knows what it wants and wants what it knows." At the Cultural Convention Hitler declared that the ancient Greeks were akin to the Nazis. Jewish intellectualism was dead (again). "Cultural stutterings and stammerings" were ended. "The nervous nineteenth century has reached its end. There will not be another revolution in Germany for a thousand years. . . . If foreigners imagine that the four million 'No' votes constitute a dangerous opposition, they are privileged to smile. . . . Our next attack will demolish the opposition." On September 7 the congress reached its climax when Hitler reviewed 185,000 party functionaries and a torch-light parade ten miles long. On the 9th Hitler reviewed 136,000 storm troopers and Schutzstaffel men, absolved them of all blame for the events of June, and declared that "Nationalsocialism stands firm together with its S.A. and S.S." On September 10 the congress adjourned after military manœuvres and sham battles. Hitler was again elated by the wide acclamation, the dramatic parades, the cheering throngs, the smiling children, the old women weeping for joy at a glance from the Reichsführer.

"It is wonderful," he said to a foreign correspondent. "To know that one is thus carried on by the love of one's people helps a public man over many dark hours. But one can keep the affections of a people only if one works continually with them. They must ever be won anew. One must never lag." [1]

In all this there was nothing new—no new program, no new idea, no new solutions for the Reich's economic problems—only the old clichés, the old pageantry, and the old mysticism. But it still wove its spell over the masses—almost, if not quite, as effectively as ever.

The Nazi dictatorship entered quietly upon its second winter. Hitler again greeted seven hundred thousand peasants in the great harvest festival at Bückeburg on September 30. On October 9 he opened the winter relief campaign, warning the rich to give more than the poor. A superficial veneer of prosperity concealed symptoms of disillusionment. Politically all was calm. Rumours of rifts between Hitler and Göring and between Schacht and Goebbels were denied and denounced. Papen remained Vice-Chancellor *in absentia*. Hitler appointed no one as his deputy in his capacity as Reichsführer, though Hess remained his party deputy. Göring, Hess, and Blomberg were

[1] AP dispatch, September 10, 1934; cf. *News in Brief* (Deutscher Akademische Austauschdienst), No. 17 (September 1934).

spoken of as a triumvirate to succeed him, should he become incapacitated. Hitler was secure, with popular support still overwhelming under the spell of a magic which neither bloodshed nor privation had yet been able to break. The powers in his hands, undreamed-of by the most despotic of autocrats, seemingly assured his control of the Reich for life. His position was well described by Dr. Lammers, Secretary of the Chancellery: [1]

"There is no need for a constitution regulating the conduct of affairs of State; at any rate, there is no need for a written constitution. One thing suffices in the Nationalsocialist State: a fanatical will, based on faith in the principle of leadership and loyalty to Der Führer and those whom he leads, to possess a German State which will unite all Germans in a national and social community. . . .

"The union of the offices of Reichspresident and Chancellor after the death of President von Hindenburg meant a lapse of the electoral provisions of the Weimar Constitution and of responsibility to the Reichstag. Political and moral responsibility to the people has now taken its place. The new law has also abolished the constitutional provision prescribing the term of office of the Reichspresident. Herr Hitler has joined the functions of the President with those of the Chancellor and holds the joint offices for the period of his life."

But the omnipotence of Der Führer did not of itself furnish a solution of the problems with which he was confronted. The liquidation by terror of the socialistic "Left opposition" did not remove the necessity of combating rising prices and of criticizing and regimenting the industrial plutocracy for the purpose of maintaining, to some degree at least, the fiction that the dictatorship was serving the interests of workers and consumers. Dr. Karl Goerdeler was appointed Reich Price Commissar on November 5, 1934. He assumed full control over all cartels. "Superfluous" middlemen were threatened with extinction. Producers and merchants who sought to raise prices were denounced as bitterly in the party press as consumers who hoarded produce in fear of inflation or further increases in prices. Competitive price-cutting was likewise forbidden. These efforts to "freeze" the price structure were not conspicuously successful.

Such measures did not meet with the general approval of German Big Business. Industrial and financial circles were alternately alarmed and reassured by the government's course. At the end of November

[1] *The New York Times,* October 21, 1934.

Julius Streicher and his chief aide, Karl Holz, took over the Strauss department store in Nürnberg and converted it into a semi-public corporation. The fact that the former owners were denounced by Streicher as "Jewish bastards" did not wholly allay the apprehensions of large Aryan retailers. The NSHAGO, however, declared that this was a "purely local" development and did not foreshadow any general elimination of private department stores. Business was further reassured by the report of the commission of inquiry on banking, made public on November 29. It flatly rejected all thought of nationalizing the banking system and merely suggested certain administrative reforms. The new decrees of December 4, on the other hand, increased governmental control over credit transactions, reduced the number of stock exchanges from 21 to 9, limited cash dividends to six per cent, and required the diversion of excess corporate earnings into a forced loan fund. The announcement of these measures led to a marked slump on the stock market. Krupp resigned as president of the Reichstand der Industrie and was succeeded by Ewald Hecker. At the same time Thyssen went to South America "to look after his private interests." These events suggested increasing dissatisfaction in upper bourgeois circles with the economic policies of the Fascist State.

By way of counterbalancing these tendencies and conciliating the industrialists the party radicals were subjected to new repressions. On December 4 Helmuth Brückner, Governor of Silesia, was deposed by Hitler, ousted from his various posts, and expelled from the party. He was succeeded by Joseph Wagner as Silesian regional leader of the NSDAP. On December 6 Gottfried Feder, author of the party program and the party "catechism," was likewise compelled to relinquish his various offices and go into retirement, presumably because of the opposition of Schacht, Krupp, and Thyssen to his anti-capitalistic tendencies. Two weeks later the conservative Hans Frank became Minister without Portfolio in the Reich Cabinet. On December 30 it was announced that Walter Darré's radical agrarian organ, the *Deutsche Zeitung,* and Ley's Labour Front journal, *Der Deutsche,* would both suspend publication on January 1. Darré fell under a shadow. Ley, in a chastened mood, declared in the New Year's Day issue of the *V.B.* that the "corporate State" envisaged in Point 25 of the program could not be realized in the near future.

These developments represented further triumphs of the conservative business elements in the party leadership over the social radicals. They were accompanied by a grant of still wider powers to Hjalmar Schacht. On September 7, 1934, he forbade the establishment of any new financial institutions until the end of 1936, thus giving a monopoly to the existing banks. He fostered credit expansion, but rejected all proposals for currency inflation. For the purpose of evading payment to Germany's creditors abroad, he had reduced the gold holdings of the Reichsbank from 882,383,000 marks in March 1933 to 74,973,000 marks by September 1934, when the note coverage stood at 2.1 per cent. But the fictitious "gold standard" was nevertheless adhered to. *"Federgeld"* was relegated to the limbo of forgotten things along with its inventor. Schacht also became supervisor of the Reich Chamber of Business, established on December 4, 1934 as a central union of all chambers of commerce, industry, and trade. He appointed Hecker as his immediate subordinate. The new organization was hailed in business circles as marking the end of interference with private enterprise by party radicals and as creating an effective counter-weight to the Labour Front. Hitler seemed disposed to grant Schacht dictatorial powers in the economic sphere. Schacht was perfectly acceptable to most of the business community.

The role of guardian of monopolistic industry and finance required Hitler to exercise constant viligance lest the remaining national Socialists in the party seek to upset the status quo. The Labour Front was kept under firm control. After January 1, 1935, youths under twenty-five could be employed in enterprises only with the consent of the Employment Office. The introduction of compulsory universal labour service was planned for the spring, under conditions approximating military conscription. The further reduction of the S.A. proceeded quietly during the course of the winter. The more "reliable" storm troopers were absorbed into the S.S. or the Reichswehr. On December 17 secret police and S.S. men arrested six hundred people in Berlin and its environs for "immorality." The victims included many S.A. homosexuals. The eventual elimination of the S.A. as a significant political and military factor in the régime seemed assured.

Meanwhile rivalry between the S.S. and the Reichswehr reached disturbing proportions. Heinrich Himmler and Baron Werner von Fritsch became rivals for Der Führer's favour, with the Junker high command insisting that the Reichswehr alone must be the arms-bearer of the nation. On January 3, 1935, Hitler summoned a secret conclave of party, army, and government leaders in the State Operahouse in Berlin, under the chairmanship of Hess. This new "demonstration of solidarity" was allegedly called "to combat foreign lies." It was accompanied by a new and violent campaign against the foreign press. The meeting was in fact designed to reassure the Reichswehr and to restore harmony between the S.S. and the regular army. Amid much mystery and many rumours, it was reported that Fritsch and other high Reichswehr officers exacted an admission from Hitler that Schleicher had been innocent of treason. It was likewise reported that the S.S. would be disarmed. In any case Der Führer bowed to the Reichswehr. Again he sacrificed the interests of the party to the demands of the feudal-military ruling class which had helped to place him in power. The S.A.-S.S. feud was apparently not to be followed by an S.S.-Reichswehr feud if Hitler could avoid this by liquidating his special guards as he had already liquidated his storm troopers.

At the beginning of its third year of power the dictatorship was thus in process of becoming, even more obviously than before, a régime dominated by Big Business, *Hoch Finanz,* the Junkers and the Reichswehr. The anti-aristocratic and anti-capitalistic *Kleinbürgertum* in the NSDAP was being pushed farther and farther away from the seats of power. The resulting disillusionments and resentments were being intensified by the progressive impoverishment of the subjugated proletariat. Growing popular unrest threatened to reflect itself in new feuds between the mercenaries or in new clashes between the party leaders and their disgruntled followers. More violence, reprisals, and repressions were in the offing. But so long as Hitler and his aides continued to serve the interests of the old ruling classes with some degree of success, it seemed improbable that these tensions and disturbances would seriously undermine the régime.

5. THE THIRD YEAR AND BEYOND

A HUNDRED years ago Germany's greatest Romantic poet, Heinrich Heine, spokesman of liberalism, foresaw the ultimate results of that reactionary, militaristic fanaticism which drove him out of his Fatherland into exile. With uncanny insight he predicted the anti-rationalistic paganism and the war-mad megalomania of the Third Reich. One of the passages in the first volume of his literary history of Germany will bear careful re-reading today:

"The philosopher of Nature will be terrible because he will appear in alliance with the primitive powers of Nature, able to evoke the demoniac energies of old Germanic Pantheism—doing which there will awake in him that battle-madness which we find among the ancient Teutonic races who fought neither to kill nor to conquer, but for the very love of fighting itself. It is the fairest merit of Christianity that it somewhat mitigated that brutal German *gaudium certaminis* or joy in battle, but it could not destroy it. And should that subduing talisman, the Cross, break, then will come crashing and roaring forth the wild madness of the old champions, the insane Berserker rage, of which the Northern poets say and sing. That talisman is brittle, and the day will come when it will pitifully break. The old stone gods will rise from long-forgotten ruin and rub the dust of a thousand years from their eyes, and Thor, leaping to life with his giant hammer, will crush the Gothic cathedrals! But when those days shall come and ye hear the stamping and ring of arms, guard ye well, ye neighbours' children, ye French, and put not forth your hands into what we are doing in Germany, for verily evil will come upon you for that. Beware lest ye blow the fire, and take good care that ye do not quench it; ye can in so doing all too easily burn your fingers. . . .

"There will be played in Germany a drama compared to which the French Revolution will be only an innocent idyll. . . .

"You have more to fear from Germany set free than from all the Holy Alliance with all the Croats and Cossacks. . . . I have the kindest feelings for you, and I was almost alarmed when I read lately that your Minister proposed to disarm France.

"For, despite your present Romanticism, you are born classics, you know Olympus well. Among the naked gods and goddesses who there make merry over nectar and ambrosia, you may see one goddess who, though surrounded by such festivity and gaiety, ever wears a coat of mail and bears helmet on head and spear in hand. It is the Goddess of Wisdom."

In the third year of the Third Reich the Goddess of Wisdom gave ill counsel to Germany's neighbours. But the Nazi dictatorship moved perceptibly nearer to that day of fury which Heine prophesied.

Intolerance and war are concomitants of every Fascist régime because of Fascism's inability to resolve the economic dilemma of its own creation. In 1935 Italian Fascism shrank from the abyss of bankruptcy and launched a war of glory and desperation against Ethiopia.

In 1935 German Fascism drifted closer to the same destination. The economics of monopoly continued to effect a temporary enrichment of the classes and a permanent impoverishment of the masses. Popular unrest was met by terror and by intensified anti-Semitism. A breakdown continued to be averted by huge expenditures of public funds. When the wells of credit should run dry in another two or three years, there would loom State bankruptcy, disastrous inflation or catastrophic deflation, undermining the psychological and political foundations of the dictatorship. Before that day the dictators would take the sword against the neighbours of the Reich as the only remaining means of protecting themselves from their own subjects.

The economic impasse of Fascism [1] was reflected less in Germany's international-trade situation than in the condition of domestic business. By the close of 1934 heroic measures to restrict imports and promote exports had achieved an approximate equilibrium in foreign commerce and halted the outflow of gold. But in the early months of 1935 imports increased again and exports slumped to unprecedentedly low levels. The total unfavourable balance for the first half of the year was 163,900,000 marks, as compared with 297,000,000 marks for the entire year 1934. This critical situation led to new restrictions on imports and to the adoption of a billion-mark subsidy scheme to increase exports. By the close of 1935 a favourable balance of 124,200,000 marks had been obtained, with annual exports totalling 4,269,600,000 marks and imports 4,145,400,000 marks. This "miracle" of Dr. Schacht was achieved by continued transfer moratoria on foreign debts, the repurchase at greatly depreciated prices of German securities held abroad, large subsidies to exports (ranging from twenty-five to fifty per cent of the purchase price and financed by a levy on German industry as a whole), and rigid limitations on imports, especially of foodstuffs.

In the internal business situation were to be found clearer indications of the economic consequences of Fascism. The apparent recovery of some degree of prosperity was due less to any restoration of normal markets than to large government orders and subsidies. While the significant details of the Reich's budget are no longer made public, it was officially conceded that expenditures for the fiscal year 1934–5 totalled 8,220,500,000 marks, as against receipts of 7,806,500,000 marks,

[1] Cf. pp. 417–19 above, and M. T. Florinsky: *Fascism and National Socialism* (New York: Macmillan; 1935).

leaving a deficit of 414,000,000 marks. But the ordinary budget did not include special expenditures for public works and armaments, roughly estimated at 17,000,000,000 marks from July 1932 to June 1935. These sums were raised by short-term public loans, only a portion of which were acknowledged as part of the public debt. These "frozen" obligations were forced upon banks, insurance companies, and other corporations. In the rigidly regimented Fascist economy of the Reich, government spending did not promote a recovery of private capital investments to any appreciable degree, despite Nazi appeals to business to rely upon private enterprise rather than upon government orders. While it was clear that the "State boom" could continue to be financed for some time by forcing government notes on credit institutions, it was equally clear that a definite limit to this process must sooner or later be reached.

The exact size of the German public debt cannot be estimated with any degree of accuracy. The *Institut für Konjunktur Forschung*, in its report of November 13, 1935, contended that public spending had increased the government debt by only 4,340,000,000 marks, bringing it to a total of 29,800,000,000 marks by June 1935. It likewise denied allegations that the actual debt was over 40,000,000,000 marks and asserted that "the present German public indebtedness is not excessive." But all such estimates must be received with caution. The decrees of early December 1934 limited corporation dividends to six or eight per cent and required that all additional earnings be turned over to the Gold Discount Bank for investment in government loans. On February 21, 1935, the Ministry of Finance was authorized to float a billion-mark loan to convert short-term obligations into long-term bonds. A billion-mark loan at 4½ per cent was announced on August 23. Despite pressure on potential lenders, increasing though unadmitted difficulties in borrowing were apparently being encountered by the close of the year. Foreign borrowing was precluded by past defaults. Tax revenues, while increasing with more and heavier levies, offered no promise of ultimate solvency without a restoration of privately financed prosperity. This seemed impossible without a prosperous domestic market endowed with sufficient purchasing power to take the place of government orders and subsidies. Without this the Nazi State faced the dilemma of government bankruptcy versus inflation or deflation.

Symptoms of a decline in the "State boom" became apparent during 1935. Each year the rate of business recovery was slower. Each year it was clearer that the recovery had no sound basis in enhanced consumer purchasing power. But so long as government spending continued, there was a measure of temporary recovery. The increased profits of industry tempered the resentment of employers against Nazi bureaucratic control. Dr. Schacht continued to enjoy Der Führer's confidence and to protect business from the anti-capitalistic party radicals. In an address of November 30, 1935, he asserted that "nothing more urgently demands a capitalistic basis than a modern army. Guns, airplanes, submarines—everything belonging to modern defence—are unthinkable without the highest industrial development in a capitalistic sense. . . . The urge for acquisition is and remains the natural foundation of all economic life; it remains the strongest spur for economic achievement. . . . The State must not engage in business itself."[1]

But the protection of profits at the expense of wages meant a progressive decline of living-standards, which in turn threatened further depression when government orders should diminish. German labour had little share in the new "prosperity." Its chains hung heavy. In February 1935 it was announced that the unemployed would be reduced to 800,000 by driving women and young workers from the labour market. On June 26 the long-promised compulsory labour service was decreed by the Cabinet, with six months of service required of all youths at the age of nineteen. German labour continued to enjoy vacations arranged by the Strength Through Joy Organization of the *Arbeitsfront*. The hungry shared in the blessings of the annual winter relief drives, with tin cups on every street corner, collectors in every theatre, office, and apartment building, and irresistible pressure put upon the poor to save those still poorer from starvation. Wage-earners continued to be treated to great labour festivals. May Day of 1935—"the Festival of the Nation"—found the usual millions marching through the slush and listening, with dampened enthusiasm, to the usual speeches about "honour," "duty," "national solidarity," and the "beauty of sacrifice." "We shall not rest until we give to the last German his daily bread," bellowed Hitler on Tempelhofer Feld. But he made no mention of the anticipated promises of wage increases. "Demonstrate to the world your faith in your people and your State. My will must be your confession. I serve my people with my life."[2]

[1] *New York Times,* December 1, 1935. [2] *V. B.,* May 2, 1935.

In actuality the economic status of the German workers continued to decline. By the end of January 1935 the number of officially registered unemployed had increased by 705,000 since October to a total of 2,973,000. By the end of July the total was again reduced to 1,754,000. The increase in unemployment in the winter of 1935–6, however, was the largest recorded since the establishment of the régime. In December the ranks of the jobless were swelled by 522,000, the largest monthly increase since 1932. By the end of January 1936, 814,000 workers had lost their places since September. The total of 2,520,000 was almost half a million smaller than the corresponding figure for 1935, thanks to military and labour conscription, but it was evident that the ultimate goal was farther than ever from attainment.

More significant than the relative decline in the rate of re-employment was the steady rise of prices and the progressive impoverishment of proletarian and petit-bourgeois consumers. Dr. Karl Goerdeler, Reich price commissar, fought valiantly but in vain to prevent price increases. The rise was retarded by the arrest of butchers, bakers, and grocers, but not halted. By August 1935 soaring prices of foodstuffs, accompanied by actual shortages of some commodities, caused Walter Darré to decree arbitrary reductions in retail prices of pork, beef, lard, tallow, veal, potatoes, and cheese. Joseph Buerckel, new Governor of the Saar, warned that "peasant blood has its obligations. The greed of individuals who disgrace the whole peasant class will become a crime unless this insanity is stopped. . . . Increases in food prices mean a reduction in the standard of living, especially for the wage-earner. This produces bitterness."[1] An acute shortage of butter and fats developed in the autumn. Göring mobilized the *Gestapo* in December to combat "passive or open resistance of individual peasants" and compel butter and milk deliveries at fixed prices. "Sabotage of this milk delivery," he declared, "is treason to the people's nutrition and also to the nation and Fatherland." Even the favoured peasantry was thus obliged to pay the price of Fascism.

Goebbels pompously informed the indignant hausfraus: "We are making history, not butter!" On January 17, 1936, he made a plea for the return of the German colonies and declared: "When one does not know how a nation is to be nourished in the long run that fact becomes eventually a threat to the whole world. . . . We can get along without butter, but never without cannon." According to of-

[1] *New York Times,* August 29, 1935.

ficial figures, in many communities the retail prices of beef and pork in January 1936 were 23 per cent above the figures for the preceding year, of veal 38 per cent, of ham 40 per cent, and of beef filet 70 per cent. Retail trade suffered and the consumption-goods index began to fall below the producers' goods index. During 1935, as compared with 1934, Germans consumed less meat, sugar, coffee, fruit, clothing, and household goods and more beer, cigars, radios, and automobiles. Champagne-consumption tripled since 1932. In short, the rich were better able than before to purchase luxury goods and the poor were less able to buy the elementary necessities of life. In the fifty-five largest cities there were only 217,252 marriages in 1935, compared with 252,863 in 1934. The birth-rate had also begun to slump by the end of the year, despite Nazi inducements to matrimony and reproduction. For these problems the Academy of Reich Planning, established in October 1935, seemingly had no solutions.

While the economic dilemma suggested by these tendencies made a major social and political crisis ultimately inevitable, this crisis did not assume acute form during the third year of the dictatorship, nor did it seem likely to during the fourth. The NSDAP could still protect itself by strengthening its grip upon all the instrumentalities of power in the Reich. Growing dissatisfaction could still be met through more savage persecution of scapegoats, more fanatic inculcation of racial and national conceit, and accelerated preparations for the final bloody catharsis of war.

A review of the political developments of 1935–6 reveals no major changes of policies or personnel in party or government.[1] The liquidation of the S.A. proceeded apace, until the party storm-troopers were reduced to a purely ornamental role. In February 1935 it was indicated that the S.S. would be reduced and reorganized, with only 20,000 out of a membership of 200,000 permitted to carry rifles. On November 16, 1935, Heinrich Himmler announced that only a special branch of the S.S., estimated at 12,000, would carry arms—for the purpose of fighting Communism, exercising police functions in war-time, and keeping watch over the S.A. and the Reichswehr. The rivalries between the various semi-military political organizations of Germany were further reduced by the final liquidation of the Stahlhelm or N.S. Front Fighters' League. Friction between the remnants of the Stahlhelm and of the S.A. increased in the spring of 1935.

[1] For an excellent brief treatment of the constitutional system, see Fritz Morstein Marx: *Government in the Third Reich* (New York: McGraw-Hill; 1936).

On August 8 the *Gestapo* announced the suppression of the Stahlhelm branches in Berlin, Brandenburg, and Pomerania, simultaneously with the dissolution of the remaining Masonic lodges in the Reich. Five days later Hitler received Seldte, Stahlhelm commander, at Berchtesgaden, but such pleas as the Minister of Labour may have made only served to delay the end. On November 7, 1935, the Chancellor decreed the complete dissolution of the organization. The members submitted to their extinction as an organized group as meekly as the Students' corps had done two weeks earlier. On December 21 it was announced that all men who passed through the Reichswehr would be gathered into a non-political "Soldiers' League." Thus the army command not only triumphed over the S.A. and S.S., but secured control of ex-soldiers as well.

Hitler thus yielded once more to the Junker militarists at the expense of his own party organizations, as he had often yielded to the industrialists at the expense of the Nazi radicals. Blomberg and Fritsch remained his liaison with the Junkers, as Schacht was his liaison with Big Business. Here, as always, he exhibited a realistic sense of the actual sources of power in the Third Reich. Der Führer continued to wield his authority with undiminished vigour, despite occasional throat trouble giving rise to rumours, probably unfounded, of cancer or other serious physical disorders. Other rumours had it that Hess, Göring, and Blomberg were to become the ruling triumvirate, should Hitler be incapacitated.[1]

Since eternal vigilance is the price of dictatorship, the NSDAP intensified espionage and repression in the face of a slowly rising tide of disillusionment. Catholics, Communists, monarchists, liberals were under the unsleeping eye of the *Gestapo* at all times. Following extensive raids on alleged traitors of Catholic or Communist persuasion in the Rhineland, the State secret police was empowered on February 12, 1936, to issue orders directly to civilian authorities. Its acts were in law, as well as in fact, removed from the possibility of review by the administrative courts. By the new decree the *Gestapo*, still commanded by Himmler, head of the S.S., was placed under the joint control of Göring, as Premier of Prussia, and Frick, as Minister of the Interior.

Prominent among the new measures of repression was a series of

[1] The most comprehensive life of Hitler thus far published is Konrad Heiden's *Adolf Hitler—Das Zeitalter der Verantwortungslosigkeit* (Zurich: Europea Verlag; 1936).

decrees aimed at non-Nazi newspapers. In April 1935 Max Amann, president of the Reich Press Chamber and director of the Eher publishing house, issued orders designed to eliminate from the world of journalism those who would "degrade the newspaper to a mere business." An "Ordinance for Safeguarding the Independence of the Newspaper-Publishing System" required that papers must henceforth be published only by individuals or partners, with verified Aryan ancestry back to 1800, and no longer by anonymous stock companies. All publishers and editors, save those of the party press, were made subject to appointment and dismissal by Amann, Another "Ordinance for Closing Newspaper-Publishing Concerns to Eliminate Unhealthy Competition" authorized Amann to suppress papers competing with the party press. A third "Ordinance for the Removal of the Scandal Press" prohibited papers damaging the "dignity of the press."[1] Rosenberg naïvely explained these ordinances by saying that the party press had been under an economic disadvantage in competing with other papers. By the end of the year many surviving non-Nazi papers had been forced out of business.

Brutal and ruthless punishment of "enemies of the State" continued under a thinly disguised judicial terror. Minister of Justice Guertner outlined the new penal code in May 1935. "The criminal shall again learn to tremble before just punishment," asserted Hans Frank, the guiding spirit of the legal regeneration. The new code was based upon tribal loyalty to "the German community of blood and destiny." Wide latitude was allowed for penalizing offences not specifically defined in the code. Treason was made "the most dastardly crime." In the spirit of the new jurisprudence, one German out of every 203 was imprisoned between June 1933 and June 1934, 212 were beheaded, 184 were "shot while attempting to escape," 49,000 were sent to concentration camps, and 280,308 received court sentences of one kind or another. Figures for 1935 and 1936 are not yet available, but will no doubt reveal even more impressive totals. Humanitarian opinion in the west was especially shocked by the beheading on February 18, 1935, of Baroness Benita von Falkenhayn and Frau Renate von Natzmer for high treason, the more so as Baron George von Sosnowski, the Polish officer who was ringleader of the espionage group of which the two women were members, was given a life sentence and later exchanged for a German spy in Poland. Periodical decapitations of Communists continued. The number of arrests, im-

[1] *V. B.*, April 25, 1935.

prisonments, and executions increased with the spread of unrest in the autumn and winter.

Short of war, however, the sovereign remedy for popular dissatisfaction in the Third Reich continued to be anti-Semitism. The beating of the Nazi drums of racial hate grew ever louder as prices rose and living-standards declined. On December 13, 1934, Julius Streicher announced his discovery that "the blood corpuscles of Jews are quite different in form from those of Nordics. . . . Sexual intercourse between a Jew and a non-Jewish woman must be punished with death."[1] On his fiftieth birthday the arch-priest of anti-Semitic pornography was visited by Hitler, who declared: "I am happy to know I have in Julius Streicher one man on whose whole-hearted support I can rely in every situation." The Reich Health Office protested to Der Führer over Streicher's efforts to abolish vaccines and serums (another of his remarkable discoveries was that the Wassermann test was devised by Jews to secure Christian blood for ritual purposes), but Streicher's star was in the ascendancy. He staged an international anti-Semitic Congress in Nürnberg early in May 1935. Late in June, at a pagan fire-ceremony for the Hitler Jugend on Hesenberg mountain, Streicher called upon the German youth to dedicate itself to hatred of the Jews, to avoid priests and confessions, to come to him for absolution of sin, and to make the next war a world crusade against Jewry.

The new campaign assumed violent form in the summer. On the night of July 15, 1935, Nazi rowdies beat up numerous Jews on the Kurfürstendamm in Berlin. Under the eyes of the idle police, men and women were assaulted and kicked bloody and unconscious. Similar disorders followed on ensuing days. On July 19 the violent anti-Semite and terrorist Count Wolf von Helldorf was appointed Police President of Berlin to succeed Admiral Levetzow, after Streicher had been considered for the post. This step was taken, said the official pronouncement, to ensure "intimate co-operation of the police, S. A., party functionaries, and the municipality" in fighting "reactionary plots, Bolsheviki, Jewish usurpations, and Communist conspiracies to undermine the régime." Throughout the Reich persecution of Jews was everywhere intensified.

An outburst of indignation abroad, coupled with the alarms of Dr. Schacht and other business spokesmen, compelled Hitler to discourage open violence against the Jews and to adopt more subtle

[1] Address to the German Jurists' Association in Nürnberg.

methods of degradation. On July 24 Senator William King of Utah suggested that the United States protest by severing diplomatic relations with Germany. Two days later a crowd boarded the liner *Bremen* in New York and tore down the Swastika flag. When Magistrate Louis Brodsky freed the arrested rioters and referred to the Nazi banner as "the black flag of piracy," Ambassador Luther was instructed to protest to the State Department. Secretary Hull tendered a formal apology, but there was no doubt as to the temper of American opinion. Mayor La Guardia of New York denounced the Nazi régime vigorously. After the Massachusetts legislature passed a resolution of censure, Governor James Curley, on August 13, rejected the protest of the German Consul General and asserted that the Nazi persecutions were "abhorrent to right thinking men and women the world over." Though the Nazi press raged at these "insults," Schacht hinted that further disturbances would mean "ruin." The desire of the Nazis to forestall a possible cancellation of the Olympic games of 1936, scheduled to be held in Germany, also contributed to the cessation of open attacks in August. Streicher was permitted to deliver an indecent anti-Semitic harangue in the Berlin *Sport-Palast* on August 15, but Schacht continued his objections, even going so far as to defy Goebbels's censorship.

The result of these developments was the adoption of a definitive policy of driving all Jews out of business, their last refuge, of excluding Jewish children from the public schools, and of reducing the Jews in law as well as in fact to the status of pariahs. Despite Schacht's opposition, many Jewish business men were compelled in the autumn to sell their establishments at nominal prices to Aryans, who were supplied with funds for the purpose through the *Arbeitsfront*. Frick pledged the full support of the State in the liquidation of Jewish businesses, as an alternative to the extermination of the Jews by violence.[1]

The new policy was implemented at Nürnberg in September. The annual conclave of the NSDAP for 1935 was designated as the "Congress of Freedom" to symbolize the breaking of the military shackles of the Treaty of Versailles. Again three-quarters of a million of the faithful descended upon the ancient city and again there were flags, speeches, parades, and ceremonies without end. On September 15 Hitler addressed the Reichstag, called to Nürnberg for the occasion.

[1] Address at Saarbrücken, October 13, 1935.

The Chancellor reiterated his devotion to peace, but threatened Lithuania with punishment for the "robbery" of Memel and denounced Moscow, the Comintern, and the Jews. The obedient deputies unanimously enacted the legislation which Der Führer demanded. The anti-Semitic *Hakenkreuz* banner of the party was made the single official flag of the Reich to avenge the "insult" of the *Bremen* riot. A new swastika war-flag, designed by Hitler himself, was unfurled over all army, navy, and aviation centres on November 7. Other laws deprived all Jews of citizenship, thus at long last fulfilling plank four of the party platform; forbade under severe penalties all marriages and extra-marital sexual relations between Jews and Aryans; prohibited the employment in Jewish households of Aryan female servants under forty-five years of age; forbade Jews to display the national flag; and provided for the exclusion of Jewish children from German schools after March 1, 1936.

This legislation was supplemented by two decrees of November 15, 1935. One, dealing with citizenship, abandoned the familiar distinction between "Aryans" and "non-Aryans" in favour of "Germans" and "Jews." Persons with only one Jewish grandparent (twenty-five per cent Jews) were declared eligible to citizenship. Persons with four or three Jewish grandparents (one hundred per cent and seventy-five per cent Jews) were declared ineligible. Those with two Jewish grandparents might become citizens unless they belonged to a Jewish congregation or were married to Jews or were children of seventy-five or one hundred per cent Jews. The second decree forbade marriages between Germans and Jews. Half-Jews might marry Germans only with the consent of Hess and Frick. Marriages between twenty-five per cent Jews were banned. Extra-marital relations between Jews and Germans were heavily penalized. It was further provided that German female servants might continue to work in Jewish households only if they were above twenty-five years of age. About one million persons were affected by these decrees. With the Jews thus confronted with complete economic ruin and social degradation, the external manifestations of anti-Semitism were somewhat modified in preparation for the Olympic games. Below the surface, however, the "cold pogrom" continued unabated. Mayor Sahm of Berlin was forced out of office in November for having traded at a Jewish store. Hess appealed to the peasant congress at Goslar on November 17 to save the peasantry from "Jewish plots."

The League of National German Jews, pledged to loyalty to National-socialism, was dissolved, and its leader, Dr. Max Naumann, arrested. More "ghetto decrees" followed.

That the new measures would leave the Jews of Germany no alternative save starvation or mass emigration was clear by the close of the year. In tendering his resignation as League of Nations High Commissioner for Refugees from Germany on December 27, 1935, James G. McDonald declared that "the intensified persecution in Germany threatens the pauperization of hundreds of thousands." He called for reconsideration of the whole refugee problem and collective League action to intercede with the Hitler régime.[1] The Nazi press accused McDonald of "prejudice." Plans were broached in January 1936 for a mass exodus of German Jews, to be financed by world Jewry through the sale of German goods abroad, but this scheme of international blackmail seemed unlikely to be accepted. No salvation for the victims of Nazi intolerance was in sight in the spring of 1936. On February 4 Wilhelm Gustloff, Nazi leader in Switzerland, was assassinated by a Jewish student in Davos—the first instance to date of a prominent Nazi leader being slain by a victim of anti-Semitism. Hitler proclaimed Gustloff an "immortal martyr," accused the Jews of all of Germany's misfortunes since 1918, and "accepted the challenge" hurled by "the hateful might of our Jewish foe."[2]

Throughout the third year of the Nazi régime it was increasingly appreciated by the holders of power—albeit dimly and with that warped perspective characteristic of fanatics—that neither terrorism nor persecution would avail to forestall catastrophe when the ultimate disintegration of Fascist economy should become imminent. In the end there would be need for another solution: an imperialist war of aggression, in which again necessity would know no law and a desperate effort would have to be made by the rulers of the Reich to hack their way through by the sword. Preparations for that war served the purposes of the dictatorship in several ways: the militarization of the nation facilitated the maintenance of totalitarian power

[1] *New York Times,* December 30, 1935; cf. Norman Bentwich: *The International Problem of Refugees,* FPA report, February 12, 1936.

[2] The intensified persecution of other scapegoat groups, especially of the Catholic clergy and of the Lutheran opposition, cannot be reviewed here. Cf., for a Catholic view, George N. Shuster: *Like a Mighty Army—Hitler vs. Established Religion* (New York: D. Appleton-Century Co.; 1935).

by the NSDAP; it reduced unemployment and afforded huge profits to the industrialists who supplied the weapons of conquest; it likewise meant jobs and glory for the Junker militarists of the east, whose command of the new army was now unchallenged. In the event of victory, the subjugation of the Danube basin and the Ukraine would further enrich industrialists and Junkers and afford temporary salvation from economic strangulation. In the event of defeat, all would perish in a common débâcle. Collective murder and suicide would exalt the frenzied *Kleinbürgertum,* drunk with the thunder of trumpets and drums, and would resolve the intolerable tensions of minds gone mad. In any case: Forward to Glory!

"To forge a mighty sword," wrote Der Führer in *Mein Kampf,* "is the task of internal political leadership; to protect this forging and to seek allies in arms is the task of foreign policy."[1] To this task the Third Reich devoted itself with extraordinary energy and enthusiasm in 1935–6. The search for allies was apparently unsuccessful. But the Nazi State found it easy to take advantage of the governments of prospective enemy countries, for these governments with few exceptions displayed such disunity, short-sightedness, timidity, irresolution, and panic-stricken impotence in the face of Nazi defiance as to play directly into the hands of Hitler, Rosenberg, Neurath, and Ribbentrop at every turn of events. France was checkmated; Britain was half-converted to collaboration with Berlin; Poland was friendly; Italy was preoccupied with imperial dreams of conquest in Africa. The Nazi diplomats and strategists thus had almost a free hand to do what they would to prepare the Reich for the coming war of liberation. Only two international developments caused genuine anxiety at Berlin: the new Franco-Soviet alliance and the possibility that the League system of collective security, at last mobilized against Fascist Italy, might become sufficiently powerful to halt aggression everywhere. But Moscow was in any case the enemy. And the League powers, despite unprecedented gestures of economic coercion, showed themselves in the spring of 1936 to be still reluctant to pay the price of preserving the Covenant. If Mussolini's defiant bluffing could forestall united and effective action against him, then Hitler could safely count on comparable disunity and acquiescence, at least up to the point of open armed attack.

[1] Cf. pp. 128–9 above.

A brief review of the successive diplomatic crises of the period will substantiate these generalizations. On January 7, 1935, Laval and Mussolini concluded a colonial agreement in Rome (later alleged by Il Duce to constitute French assent to his contemplated attack upon Ethiopia), in which among other things they agreed to guarantee the independence of Austria against the Nazi menace and to oppose any unilateral denunciation by the Reich of the military clauses of the Treaty of Versailles. On February 3 an Anglo-French accord promised Germany equality of armaments on condition that Berlin sign an "air Locarno" with London and Paris, guarantee Austrian independence, accept an eastern Locarno, and return to the League and the Disarmament Conference. Italy, the Little Entente, and the Soviet Union approved of this scheme. In short, the other powers, united in common fear of Nazi arms, were prepared to legalize the increase of these arms if Hitler would promise not to use them for aggression. Sir John Simon prepared to go to Berlin to negotiate. But Der Führer had other plans. In the sequel—worthy of Gilbert and Sullivan, were it not so tragic—Laval and Simon both forgot two basic rules of diplomacy: never offer to sell for a price something which the purchaser can take for nothing; never forbid a rival to do something which he has already done unless you are prepared to stop him by force. Hitler, on the other hand, remembered and applied the rules that one should never pay for something that is to be had gratis and one should never regard a warning as a threat if it is clear that those who warn are unprepared to resort to violence.

On March 16, 1935, Der Führer swept the diplomatic chess-men from the board and hurled his second great thunderbolt, comparable to the withdrawal of the Reich from Geneva on October 14, 1933. Part V of the Treaty of Versailles was openly repudiated by a "Law for the Reconstruction of the National Defence Forces," which reintroduced universal military conscription and provided for the enlargement of the Reichswehr to twelve army corps of thirty-six divisions. The Quai d'Orsay at once moved to dissuade Simon from going to Berlin, to prepare a joint Anglo-French-Italian protest, and to appeal to the League Council. But Simon insisted on going to Berlin regardless, though there was now nothing more to negotiate about. Britain protested independently on March 18, in very mild language, and solicited a renewal of the invitation to the British

Foreign Minister. On March 20 the chagrined Laval presented a separate French protest to Wilhelmstrasse, and Italy did likewise. Germany rejected the protests on the correct assumption that nothing was to be feared. After a week of wrangling the war-time Allies established a semblance of unity through a meeting in Paris on March 23. But the "unity" was without substance.

Simon conferred with Hitler in Berlin from the 24th to the 26th of March, with no result. His Cabinet colleague, Captain Anthony Eden, proceeded to Moscow and established a community of views with Stalin and Litvinov. He likewise visited Warsaw and Prague. On April 11, British, French, and Italian representatives met at Stresa, where it was announced on the 14th that they had agreed to approve common action at Geneva against the Reich. On the same day at the Quai d'Orsay presented an indictment of German treaty-breaking to the League Council. On April 17 the Council unanimously condemned Germany for failing "in the duty which lies upon all members of the international community to respect the undertakings which they have contracted"; decided that the repudiation of treaties should "call into play all appropriate measures on the part of the Members of the League"; and requested a committee of thirteen States to propose economic and financial measures "which might be applied should a State in the future . . . endanger peace by the unilateral repudiation of its international obligations." Such threats were fruitless. Italy was already preparing to repudiate her own obligations toward Ethiopia and the League. Germany denounced Britain's "betrayal" on the 18th and two days later, on Hitler's birthday, rejected the League resolution in a note to the powers. No sanctions followed. The Reich could safely scoff at the "Stresa front."

On May 2, 1935, however, a Franco-Soviet pact was signed in Paris. It provided that if either party were threatened with aggression by any European State, they would consult on measures to enforce Article 10 of the Covenant; that if either were a victim of unprovoked aggression, they would at once come to one another's aid and assistance under Article 16. This was a defensive military alliance within the framework of the League system of collective security, open to Germany and other nations. Czechoslovakia signed a similar pact with Moscow on May 16, and negotiations were initiated for a comparable Soviet-Rumanian pact. Without the adherence of these

States or others adjacent to Germany, the Red army could of course be of no use to France in the event of war. Somewhat sobered by this threat, Hitler adopted a conciliatory tone in his Reichstag address of May 21, promising to respect the other clauses of the treaty, including those relating to the demilitarization of the Rhineland, and offering to conclude non-aggression pacts with all the Reich's neighbours save Lithuania. The U.S.S.R., not being contiguous, was not a neighbour. He also offered to sign a naval agreement, limiting the new German fleet to thirty-five per cent of the British fleet.

Downing Street fell into this trap. On June 18 a British White Paper announced that the new Foreign Minister, Sir Samuel Hoare, and Joachim von Ribbentrop had exchanged notes providing that Germany should have a fleet thirty-five per cent as large as the British, with submarine strength at forty-five or even a hundred per cent, at the option of the Reich. The British government, without consulting France or Italy, thus supported Berlin in scrapping the naval clauses of the treaty. The new Reich navy would, of course, be directed against the Soviet Union. Moscow and Paris objected, but in vain. "Perfidious Albion" has again played Der Führer's game. The Stresa front, moribund at birth, was now dead.

Meanwhile most of the British fleet moved to the Mediterranean with the apparent object of scaring Mussolini out of his African war. But Il Duce, like Hitler, was adept at calling diplomatic bluffs and launched his war in defiance of Britain and the League on October 3, 1935. League economic sanctions against Italy and mounting tension in the Mediterranean were grist for Hitler's mill. Still better, the French government, which for fifteen years had championed League sanctions against aggression, followed the British lead against Italy with the utmost reluctance and delayed ratifying the Soviet pact. Laval was dominated by Fascist sympathizers among French conservatives and reactionaries and hoped to keep the support of one aggressor (Italy) against another potential aggressor (Germany). On December 8 Hoare and Laval concocted a preposterous scheme, in the name of "peace," for the cession of much of Ethiopia to Italy, thus reducing the Covenant and the pretence of collective security to an absurdity. Liberal indignation, to be sure, forced Hoare's resignation on December 18 and led to the fall of the Laval Cabinet on January 22, 1936. Baldwin appointed Eden as Britain's new Foreign Minister. Flandin become French Foreign

Minister in the Sarraut Cabinet. There was still a possibility that the Geneva experiment in sanctions might, in new hands, develop into an effective weapon of defence against aggression everywhere. But with Flandin, like Laval, bespeaking "conciliation" with Mussolini, this prospect grew increasingly remote. The Third Reich could proceed with its preparations for conquest undeterred by Geneva and benefited by the endless bickerings and equivocations among the States committed to peace and the status quo.

The construction of a huge German war-machine proceeded apace. Steel-production boomed. Thyssen's profits soared. Tanks, artillery, bombing planes, machine-guns, rifles, cruisers, submarines, high explosives poured forth from German factories in a flood. The General Staff was reconstituted on October 15, 1935, with General Ludwig Beck as its chief. On November 1 the first class of the new conscripts reported for duty and a new Air War Academy was opened near Berlin. A decree of November 28 made all men between the ages of eighteen and forty-five army reservists. On January 4, 1936, Baldur von Schirach announced plans for the conscription of all German youths between ten and eighteen. Throughout the land war-flags flew, conscripts goose-stepped, battle-planes droned, armoured cars rattled through the streets, and a whole nation forgot its economic problems in an orgasm of super-patriotic militarism. The annual report of the Krupp firm declared that it "had the honour again of filling armament contracts for the government after a long pause in this branch of its activities." Krupp's annual profits for 1935 were 9,700,000 marks, compared with 6,700,000 in 1934. Blue-blooded Junkers rejoiced in the new dispensation no less than hard-headed industrialists.

Hitler's third thunderbolt fell on March 7, 1936. The Chamber of Deputies had at last ratified the Soviet pact, and Berlin had abandoned hope of blocking the new Franco-Russian alliance. On March 2 Eden at Geneva had proposed oil sanctions against Italy if Il Duce refused to make peace. Flandin secured a week's grace for the Roman dictator. Mussolini must accept League conciliation by March 10 or face new penalties. The Italian government, flushed by widely advertised victories over the forces of Haile Selassie, hinted darkly at denunciation of the Locarno treaties and withdrawal from the League. While Hitler had apparently rejected Italian overtures for an "understanding," he saw in the impending crisis another golden opportunity. Should Mussolini, in fear of further sanctions, accept peace, the Stresa front might be reconstituted to Germany's disadvantage. Should Il Duce reject the League "ultimatum" or attach impossible conditions to acceptance, the sanctions system might be developed to a point where it might not only bring Italy to her knees but also become a League weapon against the Third Reich. Berlin, dreaming of a German-Italian-Japanese-Polish-Austro-Hungarian-Bulgarian coalition, could well afford to aid Italy by distracting British and French attention elsewhere and weakening the Geneva adventure in sanctions. Or, if Rome refused all compromise on Austria, Italy too might be contemptuously defied, since Mussolini was now neither able nor willing to act with France and Britain against the Reich. Another dramatic gesture of defiance, moreover, would reawaken waning loyalties to the NSDAP at home and enable Der Führer to score another domestic triumph. There were risks, of course. Anglo-French timidity and lethargy in the face of Fascist aggression might be resolved by a new threat from Berlin, and the net result might be a further development of sanctions. But the probabilities were against this. Hitler had learned to count upon disunity and impotence among his foreign foes, as among his domestic enemies. In any case, the new army could probably already give a good account of itself if the worst came. With his usual political astuteness, Der Führer acted—explosively, dramatically, decisively, but not without shrewd calculations of the consequences.

Before the suddenly convoked Reichstag, on Saturday, March 7, Hitler professed his love for peace, announced the abrogation of the Locarno Treaties of 1925, whereby Britain, France, Germany, and Italy guaranteed the French, Belgian, and German frontiers, and proclaimed the remilitarization of the Rhineland, contrary to Locarno and to Articles 42 and 43 of the Treaty of Versailles. He likewise ordered a new Reichstag election for Sunday, March 29. While twenty-five thousand troops goose-stepped across the Rhine bridges, German patriots once more grew hysterical in a bathos of exaltation and perceived once more that power and glory were to be valued above bread and butter. As in October 1933 and in March 1935, the whole nation rallied to the régime, hypnotized anew by the old clichés and ready to follow Der Führer wherever he might lead. Were Hitler's *Volksgenossen* dissatisfied, resentful, disillusioned with Nationalsocialism? Let them hate and hound the Jews. And let them all, including those insufficiently permeated with the Nazi *Weltanschauung* to enjoy Jew-baiting, hurl hatred and defiance against Frenchmen and Russians, against liberals and Communists, against Bolshevism and the damnable *Diktat von Versailles.* And let them glory in guns and marching soldiery and learn again to love and obey the State which gave them these pleasures.

His voice choking with emotion, tears flowing down his cheeks, his fists beating the air, his crescendos arising anew to hoarse delirium Hitler wove his old spell as he addressed the deputies in the Kroll Opera:

"*Pflicht und Ehre! . . . Freiheit und Brot! . . . Frieden und Gleichberechtigung!* . . . I do not want the horrors of communistic international dictatorship and hate to descend upon the German people. There is deep tragedy inherent in the fact that as a conclusion to our sincere efforts, covering many years, to win the confidence, sympathy, and affection of the French people, a military alliance should be concluded whose beginnings we know today and whose end, however, will be attended by unpredictable consequences unless indeed Providence once more again proves more merciful than men deserve. . . .

"The Russian army has a peace strength of 1,350,000 men, it encompasses 17,500,000 in war strength in reserve, it is equipped with the greatest tank weapons in the world, and has the greatest air force. . . .

"In this historic hour, when in the western provinces our German troops are at this moment moving into their future garrisons of peace, we all unite in two holy confessions.

"First, in a solemn oath to recede before no power and no force in re-establishing the honour of our people, and rather to succumb honourably to the heaviest privation than ever capitulate before it.

"Secondly, in a determination now more than ever to help bring about understanding among peoples of Europe, especially among our western peoples and neighbours.

"Thus, after three years, I believe I can consider with today the fight for German equality as concluded."

Hitler's blow was no less a political masterpiece from the point of view of the international situation than from that of mass psychology in the Reich. A long, legalistic memorandum was transmitted to the powers, arguing that the Franco-Soviet alliance was a violation of the Rhine Pact of Locarno on the part of France. Germany was therefore released from her obligations. At the same time the Reich made a series of ingenious "peace" proposals: Germany was willing to join France and Belgium in a twenty-five-year non-aggression pact, guaranteed by Britain and Italy, and in an arrangement for a bilateral demilitarized zone on both sides of the frontiers; Germany was willing to sign a non-aggression pact with her eastern neighbours, including Lithuania, but, of course, excluding the U.S.S.R.; Germany was willing to return to the League of Nations and to negotiate at Geneva for colonial equality and for the separation of the Covenant from the Treaty of Versailles. Hitler probably had no expectation that these overtures would be accepted, for at the Quai d'Orsay there were still a few realists. Bilateral demilitarization of the frontiers would require the scrapping of the new French and Belgian border fortresses, built at enormous cost, and would open all northern France and Belgium to the German armies. A promise of non-aggression for twenty-five years could mean nothing. Hitler had promised Treaty fulfilment in October 1933 and had torn up Part V of the Treaty sixteen months later. Hitler had promised to respect the demilitarization of the Rhineland in May 1935 and had openly violated it ten months later. Such pledges were meaningless to Paris.

But they would win a certain degree of British and Italian sympathy. Hitler calculated that neither pacific Britain nor embittered Italy, penalized by League sanctions, would support France and Belgium in any military moves against the Reich, even though Article 4 of the Rhine Pact (the Treaty of Mutual Guarantee of 1925) required them, in the event of a breach of Articles 42 and 43 of the Treaty of Versailles, to come immediately to the assistance of France and Belgium. Paris and Brussels would probably not resort to military reprisals alone. Poland was reassured. In his Reichstag address Hitler once more disclaimed any designs on the Corridor. If the German proposals were by some miracle accepted, Germany would be secure in the west and would have a free hand in the Danube valley and against the U.S.S.R. If they were rejected, nothing would follow save verbal denunciations, and German troops would again stand guard on the western frontiers. On the same day Mussolini "accepted in principle" League conciliation in the Ethiopian war, on condition that continued hostilities, generous Italian annexations, and the reduction of Ethiopia to helplessness were assured. While Flandin denounced the German move as "a hostile act," Rome scoffed at French indignation against Berlin (not without some anxiety over Austria and the Brenner Pass) and offered "co-operation" in return for an end of sanctions. London saw "hope" in the German suggestions. France was alone. The Geneva system would be weakened, perhaps fatally. The loyalty of the Little Entente to Paris would be shaken by French inaction. Poland's doubts as to where her future lay would be resolved. The whole French bloc would suffer a damaging loss of prestige. Italian and German Fascism would be the beneficiaries. Only Fascist dictatorships can act resolutely, ruthlessly, without regard to world opinion. Democratic governments must be tentative, open-minded, conciliatory, solicitous of peace. If short-run solicitude for "peace" should inhibit reprisals until *Der Tag* when the Reich should be ready to strike, so much the worse for liberalism.

As these pages go to press it seems clear that Hitler's calculations were once more correct. Another overwhelming victory in the referendum of March 29 was certain. French and Belgian threats remained impotent gestures, wholly inadequate to stop the Nazi war-machine in its inexorable march. Having thrice successfully defied the western powers and created the weapons of military conquest, the Third Reich would now find allies. A coalition of the unsatiated Fascist powers would emerge to confront the *status quo* bloc, since the States committed to peace and security lacked courage and determination to crush the menace while it could still be crushed. In its death-agonies Fascism would destroy European civilization in a second world war, to be initiated at a time and on terms chosen by the aggressors themselves. Forward to Armageddon!

6. THE WAY OF FASCISM

ORACLES of despair and enemies of the NSDAP addicted to wish-fulfilment thinking could, at the close of the third year of the dictatorship, point to many elements in the German situation which promised failure and ultimate collapse. The economic dilemma was wholly unresolved. For the masses it threatened further maladjustments and crises, accompanied by greater privations and lower living-standards; for the classes—smaller profits, less security, and something akin to economic strangulation. That the inexorable pressure for markets would lead to a bold policy of imperialistic aggrandizement at the first favourable opportunity seemed probable. The favourable opportunity drew ever nearer. Within the Reich the aristocracy, the plutocracy, and the peasantry remained fairly content with the régime. In the still enchanted masses of the *Kleinbürgertum* and the proletariat symptoms of disillusionment were beginning to appear. Unrest and potential opposition were increasing. Under these circumstances, those bent upon predicting ruin for the Third Reich could find much support for their prophecies of doom.

On the other hand, the extraordinary capacity of the German masses for asceticism and for self-hypnosis offered assurances that the régime would be secure for several years—barring catastrophic accidents and "acts of God." The revolution had constituted no catharsis for the neuroses of the *Kleinbürgertum*. The mass orgies of paranoia and megalomania had generated symbolisms and patterns of behaviour which were likely to be permanent until shattered by some world-shaking, nation-destroying convulsion. The persistence of hallucination and fantasy promised to set at nought the predictions of those historical materialists who perceived in the economic dilemma of the Third Reich the "inevitable" seeds of its own destruction. This dilemma merely threatened impoverishment, economic and cultural decline, dangers of international conflicts, a prospect of possible collapse in war, or a certainty of a long retrogression in peace toward a simpler, poorer, more brutal, and more mystical mode of life.

Only a social revolution can destroy the Fascist State. Only an upheaval in which the power of the ruling classes is permanently broken by mass revolt from below can offer hope of weakening the grip upon the sources of power of the totalitarian dictatorship. The new absolutism is the only possible form of power for the plutocracy and the aristocracy in the age of monopoly, since it protects their interests far better than any imaginable alternative. The Fascist State can therefore be destroyed only by a political movement aiming at the destruction of the classes which called it into being. Such a movement can probably come only from the ranks of the least-privileged class in the community—that is, the proletariat.

An effective proletarian movement aiming at social revolution is not yet on the German horizon. The KPD, now driven underground, accepts the view of the situation here suggested. But the false conviction of its leaders that the democratic bourgeois State was as much their enemy as the Fascist bourgeois State, and that Fascist dictatorship would "inevitably" be followed by Communist dictatorship, prevented them from opposing Fascism effectively while there was still a possibility of mass action. This failure to act can be readily "explained" in terms of "Social Democratic treachery," of trade-union lethargy, of mass paralysis even among the ranks of the KPD itself. Social Democracy, not Communism, had in its hands the instruments of proletarian power. But the Socialist leaders were still hypnotized by liberal bourgeois conceptions of "legality," long outgrown by the bourgeoisie. They failed to use these instruments in their own defence. This failure, too, can be "explained" in terms of "Communist treachery," financial weakness, and collective impotence. The explanations, however, are irrelevant. An autopsy over a corpse may lead to accurate and logically satisfactory deductions about the condition of the deceased. But for the patient who has expired it is a poor substitute for a diagnosis and a cure.

The German proletariat has been reduced to helplessness. Its political and economic organizations have been destroyed. Its revolutionary symbolism has been suppressed. Its revolutionary leaders have been slain or imprisoned. Are revolutionary sentiment and action likely to be revived on a mass scale among German wage-earners in the years ahead? The progressive impoverishment of the proletariat offers a prospect of disenchantment and radicalization. But impoverishment is a poor preparation for a struggle for power. Social revolutions are made by classes which are economically ascendant, not by those doomed to a permanent place at the bottom of the social pyramid. In war mere weight of numbers means nothing. Organization, discipline, enthusiasm, unity, determination, ingenuity, generalship, resources are decisive. These are the qualities which are conspicuous by their absence in such revolutionary proletarian circles as still remain articulate in the face of Nazi repressions and diversions. The scattered remnants of Social Democracy still continue to think and act in terms of a restoration of "democracy." The vestiges of the KPD are without effective means of infusing revolutionary sentiments into the working masses. The two groups are still at odds, fighting, as it were, inside of the coffin in which they have been buried by their common enemy. The future may bring changes here. The present offers no hope of early resurrection.

It must be remembered, moreover, that even a well-organized, disciplined, revolutionary proletariat cannot, of itself, initiate a social revolution with any chance of leading it to a successful conclusion. The economic and military power of the enemy classes must first be broken. In all recorded instances of proletarian revolutions which have achieved some measure of temporary success, the plutocracy and the aristocracy have been demoralized by catastrophic defeat in foreign war—for example, the Paris Commune of 1871, Russia in 1905 and 1917, Hungary and Bavaria in 1919. In each of these cases a portion of the shattered military forces of the State went over to the revolutionary cause. Even under these circumstances victory is impossible unless other major social groups rally to the proletariat. Only in Russia has such a final victory been won. Here the lower middle classes were small and weak, and the peasants fought with the workers for the revolution. Elsewhere such attempts have been drowned in blood by the old ruling classes, supported passively, if not actively, by the peasantry and the petty bourgeoisie.

It follows that the reappearance of a large, well-organized, revolutionary labour movement in the Third Reich would constitute but the first step toward the overthrow of Fascism by social revolution. The *Kleinbürgertum* would have to be won away from its stubborn, if pathetic, allegiance to the NSDAP. The peasants and rural workers would have to be permeated sufficiently with revolutionary symbolism to prevent their rallying to the defence of the status quo. With these allies a revolutionary proletarian party (which must necessarily be Communist, not Social Democratic) might build up a powerful underground organization, convert urban labor to its cause, and secure considerable support among other segments of the population. If such a party developed an able leadership, if it did not shrink from terrorism at crucial junctures, if it evolved some Lenin capable of accurate political analysis and gifted with a genius for knowing when to retreat, when to advance, and how to hold his followers together, a German social revolution to overthrow Fascism might be possible . . . *if* the unity of the NSDAP were broken, *if* the armed forces of the State were disintegrated, and *if* the moneyed and landed élite were shattered by some swift and relentless national catastrophe.

While it is idle to speculate about the physiognomy of events not yet conceived in the womb of time, it is clear that for the immediate future none of these developments is in the least probable. The German peasantry, for all its reduction to semi-serfdom, is relatively prosperous under Nazi protection. It shows few signs of being won to the cause of revolution by the only slogan which could possibly appeal to it effectively: that of the expropriation and division of the Junker estates. The *Kleinbürgertum,* despite its betrayals and frustrations, is indissolubly wedded to the ideology of property and profits. It continues to identify itself emotionally with the values of its social superiors. It will probably remain loyal, to the bitter end, to any régime committed to the championship of profits and property, of morality and religion, of the Church and the home. Even in the event of its ultimate reduction to the economic level of the proletariat, its own symbolic definition of itself as a class superior to workers and akin to the plutocracy, at least in aspiration, will probably persist for decades. No historical instance has yet been recorded of the lower middle classes being converted to the cause of proletarian revolution. In Russia this group had to be exterminated along with the nobility and the *haute bourgeoisie*. But in any case the first step toward the end of Fascism has not yet been taken in the Reich. There is no revolutionary labour movement worthy of the name, save in the imagination of émigrés and exiles.

This is not to say that the Nazi dictatorship may not undergo new "crises" and experience bloody and revolutionary transformations. Unrest will reflect itself in intra-party rivalries. Some socialistic radicals still survive in party posts despite "Bloody Saturday." S.S. and Reichswehr remain rival aspirants to military ascendancy. In the absence of other effective means of reconciling differences, terror will remain the ultimate political weapon. After June 30 it will be clear to all leaders in the next major convulsion that victory and life itself require one to shoot first and to shoot straight, as the only alternative to the crematory. If tensions are aggravated and new deprivations breed new aggressions, a long vista of periodical massacres and assassinations may stretch out before the NSDAP. But it seems safe to assume that money and guns will remain in the hands of those who best serve the industrialists and the Junkers. The social and economic bases of the dictatorship will be only slightly disturbed by these homicidal outbreaks at the top of the political hierarchy. If these be its only dangers, the dictatorship may survive for generations.

Should this come to pass, life in the Third Reich as in other Fascist States will doubtless become something quite different from anything known in the western world for several centuries. The nation will become economically self-contained, poor but secure, like a new mediæval manor on a larger stage. Technological development and scientific discovery will at first be intensified to provide substitutes for goods once imported, and will then fall into decay. There will be no market in which to sell the output of new machines, and what remains of the home market must be conserved by preventing further technological unemployment. Population will become stationary and will then slowly decline. A new caste system will emerge. Each citizen will be bound to his job and will have only such rights and obligations as the members of his vocation possess. Economic freedom and motility will disappear completely, giving way to mediæval patterns of hereditary professions and guilds. The monopolistic economy will be "frozen." Wages, rents, interest, and even profits will be rigidly fixed by law and tradition. Social relationships of contract will again give way to relationships of status. Mass poverty and exploitation will again become customary, though the new Robots, unlike the wage-earners of the early nineteenth century, will doubtless receive as much consideration as masters of serfs and slaves have always given to their human property. In government Cæsarism will once more be buttressed by mass religiosity. The multitudes will play no part in the feuds of the *condottieri*. Resentments will be discharged or sublimated through racial intolerance, religious bigotry, folk-pageantry, mysticism, and witchcraft.

Must such a social order perish because it would be subversive to all progress? The very idea of "progress" is already dying in the western world. It is in process of being replaced by the values of security and immobility in an economy which will be static and unadventurous. Must such a social order decay because it leaves mankind without hope? Comparable social orders have survived for centuries in the decadent periods of many civilizations—ancient Egypt, the Byzantine world, the late Roman Empire, modern India and China, and the "dark ages" of western culture. Hope of salvation is offered beyond the grave. In the world of mortals there are dreams—and a low level of material security in a society in which each knows his place. Science and machine technology may cease to be dynamic forces of social change. Man may "conquer the machine" at last. In the perspective of the centuries such a pattern of social organization as is here suggested may well be regarded as "normal." The libertarian, productive, restless, unstable, "progressive" age of the West between the sixteenth and the nineteenth centuries was perhaps but an episode, leaving behind a bright memory of cultural values and material achievements, but doomed like all its predecessors to vanish into the shades. Other satisfactions, reminiscent of the thirteenth century or of the ninth, will replace those current during the period between Adam Smith and Hjalmar Schacht, between Jeremy Bentham and Alfredo Rocco, between Jean Jacques Rosseau and Alfred Rosenberg. The new mediævalism will afford perhaps richer spiritual and æsthetic fare to those who survive to eke out a bare existence in the new age of poverty than that to be derived from "modernism" by the unstable, neurotic personalities of the early twentieth century. In the words of Giovanni Gentile:

"Fascism embodies what may be called its own characteristics: namely, taking life seriously. Life is toil, effort, sacrifice, hard work; a life in which we know perfectly well there is neither matter nor time for amusement. . . . Fascism is war on intellectualism. The Fascist spirit is will, not intellect. . . . Fascism is and should be an enemy without truce or pity, not against intelligence, but against intellectualism, which is a disease of intelligence. . . . For intelligence too is will, and Fascism at least feels this, disdaining the culture that is an ornament or adornment of the brain and longing for a culture by which the spirit is armed and fortified for winning ever new battles. And this may be, this should be, our barbarity, a barbarity, moreover, of intellectuals! Against science and above all against philosophy; but, of course, against the science and philosophy of decadents, of the spineless, of those who always stand at the window and are satisfied to criticize as if it were no affair of theirs! . . .

"Fascism is art. . . . Certainly because of its spontaneity and originality Fascism is art. . . . Fascism . . . is a religion." [1]

This prospect, however, will be realized only if the Fascist States are left in isolation and in peace. A prolonged period of peace is highly improbable. Still less probable, despite efforts at autarchy—intellectual as well as economic—is a long epoch of self-contained isolation. No prognosis of the future of the Nazi dictatorship can

[1] *Che cosa e il fascismo,* translated in H. W. Schneider: *Making the Fascist State* (New York: Oxford University Press; 1928), pp. 351–2.

leave out of account its relationships with great neighbouring communities, committed to other ideologies and other State-forms. The reconversion of the German ruling classes to "democracy" by the pressure and the example of Great Britain, France, and America may be dismissed as fantasy. Wilsonian idealism and the crusading ardour of 1918 are dust, too dead ever to stir again with a new breath of life. By no magic can Fascism be transmuted back into liberalism. This truth was well stated by Mussolini over a decade ago:

"Men are tired of liberty. They have had an orgy of it. Today liberty is no longer the chaste stern virgin for whom the generations of the first half of the last century fought and died. For the youth that is intrepid, restless, and hard, that faces the dawn of the new history, there are other words of much greater power, and they are: order, hierarchy, discipline. This poor Italian liberalism that is groaning and battling for a wider liberty is singularly behind the times. It is completely incomprehensible and impossible. They talk of the seeds that will bring back the spring. Jesting! Some seeds die under the shroud of winter. Fascism that was not afraid of being called reactionary while many of today's liberals lay prone before the triumphant beast, has no hesitation today in calling itself illiberal and anti-liberal. Fascism will not fall victim to this kind of vulgar play.

"Let it be known therefore once and for all that Fascism knows no idols and worships no fetishes; it has already passed over and if necessary will turn once more and quietly pass over the more or less decayed corpse of the Goddess of Liberty."[1]

The extension of Fascism to other bourgeois States still committed to liberty is by no means improbable. This development, should it materialize, will not be a consequence of propaganda emanating from Rome or Berlin. Fascism, declared Mussolini, is not an article of export. The Third Reich, declare the Nazi leaders, has no desire to "make its enemies strong" by curing them of democracy. These attitudes do not, of course, preclude propaganda activities designed to manufacture sentiment favourable to Fascism, nor do they prevent manifestations of pleasure at all indications that the western democracies are following the German and Italian examples.[2] What

[1] *"Forza e Consenso," Gerarchia,* March 1923; translated in Schneider, op. cit., p. 342.

[2] See, for example, the Nazi press of September 18, 1934, with approving comments on the incarceration of textile-strike picketers in a concentration camp near Atlanta, Georgia.

is more significant, however, is the fact that the social tensions which bred Fascism in central Europe are operating in the West to disintegrate established loyalties to the democratic way of life and to infuse into the petty bourgeoisie and the ruling classes a deep longing for the "peace," the order, the security, the authoritarian benevolence of an omniscient and omnipotent Messiah which Fascism is imagined to provide.

Fascism is the social philosophy and the State-form of the bourgeoisie in the monopolistic epoch of late capitalism.[1] It emerges first, not in the lands where monopolistic enterprise has reached its highest point of development, but rather where the deprivations produced by the dilemma of an economy strangling for lack of markets first manifest themselves most acutely. The dictatorship of the proletariat arrived first, not in Great Britain or the United States, where capitalism was oldest (and therefore in Marxist theory most ripe for the revolutionary transition to socialism), but in backward Russia. Here the moneyed élite was feeblest. Here the proletariat was most bitterly exploited and oppressed and at the same time most revolutionary, most disciplined, most unified. Here, above all, the impact of the First Imperialist War produced the most disastrous social and economic consequences, shattering the power of the State and of the ruling classes and opening the way for the seizure of power by the Bolshevists.

Similarly the dictatorship of Fascism arrived first, not where monopolistic industry had evolved most elaborately, but in backward Italy. The Italian élite in 1920–3 felt itself most acutely menaced by proletarian and peasant social revolution—whether justifiably or not is irrelevant. The Italian petty bourgeoisie was numerous, poor, embittered. In Italy the impact of the Great War led to a degradation of national symbols and to painful frustrations of patriotic expectations. Italy had "won the war, but lost the peace." Mass paranoia and megalomania, combined with the fear and desperation of the ruling classes, enabled the black-shirts of Mussolini to seize power.

A decade later Germany succumbed to the same disease of a sick society. Here trusts, monopolies, and cartels had long been features of industrial organization. Even before 1914 acute observers—for

[1] Cf. John Strachey: *The Coming Struggle for Power* (New York: Covici-Friede; 1933), and E. Palme Dutt: *Fascism and Social Revolution* (New York: International Publishers; 1934).

example, Brentano and Rathenau—were noting that industrial combinations were becoming more powerful than the State and were assuming State functions. During the blood-bath which followed Serajevo, the State, the General Staff, heavy industry, and the landed nobility were so closely integrated as to become one. After 1919 the industrial and landed élite was obliged to rule through a tepid, imported democracy for which it had scant respect. The loyalty of the masses to Weimar was destroyed by the inflation and by the diplomatic and military impotence of the republic. The *Kleinbürgertum* had long since begun to exhibit neurotic symptoms of a class suffering chronically from material and psychic insecurities. These insecurities were enormously multiplied by the economic consequences of military defeat. Here, as in Italy, poverty in natural resources made the margin between prosperity and depression a narrow one and caused economic and social maladjustments to reflect themselves more immediately in psychological and political disorders than where comfortable reserves of wealth can be drawn upon in a crisis—for example, the United States. Germany, like Italy, was economically a "marginal" State. Here Fascism blossomed into full flower as a demagogic movement bred of petty-bourgeois neuroses and as an instrument of power used by the ruling classes to serve their purposes. Here the Fascist State is most clearly the coercive and co-ordinating agency of the plutocracy in the age of monopolistic capitalism.

It is worthy of note, moreover, that Fascism appears first not only in "marginal" nations, but in "marginal" classes and "marginal" industries. It is nurtured by the social groups which are affected first and most severely by the maladjustments of a diseased economy. The petty bourgeoisie is everywhere in the West the least sharply defined and the most insecure segment of the social hierarchy. Its social status is most ambiguous. Its defences against pressure from above and below are weakest. Its identification with the symbols of nationalism is most intimate and its psychic frustrations are most acute when these symbols are debased. On the other hand, investment banking and heavy industry—that is, iron, steel, shipbuilding, armaments, and construction—are the economic activities which are first affected by down swings of the business cycle and the last to recover in up swings. These are the most sensitive centres of financial and industrial power in highly developed capitalistic societies. Bankers and heavy industrialists are most prosperous when capitalistic economy is expanding and least prosperous when it is contracting. It is here that competition first becomes destructive with the shrinking of the market. Here governmental aid, foreign markets, protective tariffs are demanded first and most insistently. Here trusts, cartels, holding companies, interlocking directorates, and all the other devices of monopoly first become general. Both Mussolini and Hitler were heavily subsidized by the powers of iron and steel, banking and investment. Thyssen and Krupp, Schroeder and Schacht constituted the liaison between these powerful but "marginal" business groups and the NSDAP. Without this alliance the Fascist State would never have come into being.

The seeds of Fascism are obviously falling upon fertile soil in other nations similarly afflicted with the dilemma of late capitalism. In Japan "economic planning," State control of business, militant nationalism, and belligerent imperialism marched hand in hand with industrial capitalism from the beginning. Japan effected the transition from an indigenous feudalism to an indigenous Fascism without the intervening phase of democratic liberalism. In the Britain, the France, the America of the Great Depression heavy industry and investment banking are likewise prostrate. Here, too, the lower middle classes are reduced to desperation, while workers and farmers suffer unemployment and impoverishment and sink to a level of misery which paralyses all will to action. In all of the western States democratic governments continue to wrestle with the problems of depression by the application of half-hearted, tentative, and "temporary" policies which have been carried to their logical conclusion by Fascism: business codes, price-fixing, production quotas, imports and export quotas, restriction of competition, subsidies to agriculture, work-creation schemes, and the like.

In all of the western States the failure of such steps to effect a restoration of prosperity has bred incipient Fascist movements which need for their rapid development only financial support from business and a further disintegration of democratic ideology among the masses. The spread of Fascism in these States has not been thwarted save in France by any greater powers of resistance on the part of the proletariat, but only by the greater antiquity and stability of the democratic tradition. The temporary success of the new experiments, such as the NRA, or another "automatic" up swing of the business cycle in spite of the new experiments, may delay the advent of Fascism in the western democracies for a considerable period. But if the analysis of the genesis and import of Fascism here essayed has any validity, these developments will not prevent the adoption by the ruling classes of such political and economic techniques as are necessary for the preservation of capitalistic economy in the epoch of business contraction and monopoly. Neither will they prevent the emergence of political ideologies and State-forms comparable in fact, if not in name, to those of Italy and Germany.

Even in this event, however, the slow descent of the Fascist societies toward the new mediævalism can by no means be forecast with any degree of certainty. The continuity of economic and cultural retrogression is far more likely to be interrupted by the advent of the Second Imperialist War. In the Third Reich the aristocracy is driven toward conquest by hunger for land and glory. The plutocracy is driven toward conquest by the shrinking of its markets, by the diminution of its profits through the impoverishment of domestic consumers, by the bright prospects of gain to be got by forging the weapons of war and by using them to conquer new markets in the East. The neurotic middle-class masses are driven toward conquest by nationalist megalomania, by hero-fantasies, by morbid longings for murder and suicide bred of the insecurities and tensions of a diseased society. The Nazi leaders are driven toward conquest by all these pressures and by the exigencies of internal politics in a dictatorship which must become increasingly unstable and insecure with the further disintegration of the economic and social order of monopolistic capitalism. Salvation is to be had only through economic expansion in new markets. New markets are to be had only by the military subjugation of the Danube basin and of such portions of the Soviet Union as can be conquered from Communism.

Fascism is driven toward war by its own ideology and by the tightening ropes of economic strangulation in which its ruling classes are entangled. Fascism was born of the trauma of the First Imperialist War. It may perish in the trauma of the Second Imperialist War. War again on a world-wide scale would doubtless bring irremediable catastrophe in its wake. Neither Britain nor the United States could long remain aloof if Russia were attacked or if two Continental coalitions fell upon one another's throats. Japan would seek to seize Siberia and to oust America from the western Pacific. The U.S.S.R., if compelled to fight, would fight with all possible weapons, including colonial revolt and proletarian revolution organized by the Comintern. Finally might come a long and bloody descent into chaos for western civilization—or world-wide social revolution—or both.

The decadent empire of Rome was not suffered to spin out its dead centuries in sleepy quiet. The barbarians broke through the gates and overwhelmed the empire in ruin. Half a millennium ensued of economic and cultural decay, social dissolution, governmental impotence, neighbourhood warfare, anarchy, darkness, and despair. The decadent empires of the twentieth century may not be suffered to decline in peace toward the new Middle Age. In dying, their own convulsions may bring bloodshed, starvation, and horror upon such a scale that a rapid passage to pre-feudal savagery may take the place of slow descent into mediæval night.

The prospect may give pause to the preachers of war. But for the ruling classes of the West war is still profitable. Conquest may still be lucrative after all other economic activity has ceased to pay dividends. When the armed pilgrims on Fascism's road reach this goal, when pathological hatreds, lusts, and longings for extinction create the means of their own satisfaction, the great guns will again thunder their doom, the terror of the skies will sow fire over the earth, and the shells will shriek their dirge over a world in agony. Fascism itself will be consumed by its war-mad sons. With it will perish the remnants of an age that has outlived its time. And over the ashes will preside not the young Siegfried, heralding a new dawn, but the Fates and the Furies, celebrating the end of the gods and the destruction of Valhalla. Here will the solemn Norns, under withered trees, and the dwarfed Nibelungs in their holes and caves keep tryst with death.

APPENDICES AND INDEX

APPENDIX I

GLOSSARY OF ABBREVIATIONS

APA: *Aussenpolitische Amt der NSDAP:* The Foreign Policy Bureau of the Nazi Party

Gestapo: *Geheime Staats Polizei:* Secret Political Police

HJ: *Hitler Jugend:* the Hitler Youth adjunct of the NSDAP

KPD: *Kommunistische Partei Deutschlands:* Communist Party of Germany

NSBO: *Nationalsozialistische Betriebszellen Organisation:* the Shop-Cell Organization of the Nazi Party

NSDAP: *Nationalsozialistische Deutsche Arbeitspartei:* the Nationalsocialist German Workers' Party, official name of the Nazi Party

NSHAGO: *Nationalsozialistische Handels und Gewerbe Organisation:* the Nationalsocialist Trade and Industry Organization

OR: *Oberste Reichsleitung:* the Central Directorate of the NSDAP

OSAF: *Ober S.A. Führer:* High Storm-troop Leader

P.G.S.: Preussische Gesetzsammlung: the official publication of Prussian statutes and decrees

PO: *Politische Organisation:* the Political Organization of the Nazi Party

R.G.B.: Reichsgesetzblatt: the official publication of German federal statutes and decrees

RPA: *Rassenpolitische Amt der NSDAP:* the Race-Policy Bureau of the Nazi Party

S.A.: *Sturmabteilung:* the Storm Division of the NSDAP, consisting of the brown-uniformed storm troopers

S.S.: *Schutzstaffel:* the Protective Staff of the NSDAP, consisting of the black-uniformed Special Guards

SPD: *Sozialdemokratische Partei Deutschlands:* the Social Democratic Party of Germany

V.B.: *Völkischer Beobachter:* the "Racial Observer," leading Nazi daily, published in Berlin and Munich

WPA: *Wehrpolitische Amt der NSDAP:* the Defence Policy Bureau of the Nazi Party

APPENDIX II (A)

TABLE OF REICHSTAG ELECTIONS—1919–28

Election Dates	JANUARY 19, 1919		JUNE 6, 1920		MAY 4, 1924		DECEMBER 7, 1924		MAY 20, 1928	
Total Valid Ballots Cast (in thousands)	*30,400*		*28,196*		*29,282*		*30,290*		*31,160*	
Total Deputies Elected	*421*		*459*		*472*		*493*		*491*	
MAJOR PARTIES	SEATS WON	POPULAR VOTES (*in thousands*)	SEATS WON	POPULAR VOTES (*in thousands*)	SEATS WON	POPULAR VOTES (*in thousands*)	SEATS WON	POPULAR VOTES (*in thousands*)	SEATS WON	POPULAR VOTES (*in thousands*)
COMMUNIST PARTY			4	*590*	62	*3,693*	45	*2,709*	54	*3,263*
SOCIAL DEMOCRATIC PARTY										
Independent Socialists	22	*2,317*	84	*5,047*		*235*		*99*		
Majority Socialists	163	*11,509*	102	*6,104*	100	*6,009*	131	*7,881*	153	*9,151*
GERMAN DEMOCRATIC PARTY (STATE PARTY)	75	*5,642*	39	*2,334*	28	*1,655*	32	*1,920*	25	*1,504*
CENTRUM	91	*5,980*	64	*3,845*	65	*3,914*	69	*4,119*	62	*3,711*
BAVARIAN PEOPLE'S PARTY			21	*1,239*	16	*947*	19	*1,134*	16	*945*
ECONOMIC PARTY	4	*275*	4	*219*	10	*694*	17	*1,005*	25	*1,396*
GERMAN PEOPLE'S PARTY	19	*1,346*	65	*3,919*	45	*2,694*	51	*3,049*	45	*2,678*
GERMAN NATIONAL PEOPLE'S PARTY	44	*3,122*	71	*4,249*	95	*5,697*	103	*6,206*	73	*4,380*
NSDAP					32	*1,918*	14	*907*	12	*810*

APPENDIX II (B)

THE PRESIDENTIAL ELECTIONS OF 1925

Election of March 29, 1925

Candidates	*Popular Votes Received*
Karl Jarres	10,416,658
Otto Braun	7,802,497
Wilhelm Marx	3,887,734
Ernst Thälmann	1,871,815
Willy Hellpach	1,568,398
Heinrich Held	1,007,450
Erich von Ludendorff	285,793

Election of April 26, 1925

Paul von Hindenburg	14,655,641
Wilhelm Marx	13,751,605
Ernst Thälmann	1,931,151

APPENDIX III

THE PROGRAM OF THE NSDAP[1]

The Program of the German Workers' Party is limited as to period. The leaders have no intention, once the aims announced in it have been achieved, of setting up fresh ones, merely in order to increase the discontent of the masses artificially and so ensure the continued existence of the party.

1. We demand the union of all Germans to form a Great Germany on the basis of the right of self-determination of nations.

2. We demand equality of rights for the German people in its dealings with other nations, and abolition of the Peace Treaties of Versailles and Saint-Germain.

3. We demand land and territory (colonies) for the nourishment of our people and for settling our superfluous population.

4. None but members of the nation (Volksgenossen) may be citizens of the State. None but those of German blood, whatever their creed, may be members of the nation. No Jew, therefore, may be a member of the nation.

5. Anyone who is not a citizen of the State may live in Germany only as a guest and must be subject to laws for aliens.

6. The right of voting for the leaders and laws of the State is to be enjoyed by the citizen of the State alone. We demand therefore that all official appointments, of whatever kind, whether in the Reich, in the Länder, or in the smaller localities, shall be granted to citizens of the State alone.

We oppose the corrupting custom of Parliament of filling posts merely with a view of party considerations, and without reference to character or capability.

7. We demand that the State shall make it its first duty to promote

[1] *Das Programm der N.S.D.A.P. und seine weltanschaulichen Grundgedanken,* von Gottfried Feder (München: Eher; 115. Auflage, 575. Tausend, 1933), pp. 19–22.

the industry and livelihood of citizens of the State. If it is not possible to nourish the entire population of the State, foreign nationals (non-citizens) must be excluded from the Reich.

8. All further non-German immigration must be prevented. We demand that all non-Germans who entered Germany subsequent to August 2nd, 1914, shall be compelled forthwith to depart from the Reich.

9. All citizens of the State shall be equal as regards rights and duties.

10. It must be the first duty of each citizen of the State to work with his mind or with his body. The activities of the individual may not clash with the interests of the whole, but must proceed within the frame of the community and be for the general good.

We demand therefore:

11. Abolition of incomes unearned by work.

Breaking of the Bonds of Interest Slavery

12. In view of the enormous sacrifice of life and property demanded of a nation by every war, personal enrichment due to a war must be regarded as a crime against the nation. We demand therefore ruthless confiscation of all war gains.

13. We demand nationalization of all businesses which have been up to the present formed into companies (trusts).

14. We demand that the profits from wholesale trade shall be shared out.

15. We demand extensive development of provision for old age.

16. We demand creation and maintenance of a healthy middle class, immediate communalization of department stores, and their lease at a cheap rate to small traders, and extreme consideration for all small purveyors to the State, district authorities, and smaller localities.

17. We demand land-reform suitable to our national requirements, passing of a law for confiscation without compensation of land for common purposes; abolition of interest on land loans, and prevention of all speculation in land.

18. We demand a ruthless struggle against those whose activities are injurious to the common interest. Common criminals against the

nation, usurers, profiteers, etc., must be punished with death, whatever their creed or race.

19. We demand that the Roman Law, which serves the materialistic world order, shall be replaced by a German legal system.

20. With the aim of opening to every capable and industrious German the possibility of higher education and of thus obtaining advancement, the State must consider a thorough reconstruction of our national system of education. The curriculum of all educational establishments must be brought into line with the requirements of practical life. Comprehension of the State idea (civic training) must be the school objective, beginning with the first dawn of understanding in the pupil. We demand development of the gifted children of poor parents, whatever their class or occupation, at the expense of the State.

21. The State must see to raising the standard of health in the nation by protecting mothers and infants, prohibiting child labour, increasing bodily efficiency by obligatory gymnastics and sports laid down by law, and by extensive support of clubs engaged in the bodily development of the young.

22. We demand abolition of a paid army, and formation of a national army.

23. We demand legal warfare against conscious political lying and its dissemination in the press. In order to facilitate creation of a German national press we demand:

(a) that all editors and their co-workers on newspapers employing the German language must be members of the nation (Volksgenossen);

(b) that special permission from the State shall be necessary before non-German newspapers may appear. These must not be printed in the German language;

(c) that non-Germans shall be prohibited by law from participation financially in or influencing German newspapers, and that the penalty for contravention of the law shall be suppression of any such newspaper and immediate deportation of the non-German concerned in it.

It must be forbidden to publish papers which do not conduce to the national welfare. We demand legal prosecution of all tendencies in art and literature of a kind likely to disintegrate our life as a nation, and the suppression of institutions which militate against the requirements above-mentioned.

24. We demand liberty for all religious denominations in the State, so far as they are not a danger to, and do not militate against the moral feelings of, the German race.

The party, as such, stands for positive Christianity, but does not bind itself in the matter of creed to any particular confession. It combats the Jewish-materialist spirit within us and without us and is convinced that our nation can only achieve permanent health from within on the principle:

The Common Interest before Self

25. That all the foregoing may be realized, we demand the creation of a strong central power of the State. Unquestioned authority of the politically centralized Parliament over the entire Reich and its organization; and formation of Chambers for classes and occupations for the purpose of carrying out the general laws promulgated by the Reich in the various states of the confederation.

The leaders of the party swear to go straight forward—if necessary to sacrifice their lives—in securing fulfilment of the foregoing points.

Munich, February 24, 1920

INDEX

A NOTE ON THE TYPE
IN WHICH THIS BOOK IS SET

DEVICE OF
ROBERT GRANJON

This book is set in Granjon, a type named in compliment to ROBERT GRANJON, *but neither a copy of a classic face nor an entirely original creation. George W. Jones drew the basic design for this type from classic sources, but deviated from his model to profit by the intervening centuries of experience and progress. This type is based primarily upon the type used by Claude Garamond (1510-61) in his beautiful French books, and more closely resembles Garamond's own than do any of the various modern types that bear his name.*

Of Robert Granjon nothing is known before 1545, except that he had begun his career as type-cutter in 1523. The boldest and most original designer of his time, he was one of the first to practise the trade of type-founder apart from that of printer. Between 1549 and 1551 he printed a number of books in Paris, also continuing as type-cutter. By 1557 he was settled in Lyons and had married Antoinette Salamon, whose father, Bernard, was an artist associated with Jean de Tournes. Between 1557 and 1562 Granjon printed about twenty books in types designed by himself, following, after the fashion of the day, the cursive handwriting of the time. These types, usually known as "caractères de civilité," he himself called "lettres françaises," as especially appropriate to his own country. He was granted a monopoly of these types for ten years, but they were soon copied. Granjon appears to have lived in Antwerp for a time, but was at Lyons in 1575 and 1577, and for the next decade at Rome, working for the Vatican and Medici presses, his work consisting largely in cutting exotic types. Towards the end of his life he may have returned to live in Paris, where he died in 1590.

This book was composed, printed, and bound by H. Wolff Estate, New York. The paper was manufactured by S. D. Warren Co., Boston.